THE FABER BOOK OF ESPIONAGE

The Faber Book of
ESPIONAGE

edited by
NIGEL WEST

faber and faber
LONDON · BOSTON

First published in 1993
by Faber and Faber Limited
3 Queen Square London WC1N 3AU
Photoset by Wilmaset Ltd, Wirral
Printed in England by Clays Ltd, St Ives plc

Nigel West is hereby identified as author of this work in
accordance with Section 77 of the Copyright, Designs and
Patents Act 1988

A CIP record for this book is available from the British Library

ISBN 0–571–16854–X

2 4 6 8 10 9 7 5 3 1

Dedicated to the memory of Wulf Schmidt (1911–1992)

Born in Abenra, Schleswig-Holstein, Wulf Schmidt adopted the identity of Harry Williamson and parachuted into Cambridgeshire in September 1940 as a spy for the German Abwehr. After his capture by MI5 Wulf was codenamed *Tate* and became one of the most successful double agents of the Second World War. He died at his home in Watford on 19 October 1992.

Contents

Introduction

Writers of thrillers tend to gravitate to the Secret Service as surely as the mentally unstable become psychiatrists, or the impotent pornographers.
Malcolm Muggeridge, The Infernal Grove

Britain has long been blessed with gifted espionage writers. John Buchan, Dornford Yates, Rudyard Kipling, Eric Ambler and Len Deighton are all authors whose reputations were established by their tales of the daring exploits of intrepid Secret Service agents. Yet, paradoxically, none of these five ever enjoyed any first-hand experience of the world of espionage. Similarly Lord Baden-Powell, the founder of the international Scout movement, is widely believed to have been a professional intelligence officer, yet he never was. However, there are impressive numbers of writers, some of them of world stature, others rather more obscure, who have operated either as agents or case officers, and it is to the publications in their names (or pseudonyms) that this anthology is devoted.

Whereas one might expect to find the best-known spy writers in an anthology of espionage, this one concentrates on the authors who really know their subject and have had first-hand experience of their craft. Sometimes, as was the case with W. Somerset Maugham (*Ashenden*), the link was well recognized and even exploited to his advantage by the individual concerned. In other examples, like that of John Dickson Carr (*Most Secret*), the author's involvement in the authentic intelligence world will be a revelation. Immediately, several questions arise. To what extent did the fiction writers base their books on true life? Are there clues in the work of Alec Waugh (*A Spy in the Family*) or Kenneth Benton (*Sole Agent*) to their undercover activities? Does the disclosure that biographers of the calibre of Brian Montgomery (*A Field Marshal in the Family*) and Donald Prater (*A Ringing Glass*) were career SIS officers shed new light on their work?

Since the creation of the British Secret Service in 1909 a rich literary tradition among its membership has developed in both fiction and non-fiction. Several intelligence officers – including A. E. W. Mason (*The Witness for the Defence*), Malcolm Muggeridge (*Affairs of the Heart*) and David Cornwell (John Le Carré; *The Spy Who Came in from the Cold*) – have achieved considerable fame as novelists. Of those who have written on the ever-popular topic of espionage, most have capitalized on their own first-hand experience of the intelligence community, but there are a few examples of writers, such as Valentine Williams (*The Man with the Clubfoot*) and Graham Greene (*The Confidential Agent*), who had already established themselves in the espionage genre before they were recruited into SIS. Paradoxically, Ian Fleming, the author who created James Bond and is probably the world's best-known spy writer, was never formally a member of either MI5 or SIS. Nor did his wartime exploits extend much beyond a desk in the Admiralty. 'He wasn't James Bond. He was a pen-pusher like the rest of us,' said his secretary. 'Ian's war had plenty of sweat and toil and tears but no real blood.' Nevertheless he did work for the Naval Intelligence Division and, as personal assistant to its Director, Admiral John Godfrey, developed a close relationship with SIS; he thereby deserves to be included in this anthology, not only for his unique and lasting contribution to espionage fiction.

Concerning the identity of the model for James Bond, there are several candidates, but the best claim is either that of the Yugoslav double agent Dusko Popov, or that of Fleming's pre-war skiing companion, Conrad O'Brien-ffrench. While the latter has the edge on physical appearance, there can be no doubt that Popov met Fleming and that the author knew of his extraordinary story long before it was published. What remains indisputable is that Fleming himself was never in any physical danger during the war.

Similarly, Dennis Wheatley (*Codeword Golden Fleece*) never formally worked for MI5 – as did his wife, stepson, stepdaughter and secretary – but his relationship with the Security Service was so close that he too qualifies for inclusion in these pages. He was regarded as something of a part-time agent by MI5; he willingly participated in quite a few important counter-espionage investigations and provided invaluable cover for some of its most sensitive operations. His wife Joan Grant had written six novels under the pseudonym Eve Chaucer (*No Ordinary Virgin*) before she joined MI5, and her son William Younger wrote three books of poetry while employed by the Security Service prior to the adoption of the pen-name William Mole for his detective fiction.

Another family with strong Security Service connections is that of Lord Clanmorris, better known as the thriller writer John Bingham, who spent thirty-seven years in MI5 until his retirement in 1977. Younger and Bingham served much of their covert career working together in the same MI5 sub-section and it is a curious coincidence that both wrote detective fiction . . . and both were criticized for the anti-police bias of their books. Not only did Bingham's wife, the biographer Madeleine Bingham (*Peers and Plebs*), also work for MI5 during the war, but his daughter Charlotte (*Coronet among the Weeds*) joined while a débutante and endured a brief but colourful career in MI5's famous registry.

There is a less well-recognized group of members and former agents of Her Majesty's Secret Intelligence Service that has defied the convention that nothing should ever be written of their exploits. Some, like Henry Landau (*All's Fair*) and Leslie Nicholson (*British Agent*), were obliged to write their memoirs from the safety of America so as to avoid the kind of criminal prosecution experienced by Sir Compton Mackenzie (*Greek Memories*), who was convicted of offences under the Official Secrets Acts in January 1933. Others – such as Allan Monkhouse (*Moscow 1911– 1933*), Hugh Trevor-Roper (*The Philby Affair*), Dick Ellis (*Transcaspian Episode*) and Nicholas Elliott (*Never Judge a Man by His Umbrella*) – have been authorized to publish rather more discreet versions of their activities. Nicholson had good reasons to be disenchanted with SIS, as had Sigismund Best (*The Venlo Incident*), for they both felt they had been badly treated by SIS's chief, Sir Stewart Menzies. Nicholson adopted a pseudonym to write *British Agent*, which bore a brief endorsement from his wartime colleague, Henry Kerby MP. Six years after Nicholson's revelations another of his erstwhile subordinates, Kenneth Cohen, contributed a preface to the English translation of *Noah's Ark*, the memoirs of his key agent in occupied France. Like Nicholson, it is likely he did not bother to seek official approval before publication. He too was a disappointed man, having suffered a demotion not long before his premature retirement.

The edict that British intelligence personnel should never reveal details of their work extended to individuals who were not strictly intelligence professionals but operated in the field as agents and survived to tell their stories. Among them are five celebrated anti-Bolsheviks: Sir Paul Dukes (*The Story of 'ST-25'*), William Gibson (*Wild Career*), Augustus Agar (*Baltic Episode*), Sir Samuel Hoare (*The Fourth Seal*) and the legendary George Hill (*Go Spy the Land*). To this category of books should also be added the remarkable *Sidney Reilly*, the autobiography of SIS's self-styled master spy which was completed by his widow, Pepita, and released after her husband's mysterious disappearance in Moscow. The Allied intervention in the Russian revolution and civil war remains a matter of some sensitivity more than three-quarters of a century later. Reginald Teague-Jones, sentenced to death for his role in Britain's anti-Communist campaign in the Caspian region, spent eighty years hiding from Soviet death squads, and his memoirs (*The Spy Who Disappeared*), based on his daily journal, were released only after his death in 1988.

A few brave professionals have ignored the comprehensive ban on publication and risked the opprobrium of colleagues by giving factual accounts of their clandestine work. Sir James Marshall-Cornwall (*Wars and Rumours of Wars*), John Cross (*Red Jungle*), George Young (*Who is My Liege?*), David Smiley (*Albanian Assignment*), Philip Johns (*Within Two Cloaks*), Fred Winterbotham (*The Ultra Secret*), R. V. Jones (*Most Secret War*) and Monty Woodhouse (*Something Ventured*) have either obtained official permission to publish or, in most cases, have simply been too senior or too highly decorated to be hauled before the courts and subjected to an embarrassing trial. Indeed, in the cases of Nigel Clive (*A Greek Experience*), Xan Fielding (*Hide and Seek*), Patrick Whinney (*Corsican Command*) and Adrian Gallegos (*From Capri into Oblivion*), they had scarcely alluded to SIS, if at all, and had generally confined their comments to a wartime context, avoiding any mention of their post-war employment by SIS.

To have prosecuted the Hon. Monty Woodhouse MP would have been profoundly awkward, not least because it would have drawn unwanted attention to SIS's peacetime existence, a fact unacknowledged by successive governments. Nor, indeed, was Woodhouse breaking ranks. When he was in the Commons he had several colleagues on both benches who had written books, albeit of a rather more prosaic nature. Jack Cordeaux, once one of SIS's Deputy Directors, published a somewhat autobiographical novel, *Safe Seat*, soon after he lost his Nottingham Central constituency at the 1964 general election. One of his wartime subordinates had been his front-bench colleague Aubrey Jones MP, the head of SIS's office in Bari until 1945, who had stuck to economics in *The Pendulum of Politics*. Sir Stephen Hastings, who went straight from conducting hazardous undercover operations during the Cyprus Emergency to fight the Mid-Bedfordshire by-election in November 1960, a constituency he retained until 1983, wrote *The Murder of TSR2*, a bitter attack on Denis Healey's decision to scrap Britain's strategic bomber project. From the Labour side of the House, Sir Kenneth Younger, once the head of MI5's wartime French country section, wrote several works of non-fiction, including *Changing Perspectives in British Foreign Policy*.

Even if a government was sufficiently misguided even to contemplate the prosecution of an indiscreet former SIS officer, there was always one particular group of wartime heroes, the escapers, who inevitably would be exempt from the usual conditions of secrecy imposed on their colleagues in more sensitive branches of intelligence. Airey Neave became a national figure following his daring trek across Europe from Colditz, and after the war he wrote an account of his adventures (*Saturday at MI9*) as did his colleague Jimmy Langley (*Fight Another Day*) who had worked in the same SIS sub-section dedicated to helping other evaders. Designated P15, this unit was better known by its military intelligence cover designation of MI9, and managed the escape lines which stretched across occupied Europe and communicated with its organizers in the field either by radio or through couriers. One of Donald Darling's more memorable agents, who certainly defied the rule that spies should be inconspicuous, was the Armenian oil tycoon Nubar Gulbenkian who refers in his memoirs *Pantaraxia* to his clandestine role and in particular to his controller whom he identifies only as 'Didi'. For those who knew that Donald Darling had been his case officer, putting a name to 'Didi' was easy, as Darling himself acknowledged in his memoirs, *Secret Sunday*, which prudently made no mention of his post-war employment by the Consular Service in Brazil. Another highly successful escapee and SIS agent, though not a member of P15's organization, was Roland Rieul (*Soldier into Spy*) who broke out of his PoW camp in Germany and made his way to Basel. There, to his surprise, instead of being repatriated he was recruited into SIS's local network which infiltrated occupied France from Swiss territory. John Brown (*In Durance Vile*) maintained contact with MI9 from his PoW camp deep in Silesia by concealing coded messages in his letters home, and upon his release he was debriefed by his SIS case officers.

Some within the closed world of the intelligence bureaucracy prefer to pretend that the disclosure by insiders of their secret careers is a quite new phenomenon, a regrettable departure from a long-respected custom of maintaining a laudably absolute silence about such matters. However, as we shall see, there is actually a long tradition of the *cognoscenti* giving accounts of their confidential activities, a practice which dates back to Captain Weldon's *Hard Lying*, published in 1925. This memoir, in which the author recalled his officially sponsored espionage on behalf of SIS in the eastern Mediterranean during the First World War, set an awkward precedent. Although one might not think so, judging by the behaviour of successive British governments and the harsh words of Treasury counsel seeking bans on particular publications, there is probably more in print about the British secret services than about any of their foreign counter-parts, and a fair proportion has been produced by authors with direct, first-hand knowledge of their subject.

Occasionally governments have been sufficiently motivated to preserve the integrity of their *sub rosa* departments by seeking counter-productive injunctions intended to restrain the publication of particularly sensitive titles. Anthony Cavendish's privately published *Inside Intelligence* was the subject of lengthy litigation with the Attorney-General in 1987 and, three years before its general publication, Joan Miller's *One Girl's War* was published posthumously, in Ireland, after the Treasury Solicitor had imposed a ban in Britain. This is in distinct contrast to the intense pressure applied two decades earlier by the intelligence establishment to excise embarrassing chapters from the autobiographies of two former MI5 officers who, coincidentally, had both been recruited from the ranks of the police: Sir Percy Sillitoe (*Cloak without Dagger*) who was, of course, MI5's first post-war Director-General, and Leonard Burt (*Commander Burt of Scotland Yard*), who headed the Metropolitan Police Special Branch after the war. Sillitoe and Burt had sought to supplement their meagre pensions by drawing on the more saleable episodes of their long careers but separately they ran into the opposition of the incoming Director-General, Sir Dick White.

Despite his academic background White, who ran MI5 between 1952 and 1956, and then headed SIS until 1968 (and thereafter exercised a considerable degree of influence over policy through his post as intelligence co-ordinator in the Cabinet Office), kept a tight rein on the release of information and muzzled Burt and Sillitoe. This memory may have caused him some embarrassment when the American publishers William Morrow announced in 1990 that Andrew Boyle had been commissioned to write his biography ... and that their author had received unprecedented co-operation from his subject. Although White himself is not known to have written anything for public consumption, his Deputy Director-General and successor, (Sir) Roger Hollis, had already made a brief contribution when he joined MI5 in 1938. A few months earlier, in October 1937, Hollis had given an address on the topic of the Sino-Japanese conflict to the Royal Central Asian Society, and his remarks were later reproduced in the Society's journal. When Hollis subsequently came under suspicion as a possible Soviet mole, special attention was given to this document in the hope that it might shed light on his political sympathies.

It was while Hollis was Director-General of the Security Service, and White was his SIS counterpart, that the Soviet spy Oleg Penkovsky was recruited. A GRU source of enormous importance, Penkovsky haemorrhaged to the West a vast quantity of secrets from the Kremlin, using a British businessman, Greville Wynne, as a conduit to SIS. Curiously, when Wynne announced that he was to release his memoirs, *The Man from Moscow*, neither MI5 nor SIS made any attempt to prevent publication ... on the grounds that most of what he intended to divulge was completely fictitious!

When one considers the lengths to which governments have gone to suppress the memoirs of apparently sensitive individuals, with more than £2.5m of public funds being spent to prevent the circulation of Peter Wright's controversial *Spycatcher*, one is bound to wonder at the selectivity of the advice given to ministers by their secret servants. After all, Arthur Martin and Stephen de Mowbray, both now famous as veterans of the Cold War and its controversial molehunts, contributed a foreword to *New Lies for Old*, the bizarre political analysis written by the KGB defector Anatoli Golitsyn. Admittedly neither was entirely unknown. Martin's identity had been revealed years earlier by Kim Philby in his memoirs, *My Silent War*, and de Mowbray had featured in *Their Trade is Treachery*, the book written by Chapman Pincher in 1981 based on data supplied by its co-author, Peter Wright. Were the authorities deterred from preventing their attributed contribution to Golitsyn's book by a reluctance to provoke a fight with a pair of molehunters who, arguably, harboured between them more inconvenient secrets than Peter Wright could have dreamed of? MI5 veteran George Leggett also capitalized on his knowledge after his retirement in *The Cheka: Lenin's Political Police* which was published a decade after his abrupt departure from the Security Service, but he discreetly omitted his biographical details.

An even smaller handful of authors have written on topics entirely unconnected with their secret lives, without even their publishers realizing their double life in the secret world. An early example is that of the playwright Edward Knoblock who worked for SIS in Switzerland and Greece during the Great War. Into this category also fall the academics Robert Cecil (*A Divided Life*); Robert Zaehner (*Hinduism*); Robert Carew-Hunt (*The Theory and Practice of Communism*); and Professor Hugh Seton-Watson (*Neither War nor Peace*). Two others who could be included in this group of distinguished academics are Reginald Fletcher, the Labour MP and SIS staff officer who shortly before the war contributed a chapter entitled 'Britain's Air Strength' to *The Air Defence of Britain*, in which he had argued for an expansion of the RAF to counter

Germany's growing airborne power; and David Footman (*Dead Yesterday*), already a novelist when he joined SIS in 1935, and later an historian of note at St Antony's, Oxford.

Two more recent SIS officers, both experts on the Far East, are Donald Lancaster and John Colvin. Neither divulged his covert role when he released his book: Lancaster capped a lengthy career in the Orient with *The Emancipation of French Indo-China* and John Colvin wrote his highly entertaining autobiography, *Twice Around the World* without giving his readers anything more than the slightest hint of his true calling. Nevertheless, careful study of both texts reveals what might be termed an oblique pointer to their authors' actual vocation.

Of course it is now public knowledge that some notables among the British intelligence personnel who undertook wartime work in SIS owed their true loyalties to Moscow. George Blake (*No Other Choice*) and Kim Philby are probably the best known, but long before the latter released his own mischievous autobiography he anonymously ghosted a history of a publishing firm, *The David Allens*. One passage in particular, quoted herein, gives the strong suggestion of a very private and dangerous joke, with the author describing a concealed political commitment. Similarly, John Cairncross operated as a Soviet spy until he was eventually unmasked as a key source for the NKVD, initially inside GCHQ and then in SIS. His collection of poetry, *La Fontaine Fables and other poems*, is highly regarded by critics. Nor by any means were Blake, Philby and Cairncross alone in their treachery. Anthony Blunt successfully penetrated MI5 on behalf of the KGB and, while for understandable reasons of self-preservation he never wrote about that part of his life, he did contribute a noteworthy valedictory tribute to Tomas Harris, a former colleague in the Security Service who happened to be a gifted artist and collector as well as an exceptionally brilliant counter-intelligence operator. Harris was also to become something of a public figure and, although he never divulged any aspects of his war service, he did write extensively about his favourite painter, Goya.

A mutual close friend of Harris and Blunt was Guy Burgess, the BBC radio producer who not only joined Section D of SIS, but went on to become an important MI5 agent. At the end of the war Burgess joined the Foreign Office and while working for the Minister of State, (Sir) Hector McNeil, ghosted his history of the Labour Party. Immediately after Burgess's defection in 1951 his old ally Goronwy Rees, who was then an SIS officer, alerted Blunt to his disappearance, warned David Footman of the awkward situation that had arisen, and thereby brought suspicion upon himself. In his autobiography *A Chapter of Accidents*, Rees described this episode but concealed the names of Footman and Blunt, and remained silent on the issue of his own duplicity. This passage takes on a special significance when one realizes the personalities to whom he was alluding, and the astonishing fact that Rees himself was then not only a mole, but also a serving SIS officer.

Others too have emerged briefly from their secret life to write on what, at first glance, appear to be entirely unrelated subjects but which upon closer examination reveal a hidden link with espionage. Take, for example, MI5's renowned expert on the KGB, Charles Elwell, who released his travelogue *Corsican Excursion* soon after joining the Security Service, and evidently could not resist describing the case of a Napoleonic spy. Nevertheless, it was only the tiny circle of his MI5 colleagues who knew that Elwell was not a minor functionary in the War Office, as he and his family told acquaintances. Certainly no one reading his book would be given any reason to guess his *métier*. There have been occasions when an author who has subsequently entered the intelligence profession has been disadvantaged by what he had written previously. The classic case is that of Archie Lyall, the monocled traveller and linguist whose reputation was established with *The Balkan Road*, and half a dozen other titles, before he joined SIS. When doubt was cast on his post-war loyalty, close attention was given to his observations of Soviet life in *Russian Roundabout* which, in effect, became the brief for his accusers.

Not all the books written by insiders can be seen to contain indications to an author's livelihood. Brian Stewart, for many years SIS's resident Far East expert, edited an anthology of Chinese proverbs entitled *All Men's Wisdom*; laudably self-effacing, he described himself in the brief biographical notes merely as a humble member of his country's Diplomatic Corps, not mentioning his bid to succeed Sir John Rennie as SIS's chief in 1973. As might be expected, others have exercised an equal degree of caution when discussing their own life's work, although their motives have been extremely varied. Once chairman of the Labour Party, Tom Driberg omitted to describe his role as an MI5 double agent in his otherwise candid autobiography, *Ruling Passions*, and concealed his intelligence connections so successfully that some of his closest friends still find it hard to believe that he was ever a valued source for the Security Service . . . and for the KGB. SIS officer Ruari Chisholm's *Ladysmith*, an acclaimed account of the Boer War siege, was written while he undertook two tours of duty in Pretoria, and his colleague Theo Pantcheff was equally discreet about his occupation when he wrote a fascinating book,

Alderney: Fortress Island on the Nazi occupation of Alderney in the Channel Isles. None of these books gives any indication that the author has led a rather more interesting life than that suggested by the wholly misleading biographical details offered by the publishers.

Naturally there are often good reasons for the publishers to be disingenuous, even when they themselves have realized their author is not quite what he seems. Shortly before the war a group of enterprising and patriotic young Britons was recruited into SIS's sabotage section to undertake a variety of secret but ill-fated missions in central Europe, and some of them operated under journalistic cover. It would never have done for Alexander Rickman's editor at Faber & Faber to have compromised his author by pointing out that his book, *Swedish Iron Ore*, was nothing more than a conveniently plausible excuse to research that country's mineral assets and transport infrastructure so they could be demolished. Geoffrey Household had only just published his best-selling thriller *Rogue Male* when he was despatched to Bucharest on a mission to wreck Ploesti's oilfields. And both David Walker (*Lunch with a Stranger*) and Basil Davidson (*Special Operations Europe*) used their credentials as genuine journalists to reconnoitre Yugoslavia and Romania for Section D. They were joined by Walter Stirling (*Safety Last*) and Julian Amery (*Approach March*) who have given brief accounts of their illicit activities in the Balkans, which were directed from London by a banker, Bickham Sweet-Escott (*Baker Street Irregular*). Their equipment and explosives were delivered by the distinguished solicitor (Sir) Gerald Glover (*115 Park Street*) who distributed *matériel* while travelling as a King's Messenger. Most of these adventurers graduated to Special Operations Executive, but not all. The barrister and biographer H. Montgomery Hyde (*Secret Intelligence Agent*) was based in Gibraltar and Bermuda, and ended up in New York, where he was reunited with one of the more improbable of Section D's recruits, the theatrical producer Eric Maschwitz (*No Chip on My Shoulder*).

Competing with SIS's literary accomplishments are the relatively few former members of the Security Service, Britain's domestic intelligence agency better known as MI5, who have worked undercover. Derek Tangye (*The Way to Minack*); William Magan (*Umma-More*); Stephen Watts (*Moonlight on a Lake in Bond Street*); Cyril Mills (*Bertram Mills Circus: Its Story*); Lord Rothschild (*Meditations of a Broomstick*) and Peter Wright (*Spycatcher*) all served in MI5 and, to a greater or lesser extent, based their books upon their experiences. Only three wartime members of the Security Service had already established a literary reputation, of sorts, before their recruitment: Mark Pepys, the sixth Earl of Cottenham and the author of *Motoring without Fears*, who was drafted into MI5 in 1939 to head its transport section; Maxwell Knight, the man once described as 'the most mysterious member of MI5', who had published a thriller in 1934, *Crime Cargo*; and (Sir) Roger Fulford whose *Royal Dukes* had been published in 1933. Only in the erudite work of H. L. A. Hart QC, Professor of Jurisprudence at Oxford, can one find absolutely no hint of his wartime career in the Security Service's counter-espionage branch.

MI5 is often described as being a wholly domestic security agency, but in fact the organization has a long tradition of running parallel bodies overseas. During the war these representatives were known as Defence Security Officers, and for a short time afterwards Security Intelligence Middle East (SIME) was effectively MI5's regional branch, staffed by personnel transferred from London or recruited locally. Into the latter category falls the eminent historian and biographer Alistair Horne who spent three years in SIME as a very young officer.

Although the Security Service has sought to maintain the polite absurdity that it never co-operates with authors, the opposite is the truth. When Dennis Wheatley started to research the life of the Bolshevik defender of Stalingrad, Marshal Voroshilov, he turned to MI5 for help. The result was *Red Eagle*, published in 1937, which was based on classified material authorized for release to Wheatley by the then Director-General, Sir Vernon Kell. Other examples include *Handbook for Spies*, the autobiography of Allan Foote, the corn merchant's clerk from Liverpool who defected from the GRU at the end of the war. Foote surrendered to the British authorities in Berlin rather than undertake a mission to the United States for his Soviet controller, and his book was largely written by his MI5 debriefer, Courtney Young, with the consent of his Director-General, Sir Percy Sillitoe. In another example, Sillitoe ordered another MI5 officer, Jim Skardon, to co-operate with Alan Moorehead, the distinguished war correspondent who was researching the treachery of the atom spy Klaus Fuchs for his standard work on the subject, *The Traitors*. Nor was this kind of unofficial co-operation limited to SIS. After the war Malcolm Muggeridge maintained a close relationship with his former employers and was in the habit of reading their files while preparing the weekend lectures he gave to new recruits. Following a visit to SIS's headquarters in September 1949 he noted contemptuously in his diary, 'Nothing in the reports I saw from behind the Iron Curtain countries which could not have been got from the newspapers.' Nor does the supposed distaste of the secret services for the printed word extend to publishers, for there are a few former intelligence officers who have taken up the occupation with some success, not the least being Derek Verschoyle, formerly the *Spectator*'s literary editor and author of *The English Novelists*, who had been engaged on especially disagreeable and dangerous work in the Adriatic after the Second World War, and whose publishing list was later to include Randolph Churchill. Similarly James MacGibbon, whose firm MacGibbon & Kee was to publish Philby's autobiography, had also served as a wartime intelligence officer.

In contrast to MI5's case officers, who almost to a man maintained their silence, their wartime double agents have been prolific in their output. Eddie Chapman (*The Real Eddie Chapman Story*), Lily Sergueiev (*Secret Service Rendered*), Juan Pujol (*GARBO*), John Moe (*John Moe: Double Agent*), Roman Garby-Czerniawski (*The Big Network*) and Dusko Popov (*Spy CounterSpy*) all duped their Abwehr controllers and co-operated with the British Security Service in a sophisticated deception operation. Into this category must also fall Wolfgang zu Putlitz (*The Zu Putlitz Dossier*), the homosexual press attaché at the German Embassy in pre-war London who kept MI5 and SIS in touch with the mission's internal politics, and who was eventually forced to defect to the British to escape the Gestapo. Two other significant MI5 sources should also be mentioned in the context of agents: the biographer Harald Kurtz (*The Empress Eugénie*) and the journalist E. H. Cookridge (*The Third Man*), both of whom worked undercover as MI5 informers in internment camps among enemy detainees.

The extraordinary contribution of these agents to the successful prosecution of the war can hardly be exaggerated, but virtually nothing would be known of their work if it had not been for the determination of Sir John Masterman (*On the Chariot Wheel*), who defied the establishment and published a copy of a history that he had been commissioned to write at the conclusion of hostilities. Intended for internal consumption only, his account of the double-cross system became a textbook for the manipulation of double agents and the development of deception campaigns. Masterman eventually won Whitehall's grudging approval to publish in 1972, and this landmark event was to be followed seven years later by the release of the first volume of official histories in the *British Intelligence* series. These heavy tomes qualify for a mention here because the team of historians selected to write them contained some MI5 and SIS professionals, including Charles Ransom, formerly SIS's man in Rome, and Anthony Simkins, latterly the Deputy Director-General of the

Security Service. In addition, Ronald Reed, from MI5's technical support branch, made an anonymous contribution to the penultimate volume of the series, entitled *Security and Counter-intelligence*. Neil Blair was commissioned to write SIS's wartime history after his retirement from SIS in 1967, and recently another retired SIS officer has embarked upon a post-war version. Neither document is ever likely to emerge from the Cabinet Office.

As recently as 1989 Parliament passed a law to prevent former insiders from disclosing the secrets of their trade. Although there was a time when practitioners of the arcane arts were hesitant to admit their Secret Service connections, or disclose the details of their involvement however banal, times have changed. Indeed, Gilbert Highet, the professor of Greek and Latin at Columbia University, who was married to the novelist Helen MacInnes, often protested that none of the authentic-sounding material in her first best-selling spy thriller *Above Suspicion* had come from his lips, which had been sealed the moment he had been recruited into British Intelligence. Highet had worked in the intelligence field for the British both in the US in 1942 and in Germany immediately after the war. It was only following his death in January 1978 that his widow's publishers were permitted to describe him as 'a high-level member of British Intelligence'. Professor Highet may have exercised discretion but others, as shall be seen, did not, which merely serves to demonstrate that throughout this century the law has been chronically unsuccessful in stemming the flow of classified material.

At the outbreak of war Britain's secret services were anxious to acquire intelligence officers, preferably from what was termed suitable backgrounds. As most physically fit young men were rather more keen to join the fighting services, MI5 and SIS found themselves employing some unusual characters, drawn mainly from the City, the universities, Fleet Street, the law, the lame and, in the case of Christopher Rhodes, the theatre. One explanation for the apparently disproportionate number of journalists, novelists and academics attracted to the intelligence world is that the skills of these professions are ideally suited to the essential core activity of any security agency: the acquisition, collation, analysis and distribution of information. Newspaper reporters are trained to cultivate sources, check material against what is already held on file, and compile reports for their editors. Apart from the knowledge that the data is likely to appear in the public domain, the attributes of the journalist and the process by which he develops a story are virtually identical to that of the intelligence professional. Indeed, there are in these pages numerous examples of journalists adopting the profession of intelligence. Until March 1940 Graham Greene wrote film reviews for Derek Verschoyle of the *Spectator*, and both subsequently joined SIS where other contributors such as Archie Lyall and Goronwy Rees were to find a niche. Their Fleet Street colleagues included Derek Tangye (*Daily Express*); Aubrey Jones (*The Times*); Valentine Williams (Reuters); Graham Mitchell (*Illustrated London News*); Malcolm Muggeridge (*Manchester Guardian*); Stephen Watts (*Sunday Express*); Dick Ellis (*Morning Post*); George Young (*Glasgow Herald*); David Walker (*Daily Mirror*); Basil Davidson (*Economist*); Dick Brooman-White; and even Kim Philby who left *The Times* for SOE and then SIS, and two decades later joined the *Observer*. Xan Fielding worked on the *Cyprus Times*, and both John Bingham and his MI5 colleague Norman Himsworth started their careers on provincial newspapers.

The link between what was Fleet Street and Britain's intelligence apparatus was the subject of intense speculation by the KGB, an organization that was never able to distinguish between journalism and espionage. In December 1968 *Izvestia* devoted two full pages to denouncing Lord Arran of the *Daily Mail*, Brian Crozier, formerly of the *Economist*, Lord Hartwell of the *Daily Telegraph*, Charles Curran of the BBC and David Astor of the *Observer* as having close connections with SIS, and even disclosed what purported to be the code numbers used to identify individual newspaper proprietors. While the Soviet accusations were slightly wide of the mark, there was and remains a proximity between the two professions. Anthony Cavendish, who joined UPI after his premature departure from SIS, confirms that 'at the end of the war a number of MI6 agents were sent abroad under the cover of newspaper men. Indeed, the Kemsley Press allowed many of their foreign correspondents to co-operate with MI6 and even took on MI6 operatives as foreign correspondents.'

Academics also practise much the same discipline in analysing information, even if they would claim to adopt more rigorous standards. Nevertheless, their function at university as well as in an intelligence agency is to acquire and disseminate knowledge. This also accounts for the high proportion of men like Freddie Ayer, Bob Carew-Hunt, Hugh Seton-Watson, Victor Rothschild, Herbert Hart and Reg Jones whose brainpower was harnessed.

One curiosity about Britain's secret establishment is how the characters that are to appear in these pages are interlinked. Some of these connections are as one might expect, such as the molehunters Peter Wright and Arthur Martin investigating the antecedents of suspected spies like Dick Ellis and Robert Zaehner. Similarly, J. C. Masterman's position at Oxford led him to teach several students, including Dick White and Bill Younger, who were both to become intelligence officers. The chain of coincidence can be fascinating. For example, the veteran SIS agent George Hill was in later life befriended by the author Dennis Wheatley, whose near neighbour in Queen's Gate was Tom Driberg, whose *Daily Express* colleague was Derek Tangye, who attended an intelligence course at Swanage with Alec Waugh, who wrote in his autobiography of having been influenced by Compton Mackenzie's notorious novel *Sinister Street*. After World War II Mackenzie tried to help the publication of Eddie Chapman's story, the wartime double agent whose wireless transmissions were supervised by Ronnie Reed, MI5's radio expert. His close colleague was the technician Russell Lee who was later appointed personal assistant to the Director-General and ghosted Sir Percy Sillitoe's memoirs.

These chains can produce some surprising results. Graham Greene's sister Liza assisted Malcolm Muggeridge's entry into SIS, soon after he had attended as an observer the Old Bailey trial at which Joan Miller played a key role for the prosecution. She had been recruited into MI5 by Maxwell Knight who also ran Harald Kurtz as an *agent provocateur*, and was responsible for the entrapment and imprisonment of Graham Greene's cousin Benjamin. One of Knight's books was illustrated by David Cornwell, who was to work alongside John Bingham when he joined MI5.

The coincidental and the improbable, both alien traits to the novelists' quest for verisimilitude, have their place in real life. As Winston Churchill observed on what he had learned of intelligence operations during the Great War, 'In the higher ranges of Secret Service work the actual facts in many cases were in every respect equal to the most fantastic inventions of romance and melodrama. Tangle within tangle, plot and counter-plot, ruse and treachery, cross and double-cross, true agent, false agent, double agent, gold and steel, the bomb, the dagger and the firing party were interwoven in many a texture so intricate as to be incredible yet true.'

Author's Note

Aficionados of intelligence literature may wonder about the criteria employed for the selection of titles for inclusion in this anthology. As well as containing works that have a relevance to the subject of espionage, written by intelligence professionals, and even a handful that boast only the indirect connection of having been written by an intelligence officer or agent, it omits a few well-known books. Their exclusion is deliberate because, despite the claims made by their publishers, and following exhaustive research, no evidence has been found to suggest that their authors had ever worked for either the Security Service or the Secret Intelligence Service. Similarly, accounts written by the agents and officers of Allied wartime intelligence services are omitted, even if a particular individual, such as the French agent Gilbert Renault (*The Silent Company*) or the head of the Czech Deuxième Bureau, General Frantisek Moravec (*Master of Spies*), worked very closely with British personnel.

Also excluded are the foreign-language books written by former British agents, an example being *Invisible Soldiers*, the memoirs as yet published only in Norwegian of Björn Rörholt DSO, who has documented the 147 wireless sets which operated for SIS in Norway during the war.

Two other categories are also excluded: those MI5 or SIS officers who were elected to the Commons like Dick Brooman-White, Henry Hunloke, Niall Macdermot, Cranley Onslow and others who have been reported only in *Hansard* or, like Paddy Ashdown, have only written minor political pamphlets that have not received wide circulation; and the intelligence personnel whose writing is limited to official reports that they wrote as servants of the Crown which have been released to the Public Record Office or, like the historic report on Imperial Defence written by Sir Eric Holt-Wilson in 1941, were declassified and made available in the US National Archives.

Future editions will be amended to include references to any titles that have been inadvertently overlooked or any untraced articles, like those known to have been contributed to various newspapers by SIS's old Middle East hand, John Teague, and the botanical sketchbooks of garden design written and illustrated by John Codrington.

Abbreviations

GRU	Soviet Military Intelligence Service
ISLD	Inter-Services Liaison Department
KGB	Soviet Intelligence Service
MI-1(c)	British Secret Intelligence Service
MI5	British Security Service
MI6	British Secret Intelligence Service
MI9	British Escape and Evasion Service (P15)
NID	Naval Intelligence Division
PIDE	Portuguese Security Service
P15	British Escape and Evasion Service (MI9)
SIS	British Secret Intelligence Service (MI6)
SOE	British Special Operations Executive

CHAPTER I

The First World War

*The day before we left C presented me with the swordstick he himself
had always carried on spying expeditions in time of peace. 'That's
when this business was really amusing,' he said. 'After the War is over
we'll do some amusing secret service work together. It's capital sport.'*
Compton Mackenzie, Greek Memories

The modern British Secret Intelligence Service, which started life in 1909
as the Secret Service Bureau, is an organization about which really very
little is known. Indeed, the fact that Britain even possessed a clandestine
overseas intelligence-gathering agency in peacetime was not officially
acknowledged by any government until May 1992, when Prime Minister
John Major addressed the new Parliament to open the debate on the
Queen's Speech and broke the long-standing convention that no admission regarding SIS could ever be made by any administration, whatever
the circumstances. This expedient had enabled ministers to neatly sidestep
awkward questions about a department of state that did not appear to
exist. The arrangement proved so convenient that it was maintained over
a period of eighty years, with the single concession that SIS had operated
during the Second World War as MI6, the unstated and misleading
implication being that it was a branch of the War Office's military
intelligence establishment. As for the First World War, no such admission
was made, although the Secret Service Bureau was to evolve into the
modern SIS and adopt temporarily the military intelligence designation of
MI-1(c).

Very little has emerged about the early days of SIS apart from the names
of some of the senior staff and the character of its first chief, Captain Sir
Mansfield Smith-Cumming. A retired naval officer whose career had been
handicapped by chronic seasickness, Smith-Cumming had a magnetic
personality, a love of flying, and a devotion to his only son Alexander who
was killed when their car hit a telegraph pole in France in October 1914.
In the same accident, which occurred at night near the front while he was

driving with dimmed lights on a tour of inspection, Alexander's father broke both legs and sustained such severe injuries that his left foot had to be amputated.

Edward Knoblock described Smith-Cumming as 'short, stocky, stout, dapper with a pair of piercing grey eyes under bushy eyebrows and a round shiny bald head'. Having acquired a substantial fortune from both his rich wives, he was a wealthy man and collected the rights to strange inventions which might have an application in the espionage field, such as powerful telescopes and signal lamps. He was also something of a voyeur and occasionally allowed an agent to look at an illustrated portfolio of *Le Nu en Salon* that included what he called 'tempting' reproductions of Bouguereau's 'Venus Arising from the Sea' – an opportunity to admire the 'female form divine'.

Smith-Cumming and his eccentrically sited headquarters, perched on the roof of Whitehall Court, were to prove a gift to writers who were later to describe their encounters with the mysterious but kindly old naval officer with his disconcerting habit of stabbing at his wooden leg with a paper knife. While William le Queux and E. Phillips Oppenheim made their fortunes inventing preposterous spy stories, the truth was actually much more bizarre than they could have imagined. Known to insiders simply by the initial C, which added to the mystique surrounding him and his unavowable organization, Smith-Cumming recognized that writers had many of the attributes of the intelligence officer, and he actively recruited a number into his fledgeling Secret Intelligence Service. Among them were the young novelist Willie Somerset Maugham, who was later to base *Ashenden* on his own experiences, and A. E. W. Mason, who was widely regarded as one of the best story-tellers of his generation. When Maugham's mission to Switzerland was concluded his duties were taken over by the American-born playwright Edward Knoblock, who later worked with Compton Mackenzie in Greece.

It is now clear that at least Maugham, Mason and Mackenzie used their own wartime adventures for their subsequent fiction, although the public could never be sure exactly how accurate their tales really were. Indeed, some were so bizarre that few could have dreamed that they were almost wholly authentic. However, there was a single example of an intelligence officer giving an authentic non-fictional account of his secret work. Seven years after the armistice Captain L. B. Weldon MC used his wartime diaries to write *Hard Lying*, a fascinating and unique insight into the management of British agents in the Eastern Mediterranean, and arguably the first authoritative disclosure of its kind. Serving alongside Weldon as an intelligence officer in the same British seaplane squadron was his fellow countryman, Erskine Childers, the Irish nationalist and author of the espionage classic, *The Riddle of the Sands*. As Weldon pointed out, it was typical of the British intelligence authorities that an expert on the North Sea should have been posted to the Mediterranean.

Following the First World War several SIS officers published their memoirs, but in only one case did the government decide to obtain an injunction to restrain distribution and prosecute the offender. That is not to say that the other disclosures were entirely welcome or even authorized. Henry Landau's revelations, made from the safety of the United States, accurately described SIS's wartime intelligence operations on the Western Front and identified some of his colleagues by name. (Sir) Compton Mackenzie's offence, which was to bring him to the Old Bailey, was to have written comprehensively about SIS's operations in the Mediterranean, where several of the people mentioned were still active a decade later.

Sir Compton Mackenzie

During the Second World War many more people discovered that those responsible for Secret Intelligence do, in very fact, as often as not behave like characters created by the Marx brothers. Duck Soup, for instance, appealed to me as a film of stark realism.

Water on the Brain

In October 1932 Compton Mackenzie attempted to publish the third volume of his war memoirs, entitled *Greek Memories*, in which he gave a detailed account of his work for SIS in the Aegean in 1917. Not only did Mackenzie reveal that Smith-Cumming was known within Whitehall by the initial C, but he identified dozens of officers with whom he had served during the war, including a few who remained active in the region after the conclusion of hostilities. Mackenzie's book – which had been preceded by *Extremes Meet*, in which he had described his experiences in fictional terms without encountering any difficulties – was instantly the subject of a ban and a short time later the author was charged with breaching the Official Secrets Act. What made the prosecution's case awkward was the fact that Mackenzie had received an informal consent to publish from Sir Eric Holt-Wilson, one of his former colleagues in the Near East who subsequently had been appointed Deputy Director-General of the Security Service. Holt-Wilson, whose name appeared in the text, sat in the well of the court during the proceedings and saw Mackenzie plead guilty and be fined £100.

Mackenzie was deeply resentful of his treatment and later wrote the hugely popular *Water on the Brain*, a wickedly entertaining satire on the Secret Service, to pay the costs of his defence. It was not until 1938 that a sanitized version of *Greek Memories* was published with SIS's permission. It was to be nearly fifty years before University Publications of America acquired a rare copy of the first, unexpurgated edition and released it with the offending passages highlighted in bold print. The first volume of Mackenzie's memoirs, *Gallipoli Memories*, was published without difficulty and the prequel to *Greek Memories*, *First Athenian Memories*, was released in March 1931. The third of ten, *Aegean Memories*, was published in 1940 and dedicated to a brother officer and lifelong friend, Edward Knoblock.

Mackenzie joined SIS in 1916, aged thirty-three, having been invalided out of the Royal Marines after being wounded in the Dardanelles offensive. He was by then, of course, already a successful author, having made his name with *Sinister Streets*. Born in West Hartlepool, and not Scotland as his name would suggest, he had read modern history at Magdalen College, Oxford, and had joined the 1st Hertfordshire regiment in 1900. Among his many later literary successes were *Extraordinary Women* and the comedy *Whisky Galore*, which was based upon the true story of the wreck of a freighter loaded with a cargo of whisky during World War II. After the war, which Mackenzie spent on the island of Barra, he helped one of his former subordinates, Wilfred Macartney, to publish the story of Eddie Chapman, the MI5 double agent codenamed Zigzag, but the enterprise failed. Macartney had been convicted of espionage on behalf of the Soviets in 1928, but this did not prevent Mackenzie from giving him support when he attempted to publicize Chapman's remarkable story.

Mackenzie was always willing to back unpopular causes – he was one of the few to back P. G. Wodehouse when the latter was in danger of being prosecuted for his unwise broadcasts for the Nazis. He married thrice and died in Edinburgh in November 1972, twenty years after he had received his knighthood, having published his tenth volume of autobiography.

Greek Memories

We had tangible evidence of Holt-Wilson's rescue work by the middle of the month when Wilfred Lafontaine, who was in private life a chartered accountant in Constantinople, arrived from Alexandria to act as our cipherer and accountant. He had a gentle and charming personality, and his presence was of immediate help to the smooth working of the Annexe offices, for I was able to put him in charge of all the departmental side and thus release Tucker from the strain of clerical work, which was beginning to tell even on his plump figure.

With the arrival of Lafontaine we were given leave to communicate directly in cases of urgency with other Mediterranean centres of Intelligence, and at the same time all political information was transferred from Matthews to myself. In connexion with this I have an amusing note from Matthews:

Dear Z:
The Minister thinks you ought to report on local matters with the
exception of Military Intelligence. Buck up therefore, and try and let
V have something really hair-raising.

Yours,
M

Matthews was much cheered up by no longer having to encode all our telegrams. This released poor Hasluck from his mushroom-like existence in the cellar of the Legation, and gave him more time to spend on making duplicates for the B branch of the EMSIB in Alexandria of the cards in what was by now an index of more than three thousand names, and increasing daily at a great pace.

One morning, at the end of the month, Tucker came into my room and announced: 'Miss Chapman and Miss Cook would like to speak to you.'

Even as I asked, 'Who the hell are Miss Chapman and Miss Cook?' Miss Chapman and Miss Cook entered close on Tucker's heels before I had time to remove my legs from the desk on which they were resting.

Miss Chapman, who was tall, with gold pince-nez and what at first seemed like the manner of a head-mistress, was inclined to be a little ruffled by my not knowing who she was or whence she came. During the many months that Miss Chapman remained with us the story of that first reception was gradually elaborated by her into a one-act farce. Actually I believe that on hearing she had been sent out to me from London as a confidential secretary I assured her warmly that the unexpectedness of her advent did not make her any the less welcome. I must have tried to display *some* politeness, for her manner grew less severe.

Miss Cook, who was the fastest and most accurate stenographer to whom I have yet dictated, had been in Cox's Bank. She was in every way the antithesis of Miss Chapman ... but let both their personalities gradually emerge as my memories prolong themselves. I made her services over to Tucker in the Passport Bureau, and for what she must have saved in the way of mistakes he owes an eternal debt. Before the whole organization was wound up in August, 1917, she was to have completed the necessary clerical work in connexion with over 60,000 passports without making a single mistake or involving me in a single letter or telegram of explanation through her fault.

As yet another addition to my clerical staff, Miss Hasluck was sent out from London.

It must have been in April, too, that Yanko Poseidon joined our service. For weeks he had been one of the stars in our card-index of suspects, and his record dated back to the first cards filled up at the British School last autumn. Indeed his was one of the rare crimson cards which in those days represented the deepest dye of guilt.

One day Zanardi came to me and said that if I would give Poseidon an interview he would be able to clear himself of any accusation that he had ever been working in the interests of the Central Powers. What he had done, which he was willing to admit, was to run more contraband of war into Turkey along the Asia Minor coast than any other smuggler. Zanardi assured me he was convinced of Poseidon's sincerity, and that if I would engage him on a monthly salary I should find him loyalty itself. In view of the fact that a meeting between myself and so notorious an alleged agent of the enemy might rouse a premature curiosity among some of our own agents who with very little success had been trying to check Poseidon's contraband activities, Zanardi suggested that the meeting should be held in some place out of Athens. I am under the impression that in the end the meeting was arranged in the garden of a hostelry near Marathon. Anyway, I remember clearly that it was in some pleasant rustic spot, and that we sat in an arbour, partaking of the refreshment which Poseidon himself had with his usual grand air of courtesy provided.

When Zanardi and I reached the place of assignation, I saw a small dark man with a round sleek head and a pair of long jet-black moustaches like the horns of a bull. He was dressed neatly in black, and he spoke English well, but slowly. Yet this slowness far from being tiresome was attractive, for it lent his speech a gentle meditative air, which was enhanced by the peculiar charm of his suave voice. On me he made an immediately favourable impression. His actions might be the actions of a smuggler and a contrabandist: his aspirations were the aspirations of an artist. Over *retzinato* wine and coffee we discussed past iniquities, and in the end, subject to a few more inquiries, I offered him work at a salary of five hundred drachmas a month.

Back in Athens I talked the matter over with Sells and Hill, and we decided that the experiment of employing him might well be justified. Contraband running was by no means easy nowadays. No doubt the king of smugglers had decided to abdicate while he could do so with dignity.

About a fortnight after Poseidon had entered my service Zanardi came to say that the new agent wished to speak to me on a matter which gravely affected his honour, if I would spare him a few minutes.

'My captain,' said Poseidon, when he entered, 'I have been told that Mr Hasluck still keeps the card of informations about me before I am coming into your much loved service. This has hurt me very much here,' he pointed to his heart. 'Because I am feeling that my honour has much damage from such a business. My captain, if you are content with my works for you, I beg you will give orders that the card of informations about me can be removed from Mr Hasluck and put into your safe, so that if ever I do bad works for you it must be put back.'

There was moisture in Poseidon's bright dark eyes as he spoke, and never had his voice trembled with such mellow emotion.

I went into the next room and asked Hasluck for the card.

'Up to tricks again, guv'nor?' Hasluck inquired, cocking his head on one side.

'No, no. The recording angel, while not yet prepared to obliterate Poseidon's list of evil deeds, has issued a decree nisi, and his card is to be put in my private safe. And make a note, will you, Hasluck, to notify all Intelligence branches which receive our Black List that Poseidon's name has been expunged.'

In due course every Intelligence branch was notified; but those who keep black lists during wars do not rejoice like Heaven over one sinner that repenteth. Could I get Poseidon's name expunged from any other list? I could not. A year after he had been in my service and after his salary of five hundred drachmas had been paid to him in his own name and entered every month in my accounts, Alexandria wrote:

> We have not heard much of Poseidon lately. What is this man doing now? We are revising our black list and should like all latest information.

Six months after he had been working for me I was receiving reports from Salonica of his nefarious activities miles away at the other end of the Ægean.

Finally, in the summer of 1917 an official black list of MI5 was sent to me from London, and there was Yanko Poseidon's name as a star turn. It seemed easier for a rich man to enter the Kingdom of Heaven than for a reformed suspect to escape from the malefactors' bloody register.

Henry Landau

When arrests occurred in our secret organizations, they came with lightning rapidity; in most cases, the Allied secret services had no idea what had happened.

Born in South Africa of Anglo-Dutch parentage, Henry Landau graduated from Cambridge shortly before the outbreak of the Great War. He volunteered for military service and was commissioned in the Royal Field Artillery but in 1916 he received a summons to Captain Smith-Cumming's headquarters in Whitehall Court. Fluent in German, Dutch and French, Landau was instructed to rebuild SIS's train-watching service in Belgium which monitored the enemy's troop movements right across the Western Front. The ring operated behind the German lines and was codenamed White Lady, which became part of the title of Landau's second book, *Secrets of the White Lady*, published in 1935.

After the war, following the success of his train-watching activities, Landau moved to America where he was out of reach of the British courts. No action was taken against *All's Fair* which was released in 1934 but the government apparently threatened to place a ban on the distribution of the sequel. In it he admitted that he had not attempted to disguise the names of Allied agents. 'My friends in Belgium and France assure me that if damage could be done by divulging them, it was done years ago when a complete list of agents' names was published in the various decoration lists.' His other books were *The Enemy Within* (1937) and *Spreading the Spy Net* (1938), both of which dealt in some detail with his experiences in SIS and can today be recognized as the first in a genre. SIS's embarrassment at the publication of *Secrets of the White Lady* was enhanced considerably by the author's assurance that the documents quoted in the text 'have been taken from secret service records which have hitherto been unavailable for publication'.

Secrets of the White Lady

On a hillside which dominates the city of Liège, lies the suburb of Thier-à-Liège. Here in one of those small brick houses with low, violet-tinted, slate roof, and diminutive garden, so typical of the area, Dieudonné Lambrecht was born, May 4, 1882, and grew to manhood, watched over by his parents, devout Catholics. In addition to giving him the best education their meagre purse could afford, they instilled the Christian qualities of that peaceful community.

For a few years he worked in one of the Belgian administrations, but his ardent nature revolted against the narrow, hide-bound, official routine of a government office. With his brother-in-law, he established an engineering workshop, which soon grew into a small factory, producing high grade precision machinery. Happily married, blessed with a small baby girl of four months, a permanent income assured, a keen participator in all church activities, Lambrecht's life was fixed. The vista of a peaceful existence stretched before him.

All this was suddenly changed by the War. Into the turmoil of that conflict went all that he had built up.

He resolved to consecrate his intelligence, his fortune, his influence, his life itself if necessary, to the task of freeing his country's soil from the German invader. Naturally, his first thought was to join the Belgian Army.

But, as happened to so many Belgian refugees, as soon as they reached Dutch soil, he was approached by one of the Allied secret service agents who swarmed in Holland at that time. It was into the hands of Afchain, a Belgian in the employ of Major Cameron, chief of an intelligence service connected with British General Headquarters, that Lambrecht fell.

Now a man of thirty-two, his sensitive mind keenly alert, Lambrecht listened attentively to Afchain, weighing how best he could serve his country. It needed little persuasion to get him to return to Belgium for the purpose of organizing an espionage service.

In the Catholic circles of Liège, Lambrecht found support. Two Jesuit priests, Father Dupont, and Father Des Onays, and his brother-in-law, Oscar Donnay, helped him recruit a number of former railway employees. With this band of faithful followers, train-watching posts were soon established at Liège, Namur, and Jemelle, from which all troop movements by rail through these important centres could be observed.

The most dangerous work Lambrecht reserved for himself. In spite of rigid surveillance by the Secret Police, he travelled around the country enrolling new agents and identifying German divisions in the various rest areas. As far afield as Belgian Flanders he went spying and recruiting; he even penetrated into the Grand Duchy of Luxemburg. On one occasion, at Jemelle, a heavy westward movement of German troops was in progress for several days from the Eastern Front. Realizing that concentration for an offensive was probably under way, Lambrecht, without hesitation, jumped on the buffer of a passing troop train, and accompanied it through the night, until he had definitely established its destination. The very boldness of his act outwitted the German Secret Police – a troop train was the last place to look for a spy, as Lambrecht cleverly realized.

In addition to this hazardous work, he often acted as his own courier, the most dangerous rôle in war-time spying. Slipping past the frontier guards at night, and avoiding the revealing rays of the searchlights, he carried the precious reports, written with a mapping pen on fine tissue paper, and sewed into the interior of the cloth buttons on his clothes, through to Holland. A friend manufactured these buttons in Liège, and it was an easy task to substitute the filling. Good as the concealment was, however, it only protected him in case of a casual search in Belgium itself. Caught at the frontier, his fate would have been sealed – the knives of the German Secret Police would soon have laid bare the compromising contents of those ingenious buttons.

For eighteen months Lambrecht and his faithful assistants kept watch. Night and day, every train passing through the railway centres of Liège, Namur, and Jemelle, every troop movement through Belgium between the Eastern and Western Fronts, was reported to British General Headquarters. These reports definitely announced coming offensives, and were far more valuable than any information obtained from stolen or captured documents. The documents might be false, or the Germans might have changed their plans after the dispatches or orders had been written, but the troop movements were established facts which could not be altered.

To Lambrecht also belongs the credit that he helped to devise these means of controlling troop movements. Train-watching posts had never been used in any previous war, and it was the initial reports of such pioneers as Lambrecht which enabled Intelligence Officers at British General Headquarters to work out from the number of constituted units passing by a given train-watching post, their accurate system of gauging the exact volume of a troop movement.

The mass of information transmitted by Lambrecht to British General Headquarters is astonishing.

In May, 1915, for example, his train-watching posts at Jemelle and Namur rapidly and accurately reported the transfer of several German divisions from the Serbian Front to Flanders. This was of vast importance because it was an indication that all the German divisions on the Serbian Front were being transferred to France. In August 1915, his posts caught a heavy movement of troops from the Eastern Front to Champagne. This concentration of troops was intended to parry the offensive which the Germans knew the French were preparing in this sector. As a result of this information, the French advanced the date of their offensive several days.

Lambrecht also accurately reported the German preparations for their attack on Verdun. Much of the information he obtained through the indiscretions of a German major, billeted in his sister's home. But not satisfied with this, he sent agents into occupied France to determine the destination of the troops which were pouring past his train-watching posts in a westerly direction.

The following letter from Afchain, Major Cameron's representative in Holland, dated January 26th, 1916, speaks eloquently for the valuable services rendered by Lambrecht and of the high hopes entertained of him:

> I have just received a telegram of congratulations from our Chief at British General Headquarters. The 26th Division, which you reported passing through Jemelle, on December 15th, coming from the Eastern Front, has been contacted in the front line.
>
> Do your best to establish train-watching posts in the Grand Duchy of Luxemburg, and in occupied France. I know how difficult this will be; but the merit will be all the greater, if you are successful. Knowing your great tenacity, I am sure if any one can succeed, you will.

Events now began to move quickly.

Eighteen months of experience had taught the German Counter-Espionage Service all the tricks used by refugees, and by the Allied secret services, and efficient means had been devised to seal the Belgian-Dutch frontier. In the interior, every Belgian, man and woman, was forced to carry an identity card, with photograph, name and address attached; and special permission had to be obtained to travel from one town to another. At the frontier, a high-voltage electric wire, a cordon of sentries every hundred yards, mounted patrols, police dogs, and, finally, an army of plainclothes secret police, guarded its entire length.

The Belgian refugees in Holland who had dabbled in secret service could well shut up shop. And it was good riddance – they had exploited the patriotism of their countrymen in the interior, and they had sold their information to the highest bidder among the Allied secret services, sometimes to several of them at the same time. The results cost the life of many a brave man or woman in the occupied territories.

But the secret service game had become a problem even to the official services. After months of fruitless effort many of their representatives were recalled from Holland, to leave the field clear for the few who still seemed to have the chance of success. There was a period in 1916 when no information of any kind was coming out of the occupied territory. The Allied secret services had lost their initiative. New methods had to be devised to penetrate the formidable barrier which the Germans had built up at the Belgian-Dutch border.

It was not surprising, then, that Lambrecht found himself suddenly cut off from all communication with Holland. His precious information piled up only to become valueless as the days dragged by. Frantically, he waited for a courier from Holland to pick up his reports at the 'letter-box', which he had established in Liège.

In Holland, Afchain was working feverishly to find some means of reaching Liège. He could no longer pick a trusted courier from a dozen volunteers. He would be fortunate if he could find anyone at all to undertake the dangerous mission. His chief at British General Headquarters wired him impatiently. He took a risk. Whether he handed a letter for Lambrecht to an intermediary, who was duped, or whether he himself was tricked, is not known exactly. The letter, however, fell into the hands of Keurvers, a Dutchman in the employ of the German Counter-Espionage Service.

Lambrecht's 'letter-box' in Liège was a small cigar store owned by one of his relatives, a man called Leclercq. While Leclercq was out Keurvers called at the store and introduced himself to Madame Leclercq as a Dutchman who had just arrived from Holland with an urgent letter for her husband. Madame Leclercq, fully aware of her husband's dangerous activities, was suspicious. This man with his red, bloated face, and small vicious eyes, repulsed her; besides, his accent seemed more German than Dutch. She refused to accept the letter. But Keurvers, not to be put off, countered with the password: 'The seven boxes of tricolour cigars have arrived safely.' Madame Leclercq was nonplussed: she recognized the words, but still she could not bring herself to trust the man. After some hesitation she replied that her husband had told her nothing about the cigars, and that they were not expecting any letters from Holland.

As soon as Keurvers was out of sight, she hastened to Lambrecht with the news. To her surprise, instead of praising her discretion, he scolded her for being overcautious. 'He gave the right password, didn't he? What more did you want?' Thoroughly dismayed, she hurried back to the store, where she found Keurvers had returned in her absence and left the letter with her servant together with a message that he would be back the next morning at ten o'clock. The message and the letter were quickly conveyed to Lambrecht.

Lambrecht eagerly opened the small roll containing the letter, and found that it was in Afchain's familiar handwriting. It was dated February 24th, 1916, and contained the following message:

> I confirm the long list of merchandise orders delivered to you, January 28th, care of our friend Dupont (Leclercq's service name), but regret having received no reply.

Our delivery man, who brought you the above orders, being unable to continue with his duties, I am using the present carrier, who will contact you once a week. I believe he is the only one who can do this at the present moment. I hope you will be able to pull us out of our present critical situation by giving him a report, as complete as possible, of all the merchandise in your store. It is absolutely necessary to make use of the present opportunity, as none of our competitors are in a position to deliver.

If Madame Leclercq had sowed any doubts in his mind, they were quickly dispelled by Afchain's letter, which was undoubtedly genuine. Lambrecht was ready to welcome Keurvers with open arms, so relieved was he that regular communications with Holland had once more been established. His thoughts immediately turned to the accumulation of six weeks' reports, which he had in his possession. He knew they would be too bulky as they were, and so the night was spent making a résumé of all but the most recent ones.

At ten o'clock next morning, Lambrecht was at the Leclercq cigar store, in the rue de Campine. As he entered, he saw a man in conversation with Leclercq. It was Keurvers. Leclercq immediately called Lambrecht aside into the small parlour at the back of the store. He, too, shared his wife's suspicions of this man. But Lambrecht could not be persuaded: there was Afchain's letter, and the man had given the right password. So Keurvers was called into the back room, and the reports were handed over to him.

On his way home Lambrecht noticed that he was being followed. Such was his trust in Keurvers and his solicitude for his men that his immediate thoughts were not for his own safety, but for that of the courier, and the precious reports in his possession. By jumping on to a passing street car, he managed to get rid of the man who had been following him.

Lambrecht knew that he had a chance of finding Keurvers in one of the cafés on the Grand' Place, for most visitors in the city gravitated to this centre. As he looked through the large windows of the Café du Marronnier, he saw Keurvers sitting with Landwerlen and Douhard, two of the German Secret Police, whom Lambrecht knew only too well by sight; they had figured in nearly every spy arrest in the city.

Instantly Lambrecht knew he was trapped, that the Secret Police were following him to discover his associates. He had a chance to get away. He had shaken off the man who had been on his trail. He had a number of friends who would gladly have hidden him until an opportunity presented itself to get across the frontier. But Lambrecht decided to return home to advise his wife, and to get her to warn Leclercq. He thought he could get there before the police.

It was a fatal step. As Lambrecht walked in at the front door, the Secret Police were waiting for him on the inside – his wife had been arrested shortly after he had left for his rendezvous with Keurvers. It was known afterwards that the Secret Police had been watching the Leclercq cigar store for several days before Keurvers presented himself there, that they had photographed Afchain's note, and, of course, had understood its meaning. As usual, their object had been to track down associates, and above all to secure the reports – the evidence to convict.

Lambrecht knew he could not save himself. He could, however, save the thirty-odd agents who had been working for him. (The Leclercqs did not know their names.) His one care now was not to betray them. Every third-degree method familiar to the Germans was employed to break down his resistance, but Lambrecht allowed no name to escape him. He even succeeded in proving to the Secret Police that his wife had no idea he was engaged in espionage activities, and that the Leclercqs did not know the purport of his correspondence with Holland.

His friends did everything within their power to save him. Brand Whitlock, the Marquis de Villalobar, and van Vollenhoven, the various neutral ministers to Belgium, were all persuaded to intercede with von Bissing, the German Governor-General of Belgium. Even the German chaplain of the prison was so moved by the heroic attitude of Lambrecht that he wrote to the German Cardinal von Hartmann, at Cologne, asking him to intervene.

All these efforts were in vain. Lambrecht was condemned to death.

Lambrecht faced his death with sublime resignation. The following letter, written to his wife on the eve of his execution, reveals his nobility:

> April 17th, 1916,
> The citadel of the Chartreuse.
>
> My well beloved Jeanne:
> I have just been transferred here from the prison of St Léonard. As I suspected, it was to inform me that the sentence of death, which was passed on the 12th, has been confirmed, and that the various petitions for mercy have been refused.
> God calls me to Him – Let His will be done. We can only but incline ourselves before His supreme wisdom.
> Oh! my well beloved, what a terrible blow to you, who had such

high hopes! Poor wife! Poor parents! My soul is filled with intense sadness thinking of you all.

He who dies is quickly rid of his pain. But for you others, how much suffering! Let my resignation be a comfort to you. May God give you the courage, which He has never ceased to grant me, so that your suffering may be less.

In heaven, I will watch over you, and will pray to God, to reserve for you those happy days which I myself had hoped to provide you. God has not permitted me to do this – let us incline ourselves before His wishes. If He causes us to suffer now, it is but to reward us better later on, when we are near Him.

Think of my life as having been given up for my country – it will make my death seem less painful to you. After my faith, my country is what I hold most dear; in sacrificing my life for it, I am only doing what so many have done before me, and will do again.

Life passes so quickly here below – it lasts but a moment. We will meet in a better world. It is in moments such as these, through which I have just passed, that one appreciates the inestimable good that parents do their children in giving them a Christian education, and faith in God.

Console my poor parents for whom the blow is going to be terrible. Draw from your love for me, the necessary force to show them an example of courage.

Take refuge in prayer, my beloved. I will leave you, as a last souvenir of me, the cross you sent me, and I will place on it kisses for you, Riette, and my parents. I will join to it my wedding ring.

Jeanne, in heaven we will meet again. For our darling little daughter, for my parents, and for you, receive on this letter, the last affectionate kisses of he, who was

Your Donné

Lambrecht was shot April 18th, 1916.

After the Armistice, Lambrecht was posthumously decorated with the OBE by the British, and was mentioned in dispatches by Field Marshal Sir Douglas Haig. King Albert bestowed on him the Chevalier of the Order of Leopold, with *lisérés d'or*; he was also mentioned in the order of the day of the nation, and was accorded the Civic Cross, first class.

Valuable as his work had been during the eighteen months he had faithfully served the Allies, it was in death that he exerted his greatest force. His example was an inspiration to others to carry on his work; his friends swore to avenge him, and out of the scattered remnants of his espionage service emerged 'The White Lady', the greatest spy organization of the War.

L. B. Weldon

We were on the whole extraordinarily lucky with our agents. I don't think more than seven were actually captured. Six of these were hanged and one had his head cut off.

When the Great War broke out Weldon was working for the survey department of the Egyptian government and he was quickly transferred to the intelligence branch of the General Staff as a map officer with responsibility for the preparation and distribution of accurate maps to British forces in the Middle East. His direct superior was Colonel Gilbert Clayton, the regional chief of MI-1(c), the military cover title of the Secret Intelligence Service. Gradually Weldon's post changed into one of liaison and in January 1915 he was appointed intelligence officer aboard the *Aenne Rickmers*, a confiscated German cargo boat that had been converted into a spyship equipped with a pair of French Nieuport seaplanes. Weldon's assignment, which was to last two years, consisted of cruising off the Syrian coast and launching reconnaissance flights inland over the Turkish lines to report on troop movements. In addition the *Aenne Rickmers* carried British agents from Port Said and dropped them ashore on short-term missions to infiltrate enemy positions.

Initially Weldon started his mission under the auspices of the Egyptian Ports & Lights Administration, acting for the GOC Egypt, which would have left him vulnerable as a civilian if he was captured by the Turks. The solution was to transform the *Aenne Rickmers* into a Royal Fleet Auxiliary and to give Weldon a commission in the Royal Naval Reserve. He operated in the eastern Mediterranean and in January 1917 he joined the *Managem*, a smaller, less conspicuous steam yacht which routinely infiltrated agents, and carrier pigeons, into enemy territory.

Weldon's memoirs, published in 1925, were entitled *Hard Lying*, after the special allowance paid to naval personnel serving on destroyers and torpedo boats. After the war Weldon became Surveyor-General of Egypt and retired to England where he relied upon his diaries to recall his service with MI-1(c). In this extract Weldon recalls some of the operations he supervised off Athlit in October 1917.

Hard Lying: Eastern Mediterranean 1914–1919

At this time of the war, while I was carrying out an espionage on the Syrian coast, Lieut. Salter, who was attached to our Intelligence office in Cyprus, was carrying out similar work on the Asia Minor coast. As we only had the one ship, he used to do his landing from French trawlers. All the French battleships and large cruisers comprising the blockading squadron of the Syrian coast had, since the submarining of the *Amiral Charnier*, been replaced by destroyers and trawlers. These latter were commanded by junior French naval lieutenants, and very decent fellows they were – most willing and obliging. While we were lying in Famagusta, one of these French trawlers came in with Lieut. Salter, who had just landed an agent successfully at Mersina. This agent was to get in touch with a 'friendly' (at a price) person at Adana, who, once a month, would send a report down to the coast, to an agreed spot, where we could land and collect it. It was extremely important to have an agent watching the railway before it reached Aleppo, as we were thus able to calculate, by referring to our reports of movement on the Syrian-Palestine line, how many troops had been sent down towards Ras el Ain to reinforce the enemy in Mesopotamia.

The French boat *Laborieux*, with Captain Picard on board, now came in. This officer was in charge of the French intelligence. He was a good fellow, and we were great friends.

On the 28th May, while we were still weather-bound in Cyprus, a German aeroplane flew over the harbour at a height of about five thousand feet and proceeded towards Larnaca. It had come, presumably, to observe if any military camps, etc., were being formed in the island. This was the first appearance of an enemy's aeroplane over the island, and it was up to us to find out whence it came. This we did later, receiving from our agents the information that an aerodrome had been erected at Selefke, on the Asia Minor coast, just north of Cyprus.

On the 29th we sailed for Port Said, hugging the Syrian coast and picking up signals at Athlit, which informed us that 'all was well' with our friends ashore there. On the morning of the 31st, when about twenty-five miles off Port Said, we sighted a large steamer which appeared to be slowly sinking. We closed with her and found she was the BI boat *Ozarda*, which had just been submarined. Her crew were in the boats alongside, and as she had two or three small steamers from Port Said to assist her, we steamed on into harbour. Eventually the *Ozarda* was towed in and grounded.

As we were going to be in Port Said for a few days, I took the train to Alexandria and visited various departments at the harbour in search of a suitable boat for surf work. But there was nothing doing, so I returned to Port Said and sailed in the *Managem* on 13th June.

This trip I took with me some carrier pigeons to try, and when off Abu Zebora, we let them go. They all reached Port Said safely. On the night of the 15th we ran in towards Athlit. I went away in one boat with the agents, and another filled with stores (which consisted of bombs, rifles and ammunition) followed. I instructed the boat with stores to anchor about three hundred yards off the beach, and then went ashore with 'Sarah' and Yussef (our agents). They walked up to the house to bring down help to unload and conceal the stores, while I remained on shore. After about an hour and a half they returned, and I then pulled off to the stores boat, brought all the stuff on shore, and handed it over to them. Luckily there was not much surf. Having received all the reports for the last three weeks I returned to the ship. In connection with this landing I might mention that it was the only time I ever took a British bluejacket with me, and even then I only left him in the stores boat and never asked him to land. Yet, when we came to censor the man's letters, we found that he had written a marvellous account of the night. According to him, both he and I had landed under heavy rifle fire, concealed ourselves behind rocks, returned enemy's fire, driven off enemy, and then swam out to the boats, having to sink our rifles on the way, and had been hauled on board in an exhausted condition. We had – according to him – slain several Turks. He appeared to be very bloodthirsty; but this was accounted for, perhaps, by the fact that before the war he had been a ship's butcher!

From Athlit we ran to Famagusta, where I spent the day coding and cabling to GHQ the reports I had brought off – or, at any rate, the most interesting items of them concerning movements of troops, etc. Next day (18th June), having shipped another 'agent' ('agent' sounded nicer than 'spy'), we sailed for Es-Surr (Tyre). The sea began to get up, and the Captain thought it would be impossible for me to make a night landing, and that we ought to return to Famagusta. But we consulted Sasseen – my best boatman – and he advised going on, as we would be sheltered by the reef when landing. So go on we did; and although there was still a heavy sea running when we got there at 10.30 p.m., we lowered our boat, and I pushed off for the town with the four Syrians pulling. We took a ladder with us and, on getting into the little harbour, put it in the water – leaving the boat lying about 150 yards off the shore – and three of us swam to the land. Then we crawled with our ladder to a house in which lived one of

Sasseen's friends. Here we put up our ladder, which Sasseen climbed and tapped at the window until it was opened. He was recognized at once, and we found no difficulty in getting into touch with the people of the house. They were quite willing to get us the information we wanted, and I told them when to look out for us again. One of the girls of the house very pluckily went out into the town and brought back one of Sasseen's sisters, who naturally was delighted to see him. We found out from her that the old 'Agooz' was still alive and well, and I gave her instructions for him which included arrangements to get him away. Then, having finished everything to my satisfaction, we took down the ladder, swam back to our boat, and eventually reached the *Managem* without having been seen by the enemy. We had been right inside a town held by the Turks and had stayed there for some time. However pleasant such a stunt may be to read about in a book of adventure, it is not the kind of thing actually to do for a holiday amusement.

We now sailed for Port Said and called at Athlit *en route* to pick up reports. I went in as usual in the boat with an agent, but when we reached the edge of the surf we found that the broken water was too rough for the boat to get through it; so one of my boatmen volunteered to swim ashore and take the agent with him. This he did, and both men reached the beach in safety, returning after about a couple of hours. Just as the agent was alongside he suddenly started to shriek at the top of his voice that he was drowning. There was nothing for it but to reach out and hold his head under water, so that he could not be heard on land. When he had quieted down a bit I hauled him on board – but not before. It took him some time to recover, and we were back on the *Managem* before he could tell me that the report had not yet arrived, and that our friends had asked that we should return a couple of nights later.

To fill in the time we ran to Famagusta and returned to Athlit on the 26th June. I landed with two men and walked to the rendezvous, but no one was there. We waited for some time and then decided to return to the boat. But on the way back we were given a good scare. Suddenly shots were fired at us, and the bullets whistled uncomfortably close to our heads. It was one of the many moments when I felt a cold distaste for all warfare – and especially for agent-running. But our attackers did not show themselves, and we got safely away. Yet I felt very friendly towards Port Said harbour when we arrived there a day later. I had had enough excitement to last me for some little time.

There is one thing of interest I think I should mention in connection with cruising in the *Managem*. Once, when returning to Port Said and when half-way between Cyprus and that port, we sighted a curious looking object one afternoon at a great height up in the sky. It was not an aeroplane. Suddenly it dawned on us what it was; nothing more or less than a 'Zeppelin'! We reported what we had seen on our arrival and heard no more about it. I don't think our report was believed at the time. As a matter of fact, this was the Zeppelin that made the famous flight from Bukarest to German East Africa and back via the Libyan Desert, Khartum and Sudan. In my opinion, one of the most wonderful achievements of the war.

A. E. W. Mason

Slingsby was an intelligence officer as well as an officer of intelligence.

Aged fifty when war broke out, and having lost his Coventry constituency in 1910, Mason wasted no time in volunteering for military service, and he joined up with the Manchester Regiment. However, after training at Aldershot and Morecombe, he was invited to an interview in London which he described with a degree of circumspection in the novel *The Summons* when Martin Hillyard is taken to a dingy house in a back street near Charing Cross to meet Commander Graham, the head of the Secret Service whose office is at the top of 'many little flights of stairs'.

Following his recruitment Mason, who had been educated at Dulwich College and Trinity College, Oxford, transferred to the Royal Marine Light Infantry and thence undertook his first secret mission, to Spain. Unlike the conventional intelligence officer, posted under some semi-transparent diplomatic cover to an embassy abroad, Mason adopted the lifestyle of a wealthy expatriate, cruising the Mediterranean in an impressive motor yacht. Exactly what occurred during this period, when he sailed between Spain, Morocco, Gibraltar and the Balearics, is obscure but there are some clues to be found in two of his subsequent publications. In *The Four Corners of the World*, which has a definitely autobiographical flavour, Anthony Strange consulted Major Slingsby of the British Secret Service about neutral ships that were loading large quantities of a cargo that purported to be bicarbonate of soda. Working together, Slingsby and Strange established that the suspect barrels contained fuel for enemy U-boats and a trap was laid for a submarine attending an illicit rendezvous in a secluded bay in supposedly neutral waters. Strange had fitted his yacht with a gun disguised as a capstan and when the German vessel approached to refuel, it was sunk by Strange's accurate shelling. This tale bore a strong resemblance to an incident in Cartagena where Mason had photographed a U-boat refuelling and had circulated the pictures as postcards, much to the embarrassment of the Spanish authorities.

In another episode recounted in *The Four Corners of the World*, Mason told the story of a German saboteur whom he had first met in Lisbon. At a second meeting, in Alicante, 'Peiffer' offered to defect and sought permission to enter Gibraltar. Peiffer was later arrested as he tried to leave the Rock and was interned, the suspicions of Slingsby and Strange having been justified. The German was indeed a dangerous spy, trained in Hamburg, and had planned with a Spanish accomplice to mount a surprise aerial attack on the undefended part of Gibraltar under cover of an air race.

In October 1916 Mason returned to London via Paris, where he was a witness at the execution of Mata Hari. His second assignment took him back to the Mediterranean on Lord Abinger's yacht, the *St George*, together with a group of guests who included Professor W. E. Dixon, the noted pharmacologist upon whom the character of Bendish is based in *The Summons*. Bendish was described, accurately, as an expert on the detection of secret ink and the opening of suspect mail without leaving a trace.

In January 1917 Mason was recalled to London where he received a promotion to the rank of major, but succumbed to bronchitis. The remainder of his military service was spent in convalescence and the preparation of *The Four Corners of the World*.

After the war Mason continued to write his series of highly successful detective mysteries featuring Inspector Hanaud. He never married and was believed to have declined the offer of a knighthood. He died in London in November 1948. In this episode Major Slingsby enrols Strange and his yacht, the *Boulotte*, into the Royal Naval Volunteer Reserve in the hope of ambushing a U-boat.

The Four Corners of the World

'Hallo,' said Slingsby. He looked into a letter-tray on the edge of his desk and took a long envelope from it and handed it to Strange. 'You might have a look at this. I'll come on board tomorrow morning. Meanwhile, if I were you I should go to bed, though I doubt if you'll get much sleep.'

The reason for that doubt became more and more apparent as the evening wore on. In the first place, when Strange returned, he found workmen with drills and hammers and rivets spoiling the white foredeck of his adored *Boulotte*. For a moment he was inclined, like Captain Hatteras when his crew cut down his bulwarks for firewood, to stand aside and weep, but he went forward, and when he saw the work which was going on his heart exulted. Then he went back to the saloon, but as he stretched himself out upon the cushions he remembered the envelope in his pocket. It was stamped 'On His Majesty's Service', and it contained the announcement that one Anthony Strange had been granted a commission as sub-lieutenant in the Royal Naval Volunteer Reserve. After that sleep was altogether out of the question. There was the paper to be re-read at regular intervals lest its meaning should have been misunderstood. And when its meaning was at last firmly and joyfully fixed in Strange's mind there was the paper itself to be guarded and continually felt, lest it should lose itself, be stolen, or evaporate into air. Towards midnight, indeed, he did begin to doze off, but then a lighter came alongside and dumped ten tons of Welsh steam coal on board, all that he could hold, it's true, but that gave him ten days' steaming at ordinary draught. And at eight o'clock to the minute Slingsby hailed him from the quay.

'You will go back now to your old harbour,' he said. 'You have been a little cruise down the coast, that's all. Just look out for a sailing schooner called the *Santa Maria del Pilar*. She ought to turn up in seven days from now to take on board a good many barrels of carbonate of soda. I'll come by train at the same time. If she arrives before and takes her cargo on board, you can wire to me through the Consul and then – act on your own discretion.'

Strange drew a long breath, and his eyes shone.

'But she won't, I think,' said Slingsby. 'By the way, you were at Rugby with Russell of my regiment, weren't you?'

'Yes.'

'And you know Cowper, who was admiral out here?'

'Yes, he's my uncle.'

'Exactly.'

Strange smiled. It was clear that a good many inquiries must have been made about him over the telegraph wires during the last week.

'Well, that's all, I think,' said Slingsby. 'You'll push off as soon as you can, and good luck.'

But there was one further ceremony before the *Boulotte* was ready for sea. The small crew was signed on under the Naval Discipline Act. Then she put out, rounded the point, and headed for her destination over a smooth, sunlit sea, with, by the way, an extra hand on board and a fine new capstan on her foredeck. Two days later she was moored in her old position, and Strange went to bed. The excitement was over, a black depression bore him down; he was deadly tired, and his back hurt him exceedingly. What was he doing at all with work of this kind? If he had to 'act on his own discretion', could he do it with any sort of profit? Such questions plagued him for two days more, whilst he lay and suffered. But then relief came. He slept soundly and without pain, and rose the next morning in a terror lest the *Santa Maria del Pilar* should have come and gone. He went up on to the deck and searched the harbour with his glasses. There was but one sailing boat taking in cargo, and she a brigantine named the *Richard*, with the Norwegian flag painted on her sides. Strange hurried to the Consul, and returned with a mind at ease. The *Santa Maria del Pilar* had not yet sailed in between the moles. Nor did she come until the next afternoon, by which time Slingsby was on board the *Boulotte*.

'There she is,' said Strange in a whisper of excitement, looking seawards. She sailed in with the sunset and a fair wind, a white schooner like a great golden bird of the sea, and she was nursed by a tug into a berth on the opposite side of the harbour. Slingsby and Strange dined at the Café de Rome and came on board again at nine. The great globes of electric light on their high pillars about the quays shone down upon the still, black water of the harbour. It was very quiet. From the cockpit of the *Boulotte* the two men looked across to the schooner.

'I think there's a lighter alongside of her, isn't there?' said Slingsby.

Strange, whose eyesight was remarkable, answered:

'Yes, a lighter loaded with barrels.'

'Some carbonate of soda,' said Slingsby, with a grin. They went into the cockpit, leaving the door open.

It was a hot night, and in a café beyond the trees a band was playing the compelling music of *Louise*. Strange listened to it, deeply stirred. Life had so changed for him that he had risen from the depths during the last weeks. Then Slingsby raised his hand.

'Listen!'

With the distant music there mingled now the creaking of a winch. Strange extinguished the light, and both men crept out from the cockpit. The sound came from the *Santa Maria del Pilar*, and they could see the spar of her hoisting tackle swing out over the lighter and inboard over the ship's deck.

'She's loading,' said Strange, in a low voice.

'Yes,' answered Slingsby; 'she's loading.' And his voice purred like a contented cat.

He slept on a bed made up in the saloon that night, Strange in his tiny cabin, and at nine o'clock the next morning, as they sat at breakfast, they saw the *Santa Maria del Pilar* make for the sea.

'We ought to follow, oughtn't we?' said Strange anxiously.

'There's no hurry.'

'But she'll do nine knots in this breeze.' Strange watched her with the eye of knowledge as she leaned over ever so slightly from the wind. 'She might give us the slip.'

Slingsby went on eating unconcernedly.

43

'She will,' he answered. 'We are not after her, my friend. Got your chart?'

Strange fetched it from the locker and spread it out on the table.

'Do you see a small island with a lighthouse?'

'Yes.'

'Four miles west-south-west of the lighthouse. Got it?'

'Yes.'

'How long will it take you to get to that point?'

Strange measured his course.

'Five to five and a half hours forced draught.'

'Good. Suppose we start at six this evening.'

The *Boulotte* went away to the minute. At eight it began to grow dark, but no steaming light was hoisted on the mast, and no side-lamps betrayed her presence. In the failing light she became one with the sea but for the tiniest wisp of smoke from her chimney, and soon the night hid that. A lantern flashed for a while here and there on the forward deck in the centre of a little group, and then Slingsby came back to Strange at the wheel.

'It's all right,' he whispered softly.

Nights at sea! The cool, dark tent of stars, the hiss and tinkle of waves against the boat's side, the dinghy, slung out upon the davits, progressing above the surface of the water, the lamp light from the compass striking up on the brasswork of the wheel and the face of the steersman; to nights at sea Strange owed all the spacious moments of his crippled life. But this night was a sacred thing. He was admitted to the band of the young strong men who serve, like a novice into the communion of a church; and his heart sang within his breast as he kept the *Boulotte* to her course. At a quarter past eleven he rang the telegraph and put the indicator to 'slow'. Five minutes later he stopped the engine altogether. Four miles away to the north-eastward a light brightened and faded.

'We are there,' he said, and he looked out over an empty sea.

Under Slingsby's orders he steamed slowly round in a circle, ever increasing the circumference, for an hour, and then the new hand – who, by the way, was a master gunner – crept aft.

'There it is, sir.'

A hundred yards from the port bow a dark mass floated on the sea. The *Boulotte* slid gently alongside of it. It was a raft made of barrels lashed together.

'We have seen those barrels before, my friend,' said Slingsby, his nose wrinkling up in a grin of delight. Before daybreak the work was done.

Fifty empty barrels floated loose; there was a layer of heavy oil over the sea and a rank smell in the air.

'Now,' said Slingsby, in a whisper, 'shall we have any luck, I wonder?'

He went forward. The capstan head had been removed, and in its place sat a neat little automatic gun, which could fling two hundred and seventy three-pound shells six thousand yards in a minute. For the rest of that night the *Boulotte* lay motionless without a light showing or a word spoken. And just as the morning came, in the very first unearthly grey of it, a wave broke – a long, placid roller which had no right to break in that smooth, deep sea. Slingsby dipped his hand into the cartridge box and made sure that the band ran free; the gunner stood with one hand on the elevating wheel, the other on the trigger; eight hundred yards away from the *Boulotte* there was suddenly a wild commotion of the water, and black against the misty grey a conning tower and a long, low body of steel rose into view. U-whatever-its-number was taken by surprise. The whole affair lasted a few seconds. With his third shot the gunner found the range, and then, planting his shells with precision in a level line like the perforations of a postage stamp, he ripped the submarine from amidships to its nose. Strange had a vision for a second of a couple of men trying to climb out from the conning tower, and then the nose went up in the air like the snout of some monstrous fish, and the sea gulped it down.

'One of 'em,' said Slingsby. 'But we won't mention it. Lucky you saw those red streaks, my friend. If a destroyer had come prowling up this coast instead of the harmless little *Boulotte* there wouldn't have been any raft on the sea or any submarine just here under the sea. What about breakfast?'

Strange set the boat's course for Marseilles, and the rest of that voyage was remarkable only for a clear illustration of the difference between the amateur and the professional. For whereas Strange could not for the life of him keep still during one minute, Slingsby, stretched at his ease on the saloon sofa, beguiled the time with quotations from the 'Bab Ballads' and 'Departmental Ditties'.

W. Somerset Maugham

The work of an agent in the Intelligence Department is on the whole extremely monotonous. A lot of it is uncommonly useless.

Maugham was already a well-known and successful writer when, in September 1915, he was approached by Sir John Wallinger with the suggestion that with his knowledge of German and French, his occupation would provide useful cover for an intelligence officer operating in a neutral country. Would he be willing to travel to one on behalf of the Secret Intelligence Service? At that time Wallinger, who was never directly identified by Maugham in any of his books, was in charge of SIS's operations in southern Europe. He had previously served in the Indian Police and, like his one-legged brother Ernest, for whom Sigismund Best worked, was a senior figure in SIS. Aged forty-one, Maugham – who was too old for military service but had already served on the Western Front in a Red Cross ambulance unit – was anxious to leave London where his mistress's impending divorce from her husband on the grounds of her adultery was set to create a scandal.

It was agreed with Wallinger that Maugham would go to Switzerland, ostensibly to complete his play *Caroline*, but actually to re-establish contact with some of SIS's agents. However, his first assignment was to watch an Englishman with a German wife who was living in Lucerne. He took a room in the Hotel Beau Rivage in Geneva and filed his weekly reports by taking the ferry across the lake to the French side. Maugham was back in London early in the New Year to see *Caroline* open in the West End, and then in March he resumed his duties in Switzerland, accompanied by his newly divorced mistress, Syrie Wellcome. They stayed in Switzerland until June when they moved to the French spa of Brides-les-Bains for a brief holiday, and then returned to London where Maugham asked Wallinger to release him from SIS.

Maugham did not write about his melancholy experiences in Switzerland until 1928 when he released *Ashenden* which unfortunately coincided with the publication of his friend Compton Mackenzie's spy novel, *Extremes Meet*, which was also based on his wartime services in SIS. In 'The Traitor' Ashenden travels to Lucerne to investigate an English expatriate who is married to a suspected enemy agent and he lures him on to French territory so he can be arrested, a tale that is very close to the first assignment Maugham undertook in Switzerland for SIS. Maugham conceded that his stories were 'on the whole a very truthful account of my experiences' but not all the episodes in *Ashenden* are directly attributable to Maugham's own adventures. Three, for example, originated with another close friend, the Irish painter Gerald Kelly who had operated for SIS in Spain. 'The Hairless Mexican' and 'The Dark Woman' describe how a Mexican general is hired to assassinate an enemy agent but mistakenly kills the wrong person, an incident that the Old Etonian Kelly later acknowledged had been close to something that had happened to him.

The *Ashenden* stories were sufficiently authentic to alarm Winston Churchill, who declared that they were a breach of the Official Secrets Acts. Accordingly Maugham burned fourteen of the remaining unpublished manuscripts. The others tell of an encounter with one of his sources who was also selling information to the Germans. Another agent threatens to denounce Ashenden to the Swiss police when he is refused an increase in pay, and a suspected Indian agitator who has been spreading anti-British dissension commits suicide before he can be intercepted. All were based on fact although in his preface Maugham claimed 'this book is a work of fiction, though I should say not much more so than several of the books on the same subject that have appeared during the last few years and that purport to be truthful memoirs.'

In August 1916, almost as soon as he returned to London, Maugham set off on a long voyage to the Pacific, but as he made his way back through New York in June 1917 he received another request from SIS, this time through Sir William Wiseman, the Service's representative in the US. Wiseman's proposal was that Maugham should travel to Petrograd and deliver a large sum of cash to the Mensheviks in the hope of keeping Russia in the war. Reluctantly Maugham agreed to the mission and in July arrived in Vladivostok by steamer from Tokyo and embarked on the Trans-Siberian Express bound for the Russian capital. Once again his cover was that of a writer, which proved convenient as Maugham spent much of the day learning Russian and most of the night enciphering reports to London. In his coded messages Maugham referred to himself as 'Somerville', the name adopted by Ashenden while in Switzerland.

In October 1917 Maugham was invited to meet the Prime Minister, Alexander Kerensky, who asked him to travel immediately to Lloyd George in London with a secret plea for political support and, more importantly, for weapons and ammunition. Maugham promptly left for Oslo where he was met by a destroyer which took him to Scotland. The following day he was in Downing Street but the Prime Minister was unwilling to help Kerensky. As Maugham contemplated how he should break the news to the Russians the Bolsheviks seized power and the issue became academic. SIS asked Maugham to go to Romania instead, but he declined, pleading poor health.

Having recovered from tuberculosis, Maugham continued his literary success and scoured the world for tales to entertain. His *Ashenden* stories, which also included some based on Maugham's work in Petrograd, certainly influenced many later spy writers, including le Carré and Ian Fleming. Le Carré was later to agree that Maugham 'was the first person to write about espionage in a mood of disenchantment and almost prosaic reality'.

Soon after the outbreak of the Second World War Maugham returned to London from his home on the French Riviera, and, now aged sixty-five, volunteered his services to an intelligence contact, Ian Hay, in the hope of working for SIS again. Maugham's offer was politely declined but he did travel to the United States at the request of the Ministry of Information to improve Britain's propaganda. After the war he returned to his home in Cap Ferrat where he died in December 1965. In this extract from *Ashenden* Maugham describes his hero's first encounter with 'Colonel R'.

Ashenden

It was not till the beginning of September that Ashenden, a writer by profession, who had been abroad at the outbreak of war, managed to get back to England. He chanced soon after his arrival to go to a party and was there introduced to a middle-aged Colonel whose name he did not catch. He had some talk with him. As he was about to leave this officer came up to him and asked:

'I say, I wonder if you'd mind coming to see me. I'd rather like to have a chat with you.'

'Certainly,' said Ashenden. 'Whenever you like.'

'What about tomorrow at eleven?'

'All right.'

'I'll just write down my address. Have you a card on you?'

Ashenden gave him one and on this the Colonel scribbled in pencil the name of a street and the number of a house. When Ashenden walked along next morning to keep his appointment he found himself in a street of rather vulgar red-brick houses in a part of London that had once been fashionable, but was now fallen in the esteem of the house-hunter who wanted a good address. On the house at which Ashenden had been asked to call there was a board up to announce that it was for sale, the shutters were closed and there was no sign that anyone lived in it. He rang the bell and the door was opened by a non-commissioned officer so promptly that he was startled. He was not asked his business, but led immediately into a long room at the back, once evidently a dining-room, the florid decoration of which looked oddly out of keeping with the office furniture, shabby and sparse, that was in it. It gave Ashenden the impression of a room in which the brokers had taken possession. The Colonel, who was known in the Intelligence Department, as Ashenden later discovered, by the letter R., rose when he came in and shook hands with him. He was a man somewhat above the middle height, lean, with a yellow, deeply-lined face, thin grey hair and a toothbrush moustache. The thing immediately noticeable about him was the closeness with which his blue eyes were set. He only just escaped a squint. They were hard and cruel eyes, and very wary; and they gave him a cunning, shifty look. Here was a man that you could neither like nor trust at first sight. His manner was pleasant and cordial.

He asked Ashenden a good many questions and then, without further to-do, suggested that he had particular qualifications for the secret service. Ashenden was acquainted with several European languages and his profession was excellent cover; on the pretext that he was writing a book he could without attracting attention visit any neutral country. It was while they were discussing this point that R. said:

'You know you ought to get material that would be very useful to you in your work.'

'I shouldn't mind that,' said Ashenden.

'I'll tell you an incident that occurred only the other day and I can vouch for its truth. I thought at the time it would make a damned good story. One of the French ministers went down to Nice to recover from a cold and he had some very important documents with him that he kept in a dispatch-case. They were very important indeed. Well, a day or two after he arrived he picked up a yellow-haired lady at some restaurant or other where there was dancing, and he got very friendly with her. To cut a long story short, he took her back to his hotel — of course it was a very imprudent thing to do — and when he came to himself in the morning the lady and the dispatch-case had disappeared. They had one or two drinks up in his room and his theory is that when his back was turned the woman slipped a drug into his glass.'

R. finished and looked at Ashenden with a gleam in his close-set eyes.

'Dramatic, isn't it?' he asked.

'Do you mean to say that happened the other day?'

'The week before last.'

'Impossible,' cried Ashenden. 'Why, we've been putting that incident on the stage for sixty years, we've written it in a thousand novels. Do you mean to say that life has only just caught up with us?'

R. was a trifle disconcerted.

'Well, if necessary, I could give you names and dates, and believe me, the Allies have been put to no end of trouble by the loss of the documents that the dispatch-case contained.'

'Well, sir, if you can't do better than that in the secret service,' sighed Ashenden, 'I'm afraid that as a source of inspiration to the writer of fiction it's a washout. We really *can't* write that story much longer.'

It did not take them long to settle things and when Ashenden rose to go he had already made careful note of his instructions. He was to start for Geneva next day. The last words that R. said to him, with a casualness that made them impressive, were:

'There's just one thing I think you ought to know before you take on this job. And don't forget it. If you do well you'll get no thanks and if you get into trouble you'll get no help. Does that suit you?'

'Perfectly.'

'Then I'll wish you good afternoon.'

Edward Knoblock

If people think that being attached to 'Secret Service' means a life of continual 'hair-breadth escapes' let me tell them at once they are sadly mistaken. It means hours of infinite drudgery in which, only very rarely there occur moments approaching the dramatic.

Born in New York in 1874, Edward Knoblock was educated at Harvard. His first play was *Faun*, published in 1911, and the following year he co-wrote *Milestones* with Arnold Bennett. Fluent in French, he lived in both Paris, where he had an apartment overlooking the garden of the Palais-Royal, and rooms in Albany, London.

Early in 1916 he was introduced to the War Office's military intelligence branch by Somerset Maugham and worked for Sir John Wallinger in Switzerland where he took over the duties of Maugham. In the autumn he transferred to the Mediterranean theatre where he served with Compton Mackenzie. Little is known about his clandestine work in Switzerland although Mackenzie gave an entertaining account of Knoblock's recruitment by him into SIS in October 1916, apparently at a party. Captain Smith-Cumming, whom Knoblock referred to as 'the skipper', seemingly promised him a commission in the RNVR but it was soon discovered that as an American citizen he was ineligible. Instead a commission in the Royal Naval Air Service was suggested but no sooner had the playwright bought the uniform than he was obliged to accept a General Service commission and change his naval uniform for the khaki and green tabs of an intelligence officer. Mackenzie recalled that 'as we were due to leave England on November 3rd and as Knoblock's commission could not possibly be gazetted until long after that, we decided it would be safest to take all three uniforms out to Greece, and possibly dispose out there of the superfluous equipment when it was settled which service he was to join. In his enthusiasm he even bought two swords, a naval and a military one.'

Mackenzie and Knoblock shared the train journey to Greece, taking the boat train to Paris and crossing the Italian frontier at Modane. After a couple of days' rest in Rome they continued to Taranto where Mackenzie, in the role of a King's Messenger, went ahead to Piraeus on a French destroyer, while Knoblock waited for a French despatch boat, the *Fauvette*, which took him to Corfu and then Patras. Upon his arrival in Greece Knoblock was installed at the British Legation's annexe where SIS operated under Port Control cover. Soon afterwards Athens was turned into a battleground as the supporters of Venizelos made a vain attempt to dethrone the king and seize power.

After this exciting episode Knoblock, acting as Mackenzie's deputy, moved to the island of Syra which had recently been occupied by the Turks. In *Aegean*

Memories Compton Mackenzie recalled that 'Even the indefatigable Knoblock was wilting under the strain of coding and decoding, for the Secret Service cipher was a diabolical device to torment the mind of man.' During their four months on Syra, broken only by Knoblock's occasional visits to Salonica and Athens, the two writers collaborated on a play, *All's Fair*. By July 1917 Knoblock was struck down by dysentery and, when his weight dropped to seven stone, was repatriated.

After two months' sick leave Knoblock returned to work for Smith-Cumming, and until May 1918 was accommodated in an office next to that occupied by the singer Kennerley Rumford. Thereafter he spent a greater part of his time in France, either carrying despatches between Paris and London, or working from an SIS outstation known as 'the Nunnery' somewhere in the French Alps. He was there when the armistice was declared and later was assigned the task of supervising the return of British PoWs from Germany. He represented his chief at the French victory parade at Strasbourg and attended the Paris Peace Conference on behalf of SIS. He returned to civilian life in January 1919, but not before he had expressed a wish to stay in SIS permanently. As he told Smith-Cumming, 'one doesn't have to think. You do the thinking for us. We just obey orders. That's the beauty of the service. I almost wish I could remain in it for the rest of my life.'

Knoblock died in July 1945, six years after the publication of his autobiography, *Round the Room*. In this extract he describes an encounter with a mysterious enemy agent in an unidentified country which is almost certainly Switzerland.

Round the Room

I was sent off to a certain neutral country to bring back a secret document which had been brought 'across the enemy frontier'. It was given to me with instructions to deliver it at a certain place. I got on the train at about half-past eight at night. There were only two first-class compartments in this corridor train and when I entered the carriage I noticed that one of them had a dressing-case, an umbrella and a novel lying on the seat. The umbrella looked as if it might belong to a lady. The compartment was empty. So evidently the person occupying it was having dinner. I had already had mine, so I decided, as I was very tired, to sit in the compartment adjacent to the one already occupied by the unknown person. I settled down in a corner of my own compartment and switched off the electric light. The next stop was not for about an hour. I would try and sleep.

I was just dozing off, when a few minutes later I heard the creak of the swing door to the second-class corridor and a moment after a man with a dark up-turned moustache looked into my compartment for a second –

then I heard him settle down in the one next to mine. I thought what an odd man he must be to possess such a feminine umbrella, and then closed my eyes again.

I hadn't been sleeping very long when someone rapped on the window of my compartment. I woke up and saw a neatly dressed woman of about thirty-five before me – evidently a lady.

'Excuse me, sir,' she asked in a strange sort of French, the accent of which I couldn't place, 'have you been in my compartment?'

'I only glanced into it,' I said, 'and as I saw it was occupied I came in here.'

'Well, someone's been in it,' she said in great agitation. 'All my jewels are gone. Come and look!'

I sprang up and went with her. She opened her dressing-case and revealed the slash of a knife across a locked pocket inside the flap.

'The man with the black moustache,' I exclaimed. And then proceeded to tell her what had happened during her absence.

She looked at me half credulously, but with a faint touch of suspicion in her eye. And all at once I realized the ugly position I was in. Supposing she thought that *I* was the thief? She'd have me arrested and searched and the secret document I had in my pocket would be found! I couldn't allow that to happen – not at any price.

For quite apart from the importance of delivering the document safely into the hands of the War Office, the discovery of it was bound to lead to very serious complications. I was in a neutral country engaged in war-work. In other words I was breaking the neutrality of that country. And that would mean endless examination into the reason for my presence there, which might end in 'blowing up' the entire organization of that particular branch of our service. And, of course, it would spell prison for me – not a pleasant prospect at best. For the prisons of that country were reputed to be icy, almost all prisoners ending by developing tuberculosis. I didn't exactly relish the idea of that.

All these various reasons shot into my mind while the lady was still eyeing me.

'I'm on my way to see my little boy,' she said all at once. 'He's very ill – with a specialist. I only brought the jewels because he loves to see me wear them.' This sounded a bit odd to me, but she seemed sincere enough. It might be true. Or was the whole thing an invention? And was she an enemy agent who was trying to catch me?

'I'm sorry your boy's ill,' I answered politely. 'And it's dreadful about the jewels. I wish I could help you.'

She now began to look extremely suspicious. And I must say my voice began to sound unconvincing to my own ears. At that moment the swing-door to the second-class opened and the conductor, a huge fat man, appeared. We both turned to him and poured out our story simultaneously.

'I know what we've got to do,' I finally said. 'I'll identify the man with the black moustache. I can do so easily.'

The conductor agreed with me. So did the lady, though somewhat reluctantly.

'Come with me,' he said.

I followed him. We went through the entire train which was very crowded in the second-class and third-class compartments. As luck would have it, there were about twenty men with fierce up-turned moustaches. I indicated one here and one there to the conductor – but was frankly uncertain which was the right man. We returned to the first-class, where the lady was waiting anxiously.

I explained the difficulty to her.

'We'll be arriving at the station in another fifteen minutes,' I added. 'We'll get the conductor to bring both the men here, if you like. And then when you get out you can see the Station-master.'

'But I'm not getting out at the next station,' she answered. 'My little boy's at L—, two hours from the next station. And the thief is bound to get off at the next stop.' Then she turned to me and asked very pointedly, 'Are you getting off?'

'No,' I answered. For luckily I was not.

This reply puzzled her for a second. And I could see that she thought it merely a clever move on my part. She now gave me an extremely suspicious look.

And just at that moment the swing-door opened again and a man with a black moustache came through it.

Whether this was the same man who had first looked into my compartment, or whether it was merely an innocent traveller walking along the corridor of the train, I shall never know. But I felt here was my salvation and turned abruptly on the fellow.

'That's the man,' I said, pointing to him. 'He's the one I saw!'

The man naturally started back at this sudden attack, and what helped me enormously was the conductor turning on him at the same time and asking him to produce his ticket. It was a second-class one.

'What are you doing in the first-class?' the conductor shouted.

'That is the man,' I repeated, facing the lady. 'He's the thief! You'd better get out at the next stop and have the man arrested.'

'But that would mean delay. And my little boy is ill. I must reach him as soon as possible. What *am* I to do?'

'Well, it's obviously a choice between your jewels and your boy,' I said bluntly. 'It's a matter for you to settle.'

We were drawing closer and closer now to the first stop. All four of us, the lady, the conductor, the man with the moustache and myself were standing wedged together in the corridor.

I kept working up her suspicions against the black moustache. Innocent or guilty I felt this was my only salvation – for unless I diverted all her doubts from me, she might swing round again and think me the thief instead of him.

The scene went on for quite ten minutes or more when we at last drew into the station.

'Now which is it to be?' I said. 'The child or the jewels? For remember if you get this man arrested there will be formalities to fulfil which will keep you here for a day or two at the very least.'

And with that the train stopped. She stood there still hesitating, when the black-moustache opened the train door, jumped out and disappeared amongst the crowd on the platform.

'There now!' I exclaimed, 'you've let him go. But how right of you. After all your boy's of far more importance to you, I'm sure, than all the jewels in the world.'

The train moved out again. I came and sat in the lady's compartment opposite her. I thought it safer not to let her out of my sight. She might still think me the thief. So for two solid hours more I had to continue to convince her of the villainy of the black-moustachio and how noble she had been in sacrificing her precious heirlooms for the sake of her dear child. I got her on to the subject of his illness and enlarged on children in general. I tried very hard to find out where she had come from. 'From very far – a day's drive in a carriage before I reached the train,' she said. But whether it was Sweden, or German Poland or Lithuania I could not find out. She had a coronet on her bag and was obviously a woman of position. At last, by much manoeuvring, I convinced her of my own respectability. When we finally reached her destination she held out her hand to me.

'Thank you for having been so sympathetic about my loss' – and with a smile she added, 'and my little boy.'

She left the train and I breathed again. I could see her on the platform talking to a porter. As the train started once more, a wild desire seized me to lean out of the window and shout:

'*I've* got the jewels.'

But of course I wasn't an idiot. I had my precious papers to think of. I delivered them safely early the next morning.

When I told my adventure to my chief he said he was convinced that the woman was a German agent and that she was only trying to pump me. But then why didn't she have me arrested, which she might easily have done? No, I believe the stealing of her jewels was genuine enough. And the more I think of it, the more I think that black-moustache was really the thief. Why else should the man have come to the first-class part of the carriage unless he hoped to steal still more out of her dressing-case?

Erskine Childers

Secrecy is rendered impossible, and secrecy is vital.

After Haileybury and Trinity College, Cambridge, Robert Erskine Childers worked in the House of Commons as a clerk, but in 1899, aged twenty-nine, he was one of the first to respond to the call for volunteers to go to South Africa. He fought in the Boer War with the Honourable Artillery Company and wrote an account of his experiences, *In the Ranks of the City Imperial Volunteers*. He and his wife were keen sailors and in 1903 he achieved tremendous success with his novel of espionage along the German coast, *The Riddle of the Sands*. The book contained detailed topographical observations and, based on his own experiences while sailing his yacht in German waters, gave an authentic flavour of an agent conducting a clandestine survey. It was reprinted shortly before the Great War and captured the public's imagination, even if there was no realistic possibility of Germany launching a raid or invasion, as portrayed in the thriller.

In 1910 Childers resigned his post in the Commons to devote himself to Irish affairs, advocating dominion status for Ireland, and in July 1914 he sailed his yacht, the *Asgard*, with a cargo of weapons to a port just north of Dublin to arm the National Volunteers.

Soon after the outbreak of war Childers joined a seaplane carrier, HMS *Engadine*, as an RNVR officer and an expert on reconnaissance work. He participated in the Cuxhaven raid in November 1914 and was later posted to the Mediterranean where he found himself employed by SIS's Near East branch, running agents up the Turkish coast and flying intelligence missions. He trained officers for the Royal Naval Air Service, which brought him into contact with Captain Weldon, the author of *Hard Lying*. By the end of the war, when the RNAS had amalgamated with the Royal Air Force, Childers was a major and had been awarded the DSC.

When he returned to civilian life in March 1919 Childers settled in Dublin and committed himself to the republican cause. He protested strongly about the British government's use of the 'Black and Tans' and was appointed minister of propaganda in the self-constituted Dáil Éireann which was formed in May 1921. He accompanied Éamon de Valera to London to negotiate with the British cabinet but stubbornly resisted any compromise treaty that fell short of complete independence for a republic. At this stage, as a hardliner, Childers joined the republican army's mobile columns to oppose the new Irish Free State government. In November 1922 his home in County Wicklow was surrounded by Free State soldiers, he was court-martialled, and executed by a firing squad at Beggar's Bush barracks. Moments before his death he shook the hand of every member of the firing party.

In this epilogue from Childers's famous tale of espionage the author describes the consequences of the mission undertaken by Carruthers and his friend Arthur Davies.

The Riddle of the Sands: A Record of Secret Service Recently Achieved

An interesting document, somewhat damaged by fire, lies on my study-table.

It is a copy (in cipher) of a confidential memorandum to the German Government embodying a scheme for the invasion of England by Germany. It is unsigned, but internal evidence and the fact that it was taken by Mr 'Carruthers' from the stove of the villa at Norderney, leave no doubt as to its authorship. For many reasons it is out of the question to print the textual translation of it, as deciphered; but I propose to give an outline of its contents.

Even this must strain discretion to its uttermost limits, and had I only to consider the instructed few who follow the trend of professional opinion on such subjects, I should leave the foregoing narrative to speak for itself. But, as was stated in the preface, our primary purpose is to reach everyone; and there may be many who, in spite of able and authoritative warnings frequently uttered since these events occurred, are still prone to treat the German danger as an idle 'bogey,' and may be disposed, in this case, to imagine that a baseless romance has been foisted on them.

A few persons (English as well as German) hold that Germany is strong enough now to meet us single-handed and throw an army on our shores. The memorandum rejects this view, deferring isolated action for at least a decade; and supposing, for present purposes, a coalition of three Powers against Great Britain. And subsequent researches through the usual channels place it beyond dispute that this condition was relied on by the German Government in adopting the scheme. They realised that even if, owing to our widely scattered forces, they gained that temporary command of the North Sea which would be essential for a successful landing, they would inevitably lose it when our standing fleets were concentrated and our reserve ships mobilised. With its sea communications cut, the prospects of the invading army would be too dubious. I state it in that mild way, for it seems not to have been held that failure was absolutely certain; and rightly, I think, in spite of the dogmas of the strategists; for the case transcends all experience; no man can calculate the effect on our delicate economic fabric of a well-timed, well-planned blow at the industrial heart of the kingdom, the great northern and midland towns, with their teeming populations of peaceful wage-earners. In this instance, however, joint action (the occasion for which is perhaps not difficult to guess) was distinctly contemplated, and Germany's role in the coalition was exclusively that of invader. Her fleet was to be kept intact, and she herself to remain ostensibly neutral until the first shock was over and our own battle-fleets either beaten, or, the much more likely event, so crippled by a hard-won victory as to be incapable of withstanding compact and unscathed forces. Then, holding the balance of power, she would strike. And the blow? It was not till I read this memorandum that I grasped the full merits of that daring scheme, under which every advantage, moral, material, and geographical, possessed by Germany, is utilised to the utmost, and every disadvantage of our own turned to account against us.

Two root principles pervade it: perfect organisation; perfect secrecy. Under the first head come some general considerations. The writer (who is intimately conversant with conditions on both sides of the North Sea) argued that Germany is pre-eminently fitted to undertake an invasion of Great Britain. She has a great army (a mere fraction of which would suffice) in a state of high efficiency, but a useless weapon, as against us, unless transported overseas. She has a peculiar genius for organisation, not only in elaborating minute detail, but in the grasp of a coherent whole. She knows the art of giving a brain to a machine, of transmitting power to the uttermost cog-wheel, and at the same time of concentrating responsibility in a supreme centre. She has a small navy, but very effective for its purpose, built, trained, and manned on methodical principles, for defined ends, and backed by an inexhaustible reserve of men from her maritime conscription. She studies and practises co-operation between her army and navy. Her hands are free for offence in home waters, since she has no distant network of coveted colonies and dependencies on which to dissipate her defensive energies. Finally, she is, compared with ourselves, economically independent, having commercial access through her land frontiers to the whole of Europe. She has little to lose and much to gain.

The writer pauses here to contrast our own situation, and I summarise his points. We have a small army, dispersed over the whole globe, and administered on a gravely defective system. We have no settled theory of national defence, and no competent authority whose business it is to give us one. The matter is still at the stage of civilian controversy. Co-operation between the army and navy is not studied and practised; much less do there exist any plans, worthy of the name, for the repulse of an invasion, or any readiness worth considering for the prompt equipment and direction of our home forces to meet a sudden emergency. We have a great and, in many respects, a magnificent navy, but not great enough for the interests it insures, and with equally defective institutions; not built or manned methodically, having an utterly inadequate reserve of men, all classes of which would be absorbed at the very outset, without a vestige of preparation for the enrolment of volunteers; distracted by the multiplicity of its functions in guarding our colossal empire and commerce, and conspicuously lacking a brain, not merely for the smooth control of its own unwieldy mechanism, but for the study of rival aims and systems. We have no North Sea naval base, no North Sea fleet, and no North Sea policy. Lastly, we stand in a highly dangerous economical position.

CHAPTER II

Anti-Bolshevik Operations

The Bolsheviks are generally courteous if one does not interfere with their business.
William Gibson, Wild Career

British opposition to the Bolsheviks was a policy enthusiastically pursued by Captain Smith-Cumming throughout the latter part of his career and this accounts for the degree of paranoia manifested by the Soviets between the wars. They had good reason to believe that the perfidious British were sending spies and saboteurs to Moscow, and the only surprising aspect to the operations undertaken at that time was the apparent willingness of all the participants to publicize their clandestine activities. These were not limited simply to the adventures of a few individual agents such as the redoubtable William Gibson and Paul Dukes. The Allied intervention of 1920 was a full-scale military operation and the war against the Communists was fought across a wide front. Dick Ellis, who later became a senior SIS officer, gave a detailed account of his experiences in the southern theatre in *The Transcaspian Episode*, although he never acknowledged his intelligence role. He and William Gibson survived relatively unscathed, but neither Sidney Reilly nor Reginald Teague-Jones was so lucky.

Even following the collapse of the Soviet Union in 1990, the mystery that surrounded Reilly's death remains. His memoirs were released in England after his death had been announced in Moscow, but at that time his exact fate had not been ascertained and Soviet sensitivity regarding the so-called Allied intervention remained high. The Kremlin of course had good reason to resent British interference in the revolution and the subsequent civil war. Reilly and George Hill were believed to have been key players in the Lockhart plot, the assassination attempt made on Lenin by Dora Kaplan, and both men had gone into hiding from the Cheka before fleeing the country. For years afterwards the Soviets portrayed the British Secret Service as staffed by shrewd and resourceful anti-Bolsheviks dedicated to the destruction of Communism. On the military front Teague-Jones had been sentenced to death *in absentia* by the Soviets for his alleged complicity in the massacre of twenty-six captive Bolsheviks from Baku, and Augustus Agar received the highest British decoration for gallantry after he sank single-handed the cruiser *Oleg* off Kronstadt in 1919. Both officers, despite their celebrity status, worked for the Secret Intelligence Service, thereby adding substance to Lenin's suspicion of the British.

One of Agar's contacts in Stockholm was Conrad O'Brien-ffrench, a swashbuckling figure with an exotic background. He had been recruited into SIS by Stewart Menzies, who was to be one of Smith-Cumming's successors as chief, and had arrived in Sweden in January 1919 under assistant military attaché cover. He was later to transfer to Helsinki, and he was to maintain his link with SIS for many years thereafter, as he admitted in his candid memoirs.

Earlier in the war Captain Smith-Cumming had sent Sam Hoare to liaise with the Russian authorities on counter-espionage matters, but the MP had found the situation chaotic and had received very little co-operation. The Soviets became intensely suspicious of British motives and, having failed to catch Dukes, Hill or Agar, waited a decade to wreak their revenge on Allan Monkhouse, the Metro-Vickers representative in Moscow. Accused of being an SIS agent, the engineer always denied the charge, even though he pleaded guilty at his trial to a lesser charge of bribery. After his deportation he published an account of his harrowing ordeal and thereby joined the expanding group of SIS agents who had written of their experiences.

The officers sent to Russia by Smith-Cumming were each assigned a codenumber, and Paul Dukes was to use his, ST-25, in the title of his memoirs. Reilly was ST-1, Hill was IK-8. Agar was ST-34, and Conrad O'Brien-ffrench was designated ST-36. Together they represented the first manifestation of SIS's ill-fated quest to strangle the Communist movement at birth, or at least contain it.

Sir Paul Dukes

The business of war was to delude, to circumvent, to outwit, and to conquer, and deception of the foe was one of its main arts in which every soldier was trained.

Before the Great War Paul Dukes, the son of a clergyman, had been studying music at the St Petersburg Conservatoire in the hope of becoming a conductor. However, soon after the Anglo-Russian Commission was established in 1915 Dukes joined it and liaised with the Russian press covering the war. When, in July 1917, there was a need for the Commission to install a representative at the Foreign Office in London Dukes was selected for the task, and there he worked under the supervision of John Buchan, then Lloyd George's Director of Information.

Dukes remained in London during the October Revolution but became increasingly determined to return to Russia. In December 1917 he got an opportunity, having volunteered as a King's Messenger to deliver despatches to Oslo, Stockholm and Petrograd. While in Russia Dukes joined an American relief mission to Samara but was recalled to London for a meeting with Captain Smith-Cumming who invited him to join SIS and fight the Bolshevks. Dukes accepted the assignment and the codename ST-25, and made his way to the Allied 'intervention' headquarters in Archangel where he adopted the disguise of a Serbian commercial traveller for a further journey to Finland to be smuggled over the frontier into Russia. Once on Soviet territory Dukes acquired the identity of a Ukrainian officer in the feared Cheka, and this lent him some protection.

He remained in Soviet Russia until September 1919 and maintained contact with SIS by meeting Agar's fast motorboats which routinely slipped across the Gulf of Finland from their clandestine base on neutral territory. As his colleague Conrad O'Brien-ffrench remarked, 'Dukes was the answer to a spy-writer's prayer.' When Dukes finally emerged from his adventures in Latvia he reported to the British Legation in Riga and was swiftly shipped to Helsinki and across the North Sea. Upon his return to London he was reunited with Augustus Agar and in 1920 knighted by the King.

The Story of 'ST-25': Adventure and Romance in the Secret Intelligence Service in Red Russia, dedicated to Mansfield Smith-Cumming, 'the chief', was published in March 1938 and was the first authoritative account of the activities of the musician who had become embroiled in espionage almost by accident. In 1940 he wrote *An Epic of the Gestapo*, his further adventures against another totalitarian regime, and after the war wrote *Come Hammer Come Sickle*, advocating greater understanding of the Soviet regime.

Dukes died in August 1967. In this extract from his autobiography he describes his first meeting with Mansfield Smith-Cumming, the mysterious chief who lived in a series of apartments on the roof of Whitehall Court.

The Story of 'ST-25'

One day in June, 1918, when I was far away in Samara, I received a wire from the British Consul-General, Mr (later Sir John Oliver) Wardrop, who had not yet left Moscow, asking me to return to the capital urgently. When I arrived he handed me a mysterious telegram from the Foreign Office. It said I was wanted at once in London. I had misgivings. I suspected that my roving mission had been a failure and that neither the information or suggestions I had been sending had been acceptable. My first impulse was to refuse to go, but the Consul-General counselled submission. I set out for Archangel – it was a long way round from Moscow to London in those days. The Russian capital (the Bolshevist Government had moved from Petrograd to Moscow) with its turmoil, its political wranglings, plots and counter-plots, its increasing misery and want, was left behind.

Leaning over the side of the White Sea steamer I wondered what London had in store for me. I stood and watched the sun dip low to the horizon, hover, an oval mass of fire, on the edge of the blazing sea, and without disappearing mount anew to celebrate the triumph over darkness of the nightless Arctic summer. Then – Murmansk and perpetual day, a destroyer to Petchenga, a tug to the Norwegian frontier, a ten days' journey round the North Cape and by the fairy land of Norwegian fjords to Bergen, with finally a zigzag course across the North Sea, dodging German submarines, to Scotland.

At Aberdeen the control officer had received orders to pass me through by the first train to London. At King's Cross a car was waiting, and knowing neither my destination nor the cause of my recall I was driven to a building in a side street in the vicinity of Trafalgar Square. 'This way,' said the chauffeur, leaving the car. He had a face like a mask. We entered the building and the lift whisked us to the top floor, above which additional superstructures had been built for war-emergency offices.

I had always associated rabbit-warrens with subterranean abodes, but here in this building I discovered a maze of rabbit-burrow-like passages, corridors, nooks and alcoves, piled higgledy-piggledy on the roof. Leaving the lift my guide led me up one flight of steps so narrow that a corpulent man would have stuck tight, round unexpected corners, and again up a flight of steps which brought us out on the roof. Crossing a short iron bridge we entered another maze, until just as I was beginning to feel dizzy I was shown into a tiny room about ten feet square where sat an officer in the uniform of a British colonel. The impassive chauffeur announced me and withdrew.

The Colonel, to my stupefaction, informed me immediately that I had been recalled to London because I was to be invited to work in the Secret Intelligence Service.

He gave me time to recover, and spoke very kindly. 'We have reason to believe that Russia will not long be open to foreigners,' he explained. 'We want someone to remain there to keep us informed of the march of events.'

I referred to my work with the Foreign Office. He said that question had already been arranged, and that under war regulations my service could be requisitioned. 'Of course,' he added, 'if the risk or danger . . .'

I forget what I said, but he did not continue.

'Very well, then,' he proceeded, 'consider the matter carefully and come back tomorrow afternoon.'

He rang a bell and a charming young lady appeared to escort me out, threading her way with what seemed to me marvellous dexterity through the maze of passages.

I went out and sat down in St James's Park. With whirling emotions I reflected on the invitation that had been made to me. It was an invitation that I felt to be of the nature of a command. But the Secret Service was to me an utterly unknown quantity, and in so far as I could imagine it at all, I could not conceive that I had any aptitude for it whatsoever. And yet, would not ninety-nine per cent of the men in the trenches formerly have thought exactly the same of the duty of killing Germans? The business of war was to delude, to circumvent, to outwit, and to conquer, and deception of the foe was one of its main arts in which every soldier was trained. Hitherto what had I been for three years – an observer, a reporter, a critic? Now, at last, I was called upon to be a soldier, a soldier who must fight alone and whose weapons were his wits! I would play my part to the utmost of my ability. And just as, over there in Flanders, hundreds of thousands of my countrymen were prepared, in violation of every humane instinct, but for service, systematically to delude, capture, and kill, so I also, for service, must be prepared systematically to play a part, and obtain that information regarding the adversary which my leaders would require.

There was exhilaration in my heart as I was whisked skywards in the lift to the roof-labyrinth next day. Another young lady escorted me up and down the narrow stairways and ushered me into the presence of the Colonel.

He appeared to take it for granted that I accepted the post. He said that as my qualifications were on the political and general side rather than the military, he would take me to the head of the political section who would give me all further explanations. I followed him downstairs to another apartment, where we found the head of the political section seated at his desk. This room was large and comfortably furnished. It appeared to be part of the main building and not of the superstructure.

In my first account of these events, written in 1920, it was suggested to me that I should make no reference whatever to this gentleman, as he was then conducting delicate diplomatic negotiations for Great Britain with representatives of the Soviet, and I cut out this paragraph and ascribed the conversation to the Colonel. For the benefit of those who may pose the question I may say that the anonymous official was not Sidney Reilly, though it was in his room that I first met that interesting personage. They were great friends and had much in common, including erudition, tastes, and possibly race. In the early years after the War the head of this section was, I believe, several times entrusted with diplomatic missions of which the public never heard. In 1920 he was knighted. During the period that I was being 'put through my paces' I had more to do with him than with any other person in the roof-labyrinth, sometimes seeing him there and sometimes at his rooms in the Albany.

Never having received permission to name this distinguished gentleman in connexion with the roof-labyrinth, I regret that he must remain anonymous, but I cannot refrain from quoting the following extract, in itself sufficiently striking, from the obituary notice in *The Times* when he died, a few years later: '. . . he served . . . on "special duty" for the War Office. The duty was of a particularly important and dangerous character, for it was the tracking down of enemy and anarchist conspiracies, of defeatism and assassination. In 1915 he discovered the anarchist plot, hatched in Switzerland and financed from Germany, for assassination of every one of the heads of the Allied nations. . . . The work carried him into many lands and dangerous situations. He could be silent as the grave. Even his intimate friends thought he was doing little more than keeping the War Office informed on Indian conspiracies.'

'He could be silent as the grave. . . .' Even his intimate friends, perhaps, knew little if anything of his activities and his methods, or that his work was that of the roof-labyrinth.

He was one of those who, during and after the War, contributed to found and firmly establish that high tradition of the silentest of services which exists today, and has made 'British Intelligence' a symbol throughout the world of thoroughness, accuracy and reliability in political and every other kind of reconnaissance, the best of allies and an object of oft-expressed admiration to our friends, a source of constant fear and apprehension to our adversaries and to all foreign intriguers.

He was very simple, kindly and reserved in manner. Receiving me warmly, he made me feel at ease at once.

'When I have briefly outlined what we want,' he said, 'I will take you up to meet – er – the Chief.'

Besides general conditions, he told me, I should have to report on changes of policy, the attitude of the population, military and naval matters, what possibilities there might be for an alteration of regime, and what part Germany was playing. As to the means by which I should re-enter the country, under what cover I should live, and how I should send out reports, it was left to me to make suggestions.

He expounded his own views on Russia, and mentioned the names of a few English people I might come in contact with. 'I will see if – er – the Chief is ready,' he said finally. 'I will be back in a moment.'

I rose to look at the pictures on the walls and the miscellany of books on the shelves. The owner was evidently a collector. Impelled purely and simply by an artistic interest in books, I picked out one or two volumes to look at the bindings and illustrations. Among others was a set of Thackeray in green morocco. When I took down *Henry Esmond* it turned out to be a dummy. There was nothing to distinguish it outwardly from its fellows. I was about to put it back quickly when, my finger accidentally touching a catch-spring, the cover opened and a few sheets of paper fell out. As I hastily gathered them up I noticed the heading *Kriegsministerium Berlin*, and minute handwriting in German. Feeling very guilty and confused – I had had no intention to do any 'spying' – I wondered whether I ought to admit that 'quite accidentally, etc.' Barely had I replaced the volume when the head of the department returned.

'The – er – Chief is not in,' he said, before I could say anything, 'but you may see him tomorrow. You are interested in books?' he added, seeing me looking at the shelves. 'I collect them. That is an interesting old volume on Cardinal Richelieu, if you care to look at it. I picked it up in Charing Cross Road for a shilling.' The volume mentioned was immediately above the dummy *Henry Esmond*. I took it down warily, expecting something uncommon to occur, but it was only a musty old volume in French with torn leaves and soiled pages. I pretended to be interested.

'There is not much else there worth looking at, I think,' he said casually. 'Well, good-bye. Come in tomorrow.'

I wondered mightily who 'the Chief' of this establishment could be and what he would be like. The young lady smiled enigmatically as she showed me to the lift. I returned again next day after thinking overnight how I should get back to Russia – and deciding on nothing. My mind seemed to be a complete blank on the subject in hand, and I was entirely absorbed in the mysteries of the roof-labyrinth.

I was shown into the same sitting-room. My eyes fell instinctively on the bookshelf. My preceptor was in a genial mood.

'I see you like my collection,' he said. 'That, by the way, is a fine edition of Thackeray.' My heart jumped! 'Would you like to look at it?'

My questioner's face was blank. I took it that he wished to initiate me into the secrets of the department. I rose quickly and, of course, took down – as I thought – the dummy *Henry Esmond*, which was in exactly the same place as it had been the day before. To my utter confusion it opened quite naturally and I found in my hands nothing more than an edition *de luxe* printed on India paper and profusely illustrated! I stared bewildered at the shelf. There was no other *Henry Esmond*. Immediately over the vacant space stood the life of Cardinal Richelieu as it had stood yesterday. Had I *dreamt* the dummy of the day before? Had I been observed when left alone in the room? And would my natural curiosity be approved or disapproved? Was the dummy a real *cachette* for secret papers? Or was it itself a mere blind, a sort of dummy dummy, put there to fool inquisitive pryers? Were others of the volumes dummies too? Did still further mysteries lie hidden in these books and pictures? All these questions rushed through my mind. Were they ever answered? Perhaps they were – but the sympathetic reader will understand that I have no desire, by revealing the solutions, even were that permitted, to earn the posthumous disrespect of one who himself preferred in life to be 'as silent as the grave'.

I replaced the volume, trying not to look disconcerted, but feeling as foolish as a cricketer who has got stumped for a 'duck' because he didn't know the wicket-keeper had the ball. The expression on the face of my kindly 'wicket-keeper' was still quite impassive, even bored.

'It is a beautiful edition,' he repeated. 'Now if you are ready we will go and see – er – the Chief.'

I stuttered assent and followed. As we proceeded through the maze of stairways and unexpected passages which seemed to me like a miniature House of Usher, I caught glimpses of tree-tops, of the Embankment Gardens, the Thames, the Tower Bridge, Westminster. We seemed to be gyrating in a limited space, and when we entered a spacious study – the sanctum of er – the Chief – I had a feeling that we had really moved only a few yards and that this study was just above the sitting-room.

My guide knocked and entered, and I followed, painfully conscious that at that moment I could not have expressed a sane opinion on any subject under the sun. From the threshold the room seemed bathed in semi-obscurity. Against the window everything appeared in silhouette. A row of half a dozen extending telephones stood at the left of a big desk littered with papers. On a side table were maps and drawings, with models of aeroplanes, submarines and mechanical devices, while a row of bottles suggested chemical experiments. These evidences of scientific investigation only served to intensify an already overpowering atmosphere of strangeness and mystery.

But it was not these things that engaged my attention as I stood nervously waiting. It was not the bottles or the machinery that attracted my gaze. My eyes fixed themselves on the figure at the writing-table. In the swing desk-chair, his shoulders hunched, with his head supported on one hand, busily writing, there sat in his shirt-sleeves 'er – the Chief'.

This extraordinary man was short of stature, thick-set, with grey hair half covering a well-rounded head. His mouth was stern, and an eagle eye, full of vivacity, glanced – or glared, as the case might be – piercingly through a gold-rimmed monocle. The coat that hung over the back of his chair was that of a naval officer.

As first encounter he appeared very severe. His manner of speech was abrupt. Woe betide the unfortunate individual who ever incurred his ire! Yet the stern countenance could melt into the kindliest of smiles, and the softened eyes and lips revealed a heart that was big and generous. Awe-inspired as I was by my first encounter, I soon learned to regard 'the Chief' with feelings of the deepest personal admiration and affection. He had only one leg, but this did not deter him, as I afterwards discovered, from driving his high-power car at breakneck speed about the streets of London to the terror of police and pedestrians alike. To his subordinates and associates he was invariably known and signed himself by a single letter of the alphabet in ink of a particular hue. I was told at the time that his name was Captain So-and-so, but I soon discovered that at least half a dozen persons either in the roof-labyrinth or associated offices were all called by that same name! It was eighteen months before I was allowed to know his real name and title, and even then I was careful never to use it. He read and approved of these pages and all I have here related about him and the roof-labyrinth, but I never received permission to mention his name, which probably would have been little known to the general public anyway. Never having received that permission, I cannot quote it, though he has now passed beyond. 'The Chief' was a British officer and an English gentleman of the very finest stamp, fearless, gifted with limitless resources of subtle ingenuity, and I counted it one of the great privileges of my life to have been brought within the circle of his acquaintance.

In silhouette I saw myself motioned to a chair. The Chief wrote for a moment and then turned abruptly with the unexpected remark: 'So I understand you want to go back to Soviet Russia?' as if it had been my own suggestion. The interview was brief and concise. The words Archangel, Stockholm, Riga, Helsingfors, recurred frequently, and the names were mentioned of English people in those places and in Petrograd. It was finally decided that I alone should determine how to regain access to Russia and how I should despatch reports.

It was also made quite clear to me that once over the frontier I should be left entirely to my own resources, and that if I got caught it would be impossible to do anything to help me.

'Good luck,' said the Chief in conclusion. 'You will see that he is instructed in ciphers,' he added to the official who had introduced me, 'and take him to the laboratory to learn the inks and all that.'

We left the Chief and arrived by a single flight of stairs at the door of the sitting-room. My companion smiled. 'You will find your way about in course of time,' he said.

I am obliged here to draw a veil over this remarkable department. Nevertheless, to satisfy the curious who ask if the roof-labyrinth still exists, I think I may, without undue indiscretion, add that it doesn't need to be on a roof nor does it need to be a labyrinth, but that suburban villas may do just as well. The last sanctum in which I visited 'er – the Chief' before his death was nowhere near Trafalgar Square, and for all you (or I) know, you may have his eminent successor housed somewhere close to you now. You would certainly never be aware of it.

Dick Ellis

In the Soviet view, however, the presence of British and Indian troops in Transcaspia and the Caucasus was a deliberate act of aggression aimed at securing political and even territorial advantage at a time of Russian weakness.

Born in Australia, and educated at the universities of Melbourne and Oxford, C. H. Ellis was recruited into SIS after his military service which was spent in the Near East. His first posting was to Berlin in October 1923 where he posed as a British Passport Control Officer while helping to run the local SIS station. Later he switched to Paris and, with the help of his White Russian wife's family, started to collect intelligence from the émigré community. Unfortunately this also brought him into contact with the Abwehr and, short of cash, he sold many of SIS's secrets. In 1939 he moved to London and was placed in charge of the illicit telephone tap that had been installed on the German embassy's external lines. Strangely, this particular source, once valued as a window into Ribbentrop's activities, was compromised soon after Ellis had been indoctrinated into it.

After a brief spell in cable censorship in Liverpool Ellis was posted to the SIS station in New York where, for the duration of the war, he was deputy to (Sir) William Stephenson, the head of British Security Co-ordination. At the conclusion of hostilities BSC was wound up and Stephenson returned to the business world but Ellis opted to continue his SIS career, being appointed Regional Controller for the Far East, based in Singapore, and then Chief Controller Pacific in London. It was not until after Ellis had resigned from SIS, ostensibly to work for SIS's Australian counterpart in Sydney, that a molehunt in London accidentally discovered his pre-war treachery. Ellis, who was then working on his book *The Expansion of Russia*, was confronted with his duplicity and provided a limited confession which failed to convince all who saw it that he had been entirely candid about his relationship with the Abwehr, or possibly with the KGB who were suspected of having blackmailed Ellis after the war.

The fact that Ellis had betrayed SIS was kept a closely guarded secret and he was never prosecuted, an omission which led some of his supporters, including his ageing former colleague Sir William Stephenson, to disbelieve the inevitable leak when it occurred. The news that Ellis had partially admitted his guilt was revealed by Peter Wright who also subscribed to the view that the KGB would have been bound to exploit his treason immediately after the war, if not sooner. Wright was convinced that because Ellis's first brother-in-law was a known Soviet agent it was almost a certainty that he had succumbed to a KGB threat to expose him.

Whatever the truth of the matter – and Ellis died in Eastbourne in July 1975 without telling even his family of his disgrace – there is no hint in his pre-SIS memoirs of his subsequent intelligence career. Nor is there in his later books, *Soviet Imperialism* and *Mission Accomplished*. In 1962 Ellis published an account of his own experiences with the Malleson mission to Meshed and Transcaspia, the notorious British intervention. In this passage Ellis, then attached to General Dunsterville's command, defends his SIS colleague, Reginald Teague-Jones, who was alleged by the Soviets to have been present when twenty-six commissars were shot in September 1918. Teague-Jones felt sufficiently vulnerable to change his name to Ronald Sinclair and it was under that name that he served with Ellis during the Second World War in British Security Co-ordination in New York.

Transcaspian Episode

As it became clear that no further resistance was to be expected from government forces, Dunsterville decided to evacuate the whole of his force.

As night fell, all British troops were withdrawn to the docks. Despite a threat by the commander of a government gunboat to prevent the departure of the British, several ships, with the whole of the British force, including its sick and wounded, crept out of the harbour in the darkness, while the crash of bursting shells reverberated among the rooftops of the stricken city.

A considerable quantity of artillery and ammunition had been evacuated with the troops. By agreement with Malleson part of this equipment was later sent to Krasnovodsk with a small detachment of artillerymen and naval personnel to help build up the defences of that port against a possible Turkish attack.

By withdrawing the best of the Caspian ships, several of which had been armed as auxiliary cruisers, Dunsterville sought to keep control of the southern waters of the Caspian, while at the same time depriving the enemy of the means of transporting large numbers of troops and military equipment to Krasnovodsk.

The fall of Baku, although not unexpected, aroused the Ashkhabad Committee to a sense of the danger to which it was now exposed from two sides. As so often happened when Allied forces intervened during the civil war period, there was a tendency on the part of the local authority to sit back and leave the brunt of the fray to Allied troops.

In Meshed, where General Malleson's headquarters staff was still located, news of the withdrawal of Dunsterville's troops brought with it recognition of the dangerous position of the small mixed force strung along the length of the Central Asian railway.

Messages received from liaison officers at Ashkhabad were indicative of the state of near panic in Transcaspian circles. Plots against their own security were suspected, and drastic action against suspects was already taking place.

On the morning of September 18th the Ashkhabad Committee's liaison officer in Meshed, Dokhov, called on the Mission in a state of great excitement. He announced that he had received a telegram from Ashkhabad on a matter of great importance and urgency, and that he had been instructed to communicate its contents to General Malleson and ask for his comments and advice.

Without producing the actual telegram, Dokhov informed General Malleson, in the presence of two of the General's staff officers, that a party of Bolshevik Commissars, former members of the Baku government that had been replaced by the Centro-Caspian Directorate at the end of July, had arrived at Krasnovodsk on the steamship *Turkman* and were being held under arrest by the Krasnovodsk Town Commandant, Kuhn. The Commissars, about thirty in number and including Shaumian, the former head of the Baku government, Korganov, Fioletov, Petrov and other prominent Bolsheviks, had been imprisoned by the Centro-Caspian authorities at the time of the evacuation of Soviet Russian forces to Astrakhan on August 14th, but had been released, or had escaped on the eve of the Turkish entry into Baku. According to Dokhov's account, the Commissars had left by sea that same evening, intending to go to Astrakhan, but for some reason, unknown to Dokhov, the ship had brought them to Krasnovodsk.

Their presence in Krasnovodsk was a matter of great concern to the Ashkhabad Committee, the members of which were seriously alarmed that opposition elements in Transcaspia might take advantage of the presence of the Commissars to stage a revolt against the government. The chairman of the Committee therefore requested General Malleson to state his views as to what should be done.

Questioned by General Malleson, Dokhov was unable or unwilling to add very much to the message he had been instructed to convey. He admitted that his government was alarmed by the fall of Baku and was nervous about the revival of opposition to its authority in Ashkahbad, Krasnovodsk and elsewhere. They considered that the presence of the Commissars, even under arrest, constituted a danger, particularly at a time when the situation in the Caspian area was uncertain and the Merv area was still in Bolshevik hands.

General Malleson replied that he considered that in no circumstances should the Commissars be allowed to proceed along the railway to Ashkhabad. While it was a matter for the Committee to decide what steps they proposed to take to prevent this, he suggested that the best course would be for the Committee to hand the prisoners over to him to be held as hostages for British citizens imprisoned or held under restraint by the Soviet government. He saw some difficulty in determining a convenient point for the prisoners to be handed over, but thought this could be arranged.

Dokhov seemed to be dubious, but undertook to inform his government of General Malleson's suggestion, though adding the words: 'If it is not already too late.' Asked what he meant, Dokhov said his government might already have decided what steps to take. He then left.

Immediately afterwards General Malleson sent a telegram to his representative in Ashkhabad, Captain Teague-Jones, informing him what Dokhov had said and instructing him to get in touch with Zimen, the Foreign Minister, ascertain what the position was and telegraph a reply without delay. The General then telegraphed a summary of the conversation with Dokhov to his chiefs at Simla, notifying them of his suggestion that the Commissars be taken over by him and conveyed to India for internment as hostages and asking for instructions.

On the same evening Teague-Jones replied that he had been informed by Zimen of the arrival in Krasnovodsk of the Commissars and their arrest there. Zimen had undertaken to keep him informed and had said that the Committee was considering the matter that night. Teague-Jones added that Zimen was in a very nervous state but had given no indication of what the Committee had in mind.

As was subsequently ascertained, the Committee, consisting of Funtikov, Kurilov, Zimen and Dorrer, sat until a late hour that night, apparently without reaching an agreement. Teague-Jones endeavoured to keep in touch with Zimen, but when the latter, together with Dorrer, left the meeting after midnight Teague-Jones was told that the question had not yet been settled, and it was hinted that there was disagreement between the members as to the course to be taken. Teague-Jones also ascertained that Kuhn had been pressing for a decision, as he feared there might be a local insurrection to secure the release of the prisoners. Funtikov was in a semi-intoxicated state and suspicious of British motives in suggesting that the Commissars be held as hostages.

On the following morning Teague-Jones tried to get into touch with Zimen but without success. That evening he approached Funtikov personally, and found him still in a state of intoxication and not disposed to discuss the matter. Finally, when pressed, Funtikov admitted that it had been decided to shoot the prisoners, and that he had sent Kurilov to Krasnovodsk on the previous night to instruct Kuhn and make the necessary arrangements. He declined to discuss the matter any further.

Teague-Jones immediately informed Malleson, who sent for Dokhov. On presenting himself at the office of the Mission, Dokhov, who was in one of his taciturn moods, said in reply to Malleson's questions that he had 'just been notified that the prisoners have been shot; that the Committee has decided to take this action in view of the seriousness of the situation, and the difficulties involved in acceding to General Malleson's proposal'.

General Malleson's reply to this was that in his opinion they were 'all alike – Red or White' – and that Dokhov could inform his chiefs that he, Malleson, was 'horrified at the action taken'.

Dokhov, who was clearly shaken by Malleson's outburst, withdrew without any further comment. Neither at that time nor subsequently did he intimate that he had had any prior information about the Committee's intentions concerning the shooting of the prisoners.

Teague-Jones was thereupon instructed to pass to Zimen the same comment given to Dokhov. When he did so, Zimen, in a state of extreme agitation, stated that the decision was Funtikov's; that he (Zimen) and

Dorrer were opposed to having the Commissars shot, and that Funtikov and Kurilov had taken matters into their own hands after the meeting and had given the order.

It transpired that on receipt of this order Kuhn had brought the Commissars, twenty-six in number, under guard from the prison late at night, indicating that they were being sent to Ashkhabad by order of the government authorities there. The train proceeded to a point some 200 kilometres east of Krasnovodsk, where it stopped. The prisoners were taken a short distance into the desert, and there, in the early morning of September 20th, were summarily shot. Exactly who carried out the shooting never became known, nor is it certain that any emissary of the Committee at Ashkhabad was present.

Every effort was made by the Ashkhabad Committee to keep the matter secret, and some time elapsed before rumours of what had happened reached the public. Members of the Committee, including those directly involved, began to show a disposition to dissociate themselves from Funtikov's views, and then and later sought a convenient scapegoat on whom responsibility for the shootings could be placed.

Several days after this episode took place, General Malleson was informed in reply to his telegram to Simla that they agreed with his suggestion that the Commissars be sent to India. Although it was already too late, the authorities in London, still unaware of what had happened, were considering the possibility of exchanging the Commissars, as well as other Bolsheviks who were in British hands, for British diplomats and officials who had been imprisoned by the Soviet government. At a later date, when the Soviet Foreign Commissar, Mr Chicherin, sought information through neutral channels regarding the whereabouts of the Commissars, the Soviet government was informed that they were not and had never been in British hands.

Although anticipating the course of events it would be useful at this point to relate briefly what subsequently happened in relation to this affair. The fate of the Twenty-six Commissars did not become known in Moscow until early in the new year, or, if it was known, no public announcement was made. A short time after the reoccupation of Baku by British troops from Enzeli, following the Turkish capitulation, a Socialist-Revolutionary journalist, Vadim Chaikin by name, who had played some part in Soviet domestic affairs in Tashkent, and now evidently seeking to ingratiate himself with the Bolsheviks, visited Transcaspia from Baku, and there interviewed Funtikov in prison. On his return to Baku, then in British occupation after the Turkish withdrawal, he published an article in a local newspaper in which he accused the British of being responsible for the arrest and execution of the Twenty-six Commissars. He followed this up later with a book, published in Moscow, elaborating this theme, making the accusation that British officers were directly involved, and that the shooting had been carried out on British orders. He cited the 'confession' of former members of the Ashkhabad Committee, including Funtikov, as evidence.

Although Chaikin produced no factual evidence to substantiate his assertions, the Soviet government now publicly accused the British government of responsibility for the evacuation of the Commissars from Baku and for their subsequent arrest and execution. Statements contained in Chaikin's article and book were cited as 'evidence'. Reports of the shooting of the Commissars were broadcast by the Soviet Radio, while the Soviet Press was filled with articles describing how the Commissars were supposed to have met their end.

Since that time the Soviet government has persisted in this charge, and has declined to accept any assurance from the British government that the facts are otherwise than as stated by Chaikin and other Soviet spokesmen at that time. The case of the Twenty-six Commissars now forms part of the epic story of the Soviet revolution. The version presented by Chaikin has become Soviet official history, so that it is included in the *Great Soviet Encyclopaedia* as a factual account of the episode, and paintings by Soviet artists and illustrations to books dealing with the civil-war period depict British officers as being present at the execution.

In fact no British officer was in the vicinity, nor was any British officer or official aware of what was happening to the prisoners until information was extracted from a drunken Funtikov after the event.

The circumstances in which the Commissars were brought over from Baku have never been satisfactorily cleared up. It is uncertain whether the Centro-Caspian authorities ordered their release, or whether friends rescued them from prison during the chaos that prevailed on the eve of the Turkish occupation of the city. Various Soviet personalities claim to have effected their release, but there seems to be some mystery surrounding their departure on the *Turkman*. The captain of the vessel informed the authorities in Krasnovodsk that the ship was bound for Astrakhan when it left port, but that the crew declined to take it here, ostensibly because of fuel shortage. In all probability, some members of the crew were uncertain what fate held in store for them on their arrival in Astrakhan. In any case, the arrival of the ship was quite unexpected in Krasnovodsk, and it was only through the action of the guard-ship from which a message was sent ashore to Kuhn that the latter was able to apprehend the Commissars before they were able to land.

The full impact of this unhappy episode on relations between the Malleson Mission and the Ashkhabad Committee, and subsequently between the Soviet and British governments, was not to make itself felt for some time. Funtikov's action in disregarding Malleson's advice completely destroyed any reputation he may have enjoyed in the General's eyes. Malleson had no high regard for revolutionary leaders, whether Bolshevik, Menshevik or Socialist-Revolutionary. He considered them to be unprincipled demagogues, self-seeking leaders of the ignorant mob, all equally untrustworthy. If he had had any knowledge of the Russian language his attitude, forcibly expressed in public as well as in private, might well have added to the difficulties experienced by his Russian-speaking staff in their relations with members of the Committee and its representatives.

William J. Gibson

The circumstances of my case were exceptional, and I had been indiscreet in the past. The Russian Secret Service always was second to none, and even today Moscow knows full well the names of all those who are her friends and those who are the enemies of Russia.

Born in Canada, William Gibson was with his parents in St Petersburg when war was declared in August 1914. Upon hearing the news he went to the British Embassy to demand a commission and, having been turned away by the military attaché, volunteered for the Russian army as a motorcycle despatch rider. Gibson fought in Poland and on the Russian–Bulgarian border until the end of 1915 when he took his German fiancée to London. There, in March 1916, he visited the War Office and offered his services. 'Eventually I was received in one of the offices with great courtesy by an impressive-looking Intelligence colonel, who informed me after a little conversation that I was exactly the man who was wanted, and that all I had to do was to go back to my hotel and await instructions. Full of joy, I did as he requested – and I was still sitting in my hotel five weeks later.'

Instead of working for the War Office Gibson accepted a job with a small trading company and was told to return to Petrograd and have the 'office in running order by the time my chief, C—, arrived on the scene.' Gibson, accompanied by his wife, arrived in Petrograd in March and his 'reputation of "mystery man" grew by leaps and bounds, as we learned later. As a matter of fact, I was, unknown to myself, about to become a real mystery man.' The cause of the mystery was Colonel Sergei Rudniev's offer to Gibson to join the Russian Secret Service, a proposition that the young man accepted. Thus Gibson embarked upon a mission to Tashkent in Central Asia as an SIS agent, and as 'Spy upon spies Number 41' for Colonel Rudniev.

Gibson succeeded in his assignment and in mid-1917 was back in London, ready for a new mission. He travelled to Finland and was then smuggled over the frontier into Russia to re-establish contact with Rudniev who had retained his post in the secret police under the new regime headed by the Social Democrats. The Colonel supplied Gibson with papers identifying him as a police commissar which allowed him the freedom to travel but, when Rudniev was himself arrested by the Cheka, Gibson fled to Finland.

Once back in London Gibson received a commission from the Air Ministry and was posted as an intelligence officer to Taranto, in Italy. He complained about his new job, and was sent to another backwater, Malta. Finally, in November 1918, he was transferred to Sir Hugh Trenchard's air intelligence staff in Paris.

In February 1919, following the armistice, Gibson was demobbed and obtained a job as the Mond Nickel Company's representative in the Black Sea region, selling copper sulphate. This took him across Asia Minor, and in 1920 he was back in London, ready to undertake another mission to Russia, buying gold in Moscow and smuggling it to Sweden. Gibson's adventures continued in the southern Soviet republics, where he traded in valuable commodities, experienced suspicion and hostility and on one occasion endured arrest and interrogation at the hands of the Cheka.

In his autobiography, *Wild Career: My Crowded Years of Adventure in Russia and the Near East*, published in 1935, Gibson recalled his commercial activities, which left him nearly bankrupt in Istanbul following the collapse of one of his business partnerships, and describes the complexity of operating as an agent for two separate intelligence services.

Wild Career

At the conclusion of our meeting, which lasted all the morning and ended with lunch, I told Colonel V— that, having considered the matter carefully, I felt that, as I was under contract to the Asiatic trading company, it was my duty to inform my manager, C—, that I was also working as a Russian agent. It was possible, I pointed out, that complications might arise. Knowing C— to be a patriotic Englishman, however, I assured the Colonel that he need have no fear of the outcome. The giant replied that he had no objection to this.

There are, perhaps, in the last few paragraphs hints of sensational and sinister material sufficient to develop into a series of breath-taking espionage novels. Real-life espionage is not like that. It means hard work, hard thinking, and alertness more than anything else. At least, that is what it meant in my case. I do not intend to dwell upon my three months as a business-man-cum-Russian-secret-agent in Turkistan, but the interlude had its interesting, exciting, dangerous, and amusing experiences, and I think that some of these are worth recording.

On that first afternoon I met Arnold B— at the local office which he had established for us. Here we discussed details both of our special work and of the commercial side of the mission. We decided to use the symbols of the Morse code as a means of communication on the trucks, since a few dots and dashes in chalk on the rear of a truck would not particularly attract those not in the secret.

Then we turned to the question of our staff for the expedition. At times we should need a fair number of men to act as drivers of pack-animals and for various manual duties, and Arnold B— advised me to hire these locally as required. But he advised me, too, to employ a first-class permanent head man to run the expedition – and to pay him well. He said that he had waiting outside just such a man as I needed, in whom I could place 'complete and absolute' confidence. Here he winked, and then added that such a man and any special men whom the head man might request me to take along with him would be invaluable in gleaning the gossip in the native bazaars. Arnold B— then called into the room a tall, broad-shouldered Tartar, with long, dangling moustaches and a flat, hideous, and utterly expressionless face. He was introduced as Baron 'Karapet,' and bowed with stately grace.

I was rather surprised at hearing this person called 'Baron'; his flowing garments were faded and rather greasy – not suggestive of aristocratic idleness. However, I soon learned that in Turkistan it is not so difficult to become a baron as it is in many other parts of the world. All you have to do is to acquire a flock of forty goats; and if you are clever you can steal these from somebody else. Unfortunately, Baron 'Karapet' had awakened one morning to find that his flock of goats had disappeared at the hands of he knew not whom; so, being no longer a man of means, he had gone to his friend Arnold B—, with whom he had had former dealings, and here he was, ready to swear 'eternal loyalty' to me for a wage which would be absurdly small in European countries. When he talked and smiled his ugly face became pleasantly animated, and he seemed to me likely to prove a stout and capable man, moreover, with an excellent knowledge of Russian; so I accepted his services.

'Karapet' recommended me to hire six friends of his as henchmen. They would act as guards, taskmasters, batmen, and, as necessary, cooks or assassins. I replied that I should like to interview these handy men on the morrow, but the Baron burst out enthusiastically with the information that I could see them on the instant, as he had them waiting outside, knowing that I should 'be gracious enough to give them employment.' A moment later six hideous Tartar giants, exactly like 'Karapet,' were filing into the room and making obeisance with solemn faces. They were magnificent men, and I felt that any man should feel confidence with these seven tall horsemen of the steppes at his back. I placed the six at the disposal of 'Karapet,' whom I sent to bargain for camp equipment, horses, and other necessities for the expedition, knowing that he would contrive to provide these at about half the price at which I should be able to do so.

I had meant to tell C— after dinner that evening about my secret activities, and had been awaiting the moment with some uneasiness; not that I thought he would object. As it turned out, owing to an unforeseen happening, the information, far from being a confession, formed the climax to a comedy.

It was an exceedingly warm evening, and we were sitting at the table in C—'s room, high up in the hotel, discussing estimates. The door was shut, and the table was between C— and the door. All at once C— became silent, and I saw that he was sitting bolt upright, as if listening intently. Then, to my amazement, he suddenly disappeared under the table, crawled beneath it, and, a moment later, still on his knees, was crouching with his hand on the knob of the door. He leaped to his feet and jerked the door open. A ragged Turkoman in a huge scarlet turban lurched into the room, and landed with a startled grunt on his hands and knees. C— attempted to seize him, but the man was on his feet like a flash, his teeth bared and a curved knife in his hand. As the Turkoman slashed, C— dodged to one side and became entangled with a chair. I rushed round the table, but by the time I had torn open the door, which he had slammed, the Turkoman had disappeared somewhere down the dim corridor.

'It's not worth while following him,' muttered C—. 'We should get very little out of him, I think, even if we did succeed in catching him.'

Of course, I had a guilty conscience. I thought that some information about my secret *rôle* must have leaked out, and that the man had been sent to listen to my conversation. C— had relit his pipe, and seemed to be taking the whole affair with a surprising lack of concern.

'What on earth made you think anybody would be listening at this door?' I asked curiously.

C— grinned to himself enigmatically, and settled himself comfortably in a cane armchair.

'Well,' he began slowly, 'seeing that you are my right-hand man out here, I think perhaps I should make a confession to you. You understand that what I tell you is in the profoundest confidence? But I have every reason to consider you a person of discretion, or you would hardly have got this job. I am a member of the British Service – in fact, I am the excuse for this mission, or, if you prefer, this mission is an excuse for me.'

I sat for a moment in astonished silence, and then I could not help laughing. C— had hardly expected his information to be received as a witty sally.

'I'm not trying to be funny, you know,' he said severely, raising his eyebrows.

Then I told him about my intended Russian activities. There seemed nothing to do but celebrate the occasion and toast each other's luck in the venture. Very appropriately at that juncture R— made his appearance, and who more fitted than he to conduct us on a round of the local night haunts he had discovered?

I had told C— that R— was in with me, and he agreed, therefore, that it would be as well for him to be let into the secret. It was after we had told R— of the joke Fate had sprung upon us, and before setting out, that C— disclosed a somewhat disturbing piece of news. Ever since C— had introduced himself in his true colours I had been wondering who could have come to suspect the motives of the trading mission, and now C— threw light on this without being asked.

'I may be wrong,' he told us, 'but that little occurrence at the door a few minutes ago makes me fear that we are going to be spied upon, or possibly even worse, for the rest of this trip. I put it down to a stroke of ill-luck which I had yesterday morning. I went to the Russo-Asiatic Bank to settle the financial arrangements for the mission and was informed that the manager was on holiday. The head cashier took me into the private office and undertook the necessary business for me. This man's name is F—. He spoke English in what sounded to me like a strongly marked German accent, and I didn't like the way in which he talked: his mother, whose father owned large estates in South Russia – how well her family had always treated the peasants on the land; how sad he was to be away from his beloved Russia; and how his father was such an enthusiastic supporter and organizer in the patriotic causes in Petrograd – all as if he was trying to impress me with his own patriotism and enthusiasm for the Allied cause. He kept on plying me with questions about the trading mission, and it wasn't long before I felt I was being "pumped" and made haste to get out. Then, yesterday evening, if you remember, while you and R— were amusing yourselves, I came home to write letters. The Russian clerk at the desk in the lobby looked up casually as I passed to go upstairs, and said in French, "Ah, Monsieur C—, there was a gentleman named F— who called here asking for you this afternoon, soon after you had gone out. I asked if I could take a message, but he said that his business was not of the least importance, and that it was not worth troubling you, as he might call again later. I thought you might be interested to know that somebody had called." Well, at that point I was not exactly interested in the news; I was just mildly surprised. When I reached my room, though, I became decidedly interested on the instant!

'It had been ransacked, although nothing of any value had been taken. My papers were scattered all over the room. Fortunately, I make a point of never keeping confidential papers anywhere but in hiding-places which an inquisitive person is not likely to discover – but, still, from the papers that were found an intelligent investigator could have gathered facts to raise his suspicions. I calculate that the unknown visitor came up the steel fire-escape which leads from the deserted garbage dump behind the hotel, in through the window at the end of my corridor, after which it would have been simple to enter my room with a skeleton key, which any native craftsman would make in five minutes for a song.

'My reason for thinking that F— was the culprit was because the visitor must have known the number of my room and on which floor it was situated. Now, apart from native servants of the hotel, who would not be interested in my papers, as they certainly could not read Russian, and the few white members of the hotel staff, who, I think, can be ruled out, the only person who could have known the number of my room was the cashier F—, who would have seen the number against my name on the letter-rack which hung behind the clerk at the desk. I did not mention that my room had been searched at the time, as I had not then made up my mind to tell you my true *rôle*.'

It was useless to worry over the affair, and we departed to celebrate. I am afraid I cannot remember how I was brought back to the National Hotel in the following dawn.

Two days later, having made our final arrangements, C—, R—, myself, Baron 'Karapet,' his six stalwarts, and twenty mounted tribesmen of nondescript race, with a long string of pack-animals, left Tashkent and set out across the desert steppes for Vyernyi. The whole party was adequately armed.

Vyernyi and the approach to it is one of the hottest spots to be found in Russian Asia. The only human beings we met during the sweltering days were occasional merchant caravans of camels or pack-horses, making for distant Samarkand, and wild nomad tribes with their flocks. These people are as wild and savage as they were in the days of Tamerlane, although, if properly treated, are disposed to be friendly. In appearance they are fierce, hideous, and uncouth to a degree, and their horsemanship is such that man and beast seem like one. To see them on their shaggy horses makes one realize how terrified the inhabitants of ancient Europe must have been when Attila, the 'Scourge of God,' led the hordes upon them 'so that the grass refused to grow where they had passed.'

Often when camping at oases round the water-holes we found ourselves near these people. We appeared too formidable a cavalcade to be trifled with, and therefore C—, R—, and I, as leaders, became honoured guests in their tents. These wild men did not smell overpleasant or value water for purposes of washing; lice and bugs meant nothing to them; so that a feast at their tent doors was rather a trial; but by this means we were able to get fresh meat at a reasonable price, besides cheese, milk, and eggs.

The favourite game of these people is the 'goat game,' and it presents such an astonishing spectacle that time and again we used to ask them to perform it. They always complied with the greatest good humour and eagerness. The only requisite is the corpse of a large goat. The players, usually all the male members of the tribe, mount, and, carrying the dead goat, proceed to the top of the steepest ridge within sight. Then they form a rough line, and the corpse of the goat is sent hurtling to the bottom of the ridge. Before the corpse has finished jolting and bounding on its course somebody above gives a signal, and the players launch their horses at full gallop down the ridge after it, roaring and howling like madmen. Their object is to gain possession of the goat and bear it to the top of the ridge, but as, since the game began, no man has ever succeeded in carrying the goat in a state of entirety to the starting-point, the winner in actual practice is the man who arrives at the top of the ridge with the largest portion. The goat is torn in hundreds of pieces, and clouds of dust surround an indescribable bedlam of men and horses. After one of these skirmishes the site is strewn with men and horses, like a veritable battlefield, but, considering the rough handling which is meted out liberally, the casualties recover with surprising frequency, and appear to have thoroughly enjoyed themselves.

But a less intriguing habit of these desert horsemen is their manner of honouring their holy men at death. The holy men are not placed in a grave, but merely laid on the ground and covered with earth. At their head is planted a tall pole, and on this are hung horses' tails. The more horses' tails a priest has dangling from his pole, the more holy he was in life. These holy men seem usually to be laid to rest at oases where passing travellers can meditate on their holiness, and as decomposition sets in very rapidly in those hot regions, it can be understood how we suffered at times when the desert night winds were blowing in our direction, or, worse still, when we arrived at a camping spot after darkness had come down!

There were two Bashkirs in our *entourage*. From the first C— took a dislike to them. They were certainly villainous-looking individuals, but villainous looks were not uncommon. C— said that they always seemed to be skulking about our tents and peering inside or trying to listen to our conversation. I ascertained that both men spoke Russian, although in itself that also was not uncommon, but they did seem to be always in our vicinity, both in the pack-train and in camp, when they could find an excuse to be so. Several times we found the things in our tents unaccount-ably disturbed in our absence, and once C— saw one of them appear from behind his tent when he approached, and had a fleeting impression that the Bashkir had just slipped out of it. 'Karapet' said he knew nothing about them; they were good at their job, and labour for the caravans was difficult to get in Tashkent, so we ought to be content.

When we were a little over half-way to Vyernyi I developed that most unpleasant of diseases – dysentery. I was soon in a high fever, and riding became impossible. 'Karapet' accordingly selected the two most docile pack-animals and constructed a rough litter, and I was carried along between the two horses. It was not a pleasant mode of travel, and the sun beating through the canvas shade did not help me in my weak condition.

On the second night of my illness we camped in a pleasant oasis, where the air was full of the perfume of certain little shrubs and bushes which grow on the steppes, and the scent of holy men was weak, while near by us a tribe of nomad Kalmucks had put up their shelters. As the night came on my temperature rose to 105 degrees. I could not sleep, and tossed and muttered to myself in a rather light-headed manner. C— and R—, after attending to me, had been sitting outside my tent, smoking and chatting. Their own tents were a little distance away and were unlighted. Our men had turned in for the night, and there was no sentry, as C— and R— had gone over and called on the headman of the tribe, and such is hospitality among nomad peoples the world over that this ensures safety.

At about half-past eleven the two of them entered my tent and took my temperature. Finding it to be still at 105 degrees, they gave me cooling drinks and decided to sponge me down, in hopes of lowering it in this way. After completing this operation they prepared to go to their own tents to turn in. C— was the first to leave. The moon was shining brightly. Suddenly he let out an oath, and I saw him start back in the tent opening. He shouted something at R—, tugged out his revolver, and darted out of sight. Three reports rang out deafeningly loud on the still air. Then I heard rattling, champing, and neighing from the horse lines, followed by the frantic padding of hooves on the hard sand.

The whole oasis was in an uproar. Forgetting my illness, I staggered to the tent door, to see C— and R— talking excitedly to 'Karapet.' Suddenly shots came from the direction of the nomad camp, and spurts of sand leaped up in the moonlight. Our men came rushing up, firing wildly as they ran. R— and 'Karapet' shouted, 'Don't shoot!' and eventually, by a process of punching and kicking them, succeeded in making them all lie down on their faces. Bullets continued to whistle over, and blood-curdling war-cries came from the Kalmuck encampment. C— threw down his revolver, pulled out his white handkerchief, and rushed towards the horse lines. Presently I saw him galloping towards the nomad lines, waving the handkerchief over his head and shouting, 'Peace! Peace!' in the native dialect. The firing stopped. Presently C— came riding back with the Kalmuck headman and about twenty followers. There was much shaking of hands, bowing, and apologies; tea was made in the native style and handed round, and C—'s store of cigarettes began to disappear rapidly; then the Kalmucks departed.

I returned to my camp bed, but I felt a different man and quite cheerful – in fact, my temperature had dropped to just above normal. R— made his appearance soon afterwards, and C— followed.

C— explained that as he went out of my tent he looked up and saw two natives, with curved knives in their hands, creeping into his tent. He rushed towards the tent, and they fled to the horse lines, seized two horses, and galloped away. The three shots fired by C— had alarmed the nomads, and only his prompt and risky visit to their camp had saved us from being massacred. He had found, upon examining our men, that two were missing, and they were the two Bashkirs whom we had suspected of spying. All that C— could get out of the others was that they thought the Bashkirs were ex-convicts who were in the pay of bad men in Tashkent.

Allan Monkhouse

I was not charged with anything definite, but it was obvious from the questions asked, what the nature of the charges which the OGPU had in mind was. They suggested that I was an agent of the British Secret Service.

Allan Monkhouse lived in the Soviet Union for nine years and devoted more then twenty-two years of his life to developing trade between London and Moscow. All his efforts were nullified when, in March 1933, he was arrested and accused of being part of a massive conspiracy to undermine Communism and sabotage Stalin's plans for economic reform and recovery.

Monkhouse's arrest by the notorious OGPU, together with that of forty-two others, among whom were six British engineers, did not come as a complete surprise. His Russian secretary had been detained briefly in January and a strong protest had been registered by her employers, Metropolitan-Vickers Electrical Company, which was supervising heavy engineering contracts for the installation of electricity generating plant in various Soviet power stations. After some hours of interrogation at the Lubyanka, during which he was accused of espionage on behalf of the British Secret Service, sabotage and bribery, Monkhouse and a colleague, Charles Nordwall, were released on condition they did not leave Moscow. The eventual indictment, handed to the defendants on 9 April and running to eighty-five pages, revealed that Monkhouse's secretary had made an incriminating statement to the OGPU about the activities of Monkhouse's chief engineer, Leslie C. Thornton.

At the subsequent trial, in which there were seventeen defendants, Monkhouse's lawyer pleaded his client guilty to a charge of bribery and Thornton made what purported to be a signed confession in which he admitted having worked for SIS, and named Monkhouse as the organizer of a network of twenty-six engineers, all his agents.

All our spying operations on USSR territory are directed by the British Intelligence Service, through their agent, C. S. Richards, who occupied the position of Managing Director of the Metropolitan-Vickers Electrical Export Company Limited. Spying operations on USSR territory were directed by myself and Monkhouse, representatives of the above-mentioned firm, who are contractors, by official agreement, to the Soviet Government, for the supply of turbines and electrical equipment and the furnishing of technical aid agreements. On the instructions of C. S. Richards given to me to this end, British personnel were gradually drawn into the spying organization after their arrival on USSR territory and instructed as to the information required. During the whole period of our presence on USSR territory, from the total of British staff employed, 27 men were engaged in spying operations. Of the above, fifteen men which included

Monkhouse	Annis A.
Cox	Annis H.
Thornton	Shipley
Teasle	Pollitt
Shutters	Waters
Burke	Nordwall
Riddle	Clark
Macdonald	

were engaged in economic and political spying, also in the investigation of the defence and offence possibilities of the Soviet Union. The remaining 12 men who included the following:

Jule	Gregory
Jolley	Smith A.
Cornell	Fallows
MacCracken	Nowell
Richards C. G.	Charnock
Cushny	Whatmough

were engaged in political and economic spying.

Similarly, a construction engineer, William MacDonald, conceded that he had collected and reported information for SIS from the Zlatoust Armament Works. Monkhouse, who was the senior Vickers representative and identified as the ringleader, pleaded innocent to all the remaining charges and protested that the bribery incident concerned a loan that had been written off as a bad debt. Under interrogation he also made a deposition regarding his predecessor, Anton Simon, who had worked for Metro-Vickers until his death in 1928:

> I knew that Simon had a special fund which he used for bribes. I firmly believe that he was interested in certain counter-revolutionary movements, but I did not enjoy his confidence. He did not trust me for certain personal and political reasons. I cannot give exact information about his activity in this direction. Upon Simon's death I was, immediately afterwards, appointed Metro-Vickers' manager in the USSR.

The trial was brief and was reported by a large press corps among whom, working on his first foreign assignment, was a young Reuters man named Ian Fleming. On 19 April Monkhouse was acquitted on the charge of espionage but convicted of having known of Thornton's sabotage, and of complicity in bribery. Thornton was sentenced to three years' imprisonment, Macdonald to two years. Together with his South African-born engineer John Cushny and his colleague, Charles Nordwall, Monkhouse was deported to London. Only William Gregory was acquitted on all charges. Upon his return Monkhouse was invited to Buckingham Palace to give the King an account of his experiences, and among the many journalists covering the story was a young *Sunday Dispatch* reporter named John Bingham. He was later to inherit an Irish barony and become one of the leading intelligence officers of his generation.

The British government expressed indignation at the treatment of the six prisoners from the moment of their arrest but Monkhouse's account of the episode, *Moscow 1911–33*, was not entirely candid. He omitted to mention his own experience as an intelligence officer in Russia during the 1918 Allied intervention in Archangel, service that he had shared with C. S. Richards, the export manager of Metropolitan-Vickers. At the trial the Soviet prosecutor emphasized Monkhouse's intelligence connections but in his own version Monkhouse ignored the issue entirely. In this extract Monkhouse describes how the feared OGPU deliberately instilled terror in the Soviet population.

Moscow 1911–33

There is little doubt that the OGPU themselves circulate fantastic tales of the tortures and punishments which it is alleged are employed in their prisons and places of detention. When the new headquarters of the Leningrad OGPU were recently completed, a terrible rumour was circulated throughout the city regarding an elaborate mincing-machine in which it was alleged that the OGPU destroyed their victims before washing their remains out into the Neva. Although I am convinced that there does not exist the slightest pretext for this rumour, it was nevertheless firmly believed by thousands of Leningrad's inhabitants. In Moscow one frequently hears fantastic tales of physical tortures to which the OGPU are reputed to subject their victims. Many of these alleged tortures completely eclipse the horrors of the Spanish Inquisition, but it is my own conviction that such methods are not used by the OGPU, and, in fact, I very much doubt whether many of their reputed victims are ever shot. The OGPU have a definite purpose in circulating such wild stories of their methods, and there is little doubt that, when they detain their own nationals for questioning and examination, the mere existence of these rumours is in itself sufficient to so terrify their victims as to make them comply readily with the examiner's demands without the OGPU officers themselves resorting to anything other than a little exaggerated politeness and firmness.

Whether torture and the extreme punishment are used or not, one thing is certain, and that is that the OGPU have struck terror into the hearts of the whole populace. Every dweller in the USSR walks in fear of those who preside at the Lubianka, and their agents. The mere name of the OGPU is seldom referred to audibly and openly.

The manner in which the OGPU act in obedience to the plans and impulses of the political group who dictate policy in the USSR will be sufficiently obvious from the chapters following dealing with the recent trial of my colleagues and myself in Moscow.

The importance of the OGPU being completely in the hands of the political dictators of the Kremlin cannot be over-exaggerated in Moscow's dealings with the constituent republics of the USSR. Nominally these republics are in many respect autonomous, as they possess a large measure of self-government. The constitution of the USSR clearly defines in what respects the Moscow Government's actions are limited in these outlying republics. On the other hand, the actions of the OGPU are not limited by anything in the constitution of the USSR, and, although the Moscow Government may not be constitutionally able to influence decisions in the autonomous republics of the Union, nevertheless the OGPU is in a position to take steps against the instigators of any political action contrary to the wishes of the Moscow political dictators. Thus the OGPU, in the hands of Stalin and his Party associates, constitutes one of the strongest 'unifying influences' existing in the USSR, and ensures that the constituent republics comply implicitly with the demands of the central Communist Party executive in Moscow.

Early in 1933 the power of the OGPU was greatly strengthened by a decision to place the civil police force of the whole country under its general supervision. Previously the civil police forces had been subject to the local Soviets only.

Following Stalin's speech in Moscow on January 7th, 1933, a decision was made to establish political control on the collective and State farms throughout the USSR. Many thousands of Party agents were sent into the country districts, and, as has already been stated, the Communist Party Executive recently announced that 10,139 specially chosen Party workers had been sent into the villages to take charge of the political side of the work on the farms. The relationship between these Party workers and the OGPU can probably be guessed even by those who have little knowledge of the USSR.

More recently, and following the Moscow Trial, the Government have considered it necessary to enforce the provision in the constitution of the USSR which provides that supervision of the legality of actions of the OGPU shall be carried out by the Procurator of the Supreme Court of the USSR. According to recent reports, Professor Veshinski, who as Public Prosecutor of the RSFSR prosecuted in the Moscow Trial, has been appointed deputy to Comrade Akulov as Procurator of the Supreme Court of the USSR.

All OGPU officials and troops are granted extraordinary privileges. They have their own co-operative stores, where food and commodities are always available, even when the ordinary workers' co-operatives are compelled to announce that they have nothing to sell. They have reserved seats, and, frequently, reserved compartments on every train, and the central coupé of the sleeping coaches on the International Sleeping Cars is almost invariably reserved for senior OGPU officials. The privileges which OGPU officials and secret agents enjoy are not infrequently used to induce Russian citizens to join their service as secret informers.

The OGPU does not allow its hundreds of thousands of victims to remain entirely idle. The total number of Soviet citizens who are now working under the supervision of the OGPU probably reaches many millions, of whom three-quarters at least are 'employed' in compulsory labour settlements such as those on the recently completed White Sea Canal, where returns show that nearly a quarter of a million detained citizens were compelled to work. When Mr Litvinov, speaking at the World Economic Conference in London, claimed that the USSR had no unemployment, apparently he was not aware of the unemployment which is resulting from the large reductions in works and factory staffs which have been made during recent months and he discredited entirely the number of citizens unemployed, and only partially employed, in the prisons and detention camps of the OGPU, who alone probably comprise as many as the total registered unemployed in Great Britain.

Peasants and kulaks are, as a general rule, drafted more or less straight away into the large construction camps where their services can be used. The White Sea Canal and Kuznetzstroi, may be cited as examples of great constructional works in which the OGPU have provided the majority of the technical supervision and labour employed.

Engineers, technicians and other educated people who fall into the hands of the OGPU are, in most cases, submitted to some weeks or months of solitary confinement before the subject of working is introduced. During this period of solitary confinement they are frequently subjected to protracted examinations, and are threatened, even although they may not know for what 'crime' they have been arrested. The OGPU openly state that the object of this preliminary period is to 'break' their victims. Finally, they are drafted into technical and special planning bureaux, where they work under escort and constant supervision. These technical bureaux employing arrested engineers are a definite part of the Soviet authorities' organization. In more than one case I have been called upon to supply technical information to engineers working under conditions of this nature. OGPU officials have shown me technical periodicals, written and published in their bureaux, and I had amongst my papers in Moscow a publication entitled *Bulletin of Special Technical Construction Bureau of the OGPU, No. 26*, which had a limited circulation in 1931 and 1932, and which constituted an excellent summary of modern developments in heavy rolling-mill drives based on the very latest world practice. This publication was 'accidentally' left on my desk by a man who, I now suspect, was an OGPU agent.

In conclusion, one word of praise for the OGPU. It is unquestionably the best organized and best disciplined force in the USSR, and its officers and men are obviously trained to exhibit calmness, tolerance and politeness. Although one sees soldiers of the Red Army unshaven and carelessly dressed, and with unclean boots, I have never seen an OGPU official unshaven or dressed discreditably, even in the most outlying districts. In every corner of the USSR one meets the officers of the OGPU, and, no matter where it is, the foreigner who applies to the local OGPU authorities for help will be received with politeness and get the best possible assistance that the most powerful force in the USSR can render. On many occasions I have felt profoundly grateful to the OGPU for assistance when travelling.

Finally, I would say that, even when I entered the dreaded Lubianka as a prisoner, the officers and *prison* officials with whom I came into contact showed me the utmost consideration.

The nature of my cross-examination by Belogorski made it necessary for him to continue questioning me long after he knew that I was worn out, but even he was always a disciplined, firm and studiously polite officer of the OGPU.

Somewhat closely associated with the OGPU there exists the Commissariat of Workmen's and Peasants' Inspection (RKI). This body reports to the Sovnarcom and Tsik in the same manner as that in which the OGPU reports. Its duties are to control the activities of all State organizations and officials responsible for carrying out the Government's plans. It has its officially appointed agents in every large State organization. Any irregularities, mismanagement, or failure to maintain the programme laid down in the Government's 'Control Figures,' are investigated by the RKI, whose activities are almost more feared by Government officials than those of the OGPU. The duties of the latter are confined to combating real and alleged counter-revolution and criminal plots, whereas the duties of the RKI finish with correcting inefficiency, negligence and incompetence. The RKI have no police or soldiery of their own, and when they find it necessary to regard a case which they have under investigation as one involving counter-revolutionary or criminal activities they hand the matter over to the OGPU.

Sir Samuel Hoare

The greater part of our Secret Service work was of a routine character, the signalling of suspected persons, the holding up of contraband, the transmission of agents' reports, and the exchange of departmental memoranda.

To have written between the wars of one's adventures in the Secret Intelligence Service was no great crime, particularly if the author concerned had subsequently acquired some status. In Sam Hoare's case, he had been the Member of Parliament for Chelsea when he was first recruited for intelligence duties, and he never lost the scepticism his experience during the First World War gave him. In 1930, shortly before his appointment as Secretary of State for India, he published the first volume of his memoirs, *The Fourth Seal: The End of a Russian Chapter*. His disclosures did nothing to jeopardize his political career and he was later to be Foreign Secretary, First Lord of the Admiralty, Lord Privy Seal, Air Minister and, after clashing with Churchill, British Ambassador in Madrid.

Hoare had learned Russian apparently in the hope that this would enable him to lead an interesting life and travel abroad. In March 1916 his linguistic skill had brought him before Smith-Cumming, the first chief of the Secret Intelligence Service, and he was despatched to Petrograd on a mission that he described vaguely as having to do with counter-espionage. Hoare returned to England the following year, having completed a survey of 'intelligence possibilities' in Russia, and in June was appointed head of the British Intelligence Mission to Petrograd. Once again he made his way to Russia, accompanied by his wife. He recalls that 'my first duty according to my instructions was to put myself into the closest personal touch with the chief of the Russian Secret Service. I found there was no such person. In Russia every department seemed to have a Secret Service and nobody exercised any central control.'

Hoare's further encounter with SIS took place in Madrid upon his appointment as ambassador there in 1940. He saw his task as preventing Franco from joining the Axis powers and he regarded the local SIS station as a source of potential embarrassment. Not long after his arrival the SIS representative, Colonel Edward de Renzy Martin, who was operating under military attaché cover, was declared *persona non grata* for 'attempting to obtain strategic information' and this confirmed Hoare's worst suspicions. Thus when Donald Darling arrived on a reconnaissance prior to extending the SIS station to accommodate a permanent escape and evasion expert from P15, Hoare was not just uncooperative but obstructive and ordered Darling's immediate return to Lisbon.

Hoare died in May 1959. His second volume of memoirs, *Ambassador on Special Assignment*, published in 1946 after he had been ennobled as Lord Templewood, omits all references to SIS although the first volume had given a fascinating description of his first encounter with Captain Smith-Cumming, the SIS chief who had sent him on his secret mission to Moscow.

The Fourth Seal

Each of the three Intelligence Services, at the War Office, the Admiralty, and the Foreign Office, was in the hands of a remarkable man. At the head of the Department of Military Intelligence was Major-General Sir George Macdonogh, an officer of varied training and almost encyclopaedic knowledge. On the one hand, a professional soldier of distinguished service, and a trained Staff Officer of broad experience, on the other, a man of wide political knowledge, who from the early days of the crisis grasped the new fact that the struggle was not so much a war of armies as a war of nations, that the rear was often as important as the front, and that civilians could sometimes play a part in the world of Intelligence that was denied to professional officers of more restricted training. Inevitably, some measure of professional jealousy and exclusiveness existed in the General Staff. How well could it be otherwise? Regular Officers would not have been human if they had not occasionally resented the intrusion of amateurs, who had passed none of the searching tests to which they themselves had been subjected. But, speaking generally, it may be said that of all the Departments that underwent extensive expansion during the course of the war, none was more ready to open its doors to men of every walk of life than the General Staff, and no chief was more anxious to utilise the services of politicians, men of business, and members of the civil professions than Sir George Macdonogh.

Of a very different type was the Director of Naval Intelligence. Small and very alert, his hair greyer than his years justified, his eyes as bright as any that I have ever seen, known to many as Reggie, and to even more as Blinker Hall, there had, even in 1915, gathered around him an atmosphere of drama, mystery and brilliant achievement. Of his flair for exposing spies, of the cunning with which he tricked enemy agents, of the instinct that enabled him to sift the grain from the chaff in a heap of reports, the frame was already echoing throughout Whitehall.

Like his colleague at the War Office, he opened the doors of his

Directorate to any talent that was available in the outer world. A well-known stockbroker was his right-hand man, and when I subsequently travelled from Rome to London with him, his confidants were a director of the Bank of England and a partner in a well-known brandy firm.

At the time that I was presented to him he was greatly discontented with the inadequacy of the intelligence that he was receiving from Russia. It was well that I listened attentively to his remarks, for in a few weeks' time I was to act as his liaison with certain departments of the Russian Naval Staff.

Thirdly, I come to the head of our Secret Service, a department that whilst serving many masters was technically under the Foreign Office, and to the man who was to be my immediate chief. What shall I say of this remarkable personage? If I describe him in detail, I may be charged, even though the circumstances of the work have completely changed, with disclosing secrets about the holiest of the Intelligence holies. If I pass him by with a word, it may be thought that he is not worthy to be placed as a peer in the company of General Macdonogh and Admiral Hall. Let me then confine myself to saying just enough to emphasise his qualities, but not enough to identify him or to disclose the details of his activities.

In all respects, physical and mental, he was the very antithesis of the spy king of popular fiction. Jovial and very human, bluff and plain speaking, outwardly at least, a very simple man, who would ever have imagined that this was the chief who conducted the British 'Business of Egypt' and employed secret agents in every corner of the world?

My first interview with him was typical of the man. I had expected to be put through an examination in the Russian language, and a questionnaire as to what I knew about Russian politics and the Russian army. I had imagined that I should have been almost blindfolded before being introduced into the presence of this man of mystery. Instead, there were a few conventional words in a very conventional room, a searching look and a nod to say that whilst it was not much of a job, I could have it, if I wanted it. What did it matter to me that the job was insignificant, and the surroundings of my chief so different from what I had expected? The chance would take me to Russia and plunge me into work that was certain to be of paramount interest. In the space of a few seconds I was accepted into the ranks of the Secret Service. For the following weeks I was to learn something of the work and to discover what kind of post was to engage my activities.

It is disclosing no secret, that has not long ago been divulged, to say that the Allies had Secret Service Missions in each other's countries. These

Missions were engaged upon espionage and contre-espionage directed against the enemy, and not against the allied country in which they were operating. They were duly accredited to the various governments, working in closest liaison with the Allies and usually installed with the allied army or in the offices of the allied army's General Staff. Such a Mission had in the early days of the war been sent to Russia and had for eighteen months worked with varying success in the Russian General Staff.

Being new, secret, and very indefinite, these organisations were bound from time to time to come into collision with the ordinary missions of peace-time diplomacy. Indeed, there were some who thought that the work that was being carried out might have been better undertaken by the Attachés, Military and Naval, of our Embassies and Legations. I do not myself think that these critics were right. The tradition that keeps British diplomacy free of Secret Service should not lightly be set aside, and the problem of war Intelligence was so novel both in its size and complexity that men who had been in recent and direct touch with the centre were more likely to deal successfully with it than those who, however excellent they may have been in their pre-war posts, did not always realise the new needs that the war had created. Be this as it may, the practical difficulties of organisation were considerable, and Whitehall, no less than the Chanceries of our overseas missions, often rang with interdepartmental disputes as to the exact place that Secret Service should hold in the official hierarchy. One of these controversies had been rumbling on in Russia for some time, and it seemed well to the authorities in Whitehall to send out a new officer to join the British Intelligence Mission in Petrograd, whose first duty should be to smooth away some of the difficulties that had arisen. Besides, as the war developed, the need for Intelligence other than Military became more insistent, and it was considered that a Member of Parliament like myself might be useful in obtaining information for our various war trade departments. I was, therefore, to proceed to Petrograd and to work permanently in the existing Mission as an additional officer on its staff. But Intelligence questions were necessarily in a state of flux and within a few weeks this arrangement was altered, and it was decided that I should go to Russia for two or three months, study on the spot the problem of Intelligence and the organisation of the Mission and then return to London to make a report. This alteration of plan had the advantage of bringing me back to London in a comparatively short time, and of enabling me to give the War Office my general impressions of Russian affairs at a time when the Eastern front and Russian politics were enveloped in a baffling obscurity.

During the weeks before I left England, I was passed through an intensive course in the various war Intelligence departments. One day, it would be espionage or contre-espionage, another coding and cyphering, another, war trade and contraband, a fourth, postal and telegraphic censorship. The ever-widening territory of Intelligence was broadly divided into two provinces. On the one side, espionage and Secret Service covered the many activities by which information was obtained from enemy countries. On the other, contre-espionage protected us from the multifarious attempts of the enemy to obtain information about the Allies. The mobilisation of propaganda had not yet been undertaken, nor had the dread possibilities of sabotage been fully explored.

It was upon this broad and enticing field that I had now set foot. Interview followed closely upon interview, for all the war departments in Whitehall had some commission for me to carry out in Russia. Two, indeed, of these commissions, I had to fulfil even before I left England. A foolish young Englishman had embroiled himself with enemy suspects. As he was an Attaché in the Diplomatic Service, his case looked serious in the eyes of the police. Would I go down to Brixton prison, interview him and advise the authorities as to what had better be done with him? According to the report that was given me, he was anxious to clear himself by undertaking war work of some kind and, being a linguist, he hoped to make himself useful in the field of Intelligence. My talk in the prison waiting-room sufficiently convinced me that he was very foolish, not at all dangerous, but altogether unsuitable for responsible work.

The second task was even more curious. One of the most notorious murderers of the last generation, whose capital sentence had been commuted to penal servitude for life, had been working in his leisure time at the Russian language. He now asked for an earlier release than his good conduct justified, in order that his knowledge might be used in the service of the country. As I also had learnt Russian with this same object of escaping from a monotonous life, I was not inaptly asked to judge of the qualifications of my fellow Russian student. With so much in common, I did what I could for the industrious murderer. He had learnt a remarkable amount of the language when it was remembered where and how he had learnt it, but he did not know enough for Intelligence work. He had, however, behaved well in prison and his effort was accounted to him for righteousness. Though it was impossible to employ him for his knowledge of Russian, I was able to get his release antedated, and to find a chance for him in another field of war work.

I do not say that I was able to learn much in the course of those few weeks, but I at least learnt enough to realise the complexities of the war machine that had been created in Whitehall and the personalities of the foremen who were working it.

My guide through an army of officers and officials and a labyrinth of departments was my old friend, Freddie Browning, famous upon every cricket ground and in every racquets court, the friend of more people in the world than almost anyone I knew, and at that time the chief mainstay of the office in which I had taken service. He had become a General Staff officer of the first grade. A brass hat and red tabs had banished his Zingari tie, and the game that he was now playing was catch-as-catch-can with enemy agents.

My education seems to have proceeded so satisfactorily that at one time it was intended to keep me in London as the head of a branch dealing exclusively with Russian Intelligence. Fortunately, the idea was dropped, and towards the middle of March 1916, I was allowed to proceed upon my mission.

A journey to Russia was at that time something of an adventure. It involved travelling to Newcastle, leaving at an uncertain hour, and probably in a small steamer, spending two or three days on the North Sea, an equal time in Scandinavia and two days between Tornea, the frontier point between Finland and Swedish Lapland, and Petrograd.

As an allied officer was liable to internment in a neutral country, it meant my travelling in mufti and concealing my sword in an umbrella case.

For some days before my departure I collected letters of introduction, laissez-passers and visas of all kinds upon my passport. I was to take a Foreign Office bag, and I well remember that, just before the train left King's Cross, I discovered that I had allowed the whole collection to be sealed up in the sack. I had only a few minutes to spare to hurry back to the Foreign Office, have the seals broken and replaced, the letters extracted, and to find my seat in the train with General Germonios, a General of the Russian Artillery, and two or three other Russian officers over whose return to Russia after a mission in London I was to watch as best I could.

For fear of raids Newcastle was pitch dark when we arrived and, what with the Russians who spoke no English, my Norfolk soldier servant who had never before been abroad, and an unknown number of suitcases and boxes, it was a formidable affair to manoeuvre everybody and everything on to the *Jupiter*. The *Jupiter*, the Norwegian steamer, that became very well known to travellers in Northern Europe during the war, was the best of the North Sea boats. An excellent officer, Captain Hansen, commanded her, and it fell to me upon a later voyage to present him with a gold watch as a token of the British Government's gratitude for the courtesy that he had always shown to British travellers.

No light was to be seen when we started down the Tyne, and I went to bed as best as I could in the dark. German submarines were reported to be near the mouth of the river, and not a match was lit on board. Should I go to bed, and if I went to bed, should I undress? That night I answered these questions as I answered them upon many other similar occasions during the war. I both undressed and went to bed. If there was to be a catastrophe in the night, I should at least have a comfortable hour or two's rest to my credit.

Augustus Agar

This was my first introduction to 'C' – the name by which this man was known to all who came into official contact with him. He had, of course, other names and one quite well-known in London society, but to us, or rather to those who served under him, he was always known and referred to by this single letter of the alphabet.

Baltic Episode

In the early summer of 1918 Lieutenant Agar was given command of a flotilla of fast 40-foot coastal motor boats and sent to the remote island of Osea in Essex. He had assumed that his role would be one of coastal protection, but he was asked by Mansfield Smith-Cumming to take two of his craft to Finland. Their purpose was to ferry British agents across the Baltic, and in particular give a means of escape to ST-25, SIS's star agent in Russia whom we now know to have been (Sir) Paul Dukes.

Agar's clandestine missions proved so successful that he was ordered to mount a surprise night raid on Kronstadt, across the Gulf of Finland, where the menacing Soviet fleet was anchored. Operating from an abandoned yacht club at Terrioki, Agar's CMBs sped over the water at speeds of up to 40 knots and launched their torpedoes against the Russian cruiser *Oleg* which sank soon afterwards, a feat for which Agar was to be decorated with the Victoria Cross.

His first volume of memoirs, *Footprints in the Sea*, was published in 1959, and was followed by *Showing the Flag* in 1962, and *Baltic Episode* in 1963. Agar remained in the Royal Navy until his retirement in 1943 when he was appointed Commodore of the Royal Naval College at Greenwich. He stood for the Greenwich constituency in the 1945 General Election but lost. For the remainder of his life, until his death in December 1968, he grew strawberries on his estate at

Alton in Hampshire. Here he recalls how he embarked on an adventure that would win him the Victoria Cross and the Distinguished Service Order.

Footprints in the Sea

Having despatched from Osea Island one flotilla of CMBs to the Caspian Sea for operations at Baku and prepared a second one for the Archangel Expedition, we were now getting a third ready for police and patrol duties on the Rhine when I was sent for by Captain French and asked if I would undertake a 'special mission' of great importance. He was studying charts spread out on a side table, some of which were of the Baltic coast.

'I will not ask you whether you will do this or not,' he said, 'because I know you will, but I have selected you as the first choice to take two of our smallest type CMBs (40-footers) to the Baltic. The matter is so secret that you are not to tell a soul until the details are worked out and then only the bare outline of your task. You will work as a civilian under the Foreign Office for whom you will carry despatches. Your venue will be the Gulf of Finland in the Baltic.'

He went on to tell me that I would be in sole charge and it was of the utmost importance that *no one* – not even in the Navy – must have the slightest suspicion who we were or what we were doing. I was to report next day to a Commander in the Naval Intelligence Division.

I met this Commander, as arranged, at the Admiralty. We had a short conversation about our work in CMBs at Osea Island after which I followed him out of the Admiralty through a passage and into another building which was even more of a rabbit warren, but instead of burrowing underground we ascended to the very top of this building where, almost on the roof overlooking London, was a small suite of offices. A young woman immediately came out of one and spoke to the Commander. Turning round to me and pointing to the door, he said, 'You are wanted in there,' and I went in.

Seated at a large desk with his back to the window, absorbed in studying a map with a document in his hand, was the Naval Officer to whom I had been introduced by Captain French at Osea Island. He was wearing plain clothes and I was fascinated by his large intelligent head which I could see in profile against the light. He continued his study of the map and document without taking any notice of me standing by the door; then, putting them aside and banging the desk with his hand, he said, 'Sit down, my boy; I think you will do.'

This was my second introduction to C. In London Society he was quite well known, but to us who served under him and knew him personally he was known and referred to only by this single letter of the alphabet.

C. was the head of the British Secret Service.

He had a wonderful gift of putting people at their ease and I was soon absorbed in listening to him. The subject was Russia whose frontiers were closed against us and with whom we were virtually at war. He explained how essential it was to restore the connecting links of communication between our own Allied side and those whom we knew we could trust on the other. In particular there was one man in Petrograd – an Englishman – who was of particular importance to us. It was vital for him to send out his reports at intervals. This could be done only through a chain of specially selected 'couriers' who, at the risk of their lives, brought these across the frontiers of Finland. Unfortunately, this system had broken down in the last few months and it was feared some had been captured and probably executed.

We must regain touch with this man who was in effect the centre of our Russian secret service intelligence system, and afterwards get him safely back to this country to report personally on conditions inside Russia to the Foreign Office. This was the problem.

A possible solution, he thought, might rest with our fast CMBs, which could cross the narrow gulf of Finland and land the couriers on the coast of Estonia close to the Russian frontier. From the Estonian coast they would make their way overland into Petrograd and thence to Moscow. There were many 'ifs' in this idea. First, we had to get the boats out there. Secondly, we needed a base to work from and thirdly, there was the risk of a breakdown in which case we would be captured and dealt with by the Russians. One boat was not enough; we must have a spare one, and above all SECRECY. Only the Head of our own Admiralty Intelligence would know what we were doing or where we were going.

I would receive from his Secret Service organization in the Baltic all the help they could give. I would pick my own team who must be young, keen, reliable and few in number. We were to be civilians, wear civilian clothes and have new names, new identities. Henceforth, we would be known by a letter and a number.

Our boats would be shipped to Sweden as fast speed boats for yachting purposes for which we were the salesmen. From Stockholm we would be re-shipped again to Helsingfors and off-loaded at a small port called Abo on the coast of Finland, a small pleasure resort and yachting centre. I was to return to Osea Island, pick up boats and crew and then go back to

London for final arrangements. The Naval Commander who had brought me in would give me all the help I needed in London while Captain French would do his part at Osea.

'Now go back to your base, select your crew, make your plans and return here when they are made,' C. said briskly, and the interview was at an end.

Back at Osea Island Captain French helped me to make plans. Two of the small 40 ft. CMBs were selected, given an overhaul and tried out on the river. For crews I chose three young Sub-Lieutenants, J. Sindall the senior, R. Marshall, and J. Hampsheir. All were RNR. In addition, two mechanics – one for each boat – Beeley (known always as 'faithful Beeley'), and Piper. Our team therefore consisted of six 'salesmen' which was the minimum necessary to run two of these high power boats. They were not told where we were bound but that it might be to reinforce our flotillas at either Archangel or the Black Sea. This was a reasonable explanation for our hurry, and gave rise to no particular speculation on the Island.

To divert attention we split our party into two lots of three and had the boats towed to the West India Docks in London where they were repainted and special tarpaulins made to cover them. They were consigned by previous agreement to a firm of yacht agents at Abo in Finland. For stores we shipped inside the boats the barest essentials for spare parts, and managed by a piece of good luck to get from Messrs. Thorneycroft a special compressed air charging plant which later saved our lives.

I must explain here that our boats were powered with either Fiat or Thorneycroft engines of about 250 horse power. There were no electric self-starters fitted so we had to start them with compressed air from charging bottles of which each boat carried two. If, unluckily, we had a leaky bottle, as often happened, it was just too bad and we had to rely upon the spare one until the dud bottle was taken ashore to be recharged.

From now on things began to move rapidly. I reported back to C. and explained our plan. Much, in fact everything, depended on the help we received from his agents in Finland who had to arrange for our petrol and oil, loading and unloading the boats, and so on. I intended, with their help, to select a small inlet on the Finnish coast facing Estonia from which to work. This should not be difficult since there were many of them. Then we would run the 'couriers' across to the opposite coast at night, a distance of between thirty to fifty miles which at our high speed should not take more than two hours in calm weather.

C. approved every detail of the plan. 'Two matters,' he said, 'must be considered. The first is to give you at least a sporting chance if by bad luck you either break down or are caught on the wrong side of the frontier. You can take with you – *but only in your boats* – one uniform coat and cap to put on over your overall in case of a crisis. But remember, they must never be taken out of the boat. From now on your party must assume the name and description on your new passports. You yourself will have one of our special numbers, ST34.' The number of our special man in Petrograd was ST25. When communicating with each other we were to use the single letter T.

He explained briefly that there was a force of naval cruisers and destroyers operating in the Baltic under the orders of a British Admiral, Sir Walter Cowan, who alone would be informed that I was there but not what I was doing and only in the Flag Officer's special Secret Code.

'Finally,' he said, 'how much money will you need?' Here was a poser which I had never considered nor had I ever been used to handling more than an ordinary sum of money in cash. I took a wild guess. 'A thousand pounds, sir,' I said. C. pressed one of the bells on his desk and when a secretary entered the room said, 'Make out a cheque pay cash one thousand pounds.' He went on to say they were not in the habit of handing over money casually like that, but this was a special case. I must keep only a rough account how I spent it as no details were expected of me. Any advance of pay required by our crew could come out of it, and if I wanted more his agents would give it on demand.

I was then passed on to another part of the building to be instructed in other matters including the use of special cyphers, inks and codes, also how to approach our contacts and who they were. No names were ever mentioned, and by degrees I began to get used to my new identity. We were to leave from Hull in two days and there was still much detail to arrange for the boats.

For my final interview C. took me to have luncheon at a well-known club. To my astonishment he drove past the sentries on the Horse Guards and through the entrance, explaining to me that he was one of five only who had this privilege. His hobby, and I learned afterwards his mania, was driving high speed cars which accounted for the loss of one leg. Like myself he loved sailing boats and we talked of nothing else until it was time for me to go. With a friendly pat on the back he said, 'Well, my boy, good luck to you,' and was gone.

Sidney Reilly

I express my willingness to give full and honest testimony and information on questions of interest to the OGPU concerning the organization and composition of the intelligence operations of Great Britain and, insofar as I know it, also information concerning American intelligence.

Extract from Reilly's confession to the OGPU

Born Sigmund Rosenblum in Odessa in 1874, the illegitimate son of a local Jewish doctor, Reilly adopted the surname of his first wife's Irish father and thereafter pretended to have his origins in Connemara. He was an adventurer, an arms dealer and traveller, and lived for a time in New York where he made and lost a fortune, and London, where he found a patron in Sir Henry Hozier, Winston Churchill's father-in-law.

Reilly's travels began when he emigrated to Brazil but his first marriage took place in London where he met a widow, Margaret Reilly Callaghan. A second, bigamous marriage followed to Nadine in New York where he operated as a purchasing agent of munitions for the Russian government.

In 1916 Reilly volunteered for military service and was commissioned into the Royal Canadian Flying Corps. Two years later, in March 1918 he was transferred to SIS and posted to Murmansk with the codename ST-1. His task was to foment resistance against the Bolsheviks and, together with George Hill, he played a key role in the Lockhart plot, the failed assassination attempt on Lenin. When Reilly and Hill eventually escaped to Sweden, in October 1918, they were decorated with the MC and DSO respectively.

Reilly's commitment to the anti-Bolshevik movement became something of an embarrassment to SIS although he continued to advise the Foreign Office of developments in Moscow until his eventual return in September 1925. The journey from Finland was sponsored by the Trust, a shadowy opposition group that claimed extensive support even within the Communist Party's hierarchy. In reality the Trust was a sophisticated deception, manipulated by the OGPU, which exercised control over the dissidents and occasionally enticed troublesome opponents of the regime across the frontier and into elaborate traps. Reilly's political mentor, Boris Savinkov, was just such a victim. In August 1924 he set off from Berlin, under the Trust's protection, with the intention of re-establishing contact with his supporters. He was arrested immediately upon his arrival and, after a trial at which he was sentenced to death, received a pardon which effectively marked his conversion to Communism. He is believed to have committed suicide in May 1925.

Despite Savinkov's experience Reilly was persuaded by a leading member of the Trust, Toivoi Vjahi (later identified as a senior OGPU officer, I. M. Petrov), to slip across the Russian frontier on 25 September 1925 to address a secret gathering of the Trust's senior membership. The meeting took place in a dacha at Malak-hova and afterwards Reilly was driven not, as he expected, to a safehouse, but to the notorious Lubyanka prison in Moscow. Months of interrogation followed, during which neither SIS nor his most recent wife, an actress named Pepita Bobadilla, had any news of his whereabouts. She knew he had been in Helsinki, and SIS had last heard of him via a postcard mailed from Moscow two days after he had left Finland. In fact Reilly, shaken by the speed and efficiency of his entrapment, had written a very full confession and had agreed to co-operate with his captors.

The announcement of Reilly's death was made in *The Times* on 15 December 1925 but in reality he had by then been dead for more than a month. He had been kept a prisoner, under constant interrogation, until his execution on 5 November by a single bullet in the back of the head. Documents purporting to have come from Reilly's dossier, only recently released from the KGB's archives, show that he was driven into the woods near Bogorodsk, shot, and then buried in the courtyard of an OGPU prison. There are, however, various reports of uncertain reliability, indicating that Reilly was either a Soviet-controlled double agent, a theory propounded in 1968 by a leading academic, Revolt Pimenov, or that he survived his imprisonment, a claim made to George Hill in 1943 by his NKVD contact, Colonel Ossipov.

Reilly's widow Pepita persisted in her attempts to extract information from the British authorities, and even approached Winston Churchill for help, but he insisted that her husband 'did not go into Russia at the request of any British official, but went there on his own private affairs'. Heartbroken by these rebuffs, Pepita arranged for Reilly's memoirs, which contained the names of several senior SIS officers, to be published. Her intention was to embarrass SIS and force them to help her husband, but by the time she had finished the necessary editorial work, and the book was released, Reilly could not be saved.

Sidney Reilly: Britain's Master Spy

In the spring of 1918, on returning from a mission, I found my superiors awaiting me with some impatience. I was instructed to proceed to Russia without delay. The process of affairs in that part of the world was filling the Allies with consternation. Following the breakdown of Kerenski's abortive administration and the accession of the Bolsheviks to power Russia had ceased hostilities against Germany. Germany, relieved of all apprehension in the East, was attacking in the West with reinforced troops and redoubled ardour.

Of course the part played by Germany in the Russian breakdown was well known and my instructions were to counter, as far as possible, the work being done by the German agents, and to report on the general feeling in the Russian capital. My superiors clung to the opinion that Russia might still be brought to her right mind in the matter of her obligations to the Allies. Agents from France and the United States were already in Moscow and Petrograd working to that end.

After my experiences as an espionage agent in Germany my Russian task seemed safe and easy. I knew Petrograd as a man does know the city in which he has lived from childhood to middle age. I was returning home after an absence of only two years. I had many friends in the city. I knew where I could go when I arrived there. I knew upwards of a score of people on whose co-operation I could implicitly rely. In short the whole mission promised to be the very antithesis of my adventures in Germany, where I had to keep up a perpetual disguise, where any moment might be my last, where often I had no idea where to turn or what to do next.

Accordingly it was Sidney Reilly who arrived quite openly in Petrograd to visit his birthplace and the *cari luoghi* of his youth.

I had not been prepared for the full extent of the change which had come over my birthplace. Petrograd, which once could challenge comparison with any city in the world, bore a ruinous and tumbledown aspect. The streets were dirty, reeking, squalid. Houses here and there lay in ruins. No attempt was made to clean the streets, which were strewn with litter and garbage. There was no police except for the secret police which held the country in thrall, no municipal administration, no sanitary arrangements, no shops open, no busy passengers on the pavements, no hustle of traffic on the roads. The place had sunk into utter stagnation, and all normal life seemed to have ceased in the city.

When I had last been in Petrograd in 1915, food had been scarce and bread queues a feature of the landscape. Now, in 1918, the bread queues were still there, but there was no food at all. The great mass of the people was starving.

It was impossible to obtain any sort of conveyance. Carriages were not to be had for love or money, if there were any of either at that time in Russia. I had already determined on my first port of refuge, the house of an old friend, Elena Michailovna, who lived in the Torgovaya Ulitza. It was a longish distance from the Fontanka, where I had been landed, but I walked there with as good a grace as I could muster. Everybody I passed avoided my glance and shuffled by with obvious suspicion and terror. Petrograd was in a state of panic. Slowly the atmosphere of horror, exuded from the very walls and pavements, seemed to grip at my heart, until I was in a mood to start at a shadow, and to my mingled embarrassment and amusement I was in a cold bath of perspiration when finally I reached my goal.

Watching that I was not observed I slipped into the house. It might have been a necropolis I entered and my footfall awoke a thousand echoes. I stopped at the well-remembered door and rapped upon it, my knock reverberating strangely through the silent building. I had to knock three times before I heard answering footsteps creeping silently, stealthily, on the other side of the door.

After another pause I knocked again and this time the door opened very silently, very slowly, very little upon its hinges.

The silence was unnerving, but it was Elena Michailovna's voice, which asked in tones of subdued alarm:

'Who is there?'

'It is I, Sidney Georgevitch,' said I.

A gasp of surprise answered me. A chain rattled, and the door was opened a little wider.

'You,' gasped Elena Michailovna, incredulously. 'You – back again in Petrograd,' and she began to sob quietly with relief.

And thus I came back to Petrograd.

I had already worked out a plan of campaign.

The first thing I did when I had billeted myself was to get into touch with some of the members of my old Petrograd set, whom I thought might be of service. I had to proceed with caution. Some might be fled, others dead, others under suspicion. It was not even impossible that some, despairing of the future, might have joined the Bolsheviks.

However, as it happened, my lucky star was in the ascendant. The man on whose assistance I set more store than on that of all my other potential allies, was immediately procurable. Grammatikoff was not only a scholar and a thinker, but a man of character. He had been long acquainted with me and his loyalty was above suspicion. It was a queer moment when I heard his voice over the wire. Two years had passed since last I spoke to him, and in those two years Russia had been turned upside down. It made our friendship seem immensely ancient somehow, as if we were survivors of a forgotten civilisation.

In pursuance of my policy of appearing in my own person, I fixed an appointment with him at his office and went round to see him openly. Grammatikoff gave me a very graphic and terrible account of the position of affairs in Russia. The new masters were exercising a *régime* of bloodthirstiness and horror hardly equalled in history. The most ignorant and the most vile, everybody who conceived that they had a grievance against society were in the ascendancy. Russia, Grammatikoff said, was in the hands of the criminal classes and of lunatics released from the asylums. Nobody did any work. There was a growing want of all the necessaries of life. People were starving. The vast majority were prepared to rise in revolt, but there was nobody to lead them. The terror of the Tcheka was heavy on every man.

All the higher officials of the Tcheka are members of the Communist Party, and the names of some of them are known. But who are its servants what man shall say? The man who has been your friend from infancy, the woman you love, nay, your parents or your children may be in the service of the Tcheka against you. It is a terrible, a gruesome, a ghastly thing. Nobody trusts anybody any more; no man dare commit a secret even to his bosom friend. Some of its work is done by *provocateurs*, men who deliberately foment counter-revolutionary plots, and when they have engineered a conspiracy, which is just about to burst into open flame, betray it to their masters. The streets run with blood, and one more counter-revolutionary plot is discovered and avenged.

In the foul cells of the Butyrsky at Moscow sit scores of the wretched victims of the Tcheka. The 'Investigators' employ every diabolical device, every ghastly torture ever invented by the fiendish ingenuity of man to wring from them a confession or a betrayal. They are held under examination without rest or food until the reason goes, and in their madness they reveal their complicity in plots, real or imaginary, against the Bolshevik power.

Such is the Tcheka, which ministers to the preachers of the foulest and most horrible gospel known in the history of the world. Such are the means by which, unless it is checked and that soon, Bolshevism will master every country in the world. And it can only be checked by an organisation as subterranean, as secret, as mysterious, as ferocious and inhuman as itself.

In Petrograd, however, I was but a bird of passage. The capital of Russia and the headquarters of Bolshevism were located in Moscow, whither I was now ready to proceed. But here an unforeseen difficulty interposed. Travelling by railway between Petrograd and Moscow was only possible on a pass, and passes were forbidden to all but officials. 'Divide et impera' was the Bolshevik motto.

In this difficulty I was able to avail myself of Grammatikoff's assistance. Grammatikoff had charge of a fine library, and among the Bolsheviks then in Moscow was the bibliophile General Brouevitch. Brouevitch had approached Grammatikoff with an offer to buy some of his books. At my suggestion Grammatikoff offered, if Brouevitch would secure him a pass, to come to Moscow, bringing me with him. The Bolshevik general was charmed and Grammatikoff and myself set out for Moscow under official favour. And Moscow was a city of the damned.

Something like this, I thought, Hell must be – paved with desolation, filth, squalor, fiendish cruelty, abject terror, blood, lust, starvation. The Bolsheviks were masters of Russia.

A city of the damned. Slowly it sank into stagnation; hoardings went up to cover dust and rubble and ruin, or did not go up and left dust and rubble and ruin naked. There had been looting at first, but now there was nothing left to loot. The rabble had been riotous, full of the lust of blood and destruction. Now the rabble was cowed and frightened, except for the few that were Bolsheviks. Everywhere was starvation, food-queues, that had forgotten to be clamorous, dearth, stagnation. And over all silent, secret, ferocious, menacing, hung the crimson shadow of the Tcheka. The new masters were ruling in Russia.

A city of the damned. Bolshevism, the new bantling of slow time, had been baptised in the blood of the bourgeoisie. Among its leaders were those who had been before oppressed by society – whatever they were, criminals, assassins, murderers, gunmen, desperadoes. The more serious their crimes had been, the heavier the penalties hanging over their heads at the time when all prisoners in the state prisons were released, the greater was their grievance against society and the greater was their welcome to the ranks of Bolshevism. A man who could read and write was eyed askance; the illiterates were obviously of the oppressed, and now their time had come.

The premium put on ignorance among the high Bolshevik officials was of the greatest value to the British Secret Service. Many of my agents operated with passports which were something more than dubious, and which were frequently scanned with an air of great knowingness by Commissars, who could neither read nor write.

George Hill

No longer was I a spy, an outlaw liable to be summarily shot against a wall.

Dreaded Hour

One of the more curious appointments of the Second World War was the decision in 1942 to sent George A. Hill, a legendary anti-Bolshevik, to Moscow to liaise with the Soviet intelligence authorities. Known to his friends as Peter, Hill was sent on behalf of Special Operations Executive but long before he arrived in Russia he was well known to the NKVD. Indeed, following the publication of his two volumes of memoirs, *Go Spy the Land* in 1932 and *Dreaded Hour* four years later, there could be no mistaking the man who fifteen years earlier had rescued the Romanian crown jewels from Bucharest only hours before the Red Army began its occupation. Born in Estonia, son of a timber merchant who travelled constantly in the Near East, and educated by French and German governesses, Hill could speak half a dozen languages and was a natural recruit for intelligence duties when he reached the Western Front at Ypres in April 1915 with a battalion of Canadian infantry attached to the Manchester Regiment. Initially an interpreter, Hill was soon undertaking dangerous missions into no man's land, on one of which he was badly wounded. A transfer to the War Office followed, and this in turn led to an assignment in Greece where he learned to fly and, based in Salonica, took his plane behind enemy lines to land Allied agents.

In 1916 Hill travelled to Egypt for a new assignment and en route met Compton Mackenzie who, he recalled, 'was running a brilliant secret intelligence department against the Germans'.

In July 1917, back in England on leave, he was ordered to Russia to join the Royal Flying Corps mission at Petrograd, but by the time he arrived the revolution had taken place and he found himself caught up in the strife. His main adventure began when he accepted a commission from the Romanian ambassador to rescue the Romanian crown jewels, which had been deposited in the Kremlin for safe-keeping, together with most of Bucharest's treasury, and return them to Jassy, the temporary seat of government in war-torn Romania. Thus Hill found himself escorting a train of treasure across the newly declared Soviet republic and over five or six battle fronts to the Romanian frontier. The epic journey lasted nine days and, after receiving the thanks of the Romanian prime minister, he returned to Moscow to help organize Trotsky's intelligence apparatus along the German front. During this period when chaos ruled Hill teamed up with Sidney Reilly. Hill did not fully approve of Reilly's commitment to the anti-Bolshevik Boris Savinkov and preferred to concentrate his resources on fighting the Germans in a guerrilla campaign waged in the Ukraine.

The Allied occupation of Archangel in August 1918 abruptly ended Hill's relationship with the revolutionaries and he went into hiding just before the Cheka arrived with warrants to arrest himself and Reilly. By discarding his uniform and growing a beard Hill successfully evaded the Cheka and was evacuated to Finland with the rest of the Lockhart mission in October 1918. Hill undertook one further, brief undercover assignment into Soviet Russia, lasting three weeks, and was back in England by Armistice Day. Upon his return to London Hill was welcomed by his Chief and by Colonel Freddie Browning of SIS, and in the coming months he was to be decorated with the MBE, and be mentioned in despatches three times. In 1919 he was awarded the coveted Distinguished Service Order, appropriate recognition for an intelligence officer who had survived the most astonishing adventures at a turbulent moment in history, and was to spend a further three years in the Near East either operating for SIS or, briefly, on the staff of Sir Halford Mackinder, the British High Commissioner for South Russia.

Upon his return to London Hill found that SIS could no longer finance his escapades, so he took his wife Dorothy to live in a caravan parked in a farmer's field in Coleman's Hatch, Sussex. There he managed to survive as a technical adviser to film companies making movies about Russia, and by living off the generosity of friends. In 1930 he found a job as manager of the Globe Theatre in London, and for a short time was deputy general manager to impresario Charles B. Cochran. During this period he wrote two plays, *It is the Law* and *Release*.

Kim Philby recalled that while the jolly Hill was in the Soviet Union for SOE in 1942, 'a very belated security check of his conference room revealed a fearsome number of sources of leakage'.

After the war Hill was appointed the manager of the Apollinaris Mineral Water Co. in Germany, and for the last ten years of his life experienced a degree of comfort that had hitherto eluded him. In this extract from his memoirs Hill, who died in 1968 soon after his second marriage, describes the hazards of infiltrating agents into enemy territory by air.

Go Spy the Land

I felt that with my experience of intelligence work I could be of greater use if I learned to fly, and luckily was able to bring my chief round to the same view; and in due course I became a fully fledged pilot in the RFC.

One of my reasons for joining the RFC was to be able to drop our spies into enemy territory.

Nico Kotzov was one of my first passengers. He was a Serbian patriot who had been in the enemy's country nine or ten times and always brought back very accurate and valuable information. He was a big-boned, tall man with a long grey beard, and had a very grand manner. He wore native dress, a sheepskin cap and a heavy brown homespun cape, and always carried a shepherd's staff.

We wanted information from an inaccessible part of the country, and as this information was urgently needed it was decided to drop him by aeroplane. I took him up for a couple of trial flights, and although he did not enjoy the experience very much he was quite determined to go. He knew the country where we were going to land, and I explained to him that I wanted the landing-ground to be as much like our aerodrome as possible.

During the trial flights I asked him to point out to me, when we were flying low, grounds that he thought were suitable, and while occasionally his judgment was very much at fault, on the whole I thought that he had grasped the general requirements necessary for a landing-ground.

With luck, providing you are not attacked by enemy fighting planes, there is no difficulty in flying over strange country, but the art of dropping a spy consists in doing so unobserved. It is necessary to land your man and get away unseen, so the operation is conducted as a rule just before sunrise, after sunset, or on a very brilliant moonlit night.

The Hague regulations respecting the customs of war were drawn up before man learnt to fly, and in consequence there was no rule under the general spies clauses of these regulations regarding an airman who dropped spies in enemy's territory. But the Germans and Bulgarians had intimated that they would treat the actual pilots of aeroplanes landing spies as spies and shoot them.

This added to the risk of dropping a spy over the line, for if one made a bad landing and crashed one was for it.

General aviation had not then been developed to the perfection it has reached today, and there were no aeroplanes fitted with air brakes to make a low-speed landing possible.

Early one morning I collected Nico from the hut he had slept in and took him across to the hangars where my machine had already been wheeled out and was waiting.

Despite a large mug of hot coffee I felt very cold and shivery.

Once again I pulled out the map and worked out the course with Nico, who told me where I would find a suitable landing-field; we were to arrive a little before daybreak, when there would be just sufficient light to land.

As we climbed into the machine the sergeant in charge of the pigeons brought along a little cage with six of our best carrier pigeons in it, and at the last minute a felt cover was slipped over them to keep them warm at the altitude we should reach during our journey.

I ran the engine up. Everything was all right.

I signalled to the sergeant to pull away the chocks and we taxied out into the dark aerodrome. I opened the engine full out and we were away.

I had to do a stiff climb in the air in order to be able to cross a mountain range, and the higher I got the less I liked the job before me. The flight was uneventful. I picked up the various objectives that were serving me – together with a compass – as a guide, and got over the country that we were to land upon in the scheduled time.

It was getting light and I throttled back my engine, so that it was just ticking over, in order to land.

We lost height rapidly and I could faintly make out the ground below me, which seemed fairly suitable. As a precautionary measure I made up my mind to circle it just once more. Suddenly I noticed that the whole of the field selected by Nico for our landing was dotted by giant boulders. To land on that field would be suicide. I climbed into the air again, and when I had got sufficiently high, switched off my engine so as to be able to make Nico hear me and told him that his selection was no good as a landing-ground. He said simply that I had told him nothing about boulders, and that he imagined we would hop over them. We were in a BE2E bus and the only way to start the propeller going was to dive vertically. The force of the air drove round the propeller and if all went well one's engine started again. So I dived. The propeller started and we climbed once more into the air.

All hope of landing that morning had to be given up, but as it was rapidly getting light I hoped to be able to pick out a suitable landing-ground for the next day, and through my glasses located a dry river bed which promised to be the best place for landing, and back we went to the aerodrome.

Nico was most crestfallen at his mistake, and thought that I had been so angry with him that I had dived purposely to punish him, and it took a couple of hours of hard talk and a thorough exposition of aero engines before I could convince him that I simply had to dive to start my engine going.

Next morning we made the trip again and I safely landed my passenger. Within ten days he had dispatched all six pigeons and on the return home of the last one I took over a further cage of pigeons and dropped them from a parachute over the spot where I had landed Nico. These also returned home safely. In all I dropped Nico three times over the line.

But not all my passengers were as good as Nico.

On one occasion it was essential to drop a spy over the lines before we had even had time to give him a trial flight. The passenger was a Greek. He was looking forward to his flight and was a boastful creature.

It was a dirty morning with bad visibility and gusts of strong ground wind swept the aerodrome. My attention was fully occupied in taking off and gaining altitude. I had to climb through four layers of cloud, and in those days once one got into a cloud one was completely blinded. Now there are special instruments to make cloud-flying simple. We had been in the air half an hour before I had a moment to turn round to see how my passenger was getting on.

He was petrified with terror. His eyes were starting out of his head, and he was being violently sick. I smiled and tried to cheer him, but it was no good. I did not think it was possible for any man to be as sick so long and so regularly. I picked out the landing-ground, planed down and made a beautiful landing, but on turning round found that my passenger had gone into a dead faint and was huddled up in the cockpit. It was no good landing him in that condition and so back I went to the aerodrome. My passenger was still unconscious, and nothing ever induced him after he had recovered to go into the air again.

One of my other passengers was a man called Petrov who loved flying, and even when not being dropped over the lines would come down to the aerodrome to cadge a joy ride.

One evening, just about sundown, he climbed into his seat behind me and was given a basket with four pigeons and off we went.

He was a joyous passenger and would sing Serbian songs at the top of his voice, and even the roar of the engine could not drown the bass sounds coming from his lungs.

Those flights over the Balkans were wonderful. The mountains beneath looked like the great waves one sees in the Atlantic.

The sun had just slipped behind a mountain, and the valley in which we were to land was plunged in shadow. I spiralled down in order to lose height rapidly and circled round our landing-ground. Everything seemed clear and there was not a soul about – the conditions appeared ideal.

How often ideal conditions are a snare and a delusion! On landing we struck a furrow which jarred the bus badly, and worse still, stopped the propeller.

The only way in those days to land a spy and to take off successfully after having done so was to throttle back one's engine so that the propeller just kept turning round. As soon as the spy had landed one revved up the engine and took off again. When I first did this work it had always been a nightmare to me that my propeller might stop, for even under good conditions propeller swinging was a tricky operation and required a great deal of knack.

When learning to fly one was instructed in the art of propeller swinging, and before qualifying one was given practical tests. I was never very good at this business, principally because of my build.

I am not tall and have very short arms, I have always been rather round, and it was all I could do to reach the propeller, let alone swing it and swing myself clear in so doing. Failure to swing clear means nine times out of ten that the propeller will hit the swinger, and many a man has been knocked out at this job.

And here we were in the enemy's country with a propeller that had stopped. Petrov hopped out of the bus, and at once volunteered to swing the propeller, and I showed him how to do it.

The process in theory is quite a simple one. The pilot calls out to the swinger 'switch off,' and the swinger then turns the propeller in order to suck sufficient petrol vapour into the cylinders. When this has been done the pilot switches on the ignition and the swinger calls out 'contact,' which is the signal for the propeller to be given a sharp, quick swing and for the person doing it to step aside.

Should the engine for some reason or other not start, the man swinging the propeller calls out 'switch off,' and the process is started all over again.

For ten minutes our voices could be heard calling 'switch off – contact – switch off.'

But nothing happened, the engine simply would not fire.

Petrov was running with perspiration due to his exertion. I was bathed in the sweat of fear.

We rested for a moment, then I climbed out of my seat and went over the petrol leads and magneto points. Everything seemed in order. Then to our horror in the rapidly deepening twilight we saw a cavalry patrol approaching.

Petrov said that he would have one more swing, but before doing so we decided to release the carrier pigeons.

We had instructions in the event of likely capture immediately to get rid of the pigeons, so that the enemy could not use them to send information calculated to mislead our intelligence department. Off flew the four pigeons. And then like a demon possessed, Petrov started swinging the propeller. Still nothing happened.

The cavalry patrol had spotted us. I think at first they thought it was one of their own machines. Then they must have got suspicious, for they started trotting over towards us. Suddenly the engine fired. Petrov raced round to the fuselage and leapt into his seat. The cavalry petrol broke into a gallop and called upon us to stop. I opened up the throttle and we were away, but before we had left the ground the patrol had opened fire. Their shooting was good, for we found when we got back to our aerodrome half a dozen bullet holes in the fuselage.

Reginald Teague-Jones

My policy throughout was to be perfectly frank and straightforward in my dealings with the Russians and as time went on they certainly seemed to place entire confidence in me.

In 1917 Captain Reginald Teague-Jones was transferred from the Indian Police to GHQ in Delhi to head a section of military intelligence monitoring developments in the Persian Gulf. Although only twenty-eight, he was exceptionally well qualified, having been brought up and educated in St Petersburg. He spoke several languages fluently, including Russian, French, German and Hindustani, and his assignment to General Malleson's forces in Trans-Caspia would have been uncontroversial except for one incident. After the fall of Baku in September 1918 a group of twenty-six important Bolshevik prisoners were executed by the victorious Socialist Revolutionaries, and when the news of their deaths reached Moscow there was considerable anger among the Communist leadership. A lawyer, Vadim Chaikin, was appointed to investigate the affair and one of those he interviewed was a participant in the affair who named Teague-Jones as having instigated the murders.

Teague-Jones denied complicity in the deaths but confirmed, in a detailed report written in November 1922 for the Foreign Office, that he had been present for part of a meeting at which the fate of the prisoners had been debated by their captors. He had been asked to accept the prisoners and escort them to internment in India but when the request had been relayed to General Malleson it had been declined with the ominous suggestion that 'the Trans-Caspian authorities find some other way of disposing of them'.

Teague-Jones's supposed involvement in the executions soured Anglo-Russian relations for many years and it was a topic that Stalin would never drop. The bodies of the twenty-six were exhumed from their common grave beside a railway line and moved to a huge memorial square in the centre of Baku. In 1922 the Soviets demanded an international tribunal to prosecute Teague-Jones, which prompted the British government to issue a rebuttal of the charges laid by the lawyer Chaikin. In the formal British statement it was alleged that Malleson's intentions had been misrepresented to Teague-Jones, and that in fact the British had wanted to take the twenty-six into custody, the implication being that alive they had a value as hostages to be exchanged for British officers held by Moscow. Furthermore, in a private account of the affair written by Teague-Jones in the mid-1920s entitled *Adventures with Turkmen, Tatars and Bolsheviks*, the author leaves the impression that not only had he played no part in the executions, but he had not even been present at the controversial meeting where the Socialist Revolutionaries had discussed what to do with their prisoners.

Soon after it was announced from Moscow in May 1922 by Trotsky that

Teague-Jones had been sentenced to death for his involvement in the crime, he simply vanished, and his name disappeared from all further official British documents and lists. Nothing more was heard of him until the death in November 1988 in Plymouth of a certain Ronald Sinclair, formerly of the Secret Intelligence Service, then in his hundredth year. Further enquiries about Sinclair revealed him to be Reginald Teague-Jones who, for nearly seventy years, had lived under a false identity. Intriguingly, he left behind a journal that was published posthumously and appears to contradict some of the author's previous assertions regarding the dead Bolshevik commissars.

Little is known of Sinclair's work for SIS and MI5 before the Second World War, apart from the itinerary of journeys described in a travelogue, *Adventures in Persia*, but in 1941 he was posted to British Security Co-ordination in New York under consular cover. He retired to Miami soon after the war with his second wife, and later moved with her to Spain and eventually England. When she died Sinclair was contacted by his first wife, Valya, whom he had met in Baku, and they remained close.

In this extract from his journal Teague-Jones describes the events that led to the massacre, a version that does not entirely coincide with the account subsequently produced for public consumption by the Foreign Office.

The Spy Who Disappeared

When Baku fell, Petrov, Shaumian and party were released by their friends and hurried on board a ship, whose captain was told to make for Astrakhan. While out at sea, someone informed the captain that he had a large party of armed Bolsheviks on board, whereupon he was much taken aback and decided to make for Krasnovodsk. The Bolsheviks noticed the change in course and immediately threatened the skipper, demanding to be taken to Astrakhan. The captain was compelled to assent, but during the night secretly changed his course again and made for Krasnovodsk. He timed himself so as to arrive off Krasnovodsk at daybreak.

On approaching the harbour he started sounding the siren and thereby attracted the attention of the guardship. The latter came alongside, immediately grasped the situation and ordered the steamer to make for Ufra and come up alongside the pier there. The guardship proceeded to escort her thither, and in the meantime sent a boat into Krasnovodsk, explaining the situation. Kuhn immediately sent an armed guard down to Ufra, who covered the incoming steamer with their machine-guns. Petrov and party had come hurriedly on deck at the first sound of the siren, but the guardship was dangerously near and would have sunk them at the first sign of hostilities. The whole party put down their arms and walked sullenly ashore, where they were promptly arrested and marched off to the local jail.

The capture naturally caused a great sensation in Krasnovodsk and the news was immediately wired through to Askhabad. Kuhn and the Krasnovodsk Committee expressed anxiety to get rid of the prisoners as soon as possible as their prison was full up and the presence of such important Bolsheviks as Petrov and Shaumian would most certainly have a disquieting effect on the local Bolshevik elements, who might quite well instigate a rising and attempt to storm the prison. The Askhabad Committee were not at all anxious to take over the prisoners and came and asked my advice. They also sent a wire to their Representative in Meshed, Dokhov, with instruction to try and persuade General Malleson to take over the prisoners and deport them to India. In reply Malleson explained that it was very difficult to find the necessary guards to send them down to India and suggested that the Trans-Caspian authorities should find some other way of disposing of them. He said that he had given Dokhov his answer and asked me to inform him what action the Government eventually decided on.

That afternoon a meeting was summoned at Dorrer's house to discuss the matter. I attended. I have rather a hazy recollection of what was actually said, but I remember that Funtikov, Kurilev, Zimin, and Dorrer were present.

The question to be discussed was what was to be done with the prisoners. Kuhn had said that they could not keep them in Krasnovodsk. The Askhabad jail was full and could not hold any more. General Malleson was not keen on taking them over. There remained only the question of shooting them. There appeared a little hesitation to decide on this course. Funtikov proposed it and he was supported by Kurilev. Zimin expressed the opinion that if possible some other measures should be taken, but could not suggest any. The same attitude was adopted by Dorrer. I remained strictly neutral and took no active part in the discussion, except to repeat Malleson's message. The discussion went on for some time and eventually I left the meeting.

It was not until the next evening that, after questioning, Funtikov informed me in confidence that it had been decided finally to shoot the prisoners and that he, Funtikov, had despatched a man to Krasnovodsk on the previous night to make the necessary arrangements. On hearing this I immediately wired General Malleson accordingly. It was not until three days later that I was able to elicit any definite information from Funtikov, but upon obtaining his statement 'that the majority of the prisoners had been quietly shot', I immediately wired General Malleson in these terms.

This is the entire story so far as I am concerned. I ascertained some time afterwards that Kurilev and Kuhn had organised the execution themselves. The prisoners, twenty-six in number, had been put in a train, had been taken out and shot at a lonely spot by the wayside.

For a long time nothing more was heard about the episode and in the course of a few weeks we had forgotten all about it. The Bolsheviks did not forget, however, nor did the relatives of the dead commissars. In particular the wife of Shaumian assumed a most vindictive attitude and stirred up very considerable trouble in Moscow. The next that was heard of it was in the spring of 1919 when a certain Chaikin made a special trip to Askhabad, which was on the eve of being evacuated by the British, and interviewed Funtikov on the subject of the missing commissars.

Funtikov had at that time fallen into disfavour and was himself languishing in the Askhabad jail. Knowing that the British were about to leave Trans-Caspia and realising that the Bolsheviks would sooner or later return there, the late President was in a terrible state of anxiety. To save his skin he decided to throw the entire blame on the British in general and on myself in particular. In short, Funtikov asserted that the execution of the commissars had been insisted on by myself and that I had planned out the details of the actual execution. With this material Chaikin returned gleefully to the Caucasus and by publishing a most exaggerated version of the story, instituted an active press campaign against the British in the Caucasus. The campaign was taken up by the Moscow press and the matter has been resuscitated at odd intervals ever since. The last effort was a book on the subject recently published by Chaikin and also an article written by Trotsky.

Such is the tragedy of the twenty-six commissars. Peace be upon their souls. The Bolsheviks proclaimed that they would put to death all those who had taken any part in the execution, one individual for each of the victims. Twenty-five had already been shot and it was understood that the twenty-sixth place was being reserved for myself, but this number has now been exceeded, the total number of persons executed by way of reprisal being over forty. Whether the Bolsheviks are yet satisfied remains to be seen, but if I may make a prophecy, I feel that before the tale is quite complete, Chaikin will himself have joined the number.

Conrad O'Brien-ffrench

A secret agent must be cool and uninvolved during danger and while in the most provoking and complicated situations.

At the age of seventeen Conrad O'Brien-ffrench, an Irishman born in London, set off for Canada to become a Mountie. Shortly before the outbreak of the Great War he returned to England and was sent to France with the Royal Irish Regiment. Wounded at Mons in August 1914, he spent the next three years in a German prisoner of war camp near the Baltic where, through the use of secret writing, he established a link with British Intelligence. His contact was Cathleen Mann, who worked for SIS as one of the chief's secretaries, and, using potassium iodide purloined from the camp hospital, he kept up an illicit correspondence with her.

O'Brien-ffrench continued to use the secret writing even when he was transferred to an internment camp in Holland. The belligerents had agreed that after three years' captivity PoWs could be moved to a neutral territory; for O'Brien-ffrench this meant staying at Scheveningen and undertaking voluntary work for the Italian legation in The Hague, where the minister had responsibility for looking after the interests of Italian PoWs in Germany. Naturally this provided plenty of useful intelligence and brought the Irishman into contact with the local SIS station.

At the end of the war Stewart Menzies offered him the post of assistant military attaché at the British legation in Helsinki. This, however, was to be his cover, and he was actually to work for Major Dymoke Scale, SIS's representative in Sweden operating against the Bolsheviks. O'Brien-ffrench arrived at his new job in January 1919, and was to be introduced to Augustus Agar and Arthur Ransome. In the autumn of the following year he was transferred to Stockholm and remained there until May 1921 when his tour ended and he returned to his regiment which had been posted to India. Bored by the dull routine of soldiering, he resigned his commission in 1923 and became something of Bohemian as he studied at the Slade School of Art, and later in Paris, to be a painter, but having acquired a reputation as a playboy he spent the next few years travelling across Europe. Among his acquaintances in the art world during this period was Tomas Harris, the Goya expert who was later to join MI5. In July 1935 he was skiing in Lapland when he discovered by accident that large reserves of Swedish iron ore had been reserved for the German steel industry. This he reported to Stewart Menzies, and he was soon back on SIS's books, ostensibly running a travel company in Vienna but actually undertaking reconnaissance missions from the ski resort of Kitzbühel. Among his clients who took advantage of the low-cost ski holidays offered by Tyrolese Tours were Peter and Ian Fleming. His principal case officer was Claude Dansey, whom he disliked. 'Times had changed. British Intelligence was now run on a shoe-string budget and on my first day Claude Dansey, as new chief, had insulted me by slipping me a fiver as if he were hooking a common informer.'

At the outbreak of the Second World War O'Brien-ffrench was in Canada, having resigned from SIS because his cover had been compromised by the Gestapo, but he returned to London in the summer of 1940 and was appointed a censor in Scotland. Later he did the same work in Trinidad. He ended the war in poor health in Oxford, and soon afterwards married and moved to Canada where he bought a ranch and taught at the Banff School of Fine Arts. In his autobiography, published in 1979 when he was eighty-five, O'Brien-ffrench recalls the background to his recruitment of Rudolfo von Gerlach, his most significant agent.

Delicate Mission

In the process of organising Tyrolese Tours as my cover, I was obliged to invoke the approval and support of the National Tourist Board who had agencies across the continent. The area I had particular interest in between Innsbruck and Salzburg took a great deal of time and effort to explore for it necessitated testing various resorts along the way and *Gasthaus* accommodation for their recreational amenities in summer and winter. Many wayside inns along this road were romantically attractive. Frescos adorned the exterior and the *Weinstube*'s panelled walls and vaulted ceilings, with carved or painted furniture in the neat and clean bedrooms. Sometimes, however, there would be no indoor plumbing. In one mountain inn I asked the *Wirt* if there was running water. He assured me that there was and promptly took me to a mountain stream at the back of the house. But prices were reasonable; a bedroom and two meals for six Austrian shillings was then roughly a dollar. The extensive desk work of Tyrolese Tours was taken care of by a Mrs Sylvester, an English resident of Kitzbühel. I don't believe she had the slightest idea of what I was doing besides acting as a guide to the increasing tide of young tourists that came from England.

Maud and I based ourselves now in Kitzbühel, from where we could conveniently operate a tourist business in a triangle, with its base on the line from Innsbruck to Salzburg and its apex to the north at Munich, and eventually another triangle with the same base but with the apex to the south at Bolzano or, perhaps, eventually even Venice. Kitzbühel was an ideal place to live as it was still unspoiled and naturally charming.

In a sunny corner of the Tiefenbrunner café some friends were having coffee. Peter Fleming and his wife Celia Johnson, the actress, shared a table with Arthur Waley and Ella Maillart. Ian Fleming, a little aloof, was reading a spy novel of Buchan's when I arrived with Maud and Margarita Brambeck, a house guest, just nineteen and a dazzlingly beautiful girl. Ian sat up and closed his book and we all joined in the general badinage. It was good to associate oneself with adults while the world was playing at soldiers. It was the popular hour of the aperitif and Maud suddenly announced that it was time to leave for lunch. Surprisingly, Ian stood up and asked, 'Can I come too?'

'Of course, of course,' Maud replied, delightedly, though a little taken aback. 'I hope you will not accept too much?' she said.

'I shall accept all that I am offered,' Ian returned, laughing, evidently amused at her confusion of words. Thus began a series of sometimes near compromising contacts with Ian.

The two Fleming boys were vastly different in character; unlike Rollo and myself, Ian was jealous of the success of his elder brother and felt eclipsed, frustrated and defeated by Peter's ability to excel at whatever he did. And yet, funnily enough, when one reads the two books written by Peter and Ella, each describing their joint journey across the inner and outer Mongolian deserts, it was Ella who was the dominant personality.

These two were sons of Valentine Fleming, killed in the First World War, and grandsons of Robert Fleming, a wealthy banker in the city of London. In the presence of a husband, a mother can exercise her natural protective care and be generous with her tenderness and affection. But the responsibilities of both parents falling solely on her, she adopts a disciplinary attitude foreign to her role as a mother and very unpopular with boys. Ian's mother's anxiety over his success was evident when I lunched with her at her home in Oxfordshire in 1944. She meant him to be a credit to his family and his failure both at Eton and Sandhurst had been a personal affront to her.

The Flemings were a family of means, accustomed to leisure and being leaders in a leisured society. Yet Ian had a definite restlessness and resentfulness about him and seemed not to know how to handle it. He was ruthless with his girl acquaintances as if, by taking it out on them, he could fulfil himself. A Casanova depends upon conquest after conquest to convince himself that he believes in his true manliness. Sex, of course, can be an addiction or a means to prove something in oneself, but it is seldom done for the purpose of accepting responsibility for another. It is almost an indulgence which a witty Frenchman once described as 'l'égoisme à deux'. Nipping in and out of beds with girls is fun while it lasts, but it must never become a purpose in itself. It is rather like the hire-purchase system without the ability to conclude the deal.

That Ian was glamorous is certain. He was also nonchalant, restless, spoiled, more cynical than funny, strong willed and ambitious, and a first-class athlete. He was very much at home in Kitzbühel, having first come there in 1924 to the Forbes-Dennis's establishment at Tennerhof. Following his problems at both Eton and Sandhurst it was hoped that the Forbes-Dennis could help him to find himself. The blessing of this interlude was not lost on Ian and he was deeply grateful to this kindly and understanding couple.

At our time of meeting he was still employed by Sir Robert Jones as a Reuters correspondent and had recently returned from the Soviet Union where he had covered the then famous Metropolitan Vickers trial where two British employees were facing charges of espionage.

From now on Ian was a frequent visitor to Haus St Franziskus and I often ran into him in the town. We met at the houses of our mutual friends, at bars, or on the mountain. Kitzbühel had a few excellent ski runs and in summer there were endless excursions and, of course, the famous warm-water lake, the Schwartz Zee.

I was sunning myself there one afternoon after a swim and, as was my habit, I had changed into a pair of dry trunks. But these particular trunks had no belt. Surrounded by the rank and fashion of society, I was enjoying the interlude, when I saw Ian on the diving board. He did an exhibition dive and I thought to myself, I can do better than that. So, forgetting that my trunks had no belt, I went to the top of the diving board and executed my best swallow dive. On contact with the water my trunks came off, leaving me to swim in complete nudity. I remember how I prayed that the bloody things would float to the surface which they eventually did, but not before I had suffered some hideous moments of embarrassment.

Among the regular visitors and residents of Kitzbühel were Frau Poland, Graf Schlick, Graf Rudi Lambert, the Brackens, Captain 'Pop' Stokes, RN, the Hadows, Count de Renville, Graf 'Chappy' Silern, Prince Tassilo Fürstenburg, Prince Ferdinand Liechtenstein and my intimate confidant, Baron Rudolfo von Gerlach. Of all those who came and went during the six-and-a-half years I made Kitzbühel my home, my association with Rudolfo was most fruitful.

Ian and many others were often to be found at Reisch's Bar. Once Rudolfo and I came in and joined a party of young people, including Ian, who sat next to a German whose name was Markwert. We sat together for some time. Ian expostulated his belief that financial security was all that mattered. I was a little doubtful of his sincerity, coming from one who was a complete romantic about money. To Ian it was more a medium of freedom from the material grind. A very complicated, imaginative and subtle character was Ian, who lacked stability and staying power and yet was most intolerant of failure in others. The realities of business bored him. There had to be movement, excitement and glamour. And so it was that Ian never stayed long with any undertaking.

We moved on to the topic of books, an interest he shared with Markwert, who spoke fluent English, and they swapped names of rare editions. It was all far above my head and the subject was soon changed to women. There was intrigue in discovering the various viewpoints of others. It became obvious that Ian's interest in girls was mostly carnal, a fact he made known to them sometimes within minutes of becoming acquainted. He was something between a wolf and a rake, equipped with good looks and money, a combination fatal for the average young female.

Rudolfo and I walked home together. His only observation about Ian was '*sehr empfindlich*' (very touchy). Of Markwert he warned me, 'Watch him, I believe he is Gestapo.'

CHAPTER III

Wartime Sabotage

Moving about the Balkans during this period was a stimulating experience. It was also a strain; one knew one was being watched day and night.
Walter Stirling, Safety Last

In March 1938 Admiral Hugh Sinclair authorized the creation of a 'Sabotage Service', a new branch of SIS to be known as D, for destruction. It was to be headed by a Royal Engineers officer, Laurence Grand, and was to be funded not from the Secret Vote, which was already inadequate to cover all of SIS's expenses, but by a private donation from Grand's friend, Sir Chester Beatty. The American-born mining tycoon had many investments on the Continent, and not a few of them were concentrated in the Trepca mine in Yugoslavia.

Grand's objective was to prepare a network of agents across Europe to initiate deniable operations – especially in neutral territories – that would reduce German access to certain strategic materials. In pursuit of this ambitious plan Section D personnel were despatched to various target countries. Alexander Rickman was one of the first and he was sent to Sweden with the intention of blowing up dock facilities on the Baltic where iron ore was loaded for shipment to Germany, but the mission failed.

Section D was to recruit several other journalists, among them Basil Davidson of *The Economist* and David Walker of the *Daily Mirror*. Both were later to write accounts of their adventures, as did Julian Amery, a future Conservative Member of Parliament, and the novelist Geoffrey Household. One of Section D's more ambitious schemes was to close the Danube to the river traffic that carried Romanian oil to Germany. Like the Oxelösund fiasco, this operation was doomed to failure, but long after the war Bickham Sweet-Escott, the banker who was in charge of supervising the preparations, engaged in a struggle with the authorities for more than a decade before his version of events could be published. Other Section D agents based in Belgrade who played an active role in the plan to sabotage the Iron Gates gorge included Archie Lyall, a linguist who was to abandon his career as a travel writer in preference for a job with SIS which was to last long into the peace, and (Sir) Gerald Glover, a hugely successful City solicitor who made a post-war fortune from masterminding profitable property deals.

Another Section D man, H. Montgomery Hyde, was also to be elected to Parliament eventually, but his autobiography which describes his work first in Section D and then in British Security Co-ordination was not released until 1982. Hyde first shared an office in the Section's London headquarters with Guy Burgess, and then was posted to Liverpool where he found Eric Maschwitz, later the head of BBC Television's Light Entertainment. Unlike Hyde, Maschwitz opted for discretion when, in 1957, he obliquely mentioned his wartime work in his memoirs.

Section D's largest overseas office was in Belgrade where Amery and his colleagues plotted to create a network of saboteurs who would resist any Axis invasion of the Balkans. However, events moved so quickly that there was insufficient time to make the necessary preparations and most of Section D's enthusiastic volunteers were withdrawn to Athens, Istanbul and Cairo where they were to form the backbone of a new enterprise, Special Operations Executive. It was on behalf of SOE that Amery returned to Albania, together with another old Section D hand, Walter Stirling.

Alexander Rickman

Most of the shipments from Narvik are destined for customers in Germany and are either directed through German ports or transhipped at Rotterdam and Amsterdam to 3,000 ton steel barges for transport up the Rhine.

Long before the outbreak of war Sweden was regarded as a vital source of strategic minerals for Germany, and accordingly SIS prepared various schemes to deny the Reich's heavy industry some of its key supplies. While a group of conspirators at the Ministry of Supply plotted to bust any German blockade imposed in the Baltic, Section D concentrated on a scheme to smuggle explosives into Stockholm and then destroy the cargo-handling installations at certain selected ports.

Rickman's cover while he was surveying potential targets was his wholly authentic claim to be researching a book on Sweden's principal industry. The result was indeed released in August 1939 although the contents betray no clue to the author's true purpose. Unfortunately Section D's plan went horribly wrong at a very early stage; the saboteurs were betrayed and arrested, causing much embarrassment for the British embassy which tried, unconvincingly, to distance itself from the fiasco.

While still in the preparatory stages of the operation, which was codenamed Strike Ox, Rickman recruited two members of the British expatriate business community. One was the local British Petroleum representative, Harry Gill, and the other was Ernest Biggs, a one-legged tea importer.

Unknown to Rickman, his attempts to recruit a network of saboteurs had not gone unnoticed by the ubiquitous Swedish secret police, who placed him under surveillance and tipped off the SIS head of station John Martin. Unfortunately Martin decided to keep this information to himself, apparently for fear of compromising his Swedish contact, and in consequence Rickman was arrested while moving his cache of explosives to Oxelösund and Luleå, the principal ice-free harbours in Sweden used for loading iron ore, following the destruction of the quays at Narvik. The one-legged Biggs was caught carrying two suitcases packed with dynamite, and two other conspirators, Elsa Johansson and Arno Behrisch, were taken into custody. Rickman was sentenced to eight years' hard labour, Biggs five years and the two Swedes three and a half years.

Rickman was to spend the remainder of the war in prison but Biggs was released in October 1941 and subsequently joined SOE's French Section. In this passage from his ostensibly innocent textbook, the author can be seen to be conducting what amounted to a survey of Sweden's iron exports to Nazi Germany.

Swedish Iron Ore

Owing to its geographical position, Luleå offers by far the shortest sea route to the principal importers of Swedish iron ore, but this is offset very largely by the better climatic conditions at Narvik, where the shipment of ore can normally continue unabated throughout each month of the year. In common with Narvik, however, difficulties are encountered in the winter with trains that arrive with frozen ore, but these are effectively dealt with by a series of steam pipes that are laid along the tracks and thaw out the train loads at a rate of 48 cars in 3 hours or less, according to the temperature. The greater part of the ore that is shipped through Luleå is drawn from the mines at Gellivare, though a very small amount, up to 100,000 tons, is annually shipped from Kiruna. Its product, however, is invariably large and is subject at times to a further crushing process at this port, where a plant has been recently constructed with capacity to reduce the ore to 100 millimetres at a rate of 700 tons per hour.

The part played by Luleå in the expansion of the iron ore trade may be judged by the fact that 64,000,000 tons have been shipped through this port in the last forty-five years. Commencing with 138,950 tons in 1892, it rose by 1918 to 2,569,000 tons, owing in this case to the war and the convenience of the port to German consumers, though during the last ten years the average annual shipment has been two and a half million tons.

Ore for export from the Grängesberg mines is directed over Oxelösund and brought to this port by the TGO railway, a distance of nearly 215 miles. Owned and operated by the TGO, the port of Oxelösund is situated on the Baltic Sea, about 60 miles south of Stockholm, and is open for shipping throughout the year. Both the port and the town nearby, with a population of 3,000, are largely dependent on the iron ore export trade. A large harbour admits of an anchorage for ships, but is sometimes affected by storms, in the more tempestuous months of the winter, when the steamers are delayed in drawing up alongside the quay. A breakwater was proposed as a remedy, but rejected on the grounds that ice would then form and render the port valueless in winter. Approximately 28 feet of water is drawn at the quayside and slightly more in the main channel, whilst the equipment provides for the loading of a maximum of two ships at one time. In contrast to Narvik and Luleå, piers have not been constructed and chutes are, therefore, not used at this port. A bridge crane of American manufacture, together with a conveyor belt and machinery made in England, provide the equipment for loading. An average of 7 trains daily arrive at the port from the mines, each bringing 40 to 45 trucks of 20 to 40 tons capacity. On arrival, they are shunted and split, then hauled by steam locomotives to one of two tippers, where each truck in turn is subverted, at a rate of 16 to 18 an hour, discharging the ore into a powerful automatically propelled transfer car of 70 tons capacity, of which two are kept constantly in operation and two in reserve. The ore is then conveyed by the car on to an embankment at the side of the stock-yard and tipped on to the pile appropriate to its grade. The stock-yards have a capacity of 1,000,000 tons and vary in size in accordance with the fluctuating market and resulting rate of shipments.

Julian Amery

The British secret services have been held in high esteem all over the world by those who are interested in such matters. How do we maintain that esteem? Of course, partly by secrecy, but partly by allowing the different successes to be known after an appropriate time.
Rt. Hon. Julian Amery, MP, House of Commons, 24 January 1989

Having only just come down from Oxford, Julian Amery was touring Albania when Europe was plunged into crisis in 1939. When he arrived in Belgrade he was invited by a contact at the British embasssy to join SIS's Section D. Although his knowledge of Albania was limited to the visit he had only recently completed, Amery was represented as an expert on the country and this was to be his entrée into the secret world.

On the basis of his experience in Section D, Amery was appointed deputy head of SOE's Balkan branch, based in Cairo, and supervised the infiltration of the first British military mission into enemy-occupied Yugoslavia in September 1941. Thereafter he concentrated on SOE's Yugoslav Section and was later to join an SOE mission to the Communist guerrillas in Albania.

Amery was later to recall the solid grounding he had been given in the espionage field by reading the exploits of earlier Secret Service personnel. 'As a young member of those services, I profited a great deal from the memoirs of Paul Dukes and Compton Mackenzie and others who had been through the mill. What they had to say taught me a lot and in a sense was an inspiration.' Thus one generation of intelligence officers gave a lead to another.

After the war Amery continued his interest in Albania and was one of those consulted when SIS hired David Smiley to train and infiltrate anti-Communist guerrillas into Albania to topple Enver Hoxha's regime. Amery was elected to the Commons as the Conservative Member for Preston North in 1950 and retired in April 1992. The following month he was elevated to the House of Lords.

In this passage from his autobiography Amery describes the rather haphazard method by which he was selected as Section D's expert on Albania.

Approach March

Early in 1940, the staff of the Legation was strengthened by the arrival of an Assistant Naval Attaché, Lieutenant Sandy Glen.[1] Glen was short, prematurely bald, with small eyes glinting behind powerful spectacles. He had been to Balliol, had explored the Arctic and had worked as a banker. He pretended to know all the answers, though very much with his tongue in his cheek, and did, in fact, know quite a lot of them. We soon became friends and, presently, decided to pool our resources and take a spacious flat with a view to enlarging our circle of Yugoslav acquaintances.

Glen spoke little of his professional activities. But it was soon clear to me that they had little to do with the Navy, and were by no means as blamelessly 'diplomatic' as my own. I was, therefore, not too surprised when one evening soon after my twenty-first birthday, he told me that 'The Chief' of his 'Show' was on his way to Belgrade and would be using

[1] Now Sir Alexander Glen.

our flat as his office. Their work, he implied, was very secret. So would I please keep out of the way and not mention the visit to anyone, even to the Minister?

The Master Spy duly arrived, self-enveloped in an aura of mystery and urgency. He had grey wavy hair, thick horn-rimmed spectacles, a green complexion and long tapering fingers. He ensconced himself in the flat and proceeded to hold several meetings with Sandy and other members of the British community whom, in my innocence, I had hitherto regarded as ordinary businessmen.

I kept out of the way, apart from bed and breakfast. But on the second day of the visit, Sandy came into my office looking distinctly worried.

'The Chief,' he said, 'has asked me for a note on the situation in Albania. Of course it's got to be different from what the FO give him. I know nothing about the beastly place, and wondered if you could help me?'

The reader will remember that during the Spanish Civil War, I had had one or two talks about Albania with Sir Robert Hodgson. This was the limit of my knowledge of the country. It had seldom figured in my talks in Belgrade except as a possible base for an Italian attack on Yugoslavia. Most Serbs, indeed, were as ignorant of the Albanian mountains as most Englishmen, in the seventeenth century, had been of the Scottish Highlands. Nevertheless, Albania seemed an intriguing subject and I sensed rather than saw an opportunity of more interesting work than the press office could offer.

'Yes, of course,' I answered. 'I'll try and let you have a short memo. on the latest trends by dinner tonight.'

For a moment after the door had closed behind Sandy, I was at a loss to know how to begin. Then I rang up Ralph Parker, of *The Times*, and asked if he knew any Albanians.

'Yes,' came his imperturbable reply. 'I know two. If it's really urgent I'll try to get them round for a drink this evening.' I said it was urgent.

Accordingly, at six o'clock, I went round to Parker's flat and there was introduced, as a fellow journalist, to Gani Bey and Said Bey Kryeziu. They were the first Albanians I had ever met and I had no real idea at the time who they were. We talked for perhaps an hour; and they told me what they knew of the situation inside Albania. I then went back to the Legation and concocted a short memorandum based upon our talk. I handed it to 'The Chief' after dinner, modestly expressing the hope that 'it might throw some light on the general picture'.

The great man glanced thoughtfully at the paper. 'This,' he said, 'is very significant.' He asked me one or two questions about it; and, as he knew even less about Albania than I did, I had little difficulty in answering. He then asked if he might take the paper with him to Athens where he was going next day. I made no objection. There, as far as I was concerned, the matter rested.

'The Chief' was, in fact, Chief of the Balkan Unit of the 'D' Section. This was the creation of a resourceful Major of the Sappers, Lawrence Grand, a man gifted with unusual powers of persuading his superiors and enthusing his subordinates. 'D' Section was quite distinct from 'C' Section, the Secret Intelligence Service. Its object was to subvert the enemy's war effort in his own and in neutral territories. By subversion was meant those operations against the enemy which lay outside the province of the Armed Forces and the Departments of State. It included such things as the sabotage of enemy factories or ships, the blowing up of his communications, and the organisation and support of 'Resistance' in occupied territories.

Later in the War, as the Resistance Movements grew in importance, 'D' Section became first 'SO2' and then 'SOE', with a Minister in the Cabinet and a galaxy of generals and high officials on its establishment. But, at this time, it was still a very small and intimate club, so secret that even our heads of mission were kept in ignorance of its exact activities and personnel. Its official funds were very limited; but Lawrence Grand had persuaded his friend Chester Beatty, the mining magnate, to second a number of his staff to 'D' Section while keeping them on his payroll.

Now it so happened that Lawrence Grand and the 'Chief' had set their hearts on organising a revolt against the Italians in Albania. They believed that it would tie down large numbers of Italian troops and weaken Italy's ability to wage war. The Foreign Office, however, took a different view. We had great interests in the Mediterranean but very limited military power. Our first object was to try and keep the Italians out of the war and not to provoke them by fomenting a revolt which in their view would probably go off at half cock.

The strength of the Foreign Office position was that they were supposed to be the experts on Albania. Several of their officials had served in Tirana. No-one in the 'D' Section had ever been there. My meeting with 'The Chief' changed all this. He quickly convinced himself that he had discovered a real expert on Albania and, being an active man, set out to convince others. From Athens he penned a dispatch to Lawrence Grand which, among other doubtless more profound observations, contained the following statement: 'Our staff in Belgrade would be greatly strengthened by the co-option of Julian Amery, whose expert knowledge of Albanian affairs would be an invaluable asset to the organisation.' With it he enclosed my report which at least had the merit of containing fresh and as it happened accurate news from Albania. This was duly circulated in Whitehall, though without quoting its source, and rather inaccurately described as 'an example' of the kind of information on Albania available in the 'D' Section.

With the help of this new ammunition, Lawrence Grand managed to win this particular battle in the Whitehall war. 'D' Section was authorised to prepare plans for a revolt in Albania and to open communications with potential Albanian centres of resistance.

In the process of arguing their case, the high-ups in the 'D' Section had ended by convincing themselves that I really was an expert on Albania. Their chief man in the Balkans, Julius Hanau, was accordingly instructed to ask me to take the work in hand.

Hanau was a very experienced arms dealer, steeped in the cultures of France and Germany and learned in history. He was no less familiar with those subterfuges which, then as now, play an essential part in the sale of arms; the exploitation of personal rivalries between Ministers, the bribing of officials and the making of suitable presents to the right people. The Balkans held few secrets from him; and it was in his hands that the threads of our network throughout the Peninsula came together.

Hanau asked me to lunch and told me of his instructions. He knew much more about Albania than I did, but he was not seriously concerned by this. I was not, of course, the ideal choice for the job, but, if he were once to query my appointment, the whole decision to prepare a revolt in Albania might be put in question. Nobody knew much about Albania anyway, and the few Englishmen who did were probably quite unsuitable for the job. There was no reason why I should not quickly become an expert. Albania was, after all, a very small place and I was young enough to learn. Anyway, he added, the best revolutionaries had usually been young, and, taking down a book from his shelves, he checked that Danton and Robespierre were both only thirty-four when the guillotine fell. At twenty-one, thirty-four sounded to me like maturity, and I kept my own counsel on this and said I would do my best.

Hanau asked me to tell no-one of this new assignment but to continue my work as assistant Press Attaché. Presently, he would have a talk with my immediate chief. Meanwhile, I should just have to do two jobs and make do with less sleep. If I needed money for the Albanian project, I had only to ask. Then as I left him he said: 'Remember we want live heroes, not dead heroes, and if there are going to be any dead heroes, let them be Italians or Germans.'

Childs by this time had gone to Paris and his place as Press Attaché had been taken by Ronald Syme, the historian of the Roman Revolution. Syme was as frustrated as I was by trying to make pro-Allied propaganda for a Legation which only wanted to keep down the temperature. He was all for cloak and dagger work and gladly agreed to turn a blind eye to my new activities.

So there I was entrusted with the preparation of a revolt in Albania. It was only a few days since my twenty-first birthday, but the dreams of boyhood were coming true with a vengeance. I thought myself very lucky.

Walter Stirling

My first instructions, when I did receive them, turned out to be very vague indeed: I was simply to move about the Balkans and keep my eyes and ears open.

After passing out of Sandhurst in 1899, and receiving a commission in the 1st Royal Dublin Fusiliers, Walter Stirling was posted to South Africa with the Natal Field Force. After his arrival he was to transfer to the mounted infantry of Lord Dundonald's Brigade with whom he saw action during the siege of Ladysmith. He was highly decorated during the Boer War and at its conclusion served for six years with the Egyptian army, retiring in 1912 at the age of thirty-two and with a chestful of medals, among them the DSO.

At the outbreak of the Great War Stirling joined the Royal Flying Corps as an observer, and the following year rejoined his old regiment for the ill-fated Gallipoli offensive. For the last two years of the war Stirling served on the General Staff, having acquired a Military Cross and a bar to his DSO.

After the war Stirling was to be found in Damascus, acting as an adviser to the Emir Faisal, and later he was appointed Deputy Chief Political Officer for the Middle East. In 1920 he was attached to the Egyptian government as Acting Governor of the Sinai Peninsula, and then Governor of the Jaffa District in Palestine. In 1923 he went to Albania to reorganize and command King Zog's gendarmerie, an assignment that was to last eight years.

At the outbreak of the Second World War Stirling was appointed Chief Telephone Censor for the Continent, and it was in June 1940, while he was in this post, that he was invited to join SIS. He flew to Athens to make contact with his chief and then embarked on a tour of the region, stopping at Salonika, Belgrade and Bucharest where he participated in the Iron Gates fiasco. When Stirling reached Istanbul he was appointed Assistant Military Attaché with the task of liaising with the Albanian expatriates.

At the conclusion of his service with SOE Stirling was placed in command of a large stretch of Syria, then under the US 9th Army's occupation. When he retired, for the second time, he took up residence in Damascus but was forced to flee to Cairo following an assassination attempt in 1949. Two years later he was expelled by the Egyptian government and he moved to Tangier where he died in February 1958. In his autobiography, published in 1953, Stirling gives a heavily sanitized account of his arrival by air in Athens on his first secret mission.

Safety Last

I passed quickly through the customs on landing and drove straight to the Grande Bretagne Hotel in Athens. The first person I met in the hall there was Madame Melas, wife of the Greek Foreign Minister, whom I had known in Alexandria ever since she was a little girl of twelve. Now the Foreign Office, for some unknown reason, had issued me with a new passport in which I was described as 'Mr Stirling – Civil Servant'. As soon as the Foreign Minister noticed this he went to our legation and asked our Minister what I was doing in Greece masquerading as a civil servant when I was known to his wife as an army officer. All sorts of unnecessary suspicions were aroused by that new passport of mine.

As I went into dinner that evening a man brushed against me and whispered:

'Ten o'clock tonight. Room 267.'

This was evidently my contact, so I appeared to take no notice and walked over to my table. I afterwards kept the appointment and found that the owner of the room was an Englishman, who was to be my chief. He outlined the general situation in Athens, which was honeycombed with German espionage organisations, and told me that I should never speak to him or recognise him in the hotel and never come to his room again. He advised me to go and call on our Minister and register my name in the legation; then I should go round the sights of Athens in the normal tourist manner and enjoy myself in a thoroughly natural way. In a few days' time I should receive further instructions.

This all sounded very mysterious, but in the circumstances I felt that the Latin principle of carpe diem was not a bad one to follow, and so set about looking up some of my Greek friends. One of the first I went to see was Tony Benachi, with whom I used to do a lot of boat-sailing in Alexandria. He had now settled in Athens and was a great philanthropist, having built and donated a magnificent museum to his country. His sister, Madame Choremi-Benachi, had a lovely country house about twelve miles out of Athens to which I used to go constantly whenever I was in Athens. Here would congregate many of the most interesting people in Greece and I heard much of the inner history of these very exciting times.

My first instructions, when I did receive them, turned out to be very vague indeed: I was simply to move about the Balkans and keep my eyes and ears open. So I went to Salonika, where I visited our Consul, then on to Belgrade, where I called on our Minister, Sir Ronald Campbell, whom I had not seen since he was a small boy of seven. From Belgrade I flew to Bucharest, where I visited all my old haunts and my old friends.

The international situation had deteriorated considerably since I had left and everyone was most apprehensive. If and when Germany marched into Rumania it was vital to deny her, or at least delay, the production of oil. To this end plans were made to sabotage the oil-fields and refineries. This was too big an undertaking to carry out in secret, so the Rumanian General Staff had to be taken into our confidence and plans were drawn up with their connivance. As the German pressure increased, the Iron Guard got a footing in the General Staff and the plans were discovered. A number of Englishmen in the oil-fields were arrested and some tortured. One was suspended from the ceiling by his thumbs, another had a blowlamp applied to the soles of his feet; various other brutalities were practised by the Iron Guard, which by now was composed of the scum of Europe.

The transportation of foodstuffs from east to west was of importance to Germany, so we concentrated on disorganising their lines of communication. Friends of ours would put sand into the axle-boxes of the goods trucks; the friction resulted in a 'hot box', and often caused a fire in the truck itself. We also turned our attention to the heavy shipments which went up the Danube by barge and steamer. The Danube is a tricky river, requiring highly skilled pilots, many of whom succumbed to our offer of six months' leave in Istambul on double pay. To make matters more difficult still for the Germans we bought up as many motor barges as we could and sent them down the river through the Black Sea to Istambul, where they were laid up for the rest of the war.

From Bucharest I went to Istambul, which was to be my future operational base and where I was appointed Assistant Military Attaché, with an office in the Embassy. Part of my duties consisted in the formation of an Albanian committee to deal with external Albanian affairs and to prepare the way for the establishment of a provisional Government when and if the Italians were driven out. There were many Albanian exiles collected in Istambul to whom the Turkish Government was friendly, and there were others in the neighbourhood of Salonika. I was able to form the committee from ex-Ministers and other leading Albanians, who in their turn got in touch with some of the well-known Comitadji leaders. These were financed and armed, after which they were then sent off by devious routes to raise bands in Albania and harass the Italians.

I found myself a pleasant flat high up in a building in Ayas Pasha, next door to the German Embassy. From my sitting-room window I could look down into the garden of the Embassy, where I often saw my old friend Von Papen, who was then German Ambassador. The other side of the flat, which consisted almost entirely of window, overlooked the Bosphorus and provided one of the most beautiful views in the world.

I used to spend much of my spare time exploring the fascinating bazaars of old Constantinople, its great Byzantine walls, its mosques and, particularly, the great Mosque of Saint Sophia, the most imposing building I have ever seen. Near the northern walls there was a little church dedicated to St Mary of the Mongols, the daughter of one of the last of the Byzantine emperors, who was married against her will to the Mongol king. This lady of the Paleologus family used her influence to such good effect that she converted the king and a considerable section of the Tartars. On the death of her husband she returned to Constantinople and commissioned the leading Christian architect of the day to build a church, which was dedicated to her Christian Mongol converts. The architect, being still alive after the Turkish capture of Constantinople, was employed, as the greatest expert available, by Mohammed the Conqueror to design new mosques and to convert the greater part of the existing churches into mosques. He agreed to do so on one condition: that the Church of the Princess Mary, which he had himself built, should be allowed to remain untouched, as it still stands today.

Beautiful as Istambul appears from the outside it is a bedraggled and neglected town within. The Turkish Government has deliberately decreased its old importance and all available funds for rebuilding have been deflected to the new capital of Ankara. Most of the Greeks, the most industrious section of the population, have been chased out, and the sloth of the East seems to have enveloped the city. The lovely old Turkish palaces along the shores of the Bosphorus have been turned into coal depots and the officials seem to have no conception of the beauty they are throwing away.

On my constant tours of duty between the Balkan capitals I had many amusing experiences. I was once in a carriage alone with a German, who helped me to put my heavy suitcase on the luggage rack. It was intriguing to speculate on what he would have done had he known that it was packed full of 'limpets', those high-explosive devices used for marine sabotage.

H. Montgomery Hyde

I was then told that I was to be attached to Section D under Colonel Grand, to whom I was introduced shortly afterwards, a tall, lean man nearly turned forty, who gave me a welcoming friendly smile when he shook hands. I remember he used to smoke cigarettes through a long, elegant holder, which suggested a character out of an Edgar Wallace novel.

H. Montgomery Hyde's application to join Section D in 1939 was held up after MI5 reported the sinister news that six years earlier he had applied for a single, one-way ticket for a voyage to Russia. Did this mean he had intended to remain in Moscow, he was challenged. Hyde reassured his interrogator that he was always going to return to London overland.

Born in Ulster and educated at Queen's University, Belfast and Magdalen College, Oxford, Hyde had been called to the bar and had built up a reasonable criminal practice on the North-east Circuit when the war broke out. He had also written several books, including a major biography of Lord Castlereagh, the nineteenth-century Anglo-Irish politician. He had volunteered as a reserve officer during the Munich crisis, when he was also serving as private secretary to the Secretary of State for Air, Lord Londonderry, and this had led him to Section D, through the intervention of a friend of his wife's.

In January 1940 Hyde was assigned to a new Section D office in Gibraltar, and then in August he was transferred to Bermuda where a major examination centre was under development with the intention of submitting all the mails exchanged between America and Europe to a clandestine scrutiny. Censorship and Contraband Control in Bermuda, as it came to be known, was to employ more than a thousand examiners and scored some notable successes in tracing letters posted by enemy spies in the United States.

In May 1941, having reported to British Security Co-ordination, SIS's regional headquarters in New York, Hyde was sent on a secret mission to Bolivia. This was a reconnaissance to research a scheme for thwarting a pro-Nazi coup in the capital, La Paz, and resulted in the circulation of a forged letter purporting to come from the coup leader, then the Bolivian military attaché in Berlin. The document was never detected as a fake and its publication sparked off an anti-Nazi purge in the Bolivian government, which was exactly what had been intended.

Apart from one short visit to London and a few visits to the Caribbean and Central America, Hyde remained at BSC headquarters in New York until the latter part of 1944. He was later appointed legal adviser to the Control Commission for Austria, and in 1950 was elected the Unionist MP for North Belfast. He was an amateur criminologist and his many books brought him great success, particularly his acclaimed biography of Oscar Wilde and his studies of Victorian scandals. His 1962 biography of his former Chief at British Security Co-ordination, Sir William Stephenson, *The Quiet Canadian*, identified the wartime chief of SIS as Sir Stewart Menzies for the first time in print and led to awkward questions being tabled in the Commons.

In April 1981 Hyde published a letter in *The Times* in support of his former colleague Dick Ellis, complaining that doubt had been cast unfairly over the latter's loyalty. Prime Minister Margaret Thatcher had declined to make a formal statement to the Commons regarding Ellis, and her reluctance to vilify him had given his few remaining supporters, Hyde and Stephenson among them, the vain hope that the accusations had been false.

Hyde, who continued to make an annual visit to Stephenson at his home in Bermuda every year, died in Tenterden, Kent, in August 1989. In this passage from his memoirs he recalls the Yugoslav playboy and double agent Dusko Popov.

Secret Intelligence Agent

One of the most important of the British double agents during the war, whom I got to know quite well (and who incidentally clashed with the FBI), was a young Yugoslav of good family and education, Dusko Popov, code-named 'Tricycle'. Indeed Graham Greene, who himself worked for a time in MI6, regarded him as the most successful as well as the most important double agent in the British field. Tricycle hated the Germans who had arrested him and thrown him into prison, when he was a law student in Germany before the war, because in the course of political discussions he had been overheard praising the advantages of political freedom and democratic rule in contrast with the oppressive Nazi regime. When he was approached by a representative of German military intelligence (*Abwehr*) in Belgrade early in 1940, he agreed to work for the Germans, but at the same time he got in touch secretly with British Intelligence, getting to know Menzies, who realized his worth and took a strong liking to him. As a result of careful handling by the Twenty (XX, i.e. Double Cross) Committee, which controlled all the British double agents under Sir James Masterman, an Oxford don, Popov was built up as a valuable source in the eyes of the Germans, and during 1940 and the first half of 1941 he operated successfully between London and Lisbon. He was undoubtedly clever and always showed himself absolutely loyal to his British employers. His tastes in clothes, women, and entertainment were expensive – for example, he had a passionate affair with the French actress Simone Simon – but then the Germans were largely paying for them.

In August 1941 the Germans sent him to the United States with the object of forming a spy ring to replace the Ludwig ring, following the arrest of Ludwig and his principal associates. At the same time Popov brought with him a detailed questionnaire for military information, of which one-third was concerned with Hawaii and particularly Pearl Harbor, which the Germans told him the Japanese planned to attack before the end of the year. He also brought with him the secret of a remarkable new method of communication which the Germans had begun to use with their secret agents – the microdot. This was a speck the size of a pinhead which, when enlarged 200 times, could convey quite a long typescript message. 'You are the first agent to get it,' the *Abwehr* representative told Popov. 'This little dot will revolutionize our espionage system.' Thanks to Popov news of this invention was passed on to the Bermuda censors, who soon began to find microdots concealed beneath postage stamps and the flaps of envelopes.

All this information was handed over by Tricycle to the FBI, who had helped to get him a passage from Lisbon to New York and consequently insisted on taking him over and running him themselves. Both Stephenson and the Twenty Committee in London had strong reservations about this arrangement, which in the event were fully justified. Tricycle disliked the comparatively unsophisticated G-men who controlled him, and he was worried by their inability to produce the requisite strategic information for him to pass on to the Germans. The FBI, on the other hand, disliked what they regarded as his extravagant mode of living, and kept making the impossible request that he should reduce his personal expenses. However, in spite of these difficulties, eight letters with secret writing in invisible ink containing the right kind of data (most of which were produced by Stephenson and Ellis), were dispatched by him to Germany in the autumn of 1941, although by a mistake one of the letters was picked out by the Bermuda censors and tested for secret writing, which made its onward transmission impossible.

In November 1941 Popov flew to Rio de Janeiro and saw Alfredo Engels, the head of German Secret Intelligence there, whose cover was that of director of the major German electrical manufacturers in Brazil. Tricycle's cover was that he worked for the Yugoslav Ministry of Information, for there were thousands of Yugoslav immigrants in Brazil.

Engels also operated a powerful transmitter, code-named Bolivar, and much of the *Abwehr* traffic for the Americas was channelled through him. He told Popov that he had complete confidence in him and instructed him to return to New York and build a short-wave radio for communicating with Rio, Lisbon, and Hamburg. Of course, this suited Hoover's book since the Bureau would necessarily control the radio's use.

Tricycle returned to New York by sea, and when his ship, which was Portuguese, stopped at Trinidad he set off to explore the island with a ballerina named Dora whom he had met on board. However, he was intercepted by Freckles Wren, whom Popov knew was the local MI5–MI6 representative and who asked him to spend a day with him which he did, excusing himself to Dora. Wren had been advised of Popov's coming and had been told to get a full account of his doings in Rio. After lunch, at which they were accompanied by Wren's secretary whom Popov found 'sensationally beautiful', feasting his eyes on her while she returned his glances with what Popov called 'a knowing smile', Wren dictated a long cable to the secretary.

'I'll have to run down to the office to code this,' Wren said when he had finished dictating. 'It will take a couple of hours, but I'll leave you Jane here as a substitute for your ballerina!'

'Sorry about the ballerina,' Jane said, as soon as Wren had left. But Popov knew she wasn't. At all events, as Popov told me afterwards, Jane proved a great compensation. 'If anything, she overcompensated. Or we did!'

Shortly after the ship sailed, news of the Japanese attack on Pearl Harbor came through on the ship's radio. After his arrival in New York I had several talks with Tricycle, and I could see how angry he was with the FBI whom he was convinced had never taken any action on his earlier warning about the Japanese and Pearl Harbor. He protested to his immediate controller, who merely said, 'Things can go wrong,' and later to Sam Foxworth, head of the FBI New York office, who advised him that 'searching for truth beyond your reach may be dangerous'.

Throughout the first three months of 1942 the FBI regularly transmitted to Germany messages which purported to come from Tricycle over his short-wave radio, but they gave Stephenson and Ellis in BSC no copies of these and no details about how they were being received. Tricycle was not even taken to see the radio station which had allegedly been built for him, with the result that he was in constant danger of being caught out by a snap question from a genuine German agent in America, or by a request to send a message at short notice. Soon I learned from Tricycle that the

Germans were complaining that his reports lacked 'meat', and they must have begun to suspect that he was working under control, particularly after Engels was arrested in Brazil. It was a miracle that Tricycle was not completely blown by this time. Eventually, after a strong protest by Stephenson to Hoover, the latter appointed one of his more experienced officers to take charge of the double agent and undertook to obtain a more regular supply of suitable information from the United States armed forces for him to send the Germans; this was supplemented by data which Stephenson was able to obtain with the help of the British Army Staff Mission to Washington, to which I was attached at that time.

Nevertheless Hoover's men were unable to shed their characteristic gangbusting methods in handling Tricycle. For instance, when the Germans sent over some money for him, instead of allowing it to reach him without interference, the FBI attempted to draw the courier into a trap, which would of course, if it had been successful, have notified the Germans that Tricycle was at least under the gravest suspicion. The last straw for Popov came after the war, when he returned to New York in connection with his law business and saw an article in *The Reader's Digest* for April 1946 entitled 'The Enemy's Masterpiece of Espionage' by J. Edgar Hoover, in which the FBI chief claimed the credit for having obtained the secret of the microdot by capturing a spy, whom he described as 'a Balkan playboy', although he did not mention Popov by name. The article was illustrated by a memorandum of a telephone message from the Brazilian Ambassador to the Yugoslav government-in-exile, Alvis de Sousa. The memo only indicated a hotel-room number and the date: the recipient's name had been cut off. Popov immediately recognized the memo as having been sent to him by de Sousa when he was staying in Rio, a fact confirmed by de Sousa who happened to be in New York at the same time as Popov in 1946 and who upbraided Popov for having 'involved him in unwanted publicity'. The memo was said to have been found in the hotel room in Rio by an FBI agent who had surreptitiously gone through Popov's belongings and found the telephone memo which turned out to have a microdot on it, subsequently reflected by the light when examined in the FBI laboratory.

Popov telephoned headquarters and asked Hoover to call him back. But he did not do so. Popov called again, with the same negative result. He then flew to Washington and went straight to the FBI building at Ninth Street and Pennsylvania Avenue. When Popov explained his business to the assistant who received him, the agent said that Hoover was too busy to see him. 'You go tell Mr Hoover he'll see me right away,' Popov replied, 'or I'll hold a press conference.' The upshot was that Hoover decided he had time to see Popov after all, although when he entered his office Hoover angrily told Popov he would have him 'kicked out of the country'. However, according to Popov, Hoover eventually calmed down, and when he realized that Popov was serious in his threat to talk to the press, he undertook to get into touch with *The Reader's Digest* and try to stop publication in their Spanish and Portuguese editions. Whether he succeeded, Popov never discovered as he did not trouble to check up.

To return to 1942. By the summer of that year the FBI decided to have nothing further to do with Tricycle on the ground that he was a liar and was too expensive to justify his retention. In fact, it was a tacit admission of their incompetence in this particular instance, and an instructive illustration of how to spoil a good double agent.

Eventually Tricycle went back to London where he continued to do valuable work for the Twenty Committee right up to D-Day, when another agent, who was in Portugal, was tricked into going to Germany where he was interrogated, no doubt under torture, and almost certainly disclosed that Tricycle was really working for the British.

I once asked Popov if there was anything particular in the way of a reward for his sterling work which he would like after the war. He replied that the only thing he would like would be to be appointed Honorary British Vice-Consul in his native Dubrovnik. But, alas, that was not to be. Marshal Tito had no use for Honorary Vice-Consuls in Dubrovnik or anywhere else in Communist Yugoslavia. So Dusko Popov never went back to his native country. Instead he married and went to live in France with his wife and four sons. 'Secret agents do retire,' he later wrote. 'At the end of the war, I was issued with two suits of mufti and a change of linen, and I said good-bye to it all. I had a life to make and a living to earn.'

David E. Walker

Spy fiction is bound to be tidier than memories: each incident can be made complete, can be rounded off, ending in neat little victories or devised surprises.

As a *Daily Mirror* sports reporter with six years' experience David Walker was not an obvious choice as a saboteur, but in August 1938 he was invited to lunch at the Royal Automobile Club in Pall Mall and the first suggestion was put to him that he might like to undertake some interesting work abroad for the government. He had been abroad a few times to help out the paper's foreign correspondents, and had a limited grasp of German and French. His first assignment for SIS was to Italy where he was instructed to make contact with a retired diplomat, identified only as D. J., and then travel to Lucerne to interview a German believed to be a defector from the SS. Hans Schneider was suspected of having been planted by the Gestapo but his offer to betray the Gestapo's secrets could not be ignored. In preparation for his mission Walker recalls that he 're-read Somerset Maugham's *Ashenden*. This account of a British agent operating in and from Lucerne had long ago captured for me what seemed the authentic glow of espionage.'

It has not proved possible to identify D. J. and there is no record of either him or his wife being arrested by the Swiss police, as alleged by Walker. Nor is anything further known about the defecting Nazi, but more information may emerge as the Cold War's archives are opened for inspection.

Like Ashenden, Walker's cover was that he was a novelist writing a book, but he was warned that his rendezvous with Schneider had compromised him in the eyes of the Swiss authorities, so he quickly moved to Bucharest. There he was drawn into the fringes of the Iron Gates operation, the ill-fated attempt to sabotage the Ploeşti oilfields, which forced him in October 1940 to flee to Athens.

In Greece Walker's connections with the British government became more overt and, on one occasion, he was sent to Belgrade as a King's Messenger to deliver despatches to Archie Lyall. Over the following months Walker flitted across the Balkans, from Sofia to Bucharest, from Belgrade to Tirana. After the Axis invasion of Yugoslavia he joined up with the remainder of the British legation, which included John Ennals, another veteran of Section D, and was evacuated to Rome until arrangements could be made for their repatriation.

Once back in London Walker was transferred to SOE and then posted to Lisbon under journalistic cover, where he remained until June 1944. After D-Day he was brought back to London and then attached to the US 9th Army as a liaison officer. This took him, after the Ardennes offensive, to Berlin, and to the end of his seven-year career with SIS. In his autobiography, published in 1957, Walker reflects upon the uncertainties of being a spy in the Ashenden mould.

Lunch with a Stranger

No successful secret agent writes a book. After years of espionage his mounting knowledge and experience commit him more and more to silence. Much of his success is in any case due to an acquired or natural preference for a life behind the scenes. Not for him the blaze of footlights or the plaudits of the crowd: his place is in the wings, or high above the safety curtain, pulling strings that make the puppets dance below. Nor does a lifetime spent in the compiling of concise reports, signed with a symbol, lead naturally to the exhibitionism of the author. His written work and way of life are dedicated to the extremest privacy. In short he is usually far too modest, responsible and sensible a person to commit himself to public print.

The fact that there have been plenty of exceptions in recent years does not disprove the rule. During the last war the saboteur, the leader of clandestine resistance in enemy-occupied territory, came into his own on a scale not known before, and his adventures were not only worth recording but have been well recorded. This type of work demanded a moral courage and physical endurance beyond the limits required of the common-or-garden spy. It produced wildly improbable experiences for those engaged in it. But elderly Blimp-spies (if such exist) would argue that this was not espionage in its traditional sense. They would write to *The Times* (if they dared) to explain that all these operations should be more accurately classified as Service sorties behind the enemy lines: magnificent in every way, but not, strictly speaking, spying.

Accepting the above distinction, this book is neither flesh nor fowl. It is an account of seven years in 'Government service', beginning in Pall Mall and ending in Berlin. If I had proved myself a successful agent I would certainly not have been dispensed with when the war was over, and this would have remained another unwritten work. It is divided into three parts in an attempt to give some shape to years which in fact had none. The brief apprenticeship in Switzerland, on the nursery slopes of spying, should have lasted longer and might well have done so but for the Swiss police. The Balkan period, from early 1939 to April 1941, reflects the incoherence of a forest fire in changing winds, when half a dozen nations were swallowed in the flames. By the time I had reached Portugal, and comparative sanity, I had been switched to quite a different type of work.

That is the explanation of the book's shapelessness, rather than an excuse for it. Spy fiction, however many shots ring out, is always neat and tidy; the facts of espionage are quite the opposite. It is abundant in loose ends, false starts, and in incidents that are never quite rounded off. Any one agent, at any given time, as a rule sees only a very small corner of a much larger picture. His memories therefore are not merely disjointed: they are incomplete.

The seven years described in this book give a glimpse of the life an agent may be asked to lead, and the sort of person he meets. It cannot be dedicated to anyone by name; and how could I choose, in any case, between D. J. and his dry Martinis, Richard, the Polish girl with the golden crucifix, the pot-bellied Midget, L in Bucharest, the lovely red-haired Viennese pianist, the polyglot Terry, or even Reinhard Heydrich's former colleague in the Gestapo, Hans S? They all contributed, though some more spontaneously than others, to a liberal education.

What impressed me most during the seven years was the type of man I constantly met who neither writes a book nor can ever be named in one despite his eccentric adventures. He was always prepared to risk his life for an idea and he must always remain anonymous. A blinkered patriotism was not the motive, because more often than not he was working for a country that he had never seen; and in the vast majority of the cases I knew he never asked for money. He was part of an unknown, unrecorded but perpetual underground. The turbulence of the war undoubtedly threw him up in exceptional quantity but even in times of peace he is still there. He may be sitting beside you in the bus, live next door, or be a relative: usually cheerful, sometimes impractical, seldom outstanding: but always *there*.

On the ethics of spying anyone can write his own thesis. Much of the routine is bound to seem unsavoury. A great deal of it *is* unsavoury. The pages that follow make no attempt to defend it on high moral principles: they only express the startled surprise of the amateur at finding so many people with high moral principles engaged in it. But whatever their failings it could never be held against any of them that they were prigs.

Almost the only attribute that the Secret Service shares with royalty is that it can practically never answer back. Its mistakes invariably make headlines, and these are usually the only headlines it is ever allowed to have. As a drain on the taxpayer's purse it is perpetually suspect and frequently the subject of derision. Its discipline, though far more flexible than generally supposed, is certainly not relaxing; and its rewards are not glittering. Yet people in every country devote their lives to it.

This is no more than an attempt to throw a beam of harmless light on a shadowy world which is either fascinating or repellent according to taste. The life of the foreign agent is not always so grim as fiction paints it; nor, at the other extreme, so glamorous. It is simply not true that he is generally a swarthy, slant-eyed, Machiavellian character with daggers up his sleeve, nor is he necessarily tall and handsome, with wrists of steel. As often as not he is a chubby little man, who marries and has children. But his work is so often denigrated and condemned that it may do no harm to put him, and more particularly the life he leads, into slightly clearer focus. He is neither saint nor devil, which makes him much like anybody else; but he is engaged on work which is unusual. Although frequently half-paralysed with fear, I thoroughly enjoyed those years in 'Government service'.

Geoffrey Household

We were never actually told that defeat was probable, but it was clearly foreseen that at the very least the meeting of the main armies would produce stalemate, and that victory might be destined for the side which could produce the most ingenious methods of breaking it.

Born in 1900, Geoffrey Household was educated at Clifton College, which he detested, and Magdalen College, Oxford, which he regarded as paradise. After graduation he was offered a job in Bucharest by a fellow student's father who happened to be managing director of the Ottoman Bank. Household's branch was a subsidiary, the Bank of Romania, and there he arrived to take up his duties as a junior clerk at the end of 1922. After four years in banking, during which he had acquired a loathing of the business and a love for the daughters of one of his customers, Household moved to Paris to take up a job with Elder & Fyffe, the fruit importers famous for their bananas.

In 1927 Household was sent to Bilbao to open a Fyffe's office but although it proved commercially to be highly successful, his ambition was to travel to America to join his fiancée who lived for much of the year with her parents in New York. He was also keen to publish his short stories but could not interest anyone in them. After two years in Spain he joined a ship bound for Panama and arrived in New York by train. There he married Marina but was unable to make a living as a writer, and instead worked as an editor on a dictionary. Finally, in the autumn of 1932 he was commissioned by CBS to write a series of radio plays and thus began his literary career.

By mid-1933 Household was back in London, ready to embark on a third career, as the representative of an ink manufacturer. He was hired, through an advertisement in *The Times*, to travel across Europe to exploit the boycott which Jewish printers had imposed on their traditional German suppliers. Later he was to open up new markets in Greece, the Near East and South America, as well as achieving success with two novels, *The Third Hour*, published in 1937, and *Rogue Male* two years later.

Household's return to London coincided with the Munich crisis which prompted him to volunteer for the Reserve and, on the basis of his claim to speak German, French and Romanian, he was instructed to attend two short intelligence courses. However, it was not until August 1939 that he was to be summoned to the War Office and sent to Cairo for the Secret Intelligence Service.

SIS's objective was the destruction of the Romanian oilfields in anticipation of a German invasion, and a group of saboteurs was sent to Bucharest from Egypt via Palestine and Turkey. 'I was forbidden to travel on my current passport which gave my profession as author,' recalled Household. 'Authors, said the authorities, were immediately suspected by every security officer. Compton Mackenzie and Somerset Maugham had destroyed our reputation as unworldly innocents forever. So I was given a new passport which stated that I was an insurance agent.' At Ploeşti Household helped co-ordinate a clandestine survey of the oil installations and, once this had been concluded, was given a cover diplomatic post at the British Legation and participated in the notorious Iron Gates failure.

In October 1940 Household returned to Cairo and was appointed a security officer in the Field Security Police. His first posting was to Greece but after the British withdrawal he joined Security Intelligence Middle East and was transferred to Jerusalem to work under MI5's local representative, Henry Hunloke MP, the Defence Security Officer. Until the end of the war, as he recalled in his autobiography *Against the Wind*, which was released in 1958, he moved between Beirut and Baghdad, but never actually caught any spies. He ended up in charge of SIME's office in Haifa in 1945, and was then brought home to London with his second wife, Ilona, who was Hungarian. However, before returning to civilian life he was posted to Germany to write an account of the Guards Armoured Division's recent battles for the Ministry of Information.

After he was demobbed Household returned to writing and published several novels and books of short stories, including *Arabesque* and *Fellow Passenger*, but none achieved the success of *Rogue Male*. He was elected a Conservative borough councillor and he died in October 1988. In this episode from his autobiography he recalls his secret but futile mission to the Romanian oilfields.

Against the Wind

In February 1940 I was despatched to Egypt on a demolition course. For the first time I put on uniform, obtained a movement order instead of a ticket and was delivered to Dabaa in the Western Desert where the field company of sappers which was earmarked for use in Roumania took over my body.

I admitted that my military training had been of the sketchiest, and they were immensely kind. It is possible that we who came down to them from Roumania appeared mysterious and heroic figures, in spite of pointing out to them apologetically that our only activities were to eat in two of the finest restaurants of all Europe and to attend a cabaret every evening. Romantic vision – which exists in the eye of the observer rather than of the participant – was more solidly based upon our appreciation of them. These were the men for whose technical skill and ability to fight off interference we were only pathfinders.

A fortnight under canvas with an efficient unit of high and happy morale made me more confident that the illusion would not be detected whenever I had to play the part of captain in any straightforward War Office production. With growing enthusiasm I blew craters, cut steel, stunned fish and my wrist-watch; and though the company had created for some miles around their camp a desert more formidable than that supplied by nature, they managed to find for the completion of my training a substantial roofless building of mud and stone. I am a most incompetent electrician, and it was one of the triumphs of my personal war when, after laying and wiring the charges myself, I pressed the plunger and the building disintegrated into noise and flame, hurling a large chunk of itself – for over-keenness had brought me a little close – in tribute at my god-like feet.

Back in Bucharest our unheroic life of luxury continued; we felt like parasites upon the unhealthy back of war. Secrecy was more essential than ever, and we preserved it; but there was no sense of speed or urgency to indemnify us. Ever since the assassination of Calinescu, the Roumanian foreign minister, by the Iron Guard, German influence had been increasing; but the Roumanians believed fairly firmly in the ultimate victory of the French and British. As soon as disaster in the West showed that we were no match at all for the German Army, it was clear that the mission would not be allowed to destroy the oil-fields, and that the field company of sappers would be forbidden to land.

That brought our third scheme into operation: to do what damage we could with a handful of British oil engineers. Our objective was the high-pressure field at Ţintea. If we could destroy that, Roumanian output would be limited to the bailing and pumping wells. We believed it could be done by four or five small parties running from well to well, laying a heavy charge at the base of each Christmas tree which controlled the flow, and timing them to go off simultaneously. Whether all the wells would catch fire immediately was doubtful, though we had means of persuading them to do so. But in any case those pillars of gas and oil could never again be controlled by anything less than a specialist team from Texas.

The guards on the wells were still company guards, whose exact movements were known. We reckoned that they could be put silently out of action, partly by bluff from engineers whom they knew, partly by strong-arm methods. It was highly desirable to avoid loss of life. Since we were in a neutral country, killing was murder. When the wells went up, a score of torches lighting the eastern foothills of the Carpathians, we hoped to be racing through the night to Galatz and a waiting destroyer.

We were convinced that the plan was possible; and in theory it was. But in practice we should have been disorganised by the difficulty, which later and more professional commandos proved again and again, of any exact timing in a night operation. I think we could have sent up enough wells to make the field unworkable, and possibly to exhaust it, but the chance of the parties ever reuniting for escape was nil; so was escape without shooting.

Twenty-four hours before this spectacular act of sabotage was to be carried out, the Roumanians posted two military sentries on every well. Who betrayed us we never knew. Such indications as there were suggested that the leak was not in Bucharest or Ploeşti, but through the Roumanian Legation in London. It is possible that someone in authority had forgotten that the allegiances of major oil companies cannot, even in war, be too closely defined.

That was the end of the oil scheme for ever. In July one of our French colleagues was arrested by the Paris Gestapo while carrying a portfolio of papers which gave away much of the earlier and official plot. All the British employees of the oil companies were expelled from Roumania. We clerks at the Legation, though both the police and the liaison officers of the Gestapo who were now with them knew that our clerkliness was highly dubious, were permitted after much argument to remain.

War, if one has the temperament for it, may be enjoyable; but it is a most unsatisfactory setting for human intelligence. What is planned with infinite pains and care never happens; and what is unforeseen flurries the ant-heap to madness before petering away into unimportance like a short story which the author cannot finish. Success does not seem to depend upon the prudence which claims to control or guard against events, but upon creating an instrument which is not affected by events. The justification for our existence – if in fact there was any – came in Burma, where our techniques proved useful and two of the oil-men, by then commissioned in the Army, were decorated for gallantry.

Perhaps our studies were also of some use in the protection of oil-fields. Three years later I inspected the Kirkuk high-pressure field, drawn partly by duty, partly by curiosity, and found that the Ţintea plan had been utterly defeated by burying the Christmas tree deep in a bank of pebbles. To reach the vulnerable depths of it, the saboteur would have needed hours without interruption and a platoon of men with noisy shovels.

Bickham Sweet-Escott

Somebody, it seemed, had been reading John Buchan. My head full of forgery, murder, and Brigadier-General Sir Richard Hannay, I entered the office.

After Winchester and Balliol, Bickham Sweet-Escott joined the British Overseas Bank and throughout the 1930s he was constantly travelling across Europe. He spoke German fluently, and a book he wrote about his experiences in the Balkans brought him to the attention of SIS. Although he had been alerted to the fact that the intelligence services had earmarked him for special work in the event of war, he heard nothing until his return in March 1940 from a business trip to Italy on behalf of Courtaulds, the textile company he had recently joined.

Sweet-Escott's entry into Section D's Balkan sub-section, with responsibility for Greece and Hungary, was the start of a five-year career in clandestine operations, for he was to become a senior staff officer in Special Operations Executive when that organization was formed in May 1940. Sweet-Escott's first task was the denial of Romanian oil to the Nazis and he handled the London end of two ill-fated schemes, the first to buy up all the Danube's oil barges, and the second to blow up the river narrows known as the Iron Gates. The operation was abandoned when several key figures in the plot were arrested by the local police.

Sweet-Escott's service in SOE took him to the Middle and Far East. At the end of the war he returned to banking and became general manager of the Ionian Bank. In the autumn of 1954 he completed the first draft of his war memoirs and submitted it to the War Office which, after a delay of six months, warned him that publication would 'render him liable to prosecution'. In November 1962 the frustrated author approached Dame Irene Ward, MP, an indomitable campaigner on behalf of those seeking to research the truth about SOE's activities, and largely owing to her pressure he was allowed to release a sanitized version in 1965. It is memorable for the extraordinary compromise reached with the authorities which required all mention of SIS to be excised. Accordingly there are references to an organization known as 'Z', while 'MI6' and 'SIS' are to be found nowhere. In this passage he describes his early days at Section D's headquarters in the St Ermin's Hotel in April 1940.

Baker Street Irregular

I do not think I was wholly to blame for the appalling mental confusion from which I suffered during the next few weeks. For there were no documents or files to study which would tell me what we were really supposed to be doing. The office consisted of I suppose about twenty-five people, but most of them had joined us only a few days or weeks before me, and appeared to have as little notion as I had of what it was all about. Everyone seemed to be working at immense pressure, and the few who really did know the reason for our presence were far too busy to explain. For some time we confined ourselves to doing as faithfully as possible what we were told to do. We assumed that those who told us to do it knew better than we did what it was all in aid of. We hoped that later on perhaps some purpose or plan would begin to emerge. Neither the assumption nor the hope, as it turned out, was entirely justified.

One or two things did however become clear fairly soon. Our unit was known as Section D, but that was a phrase we must never use outside the building. To outsiders we were to describe ourselves as members of the Statistical Research Department of the War Office, an appellation which I soon found singularly unconvincing. Section D, it seemed, bore a distant affinity to 'Z'. It had been created shortly after Munich with the object of doing those things which assisted the execution of His Majesty's Government's policy, but which His Majesty's Government preferred not to acknowledge as the action of its agents. That at any rate appeared to be the theory of the thing, and as can be imagined if there had been a charter it would have covered a wide range of activities, of which sabotage, political subversion and underground propaganda were the most important. No wonder poor Arthur Goodwill had found it difficult to explain to me what I was to do. That there should be a body responsible for unacknowledgeable activities seemed to be an excellent, even brilliant, idea. The more we thought of its potentialities, the more convinced we became that we might perhaps be able to make some contribution to the war effort. But if we were to do so, everything would clearly depend on the help we got from the other agencies of His Majesty's Government, and above all on whether they recognized that we had a job to do.

The head of this extraordinary body, though I hardly knew he existed for several days and it was a fortnight or so before I actually met him, was a remarkable professional soldier, a sapper Major called Laurence Grand. He was tall and thin, with a heavy black moustache. He never wore uniform, always had a long cigarette holder in his mouth, and was never without a red carnation in his buttonhole. What was remarkable about him was the fertility of his imagination, the imperturbability of his character in the most trying circumstances, and his gift for leadership; he also had an unusually pretty wit. I have never I think met anyone who had such a fine flow of ideas about what we should do, nor anyone for whom it was easier to work. For having made up his mind that he would leave you to get on with the job he would back you through thick and thin whatever the mistakes you might make. What was wrong about the organization, as I was soon to find out, was that there was hardly any machinery whereby his ideas could be sifted and those which we might really be able to do something about translated into action; and that many of his rapidly growing band of subordinates lacked his drive and sense of purpose. He himself was only too often forced to dissipate his energies by justifying our existence before his superiors instead of getting on with the job. This however was a difficulty with which most of his successors also were confronted.

Laurence Grand, it seemed, had been head of Section D since 1938, but Treasury control had kept his organization on a blueprint basis till the war actually broke out. It was only in the early months of 1940 that the office had reached its present modest size. Its growth had been impeded also, I gathered, by the expectation that the war would open with a hail of bombs on London. In this belief its headquarters had been sited many miles away. These headquarters, which for security reasons were always described as 'the country', consisted of a large and hideous mid-Victorian house standing in its own grounds somewhere in Hertfordshire [The Frythe, just off the Great North Road between Hatfield and Welwyn]. Many of the staff still lived there, and it was only in the winter of 1939 that our main office had been transferred to its present premises over the St Ermin's Hotel.

My own humble function in all this was to work in the section which dealt with the Balkans, where it was supposed that my knowledge might be useful and might even qualify me to represent the section in Hungary or Greece, two countries I happened to know. The Balkan section was under the control of a brilliant but ruthless Australian called George Taylor, and though it was some time before we got to know each other, we have since become close friends. George had a mind of limpid clarity and knew exactly what he wanted. It was certainly due more to him than to any other one person that the theory and practice of what eventually became SOE was in the end accepted by our detractors and competitors, as well as by our supporters. What he lacked perhaps was the ability to see that other minds did not work so clearly or so quickly as his own, and this made him somewhat naturally impatient when he failed to persuade others that he was right; but his tremendous enthusiasm and unswerving sense of purpose made him a most stimulating companion. He had, it seemed, been with 'D' from the outbreak of war, and though he had not been put in charge of the Balkans until early in 1940, he had made several trips to the area and had an extensive knowledge of the problems and of the personalities with whom we had to deal.

The principle on which George had been working was that in each of the neutral countries we should recruit a number of reliable British residents who in turn would build up contacts with local elements friendly to the allied cause. It was these elements he hoped to use to do the work of subversion and sabotage which was our aim in life. An embryonic organization existed in each of the countries of the Balkans except Greece and Albania. In Budapest there were three journalists who were supposed to be working for us. In Rumania there was a naval officer and a couple or so of British businessmen. In Bulgaria too there were contacts. There was also a number of people who seemed to be incessantly on the move between the Balkan capitals sending home long and often over-optimistic reports on openings for our work.

But the main centre of our activities in the Balkans was Belgrade. Here there was a large party of people under the control of a British business-man called Julius Hanau, who had lived in the Balkans since the Salonika campaign and had a host of contacts. He was assisted by a young mining engineer from the Trepca mines called Bill Bailey, who, though entirely self-educated, had acquired a noteworthy grasp of Balkan politics. Julius Hanau was inevitably known as Caesar, and he had good friends among some of the political parties in opposition to the régime of Stoyadinovitch and the Regent, especially the Serb Peasant party and the Slovenes. His main object had been to block the Iron Gates by blowing up the cliff which towers over the Danube from the Yugoslav side. This, it was hoped, would make the river unsafe for navigation for some time and so impede the flow of Rumanian oil to Germany. But the tunnelling had been discovered by the Yugoslav police during the winter and the plan had been abandoned, not, of course, without some loss of face by poor Caesar and needless to say, by Section D. In the meantime, there were gangs at work in Slovenia putting sand and other abrasives in the axle-boxes of railway vehicles bound for Germany. Even if no major operation could yet take place, Caesar seemed to be responsible for a constant succession of minor pinpricks.

Throughout the Balkans our immediate purpose was thus to carry out the maximum interference by unacknowledgeable means with the move-ment of supplies to Germany. This meant that supplies of detonators, explosives, specially constructed time-fuses, weapons, and above all money, had to be sent to our friends in those countries from England by clandestine means. Some of these devices had been invented for the purpose. One was a contrivance called a limpet, which looked like a steel helmet, but really contained a lump of explosive which could be attached to the side of a ship by the magnets inside the helmet. At the same time it was necessary to encourage our friends and swell their numbers by suitable propaganda. As the Balkans at the time were neutral, this propaganda also had to be disseminated by secret methods.

None of this of course was clear to me when I joined the section. My first instructions were to send £200 to Budapest, where our representatives seemed to be getting a little short of money. Delighted by this first assignment, I went away to inquire which bank to use, and whether to send the money by mail or cable. But the drill, it appeared, was simply to go to our cashier, a charming girl whom I happened to have met before the war, ask for forty five-pound notes, and put them in an envelope addressed to our representatives, and send it off. Nobody in the Balkan section seemed to have bothered about accounts. There hadn't been time, I was told. However, it seemed to be a good idea to send out for a two-shilling account book. This I did, and thereafter we at least knew how much money went through our hands.

The method of keeping our people in the Balkan capitals supplied with explosives, devices and propaganda seemed equally simple, and it was on this that I occupied myself for the next few days. There was a storeroom on the fourth floor full of such things. It was under the control of another remarkable character who had been a test pilot, a gun-runner and a boxing promoter. He was the only man I have ever met who habitually and quite naturally talked in rhyming slang, and spoke always of touching his titfer. Fortunately he knew a good deal about explosives, and it was one of my duties to help him to assemble and pack them in large bags. Once they were packed they were handed over to Cornelius who knew how to tie them up in the appropriate manner. The bags were then given to dispose of as they knew best to a number of young gentlemen who had been furnished with return tickets complete with Wagons-Lits reservations to Bucharest; taxis, sometimes two or three if there were a heavy load, were summoned, the bags were loaded, and off the party went to Victoria station. They did I think have ex-Scotland Yard detectives as guards, but not always. It seemed to be a nice job, and I hoped that one day perhaps I might qualify for it. In the meantime I wondered just how much the authorities knew of it all.

This was the crucial point in those early days. There seemed to be no doubt that people in high places had said that we were to exist, though exactly who they were or when they had said it I never succeeded in finding out. There was also no doubt that at certain levels the Foreign Office was aware of the general lines of our activities. That our chief diplomatic representatives in the various Balkan capitals also knew a little about us was clear too. But none of them, so far as I was able to see, was particularly anxious to make positive suggestions about what we ought to be doing. They seemed to restrict themselves to telling us what not to do, though the intensity of their control varied greatly from country to country. The result was that most though by no means all of the ideas on which we were working seemed to have been suggested by us.

There was a further limiting factor imposed on our activities. For the work of 'D' in this field was under the general supervision of 'Z'. 'Z's' people were in a strong position because they controlled our communications, whether by letter or cipher telegram, and 'Z' was interested only in obtaining intelligence. A fundamental conflict thus arose at the start. For the man who is interested in obtaining intelligence must have peace and quiet, and the agents he employs must never if possible be found out. But the man who has to carry out operations will produce loud noises if he is successful, and it is only too likely that some of the men he uses will not escape. To use a good intelligence agent for a dangerous operation might therefore mean that the man would get caught and the flow of intelligence from him would stop. We accordingly had to recruit our own people instead of employing 'Z's'. On the whole this was a sensible solution. For the kind of man who is ready to obtain information is not necessarily of the same type as the man who is prepared to risk his life in blowing something up. It seemed to be a question of priorities. There might be cases in which operations, even in a neutral country, were more important than intelligence. But clearly if that were so, we must be told by someone who was outside both 'D' and 'Z'.

Basil Davidson

Up on the first floor the lobby in those days had a solitary chair, and in this chair there sat a man of saturnine allure, and with the right newspaper. I recognised him at once as a character from Eric Ambler.

In March 1938 Basil Davidson had been a witness to the Anschluss in Austria, and a year later he was in Paris reporting for *The Economist*. He was convinced war was inevitable but was recruited into Section D before he could join the army. He had travelled across much of Europe as a journalist and knew the Balkans, which apparently qualified him for an invitation to lunch at Simpson's in the Strand with 'a super-spy'.

Davidson joined Section D in December 1939 and was sent by train to Budapest to open a news agency as cover for more nefarious activities, the preparation of a resistance network. Unfortunately events overtook the section and in early April 1941 German troops entered Hungary, forcing Davidson to close down his operations and flee to Belgrade. There he was documented as a press attaché on the British diplomatic staff and evacuated to Rome with several other Section D veterans.

Upon his return to London, via Gibraltar, Davidson was absorbed into SOE and then despatched to Istanbul for staff duties with the Yugoslav Section.

After the war Davidson returned to journalism, working successively as Paris correspondent of *The Times*, the *Daily Herald*, the *New Statesman* and the *Daily Mirror*. He then took to academic work in Ghana and wrote a series of books about African history and culture. He also wrote two accounts of his wartime experiences, *Partisan Picture* and *Special Operations Europe*, and made a few ventures into fiction, principally with *Golden Horn*, a curious Cold War tale set in Istanbul with British and American agents attempting to infiltrate Bulgaria. Davidson remains active in the anti-apartheid movement and lives in North Wootton, Somerset, whence he continues to contribute articles to periodicals. In his second volume of war memoirs Davidson recounted his arrival in Hungary, where Section D had sent him, much to the disapproval of the Minister at the British Legation, (Sir) Owen Malley, whom the author is careful not to identify by name.

Special Operations Europe

Need it be recalled that there were next to no airlines in Europe then [1939]? You went to Hungary, or anywhere else in Europe that you could still go to, by train. Italy not yet being in the war, I went by way of Milan. There I was joined by a colleague in Section D, a tubby man with a charming air of boredom and a corresponding tendency to sleep. We came to know each other well in after times, and his company would prove a pleasant relief from anxiety. He was really one of the unsung heroes of the 1930s, being the high priest and chief attendant of Saint Rock, the patron saint of dogs. Do you remember the patron saint of dogs? Perhaps not, for the 1930s are distant now: yet countless thousands of small tin canines, built in miniature after a genial Saint Bernard and painted tastefully, were sold to grateful ladies in the suburbs and villages of England. The priest of Saint Rock should have made a fortune; only, it transpired, somehow or other he had not. This being so, he had taken to promoting pugs in New York. Joe Stillman's gym on Eighth surely knew him well, even if Damon Runyon surprisingly failed.

Our train crossed the northern plains of Jugoslavia, not yet invaded by Hungary, an invasion still sixteen months ahead, and soon approached the frontier of the Magyar kingdom of the crooked crown. South of Subotica, rather near the frontier by now, my companion awoke and looked at me with a happy smile. He pointed to the rack above my head.

'Those blue sacks. We can't have them inspected.'

But if the Hungarian customs should insist?

'You'll make a diversion. Throw a fit, threaten to jump out of the window, almost anything may do. I've got diplomatic immunity, so don't worry about me.'

Money passing, there was no inspection.

Trundling through southern Hungary towards Budapest, I asked him what was in the sacks? He smiled again, and with an expansive secrecy. 'Plastic and such, a few toys. The sort of thing, you know, that D goes in for.'

At the Budapest terminal we got hold of a taxi, loaded the sacks ourselves, and took them to the British legation near the old castle on the Buda side of the Danube. Thereby, later on, and after the import of more blue sacks, a tale would hang. But for the moment they were none of my business.

I found a hotel and felt very lost. Outside my window, across the street, a neon sign flared after dusk. Balefully it said: 'Központi Takáréki Pénztár', and no language that I knew gave any help. Afterwards, having persevered with the Magyar tongue, I learned that this meant no more than central savings bank; but in those early days I used to stare at it without hope. Belonging, it seemed to tell me, was not going to be so easy after all. This was the beginning of 1940, but the 1930s still had a chain around my leg and it tugged hard; now and for many perplexing months.

D's man in Hungary, arriving there in January 1940, had two immediate tasks. The first was to found and operate a legal and above-board news agency for the distribution of British news to the Hungarian press and radio. This was acceptable and even welcome to the Hungarian authorities. Although already under German pressure and infiltration, the Hungarian régime and government still hoped to be able to stay reasonably neutral. Gestures to the Germans were the main thing, but gestures to the British were feasible on a minor scale. Permitting this British news agency was one of them.

Kicking the 1930s out of my way, I threw myself into the work. It proved a grand experience; being wanted and belonging began, for a while, to seem easy again. I was no longer seeking employment, after all: I was now an employer myself. At the age of twenty-five, this was really something. I leased offices, comfortable and even spacious, on the Petöfi-tér beside the Danube. I took on staff, one and two and three and eventually half a dozen. Obtained from D by way of a diplomatic contact in the British legation, money proved to be no problem. It was like winning the Irish Sweepstake and the war into the bargain. I acquired an executive desk, and I sat down by the waters of the Danube and rejoiced.

The second task, below board and illegal, was less exhilarating. This was 'to promote resistance'. Hungary's passage into the nazi camp might not be avoidable; but it might be delayed.

'There is,' said my legation contact, a few weeks after my arrival, 'this parcel of money for you.' This contained a hundred crisp fivers of the large white kind of those days. The decoded instructions said that I was to use them for bribing politicians.

I sent them back, explaining that I had yet to know any politicians, bribable or otherwise, and in any case could not hope to bribe them with five-pound notes. The fivers came back again with a curt message. 'Do what you are told,' this barked. Anxiety deepened; in the end I spent them in a variety of ways and felt guilty for a time.

Another part of this second task was to find a printer willing to produce, secretly in exchange for payment, the kind of anti-nazi propaganda too hard for the régime to stomach. One useful target would obviously be the local pro-nazi party, the Arrow Cross led by a crook called Szálasi who was hoping to rule Hungary on an outright nazi pattern. Thanks to an ingenious and bold acquaintance, a scion of the old Austro-Hungarian imperial family who had once known Parvus Helfant and acquired the taste for conspiracy, a printer was found who was willing to do this work at night, when his plant was otherwise silent. A good Hungarian friend called George Páloczi-Horváth volunteered to write anti-nazi leaflets, and very talented they were, while my Austro-Hungarian assistant organised a means of scattering them broadside. The idea was to suggest the existence of a large anti-nazi organisation. Around the middle of 1940 we began this work, and at least we repeatedly stung the Arrow Cross newspapers to furious protest.

So you might well think me fortunate: my own news agency, links with the 'underground', plenty to eat and drink and money in my purse, a safe job if ever that existed: or safe at any rate for as long as one survived, and nobody can ask for job assurance in the after-life. All this I had, and more: for magically the shores of love now lost their splintering disaster. Here they were changed to gentler scenarios, transported to the hot-spring bathing pools of Buda ringed deliciously with snow as long as winter lasted, or in summer carried to the lilting lake-lapped beaches of Balaton and soothed in the wind of weekend walks through woods and meadows of the Dunantúl, hand in hand, or bejazzed and befumed in the dives and clubs of Pest, carried further in the candle-lit cellars of Három Csiri Kocza, that blessed Three Billed Duck, and other dining joints where gypsies from the Alföld strummed their violins and sang their purple songs, till brought at last to happy ending in the waiting beds of Buda. Could anyone want more, or half as much?

All this being merely by way of introduction, I will cut short these scenes of evident fulfilment. A worm, in truth, was in the fruit. Depression appeared, and gathered. Anxiety became chronic. Belonging turned into a myth. There was a sense, both dim and sharp, of having missed the point: of being, and hopelessly, in the wrong place. For now in the middle of 1940 the 1930s flopped at last to an end; but the end was a bang. The Germans over-ran France.

There came Churchill's unforgettable response, reaching even as far as our lost little colony in Budapest. We should fight on the beaches, we should never give in. Yes indeed, but not on the beaches of Balaton.

For a while, even so, life continued as before on the merry-go-rounds of Buda and of Pest, only now the gilt looked tinsel and the music failed to convince. Shouldn't one be somewhere else?

Facing nazi invasion in that autumn of 1940, the Ministry of Information in London ceased sending the long daily news wires which fed my agency; and I formed a new habit. We had daily customers in most sections of the Hungarian press, the Budapest Radio also used our bulletins: were they now to be denied their diet of truth? One could do something about that, even if it wasn't fighting on the beaches. I began to get up at six every morning so as to re-create our news service before the staff arrived. I am glad to affirm that it was a better service than before. As the weeks passed I devised a world-wide range of sources, including many prestigious names, who revealed the facts of British victory and triumph on the distant fields of Africa, discussed the deepening crisis of Germany's oil supplies, divulged the inner frailties of fascist Italy, and won the anti-submarine battle of the Atlantic at least a year ahead of time. The good Hungarians who worked for our agency, translating and date-lining and distributing all this gilt-edged news from my early morning typewriter, gravely upheld our reputation for telling the truth and nothing but. We carried on. We never closed.

The remainder of 1940 and early 1941 fell about our heads. Sorrows came not singly. London was ferociously bombed for weeks on end. Nothing went right. Hopping on one foot that was still just legal and another that was not, I lived in a misery of mind and nerve that brought the curtain almost to the floor. One should be somewhere else. Others thought so too, and all the more for knowing nothing of Section D and their instructions. What was a fit young man about, jazzing in the dives of Pest while his country burned? He should belong, he should not be content to save his skin. Applied to by code through legation contact, D were unimpressed. 'Continue,' they replied to requests for transfer, 'for as long as possible.' But continue what?

The question was given another screw from an unexpected quarter. Called to our legation as that gruesome winter of early 1941 was drawing to a close, I was hailed before the British minister. This was an Anglo-Irish gentleman of impeccable diplomacy whose views by now, well known amongst us, were that the war was probably lost and that, this being so, nothing should be done to make bad into worse, above all nothing irregular. But he had just come upon something most irregular, and in his own legation. A cherished vision of quiet retirement to neutral Ireland seemed under sudden and wicked threat. He was terribly disturbed. He told me why.

The blue sacks had continued to arrive, every now and then, and their contents went discreetly into the cellars of the legation. The idea, evolved with a colleague in another secret branch, was to keep the stuff safely there while the two of us found means to carry out London's orders for its use. These were to distribute plastic, a conveniently malleable form of high explosive, to Hungarian volunteers who would use it against enemy shipping on the Danube as and when the local balloon went up, and when no further diplomatic considerations were involved. Some of this plastic, still more conveniently, was packed inside small metal containers, known as limpets, that were magnetised and thus affixable to the outside of hulls. More or less you simply clapped them on; and they stuck there quietly, not even ticking, till their time-delay detonators set them off. These limpet 'toys' were said to work quite well.

Some progress was made in finding appropriate volunteers to stick them on, but the time for hand-out had still to come, though by now we thought it must be near. Meanwhile, given the legation's diplomatic immunity at least until the balloon went up, by which time the stuff would be elsewhere, the legation was perfectly safe. The cellars were capacious and little visited; the British minister, in any case, was not a man to give you wine. He was understood to be saving his expenses.

He allowed me to sit down opposite to him.

He was a man of natural pallor and pale blue eyes and pale spectacles rimmed in gold. All these he turned away from me, and told his indignation. His anger trembled, and with reason. He had ordered his military attaché, purely as a routine precaution, to search the legation. And this major of the British Army, whose name I will forget, had found our stuff in the cellars and informed the minister.

'I take it that this material is yours?'

There seemed nothing useful that one could say.

'Very well, I at once ordered my military attaché to take this material and throw it into the Danube. He has done this. He has thrown it into the Danube, you understand?'

What would D have said?

'And I warn you now that if you attempt to bring in any more of such material, or in any other way act in this manner, I shall denounce you to the Hungarian police.'

His anger trembled into quiet enjoyment. I looked at him and lied, but of course he knew that I was lying; he also knew that I had no diplomatic immunity.

'I shall do that, do you understand?'

Mistake, you will think: with the enemy almost on the doorstep, I should have dared him to do his worst. My colleague in the other secret branch made the same mistake in the same kind of interview; after all, we were anxious too. But beyond that we were there to prepare for what might yet be done if Hungary should become entirely lost, and now, in this small but still useful matter of limpets and such, we had nothing to prepare with. The time had passed when blue sacks could arrive, no matter what diplomatic corners the acolytes of the priest of Saint Rock, travelling as king's messengers, might be willing to cut. The minister was concerned for his diplomatic purity: well enough, but to throw our stuff into the Danube? Yet there was nothing to be done.

Archibald Lyall

On paper, Communism seemed to be the only proper, watertight political theory existing in the world today, the only one that really solved everything and accounted for everything, and then when you actually went to Russia you came back with very little doubt that the Russians were a good deal hungrier and were more unhappy and worse off all round, not only than people in Western Europe, but than they had been before the Revolution

The details of Archie Lyall's recruitment into Section D of SIS have never been disclosed but, as a traveller and expert linguist, and the author of *The Languages of Europe*, he must have been an attractive proposition to the authorities.

Lyall's pre-war books include the novel *Envoy Extraordinary*, *The Balkan Road* and *It Isn't Done*, and he enjoyed an unparalleled reputation as a bon viveur and raconteur, quite apart from his skills as a professional intelligence officer who remained in SIS long after the war. David Walker, a fellow recruit in Section D who worked alongside him in pre-war Belgrade, recalls him as an 'admirable character' who 'carried a revolver in case of accidents and a monocle in case of serious trouble'. Later Lyall was to transfer to SOE's Yugoslav Section.

What makes Lyall's case so fascinating is the fact that during the molehunting era of the late 1960s he came under suspicion as a Soviet sympathizer and a possible traitor. Years after his death in 1964 the counter-intelligence ferrets pursued several clues that suggested he might have betrayed information to the KGB. Amounting to purely circumstantial evidence were his remarks, published in 1933, regarding the Soviet system. In that year he visited Moscow with a group of committed Communists in order, as he put it, to experience the pilgrimage-like effect of religious zealots reaching their particular Mecca. The result was *Russian Roundabout: A Non-Political Journey*, in which can be found some revealing observations about the attraction of Leninism.

One of those to investigate Archie Lyall was MI5's Peter Wright who discovered that at one point in his career Roger Hollis had been Lyall's next-door neighbour. When confronted with this fact during an interrogation Hollis affected not to remember having spent two years in close proximity to a fellow British intelligence officer, a matter that Wright interpreted as highly suspicious.

In this extract from his account of his visit to Moscow in 1933 Lyall dwells upon the contrasts between capitalism and Communism, and thereby unwittingly provides the basis for a lengthy molehunt which was to be conducted in secret more than thirty years later.

Russian Roundabout

Until about a century ago, when the Americans took to inventing new sects to suit all tastes and pockets, it seemed to be a law of Nature that every new religion came from the East as surely as each new day. The law has now been reestablished. The Red Star has arisen in the East and the Hammer and the Sickle parody the Cross, where Russia has fallen under the sway of a fierce fighting faith more like the primitive religion of

Mahomed than anything else that has disturbed the world in the last thousand years.

For all that Leninism is anti-religious, it is itself in the fullest sense a religion, with its insistence on unquestioning faith, its sacred books, its missionary zeal, its persecution of infidels and heretics and, most of all perhaps, in its effect on the minds of its adherents.

I had known a man in London, drifting, frustrated, melancholy, who had been to Russia and got converted. He had come back with a purpose in life, happy, busy, going out nearly every evening to speak at Communist meetings. With a very small twist different he might have been a man saved by the Salvation Army.

I once asked another devout Communist why I never saw her in her old haunts any more.

She said: 'Oh, Party members are forbidden to go there now.'

'I should snap my fingers at the Party and go there all the same.'

'I can't do that. Why, I should be expelled from the Party!'

'Would you mind that very much?'

She gave a gasp of sheer horror.

'Oh! I don't know *what* I should do without the Party. I – I think I should *die*.'

No more shudderingly could a pious Catholic have spoken of excommunication.

That was one of my reasons for visiting Russia. Stephen Graham had gone with the Russian pilgrims to Jerusalem. I would go with the English pilgrims to Moscow and observe the devotees of what is almost certainly the most vital religion of the century. I was a little curious too – though I did not confess it even to myself – as to whether I also might not get religion in Russia and be saved like the little Jew doctor I had known. Even if I did not, it would still be exciting to watch the enthusiasm all round me, as it would be exciting to go to Lourdes or Mecca.

A second reason was that I was profoundly impressed with the apparent breakdown of Western capitalism, and I half hoped to find a practicable alternative in the new society that was being built up in Russia.

As I saw the crisis in the West, production had hopelessly outrun consumption. Now that machinery had enabled factories to turn out a hundred times as many goods for a hundredth part of the labour, I did not see how it was possible to avoid chronic unemployment. The Communists, they said, were trying to make man the master of the machine instead of allowing the machine to master man, as we had done. By regulating everything from above, they were aiming at using machinery for the benefit of mankind by a progressive reduction of the hours of labour, and this seemed to me the only way of solving the problem, short of scrapping machinery altogether.

So many utterly contradictory reports came out of Russia, and I wanted to go and see for myself what it was like, though, to be sure, I had no very solid hope of being able to find out the truth in a month's conducted tour.

My third and perhaps most important reason was that I had never been to Russia, and that, with the pound fallen over most of Europe and the Russian Government advertising cheap tours, it seemed the obvious place to go to.

The official Russian travel bureau is called Intourist (the In- being short for *inostranets* – 'foreign'), and I went round to their office in Bush House and carried away programmes of the tours. I fancied in particular one which took you (in the third class) on a Russian boat from London to Leningrad and then, with three days in Leningrad and four days in Moscow, to Nizhni Novgorod, down the Volga to Stalingrad (*né* Tsaritsin), and from Stalingrad to Rostov, Kiev, and home by way of Leningrad again. Everything was included, even down to free theatre and cinema tickets. From London back to London. Twenty-eight days for thirty-one pounds. You could not travel that distance and see that much any other way under three figures. If you wanted to stay behind when your party went home, you could do so for a pound a day.

When, therefore, an Irish friend of mine suggested that I should come with him and his wife to Russia, I accepted straight away. He would make all the difference to the trip, for he spoke Russian fluently, and had even translated one or two Russian novels. Their names were not actually Michael and Jean Curtis, but then I have altered the names of most of the people in this book.

We were sailing from London Bridge on the thirtieth of July on the motor-ship *Alexei Rykov* with every prospect of a strenuous August ahead of us. I expected to be very uncomfortable, but I hoped I could keep that from upsetting me or influencing my judgment unduly, for I had travelled third class round Spain and in the Balkans, and I did not suppose Russia would be any harder than that.

Eric Maschwitz

During the six years of the war I was personally concerned with many secret activities, some useful, some ineffective, many frankly comical. I have no doubt that if I were to plead with the authorities for a release from the Official Secrets Act, I should be allowed, like many others, to write frankly and factually about matters that have hitherto been regarded as 'hush-hush'.

In September 1939 Eric Maschwitz was thirty-eight years old, a successful (but myopic) lyricist, and married to the actress Hermione Gingold. He had graduated from Cambridge, where he had been a modern languages scholar, and later had edited the *Radio Times* and written for Metro-Goldwyn-Mayer in Hollywood. His wartime ambition was to serve in intelligence so he wrote to Admiral Sinclair, chief of the Secret Intelligent Service and a friend of his wife, offering his knowledge of French and German. Maschwitz had no idea what Sinclair's exact position was, but reasoned that admirals could achieve more than other mortals. 'I had always understood that he had something to do with Naval Intelligence and had at one time quelled a mutiny at Portsmouth with the power of his invective,' he recalled. 'If he had something to do with Intelligence then I would become an intelligence officer; I could already see myself decoding secret messages while resisting the advances of a beautiful foreign spy!'

Not surprisingly, Maschwitz received no reply to his letter, so he applied for a job with postal censorship and was sent to Liverpool where, with hundreds of other examiners, he established himself in what had been the headquarters of Littlewood's football pools.

Soon after Admiral Sinclair's death in November 1939 Maschwitz was transferred to a unit of Section D which had opened an undercover office in the Adelphi Hotel. The cover, supplied by Maschwitz, was that they were preparing a new theatrical revue, and this eventually became true with *New Faces*.

In February 1940 he returned to London and was accommodated at St Ermin's Hotel, though still managing to work on his theatrical productions. As the likelihood of an invasion increased he was sent to Beverley in Yorkshire to create a local resistance organization but by the autumn the networks were being dismantled and Maschwitz was transferred briefly to Army Welfare in London before finding himself in SOE. After a brief spell in Baker Street he was sent to New York to join British Security Co-ordination, and he remained in the United States until early in 1942, undertaking duties that he was too discreet to mention. 'I do not personally believe in haphazard revelation. Why tell the world what you have done and why you did it? There may be another enemy one day.'

Back in London Maschwitz, who had achieved fame from writing the lyrics to the hit song 'A Nightingale Sang in Berkeley Square', was released from SOE and asked to supervise radio programmes for the troops. Later he switched to the Political Warfare Executive, preparing propaganda leaflets for dropping to the enemy during the invasion, and ended the war running a broadcasting unit for 21st Army Group in Brussels.

After the war Maschwitz continued his success as a playwright and helped pioneer light entertainment on television, moving from the BBC to independent television in 1963. He died in October 1969. In this passage from his memoirs he describes a journey from the USA which was interrupted by a U-boat.

No Chip on My Shoulder

The operations with which I was concerned under a genius known as 'Little Bill', were many and curious. In them I was associated in turn with a German ex-cabinet Minister, an astrologer, a South American professor, a stockbroker, an industrial chemist, and two splendid ruffians who could produce faultlessly the imprint of any typewriter on earth. I controlled a chemical laboratory in one place, a photographic studio in another. My travels took me to Canada, Brazil and Bermuda; I spent a good deal of time in Washington, DC.

Towards the end of November, 1941, I was given an assignment that necessitated a journey by ship to Lisbon, via Bermuda, and it was agreed that after my small mission had been completed, I should travel on to London for four weeks' home leave.

One evening, when I was gambling on the 'fruit machine' in the ship's bar, the engines stopped; the ship had been hailed by a German submarine. I happened to be the only 'belligerent' on the passenger list, so the captain, fearing that the Germans would insist upon searching his ship (in which case I might have been summarily removed), returned me my passport and sent me down to my stateroom with instructions to lock the door and keep quiet!

I had only one paper with me which might, if discovered, have proved compromising, and this I decided to destroy. Touching it off with my cigarette lighter, I watched it burn until it became too hot to hold, then let it fall into the toilet. How could I have known that the toilet-seat had been coated with some inflammable material? There was a flash, a column of flame, the reek of burning cellulose ... and there I stood, with singed eyebrows, staring at an oval of charred wood!

Fortunately the U-boat had only stopped our ship for some routine enquiry and to my intense relief I heard the engines start up again. I had been spared the horrors of an underwater journey to the concentration camp, but I had the devil of a time explaining away the accident in my bathroom (the purser, I suspect, took me for some sort of psychopathic arsonist!).

Once in Lisbon I suffered the usual delay in securing an air passage home. This was all the more annoying since I was on this occasion very short of money. No Avenida Palace this time; I settled down to wait in a side-street hotel which had been recommended to me as 'secure'. In spite of the recommendation, I noticed that my baggage was regularly examined, presumably by the chambermaid (she had a heavy black moustache and might have been a Gestapo official in disguise!).

There can have been no hotel in the world as full of mice as mine was; they ran around the corridors and swept in troops down the stairs. In the bar late one night I watched a particularly talented member of the company preening his whiskers on top of the cash-register; when the bar-tender sleepily struck one of the keys, the mouse toppled over into my dry martini, like one of those circus-artistes who dive from the roof of the Big Top into a little tank of water!

I had the interesting good fortune to meet for the first time one of the greatest of English writers. Norman Douglas, having escaped from Italy without a penny in his pocket, was making a small living in Lisbon by teaching English. With him was his Italian publisher, Pino Orioli; the two friends were occupied in preparing for publication an anthology of extracts from Douglas's writings. Their editorial office was a marble-topped table in a *pâtisserie* where, stuffing themselves with cream-cakes, they pored over gallery proofs all afternoon, watched by an admiring coterie of suspiciously doe-eyed young Portuguese. I had heard much about the author of *South Wind* from Compton Mackenzie and thought his delicate wit enchanting.

In London I found life much changed since my departure. Though the 'black-out' was as stringent as ever, the bombing had ceased. Most of my friends were in uniform, Philip Jordan a war correspondent, Val Gielgud, still retained by the BBC, a gallant Home Guard. We had a new meeting place in the little Gay Nineties which Phyllis Gordon had opened recently in Berkeley Street. While spending a weekend with Judy Campbell and her family in Grantham, I heard the news of Pearl Harbour and wondered greatly what effect the Japanese attack might have had upon our work in America. That little leave was quickly eaten up in parties and theatre-going; when the time came to return to duty I was more than a little sad.

I sailed, this time in uniform, on board a troop-ship out of Liverpool bound for Halifax. We spent fourteen stormy days at sea including Christmas Day (on which I staged a revue for the entertainment (?) of the sea-sick soldiery) and New Year's Eve. On landing I changed once more into 'civvies' and set out by train for New York.

My curiosity regarding the effect of recent events upon the great United States was soon set at rest. I found New York in highly belligerent mood and swarming with uniforms. In my own organisation much had changed, most strikingly of all our relationship with the Americans; until December 7th they had been our tolerant hosts, to be handled with delicacy, now they were our allies. The FBI which had formerly kept as watchful an eye upon us as upon the Germans, (and, incidentally, recorded all our telephone calls), now worked hand in glove with us; under Colonel 'Wild Bill' Donovan there sprang up a host of organisations parallel to our own, all of them anxious to acquire the 'know how' which we had learned in two and a half years of war. The rounding up of German, Italian and Japanese agencies made our work easier; security regulations could be relaxed a little.

As far as my own type of operation was concerned, this, having been aimed at enemy forces at work in a neutral country, had to a large extent lost its purpose. For some months I tried to find enough to do to justify my remaining under 'Little Bill' but somehow the zest had gone out of life. After receiving the sad news of my father's death in Birmingham, I was neither happy nor, what was more important, of any real value. My chief was, as usual, completely understanding; he suggested that I should be released from SOE and [that I] left to find myself a job from the War Office.

Sir Gerald Glover

One could almost see people coming in and out of Queen Anne's Gate clutching daggers and wearing cloaks and large brimmed hats! It came as no real surprise to learn after the war that virtually all the MI6 workings were known to the Germans by 1940.

Gerald Glover's introduction to intelligence work took place in the Balkans in 1938 when, in the guise of a King's Messenger, he was despatched by MI6 to Budapest with a diplomatic bag full of explosives. During the following months he made three further trips, to Bucharest and Belgrade, but after the fall of France, and a couple of clandestine courier missions to Eire, he was invited to join the Security Service.

He was posted to the south-east of England in the role of Regional Security Liaison Officer. The task of MI5's network of twelve RSLOs was to liaise with the local police and military authorities, and represent the Security Service whenever the need arose. During the invasion summer of 1940 this meant co-ordinating the counter-espionage and counter-sabotage activities of the Home Guard, Chief Constable and the senior military commander from a base in a suburban house in Tunbridge Wells. After eighteen months Glover was put in overall command of the RSLOs and he remained in that post, supervising the security arrangements for D-Day, until late in 1944, when he returned to civilian life as a leading solicitor specializing in property deals. A highly successful racehorse owner, he was knighted in 1971 and his home at Pytchley became a centre of Conservative politics in Northamptonshire.

Gerald Glover died in December 1986. In this extract from his privately published memoirs, entitled *115 Park Street*, the address of his solicitor's practice, he tells of his recruitment into MI6 by his client, Laurence Grand.

115 Park Street

In early 1938 Joseph Morgan made one of his regular phone calls that invariably led to a satisfactory mortgage deal with some client. This time his client was a young artillery captain who wished to purchase a small house in the Camberley district. He had his regular pay but not much capital. I told Morgan to send him along and I would see what I could do.

Captain Laurence Douglas Grand turned out to be a tall, thin, astute-looking character but with little idea what was involved in the finances of buying a house with the aid of a mortgage. His wife also came with him that day to 115 Park Street. Besides being extremely pretty she possessed a sound business head, and it was really because of her sensible negotiations that I was able to offer to find for them a 90 per cent mortgage on a nice detached house that they later found. The couple came to see me several times during that period concerning surveyors' reports and so, once or twice the wife came alone saying her husband was overseas. On one occasion – in May I think it was – he arrived at my office in uniform and was wearing the crowns of a major. I congratulated him on his early promotion – as it was a simple matter to pose as an army officer I had taken the simple expedient of checking his name against the army list, so I knew he had not long received his captaincy. He dismissed his good fortune by simply saying that his job with the War Office required a major and he happened to be available with the right qualifications and courses behind him. It was only an acting rank and did not mean a lot.

When the time came for completion and taking possession of the house, his wife came and said that Laurence was once more temporarily overseas and would be back next week to sign the papers. This he did. It was no more than six months after the original phone call introducing him to me so I was somewhat nonplussed to discover him once more in uniform but now with the pips and crowns of a lieutenant-colonel adorning his shoulders.

I remarked that I would not mind being in his particular branch of the War Ofice as it seemed to enjoy good promotion prospects, with plenty of overseas travel. He made no comment. I put this down to a diminishing sense of humour with his rapidly elevating rank. But I did confess to him a desire for an interesting military job. I was busy and had completed my part in his domestic affairs and so dismissed him from my mind. That was in September.

At the beginning of November there was a phone call for me from the War Office. The voice the other end announced that he understood that I was interested in a job at the War Office and could he arrange an interview with that in mind. I told him he was talking nonsense and that I was not the slightest bit interested in working at the War Office. He then disclosed that his source was Colonel Grand. Curious about the turn of events I consented to meet him but was quite unprepared for the bizarre instructions that followed: I was to go to Victoria Station just before five o'clock that afternoon having first purchased a white carnation. At precisely five I was to produce the flower and insert it into my lapel button hole. The voice who was issuing the instructions said that he would be there as well and would do exactly the same thing. As soon as I spotted him I was to go up to him and say, 'Are you Caesar?'

It was so unbelievable I very nearly did not go, but for the same reason I went. To my utter amazement it all happened exactly as the mysterious voice had instructed. There under the station clock at five o'clock precisely not six feet from me with the rush hour crowds dashing all round him was a man with brown trilby hat and wearing a belted raincoat. He stood quite still, looking straight at me. He then produced the white carnation out of his pocket and solemnly inserted it into his lapel. The sight of someone looking for all the world like a Hollywood detective with a carnation in his raincoat button hole struck me as so ridiculous that I nearly burst out laughing. However, having gone so far I carried on with my part, duly attaching my carnation to my formal city suit as I approached him. Actually the carnation was quite at home as I often wore one and had only just removed that particular flower so that I could comply with the instructions. Resisting the urge to tug at his moustache to see if it was real I asked if he was Caesar.

In reply he said, 'How do you do Glover, would you be so good as to come with me to my office?'

(The delightfully absurd spy story atmosphere that surrounded the meeting was slightly spoilt when later I learnt that 'Caesar' was not a password but in fact the man's real name.)

Caesar set off out of Victoria Station at a brisk pace with me falling in step alongside. We marched – walked would be the wrong word – down Victoria Street branching off where New Scotland Yard now stands, and made for Queen Anne's Gate. We entered a semi basement door at the back of a house that proved to be 21 Queen Anne's Gate, the headquarters, I subsequently learnt, of the Secret Intelligence Service or MI6. I entered the door and a new life.

No. 21 Queen Anne's Gate is a terraced brick building of five or six storeys no doubt dating from that good queen's time. The interior gave the appearance of being an amalgam of flats. Caesar led the way to a service lift which we took to the top floor where we were met by two armed military policemen. Caesar produced a pass for himself and some documents presumably explaining my presence. Caesar handed me over to a corporal and apart from the occasional sight of him in Queen Anne's Gate I had no further contact with him.

I was ushered into the ante room of an office which contained two more armed guards and on through to meet a Colonel Wilkinson. He was an extremely young-looking dour individual who in the three years that I was associated with him I never once saw smile.

He opened with, 'Can you make yourself available, Glover, to travel within 48 hours to Budapest as a King's Messenger? It's extremely important.'

I supposed that I could, not in the least knowing how I could explain my sudden trip to Susan.

'Good,' he said. 'No one must know what you are doing. You are required to sign the Official Secrets Act and swear allegiance to king and country.'

This done I was informed that I was to take several diplomatic bags to Budapest. One was genuine which I would pick up from the Foreign Ofice in two days' time and the other four would be in the taxi that I would then find waiting for me outside the Foreign Office ready to take me to the boat train.

'The bags will contain certain materiel,' he calmly said, 'which you must hand over to our man in Budapest.'

Colonel Wilkinson explained how on arriving at the British Embassy in

Budapest I was to give the Ambassador the genuine diplomatic bag and the entire contents of my pockets – passport, wallet, keys, note books, pens, pencils – everything. He would in turn give me sufficient Hungarian currency to cover any needs. I then would leave by a side door and load the other bags into an unofficial embassy car with a driver who would drive me round Budapest for a while. Next I had to travel in a succession of taxis ending up at an address in the dockland area which I had to memorise.

I told Susan a whopping lie about urgent business in Paris, and survived a scolding from my secretary for upsetting numerous appointments.

It was a foggy winter's morning when two days later I reported to the Foreign Office carrying a weekend case – I had been told to travel light. They were expecting me and I was immediately given a sealed diplomatic bag. Outside was an ancient taxi ticking over by the kerbside, sitting in the back was a young man surrounded by more of what I now recognised to be diplomatic bags. Clearly my vehicle. On the way to Victoria Station the young man handed me a rather grand document signed by Lord Halifax explaining that I was a King's Messenger – and a first class return ticket to Budapest in a reserved compartment on the Orient Express. The young man told me that I may have to bring some normal diplomatic bags back from Budapest for the Foreign Office, which I was to do quite openly, then I was to make my way by at least two taxis to Queen Anne's Gate for debriefing – though I believe that term had not been invented them – and to hand in my special passport.

At Victoria Station the taxi driver (who obviously was not) and the young man dismissed the services of various porters and together loaded the genuine and bogus bags into my reserved compartment of the boat train, getting very hot in the process. I later discovered to my own discomfort that the four bags weighed at least half a hundredweight apiece.

The journey went very well and was the height of luxury. I was very much on edge though, and rarely left my compartment even for meals, which I had brought to me. My anxiety was for the safety of the bags, but I learnt later that it should have been for myself. There were no problems in Budapest. No one followed me from the embassy to my contact – at least I was pretty sure they did not. Unlike my encounter with Caesar we did not have passwords to exchange and apart from wishing each other good luck no more was said. I do not know what nationality he was or if he was to use the materiel himself or whether he was simply another courier like myself.

At my debriefing I learnt that the purpose of my mission was to sabotage German bound oil barges on the River Danube. On my way home I stopped off in Paris and bought a little dress for Alison and a handbag for Susan. It was a strange experience buying gifts that I would have bought anyway but which were part of my cover story – I felt very guilty.

CHAPTER IV

MI5 at War

It is a commonplace of counter-espionage work that success comes and spies are caught not through the exercise of genius or even through the detective's flair for obscure clues, but by means of the patient and laborious study of records.
J. C. Masterman, The Double Cross System

The British Security Service has long prided itself on its ability to keep secrets, and until 1972 the organization had achieved an almost unbroken record of discretion regarding its wartime activities. The exception was the journalist Stephen Watts whose memoirs contained some suitably reticent references to a deception scheme he had perpetrated on the enemy in the hope of making them believe General Montgomery had set up his headquarters in Gilbraltar when he was really masterminding the plans for D-Day. However, it was to be Sir John Masterman who made the first significant breach in the ban on former MI5 officers making disclosures about their secret employment, and publication of his *The Double Cross System of the War of 1939–1945* was to generate much friction in Whitehall. Instead of merely outlining a single operation, it gave a detailed account of the work of dozens of double agents. Not surprisingly, the authorities reacted with horror and later he was to describe his lengthy struggle to obtain permission to publish in his memoirs, *On the Chariot Wheel*.

Masterman's campaign was assisted by Christopher Harmer, a solicitor who had served in MI5 as a case officer handling German double agents. His success encouraged two colleagues, Cyril Mills and Sir Gerald Glover, to write their own accounts which were to be published privately. Mills was the son of Bertram, the founder of the circus which became a thoroughly British institution of world renown. What was less well known was Cyril's intelligence role. In the early Thirties, as an amateur aviator he regularly flew around Europe, ostensibly in search of venues for his big top or to audition an act, but actually to collect intelligence and take aerial photographs of sensitive military airfields. At sites where British air attachés were unwelcome Mills often succeeded in obtaining permission to land his de Havilland Hornet, and in August 1936 he completed his most difficult mission, an aerial survey of the Messerschmitt factory at Ravensberg.

Following this introduction to the profession of intelligence Cyril was recruited by the Security Service in 1940 and spent the first part of his clandestine career in B Division, the counter-espionage branch where he came into contact with German double agents for the first time. One of the agents he handled, using the cover name Mr Grey, was Juan Pujol, whom he codenamed Garbo in April 1942. Soon afterwards Mills was transferred to Canada as the Security Liaison Officer responsible for maintaining contact between the embryonic Special Branch of the Royal Canadian Mounted Police and MI5's headquarters in London. His specific task was the interrogation, recruitment and handling of a German double agent in Montreal who succeeded in duping his Abwehr controllers into believing that he was still at liberty even after a year of captivity. He had been landed from a U-boat on 10 November 1942 and had been arrested almost immediately because of the attention he attracted in the small coastal community of New Carlisle. The German naval officer quickly established a rapport with Cliff Harvison, the RCMP officer who had made the arrest, and once his wireless transmitter was connected to a large radio antenna, sent signals twice daily to Hamburg where they were gratefully acknowledged. Codenamed Moonbeam he continued to deceive the Abwehr until late 1943 when, as he was running short of money, his controllers appeared to abandon him. Harvison escorted him to London where he was placed in MI5's custody, and Mills continued to monitor the activities of two other double agents who had been sent to replace him. In September 1945 Mills returned to London to take charge of his family business, his wartime role remaining undisclosed until shortly before his death in July 1991.

The person to compromise Mills's post-war role was Peter Wright who revealed in *Spycatcher* that, far from retiring in 1945, Mills had continued to assist MI5 and, in particular, had allowed his house in Kensington Palace Gardens, which conveniently neighboured the Soviet embassy, to be a listening and observation post. Indeed, at the height of the Cold War a tunnel was dug from his basement, under the garden, and up to the embassy's exterior wall so that surveillance equipment could be inserted into the building. Mills was infuriated by Wright's disclosure, and mystified by Lord Rothschild's apparent encouragement for the publication of *Spycatcher*.

Lord Rothschild MI5's sabotage expert, was himself to release two volumes, one of which contains a remarkable description of the incident which led to his receiving the George Cross for gallantry. In contrast his partner in the same unit, Detective Chief Inspector Leonard Burt, was characteristically discreet about his wartime service. The solicitor responsible for recruiting Burt into MI5, Sir William Charles Crocker, was also to publish his memoirs but steps were taken to ensure they contained no breach of the British secrecy laws.

Four MI5 officers who maintained their silence, despite being prolific writers on other topics, are Derek Tangye, MI5's wartime press liaison officer, the novelist John Dickson Carr who worked closely with the service's star agent runner Max Knight, the biographer Roger Fulford and Herbert Hart.

The son of a barrister of Scottish descent, John Dickson Carr travelled to Paris after coming down from university and, instead of becoming a lawyer like his father, took up the life of a writer. Aged twenty-one in 1927, Dickson Carr's first success was *It Walks by Night* in 1930, a detective novel that was widely praised. Soon afterwards the American-born thriller writer moved to Hampstead, married an English girl and had three children.

Carr died in February 1977, eschewing personal publicity and avoiding the limelight. He divided his time between his homes in London and Long Island and became one of the most industrious writers of his generation, using at least two pen-names to write nearly fifty books. His novels were tremendously successful but his public never guessed that he had worked for the counter-espionage branch of the Security Service before and during the war, and had successfully penetrated the Communist Party of Great Britain for MI5. Quite how many of his novels, which included the titles *The Lost Gallows*, *The Case of the Constant Suicides*, *Till Death Do Us Part*, *Below Suspicion* and *The Third Bullet*, depended upon his own experience as an MI5 agent and officer is unknown. Certainly Dickson Carr had worked for Max Knight until 1942 when he joined the BBC as a playwright, writing radio thrillers 'to take listeners' minds off the blitz'.

After leaving Oxford, H. L. A. Hart practised at the Chancery Bar before joining the Security Service in 1940. Initially he was employed in pursuing rumours of espionage and some of the many denunciations received from the public alleging enemy activity, often taking the form of lights seen to flash at night, perhaps signalling German aircraft. One of his first tasks was to survey telegraph poles in the south of England after a report that many of them bore code messages for enemy parachutists. Of all the claims made that Hart investigated, only one case proved to be that of an authentic Abwehr spy, that of Jan Ter Braak, a twenty-seven-year-old Dutchman found dead in an air raid shelter in Cambridge in April 1941. Ter Braak's identity papers were forged and Hart concluded that he had shot himself when his food ran out because he had exhausted his ration book and did not want to risk buying food on the black market.

Most of Hart's work for MI5 was in B1(b), the 'special research' sub-section of the counter-espionage division which analysed enemy inter-cepts and gleaned information relevant to German spies destined for infiltration into Britain, or data regarding any of the double agents run by his colleagues in B1(a). On his staff were several barristers and academics, including a close personal friend, Anthony Blunt.

After the war Hart returned to Oxford to teach philosophy at New College and in 1952 was appointed Professor of Jurisprudence. He never discussed his wartime service in MI5 but was to be embarrassed in 1981 by the disclosure that his wife, who had worked in a sensitive post in the Home Office, had been interviewed by Peter Wright during a molehunt. Jenifer Hart was to admit that she had been a member of a covert Communist cell, and had been in contact with a mysterious Eastern European who was probably a key Soviet spy. The references to his wife in *Spycatcher* must have caused Herbert Hart some anguish but he made no public comment, even when she appeared on television to discuss her experience at the hands of the molehunters. After he retired as Principal of Brasenose, the Harts continued to live in Oxford, and Herbert died in December 1992.

Another of Max Knight's protégés was Bill Younger, a young Oxford graduate who had been stricken with polio and was unfit for military duty. A member of the Scottish brewing clan, he joined MI5 as an agent while still at university, and later wrote some detective stories using the pen-name William Mole. His cousin Kenneth was already working for the Security Service when Bill arrived.

The second son of Viscount Younger of Leckie, Kenneth was educated at Winchester and New College, Oxford before being called to the bar by the Inner Temple in 1932. He was practising as a barrister when, in 1940, he was drafted into the Security Service where he headed the French country section. He was involved in a major diplomatic incident with the arrest in 1941 of Admiral Muselier, de Gaulle's deputy who was suspected of having sold out to Vichy. Muselier was detained in prison until de Gaulle lodged a vigorous protest with Churchill and a subsequent investigation revealed that he had been the victim of an elaborate conspiracy. Despite this embarrassing episode Younger continued to liaise with the Free French authorities and was later appointed Director of E Division, the MI5 branch responsible for dealing with aliens. In 1945 Younger was elected Labour MP for Grimsby, a seat he was to represent for the next fourteen years. After his retirement from the Commons he was appointed to Lord Radcliffe's security tribunal which looked into the case of William Vassall, the Soviet spy gaoled for betraying Admiralty secrets to the KGB. He was knighted four years before his death in May 1976.

Several other members of the Younger family worked in the wartime Security Service. Bill's mother Joan was recruited into MI5's administrative branch. She had written novels under a pseudonym earlier in the 1930s, soon after her marriage (her third) to Dennis Wheatley who himself undertook some sensitive assignments for Knight. Her daughter Diana also worked for MI5, as a secretary.

When Joan Johnstone met Dennis Wheatley in 1929 she had five children, and had been divorced and widowed. Her marriage to William Younger had been dissolved, and her subsequent marriage to Hubert Pelham Burn had ended when he was killed in a car accident. Wheatley, who was then virtually a bankrupt, having seen his wine business collapse, obtained a divorce from his wife in 1931 and then married Joan.

In 1935 Joan adopted the pen-name Eve Chaucer and wrote her first novel, *No Ordinary Virgin*. This was followed by *Life as Carola*, *Return to Elysium* (using the name Joan Grant), *Winged Pharaoh*, *Eyes of Horus*, *Lord of the Horizon*, *Scarlet Feather* and finally *Silksheets and Breadcrumbs*. She also wrote two books for children, *The Scarlet Fish and other stories*, and *Redskin Morning*, as well as a travelogue, *Vague Vacation*. On the outbreak of war, at the invitation of Max Knight, she joined MI5 where her son and daughter, William and Diana Younger, both worked. She started as a driver, carrying senior personnel around London in her own car, but later she was put in charge of the allocation of petrol coupons, a post of some importance at a time when fuel was subject to strict rationing. At the end of the war she left the Security Service and took up painting and sculpting, and acquired an impressive reputation.

One of those who worked closely with Joan Wheatley in MI5's Transport Section was Mark, the sixth Earl of Cottenham. An enthusiastic driver and pilot, he worked for the aviation department of Vickers, joined the racing teams of Alvis and Sunbeam and was adviser to the Metropolitan Police driving school. When war broke out he was commissioned into the Leicestershire Yeomanry and went to work for the Security Service. Reference to Mark Cottenham's role in MI5 is to be found in Joan Miller's *One Girl's War*, but his clandestine career was to be short-lived as he was opposed to war with Germany and moved to the United States in 1941, where he died two years later, aged forty.

Cottenham had divorced his wife in 1939 and left behind two novels, *All Out* and *Sicilian Circuit*, and numerous books about motoring, including the *Steering Wheel Papers*, *Motoring without Fears*, and a travel book based on his experiences in North America in 1937, *Mine Host, America*.

Another MI5 wife who was to be published was Madeleine Bingham, who was married to Max Knight's assistant John. While her husband was running agents in London Madeleine worked as a typist at Blenheim Palace, MI5's wartime headquarters in Oxfordshire. When Madeleine Ebel married John Bingham in 1934 she was aged twenty-two and he was a reporter with the *Sunday Dispatch*, but soon after the war broke out he was recruited into the Security Service and she followed his example. After Blenheim Palace she switched to Special Operations Executive where, she later told friends, she worked in the Baker Street headquarters and kept a drawer of suicide capsules for agents. Her talent as a writer emerged after the war when her three-act comedy, *The Man from the Ministry*, written under the pseudonym Julia Mannering, was produced in 1947.

She went on to write the standard biographies of Sheridan, Sir John Vanbrugh, Henry Irving and Herbert Beerbohm Tree. Her autobiography, *Peers and Plebs: Two Families in a Changing World*, was published in 1975 and documented the unwelcome impact she had, as a Catholic with family roots in central Europe, on her fiancé's family which was fiercely Northern Irish, anti-papist. However, at no point in the book, which draws to a close with the birth of her son Simon in 1937, does she disclose her husband's career after journalism, or her occupation during the war. Her announcement, years later, that she intended to write an account of her husband's life, and that he had been the model for John Le Carré's character George Smiley, prompted a swift rebuke from the Security Service, which warned her that no such book would be tolerated. As she herself had worked for MI5 she was in a weak position to argue her case and she reluctantly dropped the project. She died in 1988, shortly before her husband.

Unique among MI5's wartime personnel was Professor Anthony Blunt, the distinguished art historian whose espionage for the Soviets was revealed publicly in November 1979. Although Blunt never wrote about his own experiences, or his work for MI5 between 1940 and 1945, he did contribute to a Courtauld Institute catalogue praising the skill of Tomas Harris, a brilliant collector of Goya masterpieces, dealer in Spanish art, painter and colleague in the wartime Security Service. In a valedictory article published in February 1975 Blunt, who gave no explanation for the depth of his knowledge, described the key role Harris had played in the running of MI5's star double agent, Garbo:

> He 'lived' the deception, to the extent that, when he was talking in the small circle of friends concerned, it was difficult to tell whether he was talking about real events or one of his fantastic stories which he had just put across to the Nazi Intelligence Service.

Blunt rarely spoke about his work in MI5 and even after his exposure he declined to answer some of the questions put to him by journalists, offering the Official Secrets Act as an excuse. As director of the Courtauld Institute, and one of the leading art experts of his generation, he wrote extensively about Poussin and other painters but only once did he agree to write about the forbidden topic of his wartime experience.

Like any well-trained agent, Blunt naturally gravitated to the branch of the Security Service where he could do the greatest harm, and he moved swiftly from the relatively innocuous military liaison section, to which he was first appointed, to the counter-espionage division. His first role in B Division was that of personal assistant to the division's director, Guy Liddell. While ostensibly carrying out research for the gullible Liddell, who counted Guy Burgess and Kim Philby among his friends, Blunt was accumulating useful information for his NKVD contact, a diplomat at the Soviet embassy in Kensington Palace Gardens. He conducted an efficient study of MI5's famed Watcher Service, the surveillance experts who monitored the movements of suspected enemy agents, and for a brief period was attached to a highly secret unit that routinely pilfered the diplomatic bags of neutral embassies in London.

Of crucial importance to the Soviets were the identities of British sources in either the Communist Party of Great Britain or, better still, in Moscow. By roaming the building during the lunch hour when MI5's St James's Street headquarters were virtually empty, Blunt slipped into the rooms of other officers and read whatever papers were left unsecured. By this simple but risky expedient he came across a top secret circular from SIS which gave details of a highly placed source in the Kremlin. Blunt passed on enough information about the spy to his Soviet case officer for the NKVD to trace the leak and arrest the culprit, the trusted secretary of the trade minister. He disappeared and was executed. Blunt's other coup was to compromise MI5's star source inside the CPGB, Tom Driberg.

Under the overall guidance of Sir John Masterman, Blunt's friend Tomas Harris was a genius at concocting complex but plausible schemes for the deception of the Abwehr. He was killed in a car accident in January 1964, and it was in memory of his skill as a counter-intelligence expert, as well as his gifts as an artist, that Blunt praised him.

Born in 1908 to a Spanish mother and an English Jew, Harris was a brilliant artist. He was educated in Spain and, at the age of fifteen, won a scholarship to the Slade School of Art in London. His father Lionel was a well-known Mayfair art dealer who operated from his sumptuous gallery at 6 Chesterfield Gardens, a property that Harris was to inherit. Tomas was an acknowledged expert on Spanish art, specializing in Goya, El Greco and Velazquez, and joined his father's business in 1930; later he was rumoured to have acted as a conduit for the marketing of important pictures looted from churches by the Republicans during the Spanish Civil War.

In 1940 Harris transferred from Special Operations Executive to the Security Service, where he was placed in charge of the counter-espionage division's Spanish sub-section, designated B1(g). Headed by Dick Brooman-White, who later switched to Section V of SIS, this small unit handled cases of suspected enemy agents arriving in Britain from Spain. One of those who was brought to England deliberately was Juan Pujol, the celebrated double agent codenamed Garbo who, aided with gifted guidance from Harris, was to perform unprecedented feats of deception on behalf of the Allies in the weeks leading up to D-Day.

Harris and his wife Hilda were popular members of London's Bohemian society and were close friends of Burgess, Blunt and Philby. He is believed to have paid for the education of Philby's son John, and certainly Philby held him in high regard as a fellow professional, describing the Garbo case as 'one of the most creative intelligence operations of all time'.

Blunt died in March 1983 but his promised memoirs were never released for publication. When he eventually confessed to his treachery, in April 1964, the current Director-General of MI5 was one of his former wartime colleagues, Sir Roger Hollis.

Much controversy has surrounded the enigmatic figure of Sir Roger Hollis, the son of a bishop, who joined MI5 in 1938 and rose to become its Director-General in 1956. Suspected of being a Soviet spy, he was investigated by several teams of molehunters, and then brought back from retirement to face a hostile interrogation. When challenged in the

Commons, Prime Minister Margaret Thatcher read a statement which, far from ending the speculation, prompted Peter Wright publicly to denounce his former Director-General as a traitor.

The question of whether MI5 ever suffered Soviet penetration after the departure of Anthony Blunt in 1945 is an issue that may be resolved only when the KGB's archives are opened to public scrutiny. In the meantime the only certainty is that both Hollis and his deputy, Graham Mitchell (another wartime colleague of Blunt's), suffered the ignominy of being accused by colleagues of having betrayed secrets to Moscow over an extended period.

Hollis was invited to join the Security Service after his return from the Far East where he had contracted tuberculosis, a disease from which he never fully recovered and which caused him to go into a sanatorium for seven months in 1942. He had left Oxford without a degree and had sought a job in journalism in Hong Kong. Later he moved to China where he was employed by the British American Tobacco Corporation as a manager. Invalided back to London, Hollis applied unsuccessfully to Roger Fulford for a job on *The Times*, was turned down by SIS where his brother Marcus went to work, and was eventually accepted by MI5.

Once there, he worked in the counter-subversion division and made himself an expert on British Communists. He earned a reputation as a diligent but dull worker who ably represented his organization on Whitehall committees. Those of his contributions that have been declassified appear banal and uncontroversial, like this comment on a paper submitted to the Foreign Office in November 1943: 'It is not in Britain's interests for the Germans and Russians to control everything.'

Hollis's route to advancement was not through the relatively glamorous counter-espionage sections, but via the more mundane counter-subversion and protective security branches. His promotion to Deputy Director-General was entirely unexpected and followed the sudden departure in 1952 of Guy Liddell who switched to GCHQ following the embarrassing defection of his friend Guy Burgess. In 1963 several senior officers became convinced that MI5 had experienced hostile penetration. The clues ranged from specific allegations made by defectors to more intangible evidence of operational failures that might have had other, perhaps innocent explanations. There followed a series of inconclusive molehunting exercises which cast suspicion on a range of possible culprits; Hollis himself was interrogated in 1970. At one stage in this abortive exercise Hollis, who was then living in Wells, in Somerset, occasionally called on David Cornwell who had rented a house near by.

Cornwell, as John Le Carré, had already achieved fame as a writer of spy thrillers; who can say how these visits coloured his subsequent stories?

Naturally the fact that a Director-General of MI5 had himself fallen under suspicion was a closely guarded secret even within the service, but news of the investigation leaked when Peter Wright, at the instigation of Lord Rothschild, decided to divulge details of his own career to a Fleet Street journalist. By the time the Hollis affair became public knowledge Hollis himself was dead, having died of a stroke at his home near Bridgwater in Somerset, in September 1973.

Whilst Hollis's observations in China did not amount to espionage, they certainly possessed an intelligence value. Graham Mitchell, on the other hand, had been employed as a journalist by the *Illustrated London News* before his recruitment into MI5 in 1938, but only one article has survived under his acknowledged authorship, an obscure item entitled 'What Was Known about Abyssinia in the Seventeenth Century – A Detailed Account in a Geography of 1670' which was published in October 1935.

Although stricken by polio as a child, Graham Mitchell excelled at sports and played tennis to competition standard and was a fine yachtsman. In 1930 he won the Queen's Club men's doubles lawn tennis championship. Educated at Winchester where he won an exhibition, and at Magdalen College, Oxford, he had a sharp mind which manifested itself in his game of chess. He specialized in correspondence chess, in which he once ranked fifth in the world, and represented his country.

After coming down from university Mitchell joined the *Illustrated London News* and was employed by the research department of Conservative Central Office. His politics at this time appear to have been to the right, for he was close to Sir Joseph Ball, the Tory politician and former Great War MI5 officer who was appointed to the Security Executive in 1940. By then Mitchell had been recruited into MI5 where, since November 1939, he worked for Roger Hollis in the F3 section of the anti-subversion F Division, concentrating on the surveillance of suspected Fascist sympathizers. At the end of the war he succeeded Hollis as Director, F Division.

Mitchell's career in the Security Service continued into the post-war period and in 1952 he was promoted to head the counter-espionage branch in succession to Dick White who had been appointed Deputy Director-General following the resignation of Guy Liddell. During the four years Mitchell held the post, until his move up to Deputy D-G in 1956, he was responsible for drafting the notorious 1955 White Paper on the defections of Donald Maclean and his old friend Guy Burgess. This extraordinary document remains to this day a lasting testament to the perfidy and incompetence of the Security Service's counter-espionage branch under Mitchell's stewardship. Not only did it contain numerous errors of fact, but it deliberately set out to mislead Parliament and the public over the sequence of events which led up to the defections. Far from not realizing until Monday, 28 May 1951 that Maclean had disappeared, as claimed by Mitchell, MI5 knew of his escape to France immediately it took place the previous Friday evening. No explanation for the many more preposterous assertions contained in the White Paper has ever been forthcoming, although this omission may be explained by the embarrassing fact that Mitchell himself was to be investigated.

Mitchell fell under suspicion in May 1963 during a molehunt conducted to identify a Soviet spy inside the Security Service, but he opted for early retirement in September, after an inconclusive enquiry codenamed Peters which lasted only four months. He died in November 1984, shortly after the revelation that he had been the subject of an investigation and confirmation that he had drafted the notorious Burgess and Maclean White Paper, whose authorship, in accordance with convention, had never been acknowledged.

Another MI5 officer to have written about the organization's wartime activities is Anthony Simkins, although he joined only after his release from a German prisoner of war camp. Soon after his retirement as Deputy Director-General he was commissioned to write an internal history of MI5's war. This was later to be incorporated as Volume V of the official history, *British Intelligence* edited by Professor Sir Harry Hinsley and his team of Cambridge historians. Of particular interest in this important book is an anonymous account of running a German double agent's wireless transmitter which was in fact contributed by Ronald Reed, a wartime Radio Security Service operator who spent the rest of his career in MI5.

Sir John Masterman

We, the amateurs, contributed (I like to think) some useful ideas, and we formed a loyal and efficient support for the professionals.

Through sheer ill-fortune John Masterman found himself in Freiburg when the Great War started in August 1914. Instead of being repatriated, as he had expected, he was interned at Ruhleben, the camp set up on Berlin's racetrack. There, despite one unsuccessful escape attempt, he was to spend the next four years. After his release in November 1918 John Masterman was invited to Whitehall Court to dine with Sir Mansfield Smith-Cumming, SIS's first chief, anxious to hear news of Kurt Hahn, the educationist who had helped Masterman avoid being sent to a prison camp after his abortive escape.

Masterman's transformation from a Christ Church don to an intelligence officer in the Second World War was brief. In March 1940 he was called up and given a commission in the Intelligence Corps. Fluent in German, he attended the interrogation course at Swanage and was then posted to the War Office as secretary to the Howard Committee which had been set up to investigate the evacuation of the British Expeditionary Force from Dunkirk. Once the committee had completed its report Masterman was transferred to the Security Service where he worked in the counter-espionage division, first at Blenheim Palace and later at Wormwood Scrubs. There he re-established contact with several of his former students, including William Younger. In December 1941 Masterman was assigned the task of debriefing the defector Dusko Popov, recently arrived from Lisbon, and it was this remarkable encounter between one of the Abwehr's star agents and his MI5 handler that led to the creation of the Twenty (or XX for double-cross) Committee, the inter-departmental body created to supervise the conduct of double-agent operations and liaise with all the appropriate services. Masterman was to chair a total of 226 weekly meetings of the committee before he was invited to write an account of its activities at the conclusion of the war. He returned to Oxford in September 1945 having completed his task in an astonishing two months. However, it was to be twenty-seven years before he revealed to his former employers that he had retained a copy of his manuscript, and that he intended to publish it in America.

He released his autobiography in 1975, two years before his death. Here he recalls the obstacles that were placed in his path by the security authorities when he announced his intention to release his illicit copy of *The Double Cross System of the War of 1939–45*.

On the Chariot Wheel

On the advice of Philip Swinton, who was always my strongest supporter and without whose active assistance XX would never have been published, I wrote a formal request to Roger Hollis, then head of MI5, and had a long discussion with him and Dick White. Once again the timing was inept and I had no success. I am, at this distance of time, uncertain why I did not press more vehemently in 1961, but I think that the reason was that I retired from the Provostship of Worcester in that year and was much occupied in changing my home. Negotiations and consultations continued but without strong pressure and the situation, from my point of view, deteriorated when the Profumo case came to occupy the first place in the minds of those in charge of the Security Service. Roger Hollis was firmly against publication and in June 1963 Alec Douglas-Home, then Prime Minister, wrote to tell me that, though he sympathized with my aim of giving the service in question a better image, he could not contemplate going against the professional advice which he had received.

I did not abandon the struggle but in December, on Philip Swinton's advice, wrote to the Secretary of the Cabinet, Lord Normanbrook, and asked if I could discuss the matter with him. We had several meetings and exchanged several letters but the upshot was that he felt that, in view of Roger Hollis's opposition and taking into account the administration difficulties, a fresh application was unlikely to succeed. If I did pursue the matter further he advised a direct approach to the permanent head of the Home Office or to the Home Secretary, as the Minister responsible for the Security Service. Once more I was obliged to accept the inevitable. I wrote to Normanbrook in March 1965:

> ... Meantime I shall follow the advice which is implicit in your letter. I certainly should not have consulted you unless I had intended to abide by what you said. In other words I shall let the matter drop for the time being though I think that I shall revive it at a later date. Among other things I should be unwilling to embarrass Roger Hollis just at the end of his time.

By this time my own views had crystallized, and my conviction that publication would be beneficial had become stronger and stronger. Some might say that it had become an obsession. This was my argument. In the first place there is a strong argument for recording as accurately as possible the chronicles of the past, and no historian would hesitate to demand that such records should be available unless there were overriding reasons to the contrary. Moreover the work of the XX agents makes intelligible certain parts of the history of the war and of enemy operations which would otherwise be ignored or misunderstood. This, however, was not my prime motive. More than anything else I was depressed by the low state of the reputation of the Security Service – or, to use modern jargon – by the poor image of the Service. Up to a point this was inevitable, for any good work done by a secret service is usually unknown, whereas any error or failure – e.g. when a previously successful spy is uncovered – receives much publicity and criticism. Here is a real dilemma, well put by Hugh Gaitskell in 1961 when, speaking of the Lonsdale case, he stressed that secrecy was essential for the Security Service but that it was also imperative to restore confidence in the Service. No doubt in Westminster and Whitehall and among those in or near to the corridors of power the merits and efficiency of the Service were well appreciated, but with the generality of people the case was otherwise. It is impossible, for reasons which must be obvious, to release secrets about operations which are very recent or still proceeding, but with each year I felt more convinced that only good could come from releasing an account of the wartime successes.

The spy cases of the 1950s and 1960s did indeed serious damage to the image of the Service, which came to be regarded as expensive, inefficient, and unnecessary. A writer as respected and admired as Rebecca West wrote in the *Sunday Telegraph*, on 26 March 1961:

> It is a tragedy on more than one level that the apparatus of security which costs us so much and so constantly impedes us, should not be more successful in preventing penetration by the forces of espionage; for if there were never another war, and they found no use for the information which they gather, they spread a moral infection, often among people not without value.

A leading article in the *Evening Standard* on the Philby case in 1963 takes the same line. 'The real culprit in this case is the Security Service. Our intelligence service has spent millions and achieved nothing but darkness.' A reviewer in the *Sunday Times* in December 1967, discussing the spy stories of the year, began his review with this sentence: 'This year saw British espionage in more than its customary disarray, hampered by the frailties of its operatives, the eccentricities of its high command . . . and a demoralising lack of belief in its own utility.' Nor is it irrelevant to remember that in 1969 the Secret Service vote was reduced by £250,000. The fact that in the public mind espionage and counter-espionage were hopelessly mixed up does not affect the issue; to most people they were simply the Secret Service, and for this much misrepresented body many people had no use whatever.

It was in these circumstances that I embarked in October 1967 on my final effort to secure leave for publication – an effort which was to be at long last successful almost exactly four years later. The omens seemed to me propitious. Dick White, who had been Director-General of the Security Service, had moved over to become Head of MI6 and had been succeeded by Martin Furnival Jones at MI5 and I was sure that they were the key men whom I must persuade to put forward my plan to higher authority. I hoped that they would support me actively or, at the worst, adopt a neutral attitude. From both I could expect (and received) a sympathetic hearing. Dick White had been my pupil at Christ Church and I had served under him in MI5 during the war. His services in MI5 and in MI6, as also his work in SHAEF with Eisenhower were outstanding, though known only to a small circle. I had kept in close touch with him since the war and he had always shown both interest in and sympathy with my plans. In October 1967 he wrote to me: 'As you know I have always been sympathetic with the idea of your XX book, though I have equally always seen grave difficulties connected with its presentation.' He added that he would contact Furnival Jones so that we could all discuss the matter. Furnival Jones himself had been a solicitor who had entered MI5 for the war years and had stayed on when the war ended. I knew therefore that I should get a fair hearing from both. Another circumstance made me hopeful – the obvious diminution of any security risk. Twenty years before it would have been culpable to have mentioned their names – in 1967 not only their names but the position of their offices and even their telephone numbers had appeared in American publications. Furthermore, another security objection had disappeared. In earlier days I had often been met with the argument that the Russians were ignorant of our methods and must so remain, even though all the secrets were by now well known in other countries. Then came the unmasking of Philby and the unpleasant knowledge that Russia knew more about our Secret Service than any other power. It seemed to me that the last security objection had disappeared. Philby himself I had met once or twice in our office when he was responsible for MI6 for the Iberian peninsula. Even at that early date I was told by both my chiefs – Petrie and Liddell – to treat him with caution and release as little information to him as possible. Dick White always mistrusted him and was the first, or almost the first, to be convinced of his treachery. Yet Philby's own account of Dick is not without perception. I think that Philby feared him instinctively and wrote of him: 'His most obvious fault was to agree with the last person he spoke to.' In this there was a measure of truth, for Dick was so fair-minded and so responsive to the views of others that he tended to agree too easily with views that were put before him. But I am tempted to add that in his official capacity it was his only fault.

It was natural, then, that I should feel optimistic in 1967 and that I should set about arranging a meeting with Dick and Furnival Jones together. The meeting did not prove easy to arrange since Furnival Jones left for Ceylon and Australia; but I had it fixed for 8 January. Unfortunately Dick White was ill on this date and so I spent some three hours alone with Furnival Jones – an interview that seemed to me highly satisfactory. He did not believe that the book would sensibly improve the image of the Service and he thought that it would come better as part of a general history of intelligence during the war, but he had some sympathy with the idea of making the public aware of the achievements of B1A and the XX Committee and was quite ready to send my proposal forward to higher authority. The only detail on which we did not agree was the form of presentation. Earlier I had thought of an anonymous production, but one adviser after another had told me that this would be wrong and that I should write under my own name. Personally either course would have been agreeable to me, provided only that publication was allowed, but Furnival Jones was not convinced about this. A day or two after our meeting I wrote a letter of thanks to him in which I said '. . . in particular I was grateful to you for your generous proposal that you should yourself take the initiative and begin to consult the authorities concerned. You may have been surprised that I did not immediately jump at this offer. My reasons for going slow were these.' I then explained that it seemed best to get the details about the method of publication settled and also to secure the agreement of Dick White. I felt reasonably confident that if all three of us worked together and put forward the plan it would get fairly quickly to the Minister and I felt, too, that if this happened it was more than likely that leave would be given.

It was not until May that the joint meeting occurred but it was agreed then that my case should go to Sir Burke Trend, the Secretary of the Cabinet, and Sir Philip Allen, Permanent Under-Secretary of State at the Home Office. Though I was pretty optimistic I felt that it was right to make provision for a refusal and I therefore constructed what I called Plan Diabolo, a plan which was only to come into operation if leave to publish was refused. Briefly the plan consisted in publishing the book in America. This, of course, would lay me wide open to prosecution under the Official Secrets Act, but of this I was not unduly afraid. At that time there could have been either a prosecution for a felony or for a misdemeanour and a study of the Act convinced me that I was only likely to suffer the smaller penalties of one guilty of the lesser offence. In fact I did not think that Government would prosecute me or that if they did they would get a conviction. I could clearly show that the main purpose of the book was to enhance the reputation of the Security Service and of MI6; I had offered 'any part or the whole' of the royalties to the department; I could produce letters from a great number of those most intimately concerned who were wholly in favour of publication in this country; the Security Service which would have been the prosecutor would have found it easy to show that I was guilty but what would be gained thereby? They would, if they did get a conviction, only give immense publicity to the book. I did not like to disguise my intentions from Furnival Jones and Dick White, but I could not well seem to press them too hard. I therefore adopted a different technique in each case. I had a talk with another old friend in MI5 John Marriott (who was himself consistently and bitterly opposed to my plan), and let him report to Furnival Jones. For Dick White I used Peter Fleming as an intermediary. Peter, who was one of my warm supporters, wrote to Dick urging publication and telling him of what Peter described as my 'diabolic plan'. 'You can rely on my indiscretion,' he wrote, adding that he hoped I should not have to put the plan into operation.

In spite of this pressure there was no progress, and I began to feel that both Furnival Jones and Dick White were becoming lukewarm. And why not? Even if they personally agreed that publication was eventually desirable they could not help feeling that all kinds of official and administrative difficulties would be avoided if my request was allowed to lapse and be forgotten. Then in October 1968 the blow fell. Furnival Jones wrote to me and told me that the Chiefs of Staff felt that they were 'insufficiently informed about the business' and that they had 'commissioned a study of the material available as a prelude to a decision'. Apparently it was felt either that my book was better kept to be incorporated in a general history of intelligence or that it should be combined with a projected history of deception. Not unnaturally I protested vehemently, both because my book was essentially a counter-espionage document and because the proposal meant an indefinite delay. In the autumn I had secured the invaluable help of Christopher Harmer (a solicitor and former colleague in MI5), who was ready to act for me as legal adviser but, as he was bound to do, advised me not to attempt an American production. I decided to press on with my attempt to have my proposal considered at a higher level, and in January 1969 I wrote to Furnival Jones and put to him two specific questions, which I quote in full.

> (1) I am particularly anxious not to misrepresent your attitude in the matter, for you have been helpful throughout. Would it be fair if I said that you held a position of 'benevolent neutrality', that is to say that, though not committing yourself to support, you would have no objection to publication if higher authority agreed to it? Please let me know if my interpretation is correct.
>
> (2) In 1964–5 Norman Brook ... advised me to approach either

'the Home Secretary personally or Sir Charles Cunningham, for it is with them that the final decision would rest.' Is Normanbrook's advice good today? Would you advise me to go to Sir Burke Trend and/or to the Home Secretary?

As usual I sent a copy of this letter to Dick White. Furnival Jones was ill, so I did not receive his answer till April when I was told that the answer to my first question was 'Yes' (though there were misgivings about the obligations of the Department to some of its agents), and to my second question the answer was 'No', since Sir Philip Allen (Cunningham's successor) was already taking part in the business. Dick White had already written to me to say that he had no doubt at all that I must meet Burke Trend and Allen and that neither he nor Martin Furnival Jones would raise security objections to publication. He reminded me at the same time that both of them were only advisers and were as anxious as I was to have a firm decision made. A meeting with Trend and Allen was arranged for June – and I felt that a real step forward had been made. The meeting itself went off moderately well. Both of the officials were courteous and sympathetic, both emphasized the practical difficulties which they fore-saw, both agreed that, though the outcome was very dubious it was worth 'trying it on the Minister'; both agreed that there should be no unreason-able delay. I felt complete confidence that they would give a fair chance to my proposal and I did not, therefore, ask even to see the shorthand record of the meeting. I do not think that I have misrepresented their views but I did underestimate the immense slowness and the complications of the Whitehall machine. Though Philip Allen wrote to me at intervals to tell me that my request was under active consideration it was not until April 1970 that I received an answer to my request – and that was that 'the final decision comes down against your request.'

I wrote to Furnival Jones and to Dick White. The former surprised me by his answer. 'As a matter of fact I did not, as you assume, know what was going on. Perhaps it is that those who adopt a neutral stance are thought to have no opinion worth hearing.' Dick's view was that I ought to use my own Memoirs for telling the story. Donald McLachlan [in Naval Intelligence during the war] took a critical view of governmental action. 'If I believed that the motive behind the policy was security I would accept it. But I am convinced that the sole object of the FO is to avoid gossip, publicity, and administrative embarrassment.' My own view coincided with his, with the exception that I should have substituted 'Whitehall' for the FO, since I felt that the multiplicity of authorities which were expected to agree was the real stumbling-block. Whatever the cause of the refusal I decided at once that Plan Diabolo, formerly something of a pipe dream, must now be put into operation. It was perhaps hubristic on my part to set my judgement against the official view, but I felt that I could not abandon a project which I had advocated for so long. Security objections had diminished almost to the point of disappearance and I was fortified by the growing support of those individuals whom I consulted and for whose opinions I had respect. These included not only many of the officers with whom I had served during the war (of these the most important in my judgement were Tar Robertson, who had been the head of B1A and Johnny Bevan, who had been in control of Deception) but also those who had concerned themselves with intelligence work in the subsequent years, including the Chief of the Defence Staff and those engaged on the official history. A letter from Michael Howard was typical of many others. He wrote:

> Speaking personally, I would like to see it published for three reasons:–
>
> (1) As a historian, it seems to me *ipso facto* desirable that chronicles of the past should be as complete and accurate as human endeavour can make them; if only because it is misleading and possibly dangerous to get things wrong. Your story not only fills in a gap in the history of the Second World War, it makes intelligible a great deal which is at present ignored and misunderstood, and will continue, until your book is published, to be ignored and misunderstood; not only by the general public but, as the wartime generation dies out, by those concerned with formulating national policy. This will be, for obvious reasons, a Very Bad Thing.
>
> (2) As an Englishman, I should like to see the full story told of something which we really did superbly well. Our record in the Second World War is not so glittering that we can afford to leave this out of it.
>
> (3) As a connoisseur of literature, I judge it a jewel of a book in its own right: beautifully written, clear, witty and wise.
>
> The argument that the story can be told as part of a broader study of 'Deception' seems a very weak one to me. Your study is something *sui generis*, even though it does overlap with Deception; and it deals with something much more important than Deception.
>
> Please feel free to show this letter to anyone and everyone.

Philip Swinton, too, urged me to go ahead.

When I had decided on an American publication my troubles were by no means over. My literary agent wrote that he could not handle the book. He had recently been involved in the *Daily Telegraph* action and had no wish to tangle once again with the Official Secrets Act. I consulted Norman Collins and he persuaded A. D. Peters, his own agent, to act on my behalf through his representative, Harold Matson, in America. At the same time I sought the help of James Osborn, eminent bibliophile and author and a great benefactor of the Bodleian. In both cases I made it clear that I had been refused leave to publish in England. I asked Osborn to sound out the Yale Press and find out if they would publish. This was in May 1970. The next few months were a time of disappointment. The first nine publishers in America refused the book – some thought it 'too British', others were already committed to other books dealing with the same topic, others thought that it would not appeal to the general public. I came to believe that Matson was trying to sell it as a 'spy book' rather than what it was – a report of some historical significance – and I urged him to concentrate on Yale. I also sent the typescript to James Osborn, who undertook to approach the Yale Press (November 1970). In March I received a letter from Matson which offered a contract for the book, which I immediately accepted and agreed further that the Yale Press should have the Canadian rights. Chester Kerr, the Director of the Yale University Press came over to see me and thus started, for me, a close friendship with him and with Ronald Mansbridge, the head of the Yale Press in London; they, together with Jim Osborn, were to prove my staunchest and most efficient helpers in the days to come. Unfortunately Chester Kerr was only able to see his solicitors on the day before he left for America, and from them he received the advice, 'do not proceed at this time.' Accompanied by Christopher Harmer I had a long interview with Jim Sandars and presented our case to him. Jim, the senior partner of Linklater & Paine, was known to me as a Director of Birfield, but of course I had no idea what advice he would give to his clients. I had, though, an uncomfortable feeling that I was about to fail again, especially when Chester Kerr told me that his committee would not make a decision until 24 June. At the beginning of June I received a firm offer from a commercial firm to take the book for America and not to raise the question of government approval. I replied that I should certainly accept the offer unless Yale decided to carry on with their publication. Then, some ten days later, came an unexpected, but to me joyful, cable from Chester Kerr. His committee had decided not to wait for their meeting but agreed to publish my book. A contract was being prepared. It seemed that, at last, I had come to the end of the road. At the same time

Chester told me that some members of his committee wished to make a direct approach to the Home Secretary and request that the book be declassified so that it could be published simultaneously in England and America. When I first made contact with the Yale Press I had not known that they published in London as well as in New Haven and though I was convinced that no publication in England would be allowed I saw no reason why the attempt should not be made. In fact it was made and a letter went to the Home Secretary immediately after I had signed the contract.

On the day when I received the contract I wrote to Philip Allen to tell him of my action and sent a copy to Furnival Jones. Something of an explosion then occurred. Two days later Alec Douglas-Home sent me a telegram asking me to lunch the next day, so that he might take me on to see the Home Secretary. Papers, I was informed, had already gone to the Attorney-General in order that he might decide what action could or should be taken against me. I cannot know what Alec did to protect me but I do know that the meeting with the Home Secretary (Maudling) was wholly successful. I had expected that the proposal to publish in England would be turned down out of hand and that the Yale letter would be answered in that sense. I was impressed by Maudling, particularly because he had obviously read and understood the book and I think that he was impressed by the letters which I showed him and which clearly indicated that the objections to publication were based, not on security risks, but on inter-departmental and administrative difficulties. Accordingly he wrote to Yale and intimated that no leave could be given unless the official experts could be satisfied that all security risks could be avoided by the excision of certain passages. I should as a matter of course be involved in the discussions about what was to be excised.

This was the turning of the tide and at last it seemed probable that the Government would allow simultaneous publication in both countries and, in fact, give approval to the book. Why did the Government change its mind? It may well be that the responsible minister was influenced by the request from Yale; it is possible that my own talk with the Home Secretary helped to secure his agreement; possibly the knowledge that the book would in any case be published in America (either by the Yale Press or a commercial firm) impelled the officials to 'make the best of a bad job' and allow publication in England; it is likely that all these factors contrived to bring about the desired result. I like to think that the outcome was a victory for common sense and depended upon the readiness of all parties to show a reasonable willingness to compromise. Undoubtedly Alec Douglas-Home's view that simultaneous publication was the most reasonable solution was of paramount importance. One hurdle remained to surmount. To secure agreement both the Yale Press and the author (myself) had to agree to any changes or excisions proposed, and it was possible that these might prove to be so extensive that we should not be able to agree. After a three-cornered exchange of letters it was settled that Chester Kerr should come from Yale and that we should meet the Home Office party in September, when a week was set aside for the conference. Assisted by Christopher Harmer I attended for the first two days, and quickly realized that it was intended that the plan should go through. After those first two days the negotiations were left, on my side, to Chester Kerr and Ronald Mansbridge, who proved themselves admirable negotiators. The excisions proposed were not extensive and after consultation we accepted them practically *in toto*.

This, however, was not quite the end of the story. When the new text was agreed and it was settled that the book should carry the words 'Copyright (C) 1972 by Yale University – Crown Copyright reserved' HMSO entered the lists and asked for the whole of the royalties which would otherwise have been paid to me. I took no part in the negotiations which followed but left them to the Yale Press and the lawyers. Eventually it was agreed that HMG should take about half. All through I had envisaged that the Department should benefit, and had on at least three occasions offered it 'any part or the whole' of the royalties, but my feelings changed when the Department took into consideration the possibility of prosecuting me. That I think was a natural human reaction. I was, therefore, quite content that half should go to HMG but a little sad that HMSO and not MI5 should be the gainer.

The final settlement gave me the greatest satisfaction. If small men may be compared to great I felt much as Gibbon did when he finished the *Decline and Fall*. There were other thoughts also. Looking back over the whole episode I realized how strange it was that I, who all my life had been a supporter of the Establishment, should become, at eighty, a successful rebel. Perhaps, contrary to the accepted view, the old are more ruthless than the young. They have little time to spare and become impatient. But the strongest feeling of all was simply this. Sometimes in life you feel that there is something which you *must* do and in which you must trust your own judgement and not that of any other person. Some call it conscience and some plain obstinacy. Well, you can take your choice. I, for my part, was convinced that I was justified to continue pressing for the publication of *Double-Cross* and I have never had any qualms at all about the rightness of my decision.

Lord Rothschild

I was very ignorant about politics and ideologies in those days, being, so I thought, too busy with my scientific work, sport and social life to have much time for anything else.

Lord Rothschild inherited his peerage in 1937 from his uncle Lionel, his own father having committed suicide in October 1923 when young Victor was not yet aged thirteen.

Recruited into MI5 in 1940, Rothschild found a niche for himself as the Security Service's resident scientist and expert on sabotage. He had become known to the service after he had submitted to the War Office a paper on the German banking system. His proposition was that Nazi intentions could be predicted by monitoring certain financial and other transactions. Little came of the idea but, as a scientist, Rothschild's skills were attractive to MI5 and he was effectively given *carte blanche* to run his own section in the counter-espionage division, designated B1(c).

An encyclopaedic knowledge of bomb-disposal techniques, which apparently included the task of ensuring the prime minister's Cuban cigars had not been tampered with, took him to Gibraltar and France, where he was billeted briefly with Malcolm Muggeridge at the Rothschild mansion in the Avenue Marigny. The acerbic journalist, also a committed Socialist, recalled this episode in his memoirs and observed, 'his disposition was a curious, uneasy mixture of arrogance and diffidence. Somewhere between White's Club and the Ark of the Covenant, between the Old and the New Testament, between the Kremlin and the House of Lords, he had lost his way, and been floundering about ever since. Embedded deep down within him there was something touching and vulnerable and perceptive; at times lovable even. But so overlaid with the bogus certainties of science, and the equally bogus respect, accorded and expected, on account of his wealth and famous name, that it was only rarely apparent.'

Rothschild's undoubted intellectual prowess made other members of the Service feel uneasy. His boast of an IQ of 184 was almost calculated to engender unpopularity, and there was considerable adverse comment when he was decorated for dismantling a highly lethal device of ten primed blocks of explosive found in a crate of onions imported from Spain. Over a field telephone line Rothschild gave a remote running commentary on how he was tackling the mechanism and his remarks were transcribed by his secretary, and future wife, Tessa Mayor. Somehow the resulting typescript of this episode reached the commander of the local military district who was so impressed by the MI5 officer's bravery that he recommended him for an award. As Rothschild was technically a 'civil assistant at the War Office' he was ineligible for a military decoration, so he received the highest medal for civilian bravery, the George Cross.

When this was gazetted it confounded some of his critics like Sir Harry D'Avigdor Goldsmidt, the Jewish MP who, ignorant of the peer's employment by MI5, had once demanded to know why an able-bodied man such as Rothschild was not serving in the armed forces like his contemporaries.

Rothschild's decoration was a blatant breach of the long-standing convention that members of the secret services should never be singled out for recognition and it drew some criticism from his colleagues. The suspicion that Rothschild had himself retained a copy of his official report on the onion-crate incident, and had ensured it received a wide but unauthorized circulation, was compounded when in 1977 he published a collection of essays which included a short account of his handling of the bomb disposal.

After the war Rothschild returned to academic life but retained close links with the Security Service. He remained on good terms with Guy Liddell, MI5's post-war Deputy Director-General, and assisted Dick White to investigate his friend Kim Philby. Rothschild was much embarrassed by his old connections with Guy Burgess and Anthony Blunt, both of whom he had allowed to live in his West End apartment during the war. In his memoirs, *Random Variables*, he described the news that Blunt had been exposed as a traitor as a devastating blow.

Rothschild died in March 1990, not long after he had been embroiled in another controversy, this time over Peter Wright. To his profound discomfort Wright disclosed that Chapman Pincher's notorious exposé of MI5, *Their Trade is Treachery*, had been based on information provided by Peter Wright, and that Wright had been introduced to Pincher by Rothschild. Perhaps even more awkward was Wright's admission that the secret financial arrangement between himself and Pincher, via a company registered in the Cayman Islands, had been organized by Rothschild.

Always a controversial figure, Rothschild himself was at one time under suspicion as a possible Soviet mole. Eventually it was concluded that the tips he had volunteered to MI5, particularly in regard to Philby's treachery, probably cleared him, but when the elderly peer demanded of the Prime Minister a formal statement confirming his innocence of espionage, her reply was so extraordinarily ambiguous and unconvincing that it haunted him until his death.

This extract from another volume of Rothschild's memoirs comprises the transcription of the on-the-spot commentary he made during the bomb-disposal incident on 10 February 1944 which gained him Britain's highest civilian award for gallantry.

Meditations of a Broomstick

'It is a crate in three compartments. The right-hand compartment has onions in it. The middle compartment also appears to have onions in it. The left-hand compartment has already had most of the onions taken out but I can see right at the bottom in the left-hand corner of the left-hand compartment one characteristic block of German TNT. Next to it is some material which looks rather like plastic explosive and in that there is a hole in one bit which is about the size that a detonator would need. It might be plastic explosive or it might be something which is to keep the bricks of TNT in position. I am now going to stop talking and start taking onions out. I am going to start with the middle compartment to see what there is below the onions there.

I can now see one block of TNT in the middle compartment, top left-hand side.

I can now see another block of TNT in the middle compartment, top right-hand side.

There are no TNT blocks in what I might call the bottom centre compartment. By "bottom" I mean the side nearest to me; by top I mean the side furthest away from me. There is no TNT on the side nearest to me. I am still on the middle. I am now going to see if there is any in the middle of the middle compartment.

I cannot find more than two blocks in the middle compartment. I am not certain about that yet, but I cannot find more than two. I am now going to go to the right-hand compartment because I am looking for the delay mechanism or initiating device. There does not seem room for it in the middle compartment, but I am having difficulty in the middle compartment because the onions have grown and are difficult to pull out.

I think I can see some of that plastic substance in the right-hand top edge, that is, the far away side of the right-hand compartment. I can just see it and I am now going to go on taking out some onions above it.

I have come to a block of TNT in the right-hand compartment, furthest side away from me to the left of the right-hand compartment. There is a sort of putty-like thing next to it. I am not sure what that is. I am going back to the extreme left-hand compartment because I want to try and get as much TNT out as I can.

I have now taken all the onions out of the left-hand compartment. There remains a cast block of TNT and a big bit of this putty-like substance. The volume of the putty-like substance is about the same as that of the cast brick. I cannot see any detonating fuse yet. I am now going very gently to take out the cast brick of high explosive.

I have taken out that and a few little bits of this putty-like material. I am now going to try and take this putty-like material out. There is something at the right-hand end which looks a little like a bit of tape.

I have taken that out and I am now going to start doing the same on the centre compartment.

There are only two bricks of TNT in the centre compartment.

I am now going to try and take out these two bricks of TNT. I shall start with the left-hand one. It seems to be a little loose.

I have taken out the left-hand block of TNT.

I have taken out the right-hand block of TNT. I am now going to go back to the right-hand compartment. The delay mechanism and detonator must be in that compartment and I am going to start slowly taking the onions away again.

I can now see a cast block of TNT, top left-hand side of right-hand compartment, at the furthest side away across the compartment. On its right, filling up the rest of the space to the right-hand end of the compartment is a chunk of that plastic material. I still cannot see any delay. I am having difficulty because the onions are jammed right in and I do not want to pull hard.

This is the last block of TNT that I can see and I am going to try very gently to move it away from the plastic with which it is in contact. I do not see the delay or the time clock. It must be inside the plastic or possibly buried underneath it, and I am going very gently to try and get this block of TNT out, but I am going to take a little of the plastic away first to see if there is a detonator sticking into the hole in the block of TNT.

I have taken out the last block of TNT and I am now going to start looking at the plastic explosive.

I have taken out the plastic explosive but I have not looked at it yet. It seems rather heavy.

There is nothing else in the crate now and I am going to bring out the blocks of TNT and then go back to look at the plastic.

I am now going to start trying to take this plastic explosive to pieces.

I see a primer inside one of them. I am going to try and take that out.

I have taken the primer out and I can now see the detonator buried in the middle of the plastic.

It is a twenty-one-day Mark II German time clock. I have unscrewed the electric detonator from the Mark II delay so that one is safe. I am now going to look at the other piece of plastic.

I can just see the other Mark II delay inside the other piece of plastic.

I have taken the other primer off.

The other detonator is off.

All over, all safe now.'

Leonard J. Burt

All my experience in the police leads me to believe that it is impossible to be a loyal Briton and a Communist at the same time.

In the early 1930s a group of enterprising arsonists offered their services to financially embarrassed businessmen, and in consequence the City's insurers found the number of fraudulent claims for fire loss escalating dramatically. The police seemed powerless to trace the culprits so some of the firms hardest hit commissioned a distinguished solicitor and future president of the Law Society, (Sir) William Crocker, to trace the fireraisers. Crocker identified a West End wigmaker, Willie Clarkson, as one of the culprits responsible for eleven separate insurance claims and accumulated enough evidence for him to be prosecuted in October 1934. Clarkson died before he could be convicted but the case dragged on for another four years until Crocker proved that Clarkson's will had been forged, and his fellow conspirator, William Hobbs, was imprisoned for insurance fraud.

Crocker's reputation as a skilled investigator with excellent contacts in Scotland Yard was established by this episode, which resulted in Lloyd's and the other insurance companies being repaid. So when, in May 1940, Churchill sacked MI5's elderly Director-General, Sir Vernon Kell, he appointed Crocker, together with Sir Joseph Ball and Lord Swinton, to a highly secret committee to supervise the transformation of the Security Service from a hidebound peacetime organization into a body more appropriate for the task of combating Nazi subversion and espionage.

Crocker died in September 1973 but not before he had written two volumes of memoirs, *Far from Humdrum* in 1967 and *Tales from the Coffee House* six years later. In neither was he allowed to describe his work on the Security Executive, but it is known from other sources that one of his first proposals was the transfer of a group of senior detectives from London's CID to a specially created unit within MI5's counter-espionage division, designated B1(b).

At the time of his invitation to join MI5 in September 1940 Chief Inspector Burt was a Vice Squad detective but he and a colleague, Detective Sergeant Jim Skardon, had worked on the Clarkson will case with Crocker. Burt moved his offices to MI5's temporary headquarters in Wormwood Scrubs, together with his deputy, Reginald Spooner. They also took Detective Inspectors Smith and Donald Fish and, under the command of Lord Rothschild, created MI5's first specialist anti-sabotage section.

Burt's transfer to MI5 took him first to Aberdeen, to investigate a case of suspected sabotage after a freighter had sunk in the harbour, and later to Gibraltar where, in February 1942, he supervised measures to deter raids by Italian frogmen operating from Spanish territory.

After the war Burt investigated several cases of collaboration with the enemy,

including those of John Amery, William Joyce and some of the misguided British
renegades calling themselves the Legion of St George. Later in 1945 Burt returned
to Scotland Yard to head the Special Branch, a post he was to hold for a record
twelve years.

In his memoirs Burt recalls his wartime visit to Gibraltar, an account
remarkable for the fact that the Security Service is never mentioned.

Commander Burt of Scotland Yard

The scene was enough to daunt anyone.

It was 14th February 1942. From the outside, Portreath aerodrome in
Cornwall was in pitch darkness. At half-past one in the morning it was
freezing hard, and even inside the Operations Room, where I sat at a table
against the farthest wall, you could have believed you were in an igloo. At
the far end of the room in the light thrown by a single bulb a Squadron
Leader stood on a table and briefed his pilots on their trip to the Far East.
There was a map on the wall. Every now and then, raising his voice above
the sound of planes taking off across the icy ground outside, he would tap
it with a pointer and warn the silent, staring men of danger to be met from
flak or enemy fighters.

I defy anyone to have a high morale in such circumstances, especially
someone like myself who was due to take off in half an hour's time for
Gibraltar in an unarmed plane with which the pilot had just told me he
was unfamiliar and which he sincerely but not too confidently hoped he
might be able to fly. He added that he'd never been to Gib before, and
knew the landing-ground was tricky.

I was going out to investigate sabotage. Our very existence in the
Mediterranean was threatened. How were we to get through to Suez and
our desperately pressed armies in the Far East if those narrow Straits were
at the mercy of the enemy?

Frankly, at the time I wanted no part in all this. I'd been seconded from
the Yard to help clear up cases of alleged sabotage in this country, but the
plain fact is that I never found a subversive act of that nature committed
by a British citizen.

They'd sent me off to Aberdeen to look into the fate of a ship that had
been blown up while lying at anchor in the harbour. I'd investigated, and
my view was that there had been no sabotage.

Any angry young rating, through ignorance, had set off the fuse of
a demolition charge, destroying the asdic equipment – a secret device
for underwater detection of submarines. And now, as soon as that

investigation had been completed, they were sending me off to Gibraltar. No – I can't say I was facing the prospect with enthusiasm.

Going out into the freezing dark didn't improve my morale. We climbed into the plane, and the only help the pilot got on his take-off was given by several men shouting and waving lanterns on the runway. You couldn't have set up a more eerie background in a Simenon novel or a French film.

At last we were airborne. The lateness of our take-off was supposed to be an advantage when it came to slipping past the enemy defences west of the French coast. But I couldn't help remembering that we were unarmed, and I couldn't help thinking of those young pilots in the Operations Room. They too would be flying through this bitter night, under Mars and Jupiter, on the long pull to the East, where their share in the doom of sun-drenched Singapore awaited them. A grim world it was for all of us on St Valentine's Night, 1942.

I settled down in my seat and checked my parachute and Mae West. Very slowly (or so it seemed to me) the plane chugged through the darkness; like an old bus on a celestial route.

And then I thought the pilot had missed his target – just as he had sworn was bound to happen! There was a crunch, a jarring of every bone in my body, a frightful lurch. And then a blessed silence, as if the whole world was suddenly frozen. The pilot had saved our bacon after all. We were 'home and dry'. And now my adventures in Gibraltar were about to begin.

They began with a visit to Field-Marshal Lord Gort, the Governor of the Rock. He went straight to the point.

'Burt, our war effort is being sabotaged here. It's dead easy for the enemy. They've got every chance to work against us from Algeciras, not to mention the opportunity of setting up bases in the mainland. Every time we lose a ship, the Spanish Press is full of it; and there are plenty of Spaniards working in our dockyards who'd like to see us lose this war. Find out what they're up to, and report to me direct.'

It was a tough assignment. It took some little time to check through the records of the 8,000 Spaniards working in the dockyards. Yes, there were enemy agents on the list. What's more, I was able to find one or two who were ready to talk. If they hadn't. . . .

'Juan,' I said to the tall, dark-haired ship's welder with the big scar running from nostril to cheek-bone, 'we know what happens when we have a convoy of forty steamers marshalled in the dockyard here. There's an explosion – a ship is lost. You know we've got enemy aircraft beaten. They can't get through our defences. Nor can the enemy navy. Very well, then, how's it done?'

He raised the palms of his hands. 'It's a mystery.'

'It's a mystery to me. It's no mystery to you. And you're going to tell me.'

'Am I? Why?'

I told him why.

It's always a job to get valuable stuff from an informer. 'Suppose you catch what you imagine to be the lot?' asked Juan. 'Don't think you'll get them all. *I* don't know them all. But they know me. They'll realise what I've told you, and where do I stand. How long will I stand, I wonder?'

I laughed. 'I know how long you'll stand if you don't give me what I'm after,' I told him.

He shrugged his shoulders. That night I saw men dressed as Spanish fishermen come over from the mainland. We sat – my men and I – in a café and watched them drink their rough red wine and their sweet brandy. When they got up to go, we ordered another round. But two men lounging outside with girls on their arms followed silently in their tracks.

Next morning I knew that Juan had told me the truth about the dockyard. Italians, disguised as Spanish fishermen, had been tipped off there and were at work as frogmen, putting limpet mines on the ships marshalled in Gibraltar Harbour.

Where did they work from?

Mark you, their job against our ships was an act of war and the responsibility of Naval Intelligence. I was concerned with the sabotage end of the show.

There was a lot of country to be charted. One evening, when out in a boat with one of my men, I stumbled on part of the answer. We were near La Linea, at Maiorga Point on the north coast of Algeciras Bay. It was a beautiful spot, with a view of the harbour, where, from half a mile to a mile and a half out, the forty ships of our convoy lay at anchor.

'Whose is that bungalow?' I suddenly asked, pointing to a lonely building near the foreshore.

My man looked at his map. 'It belongs to a Spanish couple. They're on their honeymoon.'

'It's got a complete view of the harbour.'

'No,' he said, 'there isn't a window on that side. Nothing but cages of parakeets hung against the wall.'

But I wasn't satisfied. It seemed fantastic that anyone should build a house just here and *not* put in a window overlooking the harbour. We rowed nearer.

'There *is* a window,' I said; 'those cages are just camouflage. Behind them there's a window, and they're looking out on to the Bay.'

A shot rang out. Then another. I got a glimpse of a swarthy brute dashing between the trees at the back of the house. I had found out what I had come to learn. Now there was nothing for it but to get our boat out of range.

And, of course, I couldn't demand that the police raid the house and arrest its owner. He was on Spanish soil; I was a trespasser. *I had been shot at?* I could hear him pour scorn on my story. He had been out shooting rooks, that was all. I should get no joy out of a complaint.

But I had found one strongpoint in the saboteurs' order of battle.

'Juan, have you ever been inside the bungalow?' I asked him a few days later.

'Never. I would be shot if I tried.'

'Who lives there?'

'This Spaniard and his wife, Conchita. She's ill. She has to live near the sea for the air.'

'Listen,' I said, 'I don't suppose I'm telling you anything you don't know. Antonio Ramagnino, an officer in the Italian Navy, lives in that bungalow with his Spanish wife. They're planning something. You tell me what.'

But he couldn't. The plain fact was that he didn't know. The great *coup* wasn't yet ripe. I was to leave Gibraltar in March, and they did not strike till July.

Derek Tangye

I kept wondering what these Intelligence Sections had been doing in peacetime and realized that their members, bereft of imagination, found life more rewarding spending their time writing and reading meaningless minutes.

An Old Harrovian journalist, Derek Tangye is best known for his stories about his idyllic life on a flower farm in Cornwall, but at the beginning of the war he was appointed to the intelligence section of the War Office in charge of assessing the Chinese order of battle.

This somewhat esoteric appointment came as a result of a report Tangye had written following his travels across the Far East. Shortly before the war broke out he enlisted in the Duke of Cornwall's Light Infantry but his career as a private soldier was to be brief. He was summoned to Whitehall to take charge of an inadequate card index of military units in the Pacific, and then went on an intelligence course at Swanage where he met an old friend, the novelist Alec Waugh who was destined for the Middle East.

Instead of returning to the War Office Tangye was offered a job with MI5 and was posted to Newcastle as an assistant to the local Regional Security Liaison Officer. A month later he was placed in charge of his own section with responsibility for liaising not only with Fleet Street but also handling the foreign journalists thronging London. His future wife was public relations officer at the Savoy Hotel, where many of the American newspaper men were staying, and he was thus well placed to monitor their despatches home and influence the stories they filed.

Tangye was to spend ten years working for MI5, even when, after the war, he was first a gossip columnist on the *Daily Express* and later a cartoon writer on the *Daily Mail*. His job as William Hickey, the page made famous by Tom Driberg, lasted just three days because he 'had not been waspish enough' about Alec Waugh. On the *Daily Mail* his collaborator was Julian Phipps, a gifted artist who was later to marry Joan Miller, another MI5 agent.

Tangye remained in MI5 until late 1949 when he moved away from London and settled in Cornwall where he still lives. In this extract from his memoirs he recalls his arrival at MI5's improbable headquarters in Wormwood Scrubs prison.

The Way to Minack

I had finished my travel book by the time the uselessness of my job had been realised and I had been sent on a Course to Swanage. I showed the manuscript to Alec Waugh who was on the Course too, and he liked it mainly because he had been in Tahiti too; and while the Battle of Britain was fought over our heads, and after each day of being taught World War One methods of warfare, we reminisced. 'When the war is over,' he said optimistically, 'you and I will go to Tahiti together.'

I had no faith in myself as an army officer serving in unit, and the Course was leading me that way. I did not seem to grasp the details which were essential if I were to be efficient. I was as dumb as when I used to fail at my examinations at Harrow. I also rejected blind obedience. I just could not see the point of risking my life carrying out some plan which I knew was idiotic. Hence, when towards the end of the Course I was summoned to London, to Wormwood Scrubs, temporary headquarters of MI5, interviewed by a chain-smoking lady in a ground floor cell and told ten minutes later I had been appointed to MI5, I felt thankful I was to remain an individual. I was to be a member of MI5 in war and in peace for the next ten years.

I was sent first to Newcastle where I worked as an assistant to a delightful man who exasperated me. He was an old hand in MI5 and as a novice I was clearly in no position to query his views. I found, however, that whenever I suggested a possible line of investigation, his logical arguments against pursuing such an investigation speedily deflated me. We were poles apart in our thinking. My experience as a newspaper man had taught me that hunches could lead to a big story, and I believed the same kind of hunches might lead to catching spies. Hunches first, then painstaking investigation. But my boss did not believe in such things, and in this he was like many people I have known in my life. I have been vexed so often by those who go only by the book. Those with grooved minds who obstinately refuse to be flexible.

I had been a month in Newcastle with little to do when I was ordered back to London and instructed to form a special unit where my journalistic experiences could be of value. I was given a cell in Wormwood Scrubs, a pretty secretary, and freedom to move around the various departments asking what questions I liked to ask ... for part of my new job was to produce a weekly news-sheet containing the activities of each department. I soon realised that in some quarters I was viewed with suspicion. Wasn't the fellow on the *Daily Express*? Even the *Mirror*? I was surrounded by a plethora of solicitors, barristers, dons, all of whom had arrived to augment the tiny permanent peacetime group of MI5, and I realised I was the odd man out. I had, however, the usual ace up my sleeve ... I could not be quite as bad a risk as I appeared to be because my father had been an Intelligence Officer *and* I had been at Harrow. Public schoolboys, in those days, could not be traitors. I was tolerated therefore. I was a member of the caste. The truth is that when I joined MI5, it was being geared to combat the Germans; and the Germans as an Intelligence force had the rating of a Fourth Division football team. MI5, except in one, small, ignored corner of the organisation, was bewildered when faced by the naughty deceit of the Russians. Burgess, Maclean and Philby were already in orbit ... but they could act with gay confidence. They knew their caste.

I had not been long in Wormwood Scrubs before it was decided to evacuate MI5 to the country. The bombs were falling on London and one of them could have destroyed the MI5 records; and so a place was chosen for us to move to, and the place was Blenheim Palace where the Duke of Marlborough and his family surrendered huge rooms to trestle tables.

I realised now that the time had come for me to leave 20 Elm Park Lane, and that when I did so I would in effect be saying goodbye to my youth.

There I lived the gay days when there were oceans of time in which to make mistakes and to recover from them; and to be in despair at one moment but be filled with hope the next because there were so many years ahead. I lived there the time which one never expects to end, the ebullience of being young and successful, of passing fancies, of dominating views, of believing all youth is Peter Pan. I gave in my notice to the landlord, then although this notice had a period in which to expire, I decided to take away from the threat of bombs those possessions of mine which I valued most. There was a small kneehole desk of rosewood; my personal papers; a watercolour by Adrian Daintrey; and above all a small oil painting of a plantation and a lagoon by a strange man called Gouwe with whom I had stayed on the island of Raiatea near Tahiti. These were my treasures.

I piled them into my car and drove them to Blenheim Palace, and I carried them into the room which had been chosen for me as my office. It was on the first floor of the south wing, above the archway which all of us used to reach the quadrangle. There they were, safe from the bombs, daily reminding me of normal times.

I was billeted a couple of miles away and in the morning I drove to Blenheim Palace. And one day as I neared the Palace, I saw a plume of smoke curling from the rooftops; and as I drove nearer still, I saw it was coming from a room above the archway. A crowd was standing there, a fire engine was hosing, when I pulled up. And there was also my pretty secretary.

'*Our* room,' she said, looking upwards.

Smoke was now billowing from the window.

A cleaner had inadvertently dropped a match in the wastepaper basket, and set the room ablaze.

Ronald Reed

Agents in this country using radio transmitters would be operating under difficulties.

By convention MI5 officers avoid the limelight, and Ronald Reed is one of those who would prefer his clandestine career to pass unremarked. Nevertheless he is a skilled practitioner of a highly unusual art, the ability to adopt the 'fingerprint' of another wireless operator.

Reed was the holder of an amateur licence – a radio ham – and when war came he, like many of his kind, joined the Radio Security Service on the recommendation of the Radio Society of Great Britain. His task was to monitor the airwaves for illicit enemy transmissions, but there came a time when MI5 found themselves in possession of a growing number of enemy agents, some of them equipped with transmitters.

Reed's initiation into clandestine wireless took place in October 1940 when he was driven to Camp 020 at Ham Common, Richmond, where he was introduced to Wulf Schmidt, a Nazi agent who, only three weeks earlier, had parachuted into Cambridgeshire. After dozens of hours of intensive interrogation Schmidt had agreed to switch sides and help MI5 to dupe his Abwehr controllers. Reed's role was to keep a close watch on everything Schmidt did and ensure he only double-crossed the enemy and made absolutely no attempt to warn the receiving station that he was operating under duress. At exactly midnight Schmidt tapped out his recognition callsign D–F–H, which was acknowledged by Hamburg. This exchange was to be the first of hundreds of coded messages that passed between Schmidt and the Abwehr. The final transmission took place in May 1945, just as Allied troops entered Hamburg, forcing the Abwehr operators to evacuate their base.

At first Reed's task was limited to monitoring Schmidt's wireless procedure, but when the spy went into hospital for surgery to a duodenal ulcer another RSS operator, Russell Lee, was obliged to take over the transmitter and impersonate Schmidt's style. Lee's performance was judged perfect by Reed, but to reduce the risk of detection MI5 decided to allow Lee to continue the charade with Schmidt standing close by to answer any awkward questions posed by his Abwehr controllers.

As a result of the successful deception perpetrated by Reed and Lee both men were invited to stay in the Security Service after the war. When the time came for an official history to be written of MI5's wartime achievements Reed, then in retirement, was asked to contribute a monograph on the subject of clandestine wireless. Written anonymously, this appeared as an appendix in Volume IV of the *British Intelligence in the Second World War* series edited by Professor Sir Harry Hinsley and Anthony Simkins.

Technical Problems Affecting Radio Communications by the Double-Cross Agents

1   For those used to watching colour television pictures of men on the moon, and listening to the conversation of astronauts, it is not easy to imagine the state of the art of radio at the outbreak of the 1939–1945 war. True, there was television in black and white, communication by radio throughout the world was commonplace and radio amateurs ('hams') kept in touch with each other in all countries of the world using low

power, but transistors had not been invented, computers were unknown and recording on long steel wire, not on tape, was only carried out by the BBC and other professional recording organisations.

2   Radio communication between the UK and Germany was carried out on the high frequency bands from 5–7 MHz. As the propagation of radio waves varies between night and day, frequencies should be on the low side at night and higher during the day. This meant that a radio agent should not stay on the same frequency but move up and down the spectrum for his communications to be fully effective. The snag for the receiving station was that the agent's signal had to be picked out of other interfering signals so that time might be used up establishing communication before the message began. Time on the air is danger time for being intercepted by the enemy and should be kept to the minimum. Another factor was that the most efficient aerial for these frequencies would be about 30 metres long and erected high in the air free of obstructions. The strength of a transmission is low if the aerial is close to the ground and if the transmission path is obstructed.

3   Accordingly agents in this country using radio transmitters would be operating under difficulties. In order not to draw attention to themselves they would have to erect aerials which would not be obtrusive, or excite comment, and these were likely to be inefficient. It would not be easy for a man to take lodgings, put up an aerial and lock himself in his room for a period each day while he sent messages and received replies on equipment which, if it were seen by the landlady, would certainly cause her to call the Police. Indeed, on reflection it seems amazing that the Germans could believe that a man would find it possible to arrive by parachute or boat in a country alert for spies, find lodgings and set himself up in this way.

4   Besides the difficulty of establishing and maintaining contact there were the problems presented by (a) direction finding and (b) 'fingerprinting' and control signals.

(a)   The most accurate 'fix' of a transmitting station is obtained if not less than three receiving stations are spaced round the transmitting station. The Germans could not use stations all round an agent in England, but they could get a long base line with receiving stations at Nantes and Bordeaux in the west and Hamburg and Bremen in the east. We could not therefore take any chances although there was (as always) some inability among the experts to agree how accurate 'fixes' could be. Could a station be 'fixed' within a mile radius or was it as much as 10 miles? Like many other intelligence appreciations all one could do was to play safe and assume that the Germans were at least as good as us and maybe a bit better, and that if bearings were taken every day and found consistently to point to a location other than the one from which the agent said he was transmitting, they might smell a rat. We therefore had to assume that if a German agent told them he was transmitting from, say, Aylesbury, he would actually have to be located at or close to Aylesbury.

(b) Morse sent on an ordinary morse key by an individual has individual characteristics which any one familiar with the operator's 'fist' can recognise. All the radio agents who were sent to this country had been trained by the Germans who were going to listen to them after their arrival in England. So the principle on which we had to operate was to 'turn' the agent so that he would agree to send his own messages, and to have another person, who knew the morse code, to listen to the transmission and watch carefully what was being sent so as to be sure that there was no deviation from the message agreed upon. We knew, for example, that the Germans had envisaged the possibility of some agents being 'turned' and had instructed them to agree to co-operate, but to insert 'control' signals in a message. For example, the agent might say that he was always to put the word 'greetings' at the end of his message, whereas the inclusion of the word meant that he was operating under duress. There were variations of subtlety on this theme. If an agent was under control he might add – or omit – an X or a full stop or something small. It was difficult to know whether an agent was telling the truth about this. There were precedents to be consulted in previous cases, but the Germans (sensibly) did not seem to follow any consistent pattern – sometimes a sign was to be put in and sometimes omitted – and occasionally the agent couldn't remember his instructions properly. Even when the 'control' signal was included the Germans were inclined to say that the agent must have become confused in his excitement and to take no notice of it. Because they wanted to believe his transmission was genuine (and get the credit for it) they might not even report to their HQ that the control signal had been included.

If an agent went 'bad' and refused to continue, or if we had misgivings about his truthfulness and did not think we could trust him, we had to consider whether his 'fist' should be impersonated by the operator who had sat at his side listening to him. Another possibility was to say that the agent had managed to recruit 'a friend' to do the transmitting leaving the agent more time to engage in reconnaissance. Much depended on the circumstances of the case and what we thought we could get away with. But it was always difficult to decide whether it was safe to make a change or not. If an agent was under suspicion of having been 'turned', to bring in a new operator might confirm suspicions. There are examples where agents were successfully replaced by other operators. (I do not know if there were cases where the agent became suspect through making a change of operator).

5   Nearly all the equipment made by the Germans for their radio spies could be contained in a small suitcase. The power of the transmitter was no more than 3 watts on batteries and 5/10 watts when running from a mains power supply. But the Germans realised that, although transmitters with higher power might help the reliability of communications and cut down transmitting time, higher power also presented a hazard to the agent himself in that the transmitter might cause local interference to domestic radio receivers and be more easily intercepted by the British authorities who, certainly in 1940, were bombarded with reports from all sides from people who thought they had heard 'morse' signals coming from suspicious houses. All such reports were investigated and most were discovered to be the product of a lively imagination, noisy water pipes or a central heating plant.

Anthony Simkins

No constraints have been placed on us while carrying out our research . . .
In preparing the results of our research for publication we have observed
the ruling that was laid down by the Secretary of State for Foreign Affairs.

A prisoner of war following his capture in North Africa in 1941, Anthony Simkins joined the Security Service in 1945. He had graduated from New College, Oxford, where he had obtained a first-class degree in modern history, and was later called to the Bar at Lincoln's Inn.

In December 1965, following the retirement of Sir Roger Hollis, Simkins was promoted from Director of C Branch, the protective security division, to the post of Deputy Director-General. Simkins remained as Sir Martin Furnival Jones's deputy until his retirement in the autumn of 1971, and later was invited by the Cabinet Office to write an official history of MI5's wartime work. This was never intended to be published but when Prime Minister Margaret Thatcher authorized the release of Professor Hinsley's *British Intelligence* series, some additional editorial work was done to Simkins's account to make it conform to the standard set by the previous three volumes, and it was published as Volume IV. As can be seen from the contradiction in the heading above, taken from the preface written by Anthony Simkins and Professor Hinsley, no obstacle was placed in the path of the authors while they researched Security and Counter-intelligence, but there was a ban on the disclosure of the methods employed to gather intelligence, as announced by foreign secretary Dr David Owen to the Commons in January 1978.

Soon after publication, the Australian journalist Philip Knightley thought he recognized a similarity between the official history and Nigel West's *MI5: British Security Service Operations 1909–45*, which had been published almost a decade earlier. Unwisely, in *The Second Oldest Profession* Knightley accused Simkins of having supplied West with much of his material, and in consequence found himself on the receiving end of an expensive legal action which was settled out of court, much to Simkins's satisfaction.

Throughout his career Simkins avoided controversy but a decade after his retirement he joined Sir Martin Furnival Jones in writing a letter to *The Times* in October 1981 in defence of Sir Roger Hollis. Its intention was to support the late Sir Roger from a charge of having been a Soviet mole but unfortunately all it served to do was to confirm that the former Director-General had been brought out of his retirement to face interrogation.

In this extract from the official history the interlocking roles of Zigzag (Eddie Chapman), Brutus (Roman Garby-Czerniawski) and Garbo (Juan Pujol) are described, although in terms somewhat different from those used by the agents themselves in their own accounts.

Security and Counter-intelligence

It had been assumed that, whether or not the Overlord deception programme succeeded in misleading the Germans, it would have the result that the agents taking part in it, their reporting contradicted by events, would be fatally compromised. In fact they survived with their reputations in Germany unscathed; and while some of them were phased out at different dates for a variety of reasons, several were operated till the end of the war either as a means of keeping in touch with the intentions of the German Intelligence Service or in support of further deception operations.

Few opportunities arose for deception operations in support of SHAEF's campaign in north-west Europe. A project by which Brutus would volunteer to work for the Germans in that theatre was abandoned early in August 1944. Towards the end of August, to supervise the work of the three SCIUs which had been set up to run suitable agents captured in the field as double agents, 21st Army Group, 12th US Army Group and the naval and air components of the Expeditionary Force formed the 212 Committee at SHAEF. In view of the speed of the Allied advance from that time, however, successive deception plans became out-dated as soon as they were formulated. As early as the middle of September SHAEF had decided that the double agents in the field should be used only for counter-intelligence purposes and that any further strategic deception, should it be worthwhile, would be best carried out by the established double agents in the United Kingdom. But there was no call for strategic deception on behalf of the armies in Europe even from the United Kingdom after September, when Brutus was used briefly to provide cover for the airborne attack at Arnhem; in two messages on 10 and 14 September he reported that an airborne attack was intended for 15 September, but that the target area was either in Denmark or in the Kiel–Bremen area.

From June 1944 Tate took part in a deception plan drawn up to provide the Germans with false information about the fall of the V-weapons, and from November 1944 to May 1945 he was the channel used by the Admiralty for passing to Germany bogus intelligence about the laying of a minefield to deter the U-boats operating in British inshore waters. German records obtained after the war showed that this information had been acted on despite some uncertainty in the Abwehr as to whether he could be trusted. But he appears to have retained the confidence of his control in Hamburg, which maintained contact with him till a few hours before the fall of the city. Treasure's signals, continued by an MI5 operator after her dismissal in June 1944, were also used in the V-weapons project, but their chief value lay in the assistance they gave to GC and CS; they were phased out in November 1944.

Rover was released to the Royal Navy in September 1944 after failing to make radio contact with Germany. But the Germans then began to call him and it was decided to re-establish communication using MI5 operators. From early in October Rover's signals were an important channel for deception about the fall of V-weapons. They continued till the end of the war. Gelatine and Bronx, who also remained in contact with Germany till the end of the war, were used mainly as a possible source of information about German intelligence for the future. Because of her connections, Gelatine was also a possible channel for news about any peace feelers that might emanate from Germany. Though her last letter was dated 30 April 1945, she in fact received no intelligence of any importance. Bronx, who sent with her last letter on 3 May an offer to continue her collaboration with Germany, was asked early in 1945 to report in the plain language code devised in 1944 if she obtained any information about the attack on Norway which the Germans expected.

Zigzag, the last wartime spy to reach England, as already noted, had arrived in Cambridgeshire by parachute on the night of 27–28 June 1944 with two radio sets, cameras, a large sum of money and much useful information. Notice of his arrival had been given in an ISOS decrypt of 10 June and he now revealed that his mission was to collect information on ASDIC equipment, on anti-aircraft radar, on the bases and operational plans of the US Army Air Force, on the fall of V1s and the damage they were inflicting and on a new radio frequency which, the Germans believed, might affect their operation of the V2 weapon. He was soon in radio contact with the Germans and was used for deception about the V1 offensive and in connection with the development of anti-submarine weapons. By October, however, he had become so much of an embarrassment that his contract was terminated on generous terms; it was known that he had disclosed details of his work to a wide circle of his criminal acquaintances, and there was a further problem. He had brought with him instructions as to how to contact another agent, whose identity he did not know but who was obviously Brutus, to hand over a camera and money. He had not been allowed to carry out his instructions, because of the risk that suspicion would be thrown on Brutus if the Germans began to distrust Zigzag. But if he continued to operate he could not be kept away from Brutus indefinitely.

In June the Germans had asked Brutus, who was then supposedly with FUSAG in Staines while keeping his transmitter in London, to report on the fall of V1s as a matter of urgency. But in the middle of July they had instructed him to confine himself to reports on the Allied order of battle. Towards the end of August he had advised them that he was leaving his FUSAG appointment to rejoin the Polish Air HQ. His messages, which mainly related to the dispersal of the notional forces assembled for Fortitude, had then become much less frequent. He sent the last on 2 January 1945; it informed the Germans that he was being sent on a visit to Belgium. Some of his former associates, who knew that he had made a deal with the Germans before moving to the United Kingdom, had by then been arrested, and there was considerable risk that if the Germans learned of the arrests, and if Brutus continued to operate, they would assume that he was doing so under control.

Garbo, also, greatly reduced his activity after August 1944. No sooner had he intervened personally in sending reports on the V1 offensive than a Spanish agent of the Abwehr told the SIS in Madrid that the chief German agent in England was communicating by radio to Spain and offered to divulge his name in return for money. As this offer could not be refused, Garbo took evasive action by informing the Germans that he had heard through his courier that he was about to be betrayed and that he was taking refuge in a hide-out in Wales. In German eyes he remained there till the end of the war, leaving his organisation in charge of Agent No. 3 and keeping in touch with it by courier and occasional meetings. The Germans co-operated zealously in various measures designed to convince the British authorities that Garbo had escaped to Spain, and in the discussion of various plans to effect his actual escape from Britain, and they assured him that they continued to value the work of the organisation. But the organisation was gradually run down, the Germans being informed that No. 4 was being sent to Canada in October and that other members were resigning or being paid off during the winter, and on 1 May 1945 the Germans advised Garbo to wind it up.

Garbo carried out one more mission. On 8 May, in their last message to him, the Germans hoped that he would be able to make his way to Madrid and instructed him to frequent a cafe there every Monday evening from 4 June; they warned him that it might be impossible for them to keep the rendezvous. Although Garbo turned up, MI5 being anxious to maintain contact in case the Germans had plans to continue their activities after the end of hostilities, the rendezvous was not kept. But he succeeded in tracking down his case-officer, to whom he explained how he had succeeded in getting to Spain via south America and expressed his wish to work for the Germans in any plans they might have for the future. The case-officer knew of no such plans, but he was full of praise for Garbo's past services and promised that the balance of what was owed to him would be paid. The money, 35,000 pesetas, was subsequently handed over in cash to Mrs Garbo by an anonymous intermediary.

Dennis Wheatley

From 9 April 1940 when Hitler went into Denmark and Norway, hundreds of refugees escaped in ships from those countries to England. From May onwards, thousands more flooded in from Holland, Belgium and France. It appeared utterly beyond the capacity of MI5, working night and day, to check up on all these people.

Stranger than Fiction

It was only when Dennis Wheatley's wine business failed in 1931 that he wrote his first novel, *The Forbidden Territory*, and it was an instant success. He was a popular, Bohemian character, constantly in demand at parties, and it was in the Chelsea flat of Sir Charles Birkin, then regarded as London's most eligible bachelor, that he was introduced to Maxwell Knight, MI5's star agent-runner. Both had been cadets aboard HMS *Worcester*, and from this common bond was formed a lifelong friendship.

Knight frequently used Wheatley for various clandestine purposes, among the first being the provision of cover to one of his agents, Friedle Gaertner, who had become a talented double agent. Gaertner, who was to acquire the codename Gelatine in MI5, ostensibly worked for Wheatley as his secretary, but in reality he was reimbursed her salary by Knight.

Another of Wheatley's tasks for Knight was to provide background information about the traitor William Joyce, later known as Lord Haw-Haw. Joyce had been a guest at one of Wheatley's literary parties and after he fled to Germany Wheatley's name was found among his papers by MI5. Pro-Fascist, but not pro-Nazi, Wheatley had been recommended by Joyce as a suitable candidate for the position of *gauleiter* of North-West London after a German invasion.

Using his reputation as the successful biographer of Marshal Voroshilov, Wheatley approached the Soviet embassy in 1942 on Knight's instructions with the intention of cultivating the press attaché. The contact led to a single dinner at the famous Hungaria Restaurant, but although Wheatley was later to write an article for the *Daily Mail* about Stalingrad's defender, nothing more was achieved.

Although his wife, stepson and stepdaughter were employed by MI5, Wheatley was never formally employed as an officer of the Security Service, although, through the intervention of his wife, he was later to join the War Planning Staff where he worked closely with Colonel Gilbert Lennox, one of MI5's experts on strategic deception. After the war Wheatley resumed his literary career, achieved phenomenal success as a writer and, before his death in November 1977, published more than sixty books.

In this extract from the third volume of his memoirs, *Drink and Ink*, Wheatley recalls an episode when 'Uncle Max' Knight sought out his help to watch a suspected Nazi agent. The person concerned is unnamed but Wheatley's description of her would appear to fit Judith, Countess of Listowel. She was born in Hungary, the daughter of a diplomat, and married the Labour peer Lord Listowel in 1933. They were divorced in 1945 two years after the release of her autobiography, *This I Have Seen*. However, the mystery of the Hungarian lady's identity deepens, for Judith Listowel cannot recall ever having met Wheatley, knowing anyone who fits the description of the 'Black Baroness', or even having heard of another Hungarian who married a British peer before the war.

Drink and Ink

At one of Charlie Birkin's cocktail parties [in 1939] Joan and I met a peer's wife, later known to us all as Vicki. A few days later 'Uncle', having learned by his own mysterious means that we had met her, came along and told me what MI5 believed about this very attractive little brunette.

Vicki was a Hungarian. A year or two before the war she had managed to marry the peer. By her marriage she had, of course, become a British subject and was now living in a fine flat in Mayfair. Her husband, meanwhile, had become an officer in the RAF and was stationed somewhere in the country.

'Uncle' believed that Vicki was an enemy agent and, owing to the connections she had established with many influential people, a very dangerous one. She was said to have been, before the war, the mistress of a wealthy Jewish armaments man, who now lived on a neutral ship that continued to trade between England and the Continent. Although MI5 knew enough to hang him, they had no power to have him arrested, even when the ship was in a British port; so all they could do was to keep tabs on Vicki and as far as possible prevent her passing on any information to her old boy friend. 'Uncle' wanted us to take a hand in looking after her.

Naturally we obliged and, soon afterwards, I had the interesting experience of watching a real live Mata Hari knocking back our cocktails. To keep in touch with her without arousing her suspicions proved exceptionally easy, as it transpired that she had just written her memoirs, and I was obviously the chap to assist her in securing a publisher. Thenceforth we saw a lot of her and her bosom friend, said to have been another Nazi agent, a little black-haired Baroness. We christened her 'The Black Baroness', which phrase I afterwards used for the title of my third Gregory Sallust spy novel.

To assist us in keeping an eye on these two beauties 'Uncle' agreed that we might rope in Charlie Birkin and Captain Bunny Tattersall, DSO, as both went to many parties at which Vicki and the Baroness were likely to be present. Bunny proved particularly useful in this respect, as although he was again back in the uniform of the Inniskilling Dragoons, with a beautiful green silk-lined greatcoat, he had for many years been the 'Man about Town' of the *Daily Mail*; so he knew everyone and went everywhere.

On the last day of November the Russians invaded Finland. This was a perfectly logical sequel to their having overrun the eastern half of Poland and absorbed the three small independent Baltic States of Latvia,

Lithuania and Esthonia, created in 1919/20. That should have come as no surprise to anyone who had read my book *Red Eagle*. Marshal Voroshilov had stated very clearly, that owing to Russia's geographical situation, Germany was the only power Russia had to fear; and that in the initial stages of a war the Russian army could not hope to defeat that of Germany. Therefore Soviet strategy must be to fall back, destroying as she withdrew everything that might be of value to the enemy, even if this meant leaving many important cities in ruins. By this 'scorched earth' policy a belt of territory 300 miles deep was to be sacrificed as slowly as possible to give Russia time to mobilize her huge manpower which would later defeat Germany. In preparation for this the Russians were already removing their heavy industry and munition plants from cities in this belt and creating new and larger ones a thousand miles back behind the Urals.

Stalin's seizure of half Poland, after the Germans had defeated the Polish army, was therefore the logical outcome of Voroshilov's policy. Why destroy your own bridges, railways and cities if instead you can devastate your neighbour's territory to form an obstacle for the enemy? So, too, was the annexation of the three Baltic States further north, whose largely Teutonic populations might well have favoured opening their ports to German forces in the event of Hitler's going to war with Russia. Voroshilov's invasion of Finland eliminated the risk of a German army's being put ashore at Helsinki.

In Britain people agitated for aid to be sent to the gallant Finns, who were fighting against great odds to maintain their independence. But for us to have done so would have been the height of madness. The 'aid for Finland' group would have shown more sense had they agitated for the internment of all British Communists, as the Party was still taking its orders from Moscow and its members were doing their utmost in our factories to cause munition workers to go slow.

As things turned out we had good reason to be thankful for Voroshilov's strategy. Had he not formed his 'Chastity Belt', so that the Germans had to fight their way over an additional 300 miles of Polish territory before they could reach Moscow and the Volga, Russia might well have been put out of the war in 1942, and Hitler still have had the forces to invade Britain before the United States could come to our aid.

In December we went to a most amusing party given by Vicki. Among the guests was the Turkish Ambassador and for the best part of an hour I sat with him, Vicki and a few other people at a small table discussing the war.

The Turk made no secret of his opinion that in the spring Hitler would overwhelm the French, then turn on Britain, invade and conquer her. I agreed to that possibility but gave chapter and verse about what would follow if that did happen. I maintained that there was no conceivable likelihood of our accepting terms from Hitler. Although there were not the faintest grounds for my statement, I told him that plans had already been prepared. The King and his Government would retire to Canada; so would the Navy: and that from all parts of the Empire the war would continue to be carried on. Moreover, as the United States could not possibly allow Hitler to remain dominant in Europe, with all Europe's shipyards at his disposal in which to build a Fleet that would enable him to destroy the American Navy and conquer the Western Hemisphere, it could be counted as certain that the Americans would decide to fight while they were still in a good position to do so.

How, therefore, I asked, with Russia only waiting for the chance to stab Hitler in the back, could he possibly emerge victorious? As the Ambassador conceded many of my points, by the time he left I had some reason to believe that the informal talk had caused him to take a much more optimistic view of Britain's chances.

But the really great fun of Vicki's party was its composition. Among the thirty guests who were swilling her champagne and happily devouring her *foie-gras* were Joan, Diana and me, Bill and Fritzi, Bill's colleague Grierson Dickson, Charlie Birkin, Bunny Tattersall, 'Uncle' himself and, as he told me with a finger to his big nose, several of his other aides; so cuddlesome little Vicki was more or less throwing her party for MI5.

Roger Fulford

Russia was a perpetual nightmare to British statesmen in the nineteenth century – largely because of her supposed intention to expand towards India and the East.

President of the Oxford Union in 1927, Roger Fulford was a lifelong supporter of the Liberal Party, and stood unsuccessfully for Parliament in 1929, 1945 and 1950. In 1933, aged twenty-nine, he joined *The Times* and published his first book, *Royal Dukes*. This was followed two years later by a biography, *George IV*, and coincided with his appointment as a lecturer in English at King's College, London. Fulford became a recognized authority on the history of the royal family and was commissioned by his friend Guy Burgess to give a BBC radio talk on the coronation of George V.

When the war broke out he became a censor and was soon transferred to the

Security Service where he worked in the F4 sub-section of the division led by Roger Hollis, whom he had known for some years, and whom he had once turned down for a job on *The Times*. Fulford's role was to monitor the activities of pacifists, peace groups and revolutionary movements, all of whom were regarded as potentially subversive, but after two years he switched to the Air Ministry where he was assistant private secretary to Sir Archibald Sinclair, the Secretary of State for Air, until the end of the war.

Upon his return to civilian life Fulford published *The Right Honourable Gentleman* and continued thereafter to work as a historian and biographer. Despite his election defeats his commitment to the Liberal cause was undiminished and his loyalty to the party was rewarded with a knighthood just three years before his death in May 1983.

Queen Victoria

The influence of Queen Victoria on politics in nineteenth-century England was considerable. While it is true that she never – except perhaps over the Bedchamber crisis in the early days of her reign – came to loggerheads with the Government in the sense that King George III openly quarrelled with Fox and North, she was a potent force, watchful, critical and easily roused to anger. Her influence is not therefore obvious but it was none the less effective. No Prime Minister – not even Disraeli – would have contemplated any important measure without first considering whether the Queen's approval was probable. To that extent her views affected legislation. Cabinets had to placate her – to convert her to their point of view – and it is certainly true that she caused Ministers a great deal of additional work and anxiety.

Reading her large correspondence with Ministers – swiftly written and not always decipherable with the writing running off into the thick, black margins which edged all her paper – we can see how tireless and active she really was. Any Cabinet Minister was liable to receive one of these letters – full of shrewd questions and giving a point of view which was often refreshingly original in contrast to the one prevailing in Whitehall. Indeed these probing, occasionally encouraging, letters have something in common with the letters written by Mr Churchill to his colleagues during the war. While readily admitting that Queen Victoria was often a sore trial to her Ministers, all impartial observers would have to agree that she was always prompted by a vigorous patriotic sense, by a solicitous interest in the well-being of her subjects, and she was not influenced by any selfish considerations. This is perhaps most clearly illustrated in a letter which she wrote to a close friend when Disraeli had bought for £4,000,000 the shares in the Suez Canal which belonged to the Khedive of Egypt, 'The news of to-day the Queen felt sure must be a source of great satisfaction and pride to every British heart! It is *entirely* the doing of Mr Disraeli, who has *very large ideas* and *very lofty views* of the position this country should hold. His mind is so much greater, larger, and his apprehension of things great and small so much quicker than that of Mr Gladstone.'

The gifts of character which the Queen showed in politics were no less obvious in her private life. Although by nature the Queen was warmhearted and impulsive she was a severe mother particularly with her elder children. But here again this sprang from her own high standard and a longing that they should not fall below the best. Certainly they could never complain that they did not know where they stood with her, for she was invariably perfectly blunt in what she said or wrote to them. She disapproved of what she called lounging in her sons and particularly of too much smoking, card playing, racing and gossip. When all her four sons had been staying with her at Balmoral she wrote icily, 'There are too many Princes here at once.' When the Prince of Wales was twenty-five, married and with two sons, he wished to go to St Petersburg for the marriage of his sister-in-law to the future Tsar. After clearly stating why she did not wish him to go, she added, 'These are my reasons against it, and to that I may add another, which, dear child, you know I have often already alluded to, viz.: your remaining so little quiet at home, and always running about. The country, and all of us, would like to see you a little more stationary.'

She did not at all approve of his racing and she wrote to him, 'Now that Ascot Races are approaching I wish to repeat earnestly and seriously that I trust you will confine your visits to the races, to the two days ... your example can do much for good, and may do an immense deal for evil, in the present day.' Much later when the Prince was forty she heard that he was giving a ball at his London house on a day which happened to coincide with the funeral of the Dean of Westminster. She immediately sent him a telegram complaining of his 'extreme impropriety.' In private she grumbled about his always mixing with 'heartless Society people.' Of her second son Prince Alfred – a perverse and curious character – she was outspokenly critical. She hated his excessive smoking and gave orders when he was staying at Balmoral that the smoking-room should be shut at midnight and the lights extinguished. When her third son, Prince Arthur, afterwards the Duke of Connaught, acquired a suit with long trousers she at once wrote to his Governor, 'She is sorry to see trouser-pockets. The Prince Consort *hated* hands in the pockets, and really to *see* Prince Alfred never with his hands *out* of them would be enough to cure anyone. He walks into dinner and sits at dinner with his hands in his pockets.' When Prince Arthur was twenty-eight she wrote to his Equerry, 'He must be *dosed* for he is yellow and green.'

Stephen Watts

If a man or woman walked in at the front door of the War Office, demanded to see 'Intelligence' and was interviewed either by an officer of one of the purely military branches or by the long-suffering civilians retained for the purposes of dealing with enquiries, the chances were that sooner or later he or she would wind up across the desk from me.

At the outbreak of war in September 1939 Stephen Watts, having been film and drama critic of the *Sunday Express*, was the spotter in a searchlight battery with the rank of lance-corporal. A year later he had been commissioned and was appointed editor of *War*, the broadsheet of the Army Bureau of Current Affairs. Watts stayed with this rather obscure branch of Army Education until early in 1943, when he joined the Security Service.

Watts's work in MI5 began with routine port security, vetting recent arrivals from the Continent and checking their credentials. In March 1944 he was assigned to a liaison role with the deception staff at SHAEF (Supreme Headquarters Allied Expeditionary Force) and participated in a bizarre scheme intended to persuade the enemy that General Montgomery had been posted to Gibraltar, thereby implying that the long-awaited invasion of occupied France was likely to be spearheaded from the Mediterranean. An actor with a strong resemblance to Monty was found in the ranks of the Army Pay Corps and he was flown to the Rock with a retinue large enough to catch the attention of the local Abwehr agents.

After the liberation Watts was sent to Paris to trace the source of an indiscreet newspaper article that had borne a resemblance to a classified Army Council document. Returned to civilian life in October 1945, he was later to become the London film correspondent of the *New York Times* and in 1953 was elected president of the London Critics Circle. He now lives in Chelsea. His war memoirs do not directly identify MI5 as the branch of intelligence for which he worked. In this extract Watts recalls his encounter with 'Colonel Logan', the deception staff officer who had initiated the operation codenamed Copperhead. In reality 'Logan' was Colonel Dudley Clarke but neither his true name, nor that of Watts's immediate superior, Gilbert Lennox, appear in the book.

Moonlight on a Lake in Bond Street

One afternoon in March 1944 my Colonel buzzed for me twice. Both buzzes were memorable. He was a heavily-built, restless man who usually preferred to wear civilian clothes (which our curious Intelligence status permitted) and, with cigarette ash permanently sprinkled down his rumpled blue suit, he cut a distinctly unmilitary figure. This, while natural to him, also served his purpose; he was, in fact, a regular soldier, but, although he had spent more of his adult years in uniform than out of it, 'soldier' was as unlikely a label as you would ever have hung on him by guesswork.

When I answered the first buzz, the Colonel was pacing up and down his room and he bustled me over to a wall map which showed the south coast of England and the north coast of France. With a remarkable economy of words and gestures, and therefore, the maximum drama, he put me – as the phrase was – 'in the picture' about the plan for the invasion of Europe, then timed for June 1.

I was still thinking over the implications of this dramatic news when I was summoned again by the buzzer. This time, before I was properly in the room, he barked, 'Who could impersonate Montgomery?' I was fairly new to working with this colonel – let us call him Colonel Logan, as did the film which was eventually made of this episode – but I felt I knew him fairly well. His bark was a mannerism; unless you had done something very stupid (or somebody high up had and you were catching the backwash) there was no bite. He had a strong dramatic sense and he liked to shoot startling questions, to which quick answers were required. He was a stimulating if sometimes exasperating man to work for.

'Miles Mander,' I said.

'How tall is he?'

'If he stood up straight he would be close on six feet, but he stoops.'

'Too tall. Anyhow, he's in Hollywood, isn't he? Who else?'

'Look,' I said, 'I can't produce two Montys out of a hat. Let me think about it.'

'Right,' said the Colonel, 'see you in the morning.'

I have a goodish but erratic memory and during the rest of that day something nagged at the back of my mind, as if I had somewhere an answer to this problem, if only I could dredge it up. I lay awake that night trying to search systematically for some clue or association, then, typically, the answer came all in one piece. It was a photographic memory. I had seen a newspaper page with a picture of a man in a beret. I remembered taking for granted that it was General Montgomery until I read the caption. Then I found that it was a photograph of a man who had walked on to the stage at a troop show to take his bow as producer, had been cheered by the audience as Monty, and then revealed himself as – but what he revealed himself as I could not recall.

In the morning I telephoned the Colonel and told him I was working on the problem and would not be coming into the office. Not very confidently I thought it was the *News Chronicle* in which I had seen the picture, but after an hour or two turning the pages of the files I almost decided I was wrong. Then, suddenly, I came on it. It was just as I had remembered and the man was named as Lieutenant Clifton James. Back at my office I went through the Army List, but there was no officer identifiable as Clifton James. The number of Jameses made me quail, but I started sending for their personal files in batches. For the next day or two I was invisible behind a rampart of files on and around my desk. Again I was tempted to give up, but persevered. Exactly half way through the alphabet in terms of Christian name initial I was rewarded. There was a Meyrick Clifton James serving with the Royal Army Pay Corps, who seemed about the right age and who was an actor in civilian life. He was stationed at Leicester. It was time to make a progress report to the Colonel.

'Trustworthy?' that insatiable man barked when I had finished my story.

'How should I know?' I said; 'and anyhow, what's it all about?'

All I knew at this point was that somebody was required to impersonate Monty; the Colonel filled in the whys and hows for me. Somebody – to this day I do not know who – had had the idea that while the cross-channel invasion was being mounted General Montgomery should ostensibly appear in another theatre of war.

It was becoming increasingly impossible by then to conceal the assembly of men and materials in the South of England. Enemy reconnaissance must have shown that something was in preparation and the irresistible conclusion was a cross-channel attack into France. Assuming that knowledge, the enemy must be asking two vital questions – when and where? If General Montgomery, who was bound to be one of the leaders of an Allied invasion, was reported to Berlin to be in the Mediterranean the enemy would draw one conclusion and might be tempted by one speculation. The conclusion would be that the invasion of north-west Europe was unlikely to be imminent while Monty was out of England; the speculation would be that another attack was planned – across the Mediterranean from North Africa into the South of France. Some strength would be given to the speculation by the fact that signs of preparation had no doubt been reported from North Africa, for, although on nothing like the scale of the English Channel attack, there was then being mounted in North Africa the attack which went into the South of France about two months after D-Day.

Thus our assignment was to find or create a figure sufficiently like Monty to be mistaken for him, and to exhibit the dummy (while, of course, seeming to conceal him as we would if he *had* been General Montgomery) in places where the news of his presence would be reported back to Berlin and, at the very least, cause some doubt, uncertainty, and desirable confusion as to the Allies' intentions and what should be done to counter them.

Already, although we had no 'Monty', the Colonel had decided where he ought to go. A brief call at Gibraltar and then an arrival at Allied Forces Headquarters in Algiers would, he thought, be at once logical for the Commander of our notional operation and would be likely to yield to the enemy the necessary leakage of his presence. But, although D-Day was still nearly six weeks off and our deception should be executed as close to D-Day as possible, it was urgent that we find our double and make our plans. The first step was to have a look at Clifton James, but without his realising why he was being looked at.

'I'll go up to Leicester,' said the Colonel suddenly. 'Think up some pretext.'

This was a favourite trick of Colonel Logan's. Instead of saying 'How can we have a look at James?' he was proposing something which was impracticable and, on the face of it, even foolish. He could not go unannounced and snoop around the Army Pay Office in Leicester to have a look at one junior officer; and looking would not be enough – we would have to find out what sort of man he was. It was up to me to fill the gap and make the Colonel's trip to Leicester a viable proposition.

In cases like this, a kind of elementary, brain-cudgelling logic is the only hope. Why would a senior officer from London want to interview James and not through the proper channels of his Commanding Officer? Who in the War Office would be interested in James? He was an actor. Who was interested in actors? ENSA? Army films? This kind of unbrilliant thinking sometimes produces a momentum which will make the mind jump several steps ahead to the answer. Suddenly I had it. In the Directorate of the Army Kinematograph Service David Niven was a lieutenant-colonel. In his position it seemed reasonable enough that he might want to borrow a professional actor for a part in a film. Niven had the great advantage in my eyes of being a friend who knew where I worked; his well-known name could cut two ways. It might open doors or it might create resistance. It all depended on the people in charge at Leicester. It was certainly a good enough idea to act on.

It could be said that the Monty's Double operation went into gear in the casual encounter of two officers on a corner of St James's Street one lunchtime. What David did not know was that, remembering he lunched as often as not at Boodle's, I had lain in wait for him. What I hoped to promote was best done as informally as possible. I simply told him I wanted to make contact with an officer serving in Leicester and perhaps David might act as the lever by which the man could be prised loose from his unit without too many questions being asked. He gave me a long, steady look with his bright blue eyes and then responded as ideally as though I had written the line for him. 'But, of course, old boy,' he said. 'Ring me in the afternoon and give me the details.'

The next episode is, of course, not within my personal experience but the Colonel and James described it to me later. An excited ATS telephone operator rang through to James in the Leicester Pay Office and gasped, 'Oh, sir, it's London calling. You'll never guess who it is.' On that level, the film star name produced its effect. As an ex-regular soldier, David Niven knew quite well what the 'channels' ought to have been, but he played it much more cleverly by his seeming ignorance of procedure. He simply told James that his name had come up as a possible for a part in an Army film, but that, as it was all very much in the air, he did not want to approach his CO formally at this stage. However, a colleague, a Colonel Logan, happened to be passing through Leicester next day and would James meet him for lunch and a talk? David Niven had never seen James, so he had no inkling of our purpose; but we had created a perfectly good excuse for Logan and James to come together without any need to confide in anybody.

The Colonel came back satisfied that James was, superficially at least, our man. Another telephone call from Colonel Niven to Leicester and James reported at Curzon Street House. What more natural than that after a few minutes the busy Colonel Niven should retire and leave James with his colleague, Logan? Some more talk, and James was handed a printed form. It was the relevant extract from the Official Secrets Act. James was told to read it carefully and then sign a declaration that it had been brought to his notice.

When the Colonel came back to our office it was my turn to have a spasm of canniness.

'You're sure he's all right – he won't leak?' I asked.

'I think so,' said the Colonel, then he grinned. 'Anyhow,' he added, 'it wouldn't be the end of the world if he did.'

'How?'

'Because I told him the story in reverse.'

One is always especially impressed by the twist one failed to think of one's self. Logan had told James he was to impersonate Montgomery *in the UK* while Montgomery went to the Mediterranean to launch the invasion. Suppose, at the very worst, that all James knew reached the enemy. A Mediterranean invasion was precisely the idea we wanted to sell them.

After that I saw a lot of James. While the rest of the plans were being made there was nothing for him to do but hang about. Not unnaturally, it made him restive and nervous. We did not want him seen coming and going at our office, which made it worse. I used to meet him in the mornings on a street corner and we would drink coffee in the Kardomah in Piccadilly and talk. When I had other work to do, I would pack him off to the pictures. I wouldn't like to think how many newsreels he saw in that period.

Fortunately, James was a pleasant companion and while I could do nothing to allay his nervousness by giving him the information he badly wanted about exactly what he was going to have to do I could keep him reasonably cheerful and advise him on security to cover his being in London. I came to know him well and this was reassuring because there was no doubt about his intelligence, his willingness to do what was required, and his common-sense about secrecy.

Even his nervousness was all right; what I had dreaded was an over-confident know-all who would take the thing too lightly, whose vanity would endanger security (and after all he had, as an actor, landed a plum part), and who would collapse when the time came.

Through this period, as we made our careful arrangements, letting as few people as possible into the story, I was constantly bombarded with questions about James from Colonel Logan. One day he demanded, 'Can he fly?' This hadn't occurred to me. It would be too bad if our Monty arrived at Gibraltar green-faced and rubber-legged from air-sickness. But how to establish his airworthiness if our story to him was that the impersonation was to be done in the UK? Between us, the Colonel and I worked it out that we could tell James that among his Monty duties would be to show himself in Northern Ireland, inspecting troops or something. We added colour by saying that leakage from there via Dublin was likely.

I asked the question and James told me he had never been in an aeroplane in his life. With the help of a pilot who was employed on secret missions we had James make a flight to Devon and back. It was made in a tiny two-seater plane in bad weather and James emerged successfully.

At last the deadline drew near and we had a full scenario worked out. To let James have a close study of Montgomery we transformed him into an Intelligence Corps sergeant and attached him to the General's body-guard, first on a South Coast tour and then on the fishing holiday Montgomery took in Scotland when he had everything set for D-Day.

James had a miserable time. He was not strong physically and he had to sleep in damp tents and ride in open jeeps in bad weather. Several times he was reprimanded by officers and for failing to salute or say 'sir'. He had served in two wars, but never before in the ranks.

He came back from Scotland exhausted but with a new spirit in him. He had met Montgomery, very privately, and he was now right inside the part. He had caught the distinctive carriage and expressions; he could mimic the voice excellently (though it wasn't strictly necessary), and he had picked up several mannerisms. It was when he was showing me exactly how Monty saluted that I realised something we had overlooked. James had a finger missing from his right hand. It seemed terribly conspicuous when he saluted. This snag was overcome by ingenious bandaging so that the 'General' merely looked as if he had had a slight accident.

Without any help, James made himself up — extra grey at the temples and on the moustache — so that with the double-badged beret the likeness was uncanny. At his two ports of call only the Commander-in-Chief and one other officer would be in the picture. James learned names, studied photographs, and memorised some 'in character' conversational gambits.

We held rehearsals. Chairs represented the aircraft and, although we were all very serious at the time, it must have been a funny sight, with one of my colleagues, the late Marcus Haywood, representing the Governor of Gibraltar (though we couldn't use the name as James didn't know where he was going) and Colonel Logan, in civilian clothes, as the guard of honour, presenting arms with an umbrella while 'Monty' inspected him.

We had fitted James out by this time, which was easy enough, except for the medal ribbons. For these we had to get General Montgomery himself to put in an order with his own tailor. At the latest possible moment we told James that the plan had been switched and that he was going to the Mediterranean. I think that if we had told him he was to drop by parachute into enemy territory it could not have added to his anxieties;

there is a point beyond which more worry is impossible. This did not bother me, and fortunately the Colonel too knew something about theatre people. Actors can be like jelly in the last days before a new play and rock-like the moment they step on stage. Again, I would have been worried if he had been less than petrified.

The departure was to be at night, so that evening we held a dress rehearsal in my office. The Colonel's secretary was there as a kind of wardrobe mistress, checking the clothes to be worn and those to be packed. Suddenly I realised that a tropical shirt lacked the badges of rank – and we had no spares. The Colonel blew up, justifiably, I suppose. It was too late to get Montgomery's tailor. Then the secretary, a quiet, pretty girl, spoke up. 'I believe I can help,' she said.

'How?' Logan barked. 'What d'you mean you can help?'

'Well,' she said, very diffidently, 'Daddy's a general.'

The Colonel looked as though he were going to kiss her. Instead he patted her and bustled her off to rob Daddy's wardrobe, and that problem was solved.

It had been decided that James should be accompanied by two officers – an ADC and a senior staff officer, rank of Brigadier. Here I fell disappointingly between two stools. I didn't look young enough and smooth enough to pose as an ADC and at the age of thirty-three I could not claim to look like a plausible Brigadier. Nor could I argue the casting of these two rôles. We borrowed a young man from the real Monty's entourage and he looked just right (he was, however, very airsick and had to be practically carried off the plane at Gibraltar, so as a performer he was virtually a non-starter). For the Brigadier, my colleague, Marcus Haywood, was chosen. He was perfect. A major like me, he was in his fifties. He had been a regular soldier in his youth. He was handsome, silver-haired, and moustached, not too old, not too young, and had a quiet air of senior authority to which I could not aspire. Marcus got the job, and I have seen many Brigadiers not nearly so well cast for the rank. But I had taken it for granted that as I had been closest to James from the time I 'found' him I would follow through at his side. I felt (if James will forgive the simile) like a puppet master who has to stand aside at the last moment and let somebody else manipulate the show.

CHAPTER V

Broadway

While MI5, which was responsible for home security, did an excellent job and succeeded in catching nearly every spy sent over within forty-eight hours of his arrival, MI6, which was responsible for our spies in enemy and neutral countries, was pathetic.
Dennis Wheatley, The Deception Planners

During the early months of the Second World War Britain's secret services underwent a dramatic expansion and talent of diverse suitability was recruited from the City, Fleet Street and the universities. The pre-war organization was woefully inadequate to cope with the demand for wartime intelligence with the consequence that brainpower, capable of sifting information and analysing conflicting reports, became a much sought-after commodity. These were not the people to work behind enemy lines, but rather the essential intelligence bureaucrats who would receive all the differing pieces of the intelligence jigsaw and construct an appreciation that could be understood by the military commanders. Dons, bankers, novelists and journalists found themselves at Broadway Buildings, Victoria, working alongside the professionals of the pre-war era and regular servicemen seconded to intelligence duties. Although warned to remain silent about their work, a few have divulged details of their own particular experiences, and some can be seen to have capitalized on their wartime role. John Cairncross, for example, who has written extensively on the subject of French poetry, but not on his own wartime activities, admitted having passed on SIS's secrets to the Kremlin.

Born in Glasgow, Cairncross was intellectually brilliant and studied at Glasgow University and the Sorbonne before winning a scholarship to Trinity College, Cambridge to read French. He obtained his BA in just two years, and one of his college supervisors in French literature was Anthony Blunt. While at Trinity Cairncross came under the influence of both Blunt and Guy Burgess, and after he had graduated with first-class honours in modern languages he passed top in the entrance exams into the Foreign Office in the autumn of 1936, aged twenty-three.

At this stage Cairncross, though a Communist, was not a spy, but when he transferred to GCHQ at Bletchley Park in 1942, as an analyst specializing on the German order of battle along the Eastern Front, he began passing copies of the Luftwaffe Enigma intercepts to his Soviet contacts. When in 1943 he was able to supply comprehensive details of the enemy units deployed in the battle of Kursk the Soviets exploited his information to the full and won an historic victory. In 1944 Cairncross was switched to SIS but at the end of the war he moved to the Treasury. There he remained, taking copies of classified documents to illicit meetings with his case officer until the unplanned defection of his friend Guy Burgess in May 1951.

Immediately after Burgess had fled, MI5 officers searched his flat and discovered some compromising manuscript notes hidden in a suitcase under his bed. Arthur Martin was one of the Security Service officers working on the investigation into the backgrounds of Burgess and Maclean, and fortuitously his secretary recognized Cairncross's characteristic handwriting. Cairncross was placed under surveillance and eventually questioned. He made some limited admissions but his confession was insufficient for a criminal prosecution. Instead he was allowed to resign his civil service post in the Treasury and take up a teaching position at Northwestern University in Chicago.

Early in 1964, in a further interrogation by the tenacious Arthur Martin, Cairncross made a detailed and highly incriminating statement in which he admitted having given the Soviets a mass of classified data from GCHQ and SIS during the war. He was warned that if he returned to England he might face charges so he moved to Rome where he worked as a translator in a United Nations organization, and he now lives in the south of France. The fact that he had operated as a Soviet source became known in 1982 when Peter Wright told his co-author, Chapman Pincher, about the case.

Once accepted into Broadway, Cairncross had found himself at the heart of the British secret establishment. Like Philby, he discovered that checks into the backgrounds of new recruits were at best perfunctory. It was the task of an already well-established author, Valentine Williams, to interview SIS's candidates and assign them to the appropriate sections. Williams was a wartime entrant and had joined a relatively small organization staffed with professionals of the calibre of Kenneth Cohen, Fred Winterbotham and Rex Fletcher. Cohen had transferred to SIS from the Royal Navy in 1935 and was the only one of the three to stay on after the war.

Group Captain Fred Winterbotham had been recruited into SIS in 1930 to head a new Air Intelligence section, in response to the demand from the Air Ministry for information on German aircraft production. One of his close colleagues in SIS was Rex Fletcher MP, later Lord Winster, who was to write a damning critique on the topic of the relative weakness of Britain's pre-war air power when he was still on SIS's staff. To compare his observations with what SIS was advising Whitehall is an illuminating exercise made possible by the release of the official history prepared by Professor Sir Harry Hinsley.

Another of those to be drafted into SIS after the outbreak of war was Sir James Marshall-Cornwall, a regular soldier who was to be given the specially created rank of Assistant Chief as a trouble-shooter to assuage the complaints of his colleagues on the General Staff who were becoming increasingly disillusioned about the quality of SIS's information. Another senior officer to be inserted into SIS's hierarchy at high level, also with Deputy Director rank, supposedly to impose some much needed intellectual discipline, was Jack Cordeaux, from the Naval Intelligence Division. After the war Cordeaux was elected to Parliament and while in the Commons was a fierce defender of the Secret Intelligence Service and, when Montgomery Hyde published *The Quiet Canadian* in November 1962, launched an attack upon him, demanding during questions to the Attorney-General: 'Is my right honourable and learned friend really telling the House that no breach of the Official Secrets Acts has taken place in the writing and publication of a book that describes in detail the work of one of the head agents of the British Secret Intelligence Service?'

The decision to draft in three senior officers, from the Admiralty, the Army and the RAF, was taken after numerous complaints had been made regarding the dissemination of intelligence. In an almost unique display of unity, all three services protested that SIS was consistently failing to deliver information to the appropriate quarter in a timely fashion, and the creation of a special tier of management on the distribution side was intended to rectify the situation before the Joint Intelligence Committee took more drastic action. Cordeaux's role was to enhance the links between SIS and its naval clients by supervising the extraction of intelligence with a naval significance from the production or operational branches of SIS.

Once Cordeaux had completed his task he was given a particularly sensitive assignment, and one that remains classified to this day. He was selected to head SIS's inquest into the fate of its networks in Holland, and identify the structural failures that had allowed the enemy to mount a hugely successful deception campaign which had led to the Abwehr exercising almost complete control over SOE's Dutch operations. More than forty Dutch agents perished and it fell to Cordeaux, as Controller, Northern Area, with responsibility for supervising operations across Holland, Denmark and the rest of Scandinavia, to chronicle the tragedy and apportion the blame. Neither the document he wrote nor its conclusions have ever been declassified, or even its existence divulged to the parliamentary enquiry held after the war in the Netherlands.

Cordeaux retired from SIS in 1946 and subsequently contested two elections in Derbyshire before being elected the Tory MP for Nottingham Central in 1955. He never achieved ministerial office during his eleven years in the Commons but he was a fierce defender of what he perceived to be SIS's interests. In December 1958 he launched a scathing attack on the SOE survivors who had written their memoirs, referring to them as 'these amateur spies cashing in on their war experiences by turning amateur authors'. Three years after he left the Commons he wrote a novel, *Safe Seat*, in which he told the story of 'Jack Reston', the MP for Trentham East, who was defeated in the 1964 General Election and, having been found a safer constituency, lost that too in a by-election. Cordeaux died in January 1982, leaving the definite impression among his readers that it was virtually impossible to distinguish between the wretchedly ambitious 'Jack Reston' and his creator.

Cordeaux's former brother officer in NID, Ian Fleming, was to make a rather better name for himself as a writer and the inventor of James Bond. He had arrived at the Admiralty from the City, while Robert Cecil was a diplomat who found himself moved to C's office as his assistant.

Hugh Trevor-Roper, later Lord Dacre, graduated into SIS from the Radio Security Service where he was responsible for monitoring illicit wireless transmissions. Other distinguished academics to find themselves in SIS included Robert Carew-Hunt and Professor R. V. Jones. Of these three, only Carew-Hunt has given absolutely no clue to his wartime activities but his cover was blown by Kim Philby who made a passing reference to him in *My Silent War*.

When these powerful intellects arrived at Broadway Buildings, then SIS's austere headquarters opposite St James's Park tube station, some expected to be met with a measure of hostility from a group of superannuated naval officers, for that was the organization's pre-war reputation among the less well informed. In reality SIS boasted some impressive brains in its permanent, professional staff, perhaps the most outstanding of whom was David Footman, who was later to take up an academic existence at Oxford. A gifted commentator on the world scene, and a recognized expert on political trends in eastern Europe, Footman never divulged any aspect of his operational work but wrote several novels while at Broadway. In his curiously intimate autobiography published in 1974, *Dead Yesterday: An Edwardian Childhood*, in which he gave a graphic description of an early homosexual encounter, he also described his political views: 'We were dissidents, not rebels; but cracks in the old order were already appearing and we helped to widen them. Whether or not humanity is better for the change is open to argument.'

David Footman entered the Secret Intelligence Service in 1935 following ten years with the Levant Consular Service. Educated at Marlborough and New College, Oxford, he had served in France with the Royal Berkshire Regiment during the Great War, and was decorated with the MC in 1916. After working in consular posts in Yugoslavia, Alexandria and Port Said, he left the service in 1929 to be manager of the Gramophone Company in Vienna. That job lasted three years, whereupon he moved to Belgrade to represent the London bank of Glyn Mills. His wife Joan, whom he had married in 1917 when he was aged twenty-two, divorced him in 1936.

Footman's first posting in SIS was to Section I, the political branch created to advise the chief on developments around the world. Already a novelist of some note, in 1944, while heading Section I, he published *Red Prelude*, a biography of Andrei Zhelyabov, and the first of several scholarly books on Russian revolutionary history. Two years later in *The Primrose Path* he documented the life of Ferdinand Lassalle, founder of the German Labour Movement and significant influence on Marx and Engels.

Footman remained in SIS until 1953 when he took up an academic appointment at St Antony's, Oxford where he was in charge of modern Russian studies. A close friend of many leftist intellectuals, the end of his career in the intelligence field was tainted by his connections with Anthony Blunt and Guy Burgess. Indeed, according to Goronwy Rees, when Burgess defected in May 1951 he had telephoned Footman to warn him that he believed the diplomat's disappearance was no temporary phenomenon but the carefully planned escape of a traitor. Rees's claim that Footman had dismissively brushed the assertion aside was to prove exceptionally damaging to a brilliant intelligence officer.

Footman himself was unembarrassed by what some of his more critical colleagues regarded as injudicious friendships, as was demonstrated in

1967 when he published *In Memoriam Archie*, following the death three years earlier of Archie Lyall. Footman was a prolific author while studying at St Antony's, almost all of his work concentrating on aspects of the Russian civil wars, beginning with *The Last Days of Kolchak*. In 1956 he wrote a biography of Boris Savinkov, the Menshevik leader (supported by SIS through Somerset Maugham) who had been the assassin of the Grand Duke Serge and the Czar's police chief, Dmitri Trepov. Footman retired from St Antony's in 1963 and, at the time of his death in October 1983, was still active contributing articles to journals. He had dominated the Secret Intelligence Service for nearly twenty years and had been a significant influence over his colleagues, most of whom were of rather lesser intellects.

Rex Fletcher

I have no Intelligence Service to give me precise information.

Reginald T. H. Fletcher, known to his friends as Rex, joined the Royal Navy in 1899, aged fourteen, and saw action in destroyers at the Dardanelles and with the Grand Fleet and the Channel Patrol. After the Great War he was posted to the Naval Intelligence Division where, as head of the Near East section, he served under Admiral Sinclair who was soon to be appointed chief of the Secret Intelligence Service. In 1923, as Sinclair took up his post in SIS's headquarters, Fletcher was elected the Liberal MP for Basingstoke. He lost his seat a year later and in 1929 joined the Labour Party, for whom he won the Nuneaton seat in 1935, and thereafter established his reputation as an expert on naval matters. Certainly he was well informed for he spent each morning at his desk in SIS's headquarters.

Fletcher's role in SIS was that of a G Officer, one of a small group of senior personnel who supervised the organization's overseas operations. Thus it was as a Labour MP and a senior SIS officer that in 1938 Fletcher contributed to a collection of essays and surveys, *The Air Defence of Britain*. To have made such a savage attack on the Air Ministry and the aircraft industry was itself a matter of controversy, but the really remarkable fact was that Fletcher was also a serving SIS officer, although his brief entries in *Who's Who* and the *Dictionary of National Biography* make no mention of the fact. Indeed, in the book he takes care to deny that he had access to any intelligence relating to the relative aircraft strengths of different countries and was relying upon an article in the *News Chronicle* attributed to Pierre Cot, the French Minister of Aviation. In reality, of course, Fletcher had all the relevant data at his fingertips because his principal preoccupation at SIS was this very topic.

Soon after the outbreak of war Fletcher resigned from SIS and rejoined the navy, to be posted to the London docks where he supervised the arming of the merchant fleet. He was then transferred to Grimsby, as a staff officer planning east coast convoys, but in May 1940 he returned to London as Parliamentary Private Secretary to the First Lord of the Admiralty, A. V. Alexander. At the end of 1941 Fletcher was elevated to a barony, together with three other Labour MPs, and he took the title of Lord Winster. When the Labour government was elected in 1945 Winster was appointed Minister of Civil Aviation, a post he held until October 1946 when he went to Cyprus as governor. During the twenty-eight months he was in Cyprus demands from the Greek section of the population for *enosis* led to political turmoil and the civil strife that would eventually lead to the declaration of an Emergency. Upon his return to London Winster resumed his seat in the Lords and took an independent line from the increasingly Leftist Labour Party. He died at his home in Crowborough, Sussex, in June 1961.

In this passage from his essay in *The Air Defence of Britain*, Fletcher indicts the development of the RAF and offers some comparative statistics for European air power. His figures for Germany are of particular interest for he tends to exaggerate the conclusions of the secret studies carried out by SIS at the time. The classified assessments gave an estimate in 1938 of 2640 front line aircraft in the Luftwaffe, rising to 4320 in 1939. This was based on a production level of 550 aircraft a month which was considered likely to rise to 700 a month the following year. This contrasts with what is now known to be the true position, of 3000 front line aircraft in 1938, increasing to a total of 3647 in 1939, and even more sharply with Fletcher's inflated numbers of 5200 to 5500 reserve and front line aircraft. SIS's erroneous position of 1938, to which Fletcher had contributed, is revealed in Volume I of *British Intelligence*, the official history published in 1979.

Clearly Fletcher was privy to the inter-departmental debates that were under way between the Industrial Intelligence Centre, the Air Ministry, SIS and the Committee of Imperial Defence to advise the Cabinet on the true scale of the German threat. 'After careful sifting of the evidence', Fletcher asserts that 'Germany will have an actual production of almost 600 machines a month' in 1938, which was not entirely inconsistent with the real production level of under 550 in 1938, escalating to 725–750 a month in mid-1939. Thus Fletcher's prediction regarding factory productivity in Germany was broadly accurate, while his appreciation of operational aircraft was greatly exaggerated, thereby over-compensating for SIS's figures which were themselves underestimated by a wide margin.

The Air Defence of Britain

For centuries Great Britain has been able to play a major part in European History, to engage in Europe's major wars and to win through. So long as the Navy held command of the seas, our island went untouched by an invader.

The coming of the air weapon has changed all that. Either we must succeed in organizing international law to such an extent that air forces can be dissolved, leaving order to be maintained by an International Air Police Force or, if we wish to retain immunity from attack and destruction, we must, with our friends, control the air above our island as we have controlled the seas around it.

This country is peculiarly vulnerable from the air. It is a small island; its vitally important industrial and administrative centres concentrated in a few areas, and its capital, and nearly a quarter of the population, lying close to the Continent, clearly marked by the Thames running through its centre.

The air forces employed on a limited scale in Spain, Abyssinia and China have sufficed to show the devastating effect of high explosive used in air attacks. To inflict damage on London, Birmingham, Manchester, Newcastle, so serious as to render us helpless, for some time at least, is a task well within the compass of an Air Force of the size possessed by any great Power of today, unless confronted by an effective defence.

Effective defence includes anti-aircraft artillery, balloon barrages, and ARP, as well as fighter aircraft; but our main defence from air attack must remain the strength of our own Air Force to oppose raiding squadrons sent against us and to answer raid with raid.

We can only measure the strength and adequacy of our Air Force in the same way as we have always measured the strength of our Navy; by comparing it with the Forces it may have to meet. It is difficult to ascertain the effective strength of any country's air force. Figures and facts are kept secret; and, out of such as are published, we have to sift the figures of 'first-line' strength, of immediately available reserve machines, of other reserves, and of training and civil aircraft; as well as numbers of trained pilots, state of equipment, preparedness, etc. etc.

We are only concerned with machines here in which connection the most reliable figures to which I can refer you are those recently published in the *News Chronicle* in an article by Pierre Cot, who, as Air Minister in the French Popular Front Government, would have Intelligence figures at his disposal. M. Cot says that the front-line air strength of the European Powers is as follows:

Russia	4,000	Gt Britain	2,000
Germany	3,500	Italy	2,000
France	2,500	Poland	550
		Czechoslovakia	550

Behind these first-line machines each country has a reserve of immediately available machines, largest, probably, in the case of the dictatorship Powers, which began rearming earliest. Germany and Russia, for instance, may well dispose of reserves of over 50 per cent of their first-line figures. Italy may not be so well found but she is in a better position than France or ourselves, whose air rearmament has been later and slower. The air armaments of the Great Powers, first line and effective reserve machines inclusive, may be estimated as follows:

Russia	6,200 to 6,500
Germany	5,200 to 5,500
Italy	2,300 to 2,600
France	2,200 to 2,500
Gt Britain	2,300 to 2,600

It must, however, be noted that much of the British force is spread out along our Imperial lines of communications, and we cannot rely on more than about 1,900 or 2,100 machines for Home Defence or what is sometimes called the Metropolitan Air Force.

The available data are so unreliable that I should not like to guess at the production, actual and potential, of any other Powers than this country, Germany and possibly France. But I should say that by the time this book is published, Germany will have an actual production of almost 600 machines a month, this country about 400, and France less than 300.

These figures, if approximately correct and which I have put down only after careful sifting of evidence, reveal a very serious situation for the country – remember we are only 250–300 miles from the Rhine, which Lord Baldwin called 'our frontier'.

An essential fact to bear in mind when considering questions of aircraft production and air rearmament is that we must expect a 50 per cent wastage of first-line strength per month, in actual warfare, as a very minimum. Some experts say it will be nearer 100 per cent. Our production potential per month then must be not less than half of our front-line strength for war machines only. There are trainer and other aircraft needed as well.

We cannot comfortably face the world with less than an equal strength in first-line aircraft – 'parity' as it is called – with any Power within striking distance of our shores. To achieve and maintain such parity was the aim of Lord Baldwin's Government. Looking at the figures I have set out above you will realize at once that we need a first-line strength of not less than 3,000 planes *now*, in our Home Defence Force; and, since other

Powers will be carrying on whilst we are making a supreme effort to catch up, we cannot contemplate, under present conditions, attaining parity short of the 5,000 front-line strength mark. The potential production we have to aim at is, therefore, not less than 2,000–2,500 monthly, or over 25,000 aircraft a year.

That is, I believe, roughly the arithmetic, and the logic, which inspired the *Sunday Times* to say that the aim of Sir Kingsley Wood's recently reformed Air Ministry, is a potential production of 25,000 per annum, to be reached in two years, and an actual production of half that, which will be needed to reach parity and maintain it.

Note that this means two and a half times our present actual and at least five times our present potential production.

Sir James Marshall-Cornwall

I had previously acquired a certain knowledge of clandestine operations, such as the invisible opening of sealed envelopes and the tapping of Turkish telegraph and telephone lines, but I now had to acquaint myself with other ancillary techniques, such as the picking of locks, the burgling of safes, the forging of passports and the use of secret inks. These activities were of course common to all secret service operations.

A professional soldier who rarely experienced command of troops in the field, Marshall-Cornwall was drafted into SIS with the rank of Deputy Director in the spring of 1943. The intention was to silence criticism from SIS's military clients that the organization's information was inadequate to their needs. Marshall-Cornwall learned his trade from Sir Claude Dansey and upon the latter's retirement the following year took over his post.

Born James Cornwall, he changed his name in 1927 so as to inherit his maternal uncle's estate in Scotland. By that time he had acquired a reputation as one of the most gifted linguists of his generation and had been highly decorated in the Great War when he had spent two years as an intelligence officer at GHQ in France. In January 1918 he had been appointed to head MI3, a section of military intelligence at the War Office, and then went to the Paris peace conference to represent the General Staff.

In between the wars he headed the military mission to Egypt and in 1938 was placed in charge of Britain's air defence. In 1940 he helped evacuate Allied troops from Cherbourg, and in November 1941 he took over Western Command. This posting ended in his dismissal, after he incurred the wrath of the War Office over his deployment of troops to guard Liverpool docks. Just when his career appeared to be heading into the doldrums, he was offered the opportunity to join Special Operations Executive. His task was to reduce the inter-departmental conflict between SOE and SIS, and in March 1943, after five months at Baker Street, he switched to SIS.

After the war Marshall-Cornwall, aged fifty-eight, retired from the army and became editor-in-chief of captured German archives. He later became involved in some arms trading and wrote military histories. He died in December 1985 at his daughter's home in Yorkshire.

In his memoirs, published a year before his death, he recalled the many overseas inspection tours he undertook during 1944 as SIS faced reorganization in anticipation of peace.

Wars and Rumours of Wars

SOE appeared to be liberally endowed with funds, for it rented a large number of palatial country houses, such as Audley End, as schools for training its agents, French, Belgian, Dutch, Danish, Norwegian and Polish. Indeed it was unkindly suggested that the letters SOE stood for the 'Stately 'Omes of England'. I spent a good deal of my time in visiting these training establishments all over the country as far as the Scottish Highlands to observe the methods of instructing the agents in coding and wireless transmission, and in rehearsing their cover stories. I also visited the special airfields used and saw the agents before they took off on their perilous journeys.

From January to March, 1943, I took over charge of the military side of SOE from Colin Gubbins during his absence in North Africa to arrange the establishment of the organization out there. At the end of March, after five months of experience with SOE, I was transferred to MI6, for Stewart Menzies had asked me to understudy his deputy, Sir Claude Dansey, who was shortly to retire owing to ill-health, with a view to taking over his duties. This accorded well with my original assignment to smooth over the troubles between the two organizations, and it also gave me a position of greater responsibility. The operations of MI6 and SOE were now fairly well harmonized, but it was illogical that they were still controlled by two different departments of state.

During April and May, 1943, I sat at Claude Dansey's feet at the Broadway office, and was inculcated into the methods and mysteries of MI6. Meanwhile the war in North Africa came to an end with the final surrender of 200,000 Germans in Tunisia. During this period also, I first made the acquaintance of an outstanding American, David Bruce, who had arrived in London as representative of the American 'Office of

Strategic Services' (OSS), an offshoot of the Central Intelligence Agency, which combined the functions of MI6 and SOE for the American Army. The head of OSS was General William ('Big Bill') Donovan, an energetic but somewhat eccentric chief. The Americans had of course much to learn from us about the technical problems of infiltrating agents into enemy-occupied countries, and this introduced yet another complication into our network of clandestine operations. These were already suffering from the competition of a Free French Intelligence and Sabotage Service (*Bureau Central de Renseignements et d'Action*) at de Gaulle's London Head-quarters, headed by a rather contentious officer, Colonel André de Wavrin, who bore the assumed name of 'Passy'. Thanks to David Bruce's tact and cooperation, we had less difficulty in controlling the somewhat amateurish operations of our American allies. David Bruce later became a very popular and successful Ambassador in both Paris and London.

From 25 May to 10 June I spent a fortnight in visiting Algiers, Bône, Tunis, Malta and Cairo in order to reorganize our Secret Intelligence Service throughout that region in accordance with the changing military situation. This gave me an opportunity of meeting many interesting personalities, including General Sir Harold Alexander (later Lord Alexander of Tunis, 1891–1969) and his political assistant, Harold Macmillan. Others I had to deal with were Air Marshal Tedder, General Bedell Smith (Eisenhower's Chief of Staff) and the French Generals Giraud and Georges, who were competing unsuccessfully to replace de Gaulle.

Towards the end of 1943 we were devoting much time and effort to trace the development of the German secret weapons known as V1 and V2 which were designed for the destruction of London, and of which our agents had kept us informed. The brilliant young physicist, R. V. Jones, in charge of the scientific intelligence section of MI6, contributed largely to combat this menace.

From 9 March to 10 April, 1944, I spent a month in visiting and inspecting all our secret service establishments in Gibraltar, Algiers, Naples, Bari, Cairo, Beirut, Jerusalem, Baghdad and Tehran, in the course of which I met a number of interesting men, such as our Ambassadors in Iraq and Iran, Sir Kinahan Cornwallis and Sir Reader Bullard.

After my return to London, on 18 June I was looking eastwards from my dressing-room window when I heard a loud explosion and saw a thick cloud of smoke rising. It was a V1 'doodle-bug' flying bomb which had hit the Guards Chapel, killing 120 people and wounding ninety. These flying bombs were now descending daily on London, although they were soon to be tackled with considerable success by our anti-aircraft defences under 'Tim' Pile. On 5 August my wife and I received the tragic news that our only son Jim had been killed in action in Normandy on 30 July, while commanding a troop of Churchill tanks in the 4th (Tank) Battalion of the Grenadier Guards.

This unit led an attack on 30 July by VIII Corps, commanded by my old friend, General Sir Richard O'Connor (1899–1981). The battle was known as Operation Bluecoat, which initiated the break-out of the Anglo-American Armies, which had been brought to a halt by the German armoured counter-attacks after the initial landings on 6 June. The left wing of VIII Corps consisted of the 15th (Scottish) Division, which was spear-headed by my son's armoured battalion. With his troop of three Churchill tanks he captured the Bois de Mondant, south-east of Caumont-l'Eventé, which was the key-point of the German defensive position. The Germans raised their hands and surrendered, so my son opened the turret of his tank to round up the prisoners. He was then shot through the head by a sniper from the rear. He fell at the moment of victory at the age of 22.

My son was not buried in one of the vast cemeteries of the Commonwealth War Graves Commission, with which Normandy is studded. The owner of the wood which he captured, Monsieur de Saint-Louvent, a retired cavalry officer and Mayor of a neighbouring village, kindly presented me with a quarter-acre plot, now a cider-apple orchard, close to where he fell and I had him buried there, beside the road leading from Caumont-l'Eventé to Cahagnes. I engaged an architect of the War Graves Commission to design a monument containing two bronze plaques recording in French and English the story of the battle. Every year since 1947 I have attended an anniversary memorial service at the grave with the assistance of the Mayor and Curé of Cahagnes. The last time I made this pilgrimage was on 31 July 1983.

On 15 September I left by air for Naples to inspect our establishments in Italy, staying with General Sir Henry Maitland Wilson at his villa near Naples; he and I had been fellow students at the Camberley Staff College in 1919. I then went on to Rome where we were now well established, the Germans having withdrawn to a strong defensive line farther north covering Florence. On 21 September, while driving down the Appian Way from Rome to Naples, my car skidded on a wet pavé road after a rainstorm and we crashed into a tree. It was in the days before the introduction of seat-belts and, as I was sitting beside the driver, I went through the windscreen, my head and face being embedded with glass splinters. Fortunately the accident took place not far from Naples, where I was well looked after in No. 65 General Hospital; thirty glass fragments were extracted from my skull and face. Eight days later I was discharged from hospital and flew to Cairo on 1 October.

On 6 October I flew via Malta to Bari in southern Italy, where we had a station under Air Vice-Marshal William Elliot, supporting the liaison mission under Brigadier Fitzroy Maclean, which was accredited to Tito's resistance movement in Yugoslavia. I returned to London on 11 October.

The war was now progressing satisfactorily in Europe, but our re-entry into the occupied countries involved much reorganization of our establishments and the setting up of new stations in the wake of our advancing armies. New offices, for instance, had to be opened in Vienna, Budapest, Sofia and Bucharest, and suitable persons found to man them. In this process of reorganization we had to work in close touch with SOE in order to avoid confusion through the crossing of lines. These activities kept me busy in London with administrative work, so that I had no further occasion for travel abroad.

A delicate problem which had to be tackled early in 1945 was our relationship with the Russian Intelligence Service and our future operations in that country. This of course involved close liaison with the Foreign Office. Unfortunately we were then unaware that we had a traitor in our midst, the notorious 'Kim' Philby. I did not have any occasion to deal with him personally, though I was well acquainted with his father, the Arabian explorer. He also was an eccentric character; after deserting his English wife, he became a Moslem and married a Moslem woman, perhaps to ingratiate himself with his Arab friends.

The Germans finally surrendered on 7 May, 1945, and the Japanese three months later, but the aftermath of the war involved the secret services in a vast amount of administrative work. Our agents all over the world had to be paid off and suitably rewarded, the office records had to be brought up to date, and fresh foundations had to be laid for the continuation of intelligence work abroad under peacetime conditions. On 16 October I arranged with Stewart Menzies that my service with him could be terminated, and on 10 November I finally said goodbye to my friends at Broadway.

Ian Fleming

The people behind Bond were powerful people. Bond didn't like attempts to squash him or his service.

Dr No

As an aspiring journalist Fleming visited Moscow in 1933 for Reuters and pulled off an impressive coup: he was the first reporter to telephone London and dictate an account of the outcome of the famous Vickers trial at which several Britons, including Allan Monkhouse, were convicted of espionage and sabotage.

Fleming had originally hoped to join the diplomatic service but his examination results were so disappointing, despite his having studied languages at Munich University and Geneva, that he joined Reuters. His scoop in Moscow led to an offer of correspondent in the Far East but instead he took a better paid job with a firm of merchant bankers, and later switched to stockbroking. Fleming's move from the City to Admiral John Godfrey's staff as personal assistant in the Naval Intelligence Division was gradual at first, with him initially spending just three afternoons a week at the Admiralty, and brought him into daily contact with SIS, where in 1941 he routinely met Philip Johns to exchange information. According to Merlin Minshall, an eccentric Naval Intelligence officer who participated in the failed Iron Gates sabotage in Romania, Fleming played a part in the operation by supervising the London end of the project that was to be such an embarrassment to Section D. Later in the war Fleming accompanied Admiral Godfrey to the United States and for a time he was a frequent visitor to the headquarters of British Security Co-ordination in the Rockefeller Center on Fifth Avenue.

The question of the extent to which he drew on his own experiences to develop the character of James Bond is uncertain. Some contend that Dusko Popov was a model, for the playboy Yugoslav was certainly very attractive to women, in spite of his hunchback. There have been other candidates too, including Conrad O'Brien-ffrench with whom he skied before the war in the Austrian alpine resort of Kitzbühel, but no one has answered this conundrum with any authority; it may well be that there was no single model, and Fleming simply relied upon his imagination. However, there was an occasion when Fleming stayed in neutral Lisbon while en route to the United States, and it is widely believed that the spectacle of Axis spies and diplomats playing roulette alongside their Allied counterparts may have inspired some of the scenes for his first Bond novel, *Casino Royale*, which he completed in 1952.

Certainly Fleming incorporated much of the wartime SIS into the Bond series. His M was of course C, Sir Stewart Menzies, and Miss Moneypenny was a more glamorous version of Menzies' real secretary, Miss Pettigrew. In *Dr No* he referred to the Passport Control Officer as the local SIS representative, a cover that had only recently been discarded in favour of 'Visa Officer', and described the red light that glowed outside the chief's office when he was not to be disturbed. As for the name Bond, most likely it originated with the author of the standard ornithological work on Jamaica, where Fleming built a home.

Fleming died in 1964 aged fifty-six, at the height of his fame, having published thirteen Bond thrillers. In this passage from his first Bond book Fleming describes how his hero prepares to beat Le Chiffre at baccarat, the scene supposedly inspired by Fleming's wartime visit to the Lisbon casino.

Casino Royale

Le Chiffre looked incuriously at him, the whites of his eyes, which showed all round the irises, lending something impassive and doll-like to his gaze.

He slowly removed one thick hand from the table and slipped it into the pocket of his dinner-jacket. The hand came out holding a small metal cylinder with a cap which Le Chiffre unscrewed. He inserted the nozzle of the cylinder, with an obscene deliberation, twice into each black nostril in turn, and luxuriously inhaled the benzedrine vapour.

Unhurriedly he pocketed the inhaler, then his hand came quickly back above the level of the table and gave the shoe its usual hard, sharp slap.

During this offensive pantomime Bond had coldly held the banker's gaze, taking in the wide expanse of white face surmounted by the short abrupt cliff of reddish-brown hair, the unsmiling wet red mouth and the impressive width of the shoulders, loosely draped in a massively cut dinner-jacket.

But for the high-lights on the satin of the shawl-cut lapels, he might have been faced by the thick bust of a black-fleeced Minotaur rising out of a green grass field.

Bond slipped a packet of notes on to the table without counting them. If he lost, the croupier would extract what was necessary to cover the bet, but the easy gesture conveyed that Bond didn't expect to lose and that this was only a token display from the deep funds at Bond's disposal.

The other players sensed a tension between the two gamblers and there was silence as Le Chiffre fingered the four cards out of the shoe.

The croupier slipped Bond's two cards across to him with the tip of his spatula. Bond, still with his eyes holding Le Chiffre's, reached his right hand out a few inches, glanced down very swiftly, then as he looked up again impassively at Le Chiffre, with a disdainful gesture he tossed the cards face upwards on the table.

They were a four and a five – an unbeatable nine.

There was a little gasp of envy from the table and the players to the left of Bond exchanged rueful glances at their failure to accept the two million franc bet.

With the hint of a shrug, Le Chiffre slowly faced his own two cards and flicked them away with his finger nail. They were two valueless knaves.

'Le baccarat,' intoned the croupier as he spaded the thick chips over the table to Bond.

Bond slipped them into his right-hand pocket with the unused packet of notes. His face showed no emotion, but he was pleased with the success of his first coup and with the outcome of the silent clash of wills across the table.

The woman on his left, the American Mrs Du Pont, turned to him with a wry smile.

'I shouldn't have let it come to you,' she said. 'Directly the cards were dealt I kicked myself.'

'It's only the beginning of the game,' said Bond. 'You may be right the next time you pass it.'

Mr Du Pont leant forward from the other side of his wife: 'If one could be right every hand, none of us would be here,' he said philosophically.

'I would be,' his wife laughed. 'You don't think I do this for pleasure.'

As the game went on, Bond looked over the spectators leaning on the high brass rail round the table. He soon saw Le Chiffre's two gunmen. They stood behind and to either side of the banker. They looked respectable enough, but not sufficiently a part of the game to be unobtrusive.

The one more or less behind Le Chiffre's right arm was tall and funereal in his dinner-jacket. His face was wooden and grey, but his eyes flickered and gleamed like a conjurer's. His whole long body was restless and his hands shifted often on the brass rail. Bond guessed that he would kill without interest or concern for what he killed and that he would prefer strangling. He had something of Lennie in *Of Mice and Men*, but his inhumanity would not come from infantilism but from drugs. Marihuana, decided Bond.

The other man looked like a Corsican shopkeeper. He was short and very dark with a flat head covered with thickly greased hair. He seemed to be a cripple. A chunky malacca cane with a rubber tip hung on the rail beside him. He must have had permission to bring the cane into the Casino with him, reflected Bond, who knew that neither sticks nor any other objects were allowed in the rooms as a precaution against acts of violence. He looked sleek and well fed. His mouth hung vacantly half-open and revealed very bad teeth. He wore a heavy black moustache and the backs of his hands on the rail were matted with black hair. Bond guessed that hair covered most of his squat body. Naked, Bond supposed, he would be an obscene object.

The game continued uneventfully, but with a slight bias against the bank.

The third coup is the 'sound barrier' at chemin-de-fer and baccarat. Your luck can defeat the first and second tests, but when the third deal comes along it most often spells disaster. Again and again at this point you find yourself being bounced back to earth. It was like that now. Neither the bank nor any of the players seemed to be able to get hot. But there was a steady and inexorable seepage against the bank, amounting after about two hours' play to ten million francs. Bond had no idea what profits Le Chiffre had made over the past two days. He estimated them at five million and guessed that now the banker's capital could not be more than twenty million.

In fact, Le Chiffre had lost heavily all that afternoon. At this moment he only had ten million left.

Bond, on the other hand, by one o'clock in the morning, had won four million, bringing his resources up to twenty-eight million.

Bond was cautiously pleased. Le Chiffre showed no trace of emotion. He continued to play like an automaton, never speaking except when he gave instructions in a low aside to the croupier at the opening of each new bank.

Outside the pool of silence round the high table, there was the constant hum of the other tables, chemin-de-fer, roulette and trente-et-quarante, interspersed with the clear calls of the croupiers and occasional bursts of laughter or gasps of excitement from different corners of the huge salle.

In the background there thudded always the hidden metronome of the Casino, ticking up its little treasure of one-per-cents with each spin of a wheel and each turn of a card – a pulsing fat-cat with a zero for a heart.

It was at ten minutes past one by Bond's watch when, at the high table, the whole pattern of play suddenly altered.

The Greek at Number 1 was still having a bad time. He had lost the first coup of half a million francs and the second. He passed the third time, leaving a bank of two million. Carmel Delane at Number 2 refused it. So did Lady Danvers at Number 3.

The Du Ponts looked at each other.

'Banco,' said Mrs Du Pont, and promptly lost to the banker's natural eight.

'Un banco de quatre millions,' said the croupier.

'Banco,' said Bond, pushing out a wad of notes.

Again he fixed Le Chiffre with his eye. Again he gave only a cursory look at his two cards.

'No,' he said. He held a marginal five. The position was dangerous.

Le Chiffre turned up a knave and a four. He gave the shoe another slap. He drew a three.

'Sept à la banque,' said the croupier, 'et cinq,' he added as he tipped Bond's losing cards face upwards. He raked over Bond's money, extracted four million francs and returned the remainder to Bond.

'Un banco de huit millions.'

'Suivi,' said Bond.

And lost again, to a natural nine.

In two coups he had lost twelve million francs. By scraping the barrel, he had just sixteen million francs left, exactly the amount of the next banco.

Suddenly Bond felt the sweat on his palms. Like snow in sunshine his capital had melted. With the covetous deliberation of the winning gambler, Le Chiffre was tapping a light tattoo on the table with his right hand. Bond looked across into the eyes of murky basalt. They held an ironical question. 'Do you want the full treatment?' they seemed to ask.

'Suivi,' Bond said softly.

He took some notes and plaques out of his right-hand pocket and the entire stack of notes out of his left and pushed them forward. There was no hint in his movements that this would be his last stake.

Robert Cecil

The contest between Soviet intelligence and British counter-intelligence resembles – at least until the late 1950s – a football match between Manchester United and the Corinthian Casuals in the years of the decline of amateurism.

The Missing Dimension

For the last two years of the war Robert Cecil, a regular member of the Diplomatic Corps, was seconded to SIS to act as personal assistant to Sir Stewart Menzies. In the summer of 1943 he succeeded (Sir) Patrick Reilly as 'PA/CSS', his previous experience having been as assistant to Peter Loxley, the Private Secretary to the Permanent Under-Secretary, Sir Alexander Cadogan.

After the war Cecil worked in the American Department at the Foreign Office, with a desk in the same room as Donald Maclean, a trusted colleague whom he had known in Paris in 1939. After Maclean's defection Cecil was appointed his successor as head of the American Department. He was also acquainted with Anthony Blunt and Guy Burgess, and was therefore eminently qualified to write on the subject of secret intelligence.

After his retirement from the diplomatic service Cecil took an appointment at Reading University and subsequently published *The Myth of the Master Race* and *Hitler's Decision to Invade Russia*. He has also written on the subject of intelligence, his first contribution being 'The Cambridge Comintern', a chapter in *The Missing Dimension*, edited by Christopher Andrew and David Dilks. In February 1978 he wrote a damning critique of Philby's *My Silent War* for *The Times*, ably identifying several instances where the traitor had deliberately distorted history. In this passage from his 1988 biography of Donald Maclean, Cecil – ever sensitive to Alan, Donald's brother and his friend and former colleague – gives his version of the traitor's escape in May 1951 and the innocent part played by Goronwy Rees.

A Divided Life

Before Burgess finally left the Reform Club on 25th May, he tried to telephone to Goronwy Rees. Rees was spending the weekend at All Souls and the call was taken by his wife, who knew nothing of her husband's former association with Burgess and his spy ring. Burgess was therefore obliged to speak less frankly than he might have wished, but he did make it clear that he was about 'to do something which would surprise and shock many people', and that Goronwy would not see him again for some time. Goronwy, he concluded, would understand. Rees did indeed understand and, when he returned home on the evening of Sunday, 27th May and learned of this conversation, he telephoned to Blunt, who came to see him on the following day and tried to persuade him not to tell MI5:

> He was the Cambridge liberal conscience at its very best, reasonable, sensible and firm in the faith that personal relations are the highest of all human values.

Rees felt matters had gone too far; even the E. M. Forster syndrome failed to move him. When he got to see MI5, he learnt that not only Burgess, but also Maclean, was missing.

The accumulation of instances, in which everyone delayed just too long, has fuelled the supposition that these were not coincidental and that officialdom was reluctant to act in time. The actions of officialdom, however, represent only one side of the equation; on the other side,

Burgess had plenty of time to act and plenty of warning that he should do so. That he left everything so late and got away with it is completely in character. There is no need to resort to conspiracy theory in order to explain the sequence of events; nor at this remove in time is it useful to go on hunting for scapegoats. Maclean and Burgess slipped through a net that was, admittedly, full of holes; those who would like to live in a country where the nets catch all the 'moles' should go and live in the USSR or South Africa. Sometimes the price of liberty is eternal inefficiency.

Although Maclean was out of touch with all his fellow conspirators except Burgess, he was certainly well aware before seeing Burgess that his days were numbered; the end was in sight of the two careers that had twined themselves round his life to the point of suffocation. Latterly his access to top-secret reports had been restricted; he was still receiving the normal distribution of telegrams and printed despatches sent daily to all heads of Departments and above; but boxes requiring special keys were withheld. Maclean had not been a spy for fifteen years without developing very fine antennae; he would have read the signs. If any confirmation were needed, this was provided when he became aware that, at least in London, he was being shadowed. His low spirits did not inhibit him on one occasion from playing a game with his pursuer. One of the few Under-Secretaries who was in the know recalls crossing St James's Park after lunch on a warm spring afternoon and being surprised to see Maclean following a diagonal course at great speed. This focused his attention on the spectacle of another man, with much shorter legs, moving at a similar speed, but at a fixed distance. It may have been in order to upset his 'watchers' that Maclean sometimes varied his routine by travelling to Victoria, instead of to Charing Cross. On two or three occasions when he did so, he encountered a fellow commuter in the person of Fred Everson (Sir Frederick), who had been his colleague in better days in Washington. The latter recalls:

> I was struck by Donald's shabby dress and moroseness. He wore an untidy, worn, brownish tweed coat and a crumpled trilby hat, when we were wearing Anthony Eden homburgs. He walked, untalkative, with his hands thrust deep into the coat pockets and his shoulders hunched.

Whilst Burgess dithered and delayed, Maclean tried to carry on at the office, as if no disaster impended. It must have consoled him to observe that none of those with whom he had regular dealings were treating him in an unusual manner; indeed none of us in the American Department was aware that anything was amiss. The sound reputation that he had built up in earlier years stood him in good stead. One Under-Secretary, when told that a former colleague of Washington days was about to be called in and accused of espionage, leaped to the conclusion that the suspect must be Paul Gore-Booth (the late Lord Gore-Booth). This distinguished public servant was regarded as something of an eccentric, partly because he was a strict Christian Scientist and partly because he was the nephew of Constance Markievicz, who had been sentenced to death, but reprieved, after the Easter Rising in Dublin. This association seemed to make him a more likely black sheep than the son of a former Cabinet Minister. By a curious coincidence, Gore-Booth, whilst he was serving with Maclean in the Washington Embassy, had also visited New York, where his wife gave birth to twins.

In the last, miserable week an old friend from Cairo days, Michael Maude, came back to London. At first he had difficulty in getting Maclean to return his calls, but on 22nd May they met for lunch in the Sloane Square area. Maude found his friend looking ill and unhappy, and asked if anything were wrong. Maclean replied that the Foreign Office were insisting on his having another examination at the hands of the Treasury doctor. Maude did not pursue the point, but wondered if Maclean were facing the end of his career; it was a correct diagnosis, though not in the way he thought. Three days later came Donald's thirty-eighth birthday. Either that morning or, more likely, on the previous evening, word reached him that the day of departure had come at last. He said nothing to Melinda, who was preparing a special birthday supper for his return that evening. The only other celebration was to be lunch with Robin and Mary Campbell and he decided to stick to their plan; any change might have excited questions.

For Donald Maclean that Friday was to be the longest day; he began it unusually early and was in his office by 9.15. Next door was the office of the Assistant Labour Adviser, Frederick Mason (Sir Frederick), who walked into his room with a telegram just received from Ciudad Trujillo: a prominent trade unionist in the dictator-ridden Dominican Republic had disappeared and was believed to have been kidnapped. Maclean spared it a languid glance; it was his own disappearance that was on his mind. Soon after noon Mary Campbell, driving her jeep, collected him in the cobbled courtyard of the Foreign Office. She noticed at once that he was in good spirits; the recognised sign of this was that the brim of his hat was turned up all round. He was wearing a jaunty and very unproletarian bow-tie. Some years later, when Mary Campbell was able to write to him in Moscow, she asked him whether, when they met that day, he had already known that it was the day of his final departure. Yes, came back the answer: he had known.

It is easy to understand how his spirits had risen, as soon as he knew the die was cast: after the long period of suspense the very thought that the time for action had come must have been a stimulant. His Russian friends were living up to the confidence he had long ago placed in them; on the far side of what the capitalists foolishly called the Iron Curtain he would be recompensed for his secret years of service to the cause. There he could at last lead an honest life and put behind him the precarious deceits and furtive meetings. Above all, he would not now have to face his inquisitors and the pressure to give away the names of those who had shared his clandestine struggle. No half-promises of leniency, if he co-operated, followed by renewed pressure to tell all. He could not have stood up to all that: he was too tired.

So he gave Mary his tired, but grateful, smile and she took him first to Wheelers, off St James's Square, for oysters and a half-bottle of champagne. They talked about Melinda's baby and he promised that, when she went into hospital, he would come and stay with the Campbells at Stokke. It was a 'dutch' party and, by the time Maclean had paid his share, he was out of cash; he went across Pall Mall to the Travellers' Club and cashed a cheque for £5, which in those days was the permitted maximum. They then went to Bertorelli's in Soho to meet Robin Campbell and eat the rest of their lunch. On the way they ran into Connolly and some of his friends. Donald, he thought, was

> looking rather creased and yellow, casual but diffident . . . He seemed calm and genial, and went off gaily to continue the luncheon with his friends.

By this time it was late and a certain amount of drink had been consumed. For some reason Maclean, instead of going straight back to the office, telephoned to Geoffrey Jackson, who was in charge of the Latin American section, during my absence on leave. It was, according to Jackson, a rather incoherent conversation on a bad line:

> Would I hold the fort? There followed a rather garbled explanation of meeting his sister-in-law, due at Tilbury from abroad.

Evidently Maclean was covering his tracks and accounting for his absence on the following morning, since at that date Saturday in Whitehall was a regular half-day. He did not speak again to Jackson, but he returned to the office in time to receive the visit of the Argentine Minister-Counsellor and record, with his usual accuracy, Señor Leguizamon's communication about Anglo-Argentine trade negotiations. He also signed a clear, concise letter to Sir Nevile Butler, the Ambassador at Rio de Janeiro. He had missed his usual train – the 5.19 from Charing Cross; it was about six o'clock when he put his head round the door of John Curle's room: 'I shan't be in tomorrow morning.' That's my final word, he must have thought, but it was not so. In the courtyard he unexpectedly ran into Makins (Lord Sherfield), who was also leaving, and they exchanged a few casual remarks. Sherfield's main concern was to give Maclean no ground for suspicion; he was under the impression that watch was being kept at Tatsfield, as well as in London. Maclean decided to repeat the 'cover' story that he had already used with Jackson and said that on Saturday morning he would be meeting Harriet, whom Sherfield had known slightly in Washington. Sherfield has since said, 'There was nothing fishy about him. In any case, I knew he was being tailed.' Nonetheless he decided to go back into the Foreign Office and alert Carey-Foster; but both he and his secretary, who was also in the know, had gone home. Next morning, when MI5 met the usual train and failed to see Maclean, telephones began to ring and this episode came to light.

An ill-informed academic writer, embroidering a reference I have made elsewhere to this episode, accuses me of having implied that

> Lord Sherfield was, in the final analysis, responsible for Burgess and Maclean's defection, since if he had told Carey-Foster of Maclean's request, MI5 would have been alerted and steps taken to prevent Maclean from leaving England.

This is a false deduction and one that I have never made. Even if Lord Sherfield had known that Maclean was not under surveillance at Tatsfield, there was no warrant for detaining the fugitive; to have imposed restraints at ports and airports would have required the authority of the Home Secretary. This was, in fact, obtained in the late afternoon of Monday, 28th May; but by then, of course, the birds had flown.

The fate-lines of Maclean and Burgess, which since Cambridge days had been performing a dance – now nearer, now farther – were once more converging. Burgess had hired an Austin A40 and begun to pack; he slipped in the collected works of Jane Austen; as he said later to Tom Driberg, 'I never travel without it.' At Charing Cross, Maclean, duly observed by his 'watchers', had caught his later train; the temptation to wave them goodbye must have been very strong. Melinda had cooked a ham for his birthday supper and it was awaiting him on the dining-room table; but they had scarcely begun before Burgess drove through the open gates and insisted that, if they were to catch the boat, they must go at once. He was introduced to Melinda, who had a hazy recollection of having seen him somewhere before, as 'Roger Styles'. She was incensed by his sudden appearance and Donald's failure to tell her what had been planned; her supper grew cold. Maclean raced up the stairs to say goodnight to the boys, then he was gone. They shared the driving. Even in these days of dual carriageways it is a slow cross-country journey from Tatsfield to Southampton; Burgess had left barely enough time to reach the quayside before the *Falaise* sailed at midnight. 'We'll be back on Monday,' he shouted, as they ran out of the car-park.

Donald Maclean's thirty-eighth birthday was over. The elation of the morning would have given way to a state of exhaustion and confused reactions to the drama of this last day in England. As the ferry moved out into the Channel through the darkness, he was not just between two coastlines but between two worlds. The capitalist world, which he had so often condemned, would soon be behind him; the untried world of communism, for which he was bound, had not yet taken shape in the dark ahead. How much remained of his youthful enthusiasm for life under Stalin? He would not have been human if, when no turning back was possible, some doubt, and indeed self-doubt, had not assailed him.

Hugh Trevor-Roper

The faults of SIS were the faults of a particular organization, conditioned by particular circumstances. They were not the faults of bureaucracy in general, far less of society. They were the effect of secrecy, of insulation, of immunity, of immediate circumstance – and perhaps also of popular myth.

Hugh Trevor-Roper is one of those unusual individuals who has served in both MI5 and SIS. His initiation into the secret world took place when, at the beginning of the war, he left Oxford and joined the Radio Security Service, a little-known but vital offshoot of the Security Service. As well as monitoring the airwaves for illicit wireless transmissions, the RSS also fulfilled a vital crypto-graphic role, intercepting and decoding radio messages between German agents and their controllers. Following the RSS's success in decrypting enemy signals one section was transferred in 1941 from RSS to SIS's Section V, but Trevor-Roper's task remained the same, the study of the German intelligence service, the Abwehr, from a distance using intercepts.

At the end of hostilities Trevor-Roper travelled to Berlin to investigate Hitler's fate and his report formed the basis of his subsequent bestseller, *The Last Days of Hitler*. He also hoped to publish a biography of Admiral Canaris, the Abwehr's chief, but he was inhibited from doing so because his knowledge came from unavowable experience. However, he did contribute an article about Canaris to the *Cornhill Magazine* which was published in 1950. Trevor-Roper remained discreet on the subject of his wartime service until April 1968, when he wrote 'The Philby Affair' for *Encounter*, which led to the release of monographs on Philby and Canaris under the same title.

The publication of 'The Philby Affair' was a milestone, not least because of the author's candour about his own work for SIS, but also for his indiscreet reference to 'the breaking of the "Enigma" machine'. Although there had been an oblique comment, in another book about Philby, on GCHQ's success at reading the German Kriegsmarine's wireless signals, this was the first authoritative admission of SIS's 'accidental property in "most secret" sources'.

In his book Trevor-Roper denounced Graham Greene for having been Philby's apologist, attacked John Le Carré for his distorted view of SIS, and reminded Malcolm Muggeridge that 'no man was a more zealous and persistent defender of Philby against the "McCarthyite" suspicions of his critics'.

'Whether the British Secret Service was incompetent in wartime is a question, as Sir Thomas Browne would say, too sad to insist upon,' asserted Trevor-Roper, taking the role of SIS's defender. His remarks, however, were not appreciated universally.

The Philby Affair

What, then, is the real function of secret intelligence? I believe that it can be stated quite simply. Secret intelligence is the continuation of open intelligence by other means. So long as governments conceal a part of their activities, other governments, if they wish to base their policy on full and correct information, must seek to penetrate the veil. This inevitably entails varying methods. But however the means may vary, the end must be still the same. It is to complement the results of what, for convenience, we may call 'public' intelligence: that is, the intelligence derived from rational study of public or at least avowable sources. Intelligence, in fact, is indivisible. The greater part of it must always be acquired by open or official methods. Only a relatively small area requires secret penetration, or espionage. Nevertheless, that small area may be vital. Not all official secrets need protection; but some do. The date of a surprise military operation; the details of a vital technical process, the *arcana imperii* of any political system; the identity of an agent who can supply such facts; the list of the secret codes which are read – these are all secrets which are rightly protected by one side, and rightly sought out by the other, in the contests of international power politics, which do not cease because some literary men are virtuous. This struggle for secret intelligence is the central work of any secret service, and to say that it is unnecessary is absurd – provided that its limitations are always recognised. That is, secret intelligence must always be relevant to real political or military purposes; it must always be continuous with 'open' intelligence; and it must always be verifiable – for if it is not verifiable it is, in the strict sense of the word, worthless: it cannot be believed, or used.

These limitations, as it seems to me, are of cardinal importance. All of them emphasise the constant dependence of secret intelligence on public intelligence: in definition, in acquisition, in evaluation. Almost all the errors to which secret services, by their very nature, are liable can be traced to neglect of this essential condition. Instead of continuous pursuit of information from the public into the secret sector, they indulge in sporadic petty larceny within the secret sector only. They prize material because of its secrecy rather than because of its relevance or its inherent value. They test it, if at all, within their own secret world instead of within its general context, which is partly 'public'. A report is regarded as credible because a particular spy has been graded as 'reliable' by his employers, whereas credibility really depends not on the person but on the report: on its demonstrable coherence with its known or knowable context. Finally, this very insularity, to which secret services are naturally prone, tends to lower the intellectual level within them. A secret service which sees itself as a branch of the public service pursuing, though by different means, the same ends will serve a useful purpose. A secret service which, merely because of its secrecy, severs itself from the public service will soon shrink into an irrelevancy. For ultimately all information, however obtained, is subject to the same tests, nor is there any substitute for understanding and intelligence. In the 1930s the minutes of Hitler's secret conferences would have been invaluable. So, today, would be the central documents of Russian policy. Failing such scoops – the scoops obtained by a Sorge or a Penkovsky – more can be deduced by an intelligent study of public sources than by any number of 'reliable' but unintelligent 'agents' listening at keyholes or swopping drinks at bars.

Moreover, once secret intelligence is thus divorced from public intelligence and becomes irrelevant, it tends – naturally enough – to develop a momentum of its own. Agents pursuing unimportant intelligence run into incidental difficulties. They therefore need protection. In order to protect them, further resources are mobilised, new operations are undertaken, more useless information is sought. In the end, the original purpose of such agents may be forgotten in the maze of secondary developments. Agents become fully occupied in arcane local manoeuvres totally irrelevant to their proper function, and I have known occasions on which real 'hard' intelligence has been suppressed in order to protect agents who have never produced any 'hard' intelligence at all.

*

The British Secret Service of the 1930s exhibited many of these defects. It was not a rational extension of an efficient bureaucracy of information. Perhaps it never had been. When it was set up, before the First World War, it had not been intended as such. It had been a piece of machinery designed passively to receive, rather than actively to collect, such intelligence as the friends of Britain, in foreign countries, might wish secretly to impart. For that purpose, its funds were very limited; and although the First World War saw a great temporary expansion of its activities, its basis remained always the same. Novels of clubland heroes might have given it a factitious lustre, but essentially it remained an amateur organisation with a slender budget, dependent often on voluntary assistance. As such, it no doubt performed its limited role well enough. But when it ventured outside those limits, it succumbed too easily to the inherent risks of all secret societies. It became divorced from the 'public' bureaucracy; being recruited by patronage, it acquired some of the character of a coterie; and it preserved, as such coteries easily do, outmoded habits of thought.

Recruitment by patronage is not in itself necessarily bad: it depends on the patrons. Nor are ancient traditions to be despised, provided they can incorporate new ideas. Unfortunately, after 1918, the patronage of SIS was not very intelligent, nor were new ideas very popular in it. Moreover, it seemed to look in one direction only. The main threat to British interests, in those years of unchallenged military victory, seemed to come not from other territorial powers, which were either safely allied or safely defeated, but from the pervasive international movement of revolutionary communism. Therefore the rulers of SIS seem to have concentrated their forces against this enemy – without, however, making much effort to understand its true character and ideological motivation.

The weakness of SIS in the 1920s is well illustrated by what seemed at the time its most spectacular scoop: its acquisition of the famous Zinoviev Letter of 1924. This document is now recognised to have been a forgery handed to a gullible SIS by White Russian *émigrés* in Berlin. The whole history of this episode painfully illustrates the errors which I have listed above. Particularly pitiful is the letter which Admiral Sir Hugh Sinclair, then 'C', sent to Sir Eyre Crowe reporting his 'check' on the authenticity of the letter. It amounts simply to this: our man in Riga (which was not then in the Soviet Union) says that he knows of a conversation between Chicherin and Zinoviev which proves the letter to be genuine. That so contemptible a snippet of unverifiable gossip from an unidentified and distant source – and Riga was notoriously the factory of anti-Soviet propaganda and fiction – should have been sent, as authoritative proof of fact, by the Head of the Secret Service to the Permanent Under-Secretary of the Foreign Office, shows that SIS, under Admiral Sinclair, had lost all contact with rational methods. In the one field of activity on which it had concentrated its expertise, and whose importance it regarded as paramount, it was simply the willing dupe of *émigré* forgers.

The Secret Service of 1941, which I knew, seems hardly to have differed from that of 1924, whose character I deduce. It was still, basically, the service of Admiral Sinclair, who had died in 1939, and whose old subordinates now ruled it, in uneasy combination. It was still directed against international communism, which it still misunderstood. It had not yet adjusted itself to a war against fascism, which it also misunderstood. Its permanent officers were drawn largely from two classes of men. There were the metropolitan young gentlemen whose education had been expensive rather than profound and who were recruited at the bars of White's and Boodle's by Colonel Dansey, and there were the ex-Indian policemen who were recruited, through the Central Intelligence Bureau in New Delhi, by Colonel Vivian. The former ran the espionage, the latter the counter-espionage. Neither class had much use for ideas. The former had seldom heard of them (Colonel Dansey, we have seen, did not approve of university men); the latter regarded them as subversive. In view of the rise of the new ideologies in the 1930s this was perhaps unfortunate. I doubt if there was one man among the professionals of SIS, at that time, who had read *Mein Kampf*, or more than one who had read any of the works of Karl Marx.

Colonel Dansey and Colonel Vivian, *ACSS* (or was it *VCSS*?) and *DCSS* – what old frustrations they recall to mind! All through the war these were the grandees of our Service, the Aaron and Hur who, from right and left (but with eyes steadily averted from each other), held up the labouring hands of our Moses, *CSS* or 'C', Sir Stewart Menzies. How we used to sympathize with Menzies! He held a most invidious position, responsible to an exacting Prime Minister. And yet where could he lean for support? At the beginning of the war, Colonel Dansey's 'agents' in Europe were mopped up and swept away, and in a public speech (of which the text was kept secret even within SIS), Himmler named all the chief officers of SIS, from 'C' downwards. As the progress of the war left it further and further behind, 'C''s whole empire was racked by internal tensions. The Foreign Office sought to sustain him by inserting an adviser from the rational world. The adviser – a grave Wykehamist, now an ambassador – was driven to distraction by what he found and uttered the most un-Wykehamist sentiments. When I looked coolly at the world in which I found myself, I sometimes thought that, if this was our intelligence system, we were doomed to defeat. Sometimes I encouraged myself by saying that such an organisation could not possibly survive, unchanged, the strain of war: it would have to be reformed. In fact I was wrong both times. We won the war; and SIS, at the end of it, remained totally unreformed.

Fred Winterbotham

It is characteristic of the British that when a situation grows really serious, deadly calm prevails.

The Ultra Spy

During the Great War Winterbotham served as a fighter pilot in the Royal Flying Corps, and in July 1917 was shot down over the German trenches in France and taken prisoner, to be released only in January 1919. Upon his return to England he went up to Christ Church, Oxford, where he was coached in tennis by John Masterman. After university he tried farming but when this venture failed he was persuaded, in January 1930, to join SIS and head its new Air Section set up to liaise closely with several of his old colleagues in the Air Ministry's tiny intelligence branch. During the next eight years he made numerous visits to Germany, often piloting himself, recruiting sources and making clandestine photographic reconnaissance flights over sensitive airfields.

After the outbreak of war Winterbotham's section took over responsibility for the secure distribution of the signals intelligence product that, in 1941, was to become known as Ultra. His task was to ensure summaries of the decrypts were conveyed from Bletchley Park to selected military commanders using a dedicated communications channel of specially indoctrinated liaison officers equipped with one-time pads and the latest cryptographic technology. These three-man teams, discreetly attached to individual theatre staffs, were known as Special Liaison Units, but very few outsiders knew their true function.

Winterbotham's achievement in obtaining inter-service co-operation at Bletchley Park was not without its pitfalls. The Director of Naval Intelligence, for one, proved awkward to deal with, for which Winterbotham blamed the DNI's assistant, Ian Fleming. But if he was critical of Fleming, he was full of praise for the colleague he described as his 'scientific assistant', R. V. Jones.

The security surrounding the Allied codebreakers was such that no word of the success they achieved leaked until an American journalist, Anthony Cave Brown, discovered in 1972 that Bletchley's boffins had accomplished far more than had hitherto been suspected or hinted at. Only a relative handful of the ten thousand employed by GCHQ gained an overall view of Ultra's astonishing scope and one of those was Winterbotham who, when challenged by Cave Brown to disclose what he knew, approached the authorities for permission to publish his own recollections.

Winterbotham had at this stage already, in 1969, published a suitably sanitized account of his experiences, *Secret and Personal*, which carefully omitted any reference to Ultra. His announcement that he proposed to release a comprehensive version of Bletchley's work, to pre-empt Cave Brown, was greeted with dismay in Whitehall but the decision was taken not to place any legal obstacle in his path; or, in the words of Admiral Farnhill, then Secretary of the D-Notice Committee, 'that objections to publication on the grounds of security were not sufficient to warrant his advice that publication would contravene D-Notices'.

Winterbotham's authoritative revelation that much of the enemy's cipher traffic had been intercepted and decrypted astonished the public and led to a dramatic revision of previously published histories, particularly those of the great military strategists like Field Marshal Montgomery and General Eisenhower whose own memoirs had neglected to mention the 'most secret source' of intelligence they had relied upon. Understandably, SIS was especially anxious about Winterbotham's breach of security, even though he had returned to civilian life in 1945. Certainly the organization was aware of every stage of the book's production process for his editor was herself closely connected to SIS, her sister being married to one of SIS's senior directors.

The publication of *The Ultra Secret* eventually forced the government to agree to the release of relevant material to the Public Record Office and led to a radical reappraisal of the Allied prosecution of the war. It also made the author deeply unpopular with his former colleagues, especially those he had himself reprimanded for minor breaches of wartime security. Winterbotham shrugged off the criticism and went on to publish two further volumes of memoirs, *The Nazi Connection* and his last, *The Ultra Spy*.

Winterbotham died in January 1990 shortly after the publication of his last autobiography, and although his text was bound to contain inaccuracies, because he was unable to study the original working papers at GCHQ, he did open the way for scholars to reassess the history of the Second World War with greater depth than had been possible previously.

The Ultra Secret

To be Chief of the Secret Service, a post which by long tradition had been a gift of the Monarch, was, of course, a plum job. In recent years it had been a perquisite of the Navy and now [1940] the admirals were lining up. However, Colonel Stewart Menzies had other ideas. I had worked with Stewart as a colleague for the past nine years and I think all of us in the office were anxious that he should take over rather than that we should have a new broom at this critical stage. Our only misgivings were whether he carried the weight to hold on to his chair. He had been educated at Eton, and, like so many sons of wealthy parents, he had gone into the Household Cavalry. He won the DSO and served on Haig's staff during World War I. He was a member of the exclusive White's Club and had personal contacts with the highest in the land. He was a Scot, he had a ready smile and the assurance which had come down with the profit from the millions of gallons of whisky distilled by his ancestors. His family owned the lovely Dorchester House set on an island in Park Lane, soon to become the great yellow-white edifice of the hotel, and, back in my own home county of Gloucestershire, his family estate sat quietly in secluded elegance next to that of the Duke of Beaufort. He wouldn't give in easily and, by the end of 1939, realization that something very big might come out of the Enigma cypher operation made him doubly determined to hold on. He had kept his word and personally informed me of the progress being made. But there were tremendous problems to be overcome.

In September 1939 the SIS were also evacuated to Bletchley Park, some fifty miles north of London near the main road and railway to the north-west. It was one of those large and rather ornate houses of red brick with timbered gables in the prosperous late Victorian style, probably built by one of the wealthy owners of the many brickworks which abound in this rich clay area. There must have been twenty or more rooms in the house, which was a long two-storey building, entered through a pretentious porch. There were spacious green lawns with the regulation cedar trees, a croquet lawn and a ha-ha, a sunken boundary fence that was invisible from the house and gave the idea of unbroken space. This was a favourite place later on to sit and eat one's sandwich lunch.

Bletchley was only a small town. It was not beautiful; five miles away was Woburn Park and Abbey where the Duke of Bedford lived. A number of wooden huts had been erected on the wide lawns at Bletchley and it was in Hut No. 3 that I and my small staff set up office. We lived, however, in billets in the surrounding country, and it was in another big house, which belonged to a man who owned a near-by glucose factory, that I found I had a number of backroom boys as fellow boarders. They were a cheerful lot, even if the conversation was at times well over the top of my head. I had known several of them when we all worked in the same building in London. Between them there was little they did not know about cyphers, and now that we had actually got one of Hitler's latest Enigma cypher machines, it was possible to understand with some accuracy its function and complexity. Enigma, the ancient Greek word for a puzzle, was certainly a good name for it. We could now at least get the machine accurately duplicated.

In the absence of a grey-stone quadrangle of an old university college, what remained of the green tree-studded lawns of the English country house was as good a place as any for the assembly of a pride of intellectual lions. There had come to Bletchley some of the most distinguished mathematicians of the day. Alexander, Babbage, Milner Barry, Gordon Welchman, names to whisper in the world of chess. They had been persuaded by Denniston to leave their comfortable universities and join with our own backroom boys to try to prove or disprove the theory that if a man could design a machine to create a mathematical problem, then man could equally well design a machine to solve it.

It was, I think, generally accepted that of our own backroom boys 'Dilly' Knox was the mastermind behind the Enigma affair. He was quite young, tall, with a rather gangling figure, unruly black hair, his eyes, behind glasses, some miles away in thought. Like Mitchell, the designer of the Spitfire fighter aeroplane which tipped the scales in our favour during the Battle of Britain, who worked himself to his death at the moment of his triumph, Knox too, knowing he was a sick man, pushed himself to the utmost to overcome the problems of Enigma variations (introduced by the Germans to further complicate their cyphers between 1940 and 1942). He, too, died with his job completed. J. H. Tiltman, another brilliant brain, had been borrowed from the Army. He was tall and dark with a short, clipped, military moustache, and his regimental tartan trousers eventually gave way to green corduroy slacks which were thought slightly way out in 1939. Oliver Strachey was an individualist, tall though a little stooped, with greying hair, broad forehead; his eyes, behind his glasses, always had a smile in them, as if he found life intensely amusing, except when our billetor used to stand at the foot of the stairs on Saturday mornings collecting our cheques. Oliver was also extremely musical. I believe he played several instruments, but he most enjoyed playing duets with Benjamin Britten on the grand piano in his rather untidy London flat.

Then there was 'Josh' Cooper whom I saw fairly often, as he was primarily concerned with Air Force matters. He was another brilliant mathematician. Still in his thirties, he had to use powerful glasses which often seemed to get in the way of his straight black hair. Dick Pritchard, young, tall, clean-shaven, rather round of face, with a quiet voice, could talk on any subject with witty penetration. He, too, was deeply musical. It struck me at the time how often the art of undoing other people's cyphers was closely allied to a brain which could excel both in mathematics and music. It was rather frightening playing one's evening bridge with these men. It all came easily to them and the conversation was ever interesting. I could well have spent longer in our country retreat than I did, but it soon became apparent that the phoney war would last over the winter of 1939–40, so I took my small staff back to London in order to be near the Air Ministry. I missed the professorial atmosphere of Bletchley.

It is no longer a secret that the backroom boys of Bletchley used the new science of electronics to help them solve the puzzle of Enigma. I am not of the computer age nor do I attempt to understand them, but early in 1940 I was ushered with great solemnity to the shrine where stood a bronze-coloured column surmounted by a larger circular bronze-coloured face, like some Eastern Goddess who was destined to become the oracle of Bletchley, at least when she felt like it. She was an awesome piece of magic. We were, of course, all wondering whether the great experiment could really become operational, and if so, would it be in time for the hot war which we now felt was bound to break out in the spring? Hitler had given us six months' respite. Each day had, I think, been used to the full by every branch of the nation's defences. We all knew it was too little, too late, but at least in this one vital concept the possibilities were prodigiously exciting, for we had in our hands the very encyphering machine the Germans would be using in their wartime communications.

It must have been about the end of February 1940 that the Luftwaffe, the German Air Force, had evidently received enough Enigma machines to train their operators sufficiently well for them to start putting some practice messages on the air. The signals were quite short but must have contained the ingredients the bronze goddess had been waiting for. Menzies had given instructions that any successful results were to be sent immediately to him, and it was just as the bitter cold days of that frozen winter were giving way to the first days of April sunshine that the oracle of Bletchley spoke and Menzies handed me four little slips of paper, each with a short Luftwaffe message dealing with personnel postings to units. From the Intelligence point of view they were of little value, except as a small bit of administrative inventory, but to the backroom boys at Bletchley Park and to Menzies, and indeed to me, they were like the magic in the pot of gold at the end of the rainbow.

The miracle had arrived.

Valentine Williams

Secret service has been called 'the game without rules'. The phrase is misleading. There are unwritten laws in Intelligence work which all permanent agents respect.

The eldest son of the chief editor at Reuters, Valentine Williams was to make his reputation as a journalist before turning to writing thrillers. He went to Berlin first as a correspondent for his father's news agency and then to Paris for the *Daily Mail*. He covered the 1910 revolution in Portugal and was in the Balkans when the Great War broke out in 1914. In March 1915 he was accredited to GHQ in Flanders but joined the Irish Guards in December of that year and later won the Military Cross. Two books of non-fiction documented his experiences: *With Our Army in Flanders* and *Adventures of an Ensign*.

After the war Williams travelled the world to file reports from among other events the Versailles peace conference and the expedition that discovered the tomb of King Tutankhamen. Numerous assignments in America and North Africa followed, but his fame was achieved as the author of such classics as *The Man with the Clubfoot, The Secret Hand, The Return of Clubfoot* and *The Three of Clubs*. Aged fifty-six when Hitler invaded Poland, Williams was too old for military service so he joined SIS where he checked the credentials of new recruits. One of the aspiring intelligence officers he interviewed was Malcolm Muggeridge who had worked with Valentine's younger brother Douglas on the *Daily Telegraph*. Muggeridge later recalled the encounter in which 'Williams spoke darkly of the dangers involved in a service in which, by the nature of the case, a blown agent had to be discarded.' Williams's gloomy strictures failed to deter Muggeridge who subsequently 'disappeared into the limbo of MI6, the wartime version of the Secret Service'. In his autobiography Kim Philby recalls a visit to the secret propaganda centre at Woburn Abbey accompanied by Williams who lunched well and slept for the entire drive back to London in SIS's Rolls-Royce.

In 1941 Williams was transferred to the British embassy in Washington DC but soon afterwards he moved to Hollywood to work as a scriptwriter. He wrote screenplays for 20th Century-Fox and Metro-Goldwyn-Mayer for the remainder of the war, and published two further novels, *Courier to Marrakesh* in 1945 and *Skeleton Out of the Cupboard*, which was released the following year, shortly before his death in November 1946.

In his autobiography *The World of Action*, published in April 1938, Williams recalls his friendship with Captain Smith-Cumming.

The World of Action

A small service I was able to render 'C' in the early days of the [1914–18] War, when I put him on his guard against a certain individual, not a British subject, who I knew to be a thorough-paced scamp, started a friendship between us that lasted to the day, almost to the hour, indeed, of his death. I never worked for him and he gave no secrets away to me; but he told me many stories of secret service, including one or two of his own adventures in the days before the War. Once he showed me a photograph of a heavily-built German-looking individual in most unmistakably German clothes and was entranced when I failed to recognise the party in question – it was himself, disguised for the purposes of a certain delicate mission he once undertook on the Continent before the War. He never had much use for what he called 'crepe hair and grease paint' in secret service work: but on this occasion, he informed me apologetically, disguise was indispensable. 'C' was always very friendly to me, and when I went out to France to join the Irish Guards on active service he presented me with a splendid 16-magnification Ross telescope which to this day is one of my most cherished possessions.

I used to go and chat with him at his war-time headquarters situated in the attics of a block of residential flats near Charing Cross. A private lift shot the caller up seven floors to a regular maze of passages, and steps, and oddly shaped rooms. No casual visitor ever penetrated here. The liftman was of the service, too: the organisation had its own arrangements whereby ordinary inquirers were interviewed and thoroughly 'vetted' before being admitted to the labyrinth under the roof.

The first thing to meet the eye on entering the Chief's room was a picture representing a group of French villagers facing a Prussian firing squad in the war of 1870 – a sort of 'Memento mori' in that setting. There was nothing dramatic or mysterious about the quiet study with its small windows high above the London chimney pots and the Thames, rolling along its 'liquid history', as John Burns once called it, far below. A plain work-table, a big safe, some maps and charts on the walls, a vase of flowers, one or two seascapes recalling 'C's' passion for sailing and inevitably, scattered about, various examples of the mechanical gadgets in which he revelled with boyish enthusiasm – a patent compass, a new sort of electric clock.

Forthright and four-square as the Tower of London, he would confront me. A breath of the sea, which he abandoned with infinite regret to take on this shore job, seemed yet to cling to this bluff, brawny Englishman, no longer young when, long awaited, '*der Tag*' broke thunderously to test the organisation so patiently, so skilfully built up.

A Roman head, bald of cranium with greying hair close-cropped at the sides, strapping shoulders filling the undress naval jacket, eyes as grey as the North Sea to which they had for years been constantly turned, a jutting, imperious nose, a massive chin. Lines about the rather grim mouth, the ring of authority in the voice, spoke of habits of iron discipline acquired in boyhood. But asked to name the salient characteristic of this extraordinary man, one would say his gentleness.

R. V. Jones

Gentlemanly behaviour can put any who practise it in intelligence at a disadvantage.

Reflections on Intelligence

Whereas most of the academics drafted into SIS during the Second World War were to concentrate on exploiting flaws in the enemy's cryptographic system, R. V. Jones was recruited with the specific purpose of advising the organization on developments in the scientific field. Of particular concern was Germany's progress in radar, proximity fuses and aircraft guidance devices.

One of Jones's first tasks was to study an apparent windfall from Norway, the anonymous gift of technical data which purported to describe the enemy's latest work on fuses, acoustic torpedoes, aircraft navigation aids and bomber production. While SIS was initially inclined to dismiss the document, which was to become known as the Oslo Report, as a crude exercise in disinformation, Jones undertook some practical experiments and concluded the information was largely authentic.

Jones's achievement in recognizing the Oslo Report as a genuine attempt to alert the Allies to German scientific advances enhanced his status in an organization that traditionally was suspicious of anyone manifesting technical skills. Indeed, until he joined SIS, the service possessed only one officer with a university background who had studied a scientific subject: Eric Walsh. Later Jones was to play a key role in devising counter-measures for German scientific breakthroughs: he helped 'bend' the radio beams used to guide Luftwaffe bombers to their targets, as well as developing an apparatus to jam the enemy's radar and monitoring the production of Hitler's V-weapons.

After the war Jones returned to academic life but in 1952 he was invited back to the Ministry of Defence to head a new Directorate of Scientific Intelligence, a post that coincidentally brought him into contact with Sir Percy Sillitoe, Peter Wright and the Soviet microphone codenamed Satyr. He stayed for two years before resuming his academic career in Aberdeen.

In 1978 he released *Most Secret War*, an unprecedented analysis of his contribution to the scientific war prosecuted behind the scenes by the boffins. Eleven years later his autobiography, *Reflections on Intelligence*, elaborated on some of the topics that previously had been considered too sensitive for public consumption.

His decision to publish *Most Secret War* was prompted by the discovery of various of his wartime research papers in the Public Record Office. BBC researchers who uncovered the material announced that they intended to use it in a television series with or without his co-operation, and accordingly he sought permission to write his own account of his wartime work. In this passage he describes how the German atomic scientists captured at the end of the war were accommodated in a safe-house in Bedfordshire which had been wired for sound. The resulting recordings and transcripts were only officially acknowledged and released by the British Government in March 1992, more than forty-five years after they were made, but only fourteen since Jones advocated they be made public.

Most Secret War

We had the problem of what to do with the German nuclear physicists who had been rounded up, and who were temporarily held in an American internment camp in France known as 'Dustbin'. After they had been there a short while, Welsh suggested to me that we should get them moved to Britain because he had heard that an American General had said the best way of dealing with the nuclear physics problem in post-war Germany was to shoot all their nuclear physicists. Could I therefore please intervene, and somehow have the physicists held in England? Welsh's statements were sometimes made with a hidden motive, but the danger did seem possible, and we should at least have some residual advantage if the physicists came to Britain instead of going to America. I therefore suggested to Stewart Menzies that they might be accommodated in Farm Hall, the country house in Huntingdon which MI6 and SOE had used as a staging-post for agents who were about to be flown into Occupied Territory from the RAF Station at Tempsford, and which was now vacant. Menzies agreed, and I advised that before the physicists arrived we should have the house fitted out with microphones, so that we could hear their reactions when they realized how far the Americans and ourselves had progressed. If this was an ungentlemanly thing to do, it was a relatively small advantage to be taken of the possible fact that we had saved them from being shot. The move bewildered Sam Goudsmit who afterwards wrote in *Alsos*, 'Just why these top German physicists were interned in England I never understood . . .'

By far the most interesting items that came out of the Farm Hall conversations were the reactions of the German physicists when the news of the bomb on Hiroshima reached them on 7th August 1945. Incidentally, we ourselves were almost awestruck, not so much at the power of the bomb, for this we had expected, but because the Americans had used it with so little notice. It had been clear to us that at least some Japanese authorities knew that they were losing the war, and that they were putting out peace feelers. So much so, in fact, that in March 1945 Geoffrey Tandy, of the naval section at Bletchley, had remarked to me that it was even money whether Germany or Japan would collapse first. For myself, I would have given the Japanese the chance of witnessing a demonstration before actually dropping a bomb on them, not entirely out of feeling for the Japanese who, although I have since come to like them, had conducted the war in a way (for example at Pearl Harbor and in torturing prisoners) that put them beyond the pale of normal humanity. But it was clear that with the dropping of the bomb another threshold would have been crossed, although it can still be argued that many more lives were saved on both sides by the sudden end of the war that would otherwise have been lost in its prolongation.

The transcripts of the reactions of the German physicists have never been published in full, because the official British attitude has been that they never existed. Transcripts were sent to America, of course, and they have been partly quoted both by Groves and Goudsmit. There is no dignity in denying their existence, which I myself have never tried to hide. Their historical importance lies in the light that they might throw on the question of the extent to which the German physicists had thought of making a bomb. Afterwards, Heisenberg gave the impression that he merely kept in with the Nazis because, as he explained to Robert Jungk in *Brighter Than a Thousand Suns*, 'Under a dictatorship active resistance can only be practised by those who pretend to collaborate with the regime.' And if he strove to keep control of nuclear energy in Germany, Jungk says that this was because he and his friends feared that 'other less scrupulous physicists might in different circumstances make the attempt to construct atom bombs for Hitler'.

I would accept that there was something to the comment of von Weizsäcker, one of the physicists at Farm Hall, who said, 'I believe that the reason why we did not do it was that all the physicists did not want to do it, on principle. . . . If we had wanted Germany to win the war we could have succeeded'. But against this must be set the comment of his colleague Bagge: 'I think it is absurd for von Weizsäcker to say that he did not want the thing to succeed: that may be so in his case but not for all of us'. So the reactions at Farm Hall ranged from those of one or two who regarded themselves as defeated Generals, to others such as Otto Hahn, who was so upset that his original discovery of nuclear fission had led to so much destruction of humanity that he had to be restrained from committing suicide. All this is clear from what has been published about Farm Hall.

Robert Carew-Hunt

The truth is that neither Marx nor Lenin ever seriously considered what would be the result of practising the revolutionary principles they preached.

The curious paradox about Robert Carew-Hunt's contribution to intelligence literature is that it was originally sponsored by Kim Philby and distributed, under a top secret classification, to SIS personnel only.

A distinguished academic and a fellow of St Antony's College, Oxford, Professor Carew-Hunt had joined SIS in 1940. Before the war he had published an article in the *Spectator* on the subject of the difficulties likely to confront diplomats working in Communist countries, and this was expanded and reprinted by SIS for internal consumption. It became the basic handbook of Section IX, the anti-Soviet unit created in late 1945 and headed by Philby, and in 1950 Carew-Hunt was authorized to publish a larger edition commercially. For its title he adapted John Strachey's famous 1936 study, *The Theory and Practice of Socialism*, which he described as 'a valuable introduction to Marxist theory'.

The Theory and Practice of Communism

The purpose of government, and the central problem of political philosophy is the adjustment of the claims of the individual and the community. In the last century the subjective individualism which entered Western Europe with the Renaissance and the Reformation issued in Liberalism and *laissez faire* until, in its third quarter, the tide turned in the direction of collectivism, and this has been advancing ever since. The change was primarily due to two causes – on the one hand, the extension of the parliamentary suffrage and the development of organized labour, and on the other, the growing complexity of the international world market which led the workers to believe that political rights were of little account if they failed to secure them a livelihood. Thus there arose the demand, which became intensified in the inter-war years, for such security as logically demands a State-controlled economy. Of this type of economy Russia is the most extreme example, as it is based upon collectivist principles applied with complete ruthlessness.

The ideological foundation upon which the Soviet order is founded has already been considered. We have seen that it is materialist because its fundamental assumption is the primacy of the economic factor, of which whatever else exists is held to be the reflection. It follows therefore that if society is to be reconstituted, the first step must be to change its economic basis by collectivizing the productive forces which Capitalism has been hitherto exploiting. These productive forces will now 'belong to the workers'. But the Communists are well aware that the workers are powerless to direct them, and under the new order this will become the responsibility of the Party which, by a convenient fiction, is held to represent the single class of 'toilers' to which the community will now be levelled, all of whom are assumed to possess the same class interests. Within such a framework, democracy of the western type is meaningless. One-party government alone makes sense, for there is nothing for a second party to represent; if it agrees with the official party it is superfluous; if it does not, it is counter-revolutionary. Nor can there be any limit to the powers that may be exercised by a regime which represents *ex hypothesei* the will of the single and undivided people. The individual has no status outside the group to which he belongs, and what part he can best play within it is for his leaders to decide. The law becomes an instrument for suppressing whatever they may choose to regard as subversion, as Soviet jurists have not troubled to conceal. Philosophy, literature, art and science can claim no autonomy under such a system, for their value and justification lie solely in the degrees to which they strengthen it. The family, long ago exposed by Engels as an immature form of association, will only be upheld in so far as the State may decide to make use of it, seeing that it is to society and not to its parents that the child belongs. Religion will certainly not be tolerated for long, since it theatens to create a dual loyalty in a world in which all things have become Caesar's. The engineers of the new society can brook no rival. Yet God is a serious rival; even the very thought that He may exist is unendurable. Thus the individual is completely absorbed into the collective, in which he must live and move and have his being.

To the West, democracy of this totalitarian type will appear a mockery. Yet, as J. L. Talmon has pointed out, it is a part of the European tradition, and coeval with democracy of the liberal type. Both derive from the belief entertained by the eighteenth-century *philosophes* that there existed a natural social order, the counterpart of the cosmic order of Newtonian physics, which everyone, if properly instructed, would accept because it corresponded with what Rousseau called the 'General Will'. The Jacobins shared this belief, but only to discover that their own particular specific for setting the world to rights not only failed to command universal assent, but excited violent opposition even among those whom it was intended to benefit. Clearly there could be nothing wrong with the specific itself. The fault lay with the people, who were too immature to see what their true interests were, and must therefore be induced to do so, if necessary by force. Thus the 'General Will' becomes transformed into the will of the leaders, and we find such men as Robespierre and Saint-Just using the same arguments to defend their actions as Lenin and Stalin were to employ a century and a quarter later.

The Jacobins had believed that they could realize their objectives without interfering with the rights of property. All that was necessary was to rid society of kings, priests and other obstacles to liberty, substitute good laws for bad, and educate men in the virtues of citizenship. But when Marx revived the revolutionary tradition half a century later, he made the abolition of the existing property system the precondition of the establishment of a just social order. The private ownership of the means of production was the source of all evils, and with its abolition they would disappear. Society could not be restored by constitution-making after the manner of a Sieyès or a Bentham, but only by radically changing the whole complex of productive relations, of which he held the property system to be the most important element. From the revolution that would bring this about there would eventually develop a genuine communist society in which men would agree to abandon their individuality, of which property is an expression, and live solely in and for the collective whole. Yet to believe that they will ever voluntarily do this is the very extreme of utopianism. The tension between the individual and society is a natural one, and it is not resolved by getting rid of one of its elements, any more than is the equilibrium of a pair of scales restored by removing one of its balances. There is nothing in Marx's teaching to show how this transformation of human nature will be brought about; while in *The State and Revolution* Lenin dismisses the question as one to which there can be no answer and which no one has the right to ask.

Kenneth Cohen

Reporting of intelligence had none of the glamour or the 'instant results' of sabotage, which was, together with organizing escapes, the other principal opportunity of resistance open to French patriots.

Kenneth Cohen joined the Royal Navy in 1918 and served as a midshipman in HMS *Iron Duke*. He went to staff college in 1932 and three years later was persuaded by Admiral Sinclair to join him at Broadway.

Cohen's career in SIS was always controversial, not least because in 1937 he was assigned the near-impossible task of liaising for Claude Dansey, later the deputy chief. At that time Dansey, much feared for his ruthlessness, ran a semi-independent network on the Continent known as the Z Organization and was located well away from Broadway. His purpose was to build a commercially based structure in parallel to the rather opaque Passport Control Offices which were often handicapped in their activities by having been declared to the local security authorities. While the PCO was obliged to liaise with his counterparts in the host country, the Z representative was not so limited and could undertake the kind of deniable operations that, if discovered, would compromise the PCO's status. The Z Organization was concealed behind a front company based in Bush House, Aldwych, and Cohen, calling himself Keith Crane, despatched its personnel under business cover across Europe. Alexander Korda's London Films was a favourite cover and there were others, including some bogus import-export firms, a travel agency and a company dealing in fine arts.

In retrospect the decision to amalgamate the Z Organization with the Passport Control Offices on the outbreak of war was a costly mistake. Simultaneously, in each European capital the local PCO received a signal alerting him to the identity of the local Z representative, who in turn was sent an order to introduce himself to the PCO. Thus, in Riga, Leslie Nicholson was visited by a dubious character who claimed to be an author 'engaged on writing a book about Baltic politics' and in The Hague Major Richard Stevens was astonished to find Sigismund Payne Best as his mysterious collaborator. When Stevens and Best were kidnapped by the Nazis in November 1939 the entire Z Organization was hastily wound up and Kenneth Cohen was switched to SIS's French Country Section to liaise with the embryonic Free French intelligence service.

Together Dansey and Cohen walked the tightrope of French politics and developed a remarkable degree of co-operation with de Gaulle's *Bureau Central de Renseignements et d'Action*. One of their earliest recruits and a key agent in the unoccupied zone was Marie-Madeleine Fourcade, who ran the 3000-strong Alliance intelligence network. In 1973 she wrote her memoirs, *Noah's Ark*, to which Cohen contributed a lengthy preface. After the war Cohen stayed in SIS as Director of Production but in 1953, having been demoted to Chief Controller/

Europe, retired to join United Steel Companies as their European adviser. Before his death in September 1984 he contributed many articles to various publications on the subject of European integration, and for five years was chairman of the Franco-British Society.

Noah's Ark (Preface)

Loustaunau-Lacau [under the codename Navarre, Marie-Madeleine's predecessor as boss of the network] was early betrayed, but miraculously survived the torment of Mauthausen concentration camp. He was replaced by a woman, of whom we (the British) then knew little beyond her code name, 'Poz 55'. She first made contact with the outside world when she emerged, paralysed with cold and cramp, from a sealed diplomatic bag. This had been carried in the boot of a car to Madrid by a compliant Vichy courier, who had crossed the Pyrenees in mid-winter. Reports to London that her Nefertiti-like beauty and charm (she was then thirty-two, mother of two children) were equalled by her total dedication and executive capacity proved unexaggerated. Fact had out-paced fiction in producing the copybook 'beautiful spy'. This was Marie-Madeleine.

It was not till twenty years after the liberation of France that the author started on this Homeric saga of her *réseau*'s 'daily life' under German occupation. She tells of their desperate anxieties, their suffering, their elation, their disasters, their interminable waiting for 'the landings', and of their final freedom. The various characters of whom she quickly became established as the chosen leader range, as will be seen, from the magnificent but totally aggressive 'Eagle', to the highly disciplined wireless operator 'Magpie'; from Dukes and Duchesses to *concierges* (where would 'intelligence' be without these latter?); from politicians to policemen. She allows the characters to speak for themselves and these, alas, include a traitor who was sent to her with disastrous results. This blunder did not dim her loyalty to the British alliance, and was perhaps later appropriately redeemed by the splendid record of 'Magpie', another British subject and clandestine wireless operator.

Marie-Madeleine's ability at this distance of time to recount with such evocative detail the lives of her fellow helpers is a tribute to her intellectual powers and her human comprehension. This is perhaps, in part, an explanation of her success as a resistance leader. That she did not take this success for granted is shown by her self-questioning at the time of her 'accession': '*Vont ils m'obéir?*' As a digression it might be added that on one of the two or three occasions known to the writer, when Churchill gave personal attention to the affairs of the Alliance, the qualities of a *'Grand chef'* were defined to him by a French officer. They were: (1) *Courage*, (2) *Connaissance de son métier*, (3) *Compréhension des hommes*. These qualities, in maximum or minimum degree, were then assigned to General de Gaulle, but (with a different 'mix') could readily have been ascribed to Marie-Madeleine.

With a Tolstoyan inevitability she tells of the ebb of the national spirit as the armies disintegrated in the summer of 1940, and then of the very slow turn of the tide as a permanent German hegemony became less certain. But only a minute elite (who became known to us as 'vintage 1940') were ready at that time to risk their all. Amongst these few were, of course, Loustaunau-Lacau, the founder of the network *'Oui nous les refoulerons. . . . Il* (Hitler) *fonce comme une brute avec des moyens puissants, certes, mais pas infaillibles ni éternels. Il faut prévoir la gaffe que l'Allemand commet inévitablement tôt ou tard et en attendant – tenir'*. ['We'll drive them back. Hitler will batter his way in but his resources are neither infallible nor everlasting. Sooner or later we can expect the inevitable German blunder. Until then – hold on!']

They started their work appropriately enough in Loustaunau's beloved Pyrenees. A vivid picture of his own tumultuous life there (and elsewhere) can be found in his well-named book, *Mémoires d'un Français rebelle*. His successor's, Marie-Madeleine's, attitude was more personal (and feminine?): *'Qu'est-ce que la patience? ruminais-je. Une vertu idiote faite pour les gens sans nerfs comme Diogène et Socrate . . . des ânes qui n'exige point de vengeance. Je m'examinais. Mon ressentiment ne cédait pas et je bouillais du désir de me venger.'* ['And patience, I reflected? An absurd virtue fit for a thin-blooded Diogenes or Socrates; for an ass that seeks no vengeance. I looked into my heart. My hostility remained undiminished and I boiled with a desire for revenge.']

But such personal feelings in no way diminished Marie-Madeleine's capacity to lead her 3,000 followers without any of the aids which a field commander would take for granted at his relatively safe headquarters. Her attitude towards the enemy was accompanied by a shrewd appreciation of what was 'worthwhile' in the way of information, both from the point of view of her agents' opportunities and the criteria of the Service Staffs for whom it was destined. But for her, *me venger* meant more than that, and to the dismay of her subordinates, of the British Staffs concerned, to say nothing of her immediate family, she would insist on plunging into the fray in the first person. This brought about her arrest by the Vichy police and her subsequent escape (admittedly, in this case, with some rather light-hearted collusion), her smuggled appearance in Madrid, a visit to London by a clandestine air operation, and finally a further arrest by the Gestapo, with a desperate escape to follow. Thus she stoutly combined the role of fighter and strategist.

No single French network can claim the monopoly of intelligence-gathering from occupied territory (soon to include the whole of France), but this writer would maintain that the Alliance survivors and their 500 dead had particularly well served the allied services with their emphasis on information concerning German submarine bases and, in 1944, rocket sites. Many of their sources had begun their flow in 1941, when resistance was confined to the few. Moreover, reporting of intelligence had none of the glamour or the 'instant results' of sabotage, which was, together with organizing escapes, the other principal opportunity of resistance open to French patriots. Their remarkable exploits included, incidentally, as described in the book, the organizing of the escape of General Giraud on the eve of the North African landings. Although Giraud's subsequent performance proved something of an anticlimax, General Eisenhower, it should be noted, at the time attached great importance to this delicate operation.

Marie-Madeleine describes with telling pathos the capture and eventual execution of her splendid second-in-command, Commandant Faye, and his last wishes, later found hidden in his cell, might serve as a requiem for the Alliance's sacrifices. *'Fermez les prisons, chassez les bourreaux ... Plus tard les historiens jugeront. Pour l'instant il s'agit d'union et non de représailles, de travail et non de désordre, c'est mon dernier voeu.'* ['Close down the prisons, throw out the executioners ... later the historians will give their verdict. Now we need unity, not reprisals, work and not chaos. These are my last wishes.']

I will add only a short personal postscript concerning Loustaunau-Lacau, the network's founder, and the author, his successor. As might be expected, it is not of a 'they lived happily ever after' character. With his unbelievable stamina, Loustaunau-Lacau survived three years in the hands of the Gestapo, coming back to Paris the merest skeleton of his normally bull-like frame, and, as it happened, at the height of the Pétain trial. He had been Pétain's personal assistant during the pre-war years, but this had not prevented his former chief from allowing him to be handed over by Vichy to the Gestapo. The prosecuting counsel, not knowing their man, rashly brought him forward as a promising witness. Certainly his evidence hit the headlines. Like Faye, he felt this was no time for fostering enmities and questioned in no uncertain terms whether the judges' and prosecution's own records justified their pursuing the trial: '*Vous n'allez pas refiler à ce vieillard l'ardoise de vos erreurs. . . !*' ['Don't pile on this old man the weight of your own faults. . . !'] He was not recalled to the witness box! In the few years remaining to him after his war time sufferings, this formidable man of the Right, but inveterate rebel, was to serve as an independent deputy. There he eagerly pursued the possibility of reconciliation behind the Iron Curtain – an attitude much ahead of the politics of the day.

Marie-Madeleine – like Faye – never lost faith in the regeneration of France, and I remember this attitude of hers being expressed with characteristic vividness on the evening of D-Day, when she and the acting head of the Free French special services dined in London with my wife and myself. (Owing to Gestapo raids on her *réseau* it was only some days later that she was allowed by the British authorities to return to her dangerous task in occupied France.) She was exultant over the prospective liberation, but our other guest thought more of the ravaged and embittered state of his country, as our conversation was punctuated by the detonations of occasional V2s. '*Voyons donc,*' expostulated Marie-Madeleine, '*dans les accouchements, ce sont les femmes qui sont vaillantes*'. [You see! In confinements only the women are brave.']

CHAPTER VI

Overseas Stations

The very fantasy of a spy's life, the loss of his own identity, his pursuit of pseudo-information through pseudo-relationships, makes him a sort of hero of our time.
Malcolm Muggeridge

Before the war SIS's overseas networks had been concealed under the convenient cover of British Passport Control Offices which were attached to local diplomatic premises. This arrangement, of course, scarcely fooled the Germans or, for that matter, the security apparatus in neutral countries like Portugal and Switzerland where espionage had become a growth industry. Confirmation that the PCOs had been thoroughly compromised was provided in November 1939 when Major Richard Stevens, the SIS head of station in The Hague, was abducted by the Nazis. He and another SIS colleague, Sigismund Payne Best, were seized by armed raiders who crossed the Dutch frontier at Venlo and both men were subjected to lengthy interrogation by the Gestapo. Faced with incontrovertible evidence that its European network of PCOs had been blown, SIS created several new cover organizations to provide its personnel posted abroad with more plausible cover. In the Middle and Far East it was the 'Inter-Service Liaison Department', and this was the branch Nigel Clive joined in Baghdad in 1941. In North America, where Freddie Ayer was despatched, the Passport Control Office was absorbed into 'British Security Co-ordination' which offered a useful umbrella for both MI5 and SIS. Elsewhere individual SIS officers were obliged to rely on the Foreign Office to concede an appropriate consular post. Thus Graham Greene and Malcolm Muggeridge, who were sent to Freetown and Lourenço Marques respectively, adopted the role of rather junior consular officials.

Philip Johns was 'invited' into SIS soon after the outbreak of war, and just as he had been appointed to a more orthodox naval post in Antwerp. Similarly Leslie Nicholson, who had operated as a PCO in Prague and

Riga before the war, found his cover had fooled neither the Germans nor the Russians and, after enduring several weeks of the Soviet occupation, returned to Broadway. In 1966 Nicholson adopted the pseudonym John Whitwell and gave an account of his clandestine career in *British Agent*.

Aubrey Jones began his SIS career in Section V in 1940 when he was recruited from *The Times*, the newspaper he was to return to in 1947. From London he was posted to the Mediterranean and headed SIS's office in Bari following the invasion of Italy. He was elected MP for Birmingham, Hall Green in 1950 and was appointed Minister of Fuel and Supply in December 1955. He retired from the Commons in 1965 and took numerous directorships in industry.

In July 1988 he made a contribution to the debate on public accountability, prompted by the Peter Wright affair, and argued for a system of supervision for the security and intelligence services. 'Several of my acquaintances were members of the secret agencies during and immediately after the Second World War. I doubt whether there is anything which they could say of their then experiences which would now prejudice security ... An agency whose servants are obliged for ever to keep everything secret will never develop an objective view of the world. It will see everything around it through a miasma of suspicion and therefore proffer unwarranted observations and conclusions. That is one of the more important lessons of Mr Peter Wright's book.' Jones's own publications are primarily on industrial and economic topics, but *The Pendulum of Politics*, published in 1946, gives some insight into his political views at that time.

Kenneth Benton has exercised a similar degree of discretion over his covert career. He joined SIS in 1937 after having studied languages at London University, and having worked as a teacher in Florence and Austria. It was in Vienna that he was enrolled into SIS and where he worked under Thomas Kendrick, the head of station who was to be arrested by the Nazis in August the following year. The SIS station was evacuated and Benton moved to Leslie Nicholson's station in Riga, but was withdrawn again in 1940 after undergoing three months of Soviet occupation. His lengthy return to London took him, via Moscow, by the Trans-Siberian Railway to the Pacific, Tokyo and Ottawa. After his arrival in London he was transferred to Section V and was sent as that department's representative to Madrid. In Spain Benton was embroiled in numerous adventures, including the bribery of the private secretary of Alcazar de Velasco, a notorious German spy who operated in London as the press attaché at the Spanish embassy. Benton was also involved in the abduction of a Vichy French naval officer, Capitaine de Corvette Lablache-Combier who, working for de Gaulle's Free French intelligence service BCRA, was sent to Lisbon with the identity of Paul Lewis-Claire but underwent a change of heart and offered his services to the Vichy embassy. This approach was instantly reported to SIS and arrangements were made to kidnap the defector. Lablache-Combier was invited to the British embassy on a pretext; there he was seized by Benton and Jimmy Langley, drugged, and driven in a car boot to Gibraltar, but on arrival was discovered to be dead.

After two years in Madrid Benton moved to Rome but returned to London for a headquarters post in 1948. He was back in Italy in 1950, and in 1953 returned to Madrid. Soon after the Suez crisis of 1956 Benton moved to London, and in 1963 went to Peru to be head of station in Lima. Three years later came his final assignment, SIS head of station in Rio de Janeiro. His retirement from the clandestine world took place two years later and his talent for writing spy thrillers manifested itself in the publication the next year of *The Twenty-Fourth Level*, with secret agent Peter Craig as its hero, set in a Brazilian gold mine. Numerous other thrillers followed, including two murder mysteries, *A Time for Murder* and *Greek Fire*, written under the pen-name James Kirton. When he was elected chairman of the Crime Writers' Guild, an accolade which reflected the author's high standing among his fellow writers, few reading his biography would have known that his long service in the diplomatic corps was actually a cover for a clandestine career.

In the autumn of the year that Benton retired, Nicholas Elliott swapped his desk in SIS's headquarters for a peripatetic existence at Lonrho, initially as a consultant to the chairman, Tiny Rowland, and later as a non-executive director. His hugely amusing autobiography, published in 1991, gave scarcely a clue to the fact that he had spent twenty-nine years as an intelligence officer, serving in both MI5 and SIS.

In contrast, John Bruce Lockhart has made no bones of his SIS career, which spanned thirty-five years, and is an advocate for greater openness on the part of government. His attempts to increase public knowledge of the secret world, and the way in which administrations use (or ignore) intelligence have often brought him into conflict with his successors.

SIS officers with overseas experience are likely to find their careers enhanced, if only because a period abroad is considered by the hierarchy to be an essential condition for promotion. On the other hand, too much time spent away from headquarters will act to the disadvantage of the ambitious SIS officer seeking to climb the ladder. Kim Philby was reluctant to exchange his top job in the anti-Soviet branch Section IX in late 1946 for an appointment as head of station in Istanbul, but he recognized that he 'could not reasonably resist a foreign posting without serious loss of standing in the service'. Philby's concern, of course, was that his access to classified data of interest to his Soviet contacts would diminish while he languished in Turkey but he also acknowledged that his future prospects would be increased by the tour of duty which, in normal circumstances, would not exceed three years.

These overseas postings are not as hazardous as one might expect. Indeed, none of the SIS officers who were posted to overseas stations during the Second World War was ever really at much personal risk, and only a very few were casualties as staff personnel, or anyone with a knowledge of future operations, were automatically banned from placing themselves in danger. Bill Stuart, an SIS liaison officer in Yugoslavia, was killed in May 1943 during a German air raid on Tito's headquarters, but he was an exception. Virtually SIS's only post-war casualty has been Desmond Doran, assassinated by Jewish terrorists in Tel Aviv in September 1946.

Graham Greene

Who among us has not committed treason to something or someone more important than a country?

Foreword to My Silent War *by Kim Philby*

Graham Greene's career as an SIS officer was, as he admitted, wholly undistinguished. Soon after the release of his magnificent *The Power and the Glory* Graham Greene moved from the Ministry of Information to join his sister in the Secret Intelligence Service. Elizabeth, who had married Rodney Dennys, later the Somerset Herald at the College of Arms but then a counter-intelligence officer who was to be based in Cairo for much of the war, was also responsible for obtaining a similar transfer for Malcolm Muggeridge. While Muggeridge encountered no difficulty in joining SIS, Greene's application was complicated by an adverse MI5 dossier which correctly reported that he had bankrupted a magazine by losing an expensive libel action to Shirley Temple, the American child star whom he accused of being sexually provocative.

Graham's original appointment was to Section V, the signals intelligence exploitation unit based in St Albans where his friend Kim Philby analysed intercepted enemy wireless messages and distributed them to the appropriate SIS stations in Spain, Portugal and North Africa. Following his work in the Iberian sub-section Greene was sent to West Africa where he languished in a villa overlooking Freetown's harbour until his recall to London in 1944.

While in Sierra Leone Greene wrote *The Ministry of Fear* and *The Heart of the Matter* but, despite the pre-war success of *Brighton Rock*, he was still uncertain about his financial future and in 1944 signed a contract with Metro-Goldwyn-Mayer for a series of film scripts which was to include his hugely successful *The Third Man*. During this period he sketched a treatment entitled *Nobody to Blame* about Richard Tripp, SIS head of station in an unnamed pre-war Baltic capital. The British Board of Film Censors rejected the idea with the rebuke that 'they could not grant a certificate to a film making fun of the Secret Service'. Ten years later Greene was to take his revenge with *Our Man in Havana*, a splendid spoof of SIS, but one which nearly landed him in trouble. 'There is no censorship for novels but I learnt later that MI5 suggested to MI6 that they should bring an action against the book for a breach of official secrets. What secret had I betrayed? Was it the possibility of using bird shit as a secret ink? But luckily C, the head of MI6, had a better sense of humour than his colleague in MI5, and he discouraged him from taking action.'

To what extent Greene was influenced by his long friendship with Philby is hard to determine, but their relationship survived the traitor's defection to Moscow in January 1963. Greene's decision to contribute an uncritical foreword to Philby's memoirs, *My Silent War*, enraged his former colleagues in SIS who suspected that he had played a significant role in delivering the manuscript to the offices in Paris of Philby's literary agents, and MI5 molehunters hinted darkly about Greene's dubious loyalty. The attitude of Greene himself to SIS veered from the ridicule of *Our Man in Havana* to the baseless accusation in *The Human Factor* that SIS indulged in murder.

Greene died at his home in Antibes in April 1991, and one of the last of his books published before his death was a long-forgotten novel, *The Tenth Man*, which he had written for a movie studio in Hollywood after the war. Discovered by the publisher Anthony Blond, it contained the film treatment that the censors turned down.

Nobody to Blame

I

Richard Tripp is the agent of Singer Sewing Machines in some Baltic capital similar to Tallinn. He is a small inoffensive man of a rather timid disposition with a passionate love for postage stamps, Gilbert and Sullivan's music and his wife, and a passionate loyalty to Singer Sewing Machines. Unofficially he is Agent B.720 of the British Secret Service. The year is 1938/39.

Mrs Tripp – Gloria – is much younger than Tripp and it is to give her a good life that he has allowed himself to be enlisted in the Secret Service. He feels he must spend more money on her than Singer provide in order to keep her, although she has a genuine fondness for her dim husband. She knows nothing, of course, of his activities.

At HQ in London Tripp is regarded as one of their soundest agents – unimaginative, accurate, not easily ruffled. He is believed to have a network of sub-agents throughout Germany and he keeps in touch with HQ through the medium of his business reports written to his firm. What HQ does not know is that in fact Tripp has no agents at all. He invents all his reports and when London expresses dissatisfaction with an agent he simply dismisses one notional source and engages another equally notional. Naturally he draws salaries and expenses for all the imaginary agents.

His active imagination, from which he has drawn the details of a large underground factory near Leipzig for the construction of a secret explosive, does on one occasion lead to a little trouble with the local police. From an independent source London learns that B.720 is being shadowed, and they send him an urgent warning, but the warning arrives too late.

At the end of a programme of Gilbert and Sullivan opera by the Anglo-Latesthian Society in which Tripp takes a leading part the Chief of Police, who is sitting in the front row, hands up a bouquet with a card attached and the request that he may have a drink with Tripp immediately in his dressing-room. There he tells Tripp that the German Embassy have complained of his activities. Tripp confesses to his deception.

The Chief of Police is amused and pleased that Tripp's presence will keep out any serious agents, and he accepts the gift of a sewing machine for his wife. He will ensure that Tripp's messages go safely out of the country – and to keep the German Embassy quiet, he decides, they can have a look at them on the way. London's warning comes on the heels of the interview, and Tripp sends back a message announcing that he has appointed the Chief of Police himself as one of his agents, enclosing that officer's first report on the chief political characters of Latesthia and requesting that as first payment and bonus the Chief, who he says is an ardent stamp collector, should receive a rare Triangular Cape, and when the stamp arrives of course he sticks it in his own album. This gives him an idea, and soon the Chief of the Secret Service is commenting to the HQ officer in charge of Tripp's station, 'What a lot of stamp collectors he has among his agents.'

'It might be worse. Do you remember old Stott's agents? They all wanted art photos from Paris.'

'Stott's at a loose end, isn't he?'

'Yes.'

'Send him over to take a look at Tripp's station. He may be able to give Tripp some advice. I always believe in letting two sound men get together.'

2

Stott is a much older man than Tripp. He is bottle-nosed and mottled with a little round stomach and a roving eye. Tripp is naturally apprehensive of his visit and expects to be unmasked at any moment, but to his relief he finds that Stott is much more interested in the foods and wines of Latesthia, and in the night life, than in the details of Tripp's organization. There are even fleeting moments when Tripp wonders whether it could possibly be that Stott also had run his station on notional lines, but such a thought of course can hardly be held for long.

The first evening together Stott remarks, 'Now, the brothels, old man. You've got good contacts there, I suppose?'

Tripp has never been in a brothel in his life. He has to own that he has overlooked brothels.

'Most important, old man. Every visiting businessman goes to the brothels. Got to have them covered.'

He has a night round the town with Stott and gets into trouble with his wife for returning at two in the morning. Stott moves on to Berlin, but he has sown seeds in Tripp's mind. His notional agents in future follow a Stott line. London is asked to approve in rapid succession the madame of a high class 'house', a café singer, and, his most imaginative effort to date, a well-known Latesthian cinema actress who is described as Agent B.720's (i.e. Tripp's) mistress. Of course he has never spoken to her in his life, and he has no idea that she is in fact a German agent.

3

A second crisis – needing more delicate handling than Stott's – blows up. The threat of European war is deepening and London considers that Tripp's position in Latesthia is a key one. He must have a proper staff: Singer Sewing Machines are persuaded in the interests of the nation to build up their agency in Latesthia and they inform Tripp that they are sending out to him a secretary-typist and a clerk. Tripp is innocently delighted that his work for Singer has borne such fruit and that sewing machines are booming. He is less pleased, however, when the clerk and typist arrive and prove to be members of the Secret Service sent to assist him in handling his now complicated network of agents.

The clerk is a young man with a penetrating cockney accent and an enormous capacity for hero-worship – and heroine-worship. His devotion is equally aroused by what he considers the experience and daring of Tripp and by the legs and breasts of Tripp's wife. His name is Cobb, and he has an annoying habit of asking questions. He says himself, 'You don't have to bother to explain things, Chief. Just let me dig in and ask questions, and I'll get the hang of things for myself.'

The typist – Miss Jixon – is a withered spinster of forty-four who regards everyone and everything with suspicion. She believes that even the most innocent labourer is in the pay of the secret police, and she is shocked by the inadequacy of the security arrangements in the office. She insists on all blotting paper being locked in the safe and all typewriting ribbons being removed at night. This is highly inconvenient as no one is very good at fixing typewriter ribbons. Once she finds a used ribbon thrown in the wastepaper basket instead of being burnt in the incinerator and she begins to demonstrate the danger of the practice by deciphering the impress on the ribbon. All she can make out is 'Red lips were ne'er so red nor eyes so pure', which turns out to be a line of a sonnet written by Cobb – obviously with Mrs Tripp in mind.

'He's really rather sweet,' Mrs Tripp says.

The chief problem that Tripp has to solve is how to disguise the fact that he has no sources for his reports. He finds this unexpectedly easy. He goes shopping and returns with envelopes that have been handed to him, he says, from under the counter: he makes a great show of testing perfectly innocent letters about sewing machines for secret inks: he takes Cobb for a round of the town and now and then in the restaurants points out his agents.

'A very discreet man. You'll see he won't show the least flicker of recognition.'

The monthly payments to agents present a difficulty: Miss Jixon objects strongly to the payments being made by himself.

'It's irregular, insecure: HQ would never countenance it.'

By this time, for the sake of his assistants, he has drawn up an impressive chart of his sources: with the immediate head agents who control each gang. Miss Jixon insists that from now on he shall cut off his personal contacts with all but his head agents (of whom the cinema actress is one) and that he should meet them on every occasion in a different disguise.

Disguises become the bane of Tripp's life. What makes it worse, of course, is that his wife knows nothing. Miss Jixon shows a horrible ingenuity: Tripp's make-up box for the operatic productions of the Anglo-Latesthian Society is requisitioned. He finds himself being forced to slip out of back doors in red wigs and return by front doors in black wigs. She makes him carry at least two soft hats of varying colours in his overcoat pockets, so that he can change hats. Spectacles, horn-rimmed and steel-rimmed, bulge his breast pockets.

The strain tells. He becomes irritable and Mrs Tripp is reduced to tears. Cobb is torn between hero-worship and heroine-worship.

4

Next crisis: the enemy begins to take Tripp seriously. He becomes aware that he is followed everywhere – even to the Anglo-Latesthian musical *soirée* – 'an evening with Edward German and Vaughan Williams'. Miss Jixon's security arrangements have been a little too good and the Germans are no longer able to keep an eye on the reports he sends.

She has objected to the use of the Chief of Police as transmitter and has evolved an elaborate method of sending secret ink messages on postage stamps. (There is a moment when Miss Jixon skirts shyly round the possibility of bird shit as a secret ink.) Unfortunately the ink never develops properly – single words will appear and disappear with disconcerting rapidity.

Tripp, in order to be able to fake his expenses sheet and show the expenditure of huge sums for entertainment, is forced to dine out at least three times a week. He hates restaurant meals – and in any case it would be fatal if one of his assistants saw him dining alone. He therefore rents a room in the suburbs and retires there for a quiet read (his favourite authors are Charles Lamb and Newbolt) or the writing of a bogus report, taking a little food out of the larder with him. (In his account book this appears as 'Dinner for three (political sources) with wines, cigars, etc., £5.10s.0d'.) This constant dining out had never been necessary in the old days before his assistants came, and Mrs Tripp resents it.

The domestic crisis reaches its culmination when on pay day Tripp has to pretend to visit the home of the cinema actress with pay for her sub-sources. Cobb keeps guard in the street outside and Tripp, wearing a false moustache, proceeds up to the actress's flat, rings the bell and enquires for an imaginary person. He turns away from the closing door just as Mrs Tripp comes down from visiting a friend in the flat above. His excuse that he was trying to sell a sewing machine seems weak to Mrs Tripp in view of his false moustache.

Domestic harmony is further shattered when Cobb, anxious to make peace between his hero and his heroine, tells Mrs Tripp everything – or what he thinks is everything. 'It's for his country, Mrs Tripp,' he says.

Mrs Tripp decides that she too will go in for patriotism. She begins to dine out too, and Tripp, not unduly disturbed, takes the opportunity of appointing her as agent with a notional lover in the Foreign Ministry.

'That fellow Tripp,' they say in London, 'deserves a decoration. The Service comes even before his wife. Good show.'

His notional mistress and his wife's notional lover are among his most interesting sources. Unfortunately, of course, his wife does not believe that his mistress is notional and her dinner companion, unlike the notional member of the Foreign Ministry, is a very real young man attached to Agriculture and Fisheries.

Mrs Tripp gets news of Tripp's hide-out and decides to track him down. She is certain she will find him in the company of the actress and that he will not be engaged in work of national importance.

The enemy are aware of his hide-out.

5

Tripp has got his legs up on the stove, some sausage rolls in his pocket, and he is reading his favourite poet Newbolt aloud, in a kind of sub-human drone which is his method with poetry. 'Play up, play up and play the game . . . the dons on the dais serene . . .' He is surprised by a knock at the door. He opens it and is still more surprised by the sight of his notional sub-agent, the cinema actress. Her car has broken down outside: can she have his help? Outside in the car two thugs crouch ready to knock Tripp on the head. A third – a tall stupid sentimental-looking German of immense physique – keeps watch at the end of the street. Tripp says he knows nothing about cars: now if it had been a sewing machine . . .

Mrs Tripp is coming up the road. She has obviously lost her way. Tripp by this time is demonstrating the special points of the Singer sewing machine . . . Mrs Tripp is cold and miserable. She leans against a fence and cries. A little further down the road the sentimental German watches her. He is torn between pity and duty. He edges nearer.

Mr Tripp is talking about poetry to the cinema actress . . .

Mrs Tripp weeps on the German's shoulder and tells him how her husband is betraying her at this moment, but she can't remember the number of the house . . .

The Germans in the car are getting very cold. They get out and begin to walk up and down . . . Tripp is reading Newbolt to the actress . . . 'His captain's hand on his shoulder smote . . .' Mrs Tripp and the German peer in at the window. He hasn't realized that this treacherous husband has anything to do with him. Mrs Tripp moans, 'Take me away,' and he obeys at once – in his comrades' car. Somebody – he is too sentimentally wrought up to care who – tries to stop him and he knocks him down. He deposits Mrs Tripp at her own door.

Tripp is still reading poetry when there is another knock at the door. One German pulls in the other German who is still unconscious. There is a babble of German explanations. 'He was trying to mend the car,' the actress explains, 'and it ran away from him.'

'I'll ring up the garage,' Tripp says. He goes in an alcove, where nobody has seen the telephone.

They prepare to knock him out. 'Wrong number,' he says furiously. 'It's the police.'

When he puts down the receiver again they knock him out.

6

Mr Tripp has not returned home for some days. Cobb and Miss Jixon are worried. Mrs Tripp is furious but finds consolation.

Tripp comes to himself inside the German Embassy. Enormous pressure is put on him to betray his organization, but he has no organization to betray. The threat forcibly resolves itself into this: either he will remain a prisoner in the Embassy until war starts, when he will be handed to the Gestapo as a spy, or he will send a message for them – containing false information carefully devised to discredit him – to London and then in due course he will be released. They show him films of concentration camps, they keep him from sleeping: he is shut up in a cell with the sentimental German, now disgraced, who wakes him whenever he tries to sleep and reproves him for betraying his wife.

The German Ambassador, in collaboration with the Military Attaché, plans out the message for him to send. On one sheet the Military Attaché notes the facts to be concealed: the date of invasion; number of divisions etc. On the other they note the lies to be revealed. A breeze from the open window whips the papers around. The wrong notes (that is to say the true notes) are handed to Tripp to write in secret ink. Tripp gives way. To send one more message of false information seems a small price to pay.

To make all secure and ensure that no Tripp message will ever be believed again, the Germans instruct the Chief of Police to go to the British Ambassador and expose Tripp's dealings with him – the invented messages which he used to show to the Germans before transmitting them. He gives the impression that Tripp knew that the Germans saw them.

Tripp is arrested by the police immediately he leaves the German Embassy. He is escorted home where he is allowed to pack a bag. Mrs Tripp is not there. Cobb shows him a decoded cable from London: 'Dismiss Agent XY.27 [his wife]. Intercepted correspondence to school friend shows she is carrying on intrigue with ... of Agriculture and Fisheries Ministry instead of ... of Foreign Ministry. Unreliable.'

Tripp says goodbye to his home, to Cobb and Miss Jixon, to his make-up box, presented to him by the Anglo-Latesthian Society, to his collected works of Gilbert and Sullivan. He empties his pockets of the false moustache, soft hats, spectacles. 'These were the trouble,' he says sadly to Miss Jixon.

He is put on board a plane to England.

An official enquiry awaits him at HQ. His Ambassador's report has been received, but opinion among his judges before he comes is divided. The trouble is that his reports have been welcomed by the armed forces. The whole Secret Service will look foolish if they have to recall hundreds of reports over the last two years – ones which have been acclaimed as 'most valuable'. The head of the enquiry points out that it will discredit the whole Service. Any of their agents could have done the same. None of them will be believed in future.

A message arrives that Tripp is in the outer office, and the youngest member of the enquiry – a dapper, earnest FO type – goes out to see him. He whispers to him urgently, 'Everything will be all right. Deny everything.'

'If only,' the chairman is saying, 'he hadn't sent that last message. All his other messages are matters of opinion. You remember the underground works at Leipzig. After all, they are underground – we can't be *sure* he invented them. General Hays particularly liked that report. He said it was a model report. We've used it in our training courses. But this one – it gives a time and date for zero hour, and the source claimed – the German Military Attaché himself – you can't get round that. Such and such divisions will cross the frontiers at ten o'clock today. If we hadn't been warned by the Ambassador we'd have had the whole Army, Navy and Air Force ringing us up to know who the devil had sent such nonsense. Come in, Tripp. Sit down. This is a very serious matter. You know the charges against you.'

'I admit everything.'

The dapper young man whispers excitedly, 'No, no, I said deny.'

'You can't possibly admit everything,' the chairman interrupts with equal excitement, 'it's for us to tell you what you admit and what you don't admit. Of course this last message–' The telephone rings: he raises the receiver: 'Yes, yes. Good God!'

He puts the receiver down and addresses the enquiry board. 'The Germans crossed the Polish frontier this morning. Under the circumstances, gentlemen, I think we should congratulate Mr Tripp on his last message from Latesthia. It is unfortunate that bungling in the British Embassy resulted in no use being made of it – but those after all are the chances of the Service. We can say with confidence among ourselves that the Secret Service was informed of the date and time of war breaking out.'

Tripp is given the OBE. He is also appointed chief lecturer at the course for recruits to the Secret Service. We see him last as he comes forward to the blackboard, cue in hand, after being introduced to the recruits as 'one of our oldest and soundest officers – the man who obtained advance news of the exact date and even the hour of the German attack – Richard Tripp will lecture on "How to Run a Station Abroad".'

Malcolm Muggeridge

Secrecy is as essential to Intelligence as vestments and incense to a Mass, or darkness to a Spiritualist seance, and must at all costs be maintained, quite irrespective of whether or not it serves any purpose.

Always a controversial figure who responded to any challenge, Malcolm Muggeridge volunteered for military service after an officer described one of his more satirical articles in the *Daily Telegraph* as a bluff. Muggeridge soon found himself assigned to the Field Security Police wing of the Corps of Military Police at Mytchett, near Aldershot, on the basis of his rather rudimentary grasp of the French language. Although his knowledge of French was slim, he did have wide overseas experience, having taught in India and Egypt, and having spent a year as the *Manchester Guardian*'s correspondent in Moscow.

Muggeridge's Field Security Section was attached to GHQ Home Forces where, to his embarrassment, he was given the task of monitoring the movements of the Chief of the Imperial General Staff, Field Marshal Ironside, whom he judged to be a Fascist sympathizer. His duties in London during the Blitz were not wholly onerous, and his social life revolved largely around his close friend Graham Greene, whose sister Elizabeth was already working for SIS. Through her intervention both Muggeridge and Greene obtained transfers into SIS. For Muggeridge this involved a preliminary interview with the thriller writer Valentine Williams at his London club, the Savage. Once accepted Muggeridge found himself assigned to Section V where he met a fellow journalist, Kim Philby, with whom he was to work closely.

In March 1942 Muggeridge was posted by Leslie Nicholson to the east African port of Lourenço Marques where he remained, under consular cover, for nearly eighteen months, a melancholy period during which his depression reached such depths that at one moment he attempted suicide by trying to drown himself in the Indian Ocean; at the last minute he had a change of heart and swam for the shore.

Then he was sent to the SIS station in Algiers to liaise with de Gaulle's intelligence service, followed by a posting to Paris where his formal employment by SIS ended. He went back to journalism for the *Daily Telegraph* but continued to undertake special assignments and was invited to lecture at SIS's training weekends, routinely held at Worcester College, Oxford.

Muggeridge was not only to publish two volumes of his autobiography *Chronicles of Wasted Time*, in which he discussed his work for SIS, but he had also kept a diary during the war – strictly against SIS rules. *Like It Was*, a collection of his diaries, was published in 1981 and contains a daily account of his activities from his arrival in Lisbon in 1942, en route to Lourenço Marques. Among those mentioned in the Portuguese section of the diaries is Rita Winsor, a key figure in the local SIS station and formerly a member of the pre-war SIS station in Zurich. Other SIS personalities included in the diaries were Liza Greene and two post-war SIS Chiefs, General Sir John Sinclair and his successor, Dick White.

In this extract from his autobiography *The Infernal Grove* Muggeridge describes the atmosphere at his hotel in Lourenço Marques, where the other guests included his German and Italian counterparts.

The Infernal Grove

A flying-boat carried me down the African coast, and at last I arrived at my destination, Lourenço Marques. My first impression was of a rather run-down Mediterranean resort, with bathing beaches, picture postcards, souvenirs, cafés, restaurants, and, at night, cabarets and casinos; except that the sun was hotter and the air more humid. I stayed at the Polana Hotel, overlooking the sea, and only lately completed. The idea of the Portuguese authorities was to attract clients with money to spend from Johannesburg and other cities in the neighbouring Union of South Africa by offering a style of living and of entertainment more 'continental' in character than was permissible in the Union under the aegis of the zealots of the Dutch Reformed Church. This worked even in war-time, and there was a steady influx of South Africans looking for a gamble, and even an occasional clandestine visit to a brothel.

Both my opposite numbers – the Italian Consul-General, Campini, and the German Consul-General, Leopold Wertz – also lodged at the Polana Hotel, so I was able to examine them at my leisure in the hotel restaurant, where, like me, they came for meals. Campini was a large ebullient man, who obviously tried to look as like his Duce as possible; wearing a cloak whenever an occasion offered, and given to using extravagant gestures and rhetorical flourishes. Wertz, on the other hand, was not at all like Hitler or any of his henchmen; unless it was Ribbentrop, who, as Foreign Minister, was his ostensible boss, and to whom he might have been said to bear a passing resemblance. He had the youthfulness common among Germans of his type; blond and pink and spectacled and earnest. I had occasion later on to read some of his letters home, which a friendly purser on the Portuguese ship carrying the mail gave me a sight of before sailing. They were addressed to his mother; very affectionate and filial, if not sentimental, written in a rather formless hand sprawling across page after page. After the war I also read some of his official dispatches made available from captured Abwehr archives. They, too, were decidedly verbose, and in them I appeared as a ruthless intrepid spy-master, with a chain of agents extending over the whole of Southern Africa, whom he, Wertz, was able nonetheless ultimately to pulverise. Diplomats and Intelligence agents, in my experience, are even bigger liars than journalists, and the historians who try to reconstruct the past out of their records are, for the most part, dealing in fantasy.

If, as sometimes inevitably happened, I bumped into Campini or Wertz, or passed through a door at the same time, we bowed politely, but never spoke. Or we might meet in the lavatory, there, too, maintaining a coolly distant manner. Yet, of course, we were conscious of one another, living, as we were, under the same roof, eating the same meals, sharing the same servants; not to mention bribing the same local officials and police officers. Espionage and counter-espionage, as far as the Portuguese were concerned, made good their war-time losses on tourism; we secret agents represented an invisible import, if not a capital gain. It was altogether a curious relationship I had with Campini and Wertz; a kind of wordless intimacy. Even now I feel as though, if I ever ran into one of them, it would be as an old acquaintance – 'My dear fellow, how are you?'

Ledger, the British Consul-General, a kindly low-keyed man, treated me handsomely, though it was obvious that he had considerable scepticism about my supposed duties, and disliked handing out money to me even though it did not affect his own careful accounting. The other members of the staff likewise regarded me as a kind of pampered interloper whose activities were not to be taken seriously. I had a room to myself in the Consulate-General, and there I sat, with my typewriter, and a safe, in which I kept my code-book, my invisible inks and my cash, my general assignment being to try and stop the enemy from getting information about our convoys sailing to North Africa up the Mozambique Channel, where they were being torpedoed by German submarines. This was happening on a large scale, greatly assisted by the ease with which a message could be sent from Durban to Lourenço Marques giving details of Allied shipping passing through the port. The task was daunting, and I scarcely knew where to begin, seeing I had no local contacts, and my knowledge of Portuguese was sketchy to say the least. To while away the time I deciphered a long telegram which had come for me via Ledger. It was a laborious business, and the kind of thing I have always been bad at. First, one had to subtract from the groups of numbers in the telegram corresponding groups from a so-called one-time pad; then to look up what the resultant groups signified in the code-book. Any mistake in the subtraction, or, even worse, in the groups subtracted, threw the whole thing out. I toiled away at it, getting into terrible muddles and having to begin again, but finally managed to disentangle the message in an approximately legible form.

It came from Philby, as I knew from the style, and provided a résumé of the espionage scene in Lourenço Marques in the light of Wertz's and Campini's latest telegrams. All their traffic was being intercepted and cracked at Bletchley; so I had the inestimable advantage of knowing just what they were up to – like having access to the answers at the end of the book in an arithmetic test. This benefit was available to Montgomery fighting the Battle of North Africa just as much as to me fighting the Battle of Lourenço Marques. It also meant, of course, that my activities showed in the Wertz–Campini traffic, so that any bluff, or any pretence practised on my own account without reference to London was bound to become known there at once. Nonetheless, to show at all in the Bletchley material was considered in MI6 circles to be an enviable distinction; exactly like having a leader quoted in the foreign press in my *Guardian* days. The Philby directive suggested that it might be a good idea to concentrate on infiltrating the Campini *apparat* rather than the Wertz one, since the personality of Campini, to judge from his boastful, high-flown style, seemed the more vulnerable of the two.

That evening at dinner at the Polana Hotel I looked across at Campini's table – where they seemed to be in a particularly festive mood – wondering how I could hope to plant an informer among them, or otherwise get at their secrets. Signora Campini, for instance – what about her? Might she be approachable? A short, compact lady, not particularly beautiful, but quite vivacious looking, and about a third of Campini's bulk. I began to think of her almost amorously, and after dinner, when the Italian party went for a stroll in the cool moonlight, followed at a distance, only, however, catching vague echoes of their voices and their laughter. I sent a longish message to London, ciphering with anguish late into the night. It announced my arrival and establishment at the Consulate-General, and gave an account of how things were at the Polana Hotel; as it were, setting up the board and beginning to arrange my pieces.

Like Brighton rock, a war spells out the same word wherever you bite into it; on the various fronts, from Stalingrad to the Polana Hotel, the same essential line-up. Only the scale varies; not the dramatis personae. Wertz and Campini, Führer and Duce – what's the difference? Lipski, a Polish diplomat, told me once that when he saw the accused at Nuremberg he could not believe they were the same men he had treated with so deferentially in Berlin. That shambling figure, surely not Ribbentrop; that woebegone clown couldn't be Goering. But they were; it was just that they had changed their positions on the board, moving from an attacking position, to a defensive one, and then to surrender.

So, the drama of the war was played out on the Polana Front as on any other, though it has to be admitted that actual hostilities occurred but rarely. On one occasion, a South African lurched as though by accident into Campini, and a fracas of sorts followed; on another, after a drunken party, someone went round muddling up all the Axis boots and shoes put out in the corridor for cleaning. There was also an ugly scene about which particular radio station should be turned on for the news, to the point that the management decreed that the public transmission of broadcast news bulletins, from whatever source, was forbidden. Naturally, we all believed that our rooms were bugged and our bags searched; and I occasionally prowled about the hotel corridors and peered in through windows, though the only discovery I made was that Dr Wertz wore a hair-net in the privacy of his room – an interesting, but scarcely significant, item of intelligence. It piqued me slightly to observe that when visitors from South Africa arrived in the hotel it was always Wertz and Campini they wanted pointed out to them, never me. However, I comforted myself with the thought that, in war, the enemy enjoys the advantage of being glamorous; like other men's wives.

It was through the good offices of Ledger that I recruited my first sub-agent; Camille, a Polish Jew who had managed to escape from the Gestapo and make his way to Lourenço Marques, where he subsisted largely on bridge, which he played extremely well. He came to see me often. Through his bridge-playing he had a large circle of acquaintances among Portuguese officials, including the police; and in his long conversations with me – in French, which he spoke with rather a thick accent – he always presented himself as a sort of *chevalier* or dashing cavalry officer, who, through the fortunes of war, found himself in strange, if not disreputable, company, towards whom his attitude was one of tolerant condescension, as I, a fellow *chevalier*, would readily understand. It is the measure of his essential decency, and of my fondness for him, that we maintained this fiction intact to the end of our relationship, despite the fact that money passed hands, and sometimes led to wrangling which could easily have become acrimonious, and that sometimes the information he passed to me likewise partook of the fantasy which governed so much of his life in Lourenço Marques. I can see him now – the close-cropped hair, the jaunty appearance, the carefully pressed linen suit that had seen better days and white shoes always meticulously pipe-clayed, the cane, the ravaged face liable to carry an afternoon shadow even in the morning, and, above all, the eyes peering out from this ensemble anxiously, courageously, and with a touch of sheer consternation.

Quite early on in our acquaintanceship he brought to see me one of the more senior police officers in Lourenço Marques – Inspector Y. From his colour and bearing the inspector seemed to be decidedly a local product; as, indeed, were a good proportion of the officials in Mozambique. The Portuguese, I found, had no colour prejudice as such. Any resident in their colonies who acquired money and was generous in handing it out to his betters; who adopted a name like Costa da Silva, went to Mass regularly, and generally conducted himself in a responsible, respectable way, became automatically socially acceptable. The pawn got through to the back row more easily than in other African colonies. I used to think because of this, that, had I been a black African, I should have preferred to live under Portuguese rule, despite its brutality, incompetence and corruption, than under that of any of the other colonial Powers; certainly than under the rule of Afrikaners in the Union of South Africa across the border.

Camille had given his police inspector friend a great build-up before bringing him to see me – '*Vous savez, un homme très intelligent, très cultivé, très fin. Franchement, je m'étonne; même en comparaison avec les cercles intellectuelles les plus estimeés de Varsovie. Un homme exception-nel.*' He lingered over the syllables of this last word – *ex-cep-tion-nel*. Inspector Y did not, at first glance, live up to this panegyric. He had one of those bashed-in faces which look as though lumps have fallen off them here and there; like a plaster bust which has been left exposed to the weather. As he spoke only a few words of French and English, I had no means of appreciating his wit and learning, so highly praised by Camille. Despite linguistic difficulties, I managed to convey to him the suggestion that if, in the course of his duties, he came across anything that might be of interest to the British Consulate-General, I should be most grateful if he would communicate it to me via our mutual and esteemed friend Camille. The suggestion was well received; something in the nature of a smile broke across the waste-land of the inspector's face, followed by a pause in which we all three looked at one another, aware that we had reached the heart of the matter.

Diffidently – it was my first bribe; later, I became brazen enough – I produced from the drawer of my desk an envelope in which I had put some hundred escudo notes, and mentioned that, no doubt, certain expenses would arise in connection with the assignment the inspector had so graciously undertaken which I hoped he would allow me to defray. Thereupon, I passed the envelope to Camille to pass on to his friend. Camille opened it, took out the notes and counted them, with the other's eyes closely upon him. I noticed in the inspector's face, as he watched Camille counting the notes, a faint but unmistakable look of dissatisfaction; a barely discernible shake of the head, a touch of coldness breaking in on the amiability he had previously displayed. It would not do. Camille, as ever, master of the situation, very courteously asked permission to enter into a private colloquy with me. Drawing me aside, he said in an undertone that his friend was too polite (*trop gentleman*) to say so, but the amount I had handed over was quite inadequate. Wertz, in such a case, paid at least three times as much; Campini even more, *et même les Japonais, bien plus.* As I well knew, he went on, he never cared to discuss money with me; the subject was highly distasteful to him. Where money was concerned he was *un enfant nouveau né.* Even so, in this particular case, his honour was involved, and he must ask me to increase the amount paid to his friend, even if it had to be deducted from his own paltry honorarium. I suggested another three hundred escudos; his lips soundlessly formed the word *cinq,* and *cinq* it was. I should add that Camille's notion that he disliked discussing money was scarcely in accord with the facts; we discussed little else, invariably to the disadvantage of HM's Government and the British taxpayer. Having settled the matter of the escudos, Camille and his friend departed, with many courtesies, leaving me to work out a telegram to London announcing the new recruit to my *apparat*, and seeking approval for the rate we had settled on for the job. I anticipated no difficulties.

I found that bribing, which inevitably played a large part in my Lourenço Marques activities, had as many subtleties and diversities as seduction. Thus, in certain circumstances the passing of money had to be engineered in such a way that it seemed to happen of itself, which, in seduction terms, was the equivalent of lolling or reaching out an arm as though by accident. Alternatively, there were occasions in which one yelled or banged the desk, insisting that not a cent more would be forthcoming. This might be compared with violent assault. It is interesting, incidentally, as bearing on the close relation between the two activities, that the same word is used for both – to pass money or to make a pass. I became quite an adept as time went on, knowing just when to show the colour of my (or rather HMG's) money, and how much was needed to provide the necessary incentive in this or that case. In Intelligence operations, money is an essential ingredient; even where other motives arise – as patriotism or ideological affiliations – money, however little, or its equivalent, must be dropped in, like a touch of bitter in a mint julep, to validate the deal. Only when money has passed is the mystical union fully established; it's money that makes Intelligence go round. And money, as it were, on trust. For obvious reasons, I couldn't ask Inspector Y for a receipt. In bribery there are no accounts; only good, or, more often, bad, faith.

Leslie Nicholson

A British agent is a very normal, frustrated, hard-worked ordinary person most of the time. He is hedged about by rules and regulations, bombarded with boring questions, interminable reports and assessments of his own reports. Officially he must lead a normal and discreet kind of life; He has to keep up a suitable front job and that means doing *the job in addition to* Intelligence *work.*

Whether Graham Greene had Leslie Nicholson in mind when he wrote his abortive film story *Nobody to Blame* is unknown, but it is not impossible. Nicholson was well liked by his colleagues and was known as a raconteur of entertaining and irreverent anecdotes about his experiences as an SIS officer in pre-war Czechoslovakia and Latvia.

He had been posted to Prague in 1930 and was to spend the next twenty years in

SIS. However, when his wife fell ill he asked C, Sir Stewart Menzies, for a loan. Unwisely, Menzies refused, but offered instead to commute what pension his subordinate was due. When his wife died Nicholson moved to the United States and wreaked his revenge on SIS in 1966 by publishing *British Agent*, an amusing account of his pre-war career. He recalled having been recruited by SIS in London in 1929 and being persuaded to resign his army commission. His first assignment was to Vienna to be briefed by the local head of station in Vienna, Thomas Kendrick, although he discreetly omitted his name from the text. Then he moved on to Czechoslovakia and remained there until February 1934 when he was transferred to Latvia. His eventual withdrawal to London in 1940 followed the Soviet occupation of Riga and his lengthy journey home was to take him via Moscow, Vladivostok, Japan and Canada. For much of the rest of the war he remained at Broadway and in 1945 he was sent to Bucharest to open up a new station. Although Nicholson tactfully concluded his story at that sensitive point, SIS was outraged, all the more so because another wartime colleague, Captain Henry Kerby, who had operated in Sweden in 1940 and was then the Conservative Member of Parliament for West Sussex, had contributed a short foreword. In addition, Malcolm Muggeridge had given his endorsement to the book in an introduction.

The British edition of Nicholson's memoirs was heavily censored and he was dissuaded from writing a sequel. Instead he volunteered a mass of information to Ladislas Farago, an American journalist of Hungarian origin who was to write *Game of the Foxes*, arguably the most detailed account of wartime intelligence operations yet published. Unfortunately Farago was later discredited because of his sensational newspaper stories, not the least of which was the revelation that he had found Martin Bormann alive in Argentina. Desperately disappointed, Nicholson died in New York, penniless, in 1973.

British Agent

And so there I was, in the summer of 1930, sitting in the Arlsberg Express bound for Vienna, a member of the allegedly non-existent British Secret Service. I did not feel much like one; I had not even got a symbol, though I knew what this would be when I reached Prague. As far as I can remember, I slept very well that night until a *wagon-lit* attendant rattled at my door to announce breakfast.

Vienna took a long time to appear. I had never been there before and I was looking forward to seeing it. In the afternoon the train finally pulled into the West Station and I was met, by arrangement, by our man in Vienna. He had a car outside and soon organised a couple of porters to remove and load my luggage. I had been booked in at the Hotel Sacher where he deposited me, having told me that he would be calling for me in the evening as we were going to a dinner party at which I would meet some other links in the chain.

Sacher's was the gayest and most elegant of the Vienna hotels. I noticed, however, that all the staff were in mourning and I was told that the famous Madame Sacher had recently died. Before expiring Madame had requested that the hotel should continue to function as usual. An assistant manager showed me to my room which was vast, comfortably overfurnished and had an atmosphere of faded glory. There were two hours to waste before the evening engagement and I was impatient to see something of the hotel and possibly the city. I slipped out of my clothes and turned on a bath.

Within half an hour I was walking down the soft carpeted stairs on the ground floor and entered the bar. For years Sacher's had been the rendezvous of gay Viennese society and on this evening, faithful to the late Madame Sacher's last wishes and in spite of the black crêpe it was as gay as ever. I took a stool at the long bar and ordered some brandy and soda. Then, swinging round on the seat, I surveyed the scene: the softly-glowing candelabra, the gloriously Victorian upholstery and furnishings, the intricately-carved mirrors and faded gilt wall brackets. Even in 1930 American tourists were very much in evidence; gullible, prepared to be bored for hours and buy many rounds of drinks just to be able to say on return to the States: 'I found real romance in Vienna.'

It was a wonderful scene. Young Viennese beauties were everywhere, their features and fine figures distinguishing them from other nationalities, unrivalled, except, perhaps, by the Hungarian girls. My contemplation was interrupted by the arrival of my host for the evening. An hour had passed, and I had not even noticed the time. It also occurred to me that here I was, in the middle of Vienna, surrounded by a host of potential contacts from several countries, and I had not even struck up a conversation with the barman, let alone with one of the customers. I made a mental note to be more industrious in future.

The dinner was a formal affair and the talk was mostly about the political set-up in Vienna and – which was closely connected – the state of the Austrian exchequer.

With the collapse of the Austro-Hungarian Empire, Vienna was the vast Imperial-sized capital of a tiny country. The Empire had been carved up into three main states: Austria itself, Czechoslovakia and Hungary. Czechoslovakia, where I was to spend four happy years, was really a new creation and she came off by far the best. Under the benign President Masaryk, she was the most stable and prosperous state to emerge from the fallen Empire. Her people were level-headed and hardworking, and she possessed some first-class industries. Her neighbour, Hungary, was in a less happy state. She was primarily an agricultural country but had been deprived of three-quarters of her former territory by the Treaty of the Trianon; she was clamouring for a revision of her frontiers. Fear of an Hungarian assault led to the formation of a defensive coalition between Czechoslovakia, Roumania and Yugoslavia, known as the 'Little Entente'. The Hungarian Regent was Admiral Nicholas Horthy, under whom the 'White Terror' against Jews and Communists had flourished immediately after the First World War. The Prime Minister was the chauvinistic General Gömbös. Mussolini, who had already come to power in Italy, had taken Hungary under his wing and the Hungarians also had the sympathy and support of Germany – who had similar revisionary aims.

Austria was now a tiny country, but Vienna was the former capital of an Empire and her economy formed an integral part of the financial structure of the world. In 1930 Vienna was already veering towards bankruptcy. The failure of the Credit-Anstalt, a private but important Viennese bank, in May of 1931, sparked off a chain reaction through Europe which later forced Britain off the Gold Standard.

I don't remember my first dinner party in Vienna as particularly cheerful and I had no opportunity to talk about my job; my complete ignorance of how I was supposed to operate was causing me considerable anxiety. After dinner we were all going on to a dance at the American Women's Club. I was apparently invited as well and off we went.

I met a few people at the party and my colleague regaled me with stories of my predecessors. One of these had indulged in periodic drinking bouts, when he would disappear from his office without warning and vanish for a couple of days, much to the worry of the rest of the staff, until he returned, ravaged and exhausted. On one occasion he had been picked up by the police for being offensive and put in a cell to cool off. In his briefcase, which was not locked or, it was hoped, tampered with, were all sorts of confidential documents which he had collected earlier in the day.

His successor, the product of a famous public school and a rugger blue, was a gay young man about town. He had got himself involved in a row over a girl-friend which had also attracted some rather unwelcome attention from the police. This was not at all what London wanted, and he, like his predecessor, was smartly recalled. Naturally I did not find all this very encouraging. However, I made an appointment to call at my colleague's office – to be, as I hoped, briefed on how I was to carry on the work in Prague.

My mentor was a man of great charm, a keen sense of humour and with an air of middle-aged respectability which I found reassuring in view of his stories. He gave me the run of all his files, but I could make nothing of them. The operational files contained little more than a series of questions and answers exchanged with London. They revealed nothing of how it was done and to the uninitiated reader it was almost impossible to see what they were all about.

At the end of a wearisome day I told him that I was getting nowhere with the files and he agreed that perhaps they were not much help.

'Could you give me some idea of how to begin?' I asked him imploringly. 'Are there any standard rules? . . . or could you give me some practical hints?'

He thought for a bit. 'I don't think there are really; you'll just have to work it out for yourself. I think everyone has his own methods and I can't think of anything I can tell you.'

This was appalling. I had banked on the interview – London had told me he was their best man. And now it was over and I had got precisely nowhere.

A few nights later I went out with my colleague and his wife on an evening tour of the town. In one bar on the Ring which he often frequented I made my first acquaintance with someone who was later to become an important link in my organisation. This was the Balkan correspondent of an American newspaper whose office was in Vienna. I was introduced to him and his attractive Canadian wife as we stood at the bar. After exchanging a few remarks about the international situation, the American aroused my professional curiosity.

'Vienna is the best clearinghouse for us newspapermen in Central Europe,' he told me. I gathered that he had only been in Vienna for a few months but already he had set up a little network of correspondents who, he reckoned, would keep him posted in advance of any major political moves. I think American dollars had played quite a part in all this, but, even so, I found his confidence encouraging. As we were talking a good-looking gentleman came up and greeted the American with considerable deference. He turned out to be an Austrian baron and he was anxious to offer his services to my new acquaintance.

'I have good friends in several of the Ministries, both here in Vienna and in Budapest. I am sure I could be of great assistance to you. . . .'

I did not hear any more as my party was leaving but I could see that an agent's task in Central Europe might not be as daunting as I had feared!

We went on to a well-known restaurant and here my colleague pointed out to me a swarthy-looking Austrian dining with a big party who was the Chief of the Political Police. This man had once demonstrated local methods of interrogation by striking a prisoner he happened to be questioning across the face with a rubber truncheon, much to the discomfort of my colleague who at that moment was ushered into the office. Dining here also was a striking-looking redhaired girl who was a friend of Prince Stahremberg, the leader of the Austrian Nationalist *Heimwehr* Organisation – this was a curious set-up, because although the rank and file were on first-class terms with their opposite numbers in the Nazi Party, its leaders, Prince Stahremberg and others, were by no means on good terms with the Hitler regime. Later, as relations between Austria and Germany became more and more complicated, the exact position of Prince Stahremberg and the *Heimwehr* was very difficult to diagnose.

From what I observed during my all too brief stay, the Viennese were still incorrigibly romantic; café and night life flourished in all its variations in spite of the general shortage of money. I was sorry to leave the city after a most enjoyable fortnight, but I felt that there was nothing to justify my staying there any longer. I must get on with my work, which lay ahead in Prague. I booked a sleeper on the night train and my colleague and his wife waved goodbye as my carriage moved out of the Franz Josef Station.

Nigel Clive

Far too little was known about 'the real enemy', and I was given the first of many repeated instructions to keep my nose out of politics, concentrate on the main objective, maintain the good reputation of the service with the Foreign Office and not meddle in matters which should properly be handled by the Foreign Office.

When Nigel Clive came down from Christ Church, Oxford, in June 1940 he volunteered for the army and by Christmas was in Egypt with the 2nd Armoured Division. Instead of being transferred to the Libyan desert, Clive's troop was deployed to Greece and arrived only shortly before the evacuation of April 1941. Posted to Palestine, he was recruited into SIS by Frank Giffey, formerly the head of station in pre-war Riga and now SIS's man in Baghdad. For eighteen months Clive was billeted with Freya Stark, the noted Arabist and a wartime SIS agent, and learned the rudiments of secret intelligence.

Clive was appalled by the jealousies that plagued the British intelligence structure in Iraq, where five different agencies were in fierce competition. He recalls that 'it became a commonplace to say that if fifty per cent of the day could be devoted to trying to defeat Hitler, we were doing well and might win the war.' In July 1943, disillusioned by the inter-agency sniping, Clive obtained a transfer to SIS's Yugoslav Section in Cairo where he prepared to join a military mission to Tito. At the last moment the operation was cancelled and Clive was returned to Cairo where he was assigned to the Greek Section, headed by Edward Dillon. There he experienced further delays, but in December 1943 he was finally parachuted into the Epirus region of Greece to join up with a group of anti-Communist guerrillas operating under SOE's sponsorship.

Clive remained in the mountains of Greece operating with the partisans until November 1944 when, following the German withdrawal, he reported to Cairo, only to be returned to Epirus on a second mission later the same month. He arrived in Athens in time to witness the opening rounds of the Greek civil war, but by the end of the year he was back in London, recalled to headquarters for consultations.

Having briefed David Footman, the head of SIS's Political Section, on the deteriorating situation in Greece, Clive returned to Athens in March 1945 to start what was to be a three-year attachment to the British embassy. In April 1948 he was transferred to Jerusalem and arrived in time to watch the first Arab–Israeli war but his cover was blown almost as soon as he had opened his office. Accordingly, in 1950, he was sent to Iraq to run the Baghdad station, and was back in London as Controller Middle East, in succession to George Young, to supervise SIS's contribution to the ill-fated Suez campaign. Two years later Clive was assigned to Tunis, and thereafter to Algiers. He returned to London in 1966 and was appointed head of the Information Research Department, a hybrid organization which co-ordinated anti-Soviet propaganda and developed techniques of psychological warfare.

In 1969 Clive retired and joined the Organization for Economic Co-operation and Development in Paris, and until 1980 served in the Secretary-General's private office. In 1985 his wartime memoirs were published, apparently without the knowledge or consent of his old office, but no action was taken to prevent their distribution. In this passage he recounts the tangled relationships that existed between the various competing secret organizations in the Middle East.

A Greek Experience

When the Greek office sent me alone to SOE headquarters in Cairo, it had already been agreed that my mission – code name 'Jute' – consisting of Kalousis, Katsikakis and myself would be dropped in Epirus and formally attached to SOE's Allied Military Mission under Lieutenant Colonel Tom Barnes at EDES headquarters. Once again I was warned in advance to be on my guard and not to express any political opinions, and it was stressed that my objectives were strictly confined to the acquisition of the military intelligence required by GHQ. I spent an entertaining few days in an atmosphere more reminiscent of a newspaper office than of a paramilitary headquarters. I found myself talking to people who were politically alert and whose judgments, right or wrong, were persuasively argued. In one room I heard a panegyric of Zervas and in another an anathema against him. In the space of a day, he was described as a national hero, as well as an untrustworthy ruffian with a colourful but disreputable political past whose 'splinter group', EDES, had divided an otherwise united 'democratic resistance movement'. Before such voluble briefing, it was easy to obey my instructions 'to listen and not to talk'. But although I welcomed every scrap of information that was offered to me, it was difficult to piece together so much contradictory evidence. A further problem was what to reveal and what not to reveal to Kalousis, who had an entirely legitimate interest in sharing whatever information I was gathering. During the parachute course, we had agreed that it would be unwise to jump to conclusions and more prudent to form judgments of the political situation once we had arrived. I therefore sidestepped his questions about the impressions I had gained of Zervas's reputation and standing in SOE.

When I told the head of the Greek office of the confusing accounts I had been given at SOE and how the situation should be presented to Kalousis, he merely shrugged his shoulders and repeated his set speech about keeping out of the political business and concentrating on the Germans as the main enemy and my only target. My first duty, he unhelpfully emphasized, was to escape the fate of Costa Lawrence. I must avoid, if conceivably possible, any open breach with SOE on any issue; but at the same time my mission was to be kept separate from all their activities, and I was given a string of assurances that if I obeyed my instructions, I could count on the support of the Greek office within and beyond the limits of what was possible.

When the head of the Greek office referred me upward to his superiors at SIS headquarters in Cairo, which was designated the Inter Services Liaison Department (ISLD), I found myself being interviewed by Army, Navy and Air Force officers who, for different reasons, had left their respective services before the war. Their whole professional upbringing had schooled them to treat politics as an arcane subject, best left to others. Every senior officer to whom I spoke emphasized, sometimes with undisguised pleasure, that SOE 'had made a mess of it' in Greece and this was the root cause of its turbulent relations with the Foreign Office and with the British Embassy to the exiled Greek government in Cairo. I was told that the Ambassador, Rex Leeper, was an enemy of SOE, but when I gently inquired what SOE had done to cause his enmity, the answers I received made me none the wiser. Moreover, the suggestion that I should myself call on the Embassy was politely turned aside. It therefore seemed all the more strange and contradictory to be reminded that SIS came under the Foreign Office, was both shielded by it and should be its shield against 'amateur policy-makers' – as the head of ISLD described them – whose professionalism had been lost when SOE had been allowed to break away from SIS in the summer of 1940 and set up on its own under the aegis of the Ministry of Economic Warfare.

Now that I had tested it out at different levels, I could see more clearly than in Baghdad that the child, SOE, had outgrown its parent, SIS. Even from my brief contacts with SOE it was clear that both their military and civilian members were of a quite different stamp. They had no fear whatever of trading in political commodities and knew that resistance in Europe was as political a matter as the composition of a government. Hence, in this respect SOE outgunned SIS for the simple reason that SIS had virtually no artillery. As usual, personalities also had their part to play in the rivalry between the two organizations in Cairo, which were in effect at loggerheads with one another.

Though I was not to know it at the time, the rivalry between SOE and SIS was no less fierce in London, with one vital difference. The head of SIS, Sir Stewart Menzies, operating both from his office in Broadway and his club, White's in St James's Street, was closer to the levers of power than any of his rivals and exploited to the full his direct access to the Prime Minister. He was greatly helped by Major Desmond Morton, who had been a trusted adviser to Churchill before the war while he was serving in SIS and had naturally graduated into Churchill's inner circle after 1940. No one in his right mind would have accused Menzies of being outgunned in Whitehall. But SIS's position in London was in no way reflected in the power and influence of ISLD, its regional headquarters in Cairo.

When therefore I tiptoed forward with some elementary inquiries about the politics of mountain Greece, which I would shortly be experiencing, at no level in ISLD were answers available to the following questions. Was His Majesty's Government (HMG) irrevocably committed to support the King's return to Greece after liberation? How did the exiled Greek government in Cairo maintain its links with the Resistance? What did EDES and Zervas represent? If it was true, as I had been told by Kalousis, that Zervas had a republican past, when and how had he come to terms with the King? Or was he opposed to the King's return? Obviously EAM/

ELAS was, by definition, republican; but was it partly or wholly under Communist control? In any event, what was the role of the Greek Communist Party? What were EAM/ELAS's links with Tito? On what issue and how and when had fighting broken out between EDES and ELAS? Which of the two had been the first to organize resistance? Which had done the most damage to the Germans?

These, one might have thought, were no more than the normal questions likely to be asked by any newcomer to the scene. I had hoped for brief, standard, textbook answers, but whenever I alluded to these matters, I was told again and again that I did not need this kind of information and should be concentrating all my efforts on the buildup and analysis of the German order of battle. The impression left on me at the end of my briefing in ISLD was that Lanz might have been operating, not within and part of a civil war, but across a sparsely populated desert.

Philip Johns

In my day the Secret Service resembled more an exclusive club. To all intents a band of brothers, its members recruited by invitation from an existing member.

In the autumn of 1939, as a newly arrived member of the Naval Control Service in Antwerp, Commander Philip Johns, RNVR, joined SIS's local station. 'There was no application form to join the Secret Service,' he recalled. 'There was no written examination or personal interview with any board.' Instead he was invited to volunteer for 'special service' and promptly driven by a civilian member of the Passport Control Office to Brussels where he was introduced to Edward Calthrop, the wheelchair-bound head of station.

Johns remained in Brussels until the evacuation in May the following year when he returned to London to join SIS's Naval Section. As the third most senior member of the section Johns recalls that one of his duties was to confer with Ian Fleming, his liaison contact in the Naval Intelligence Division. 'After our exchanges on duty matters, we would often lunch together, sometimes at one of his clubs, Boodle's, where he maintained (and I could not but agree) that the wartime cuisine was probably the best available in London.' Early in 1941 Johns was posted as head of station to Lisbon, the neutral capital that had become a centre of European espionage. During his two years there Johns encountered Dusko Popov, one of MI5's many double agents, and Donald Darling, the local MI9 representative who had been identified mistakenly by the notorious PIDE as head of SIS's local networks. John recalls that the arrival of the double agent codenamed Tricycle 'was reported to me and the fact that he had been given by his German controllers a questionnaire relating to the US defences of Pearl Harbor. At the time, if I remember correctly, little importance was attached to this piece of information and if of value it would have been for the Americans to assess, although of course at that time the USA had not entered the war. As it turned out, when Tricycle was handed over to the FBI on his arrival in the USA, the implications in regard to Pearl Harbor were given little credence.'

In December 1942 Johns was recalled to London for a new assignment, the supervision of a complicated shipping deal in Buenos Aires intended to transfer the ownership of Axis merchant vessels mothballed in neutral ports to front companies in Argentina. The scheme was to be financed by the Treasury but after Johns arrived and opened negotiations the project was abandoned and he was sent to Rio de Janeiro as head of station. He remained in Brazil until October 1943 when he returned to London, via New York, to take command of SOE's Belgian Section.

For the last eighteen months of the war Johns was in charge of the Low Countries Section which combined the Belgian and ill-fated Dutch country sections. It was a task requiring great skill and tact, considering the tension that had developed between the various intelligence agencies with overlapping responsibilities and the fact that they had all experienced degrees of enemy penetration. When Brussels was liberated, in September 1944, he opened a Special Forces headquarters in what had until recently been the offices of the Luftwaffe.

At the end of the war he returned to commercial life and emigrated to the United States where he now lives. His memoirs, published in 1979, were among the very first to be written by a wartime SIS officer, and were unusual because the author identified many of his SIS colleagues, although he neglected to reveal the name of his successor in Lisbon, Cecil Gledhill, with whom he had been on poor terms. Resident in Florida, Johns felt under no obligation to submit his manuscript to the authorities, and it thereby achieved some notoriety within the intelligence community.

Within Two Cloaks: Missions with SIS and SOE

Regarding the routine in the office, I was one of the first to arrive at the Embassy [in Lisbon] most mornings and the daily work schedule was followed as far as possible. First there were the incoming signals on my desk, one occasionally marked 'Personal for 24300. Decipher yourself'. Then, twice weekly as a rule, the King's Messenger would have arrived from London and his diplomatic bag would include our own individual bag from HQ. This contained appreciations of reports submitted earlier by the station, accompanied sometimes by requests for clarification or more details, new and revised questionnaires, advice regarding our personnel in transit to and from London via Lisbon with their priorities for onward travel. These would be sorted out and distributed to the officers concerned for action.

I had rid myself long ago of any ideas that the Secret Service was the glamorous and exciting career of the novelists. I had yet to see any false beards or to encounter alluring adventuresses who would seduce me from my loyalties. My car was a *casse gueule* Citroën 15 CV, several years old, instead of a shining Bristol or Aston Martin. Although I had done some pistol practice on the range in London, I did not habitually carry a Beretta strapped to my armpit, and I had no supply of cyanide ampoules to issue to our agents.

Agents inside Europe were certainly engaged in most dangerous work. Any small mistake, any lack of attention in establishing convincingly their 'cover' could well be fatal. Our own work, however, was mostly a painstaking process of obtaining and sifting secret information, and I emphasise the word secret as compared with intelligence not so classified, which passed through the channels of the Service Attachés, the Commercial Section, and the Press Attaché.

The time I had spent at Broadway had made me fully acquainted with what intelligence was required from the Station. It was my responsibility to get it from the limited sources at my disposal. It is true that theoretically we had access through officially neutral Spain to Hitler's Europe. Practically, however, just as we controlled the air services from Lisbon to London and the USA, the Germans controlled the air service to Paris and to the occupied countries and Berlin. We were restricted in practice to the use of the railway and this meant that we were in no position to take the risk of supplying the agents we enlisted with items of equipment such as a radio. Detection would have been almost inevitable. The best we could manage to arrange for communications was by secret ink and simple codes, although there were the exceptions, the few agents we knew from past experience to be completely reliable and trustworthy who were sent to contact existing networks in the field with their own wireless communications already in place. In this category also would be a few men and women recruited in London who passed through our hands for onward travel arrangements.

Volunteers were not the problem. There were many of them but few who had (a) the necessary qualifications and (b) the cover, either already existing, or to be contrived for them, which would satisfy the scrutiny of German security control. Moreover we had to be specially wary against possible plants by the German SD in Portugal. Thus the selected few comprised mostly neutral citizens who had a valid reason to travel to occupied Europe, mostly businessmen who had no special training in military matters, but could be most useful in the field of industrial intelligence. There were also potentially valuable dissidents from countries such as Austria, Poland and Yugoslavia, or nationals from such countries who found themselves isolated in Portugal when their homeland was overrun. The majority of these were incarcerated by the Portuguese at Caldas da Rainha, but there were a handful who had the financial means and necessary identity papers to continue in Portugal unmolested. A few, a very few, of these people were worthy of consideration to be briefed by SIS for missions of importance.

By far the greater volume of human traffic was in the other direction, i.e. arriving in Portugal from occupied Europe. I do not refer here to people coming through the escape lines, but to men and women who had managed to secure travel papers from the German authorities. Obviously, they were mostly suspect as probable collaborators, but there were a few known to us and trusted, such as the executive of Air Liquide referred to previously. There were also a few Portuguese, travelling in connection with the export of cork, olive oil, and fruit such as almonds, but these were representatives whose credentials could readily be checked by the Germans, and so were in most cases not available for our purposes.

Apart from these categories, there were a handful of diplomats travelling legitimately, some of them representing neutral countries and a few who were personally acquainted with members of our own embassy, so that through the latter it was occasionally possible for myself or one of my staff to be introduced. After Germany declared war on the USA in December 1941, there was a big influx of American diplomats. By this time I had built up excellent relationships with various officers in the US Legation (later upgraded to embassy status) and so came into possession of a considerable amount of up-to-date intelligence.

Of great importance to us were arrivals through the escape lines of our own secret agents who, fearing arrest by the Gestapo, had been obliged to abandon their missions. These would first of all be interviewed by the Repatriation Office when the agents usually asked to be put in touch with one of the Service Attachés. I would then be advised, would obtain full details concerning the men or women involved, and would check their bona fides with HQ in London. If verification were forthcoming, these agents would be taken over by me or by one of my staff for detailed interrogation and report to Broadway.

I held a weekly meeting with the other heads of departments. Present would be Ralph Jarvis, sometimes accompanied by Dorrington, one of his staff, a highly experienced officer who had served with Passport Control in Berlin, and who spoke German fluently. Ralph would usually represent the Repatriation Office as well as his own Section V. Jack Beevor and Paul Homberger represented SOE. The Shipping Attaché often delegated John Mockford, a lieutenant RNVR who in pre-war days was employed by me in Antwerp. Discussions were of a general nature ranging over events of the past week which were of interest to all concerned. Details of present and future operations, including identity of sources were avoided. The 'watertight door' principle applied.

The Ambassador usually expected me to spend a short time with him every week to keep him posted about any information which might interest him. Peter Garran would call and let me know at what time. I had meetings with Captain Arthur Benson, Shipping Attaché, three or four times a week. He would call, saying 'P. J. – are you free? Can you pass by the Consulate some time today?' or: 'When may I come and see you. I believe I have something of interest.' It must be remembered that we could never discuss anything of a confidential nature over the telephone. There were no 'scramblers'. As I mentioned previously, the Shipping Attaché and his staff were housed in the Consulate-General so usually when I called to see Arthur I made a point of spending at least a few minutes with Henry King. Most days I had informal meetings with the three Service Attachés.

Outside the Embassy my most important contacts were with the US Legation staff. At the time of my arrival early in 1941 the USA was neutral and the staff was small in numbers. As the weeks went by and it became obvious that there would be no early end to the conflict, the legation expanded and from Washington arrived a variety of new faces: nominees of the FBI, the US Treasury (responsible for covering drugs and narcotics), OSS (the Office of Strategic Services) were all accredited to Lisbon with diplomatic cover. After Pearl Harbor and the official entry of the USA into the war, there was further expansion and the legation was raised to embassy status.

I had found in London that there existed a profound distrust of all USA covert intelligence. Their personnel was regarded as amateurish and lacking in security. This attitude is difficult if not impossible to understand in view of our own sad experiences with Philby, Burgess and Maclean. In any event, as far as Lisbon was concerned, my relations with my various opposite numbers in the US Legation could not have been bettered, and the co-operation between our services and the Americans was close, friendly, and most helpful. I established particularly good contacts with Ambrose ('Brose') Chambers and Kenneth (Ken) Demerest, both Assistant Naval Attachés. Brose had been a member of a legal firm of international reputation with its head office in New York. Ken Demerest had also been an attorney in civilian life, practising in Brazil, so spoke Portuguese fluently. We became extremely good friends as well as colleagues.

The US Minister was Bert Fish, but I only met him on one or two occasions. I was, however, specially impressed by George Kennan, who was US Counsellor, a career diplomat of outstanding intelligence, whose advice and recommendations always went straight to the point, and who had an immediate grasp of any problem I discussed with him. He went on to rise very high in his country's service and later was appointed US Ambassador in Moscow. His subsequent book reviewing his experiences and his views on East–West relations was a masterpiece of analysis.

A younger US Assistant Naval Attaché, whom I met frequently with Chambers and Demerest, was Teddy Rousseau, whose father I had known in Paris as the manager of the Guaranty Trust Company. After the war ended Teddy took up an appointment as curator of the Metropolitan Art Museum in New York. I saw a lot of Brose Chambers in the early postwar period when he served with Averell Harriman who was responsible for the execution of the Marshall Plan. I must also mention in Lisbon another of my good contacts in the US Embassy, Burke Elbrick. He was then a Second Secretary but some years after the war he was given rapid promotion in the Foreign Service and became US Ambassador to Brazil. It was in Rio de Janeiro that he underwent an extremely unpleasant ordeal, being the first prominent diplomat to be kidnapped and held for ransom for political motives.

Mention has been made previously of Joseph Luns, Second Secretary of the Netherlands Legation, whom I saw from time to time for meetings which were always agreeable and productive. There was also Freddie Dumont, representing the Belgian Government-in-Exile, but with no diplomatic recognition. He and Jack Beevor were close associates, but I also met him occasionally. I know he made a major contribution to SOE operations in Belgium. He was a lawyer by profession and the last I heard of him was that he was expected to become shortly Lord Chancellor of Belgium.

One of the most intriguing assignments entrusted to me in London before I left for Portugal was to cultivate the acquaintanceship of Calouste Gulbenkian. It was DCSS, 'Uncle' Claude Dansey, who spoke to me about the importance of this, and he handed me a letter of introduction to Gulbenkian, handwritten by Lord Tyrell. They had known each other as members of the International Oil Commission set up under the Armistice Administration in 1918 to report on the 'black gold' to be piped and refined from the Middle East oilfields. Gulbenkian was an Armenian by birth, but had acquired Iranian citizenship, and at the outbreak of World War II he held the post of Financial Adviser in the Iranian Legation in Paris. He was the possessor of a British passport. I never knew how this originated but Gulbenkian was inordinately proud of it.

I made an appointment to call on Gulbenkian shortly after my arrival in Lisbon, where he was living in a suite at the Hotel Aviz on the Avenida de Libertade, a small, but in 1941 by far the most luxurious, hotel in the city. He occupied this suite with his wife and personal secretary. I remember him as a small, grey, wizened and stooping individual, completely unremarkable except for his bird-like piercing eyes. He was a multi-millionaire, known throughout the oil world as 'Mr Five per cent', famous on account of his 5 per cent stock-holding in the Anglo-Iranian Oil Company. This holding not only provided him with a massive revenue, but also gave him great power and leverage in the company's operations as he held the decisive vote between the other two shareholders. He lived sparsely, and I would occasionally lunch with him very frugally at the corner table in the Aviz restaurant always reserved for him, his family, and guests. In Paris he had left behind in his home or in the Iranian Legation a priceless collection of Old Masters, gold plate, rare coins and other treasures, but as Iran was neutral at the time and Gulbenkian enjoyed diplomatic privileges, his property was sealed up by the Germans when he left Paris and was recovered by him when the war ended.

Although unimpressive in appearance, Mr Five per cent was a man of exceptional intelligence, and his knowledge in everything pertaining to the oil industry was phenomenal. He had his ear very close to the ground even when exiled in Lisbon and what he did not know about the production side of the 'black gold' and its world-wide ramifications in finance and exploration would not have been worth knowing. I have often wondered what his views would have been in respect of the Arab exploitation today of their vast oil resources. His comments would certainly have been of considerable interest.

In view of the unholy alliance between Hitler and Stalin, the Secret Service was extremely anxious to have information regarding the Soviet Union's present and potential oil production and what deliveries might be made available for Germany. Gulbenkian could be a good source for such information. In spite of his isolation in Portugal he maintained his contacts with the VIPs of the oil industry all over the world, and his experience was much valued and his advice much sought after. During my stay in Lisbon he received many visits from oil executives including one or more from the president of the Standard Oil Company of New Jersey, who flew over by Pan American Clipper specially to confer with him.

For some reason, in spite of his importance to my service, and the fact that he held a British passport, Sir Ronald Campbell [the Ambassador] would never agree to receive him, and this he took almost as a personal insult. I believe he trusted me and knew that I would respect his anonymity and never disclose except to my own London Headquarters the source of the information he passed to me. He always greeted me with the impression of being pleased to see me and gave me much of his time. One piece of intelligence we were most anxious to have was an estimate, however rough, of the extent of Soviet Russia's gold production and gold reserves. Gulbenkian was unable to be of any help. I wonder how much we know now!

Apart from expressing his views and passing on information in regard to oil, and particularly the current resources and estimated production of the USSR and the Roumanian wells at Ploeşti, Gulbenkian would sometimes discuss his family affairs and in 1941 and 1942 made no secret of the fact that he was completely estranged from his son, Nubar. He told me more than once that he had no intention of bequeathing to Nubar much of his fortune, but that instead he had taken steps to set up a foundation in the interests of art. The Gulbenkian Foundation is known throughout the world for its generous contributions towards the encouragement of art, but Nubar was never given any responsibility in the administration of this organisation. I met Nubar on several occasions after the war, and according to Airey Neave's book in connection with the MI9 escape routes the former played an important part in the French network.

Nubar spent some time in Portugal in the post-war period and as I was also living there I saw him frequently with his French wife Marie, an heiress from one of the well-known champagne families. His sister was also a friend, a pleasant intelligent girl full of the joy of living, who was often to be found wandering along the miles of sandy beaches at Guincho watching the Atlantic rollers roaring and pounding the shore. Nubar was a flamboyant character, bearded and heavily built, utterly different from his father. When in London he maintained a permanent suite at the Ritz Hotel, and his transportation was either his Rolls-Royce or a special taxi converted to his own specifications, which he regarded as more practical and more suited to his bulky frame. He rode to hounds with the Pytchley and made an invariable habit of wearing an orchid in his buttonhole, freshly selected every day. This was the subject of the story that on one occasion a member of the hunt riding alongside called over to him, 'I say, old man, who would ever dream of wearing an orchid for this sort of exercise?' To this Nubar replied, 'Well for that matter I don't suppose you've ever had a bloody Armenian riding with the Pytchley before, let alone with an orchid.'

Henry Kerby

The glut of fiction written on this theme has tended to take the work of such men into the realm of the fairy tale.

Elected in a March 1954 by-election as a Tory MP for Arundel, West Sussex, Henry Kerby had worked for SIS in Malmö during the early part of the war, operating under consular cover, and latterly was regarded as a useful agent for the Security Service. In *Spycatcher* Peter Wright recalls an episode in which Kerby was to plant in the Soviet embassy in London a sophisticated listening device concealed in an ornate silver model of the Kremlin, ostensibly a gift from the MP to the ambassador. (Kerby, born in Russia, spoke the language fluently and was the official interpreter for Khrushchev's visit to England in 1956.) The scheme was dropped when the proposal was put up to the Foreign Office and vetoed.

Educated at Highgate and on the Continent, Kerby joined the army in 1933, aged eighteen, but left four years later. In 1939 he was on the staff of the British legation in Riga with the status of honorary attaché, and this was where he came into contact with Leslie Nicholson, the local SIS head of station. In 1940 Kerby was switched to Malmö, and according to his uninformative entry in *Who's Who* he spent the remainder of the war 'specially employed under War Office'. At the end of the war he received decorations from Finland, Poland, Norway, Yugoslavia and Denmark, which gives a clue to the territories he dealt with while in SIS.

Until 1966, when Harold Wilson instructed MI5 not to run MPs as agents, Kerby was a valued source for the Security Service, reporting on his many trade visits to Moscow. He was frequently to be seen as a guest at the Soviet embassy in London, and in 1952 invited Kim Philby to tea with a curious story. He claimed also to have been sacked from SIS, and offered to use his position in Parliament to attack the Foreign Office if Philby could supply him with any ammunition. According to Philby's version of this episode, in *My Silent War*, he rejected the proposition.

Kerby was widely distrusted by his own party, and after his death in January

1971, aged fifty-six, it was revealed that he had been on surprisingly close terms with the Labour leader Harold Wilson, to the extent that some regarded him as a spy for the Socialists inside the Tory camp. Nevertheless he was returned at the 1970 General Election with a huge majority, a not inconsiderable achievement bearing in mind he had suffered a heart attack in February of that year.

When Kerby's friend Leslie Nicholson announced his intention to publish his memoirs, designed to wrongfoot SIS, Kerby gave his support and contributed the following endorsement which was calculated to inflict maximum embarrassment.

British Agent (Foreword)

This is a piece of publishing history. For the first time ever, a former senior member of the service which officially does not exist tells the true facts of life as a secret agent. For security reasons the author has adopted an assumed name, but he is an old friend of mine and I can vouch for the valuable work he carried out for Britain in his highly skilled and dangerous, and in many ways thankless, missions. The glut of fiction written on this theme has tended to take the work of such men into the realm of the fairy tale. But this book is no fairy tale. I am delighted that at last a factual account is to be published, for I believe that the public are entitled to know something of the realities of this splendid service – after all, they pay for it.

A. J. Ayer

This department cared nothing for military distinctions, so that, having automatically ceased to be a local major, I changed my rank only for the worse. For all practical purposes I reverted to being a civilian, and most often wore civilian clothes.

There was probably no more improbable intelligence officer than Freddie Ayer, who gravitated into Nigel Clive's section of SIS after a series of disappointing postings. His initial efforts to join up in 1939 were thwarted because as an Oxford don he was considered to be in a reserved occupation, but when he did succeed his experiences at the Guards depot at Caterham and the officers' training course at Sandhurst did little to engender interest in regimental life. Instead, with the dubious claim to fluency in Spanish, German and French made on his behalf by the enthusiastic daughter of his landlady, he was posted to Headquarters London District with the task of interrogating enemy prisoners of war.

Following the intervention of Robert Zaehner, Ayer was offered a transfer to Special Operations Executive's branch in New York which operated under the cover of British Security Co-ordination. Ayer arrived in November 1941 and was to spend eighteen months in Manhattan collating agents' reports from South America. In mid-1943 he returned to SOE's headquarters in Baker Street in the hope of playing a more active role in the war but was instead assigned to the Executive's mission in Accra as transport officer, an appointment which was not without irony considering that Ayer had never learned to drive. Predictably this posting proved unsuccessful and Ayer returned to London to work in the French Section under the Regional Controller, (Sir) Robin Brook, 'reading and analysing the wireless messages, reports and other documents that were constantly reaching us from France'. In the autumn of 1943 Ayer was sent to Algiers where he was to come into contact with Malcolm Muggeridge working for SIS.

Late in 1944 Ayer was brought back to London and was switched to SIS. Initially he was placed in the same section as Nigel Clive but in January 1945 he was attached to the SIS station in the British embassy in Paris. This appointment lasted just a few months and, by November 1945, he was back at Oxford to establish his reputation as one of the great philosophers of the century.

Although Ayer was to give a full account of his activities on behalf of SOE in his autobiography *Part of My Life*, he never admitted his SIS connections, as can be seen in this extract. He died in June 1989, twelve years after the book was published.

Part of My Life

When I presented myself at Baker Street, to receive a mild rebuke for leaving them so long without news of me, I was told that they had designated me for a job in France, which would have brought me a step in rank, but had been over-ridden by the Foreign Office, which had claimed me for one of its own Intelligence Departments. This department cared nothing for military distinctions, so that, having automatically ceased to be a local major, I changed my rank only for the worse. For all practical purposes I reverted to being a civilian, and most often wore civilian clothes. I spent two months doing office work under the tutelage of Nigel Clive, whom I had already known and liked when he was an undergraduate at Oxford just before the war, and then in January 1945 returned to Paris as an attaché at the British Embassy.

In the meantime, my academic future had been made secure by my election to a tutorial Fellowship at Wadham. Ian Gallie's health had declined to the point of his having to resign his Fellowship and I was chosen to replace him. I heard later that Professor Lindemann had expressed some qualms, not about my ability to teach philosophy but about my holding left-wing views in politics, and that Maurice Bowra had reassured him by saying, not altogether truly, that I had very largely outgrown them.

I was already disposed to resume work on philosophy and had found time in London to write a fairly long article on 'The Terminology of Sense-data' which Moore accepted for *Mind* and published in the autumn issue of 1945. The article mainly arose out of my reading of Moore's own reply to his critics in the volume on *The Philosophy of G. E. Moore* which had appeared in the series of *Library of Living Philosophers* in 1942. I tried to show that the question, which continued to puzzle Moore, whether sense-data could ever be identical with parts of the surfaces of physical objects, could be settled only by fixing the usage of the technical term 'sense-datum'; that Moore himself had not sufficiently explained his usage of the term, but that from such explanations as he had given it clearly followed that the identification was not logically possible. The view that I took of the status of sense-data was one that I had already advanced in *The Foundations of Empirical Knowledge*. In the course of his friendly appraisal of the book in *Mind*, Henry Price had raised some objections to my proposal that sense-data should not be credited with having any properties that they did not appear to have, and I concluded my article with an attempt to answer him. The article might now be thought to suffer from its unquestioning acceptance of the role of sense-data in the theory of perception, but I still think that it contained some good argument.

I had been continuing to see Guy de Rothschild in London, and when he heard that I was going to work in Paris, he offered me the use of his house in the Avenue Foch. With servants to take care of me, I lived there very comfortably for two or three months, staying on for a short time after Guy's own return to Paris. I then moved into a room in the Hotel Castiglione, which the British Embassy had commandeered for its staff. I did quite a lot of entertaining while I was living in the Avenue Foch, and I also made considerable use of Maxim's, which had been turned into a club for British officers. There were still some food shortages in Paris, and the restaurant had not yet recovered its luxurious standard, but we were very well supplied with wines and liqueurs at controlled prices which were almost ridiculously low. I developed a taste for Verveine, which, like my undergraduate enthusiasm for Sauternes, I have never since been able to recapture.

I worked, with a secretary, in a room of my own in a remote corner of the Embassy. There was not a great deal for me to do. I compiled a card index of the leading characters in French official life, bequeathing it to the Embassy when I left. I heard later that it was thought to be inaccurate. I wrote a report on the current state of French politics, in which I compared de Gaulle to Pétain, and annoyed Duff Cooper [the Ambassador] by sending it straight to London instead of showing it first to him. I attended the weekly meetings which Duff Cooper held with his staff but seldom contributed much to the discussion. Though my relations with him were distant, I rather liked Duff Cooper. He had a violent temper and could be very rude when he was angry, but he was intelligent and courageous and there was nothing of the outlook of the petty shop-keeper in his old-fashioned Conservatism. It was some time before Lady Diana [Cooper] was aware of my presence in the Embassy, but I then took a modest place in her social circle. If I was a little lax in my attendance at Embassy parties, it was not that I did not enjoy them, but that I often had other engagements. In the earlier part of my stay in Paris I spent most of my time with a French girl of Turkish origin whom I had got to know in Algiers. She was employed by one of the French Intelligence Services, but when we were together we put our work aside.

I had many friends in the Embassy itself. Barley Alison was there as well as Brooks Richards. Charles Whitney-Smith was working in the Press Department and outdid me, if not in the pursuit of pleasure, at least in the capacity to dispense with sleep. The head of Chancery was Patrick Reilly, whose mastery of his profession made me think it understandable that All Souls had preferred him to me. Paul Willert was the air attaché. He had an attractive apartment in the Place Dauphine, which he had acquired before the war, and his remarkable gifts as a host were displayed there as fully as they had been in London. I am sufficiently stagestruck still to remember one of his parties as the occasion of my only meeting with Noël Coward. The enchanting Yvonne Printemps was there as well, with her husband Pierre Fresnay, whose career was temporarily threatened because of his acting in a film, made under the Occupation, which was thought to have shown his countrymen in an unfavourable light. A similar cloud hung over Jean Cocteau, who was reproached for admitting Germans to his friendship. No action was taken against him, but it took a little time for him to recover his prestige. On the evening when I saw him at the Embassy, he seemed unsure of himself and did not sparkle. I was more impressed by Louis Jouvet, who was the lion of one of the *salons* that were again becoming a feature of Parisian society. With his sonorous voice and measured gestures, he carried into private life the atmosphere of the Comédie Française. I felt in his presence as though I were playing the part of an extra in one of the many films in which I had seen him. Though I was fascinated by his performance, I preferred the company of Gabrielle

D'Orziat, an actress of an older generation, who was almost equally prominent in the French theatre of the time. She was witty and wise and differed from nearly all the theatrical people that I have known by her readiness to converse on subjects other than the stage.

It was through Paul Willert that I met Francette Drin and her older sister, Nicole Bouchet de Fareins, who together with their brother Jean Joba have been my friends ever since. They had been active in the resistance, which had cost Francette's husband his life when the Germans captured him. Paul brought them to lunch with me in the Avenue Foch, and from then on I was often in their company. Besides seeing them in Paris, I used to stay in Normandy in a house belonging to Nicole. Part of my book *The Problem of Knowledge* was written there ten years later. I used to work on it out of doors, alarming the gardener who thought I must be mad, as he watched me walking up and down, juggling a watch-chain and talking to myself.

Sigismund Best

For reasons of secrecy and security I had hitherto kept very much in the background, maintaining a number of links between myself and my agents in Germany, and restricting my own direct contacts to a few chief assistants.

Sigismund Payne Best was the product of an Anglo-Indian marriage that left him with an acute sensitivity about his origins and a lasting inferiority complex. During the Great War his poor eyesight and his knowledge of French, German and Flemish, which had been acquired while attending university in Munich, brought him into the Intelligence Corps. He started by interviewing Belgian refugees at the Channel ports but later was transferred to Holland to help organize the networks of trainwatchers operating behind enemy lines.

After the war, following his marriage to the daughter of a Dutch marines general, Best ran a small import-export business in The Hague dealing in Humber bicycles. He was something of a Wodehousian figure, sporting a monocle and spats, but was very well connected in the British expatriate community. He was also the local representative of a branch of SIS known as Z, a network of agents operating independently of the British Passport Control Offices, the more usual SIS cover.

Best's career as a secret agent came to grief in November 1939 when he and his SIS colleague Major Richard Stevens drove to the Dutch–German frontier with the intention of meeting a senior anti-Nazi dissident, allegedly a Luftwaffe general.

The encounter turned out to be a trap, and the two SIS officers were bundled across the border by a group of heavily armed Nazis.

Best and Stevens underwent lengthy interrogation and after the war, following their release from concentration camps, each accused the other of having betrayed SIS's most sensitive secrets. That the Germans had acquired a detailed knowledge of the internal structure of the service could not be denied. Captured documents proved as much and there were indications that, despite their protests, Stevens and Best had been skilfully played against each other.

Stevens subsequently obtained a job as a translator with NATO and died in Brighton in 1965. Best, meanwhile, having divorced his wife, embarked upon a campaign for a pension. SIS was reluctant to accommodate him and indeed warned him that he was lucky not to have been prosecuted. He was excluded from a list, drawn up in 1964, of victims of Nazi persecution eligible for compensation from the post-war German government. But Best, who had become a bankrupt, demanded to be included and his claim was eventually accepted.

The financial settlement did nothing to diminish his sense of grievance and he insisted that he had been victimized by SIS. In his submissions to the bankruptcy courts he consistently described himself as an intelligence officer, with the intention of embarrassing SIS, and made no attempt in his memoirs to shield his former employers from criticism. He died in Calne, Wiltshire, in 1978 aged ninety-three, having donated his carefully constructed but largely fictitious diaries to the Imperial War Museum. They dated back to his adventures with carrier pigeons and observation balloons in the First World War but the material concerning his networks of agents in post-1918 Germany was almost entirely fabricated.

The tragedy of Best's case was that he was innocent of the charge that he had co-operated with his Nazi interrogators. It was only much later that SIS learned that another SIS officer, Dick Ellis, had passed on secrets to the Abwehr before the war, and this was the information that was presented for corroboration to Best and Stevens separately during their incarceration and which each assumed the other had been responsible for supplying. Ellis confessed to his treachery, citing financial hardship as a motive, only in 1966, but Best was never told.

The Venlo Incident

The 9th November, 1939. I got up shortly after five although I felt very tired and much disinclined to do so, but through these daily trips to the frontier I had been forced to neglect all my other work and there were some things which I could put off no longer. As I shaved I could not help wishing that I could somehow or other dodge having to go to that beastly frontier café again. There had been something about it the previous evening which had made me feel most uncomfortable; the unpleasant looking stout man who had looked us over so carefully as we went in, then the feeling of being completely cut off from the outside world in that little side room where we had our talks with the Germans, those big glass windows which looked out on to a wall of dense undergrowth. It would be so easy for some SS men to cross the border at the back of the café and creep up so that they could shoot us through the windows as we sat in the light. Rubbish! There was no real reason for my fears. During the First World War I had been to the frontier dozens of times like this; much closer too, for the café in Limburg where I used to meet people was half in Holland and half in Germany – but yet I was uneasy, and if I could have done so with decency, would have rung up Stevens and called the whole thing off.

My wife was not up, of course, but I spoke to her before I went out and said, that perhaps I might not be back to dinner; in any case, she was not to wait for me after 7.30. She said, 'No, don't hurry back. You drive much too fast and it always makes me nervous. I have a bridge party here this afternoon and it will really be better if you have dinner out; I shall be much happier if I know you are driving carefully.'

It was a dull morning and much colder than of late; the sky was overcast and threatened rain. When I got to the office I just had time to glance at the morning paper. It carried a stop-press notice about an attempt on Hitler's life which had been made at Munich the previous day. Hitler himself had escaped as he had already left the place before the explosion, but many others had been killed and injured. Very curious, and I wondered whether this attempt had anything to do with our people and, if not, what effect it would have on their plans.

Then I plunged into my work and it was after ten before I was free to join Stevens at his house. Klop had not yet arrived. Stevens felt just as I did, that the Huns were becoming an infernal nuisance with their shilly-shallying. If the general did not come up to the scratch this time, we would wash our hands of the whole business and leave them to run their show alone. We would keep this one last appointment, and then, finis.

Stevens produced some Browning automatics and we each loaded and pocketed one – just in case. Then Klop came in. He apologized for being late but there was a bit of a scare on and he had been kept at the office. Some news had come in to the effect that the Germans might march into Holland at any moment. The story was unconfirmed and Klop did not believe it himself; nor did it agree with any indications which Stevens and I had. We talked about this for a time and then discussed what could be done to satisfy the Germans about an escape route into Holland in case of emergency. Of course it was out of the question to give them anything in the nature of a pass, so it was decided simply to give the telephone number of Klop's office; then, if they wanted to come into Holland they could ask the customs officer to ring up this number and Klop would then see to the rest.

We were just on the point of setting off when a message from the Germans started to come in over the wireless. It might be to cancel our appointment, so we had to wait until it had been transcribed and decoded. It was, though, of no importance whatever; merely a request for a change in the hours of transmission. This had delayed us quite a bit and I would have to drive all out if we were to be on time for the meeting. As we were all feeling rather tired I asked my driver, Jan Lemmens, to come with us so that he could bring the car back in case we wished ourselves to return by train.

We made such good time that we were able to stop for a quick lunch at a little road-side café near s' Hertogenbosch. While we were eating, Stevens and I talked about the possible danger that we might be raided and captured, but Klop assured us that there was nothing to be feared, especially not during daylight, as he had arranged for a stronger guard than usual to be at the frontier.

Until we stopped for lunch Jan had sat next to me, and Stevens and Klop behind. When we started off again, Stevens came and sat by me and we had a chat about what might happen if the Germans made a sudden attack on Holland and we discussed what measures would be best for the safe evacuation of the legation and other Britishers still in Holland; Stevens also scribbled down a list of people whom he knew, who would have to be got out of the country before the Germans got in. I said, 'Better destroy that list of yours before we get to the frontier. I still have a feeling that something may go wrong.' Stevens said, 'Of course,' and I believe tore up the paper and threw it out of the car.

I never like to talk when I am driving and always find that it slows up my speed appreciably; in any case, when we reached Venlo it was already four o'clock, the time set for our meeting. Although we stopped so that Klop could call at the police station and arrange about our guard, we could not wait until the men had cycled the five miles to the frontier, but pushed on ahead of them.

All the way down from The Hague we had noticed that military precautions had been intensified and we had been held up at every road block and tank barrier. Even now, between Venlo and our café, we were stopped twice. The first time the sentry said something about having orders to allow no cars to pass and although Klop showed him his authority insisted that he must first go to the guard room and speak to the NCO in charge. Both Stevens and I, I believe, felt alike and hoped that he would come back with the news that we could go no farther; but in a few minutes he was with us: 'Everything is all right. The NCO had a message for me which had been phoned through from the office. Carry on.'

The second sentry did not actually stop us, but only made signs that we should drive slowly. He was stationed at a bend in the road just before we entered the straight along which one had a view of the frontier. Somehow or other, it seemed to me that things looked different from what they had on the previous days. Then I noticed that the German barrier across the road which had always been closed, was now lifted; there seemed to be nothing between us and the enemy. My feeling of impending danger was very strong. Yet the scene was peaceful enough. No one was in sight except a German customs officer in uniform lounging along the road towards us and a little girl who was playing at ball with a big black dog in the middle of the road before the café.

I must have rather checked my speed, for Klop called out, 'Go ahead, everything is quite all right.' I felt rather a fool to be so nervous. I let the car drift slowly along to the front of the café on my left and then reversed into the car park on the side of the building farthest from the frontier. Schaemmel was standing on the veranda at the corner and made a sign which I took to mean that our bird was inside. I stopped the engine and Stevens got out on the right. My car had left-hand drive. I had just wriggled clear of the wheel and was following him out when there was a sudden noise of shouting and shooting. I looked up, and through the windscreen saw a large open car drive up round the corner till our bumpers were touching. It seemed to be packed to overflowing with rough-looking men. Two were perched on top of the hood and were firing over our heads from sub-machine guns, others were standing up in the car and on the running boards; all shouting and waving pistols. Four men jumped off almost before their car had stopped and rushed towards us shouting: 'Hands up!'

I don't remember actually getting out of the car, but by the time the men reached us, I was certainly standing next to Stevens, on his left. I heard him say: 'Our number is up, Best.' The last words we were to exchange for over five years. Then we were seized. Two men pointed their guns at our heads, the other two quickly handcuffed us.

I heard shots behind me on my right. I looked round and saw Klop. He must have crept out behind us under cover of the car door which had been left open. He was running diagonally away from us towards the road;

running sideways in big bounds, firing at our captors as he ran. He looked graceful, with both arms outstretched – almost like a ballet dancer. I saw the windscreen of the German car splinter into a star, and then the four men standing in front of us started shooting and after a few more steps Klop just seemed to crumple and collapse into a dark heap of clothes on the grass.

'Now, march!' shouted our captors, and prodding us in the small of our backs with their guns, they hurried us, with cries of 'Hup! Hup! Hup!' along the road towards the frontier. As we passed the front of the café I saw my poor Jan held by the arms by two men who were frog-marching him along. It seemed to me that his chin was reddened as from a blow. Then we were across the border. The black and white barrier closed behind us. We were in Nazi Germany.

John Bruce Lockhart

There is a danger of the counter-intelligence expert becoming so involved in the problems of hostile services, that he starts to see counter-intelligence cases through the eyes of the hostile intelligence service he has been studying so long. His judgement then goes.

Educated at Rugby and St Andrews University, John Bruce Lockhart returned to his old school as a teacher and, like several other masters at Rugby, joined SIS in 1940, being posted to SIS's cover organization in the Middle East, the Inter-Services Liaison Department, and later working in North Africa and Italy. At the end of the war he went to Paris under assistant military attaché cover and in 1948 started a three-year tour in Germany as head of the German station under the umbrella cover of the Control Commission.

Somewhat to his embarrassment, Bruce Lockhart was hastily transferred to Washington, DC, in May 1951 following Philby's recall and dismissal. This must have been an awkward assignment, bearing in mind that some Americans could not understand why Philby had not been prosecuted, and suspected a convenient establishment cover-up. Upon his return to London in 1953 Bruce Lockhart remained at SIS headquarters and retired in 1965. In September 1984 he gave a paper entitled 'Intelligence: A British View' to a Royal United Services Institute for Defence Studies conference on Anglo-American intelligence and described himself as having been 'actively involved in intelligence at a senior level'. Three years later his remarks were updated and formed a chapter (an extract follows) in *British and American Approaches to Intelligence* edited by Ken Robertson of Reading University. At present Bruce Lockhart is researching a detailed account of SIS's contribution to the Italian campaign during the latter stages of the Second World War.

'Intelligence: A British View'

'Intelligence' is an umbrella word covering a wide field of different activities and skills. It is quite arguable to maintain that 'intelligence' should be confined to the gathering and analysing of information. It is equally arguable that 'intelligence' includes covert operations, deception and agents of influence. The views given below simply represent one man's thoughts, based on practical experience.

This chapter outlines the five main areas which constitute 'intelligence', and makes comments on each area. In a short Appendix a few principles are listed that are important for an effective intelligence organization in a democracy. Two premises have been adopted: the problem is examined from the point of view of a Western democracy, with all the constraints that that implies in contrast with the position of totalitarian states, especially the Soviet Union. Secondly, the democracies, who find no difficulty in defining intelligence objectives, methods, etc. in time of war, find themselves in a dilemma in a grey period half-way between war and peace. The satisfactory solving of this dilemma is a major and pressing problem.

The five main 'areas' of intelligence are as follows:

(a) The laying down by governments of their information requirements and priorities.
(b) The gathering of information, as required by the government, by overt, secret and technological methods.
(c) Counter-intelligence and security.
(d) Covert action: the extension of government policy by secret and non-attributable means.
(e) The analysis and evaluation of all the information gathered.

Paramilitary operations should not be regarded as the function of intelligence services. Their importance in undeniable, but they require different skills and different training. It is impossible to carry out a paramilitary operation secretly and anonymously. This became clear for all to see when CIA became involved in the 'Bay of Pigs' fiasco. If the operation was viable it should have been carried out by the US Marines, or, by a highly trained paramilitary group such as the Special Air Service (SAS) who handled the Iranian Embassy affair in London so competently.

But neither CIA nor the SDECE (The French Overseas Secret Service) chose to read the writing on the wall, and thereby did themselves great damage: examples of this are the CIA in Vietnam, the SDECE in Algeria.

REQUIREMENTS AND PRIORITIES

The first 'area' is the Government's definition of its *Requirements* and *Priorities*. The importance of this has often been underrated, and often incompetently handled by democratic governments. Yet it is the starting point of all good intelligence.

In the past, intelligence services have often decided their own requirements. Individual departments of state have even laid down their own requirements without regard to the requirements of other departments. The essential point is that the resources for producing information are not limitless, and the decision about requirements and priorities must be national and not departmental.

Democracies should have a small national committee, that, once a year, issues instructions about long-term strategic requirements. This committee should also meet frequently to review any changes in shorter-term requirements. Such a committee, if it is to be effective, must include both the main user departments *and* the main procurer agencies. Only in this way can the committee as a whole be aware of the art of the possible.

THE GATHERING OF INFORMATION

The first point to make is that there is a large area of valuable information to be obtained from overt sources. Regrettably the totalitarian states, with their total censorship, must obtain great advantage from the scientific and technological papers freely published in the democracies. Nevertheless the West can gain a lot of knowledge not only from monitoring broadcasts, but also from careful analysis of official statistics in economic, industrial and agricultural publications and from newspapers. Such overt information on politically hostile countries is a major source. It is often ignored, yet it is much cheaper to collect than information which requires complex technological or clandestine methods.

Leaving, but not forgetting, information obtained from overt sources, there are four main methods of obtaining information:

(a) Information from space.
(b) Information from technological sources on sea and land.
(c) Cryptography.
(d) The classical spy, including information from defectors.

The first of these, the technology of obtaining information from space, has developed in quantity and quality to an extent that no one anticipated twenty years ago. This is fundamentally a product of US–Soviet rivalry, and there is no doubt that the quality of information will continue to improve. However, it has produced two problems. First, the sheer volume has given the analysts and evaluators a major problem to solve. This is probably as much a problem for the Soviets as for the US. Second, the US is ahead of the Soviet in the broad field of high technology. This means the KGB will do everything possible to penetrate both the governmental institutions and the large private firms working in this field. This presents the US with a great security problem.

The second includes the whole area of computer technology, radar, 'intelligence ships', early warning systems, and 'bugging' in every form. There are three brief points to make on this vital area. It is becoming more complex, more sophisticated, and more successful than anyone imagined. The new Soviet Embassy in Washington is so placed that it has an oversight view of most of the major governmental buildings in Washington. It is inexplicable that the US government could have allowed them to build an embassy on this site. It can only be presumed that when planning permission was given, the US authorities simply did not anticipate the speed and skill with which Soviet 'bugging' techniques were developing. All democracies must have 'bugging' devices of varying degrees of sophistication. This gives rise to a major political problem where genuine liberals fear the danger to the civil rights of the individual, and the militant Marxist–Leninist element have a wonderful weapon with which to beat the 'Freedom of Information', 'Accountability' drum. This they did with great, almost tragic, effect in the US in the 1970s. There are clear signs that a strong lobby of the same sort is developing in the UK.

Cryptography has always been a basic element in the gathering of information, and as a channel for deception. Thanks to Sir Francis Walsingham, it helped to defeat the Spanish Armada, and sent Mary Queen of Scots to the block. Admiral Hall's 'Room 40' in the Admiralty made a major contribution to winning World War I. Ultra was probably the best source of intelligence in World War II. So much has been written about the subject since the publication of Sir John Masterman's *Double Cross* first indicated the fact that German wartime codes had been broken, that no time need be wasted in expanding on this subject. It should be noted, however, that Masterman was liable to prosecution under the Official Secrets Act. His book was in fact first published in the US.

There is one further point concerning the costs and benefits of technical collection which must be stressed and that is, that there is no area of intelligence where the personal vetting of the recruit, and a watchful eye on his behaviour pattern is more important. In the Western democracies there is an increasing belief among government servants and others that 'patriotism' and loyalty to the elected government is no longer the sole yardstick of behaviour. 'My conscience', 'loyalty to my principles' is considered in some circles as more important than duty to one's country. One traitor in a main cryptographic centre can probably do his country more harm than in any other situation.

With this vast quantity of information coming in daily from many different technological sources, it is not surprising that the two-legged spy, the experienced counter-intelligence officer, and the agent of influence, are occasionally thought of as an endangered species! They are not. The central point of intelligence, in the fullest sense, is still the judgement of the human mind, complicated by real or irrational motives or methods. The influence of Sir William Wiseman, 10th Bart., although only a young man in his early thirties, on President Wilson and Colonel House, Wilson's trusted friend and adviser, could not have been achieved by technological means. Wiseman was the MI6 officer in the US, and the main link in 1917–18 between Wilson and House, and Lloyd George and Balfour. Northcliffe wrote to Churchill in a letter from New York, 'There is only one man, American or British, who has access to the President whenever he wants it, and that is Sir William Wiseman'.

On the other hand, the case of Richard Sorge, the Comintern Agent working against the Japanese in World War II, shows the importance of the classical spy and the limitations of even modern technology. Sorge, entirely through his own spy network, was able to tell Stalin that the Japanese had taken the decision to attack the Americans, and *not* the Soviets. The war was going very badly for Stalin, and on this information Stalin immediately moved the twenty fresh divisions which were his defence against a Japanese attack from the Eastern to the Western front. There is a case to be made for saying that the arrival of these fresh divisions when the Germans were very near Moscow and Leningrad was critical. No technology was involved in this. Shortly afterwards the Japanese took the US battle fleet by surprise at Pearl Harbor. Today with the technological intelligence available to the US government, such a surprise attack would be quite impossible.

The third point about 'the endangered species' of secret agents is that the dividing line between the two-legged operator and high technology is a grey one. We learn from the media that tiny microchip instruments can be put into foreign embassies by the KGB, even into typewriters, and that typed correspondence and, of course, discussions can be relayed through concrete walls to receiving instruments half a mile away. If this is true, it is a remarkable technological achievement; but perhaps even more remarkable is the operational skill of the agents who managed to fit secretly the tiny instrument into the typewriter in an embassy which will have erected every type of security barrier against just such an event.

Finally, in the post-war period, there has been a general tendency to think of the information gathering problem as a battle between the US and her friends, and the Soviets and their friends. This indeed is important. But if you were to take British information priorities after World War II, where quick accurate intelligence influenced decisions at government level, you would have to include Palestine, Malaya, Suez, Borneo, Kenya, Cyprus, Aden, Ulster and the Falklands. Much of the information in these 'small wars' was supplied by two-legged spies.

COUNTER-INTELLIGENCE AND SECURITY

'Counter-intelligence' and 'security' mean different things to different people.

An acceptable interpretation of 'counter-intelligence' is that it represents the function of a democratic country's secret intelligence and security services to penetrate hostile and potentially hostile secret services; and to ensure that one's own services are not penetrated. It is a battle between professionals, complex and subtle; but the stakes are high, because if you can place an entirely reliable agent in a senior position you have an asset whose benefits will stretch far beyond a mere battle between the two services. It is an operation requiring patience above all. It may take ten years for an agent to manoeuvre himself into a post where he has access to policy-decisions. Temperamentally the Russians are prepared to wait that time. Temperamentally the Latins and the Anglo-Saxons find this waiting very hard. On the other hand, the suspicion or actual evidence that your own intelligence service has a traitor within the house is the most miserable event that can happen to a service. All secret intelligence services have been through this trauma. It destroys morale, upsets judgement, destroys personal relationships, and gravely threatens inter allied confidence.

One could discuss problems such as planting agents in hostile intelligence services, spotting the genuine defector from a hostile service as opposed to a planted defector, for a long time. However, four brief points need to be made.

It has been argued that democracies should have specialist counter-intelligence agencies, independent of other intelligence agencies. I think this is unsound. The possibility of penetrating foreign intelligence services, and the possibility of seducing defectors from potentially hostile services arise in the same field. They arise most often from secret intelligence operations run by the Home Security Service or the Foreign Secret Service (i.e. MI5 or MI6, the FBI or CIA, the DST or SDECE). Counter-intelligence experts must be an integral part of all the services. Their contribution is a deep scholarly knowledge of past cases, an encyclopaedic knowledge of individuals, of the methodology, organization and policies that motivate hostile services. The moment a possible lead comes up, be it in Helsinki, Chicago or Manchester, the operational commander and the counter-intelligence experts have to work together as a team.

There is a danger of the counter-intelligence expert becoming so involved in the problems of hostile services, that he starts to see counter-intelligence cases through the eyes of the hostile intelligence service he has been studying so long. His judgement then goes. He sees ghosts where no ghosts exist. He invents ghosts to fit his theories. This has happened, and will happen again, and it can lead to disaster. Broadly speaking no highly intelligent, sensitive, counter-intelligence expert should be involved in this fascinating specialization for more than about twelve years. After that the 'Wilderness of Mirrors' starts to take over from common sense.

In the counter-intelligence world, the role of the interrogator is vital, and often underrated. Some of the best counter-intelligence operators started life as interrogators of German and Italian POWs, though obviously this source has dried up. Any serious Western intelligence service should take time and trouble to create a small group of skilled interrogators. It is doubtful whether the lie-detector, drugs or torture help this 'art'. At the top level interrogation is a battle between trained minds. There is no reason why the Western interrogator should not be as well trained, or better trained than his adversary. But it *is* important to recognize the importance of this basic skill.

Defectors probably play the largest role on the counter-intelligence stage. One works hard to procure, persuade, charm and bribe key individuals to defect. One should stress that these defectors are not only from hostile intelligence services, but anyone who has access to technological or policy making information.

Sometimes this hard work succeeds. I have no statistics, but I believe that most of the important defectors to the West since the war, just 'walked in at the door'. Moreover, I know that many tried to walk in through the door, only to be rejected, sometimes with horror, by Western diplomats. The important point is that every member of a Western embassy abroad should be briefed about the importance of defectors. Like the Catholic concept of being in a 'State of Grace', the finger of God may or may not touch you. But if you are not in a 'State of Grace' you have no chance. So it is with defectors. In practical terms never again must a man of Penkovsky's status approach Western officials and ask to be recruited, only to be rebuffed.

Nicholas Elliott

He had an ability to inspire loyalty and even affection in his staff. He was one of those people who were instinctively liked but more rarely understood.

Nicholas Elliott on Kim Philby

For a man who has participated in some of the most exciting episodes of Britain's secret history, Nicholas Elliott is remarkably reticent to reveal what he knows. The son of an Eton headmaster, he was working as an honorary attaché at the British embassy in The Hague shortly before the outbreak of war. On returning to London he was recruited into the Security Service but his tenure in B1(a), the counter-espionage sub-section dealing with German double agents, was to be brief. He was transferred to SIS and posted to Istanbul, which took him on a lengthy voyage to Lagos and a flight to Cairo. En route he encountered his colleague Graham Greene on the quay at Freetown and he remarks that 'his *Heart of the Matter* represents MI6's contribution to world literature'. In Turkey in January 1944, with the help of his wife, Elliott pulled off a remarkable coup, the defection of Erich Vermehren, a senior Abwehr official. He was also a witness to the investigation pursued in the aftermath of the Cicero affair, the theft of vital secrets from the British ambassador's private safe by his valet, Elyesa Bazna.

At the end of the war Elliott was sent to the SIS station Berne and later served in Vienna. In 1956 he was back in London, running operations from SIS's domestic station, among them being a risky mission to inspect the hull of the *Ordzhoni-kidze*, the Soviet cruiser bringing premier Nikita Khrushchev on an official visit to England. The operation proved a major embarrassment after Elliott's agent, Lionel Crabb, died in the muddy waters of Portsmouth Harbour. The incident sparked off a major diplomatic protest from the Soviets but Elliott survived the subsequent purge that cost SIS's chief, Sir John Sinclair, his job.

Elliott was switched to SIS's station in Beirut and was later promoted to regional controller for Africa. During one tour of inspection, conducted in January 1963, Elliott was asked to make a short detour to the Lebanon to confront Kim

Philby with the latest evidence of his treachery. Elliott extracted a partial confession from Philby, but the latter promptly decamped to Moscow before further action could be taken. According to Peter Wright, Elliott's final encounter with Philby had been recorded, but dismayed counter-intelligence experts discovered when the tape was played in London that the voices of the two men had been drowned by the sound of Beirut's anarchic traffic. Having placed a microphone close to where Philby was intended to sit, Elliott had apparently opened the windows of the room, thus rendering the recording valueless.

Elliott eventually retired from SIS in 1968 and joined the board of Lonhro. His eagerly awaited autobiography, *Never Judge a Man by His Umbrella*, alas omitted many of the exciting episodes of his life, apparently in the face of SIS's demand for discretion. In this passage Elliott discusses Philby, although he omits to mention they had been colleagues.

Never Judge a Man by His Umbrella

Books and articles hitherto published have all tended to concentrate on Philby the traitor rather than Philby the man. Since Elizabeth [Elliott's wife] and I knew him and his second and third wives (Aileen and Eleanor) extremely well over an extended period, I will attempt in this chapter to concentrate on Philby the man and to make some form of analysis of the personality that evolved from his unorthodox family background and his role as son, husband and father.

Philby retained the passionate loyalty and devotion of both his second and third wives, neither of whom were in any way party to his treachery. Aileen came from a conventional upper-middle-class background and met him when she was working for Marks and Spencer before the war. She was not particularly well read, had no special interest in national or international politics, but she was highly intelligent, very human, full of courage, and had a pleasant sense of humour. In those days, and with her background, it required considerable strength of character to go off, as she did, not merely to live with Philby but to start a family while he was still married to his first wife, Litzi.

Litzi was an Austrian-Jewish Communist whom he met and married in Vienna, and they were not divorced until Aileen and he had been living together for a good while. In fact the timing of the divorce provoked a curious difference of opinion between them. Aileen was in an advanced state of pregnancy and Philby wanted to marry before the child was born. Aileen however, who was outwardly the conventional one, thought it unfair for one child to enjoy a state of legitimacy which their existing children did not share, and wanted to postpone the marriage until after the birth. After considerable argument Philby's wish prevailed and a bulky Aileen was led off to the registry office. (As it turned out, they had further children after the marriage, so the complications would not have been averted anyway.)

I first knew Philby in 1941 when he was living with Aileen at a house near St Albans, close to his work. He was a formidable drinker, even in those days, but it never affected his concentration nor did it lead him into indiscretion about his clandestine work either for the British or the Russians. His theory, which he used to expound, was that serious drinkers should never take exercise or make sudden or violent movements. This was because an ullage formed at the base of their guts and, if disturbed, upset the body system, causing – among other symptoms – a violent headache.

He had an ability to inspire loyalty and even affection in his staff. He was one of those people who were instinctively liked but more rarely understood. He had an impressive clarity of mind and also, despite his stammer, of speech; his writing was a model of economy and lucidity. He appeared to take no interest in the arts (although his great friend Tommy [Tomas] Harris was a picture dealer and expert on Goya), and preferred the Crazy Gang at the Palladium to *Hamlet* at the Old Vic. For his friends he sought out the original and the unusual. He was not at home with the ultra-conventional but did not express himself caustically about them. He very rarely discussed politics and his conversation on all serious topics appeared singularly devoid of emotion. Indeed he did not strike me as a political animal. I can hardly see him as a lecturer on dialectical materialism. On the contrary he was much more a man of practice than of theory, a view that is supported by his journalistic writings and indeed his autobiography, doubtless published by courtesy of the KGB. This autobiography virtually ends with Philby's 'clearance' by Harold Macmillan, then Foreign Secretary, in a debate in the House of Commons on 7 November 1955.

Philby was a dogmatic atheist. This caused many a semi-humorous argument with Elizabeth. He did not bore and he did not pontificate. He enjoyed discussing the English batting averages and spent many a long hour watching the cricket from the Mound Stand at Lord's. Outwardly he was a kindly man. Inwardly he must have been cold, calculating and cruel – traits which he cleverly concealed from his friends and colleagues. He undoubtedly had a high opinion of himself concealed behind a veil of false modesty and thus a firm streak of egocentricity. I wonder very much if he had ever actually joined the Communist Party. His attitude would be that he accepted Marxism 95 per cent but wished to preserve 5 per cent of doubt for the sake of his own pride. Beneath his veneer of charm lay an emotional but ruthless personality. At dinner or lunch parties he did not provoke argument, but out of fun rather than of malice (and a wish to see the reaction) would make some remark well calculated to stop the conversation dead in its tracks. For example, once at a diplomatic dinner he called across the table to Elizabeth 'You know, I can never understand how you two managed to produce such good-looking children', and on another, also to Elizabeth, 'Do tell us, when you go to confession do you really have a firm purpose of amendment?' Of course such remarks, in our view, often served to lighten the atmosphere of a dreary party but when made in similar vein to others were often the cause of severe umbrage.

There was one occasion in Beirut when Philby made a remark that caused a chain reaction of offence unparalleled in my experience. It was at a cocktail party given in our flat by Elizabeth and myself when my parents, then pretty elderly, had come out to stay. We had invited some forty people, including the Philbys (my father had met Kim Philby in the past) and our very nice Ambassador, Sir Moore Crosthwaite. There was an unusual pause in the babble of conversation during which Philby was heard to remark to Moore, 'Don't you think "Anne" [the wife of a member of the Embassy staff who was standing next to him] has the finest breasts in Beirut?' Moore was undoubtedly annoyed because, quite reasonably, he thought that the breasts of the wife of a member of his staff were not an appropriate subject of conversation for a cocktail party. 'Anne', while doubtless justifiably proud of that part of her anatomy, was annoyed at having it discussed in public and in particular with the Ambassador. Her husband was annoyed as he, equally justifiably, agreed with the Ambassador that his wife's breasts were an off-target subject for cocktail party gossip. 'Jane' (the wife of another member of Embassy staff) was annoyed because she thought she had better breasts than 'Anne'. 'Jane's' husband was annoyed, possibly because he felt his wife had been slighted. Eleanor Philby was more than just annoyed because she was not particularly well endowed in that respect and comparisons are odious. And, finally, Elizabeth was annoyed because she felt the whole party was getting out of hand. In fact the only person who thought the whole episode was a huge joke was Kim Philby himself.

Other than the newspapers, essential reading in order to earn his bread and butter from the *Observer* and the *Economist*, Philby was not an avid reader. His spare time was taken up with drinking in bars and at home with his wife and friends; and presumably also with the preoccupations involved in betraying his country. Furthermore he was not particularly well read either in terms of the classical authors or the dissertations of Marx and Lenin. His favourite author was Rex Stout and he could well have taken Nero Wolfe as his chosen subject if asked to appear on the BBC's Mastermind programme. In the summer he followed the cricket scores very closely but as far as I was aware showed no interest whatsoever in any other sport; and he certainly never partook himself in any form of sporting activity – he did not even like to walk. He never owned a car (preferring taxis) and it would not surprise me if he had never learnt to drive.

Elizabeth and I had Philby to stay for a fortnight after the war. We were in Bern and the Philby family were in Istanbul. Aileen was dying of some mysterious ailment and Philby sent the details to me to inquire if I could find a Swiss specialist who might diagnose and cure her. There was a professor in Bern who agreed to treat her; so she was flown from Istanbul with Philby to Geneva and thence by ambulance to the hospital in Bern. Philby came to stay with us, having been assured by the professor when he had examined her that he was confident of saving her life.

Aileen was suffering from acute septicemia and Philby told us the cause. She had driven her car into the country and during the course of a walk had been approached by a Turk and hit with a stone. When the Turkish police insisted on bringing a series of suspects in chains to her hospital room she had expressed distaste for the procedure and said she could identify none of them. While with us in Bern Philby came back from the clinic and told us with considerable anger that Aileen's Swiss doctor had said he wished her to see a psychiatrist because he believed that the wound in Turkey had been self-inflicted. This followed an incident when he formed an opinion that Aileen had intentionally cut herself with a razor blade while under his care. Aileen's past medical history was then investigated and it was revealed that she had been known to inflict wounds on herself since the age of fourteen, when she had been put under the care of the late Lord Horder after opening an appendix cut. The arch-deceiver then had to return to Istanbul knowing that all the years he had been living with Aileen he had himself been deceived: though this is a hard word to use of a charming woman and loving wife and mother who suffered, unknown to others, from a grave mental problem. I only mention the matter in such detail because it had such a direct bearing, in my view, on Philby's behaviour as a husband. It was an intense affront to Philby's pride that he, the arch-liar, had been tricked for so many years. The biter had been bit and the marriage steadily deteriorated.

Relations between Aileen and Philby came under enormous strain when Philby was posted to the Washington Embassy. Burgess, whom Aileen openly detested, was posted there too and Philby insisted that he came to live with them. Knowing the trouble that would inevitably ensue – and remembering Burgess's drunken and homosexual orgies when he had stayed with them in Istanbul – Aileen resisted this move but bowed in the end (and as usual) to Philby's wishes. The inevitable drunken scenes and disorder ensued and tested the marriage to its limits.

After the defection of Burgess and Maclean in 1951 Philby was recalled to London and sacked. Endless surmises followed about his role in the affair. Philby was jobless and the whole family went through a bad time. They moved first to a small furnished house near Rickmansworth and later to a large and gloomy house near Crowborough. Money was a major problem since the only job Philby could eventually get was offered him by a loyal ex-colleague at £600 a year. All the public speculation about whether Philby was or was not the Third Man meant additional stress for Aileen and the children and the house at Crowborough was at times besieged by journalists. Aileen was still concerned about the difference in status between the children born in and out of marriage and expressed her concern to Elizabeth that the journalists would question them as to their birth dates. Poor Aileen – she had so many secrets to harbour and it is highly likely that she ultimately had suspicions about her husband's treachery but was too loving and loyal to express them.

Meanwhile, Philby lived with a mistress in London, visiting his family in Crowborough for a night or two from time to time and creating mayhem. Yet, strangely, he never lost his hold on the affections of either Aileen or his children. Aileen herself became so hard pressed for cash that she took a job as a cook in London to people living in Eaton Square, where she was close enough to our house in Wilton Street to spend her off duty hours with us.

After Philby returned from Washington in 1951 and was dismissed, Aileen stuck to him loyally. In 1956 he left for Beirut as the correspondent of the *Observer* and the *Economist*. There he met Eleanor Brewer, the former wife of Sam Brewer, the American journalist. Aileen died in England in sad circumstances and Philby married Eleanor. It was reported that when Philby received the news of Aileen's death in a telegram he did not conceal his pleasure. Eleanor, whom Elizabeth and I got to know well, was in many ways not dissimilar to Aileen. She had integrity, courage and humour. Like Aileen she could not be described as intellectual but she was certainly as intelligent.

What of Philby himself as a father? He was undoubtedly devoted to his children 'after his fashion', but he could still put his youngest, Harry, into a children's home for his seventh and eighth birthdays while he and Eleanor went off on a jaunt, making no arrangements for presents or celebration. According to press accounts he sent them money from Moscow. He appears to have had most, if not all of them, out to stay with him. He had no inhibitions, in the Lebanon, about getting drunk in front of them and on one occasion on a boating picnic he knocked Harry into the sea and risked fatal consequences, causing another child to upbraid him furiously. He did not appear to make any particular effort to further their education himself, such as by talking to them about current affairs, and when they came out to Beirut they were largely left to their own devices. If one of them wanted to go to the races he was free to do so. Harry was given training in the mixing of drinks and made, after trying it out himself, in Philby's words, a 'fierce martini'. Philby probably had a parental pride in being the father of five children but it is doubtful if there was much warmth or understanding between them. Neither had there been between St John Philby and his son. Philby blamed his speech impediment on his father for reasons he did not explain.

In fairness, it must be said that the family relationships of the Philbys in Beirut were outwardly very happy. The children who were at boarding school in England came out for holidays and Annie, Eleanor's daughter by her previous marriage, got along well with them. They lived in a rather ugly flat of considerable character which Eleanor had made comfortable in an original way with an assortment of furniture and bits and pieces which she had collected in the Middle East and elsewhere. A feature of it was a wide half-circular balcony on which they had installed a fox, brought back from a visit to Saudi Arabia. Philby adored the fox and was uncharacteristically shattered when on return from a trip he found it had jumped off the balcony into the street many floors below and had been killed. Apart from when his father died, this was the only occasion, in all the times I spent with Philby, that I knew him to display visible emotion.

Philby was anxious for his sons to attend a public school and my father helped over this in getting some (if not all) of them into one of which he was a governor and which, being heavily endowed, was not too expensive. Philby was determined, however, not to teach them at home anything about religion. Elizabeth pointed out that if they turned up at school never having heard of Jesus Christ they would appear pretty silly. This argument carried no weight.

I do not believe that Philby's mother had much influence on him. In her later years she was more or less abandoned by his father who spent his time between Saudi Arabia and Beirut. She left for London when St John Philby, who was a Muslim, was given a second wife, a Baluchi slave girl, by King Ibn Saud. By her he had two sons.

Philby visited his father in Riyadh from time to time where he still lived in a mud house when all Arabs of substance had moved to concrete villas. According to Philby, he was always avid to hear football news from England. He argued hotly about the education of his two half Arab sons: he wanted them to be educated in Saudi Arabia whereas Kim Philby thought they should have an English public school education (Kim himself had been at Westminster).

Philby was enormously influenced by his father though their relationship was a mixture of love and hate. He told me that his father had always impressed upon him two things from an early age. First, if he expressed an opinion his father would always say, 'Kim, where are your facts?'; and, secondly, that if you felt strongly enough about anything you must have the guts to go through with it no matter what anyone might think. The moral is there and certainly St John Philby practised what he preached. In the early days of the war he was reported for defeatist talk by one of our Middle Eastern Ambassadors; he was had up under 18B of the Defence regulations and given the chance to retract what he had said. He categorically refused to do so and was interned.

Elizabeth and I were among the few English people to whom St John Philby was prepared to be civil in his later years. He died shortly after having lunch with us in Beirut. Humphrey Trevelyan, then Ambassador to Iraq, was staying with us and we had asked him whom he would like to meet. He said he would love to see St John Philby again, hence the lunch. It was a memorable occasion because Humphrey drew the old man out into telling us the story of his relationship with Ibn Saud. He left at tea time, had a nap, made a pass at the wife of a member of the Embassy staff in a night club, had a heart attack and died early next morning. His last words in the nursing home were, 'Take me away. I'm bored here.' Philby went out of circulation for days afterwards.

Philby's relationship with Eleanor was to all outward appearances devoted. There is no question that she was deeply in love with him and had no knowledge or suspicion that he was or had been a traitor to his country. When he chose to disappear to Moscow he did so in circumstances calculated to do her the maximum hurt. Yet against the advice of friends, she bravely decided to go to Moscow to join him. When she asked for an explanation of his conduct he refused to give it.

Life became unbearable for Eleanor after Philby formed a close relationship with Melinda Maclean and she had no alternative but to leave Russia. She told Elizabeth of her final meeting with him, when he was in hospital. He said he wished to give her a most treasured possession and pulled out his old Westminster scarf from under the pillow. It had travelled far with him – from school days to exile in Moscow – and must indeed have been treasured to have been included amongst the few possessions he had fled with from Beirut. Is that a supreme example of schizophrenia? Possibly his most ardent wish was a world revolution after which Test matches would still be played for him to watch at Lord's. I wonder if he ever attempted to explain the rules of the game to Mr Andropov [Soviet president].

Eleanor told Elizabeth that in dark moments of the Moscow winter he had spoken of the holidays they would take together in Italy 'when the revolution came there'. She spoke too of how much he missed his friends in England and what a grievous blow the death of Burgess had been to him, though the legacy of his library had been a great solace. (Curiously enough, unlike the death of his fox and his father, Philby seemed totally unmoved by news of the death of his fellow traitor and expressed to me some annoyance at this legacy.)

The picture Eleanor drew of their exiled life together in Moscow was a sad one. Few friends and few joys. News of the arrival of grapefruit at the Gum store was a notable excitement and worth a three-quarters of an hour journey to catch the trophy before it went and another three-quarters of an hour journey back. Dreary people, a spying servant, drab clothes and little on which to build up a deteriorating relationship; yet I think she, like Aileen, remained fond of him to the last and would probably not have regretted the difficult and brave decision to join him in Moscow and try to make a new life together. An American journalist described him years ago in a newspaper article as having 'charm to burn'. He is said to have had it still in his life with a Russian wife with, from her photographs, a remarkable resemblance to both Aileen and Eleanor.

A burnt out case, Philby's life is now over. Before he died [in 1988] he averred in interviews that he was content, living in harmony with the last of his wives. This may have been a façade, in a schizophrenic personality with a supreme talent for deception. He certainly did not deserve contentment from the day over fifty years ago on which he decided to betray his friends, his family and his country for a creed that is now universally discredited. The world is well rid of him. But the Russians are sure to keep alive memories of their 'master spy' for many years to come.

CHAPTER VII

The Agents

A double agent cannot be summoned from the vasty deep and set upon the stage at once to play a leading part.
J. C. Masterman, The Double Cross System

Agents come in all shapes and sizes, and are driven by a variety of motives. They can be complex individuals, deliberately weaving a complicated web of deception and intrigue around them for equally complex reasons. Some are compelled by circumstance to indulge in espionage, others thrive on the excitement and the dangers.

Within the intelligence world a clear distinction is drawn between the case officers, who are the permanent, professional intelligence officers who invariably remain desk-bound, and their sources, be they temporary or of a more durable nature. The officers recruit and manage the agents, give them logistical and moral support, and ensure their information reaches the right quarters. The classic example must be that of Marie-Madeleine Fourcade who operated in France for SIS and provided Broadway with first-class intelligence. She was eventually to build a huge circuit with some 3,000 members and, unlike some less fortunate, more insecure circuits, never came under enemy control. That is the ideal but, as Graham Greene made a career of illustrating, the human condition encapsulates numerous variations. The reluctant agent whose cooperation has been obtained by coercion may resent his employer and take revenge by betraying him to his opponent. If the opposition has the initiative and the will to exploit such a person he could be transformed into a double agent, thereby turning a weapon against its original owner, sometimes with deadly effect. The phenomenon of the triple agent, whilst more rare, is a manifestation of even more Machiavellian manipulation: an agent is betrayed deliberately with the intention that he should come under an opponent's control, thereby allowing the original employer to discount the information received from the agent as being tainted and enabling him to draw the appropriate conclusions.

The technicalities of running agents are not difficult to grasp but the rules of definition are strict. George Blake and Kim Philby, for example, were never double agents. They were relatively straightforward spies who happened also to be intelligence officers. During the war SIS recruited dozens of agents abroad, and ran several who were thought by the Abwehr to be loyal to the Reich, while at home the Security Service transformed the business of supervising double agents into something akin to an art form.

After the war several spies who had operated as double agents for MI5 published their memoirs. None had known of the others' existence, for each had been run in isolation and assigned different case officers. The common denominator was that they had arrived in Britain ostensibly as enemy agents, although in reality their loyalties had never been compromised.

The first was Eddie Chapman, a notorious safe-blower who had fallen into German hands when the Channel Islands were occupied. He was in prison at the time, serving a sentence for robbery, and he seized the opportunity to return to London under the sponsorship of the Abwehr which was convinced Chapman was a willing recruit to its cause.

Eddie Chapman's extraordinary career as a German spy formed the basis of a newspaper article which was suppressed when it was first printed, on the grounds that it jeopardized national security. Although only the Security Service knew it, Chapman's story was not entirely unique, as became clear when Lily Sergueiev wrote *Secret Service Rendered*, her account of her recruitment by the Abwehr in Paris, and her subsequent encounter with Colonel Robertson of MI5 upon her arrival in London.

It was only after the release of Sir John Masterman's *The Double Cross System of the War of 1939–1945* that the autobiographies of Chapman and Sergueiev were placed in their proper context and the two spies were revealed to be just a pair of double agents out of a stable of more than forty run by MI5. Masterman's official disclosures revealed that every enemy agent sent to Britain was, willingly or unwillingly, placed under MI5's control. A sophisticated management structure was developed to co-ordinate these agents, and a case officer was assigned to supervise each one's activities. As for the technical aspects of each case, and in particular their arrangements for communicating with their enemy controllers by wireless, Masterman skated over the detail, leaving Ronald Reed to complete the job nearly two decades later in the official history.

Following the publication of Masterman's account other double agents were encouraged to give their versions of events, the first of which was *Spy CounterSpy*, written by Dusko Popov, the Yugoslav playboy who had arrived in England in December 1940 and had been enrolled by Robertson as Tricycle. He was one of those rare creatures who worked for both SIS and MI5. Soon after he had been recruited by the Abwehr Popov had approached the local SIS station in Belgrade and had received encouragement to develop his link with the Germans. When he finally reached London and MI5, he arrived with the best possible credentials: a set of instructions from his enemy controllers and an enthusiastic endorsement from SIS.

Encouraged by Popov's success with *Spy CounterSpy*, John Moe emerged from his retirement in Sweden and collaborated with Jan Moen to write *John Moe: Double Agent*. More recently, the incomparable Juan Pujol travelled from Venezuela to participate in the fortieth anniversary celebrations of the D-Day landings. Codenamed Garbo, Pujol had duped his Abwehr controllers and had played a decisive part in the deception scheme intended to persuade the enemy that the long-awaited invasion would be centred on the Pas-de-Calais region.

No less than five of MI5's double agents were to publish their memoirs but they were by no means the only Security Service agents to do so. Wolfgang zu Putlitz, the pre-war press attaché at the German embassy in London, had kept Dick White of MI5 fully supplied with inside information until he was obliged to defect. Although his case officers knew the aristocratic zu Putlitz to be a dedicated anti-Nazi, it was not until he moved to East Germany in 1952 that the depth of his allegiance to Communism was realized. Similarly, Tom Driberg was used as a straight-forward penetration agent, to supply information about the Communist Party of Great Britain and their Soviet paymasters, but his MI5 case officers never suspected he too was playing a double game. Only long after the war was it discovered that as well as operating for the Security Service, the CPGB and the KGB, he had also been in league with the Czech intelligence service! Neither zu Putlitz nor Driberg refers directly to espionage in his memoirs, whereas Roman Garby-Czerniawski does, but not in the context of his role as a double agent. His recruitment by the Security Service only followed his arrival in London in 1941, *after* he had run a network of mainly Polish agents in occupied France for SIS. His memoirs, *The Big Network*, concentrated on his ring and discreetly closed with his escape from the Germans, leaving the reader unaware of his further involvement in espionage as a spy for the Abwehr.

As well as skilfully exploiting the agents despatched by the Abwehr to spy in Britain, MI5 also employed a small group of trusted refugees who were infiltrated into internment camps to identify Nazi sympathizers among the detainees. Among those who undertook this important but unsavoury task were the Austrians Edward Spiro, better known by his adopted English name E. H. Cookridge, and the biographer Harald Kurtz. While Cookridge gained widespread respect as a political correspondent in the House of Commons, Kurtz was to be denounced in the Lords as one of MI5's more unscrupulous *agents provocateurs*.

When Harald Kurtz arrived in Britain in 1936, aged twenty-three, he was given accommodation by a Quaker agency dedicated to helping refugees. The same organization also had close links with MI5 which occasionally recruited newly arrived immigrants for its own purposes. Kurtz was one of those who volunteered to help the Security Service and he was run as an informer by Maxwell Knight, a veteran member of the counter-espionage division. Born in Stuttgart and educated in Switzerland and at Kurt Hahn's famous Odenwald School, Kurtz had a distant connection with Queen Mary which he mentioned at every opportunity. When he first arrived he was given a job at the BBC as a translator, but in his spare time he worked for Knight. Under normal circumstances Kurtz's clandestine career would have remained a closely guarded secret, buried deep in MI5's archives, but the agent's over-zealous approach to his work led to his public exposure, litigation that reached the House of Lords, and the virtual ruination of Max Knight as MI5's agent runner.

Kurtz's assignment was to work as a stoolpigeon, posing as a Nazi in civilian internment camps to identify Party members, but he operated independently on the outside, pretending to be a Fascist sympathizer with the intention of entrapping others who expressed pro-Nazi views. Once reported to MI5, the compromised suspect invariably became the subject of a detention order made under the Emergency Regulations. However, in the case of Benjamin Greene, Kurtz, who was paid by Knight on the basis of each individual he denounced, overreached himself. Greene, a member of famous Berkhamsted family and a first cousin of Graham, was arrested in May 1940 after an encounter with Kurtz but instead of meekly submitting to Benjamin's imprisonment at Brixton his brother employed the City solicitor Oswald Hickson to discover the grounds of his internment. After a lengthy investigation Hickson traced Kurtz and persuaded him to admit that he had fabricated a damaging account of an entirely innocent meeting with Greene at which the latter, a deeply religious Quaker and pacifist, had generously offered his family company's resources to help Kurtz re-establish contact with relatives in South America. When Kurtz reported the episode to Max Knight he had put the most damaging construction on it, falsely claiming that Benjamin Greene had expressed a willingness to put him in touch with a Nazi spy ring in Brazil.

Once Greene's solicitors had obtained a signed statement from Kurtz, in which he admitted having framed Greene for a bonus payment from Knight, habeas corpus proceedings were initiated in the High Court. At first the Home Office resisted the application but Greene was released when he sued for wrongful arrest and the matter was raised in the House of Lords in January 1942, Kurtz being named as the most mercenary of *agents provocateurs*. Perhaps not entirely by coincidence, Graham Greene gave the name 'Kurtz' to a villainous character in his 1950 thriller, *The Third Man*.

Following his public humiliation Kurtz was employed as an interpreter at the Nuremberg trials, and later moved to Oxford where he eked out a living as an occasional contributor to *History Today* and writing the biographies of the Kaiser, *Wilhelm II*, and of *The Empress Eugénie*. He also translated *The Unpublished Correspondence of Madame de Staël and the Duke of Wellington*, published by Cassell. As a historian he was highly regarded, and counted Hugh Trevor-Roper, then Regius Professor of History at Oxford, among his friends before he lapsed into alcoholism and experienced problems over allegations that he had purloined documents. A homosexual, his subsequent career as a teacher at a school in Kent ended abruptly, although later he was employed to give weekly history lectures at Eton. Only a handful of friends attended his funeral in Oxford in 1972, among them being Lady Pakenham, who admired his scholarship.

His friends say he always avoided talking about his background or his wartime work. Considering that he did more than any other individual to bring the wartime Security Service, and its agents, into disrepute, his reticence can be well understood.

Dusko Popov

Until recently my mouth was sealed, my pen kept dry. I couldn't reveal my wartime activities. Not so much that they had been classified secret. More insidious, they had never been declassified.

When Dušan M. Popov arrived in London as a German spy in December 1940 he was not accommodated at MI5's interrogation centre at Ham Common at

Richmond near London, the usual destination for suspected enemy agents. Instead he was driven straight to the Savoy Hotel where he was entertained by senior members of both MI5 and SIS. The reason was that although the Abwehr believed both Popov and his brother Ivo to be dedicated to the Nazi cause, they had each been recruited by SIS in Belgrade shortly before the war. Thus when the young playboy from Dubrovnik, who was known to his family and friends as Dusko, turned up at the British embassy in Lisbon, en route to England, he declared his true purpose and requested an appropriate message be sent to his SIS contact.

Dusko had been educated in Germany and it was one of his fellow students who approached him with a view to his working for the Abwehr. The Popov brothers had seen this as an opportunity to escape from Yugoslavia and both exploited the situation to their advantage. Ivo, codenamed Dreadnought by SIS, pretended to recruit many of his friends for the Abwehr, but each willingly became a double agent. Similarly, after Dusko had been installed in a Mayfair apartment by MI5 and supplied with a case officer, he recruited several sub-agents so as to enhance his status with the Germans.

In September 1941 Dusko returned to Lisbon for a meeting with his Abwehr controller to receive details of a new assignment, a mission to the United States. During the course of the year the Abwehr's networks in America had suffered a series of setbacks with the FBI arresting several key agents. Dusko's task was to complete a questionnaire relating to US military installations and set up a clandestine wireless station in Brazil, but the FBI were never comfortable about co-operating with a self-confessed enemy agent.

When Sir John Masterman's book *The Double Cross System of the War of 1939–1945* was published in 1972 Popov recognized himself in the role of the double agent codenamed Tricycle. This prompted him to publish his own account in which he changed several names but quickly found himself in trouble with two of his sub-agents, Balloon, who was a former army officer, and Gelatine, his Austrian girlfriend, who both protested about his descriptions of them. Later editions were amended, but the book will be remembered principally because of Popov's charge that his Abwehr questionnaire, which contained many queries concerning Hawaii and in particular Pearl Harbor, had been overlooked or deliberately ignored by the FBI. Instead of pursuing the objectives set him by the Abwehr he liaised with British Security Co-ordination in New York and settled down to an extravagant lifestyle with his French girlfriend, the film star Simone Simon.

Popov claimed that the FBI had been hostile to his mission and had disapproved of his admitted promiscuity. He also alleged that he had endured an awkward interview with J. Edgar Hoover before he had been sent back, empty-handed, to London. The FBI has challenged Popov's version, and has denied Hoover ever met him, but Popov's full FBI file, of nineteen volumes, has yet to be declassified for public scrutiny.

After the war Dusko continued to maintain contact with SIS, and was in touch with Nicholas Elliott when the latter was SIS's representative in Berne. He was imprisoned briefly in Marseilles when one of his commercial ventures fell foul of the law, but retired to a beautiful house in Opio in the south of France after a successful commercial career in Germany and South Africa. He died in August 1981, still locked in conflict with the FBI. Here Popov describes his first and only meeting with J. Edgar Hoover, and his subsequent plea for help to his SIS contact in New York, Dick Ellis.

Spy CounterSpy

J. Edgar Hoover encountered me. I use the word advisedly. There was no introduction, no preliminaries, no politesse. I walked into Foxworth's office, and there was Hoover sitting behind the desk looking like a sledgehammer in search of an anvil. Foxworth, dispossessed, was sitting silently in an armchair alongside.

'Sit down, Popov,' Hoover yelped at me, with an expression of disgust on his face. I sat in the chair across the desk from him. Now, if ever, was the time for diplomacy.

'I'm running the cleanest police organization in the world,' Hoover ranted. 'You come here from nowhere and within six weeks install yourself in a Park Avenue penthouse, chase film stars, break a serious law, and try to corrupt my officers. I'm telling you right now I won't stand for it.' He pounded the desk with his fist as though to nail the words into my brain.

'I don't think,' I said quietly, 'that a choirboy could perform my job, but if I've caused trouble, I pray you, forgive me.'

Hoover turned to look at Foxworth, his face grim, not quite able to judge if I was serious or pulling his leg. From over his shoulder he gave me a long, penetrating look, turned away again, saying not to me but to Foxworth, 'He may leave now.'

I lit a cigarette and settled back in my chair. The moment had come to make my play.

I gave it to him straight. 'Mr Hoover, my apologies were purely an exhibition of manners meant to take the edge off your unjustified remarks.'

Hoover turned purple and choked out, 'What do you mean?'

'I did not come to the United States to break the law or to corrupt your organization. I came here to help with the war effort. I brought a serious warning indicating exactly where, when, how, and by whom your country is going to be attacked. I brought to you on a silver salver the newest and most dangerous intelligence weapon [the microdot] designed by the enemy, something your agents have been trying to unearth for over a year and failed at. It could have done much harm if not discovered in its initial stage. But mainly, I came to help organize an enemy agent system in your country, which would be under your control and your orders. I think that is quite a lot to start with.'

'I can catch spies without your or anybody else's help,' Hoover barked. 'What have you done since you came here?'

'Nothing but wait for instructions, which never came,' I answered.

Hoover breathed in deeply and noisily. It seemed to calm him. 'What kind of a bogus spy are you?' he said accusingly. 'None of their agents have contacted you since you arrived, as far as we know.'

For a moment I was shaken. Was it possible that no one had explained to Hoover the Abwehr's purpose in sending me to the States? Or if it had been explained, could he have not understood? In either event, I was faced with the problem of explaining to that impatient and irritable man something that should have been clear to him from the beginning. I tried.

'In the last few months, you have successfully broken up the existing German information organization in the United States. Obviously, they have to replace it with a new organization. I am the one, or one of the persons, who was entrusted with that task. I am not to contact any of their old agents now or in the future, and none of them knows of my existence. I am to build an organization of my own. To stay on in the job, I must produce results; that means information and new agents. Up to now I've been permitted to do exactly nothing.'

'You're like all double agents,' Hoover interrupted me. 'You're begging for information to sell to your German friends so you can make a lot of money and be a playboy.'

'I'm not a spy who turned playboy. I'm a man who always lived well who happened to become a spy. The Germans believe, just as you do, that I work for them for opportunistic motives. They expect me to live the way I always have, and if just to please you I accept a lower standard, they'll become suspicious. But please believe me, if it helped our common cause, I would be willing to live on bread and water in the worst slum you could find.

'As for the information you say I'm begging from you, the object is obvious. You cannot expect a crop if you don't put in the seed. You cannot deceive the enemy if you don't . . .' A sneer from Hoover stopped me. He turned to Foxworth and said, 'That man is trying to teach me my job.' Foxworth didn't reply, his face was twisted into what might be taken for a smile.

I recognized the futility of it all. 'I don't think anyone could teach you anything,' I told the FBI chief, and walked toward the door.

'Good riddance,' he screamed after me.

I felt more horror than disgust, and my morale hadn't been so low since Dunkirk. There goes the ballgame, I thought to myself in American argot as I walked home. Hoover was handing the Germans a victory of incalculable proportions.

I rang Colonel Ellis to report on the fiasco with Hoover and to prepare a strategic retreat. He asked for a day or two to see what went wrong and to seek advice from William Stephenson, head of British Security Co-ordination. Stephenson, Ellis said, was the only man in British Intelligence who could handle Hoover, perhaps because he was Canadian and Hoover was less xenophobic with him than with a European.

I roamed my apartment like the caged animal I had become. Leaving seemed the only solution. I told Ellis as much when we met for lunch two days later.

'Hoover is a very difficult man,' Ellis understated diplomatically, 'but you have to understand that he rescued the FBI from the corruption into which it had fallen during the Harding administration. That was in 1924, but I think he is still obsessed with the idea that it may have a relapse. He is very mistrustful of anyone who tries to mix in his affairs.'

'Colonel Ellis,' I protested, 'those are apologies for the man. They don't do any good. They don't change the facts. And the facts are that he is obstructing some very important work.'

'I know, I know,' Ellis lamented. 'He's a heavy-handed policeman, and we've had a lot of failures in our dealings with him. Still, the man's not unintelligent and he is honest.'

'From where I sit,' I said, 'he would be more suited to Hitler's team than ours. And to all intents and purposes that's where he is.'

'Dusko!' the Colonel rebuked me.

'Sorry, that's the way I see it. There's no use my sitting around New York any more. Let's try to get me back to London with the least amount of damage.'

Ellis shook his head sadly and said, 'You are at an impasse, Dusko. You can't go back to London. Not yet. Your sudden return would ruin your reputation with the Germans, but what's more, it would compromise many of Masterman's plans and perhaps some people.'

'But if I stay here and do nothing,' I objected, 'I'll be finished with the Germans anyway.'

'True. But it would only be you. And,' he said rubbing his chin thoughtfully, 'I'm not sure that this episode has to end so badly.'

'Episode!' I exploded. 'You call that scene the other day an eposide. It was last-act curtain.'

'No, we must give Stephenson a chance. He may fix matters. It's been known to happen. You see, Hoover pulls tantrums like that every day, sometimes with his best friends.'

'Is he really the best America can offer to run an intelligence service?'

'For the moment, he is the only thing it has to offer. His is the only organization that exists. Mind you, if the United States enters the war, as looks likely, something better and more efficient undoubtedly will come along. But America is still uncommitted, and Hoover probably thought you were warmongering. Most times that is what he thinks of all of us.'

I waved my hand at him wearily. 'Please, no more excuses.'

'All right, no more excuses. But you hold tight awhile. Give Stephenson a chance. He has connections.'

I learned sometime later that the 'quiet Canadian', as Stephenson was known, had entry to President Roosevelt whenever he wished.

I returned to my vigil. It wasn't a lonely one, and but for the contretemps with Hoover, I was enjoying New York and was still impressed with the United States.

John Moe

For the most part a double agent's life was nothing out of the ordinary. In fact it tended to be rather boring, always waiting for something to happen.

When, as a young man in Oslo, John Moe was offered the chance of leaving German-occupied Norway, he seized the opportunity, even though it meant going to Britain under the Abwehr's sponsorship as a spy.

Moe's mother had been English and he had worked in the film business at Denham Studios before the war as a make-up artist. His command of the language was fluent and to the Germans he was an ideal candidate for an espionage mission. His partner was to be Tor Glad, an old friend who shared his ambition to escape. Together they were flown across the North Sea in a Luftwaffe amphibious aircraft, and then left to row ashore in an inflatable boat. On 7 April 1941 the pair landed on the Banffshire coast and soon afterwards were arrested by the local police. Once they had persuaded MI5 of their bona fides they were enrolled as double agents with the codenames Mutt and Jeff. Radio contact was established with the Abwehr and this link was to be maintained until February 1944, although the deception was not achieved without mishap.

After four months of successful co-operation, Tor Glad tired of the restrictions imposed on him by the security-conscious MI5 and broke his curfew. He was immediately summoned to MI5's headquarters and told he was to be interned for the duration of hostilities. Despite his protests Glad was escorted to the Isle of Man where he was detailed as an enemy alien. Mutt pleaded for his friend's freedom but to no avail. An MI5 wireless expert stood in for Jeff when his notional messages were due for transmission but Mutt continued to help his MI5 case officers perpetuate the deception.

Mutt and Jeff were used as conduits for some of the most important strategic deceptions of the war, in one instance persuading the enemy that Allied troops were concentrating on Scotland's east coast in preparation for amphibious landings in Norway, a ploy designed to divert attention away from the English Channel.

At the end of the war Mutt, who had joined up with the Norwegian army in exile, returned home a hero although he was to be reticent about his activities as a double agent. Jeff was not so lucky and was escorted to Oslo under police guard. After his arrival he was arrested and charged with collaborating with the enemy, and released only after a late intervention by MI5. Tor Glad never forgave his treatment in England, but in 1980 he was reunited with John Moe and agreed to discuss his experience publicly for the first time. Glad's post-war career with Norwegian Television was handicapped by the suspicion of his colleagues that he had worked for the Germans during the war. His decision to reveal the truth gave him some comfort before his death in 1985. Moe had moved to Sweden, and encouraged by the favourable reaction of friends to the news that he had been a double agent, he started work on his autobiography, *John Moe: Double Agent*, co-written with a journalist, Jan Moen. Here he describes his interrogation soon after his arrival in Scotland, conducted by the notorious Colonel Stephens at MI5's secret detention centre in Richmond, near London.

John Moe: Double Agent

We had been given no clue as to where we were being taken and could see nothing of the journey. At first I tried to follow the route in my mind's eye, which streets we were driving along, and the junctions where we stopped. After all, I knew London quite well. I had to give in. It was impossible to tell if we were heading north or south.

One of the soldiers leaned forward to ask where we were from.

'Quiet!' yelled the corporal. He was a Cockney, but I somehow felt he might not appreciate my telling him that I, too, had been born in London.

Some minutes had passed when he pulled out some scraps of paper. He paused to leaf through them and held one of the scraps towards us. It was a dreadful caricature. A few simple pen strokes displayed Hitler's unmistakable hairstyle and short moustache. The cartoon was extremely obscene, but Tor and I burst out laughing. The corporal stared at us in amazement. He hadn't expected that.

'Do you have any more?' I asked.

He was now definitely confused but showed the rest of his collection all the same. There was Goering, his piece a field marshal's baton, and Goebbels with frogs hopping out of his mouth. We couldn't help but laugh. He really couldn't come to terms with our reaction.

It was a long journey and I realised that we had to be somewhere on the outskirts of the city. The lorry came to a sudden stop. The driver mumbled something and I heard heavy gates creak open. We drove on another hundred metres and stopped. The engine died. One of the soldiers loosened the tarpaulin cover and jumped to the ground. We had halted at a large building, perhaps a country estate of some kind.

A small man approached us from the house, a captain – I could tell that from his pips. He wore riding boots and clutched his stick firmly under his arm.

'Where are we?' I asked him.

He stopped dead in his tracks and stamped his foot. 'Get down, you bloody spies!' he screamed.

'Look, we're not spies,' I explained.

'Shut up, you bastards! Nazi pigs!'

'That will do,' I said, jumping from the truck.

The furious captain continued to stamp and rage. 'Take them inside!' he screamed to the two privates. 'We'll take care of the rest.' He pointed viciously towards the rucksacks and radio pack. There was no point in arguing, the man was hysterical. If I so much as uttered a single word, he would probably resort to physical violence.

We walked towards the house flanked by the two soldiers. Once inside we were shown into separate rooms. The door was locked behind me and I sat down on the narrow bed which stood alongside the wall. Besides the bed there was a chair and a small writing desk, and that was all. The single window was barred and impossible to see through. Where on earth were we?

I lay down. I hadn't slept much on the train and thought I had better try to sleep while I had the chance. But I couldn't, I was too much on edge. What was the meaning of it all? The horrid little officer, what had he meant? Were we simply foreign agents, to him, people to despise?

A full hour passed by before the door was opened by an armed soldier. 'Come with me,' he spat.

His face told me not to ask our whereabouts or what was to become of us. I quietly followed him along the corridor. He took me into a large room where a doctor in a long white overall had been waiting for me. An eye-chart hung on the wall with set of scales and an examination couch in the corner.

When the guard had left the room I asked the doctor the meaning of our ill-treatment. I explained that we were not what they thought we were, and I would demand an apology from the coarsely behaved captain we had met.

'Name?' asked the doctor. 'Date of birth?'

I gave him the date, adding that I had been born in London. He glanced at me and then continued with his questions. What illnesses had I had; had I been ill recently; were there any cases of TB, mental illness or heart disease in the family? He then asked me to unbutton my shirt to check my heart and lungs, and noted my appendix scar. After my eyesight and hearing had been checked, he called for the guard who had been waiting on the other side of the door.

I was escorted back to my room and the door was locked behind me. I was alone once again and none the wiser. None of my questions had been answered, and I still had no idea what would happen to us.

The guard returned after a short while and this time took me to a dentist. He meticulously examined my teeth, paying special attention to those teeth which Åge Berg had filled just a couple of weeks before we left Norway. 'Your teeth seem in very good condition,' he said at last and called for the guard.

I was returned to my cell and lay on the bed feeling totally helpless. I had been shaken by the hostility of our new prison. Both the doctor and the dentist had remained coldly distant; the guard said nothing more than 'Follow me!'; and then there was the brash rudeness of the captain. How long would this go on? Had Tor undergone the same treatment? Did he feel as confused as I now felt?

The guard returned a third time. We turned into a different corridor, with me following the heavily clumping boots of my escort. We climbed a staircase and swung down another corridor towards a large double door. I was shown into the room by the guard, who saluted. 'The prisoner!' he announced loudly. He left the room, closing the door behind me.

It looked like a huge dining-room. At the far end sat a group of men at a long table, between us a seemingly endless line of wooden floorboards. Light rectangular patches revealed the spots where mats had once decorated the floor. I recalled the same dark outlines of our own floor in Oslo when the mats had been sent for cleaning. French windows were on one side of the room and a large open fireplace lay empty on the other, but I recognised our radio on the mantelpiece. I felt I could see what they wanted. We were going to attempt to make radio contact with the Germans. It would be yet another test. I would show them the transmitter, how it worked, and then relay our first message. I walked across the wooden floor to the radio. The room was deathly silent apart from the hollow sound of my footsteps.

I examined the equipment to check that it was indeed ours. 'It's ours alright,' I announced to the table. 'Would you like me to set it up? My colleague really ought to be here – he's far better on the technical side than I am.'

There was a brief, horrid silence.

'Come here!' yelled a voice. 'And in future only speak when you're spoken to.'

I moved cautiously to the table which had been placed on a raised platform. I tipped my head back to try to make out their faces.

The table was covered by a green baize, upon which glasses, jugs of water, paper and pens had been neatly ordered. The two large windows behind them looked on to a garden. I was dazzled by the light and could scarcely see the faces of my interrogators. There had to be nine of them in total, only one of whom was dressed in civilian clothing, sitting at the far end of the table. A colonel sat in the very centre of the panel. He led the interrogation. He began with the usual questions – full name, date and place of birth. He spoke in a clipped monotone and his attitude was far from favourable. It slowly dawned on me that this was the military trial of which the men at Scotland Yard had spoken.

A verdict would be reached. If I were found guilty I could be sentenced to death. This was all too real. We had treated our double-crossing of the Germans as some sort of game. It had all felt like a well-acted theatre performance – our way of fighting the oppressive injustice of the occupation. Even the flight to Scotland and our landing by dinghy had the flavour of a boy scout adventure story, even if I had been very concerned about the films I was carrying. Had the Germans discovered them we could well have been arrested and imprisoned, but I was convinced that I could have talked our way out of it. Our visits to Banff and Aberdeen had even been quite pleasant. We had been treated with some respect as we proudly related our story to a curious audience. But this was different. I would have to work hard to gain their respect and trust, but I was determined to do so. I would not lie down now. I would convince them that I had a clear conscience and that my intentions were noble.

I looked at the chairman and realised the difficulty I would have to convince him. He looked to have a similar temperament to that of the captain. I would have to tread carefully. He was already annoyed by my unbecoming behaviour as I entered the room. I couldn't afford another mistake. All I had to do was tell the truth; I had nothing to hide. It was a good feeling and helped me stay calm despite the seriousness of the whole situation. I approached the colonel as I would a challenge. I had to persuade him.

'When were you last in England?' he asked.

'September 1939,' I replied.

'Sir!' he shouted.

'September 1939, sir.'

'Where?'

'I was working in London, on the film set of *The Thief of Baghdad*, sir.'

'As an actor?' asked a major sitting beside the chairman.

'I was a make-up artist, sir.'

'Did you go anywhere else?' asked the colonel.

'Manchester, sir.'

'What were you doing there?'

'Visiting my grandfather, sir.'

'What's his name?'

'Colonel Doctor Herbert Wade. His address is Rusholme Gardens, Manchester.'

'Is he a military doctor?'

'No, he's a colonel in the army.'

'Sir!' shouted the colonel once again. 'You will address me as sir.'

'I'm sorry, sir.'

'What regiment?'

'The Ninth Manchester Regiment, sir.'

The colonel turned to whisper to the major next to him. The major called to a lieutenant who was sitting at the far end of the table. The lieutenant disappeared quickly from the room.

The interrogation came to a temporary halt. I took a good look at the judges and jury. Three of them were majors, the remainder were captains, except for the colonel and the civilian. They all sat in silence, staring at me. I felt most uncomfortable and wanted to break the silence.

'I've asked to phone grandfather,' I said. 'But I've not been allowed to.'

The colonel glared angrily at me.

'Sir,' I added.

He gave no reply and the room was silent once again. The lieutenant returned with a thick binder beneath his arm. It had to be the army register. He placed it in front of the colonel who wet his finger and leafed through the pages of the register. One of the majors got to his feet and stood looking over the colonel's shoulder.

They eventually found grandfather's name. There was an exchange of whispers and nodding. My information was found to be correct.

'Yes,' said the colonel. 'There's a Colonel Wade in the Ninth Manchester Regiment.'

'Grandfather was at Gallipoli, sir,' I added.

The colonel looked up and turned to the major. His gaze returned to me. 'You said he was a doctor?'

'His Christian name is Doctor, sir,' I replied.

'He was christened "Doctor"?'

'His father was a chemist, sir,' I explained. 'He wanted to do something to honour his best customers, the doctors. They were the people who kept him in business. That's why he christened his first child "Doctor".'

I could see one of the captains smiling. The story was so incredible it just had to be true. No German spy could get hold of that sort of information. They were beginning to believe my story. After all, it was true.

The colonel sighed and turned to the lieutenant who leaped from his chair. 'Fetch a chair for Mr Moe,' he said.

He now called me 'Mr'. It was all over. I had done it, they believed me. Now it was just the formalities.

I thanked the lieutenant and sat down. The questioning continued but the atmosphere had changed. I still answered their questions with 'sir' but the colonel had softened his tone. His attitude towards me changed as he listened to my honest answers. I was no longer a spy on trial but an important witness informing them of the situation in Oslo, the organization of Abwehr, and our training in the techniques of sabotage and telegraphy. I kept my answers precise and to the point. I now had their undivided attention. Notes were made now and then; a few details which they could follow up or a point of information they could pass on to the Intelligence Service.

'Did you want to try and make contact with the Germans? The equipment's all there. It would just take a couple of minutes to set everything up. My colleague could help.'

The colonel dismissed the suggestion with a wave of his hand. 'That can wait,' he said.

The interrogation had come to a close. I still had so much to tell them but I realized that the jury's only task had been to establish my trustworthiness; was I a spy or not?

'You can leave now, Mr Moe,' said the colonel.

'Thank you, sir,' I said. I got to my feet, bowed and turned to leave the room, treading lightly towards the door.

My guard was there, waiting. He escorted me back to my room. I smiled at him but he did not return the gesture. It didn't matter, it was all over now.

Juan Pujol

I just could not understand why the British were so difficult when the Germans were so understanding and co-operative.

When Juan Pujol, motivated by his harrowing experiences in the Spanish civil war, offered his services to the British embassy in Madrid in 1940, he was rebuffed. Dismayed by the rejection Pujol made a similar approach to the Germans, falsely claiming to be a Nazi sympathizer. The Abwehr accepted him at face value and trained him to be a spy with the intention of sending him to England where, Pujol alleged, he had strong business connections.

Although he reported to his Abwehr controller that he had reached London, Pujol had taken up residence in Lisbon from where he concocted some highly imaginative messages which were purported to be based on his observations in England. This deception went unnoticed by the Germans, eager for any intelligence from Britain, but it was spotted by MI5 which was routinely tapping into the enemy's wireless communications. As the volume of German intercepts referring to the master spy increased, so the Security Service redoubled its efforts to trace the agent.

While MI5 scoured the intercepted messages for clues to his identity, Pujol made a second attempt to join the Allies by visiting the British embassy in Lisbon. Once again he was turned down. However the American naval attaché who interviewed him on a third occasion was impressed by the Spaniard's insistence that he had been enrolled as an Abwehr agent. Signals were exchanged between Lisbon and London and the Security Service belatedly realized that the enigmatic spy codenamed Arabel in the enemy's wireless traffic was really an elaborate hoax.

In April 1942 Pujol was flown to Plymouth, together with his wife and child, where they were met by Cyril Mills. They were accommodated at a house in north London, and Pujol was given the codename Garbo, because he was 'the best actor in the world', and introduced to Tomas Harris, the head of MI5's Spanish sub-section. Harris and Pujol took to each other instantly and together they created one of the most brilliantly successful strategic deceptions of all time. Pujol stepped up his reports to the enemy and developed a wholly fictitious network of twenty-three sub-agents.

Garbo's presence in England neatly coincided with the start of a lengthy and sophisticated campaign to persuade the Germans that the long-expected invasion across the Channel would concentrate on the beaches of the Pas-de-Calais. Garbo's vital contribution to this operation was to provide the evidence to support a completely bogus Allied order of battle which included a non-existent American army located in south-east England, poised as if in readiness for an assault on northern France. When the real invasion got under way, in June 1944, Garbo assured his enemy contacts that this was a mere feint intended to divert the defenders away from the real target further north, which would be attacked a fortnight later.

Garbo's colourful messages to his Abwehr controller made a dramatic impact on the success of D-Day and were the cause of a significant delay before the Wehrmacht launched a counter-attack in Normandy. Despite his catastrophically misleading advice, Garbo was decorated by the Germans. He also received an MBE from the grateful British government. His true name remained a close secret, and was not disclosed until 1984.

After the war Pujol and his family were resettled in Venezuela, working for a British oil company, his true identity protected by the Security Service. However, in 1984 he returned to London for the celebrations marking the fortieth anniversary of the D-Day landings and was escorted to Buckingham Palace to meet the Duke of Edinburgh who thanked him for his unique contribution to the Allied victory.

Following his visit to the Normandy beaches in 1984 Garbo collaborated with Nigel West to write an account of his extraordinary career as a double agent. In this extract Pujol's entirely notional sub-agents are quoted to support the impression that Allied troops and armour were massing in the south of England in anticipation of an assault across the Channel.

Garbo

In the middle of February 1944, Garbo pretended to have undertaken a tour of the south coast of England.

On 19 February, from Portland in Dorset, Garbo posted his fifteenth letter and mentioned having spotted some American soldiers in the neighbourhood of the town. He also described their shoulder flashes: 'the number "1" in red on a khaki ground'. This was a calculated reference to a genuine unit, the 1st US Infantry Division, which had in fact been brought back to England from the Italian front some months earlier, but SHAEF was anxious to conceal the return of these battle-seasoned troops until the last possible moment before the real invasion. Garbo's intervention was designed to win him credit for passing on some legitimate news. It had been argued that so many Africa Star campaign medals were being worn on uniforms in England, with its distinctive red and yellow ribbon, that it would be impossible to keep the Division's arrival secret for much longer. Other agents supported Garbo's observation by stating that these hardened troops were engaged in training other troops, thereby promoting the idea that Allied preparations for the invasion were not particularly advanced.

Garbo explained that 'balanced forces are being held in readiness in England to occupy any part of north-west Europe against the contingency of a German withdrawal or collapse'. In his first message concerning SHAEF's strategy, which effectively marked the opening of Operation Fortitude [codename for the massive and highly successful D-Day deception operations], Garbo remarked that 'it does not require a very wise man to deduce that should the way be left free they would not hesitate to take advantage of it'. As additional evidence of the Allies' plan, he described how he had seen a pile of newly printed leaflets in the office of his contact in the Ministry of Information and had purloined a copy. Entitled *Avis à la Population*, it was despatched to Lisbon. The forgery, the only one of its kind ever printed, was marked for distribution to French civilians following a German withdrawal and urged them to co-operate with their new occupiers. As a foundation for Fortitude North [to keep German forces in Norway], Garbo reported that he had ordered his Glasgow-based deputy, Benedict, to monitor the growing number of naval exercises in the Clyde, and the Greek deserter had been instructed to find lodgings at Methil, on the east coast of Scotland. This he did on 1 April 1944, booking a room for the next six weeks. As confirmation that the British Fourth Army was still operational (and, indeed, the key to the northern campaign), Benedict reported to Garbo on 28 March 1944 that he had just returned from a trip to Dundee, where he had spotted the 52nd Lowland Division and a unit bearing shoulder flashes of a shell on a dark background. When relaying this message in a four-minute wireless transmission at 1920 hours that evening, Garbo commented: 'This insignia is completely unknown to me.' This was not entirely surprising, considering that Roger Hesketh had only just invented it!

Meanwhile, Garbo himself had been on a tour to check on some of Dagobert's informants. During a transmission at six in the evening of 7 March, he reported:

I was able to confirm last Sunday the accuracy of the recent report sent by Donny from Dover. I am, therefore, able to classify him in future as a good reporter.

In the same message he also authenticated messages receiving from Dagobert's other agents, including Dick, the Indian fanatic: 'With regard to the military report, it is completely accurate so that we can catalogue this collaborator as being good.'

On 13 April, he sent a radio message giving a good opinion of Dorick, one of the Welsh fascists who had reported seeing 'a lot of troops and vehicles of the 9th Division' passing through Norwich: 'I consider this first report of this collaborator fairly good as he tries to get details from which one is able to appreciate the interest he takes in explaining what he has seen.'

On 22nd April, Garbo received a long letter from the Abwehr, dated 3 April 1944, Lisbon, which showed that they were particularly impressed with Dagobert's sub-agents:

> I have taken note with great interest of what you have told me in your letters about the amplification of your network and the numerous messages which you have sent during the last few weeks have demonstrated to me that you have been absolutely right in your idea of nominating the old collaborators as sub-agents of their networks. In particular, the network of Dagobert appears to be the one which is giving the best results.

This message caused some celebration at Crespigny Road [the north London base of Garbo] and St James's Street, for it was the first real proof that Fortitude was off to a good start. Garbo responded by relaying a message on 30 April from Chamillus, the NAAFI waiter, who, on 27 April, had volunteered to leave the depot at Chislehurst for a secret invasion embarkation point. On 29 April, Chamillus telephoned Garbo to arrange a rendezvous the following day at Winchester railway station. At their meeting Chamillus had disclosed that his new base was Hiltingbury Camp, near Otterbourne in Hampshire. Garbo reported that, according to Chamillus,

> all the 3rd Infantry Division are concentrated here ready to embark. There are other camps full of troops ready for attack. Have identified the 47th London Division in a camp to the south of mine . . . it is extremely difficult to leave the camp. They are preparing

cold rations for two days, also vomit bags and lifebelts for troops' sea voyage.

The purpose of this particular scheme was to place Chamillus in a position where he might reasonably be expected to let Garbo know when the invasion fleet had put to sea. Both Garbo and Harris were adamant that advance notice of the invasion of just one hour would be enough to enhance his reputation with the Abwehr. The Twenty Committee accepted this idea, with some dissent, but unfortunately the atmosphere soured early the next month and the Committee's attention was temporarily diverted.

Lily Sergueiev

I will soon be able to close my notebooks and forget. After two years in Germany I know how soon one forgets.

Controversy still surrounds the case which appears in MI5's records as Treasure. She first became known to the British authorities when she appeared in Madrid in June 1943 seeking a visa to Britain. In an interview with Kenneth Benton the following month Lily Sergueiev admitted that she had been sent to England as an Abwehr spy and disclosed a mass of material about her German controller in Paris. The decision was taken to allow her to come to London and in October 1943 she reached Gibraltar where she came into conflict with the authorities over her dog which was obliged to go into quarantine rather than accompany her to England.

After a lengthy interrogation Sergueiev was enrolled as a double agent with the codename Treasure and in January 1944, with the help of Ronald Reed, made radio contact with the Abwehr. This was to be a unique event because her usual method of communication was secret writing in letters directed to an address in Lisbon. In March 1944 she flew to Portugal for a meeting with her Abwehr controller who supplied her with a new transmitter. Using the radio she re-established wireless contact upon her return but a Radio Security Service operator was substituted to replace the temperamental double agent. Lily Sergueiev subsequently joined the French army and went back to Paris after the liberation, leaving the RSS expert to transmit on her behalf for a further five months.

Although she had no knowledge of Garbo or any of MI5's other double agents, she contributed to an elaborate deception scheme designed to deceive the enemy over where the D-Day landings were likely to occur.

After the war Sergueiev married an American officer and wrote her memoirs, *Secret Service Rendered*, in which she gave a detailed account of her duplicity.

What she did not divulge was her connection with Soviet intelligence. One of her uncles was Nikolai V. Skoblin, a senior NKVD officer, and the other was Evgenni Miller, the White Russian general who was assassinated in Paris in 1937. Much later, counter-intelligence investigators concluded that she had probably operated for the NKVD throughout the period of her supposed service for MI5 and the Germans. In this passage from her story Lily recalls her first encounter with SIS, an interview with Kenneth Benton in Madrid.

Secret Service Rendered

July 17, 1943

At 10.30 I get a telephone call: 'Benton here,' says a man's voice in English. 'I am from the passport department of the British Consulate. You have made an application for a visa, giving as reference a cousin who lives in England. We would like to have some further information. Could you come round this morning?'

'All right. I will be there in an hour.'

'Mr Benton?' I ask the messenger at the door. He gives me a slip to fill in.

'In what connection?' he asks, seeing I have left a blank line.

'I have an appointment.'

'Oh! All right. Will you wait in the next room, please?'

In the waiting room I pick up an English magazine and mechanically turn the leaves over. The door opens and the office boy beckons to me. I cross the entrance hall behind him and follow him down a passage. At the end, to the left, he pushes a door and holds it open for me. A man rises as I enter. He comes towards me, hand outstretched, and introduces himself: 'My name is Benton.' He is a classic example of 'The Englishman': young, tall, slim, with a long, narrow head and a straight brow with thinning red hair.

Benton pushes up a chair for me with a creaking wicker back. 'If what I have understood is correct,' he begins, 'you wish to go to England to rejoin your family.'

'I smile: 'Not exactly. I'm going there to spy.'

Benton raises his eyebrows.

'Maybe it would be simpler if I told you everything from the beginning?' I suggest.

'I rather think it would.'

I begin my story. Benton makes notes as I talk, and several times asks me to repeat things. Time passes. The Consulate must be closed – it's Saturday. At last he gathers the scattered sheets.

'I don't think you should stay any longer, but I would like to see you again on Monday. What you have to say is most interesting,' he adds. 'I should be grateful if you would keep quiet about it. If you are right about all this, I can tell you that you have done extremely well. But, please be careful!

'You have spoken a good deal of Kliemann [her Abwehr controller] and I have the impression that you underestimate him. He has his weaknesses certainly – you think him a little absurd because he is always late for his appointments. But we know a certain amount about Major Kliemann. He's an important man in German Intelligence – quite a formidable figure, in fact. If he finds out that you've double-crossed him, he won't be late for the next rendezvous, I can promise you.'

Monday, July 19, 1943

'I want a few more details,' says Benton this morning, looking over the notes he took on Saturday. 'Firstly, I would like to know what exactly you said in your letter to your cousin in Cambridge.'

'I tried to tip off the British Intelligence people. Unfortunately, I could only use the ordinary post and couldn't explain everything very clearly.

'I told her I had been invited by "the new owners of the place where we spent a summer together" (she would know that this could only mean Czechoslovakia) to work for them. I told her that I, personally, didn't want the job but that it might be useful to "her people". If Bessie understood that the *Germans* had offered me a very interesting job, she would guess that by "her people" I didn't mean her family. I ended by telling her that I didn't know how to get in touch with her people and asked her to get them to contact me.

'As far as I can remember, I sent three letters: one through an address someone had given me – one of those where you have to use two envelopes and enclose a 5-franc note; another one through a friend going to Vichy; and the third I sent myself from Marseilles. I never got an answer. I don't know if these letters ever reached their destination.'

'We can check that. Now, before I forget, what is to be done with the two blank sheets of paper you gave me on Saturday? I forgot to ask you about them.'

'Iron them. It's lemon juice.'

'Iron them?'

'Yes, with a hot iron.'

'Ah, I see. Then I would like to know what you have written to Kliemann since you arrived in Madrid.'

I tell him.

'And what do you mean to do now?'

'I think I might telephone Miret and arrange to meet the German agent. I would hand him a letter in clear for Kliemann, in which I would appear slightly fussed. I would say that, having started up the formalities to obtain my visa, I can foresee a close interrogation and there are some missing links in my story: the name of the person who introduced me to the Hotel Matignon and the person through whom I made his acquaintance. In other words, two names to use instead of those of Yvonne Delidaise and Genty. Because Kliemann would never want me to mention those two. I would make it clear that my letter is desperately urgent, because I may be questioned at any time.

'It is possible that I may have been watched or shadowed, although I haven't noticed anything – if they have, they will have noticed my frequent visits to your Consulate. If I talk about coming here first, and say why, it will seem much less suspicious.'

Benton smiled. 'Not bad. Have you had previous professional experience, by any chance . . . ?'

'No, but don't forget that I have been acting a part for the last two and a half years!'

'I think it's a good plan, but I had better get the approval of my chief. Could you do nothing about it until tomorrow, then ring me up in the morning and ask if we have sent the telegram to your cousin or not? Depending on whether I say 'yes' or 'no', you will know if you must act or wait. If the plan has got to be modified, I will tell you that the text is not clear and that you must return to see me. But I don't believe that that will be necessary.'

July 20, 1943

'Your cable has been sent,' I hear Benton's voice on the line.

'Thanks very much.' I ring off. Then I dial another number: 51–242. With the help of a dictionary, I have prepared a sentence: Want to see your friend tomorrow at 11 at the 'Café Lys'. It doesn't sound very grammatical, but who cares about grammar? A man's voice answers almost immediately. I ask for Monsieur Miret. It is he. I say, 'Canuto,' and then very carefully I repeat my little sentence.

He has understood: amazing!

The 'Lys' is almost at the end of the Grande Via; it has a single row of tables on the terrace and one sits on very comfortable settees. I choose a secluded corner and settle down.

I think over the events of the last few days. I have the feeling that I have connected up the two ends: the English and the German. If I don't do anything silly, all should now be well.

'Good morning, Mademoiselle Solange.'

'Hello! Good morning. I didn't hear you come.'

Miret's friend sits down beside me. 'You were absorbed in your lemon juice. How about going somewhere else? I know a lot of people who come to this café and I would rather not be seen with you.'

'Let us move, then. I don't mind. I only chose the 'Lys' because I don't know Madrid, can't speak Spanish and find it difficult to talk with Monsieur Miret!'

He calls the waiter, pays for my lemon squash and we go out. My companion is dressed in a brown suit and a light-coloured shirt; he looks much less sinister than when he suddenly appeared at my hotel the night before.

'My car is just round the corner.' We get in. I make a note of the type and the registration number. On the dash-board in front of me there is a brass plate bearing the name and address of the owner: H. von Buch – the rest is indistinct. My companion takes me to a smart bar, completely empty, in an unfamiliar street.

'Here,' I say, holding out the letter which I wrote the day before. 'This must be forwarded as quickly as possible to Major Kliemann. How many days will it take to get an answer? It's very urgent.'

'Your letter will leave tomorrow by diplomatic bag. The Major should have it the day after tomorrow. If he replies immediately, he can send his letter the next day and it should be here in four days, counting from tomorrow – so that makes five days from now.'

'It's too long. What can we do to save time?'

'Send a message by radio.'

'No, it's too complicated to put into a cable. He'd better get my letter with all the details, but could you ask him to cable his reply?'

'All right. It shall be done. Could we meet here again in two days?'

'Very well. Here at 6 o'clock.'

July 25, 1943

'Here's your answer. I haven't brought the original text, which is in German. But here's a translation.'

I take the sheet of paper which is scribbled on in pencil, and read: 'You were introduced to the Matignon by a Monsieur Perault, whose address you don't know and whom you haven't seen since. He was introduced to you in a café by Madame B . . . Good luck. Octave.' Madame B . . . I think to myself: the proprietress of the 'Maisonette,' where Moustache so often has his meals.

'Is that all right?' asks the German.

'Quite. I shan't tremble every time I go to see the British.' I feel relaxed and we remain a while, chatting. I don't know in what connection, but at some stage my interlocutor tells me his name is Fingadó.

'That's not a very German name,' I remark.

'No. My family comes from Italy. We emigrated to Germany at the time of Luther and became supporters of the new doctrine. Since then my forebears have lived in Germany until my father who, after his marriage, established himself in Barcelona. I was brought up in Spain. I only returned to Germany with the rise of the Fuhrer. I joined the Party and in '39 I wanted to enlist in the army, but I was ordered to remain here. You see, I speak the language perfectly and can pass as a Spaniard. They thought I would be able to render greater service in Madrid.'

'Is your first name, at least, German?'

'If you like: Gerhard. But I call myself Gerardo, Spanish-style.'

The cable which he has passed on for me seems to have given him confidence. He tells me all about his childhood and the Nazi Party of which he is proud to be a member. Before I leave, he gives me his telephone number in case anything urgent should crop up. Miret will apparently be absent for the next few days.

Monday

'Anything new?' asks Benton, pushing up the same creaking wicker armchair.

'Yes,' I hand him Kliemann's answer to my letter.

'Perault? Do you know the name?'

'No.'

'And Madame B . . . ?'

'I know her; she is the owner of a Russian restaurant called "La Maisonette" in the Rue de Passy.'

'Good. In any case, they don't interest us; if Major Kliemann has given their names, it means he doesn't intend to use them. I'll keep this paper and have it analysed. One never knows . . . Do you know how your letter was sent?'

'By diplomatic bag, and the answer was cabled. I've got something else for you: the German is not von Buch. He is called Gerardo Fingado, and this is his telephone number.'

'Excellent. I knew it couldn't be von Buch because the description didn't tally. This is much more likely . . .

'Now, the security people have given you a full clearance and I am authorised to tell you that you can be of great assistance to us, and that, up till now, you have done extremely well. We will be delighted if you agree to work for us.'

I feel myself blushing stupidly. I have so looked forward to this moment and all I can say is: 'Thank you. That is what I most wished to hear.'

'You can get your visa any time now,' Benton goes on, 'but in the interests of probability, I think we had better wait for a bit.'

'I thought I might write to Kliemann and inform him that everything is going all right and that I am hopeful of getting my visa. I could ask him to get ready to come over here and meet me – this will certainly take him some time. After that, I might perhaps start to see about a Portuguese visa?'

'I think that'a a good idea. I would like you to keep in touch with Fingado. You might perhaps meet up with some of their other agents . . . How are you off financially? Do you need money?'

'No. So far I have enough.'

'All the same, ask for some. It will be a good excuse to see them again, and they will expect you to ask.'

'All right.'

'Keep me informed if you get anything.'

Eddie Chapman

The ignorance of the German Intelligence astonished me. Up to the time of my arrival in England, they had no idea of the most elementary details of British life.

When the Germans occupied the Channel Islands in 1940 they found in Jersey prison a convicted safe-breaker named Eddie Chapman serving a two-year sentence for burglary. Furthermore, the prisoner expressed a willingness to betray his country and on that basis he was recruited by the Abwehr with the intention of sending him home as a spy.

Chapman, of course, was working to a rather different agenda: he saw his collaboration with the enemy as the most practical method of obtaining his release and returning to London. What he could not anticipate was the degree of knowledge that MI5 had accumulated about him from intercepted wireless signals. When he was parachuted into East Anglia in December 1942 an MI5 case officer was already near the dropping zone and on hand to receive his offer to act as a double agent. He underwent a brief but gentle interrogation at the hands of Leonard Burt, but his information exactly coincided with what MI5 had already learned so Chapman was enrolled as a double agent with the codename Zigzag.

Chapman was accommodated briefly in the same north London safe-house that had been used by Mutt, Jeff and Garbo, and undertook several sabotage missions for his Abwehr controllers, all of them masterminded by his MI5 case officer. In March 1943 he boarded a ship bound for Portugal in a daring attempt to re-establish contact with his German controllers. He reappeared in East Anglia soon after D-Day, having been flown from Belgium by the Luftwaffe. He had been in German hands for more than a year and his debriefings in London offered MI5 a unique insight into the Abwehr's methods and operations. Upon his return Chapman maintained wireless contact with the enemy but this was terminated in November 1944 when MI5 suspected that Chapman had been less than discreet in explaining his new-found wealth and recent absence on the Continent to his friends.

After the war Chapman wrote an account of his adventures with help from Sir Compton Mackenzie and a former Communist and convicted spy, Wilfred Macartney. In 1946 his story was bought by a French newspaper, *Etoile du Soir*, but the article was suppressed, and the authors prosecuted for breaches of the Official Secrets Act. A further attempt to reveal his work as a double agent ended in 1952 when an entire edition of the *News of the World* was withdrawn. Chapman subsequently collaborated with an author, Frank Owen, and produced *The Eddie Chapman Story* in 1954. By this date Chapman had acquired another criminal conviction, for illegal possession of foreign currency, the fruits of an import-export business, carried on by plane and boat from Tangier. He had also spent two years in the Gold Coast (Ghana) where he had become mixed up in a corruption scandal centring on government construction contracts signed by Prime Minister Dr Kwame Nkrumah who had also allegedly received large bribes.

After this episode Eddie Chapman returned to his trading activities in the Mediterranean and was eventually to open a hugely successful health hydro in Hertfordshire. He has now retired to the Canary Islands where he is working on an another volume of his memoirs. In this extract from his 1966 autobiography, he describes his arrival in East Anglia as a Nazi parachutist and the reception he received from MI5. The 'Colonel X' was actually Colonel T. A. Robertson, the head of B1(a).

The Real Eddie Chapman

I rang the bell several times. Finally a light came on in one of the bedrooms. A window was opened and a gruff male voice demanded my business. 'I am a flyer and I have had to make an emergency landing. May I use your telephone?' I demanded. A few minutes later the door opened and a tousle haired, yawning man opened the door. He regarded me suspiciously when he saw my attire, for I was dressed in a sports coat, flannels and was carrying my little brown attaché case. However, he allowed me to enter and invited me to have a cup of tea. God, I thought, we English and our tea. I believe that when I die and whatever heaven I go to, there will always be an Englishman poised ready to give me a cup of tea.

He motioned me to the telephone. 'Help yourself,' he said. I picked up the receiver – 'Could you put me through to the nearest police station,' I asked. A voice answered. 'I am a British flyer, I have had an accident; could you send some transport to pick me up?' I got the farmer, who was now standing by my elbow with the tea, to give the necessary directions, then went into the kitchen to await the police arrival.

The farmer's wife came down and I made a few enquiries as to how things were going in England. They were full of confidence and it did me a power of good listening to their homely accents. At the same time I could not fully share their optimism. After all, I had seen a part of the mighty forces of the Wehrmacht, experiencing the terrifying efficiency with which the Germans worked and I still doubted the eventual outcome.

· The police car arrived containing a sergeant and two constables. I took the sergeant to one side – 'Don't ask me any questions now. I will answer them down at the station. Meanwhile, could you send one of your men to pick up my parachute, overalls and landing boots?' I gave the necessary instructions. The sergeant, realising perhaps there was a need for discretion, agreed. We sat around drinking tea and generalising until the constable returned with my effects.

When we arrived at Littleport police station the Chief Constable and some plain clothes police were already awaiting our arrival.

'I wish to be put in contact with British Intelligence,' I informed them. I handed in my suitcase, poison tablet and automatic, then, taking off my coat, I undid my money belt. 'I think you will find £1,000 there, check it and give me a receipt.' This they did, but not before all eyes had curiously inspected all my equipment. Telephone calls were made, whispered conversations were carried out, the station buzzed with activity. Finally, I was asked if I would like some breakfast.

Three hours later, a military staff car drew up and a major and a lieutenant from Intelligence were ushered into the station. They interrogated me in a private room. I told them as briefly as I could who I was, what I had done and the mission the Germans had given me in Britain.

'I would like to make it clear that the reason I have started all this is first of all, I would like to work for my own country, secondly, there are several charges against me. If they can be dropped, I am certain I can be of some value as an agent.'

They wrote everything down. More telephone calls.

Then I was told 'We are taking you to London.'

The drive down to London was for me unforgettable. Convoys of army vehicles, uniforms of all the free nations, the dear familiar scene of London's hustle and bustle, but, above all, the people. They all looked happy. Something seemed to have happened to them. Everyone appeared to be on friendly terms. The common threat of war somehow had welded them together in no uncertain manner. Idly I wondered about my family – what was my father doing? Where was my brother and my sister? Were they still alive? I knew that possibly both my father and brother would be back in the merchant navy as engineers, and when I thought of the *Sonder Meldings* [sic] I had heard over the German Radio announcing the loss of thousands of tons of Allied shipping, I shuddered to think of their fate.

We drove to a large house in Kensington. There, waiting, were three officers from Special Branch, led by the redoubtable Commander Len Burt who was the chief at this time. Burt is a quiet man from Wiltshire. I believe his shrewd blue eyes miss nothing. He laughs quietly, but the brain behind the laugh still ticks. His questions are always with a point and are loaded. Not for him the bullying, threatening Gestapo technique. He is rather like a fine chess player probing out the weaknesses of his opponent. On and on went the questions. Everything I said, every answer I gave, was noted down in shorthand by one of the officers. Hour after hour. My head ached. I was exhausted. Drawing paper was produced and I drew sketches of the château in Nantes where I had undergone my training, the house I visited in Berlin, the flat in Paris. Every person with whom I had come into contact since my release from Fort Romainville in Paris had to be described in detail – the whole of my life, all my criminal activities, much of what seemed to me to be useless information was demanded and given.

Finally I could no longer keep track of the hours I had spent under interrogation. I kept falling asleep then re-awakening. Burt suddenly said to me in a kindly voice, 'You must be tired – we are taking you somewhere where you can get a good night's rest.'

I was taken in a car and driven to Ham Common on the outskirts of Hamstead [sic]. Later I found out this was a small prison kept specially for spies. At reception I was handed over to a military escort and taken to see the officer in command. I stood in front of his desk and observed his colonel's pips while he inspected me through his monocle.

'So you are Chapman. Well, now you are here, behave yourself. If you get tough, we can get tough.' I flushed with temper.

'Listen,' I said, 'I came over here with the best of good intentions. I don't like being stuck in prison. Either I am going to work for you or not at all, but I am not going to stay in prison, so pass that on to whoever is interested.'

He smiled sarcastically.

'All in good time, all in good time. Meanwhile behave yourself.'

He beckoned to two guards.

'Take him away and make him comfortable.'

I was led away into the main wing of the small prison and shown into a small cell. The cell door clanged shut and the guards clad in tennis shoes padded away. There was no mattress in the cell, only two blankets. I was much too tired to worry. I slept. At least I was back in my own country in one piece and even if the fatted calf had not been killed, neither had I.

Next day, bright and early, I was woken and given a decent breakfast. Three intelligence officers were waiting for me in the commanding officer's office.

They wanted to know about my radio transmissions to the Germans. I explained how my code worked and told them of a check word which had to be included in the code. This would prove to the Germans I was not sending under duress.

They then told me to code a message saying simply, 'Well, am with friends, good landing, Fritz.'

This I did. They gave me my transmission set, the pre-arranged time for the Germans to call me arrived, I tuned in to their frequency. I could hear their signal coming through in good strength –

GWT, GWT — — · · — — — — — · · — — —

I replied with a series of interrupting dits, then gave my call sign, I was disappointed they could not hear me, knowing that I was being monitored by several German stations, and, following my instructions, I gave my message over blind.

The intelligence officers looked impressed and asked a number of questions on codes and frequencies which the Germans operated on.

Fortunately, thinking frequencies may have been of some interest to them, I had made out a list on a cigarette paper which I had hidden in the back of my tie. Also, one evening I had gone up to the room the Germans used for their radio transmissions and finding someone had carelessly left the key in the lock, I had entered and found some interesting papers which related to the code they were using. This appeared to be of absorbing interest to the officers and everything pertaining to it had to be written out in the minutest detail. Again, however, I was led back to my cell.

Next day I was again let out of my cell, and this time I got a message from the Germans saying my message had been received and understood. They ended by wishing me good luck.

From these transmissions, the Intelligence decided that my messages were being picked up in Nantes, then sent to Paris from where I received my replies.

The next few days I was supplied with several bits of information which the British authorities thought might interest the German *Hierrefy*. Meanwhile, I still had no bed and I was fed up. I asked to see my friend the colonel – it was two days before Christmas.

'Colonel, I made an offer to the British Government. If I am not out of here by tomorrow night, forget the offer. Stick me on trial, but I am not transmitting any more to the Germans.'

'Don't threaten us,' he told me.

'I am not threatening, I am just stating a fact. I've done enough punishment, so more won't affect me, but one way or the other, I would like to know which way I stand.'

I was led back to my cell.

Next morning, bright and early, I was again taken to the colonel's office, where two military officers were waiting.

'Well, Chapman, good luck! You are being released and a merry Christmas to you!' He shook my hand.

These were the first kind words spoken to me since my arrival.

From the outside of the prison I was driven to a small house in Hendon. There I was met by Colonel X. He informed me I was to come and go exactly as I pleased and to consider myself free.

'However, when you go out, we would appreciate it if you would take one of the chaps with you.'

He introduced me to three pleasant individuals who were to be my companions during the next few weeks in England.

'I am sorry about the way you have been treated, but there were quite a few straws of red tape to be straightened out before we could get you released. Unfortunately, when you had been arrested in England and in Jersey, you always gave the name Edward Arnold, and it took the police some time to verify your true identity. Now during your interrogation, you mentioned you were friendly with a Terence Young. I have a surprise for you. We are dining with him tomorrow at the Ritz. He is a major in the Guards Armoured Division and will be pleased to see you.'

From that day my life changed. Mentally I felt a great relief. At least I was back in my own country, fighting with my own people and I knew by instinct I could do it. I have always liked working alone and during the times I had been doing villainy, I was never happier than when out at night prowling around like some big cat, over walls of the sides of buildings, always quietly, silently, bent on achieving some nefarious scheme. I knew that one mistake and I would plunge from off my own particular tightrope and the resulting mess would not be pleasant.

I met Terence Young and we discussed life in general. The topic of what I was engaged on was politely avoided. During this time too, in company with one of my intelligence escorts, I went out often dining and wining. For the first time in years I saw a Christmas pantomime. I bought myself some clothes, the excellent quality of which surprised me, even though utility was the order of the day. I explored some of the bomb damage and with permission from the authorities, sent over some slightly misleading reports.

The ignorance of the German Intelligence astonished me. Up to the time of my arrival in England, they had no idea of the most elementary details of British life. I had been warned that perhaps it would be difficult for me to obtain food, for they believed this was drastically rationed in Britain. They did not know that anyone could get a meal in a restaurant without giving up coupons. London was portrayed to the German people as a mass of devastation, and even their own secret service believed this.

It was not difficult to understand why this was so. Under the twisted genius of Goebbels, German propaganda had so long deluded the master race that its sinister influence had penetrated even into the inner recesses of the Nazi war machine. It lied to everyone; even its own Special Branch did not know the truth! Accurate reports must have flowed in from innumerable neutral sources, as well as from every foreign embassy and consulate. These were received by officials high in the hierarchy, who automatically filed them away in order to continue deluding the German public, and even their own bosses. They finished by deluding themselves.

A point had been reached at which even intelligent Germans had come to believe whatever Hitler wanted them to believe, and nothing else. If the British declared that they had bacon, meat and bread in abundance, it must clearly be lies – in fact, 'propaganda'. The Germans always firmly maintained that they were in a better position than their enemies. That is why Hitler was able to keep them fighting up to the twelfth hour, in the belief that the other side would crack first. Indeed, they are still wondering why that didn't happen!

Some light can be thrown on the bungling technique of the German Secret Service by their handling of my own case. When I unpacked my money I found that the Dienststelle had forgotten to take the bands of the Deutsche Bank of Berlin from the packages; they had even left the Dienststelle number stamped on the bundle. Again, the new valves which had been fitted to my transmitter were German, and still bore their German markings. Our intelligence had a damn good laugh at this.

Edward Spiro

Fiction may be sometimes more entertaining, and readers who take their ideas about espionage work from adventure novels may be disappointed. But I thought it better to rely upon careful investigations and official documents rather than vivid imagination. In fact, the truth about the British Secret Service is often thrilling enough.

The Secrets of the British Secret Service

Before the war Edward Spiro worked as a freelance journalist for several British newspapers in his native Austria, and it was this connection which saved his life when he was arrested by the Gestapo and incarcerated in Dachau and then Buchenwald. Diplomatic pressure was brought to bear on the Nazi authorities and in 1939 he was released to start a new life in England.

Spiro's connection with SIS began in Austria after he had graduated from Vienna University and had become political editor of the city's evening paper. In 1936 he was recruited by Captain Thomas Kendrick, the SIS head of station, as a source, and this was the lever that was subsequently used to obtain his freedom and bring him to England.

Spiro arrived in London a penniless refugee but, like so many of his Jewish countrymen forced to flee to England, he was to make a great success of his second career. However, before joining the *Daily Telegraph* as a lobby correspondent in the House of Commons, or achieving distinction with his works of non-fiction, he operated as a stoolpigeon for the Security Service by infiltrating groups of suspected Nazis who had been interned under the wartime emergency regulations. Spiro's task was to test the loyalties of the German inmates and report those whom he believed to be active party members or potential enemy spies.

Following a stay at Cookham in Berkshire Spiro changed his name to E. H. Cookridge and was later employed on propaganda work for the Ministry of Economic Warfare, the government's department of dirty tricks which broadcast ingenious radio programmes to Germany. After the war he wrote extensively on the subject of espionage, publishing biographies of Kim Philby and George Blake. He had first met Philby in Vienna in the summer of 1933 when both had been active in the anti-Fascist underground, and Philby had met and married his first wife, Litzi Friedman. In this extract from his book on Philby, Cookridge, who died in February 1979, explains how their friendship, which was to last thirty-three years, began.

The Third Man

I had spent my childhood and youth in Vienna, where my father was the representative of the Manchester textile firm of Reddaway & Co. When I came down from Vienna University, where I read *rerum politicarum*, I became a junior reporter on an evening paper, and later transferred to a morning newspaper. This paper was neither owned nor controlled by the Social Democratic party; but it supported its general policy, as the *Daily Herald* and the *Daily Mirror* supported Labour in this country. I became the paper's parliamentary reporter and, eventually, at the age of twenty-five, its political editor. As a student I had been a member of the Social Democratic university club and held a minor office; later I continued my party membership without, however, taking an active part. During the February putsch, my newspaper was closed down and its editorial staff arrested. I was detained, along with many politicians and newspaper colleagues.

Compared with my experience as a prisoner of the Gestapo at Dachau and Buchenwald some years later, the detention camp of Wöllersdorf was a holiday camp. My detention lasted for only a week or two; there was no evidence against me of any 'revolutionary activities'.

After my release I discovered that I had lost my job; all socialist and liberal newspapers had been suppressed. However, I soon found employment as a book editor with a small firm publishing art books, for which I had previously done occasional work as an editorial adviser and reviewer. On the staff of this firm was another ex-Socialist Student Club member, Walter Neurath, afterwards the owner of the renowned London publishing house of Thames and Hudson, whose untimely death in 1967 was a severe loss to the British book trade.

The office of the *Oesterreichische Monographie* publisher's in the *Handelsmuseum* building (which once housed exhibitions) was to become one of several clandestine centres of the illegal socialist movement. It was in the Hörlgasse in the ninth district of Vienna. It also became for a time one of Kim Philby's anchor points, and I was responsible for the choice.

The director of the publishing firm, Alexander Stipetic, was a Labour sympathizer and an easy-going man. If he knew that among his new editor's visitors there were some suspicious characters wanted by the political police, and if he noticed that his typewriters and duplicating machines were used after office hours for the production of clandestine news-sheets and leaflets, he closed his eyes to it.

After the collapse of the Social Democratic party, its leaders, with few exceptions, were totally discredited in the eyes of their former members. Most of the prominent politicians were elderly men: Dr Karl Renner was sixty-four, and the party chairman, Karl Seitz, the burgomaster of Vienna and a revered figure, was the same age. When Dollfuss ordered the bombardment of the workers' homes, Seitz remained in the City Hall, waiting for his arrest. Most of the National Council members were arrested in their beds hardly protesting. Similarly unprotesting were almost all the trade union leaders – portly, middle-aged, dignified gentlemen, greatly resembling their colleagues in the British TUC. But among the leaders of the Social Democratic party in Vienna there were two notable exceptions. One was Dr Otto Bauer, the 'Austrian Nye Bevan', often called the father of Austro-Marxism, who was chairman of the party's executive; the other was Julius Deutsch, one of the party's prominent front-benchers in parliament and leader of the Republican Defence League. Bauer managed to escape to Czechoslovakia, disguised in workman's overalls and with a forged passport which Wenzel Jaksch, the leader of the Sudetenland socialists had brought him during the fighting. Deutsch, wounded in the face (one of his eyes was dangerously injured) also escaped across the Czech frontier. In Brno they set up an office-in-exile of the Social Democratic party, and during the next four years, until the *Anschluss*, Bauer directed the clandestine work in Austria, trying to unite the various resistance groups.

It was only natural that, after the great debacle and the wide-spread disillusion with the 'old guard', dissension should have rent the illegal groups.

The first group to establish contact with Bauer's exile-bureau in Czechoslovakia was organized by a few members of the editorial staff of the *Arbeiterzeitung*, which until the putsch was the official party newspaper. This group was led by its former editors, Oskar Pollak, and Otto Leichter. The largest group of those formed by younger party leaders was led by Karl Hans Sailer and the trade unionist Manfred Ackerman. It was organized under the name of 'Revolutionary Socialists'. This rather romantic name was chosen to emphasize that the new organization –

which eventually united the entire Socialist clandestine resistance – had discarded the timid policy of the 'old guard', which they regarded as the main reason for the February catastrophe.

Other smaller groups included *'Der Funke'* (the Spark), led by Leopold and Ilse Kulczar, the 'Red Front', the 'Febrists', and local groups emerging from the dissolved student organization and the Social Democratic Youth League. All were smaller than the Revolutionary Socialists: some advocated a united front with the Communists.

Many former party members, particularly students and members of the Republican Defence League, had gone over to the Communists. The leaders of the Revolutionary Socialist group, despite its name, rejected the idea of the direct action of sabotage or bomb throwing. Neither did they encourage strikes, which would have only meant more misery for the working masses, already suffering from brutal retaliatory actions by the government, and from arbitrary cuts in wages and unemployment benefits. All that we could do was to keep the faithful together, provide a link between them by producing clandestine newspapers and pamphlets, and organize relief actions for the families of the many thousands in prisons and detention camps.

Within weeks several underground newspapers began to appear, the most important of which was the weekly *Arbeiterzeitung*. It was printed in Czechoslovakia and smuggled in very large quantities across the frontier for distribution throughout the country. It was remarkable that this underground paper gained a larger weekly circulation than its official predecessor had when published daily. Distribution, carried out under the noses of the police, was a risky business. Anybody caught carrying a parcel of paper could except a savage prison sentence under the emergency laws.

The office of my publishers had become one of the clandestine centres of the Revolutionary Socialists. Another and more important office was a few blocks away in Hörlgasse, managed by a brave young woman, Dr Mitzi Jahoda (later a senior lecturer at Oxford and wife of Austen Albu, MP, former Minister of State for Economic Affairs). With a few helpers, she was in charge of the clandestine secretariat of the Revolutionary Socialist party, and in constant touch with Dr Bauer's exile-bureau.

Kim Philby offered his help, which was readily accepted. With his British passport he could travel to Czechoslovakia and back, whereas Austrian travellers were invariably held up at the frontier and subjected to thorough questioning and search. This applied even to innocent travellers going abroad for business or family reasons. Our couriers had to use the 'green frontier', covering the last stage of their journeys by night on foot, and returning in the same manner, loaded with clandestine literature and messages from the exile-bureau.

Philby's assistance proved invaluable, but soon doubts emerged about where his real loyalty lay. The Communists were trying every ruse to infiltrate and take over the socialist groups. They succeeded in taking over the Students' League and several clandestine trade union groups; to all practical purposes they also took over the command of the remnants of the Defence League.

One day Philby came to me with the news that he could provide a 'safe house' for meetings of the central committee, and that the owner of the house was an Englishwoman. We jumped at his offer when we heard this. She was known as 'Mary' (her real name was Muriel Gardiner), was the divorced wife of a rich American, and had come to Vienna in 1927 as a medical student. She had plenty of money, a villa in the Vienna Woods, a large apartment in the Rummelhardt-Gasse in one of the outer districts and a pied-à-terre in the Lammgasse near the University. She also had a four-year-old daughter, looked after by a nannie and maidservant. Her socialist sympathies were somewhat out of keeping with the luxurious respectability in which she lived.

She made her flats available for illegal meetings; the garden sheds at her villa were soon filled with stacks of clandestine news-sheets and pamphlets. She was a brave and kind woman and often insisted on paying the expenses of the messengers, whose fares the central committee could not refund.

Kim Philby had pretended that it was he who had enlisted Muriel Gardiner into our work; but we soon found out that in fact she had been discovered by Ilse Kulczar, one of the 'Spark Group' leaders. Looking back after more than thirty years, I assume that Kim Philby had good reasons of his own to pose as the go-between. Also, as I had already then discovered, while helping the socialist groups he was at the same time involved with our opponents, the Communist organizations.

One day Kim appeared in my office with a young man, whom he introduced as Bernhard Suchy. At that time unsuccessful attempts were being made to arrive at some arrangement with the Communists; we wanted to establish a common front against the fascist dictatorship and, even more so, against the rapidly growing Nazi movement, which threatened to replace the Dollfuss régime by an even more iniquitous one. But the Communist leaders were already pursuing the double-faced policy which was to bring them success and domination in every Eastern country after the second world war: this policy was to negotiate coalitions with socialist and democratic groups and then to swallow them one by one and assume complete superiority.

I played a minor part in these negotiations, but I soon realized that the Communists aimed at a complete take-over of our organizations, which did not, of course, escape the members of the central committee of the Revolutionary Socialists. Philby's friend Suchy reappeared some days later with Erwin Zucker, the former editor of the Communist *Rote Fahne* and his wife Betty. At that time I had found another office in Wollzeile Street, in the heart of Vienna's newspaper world. We had registered a business firm under the somewhat ironical name of 'Patria' which ostensibly dealt with heating appliances. Our 'commercial travellers' left the office carrying long oven pipes inside which were rolls of clandestine pamphlets for distribution to local groups. Philby, Suchy and Zucker suggested that they should join us at this little office. It was a somewhat gauche attempt at a 'take-over'.

Up to that time I greatly admired Kim Philby. Here was a young Englishman, determined to risk much to help the underground freedom movement in a small country, which must have been of only very limited interest to him. He had shown his personal courage when joining the defenders of the shelled council estates during the February fighting; he had shared their ordeal in the sewers, had rescued several of them, and he continued to do a good job for us as a courier.

But doubts began to dawn on me when Philby appeared as a Communist go-between and when he declared that he could provide all the money we needed for our work. He mentioned that he had close contacts with the Soviet consul, Ivan Vorobyev, and Vladimir Alexeievich Antonov-Ovseyenko, a mystery emissary from Moscow, who had arrived in Vienna after the putsch and was obviously a GB agent. The money which Philby offered could only have come from the Russians, and the last thing my friends and I wanted was to accept financial help from Moscow. Philby was told this in unmistakable terms and our relations with him and his friends came to an abrupt end.

There was no treachery amongst the members of the socialist underground, but the Communist organizations had been infiltrated by police informers. Some of their members had been persuaded by the political police to betray their comrades for paltry payments. There was a wave of arrests and some of the Communist leaders were imprisoned; others, including Erwin Zucker, managed to escape and later emerged in Moscow.

By the summer of 1934, Kim Philby must have been compromised too; he left Vienna in a hurry, warned by his friends in the GB. The treachery within the Communist ranks also had unfortunate repercussions on the socialist organizations. Some of the leaders who had conducted the unsuccessful 'common front' negotiations with the Communists were arrested, among them Karl Hans Sailer.

But the socialist underground movement persevered, and for four long years we tried to continue our fight for freedom. In March 1938, when the Gestapo and the SS descended on Austria in the wake of the German troops, most of the Revolutionary Socialists were rounded up. The Gestapo certainly proved more efficient than the police of Dr Schuschnigg.

Since 1936 I had been in touch with the officials of the British secret service attached to the British legation in Vienna. I shall describe this work later. Like many of my friends, I was arrested soon after the *Anschluss* and taken to the concentration camp of Dachau and later to Buchenwald, when I was released – after intervention by the British Government – shortly before the outbreak of the war in 1939. Many of my friends were not so lucky and perished in the torture cellars and gas chambers of the Gestapo. A few survived and, like Otto Kreisky, Dr Otto Tschadek, Karl Maisel and Karl Czernetz, became cabinet ministers and members of parliament when Austria was restored to independence after 1945.

During his momentous year in Austria in 1934, Kim Philby had received the first taste of conspiratorial activities and cloak-and-dagger work. In a sense he had already become at that time a 'third man'; self-effacing, secretive and fully dedicated to danger, leading a double life in more ways than one.

Tom Driberg

Secret work seems to have appealed to some element in his nature. At any rate, as soon as his Secret Service job ended, he got in touch with MI5, where many of his old Cambridge and Oxford friends had temporary wartime jobs.

Guy Burgess: A Portrait

Driberg is probably best known as the politician who was at one time chairman of the Labour Party and was later ennobled by Harold Wilson as Lord Bradwell. As the William Hickey columnist in the *Daily Express* he was exceptionally well informed; he heard all the gossip and rumours and was virtually a professional party guest.

He was a rampant homosexual and a long-term MI5 mole. His involvement in espionage began when he joined the Young Communist League while he was still at school. This was the membership that was to be skilfully exploited by Maxwell Knight, MI5's star case officer who specialized in the recruitment and planting of ideologically reliable agents into the Communist Party. His other key source was Olga Gray whom he had persuaded to work for various Soviet front organizations before she was taken on by the CPGB's national organizer, Percy Glading. It was her crucial testimony, given at Glading's trial in 1938, that led to the conviction of four members of the Woolwich Arsenal spy ring. Until the moment she stepped into the witness box Glading never suspected that his trusted confidante had been a deep-cover MI5 agent, reporting daily to Max Knight.

Driberg's career as one of Knight's moles was to be terminated abruptly in 1941 when he was expelled from the party. When Driberg demanded to know the reason, he was informed that he had been accused of betraying the CPGB's secrets to MI5, and being an informant codenamed M8. When Driberg, ignorant that his reports had been circulated within MI5 as having come from M8, reported this to Knight, the latter realized that only someone inside the Security Service could have compromised his agent. Knight died in February 1968 convinced of Soviet penetration of MI5 but he never learned that his colleague Anthony Blunt had been the person responsible.

In later years Driberg was tempted back into espionage by the Czechs who paid him handsomely for his political gossip, apparently never suspecting that he was routinely reporting every contact to MI5. One significant mission undertaken by Driberg for MI5 was to travel to Moscow in 1953 to interview his old friend Guy Burgess. This journey was to result in a slim but affectionate biography of the defector, *Guy Burgess: A Portrait*, which was released in 1956. Driberg succumbed to a heart attack in the back of a London taxi in August 1976. In this extract from his autobiography, *Ruling Passions*, he describes his encounter with Burgess.

Ruling Passions

I have never kept a diary – possibly because I used to write a daily newspaper column – but I have stacks of small engagement-books, dating back many years, which occasionally remind me of people or places.

Glancing through a pre-war one recently, I was surprised to see the name of Guy Burgess, for I had and have no recollection of ever having met him before the war. The first meetings with him that I recall were when he was working for the BBC at the House of Commons and chose me, several times, to do the programme called 'The Week in Westminster'. In those days this was simply a fifteen-minute talk by one MP describing, as impartially as he could, the parliamentary events of the past five days; it went out on a Saturday, if possible live. The MP doing it used to lunch and go over his script with the producer, Guy Burgess: this was obviously an easier process if the MP was a professional writer; others required rather more coaching.

Books have been written (one of them by me) about the defection to Russia in 1951 of two senior members of the Foreign Service, Guy Burgess and Donald Maclean. There is no point now in going over the whole of that business. It was in 1956 that the two men reappeared briefly at the National Hotel in Moscow, read a prepared hand-out to a few invited correspondents, and vanished again without answering any questions. At that time I was temporarily out of Parliament and therefore working more or less all of the time as a journalist (and earning much more money than I could as an MP). It occurred to me that, as I had known Burgess in London, I might be able to go to see him in Moscow and get the full story of his and Maclean's disappearance. I told this part of it in a small book, which was serialised in the *Daily Mail* and, through the formidable bargaining skill of my literary agent, the late Jean Leroy, brought me more money than any other single story I have written.

What I could not tell then was what it was like to see Guy again when I went back to Moscow to go through the proofs of the book with him. (There is a picture of us doing this in the book, which may possibly still be found in the libraries.) Maclean I did not see: Guy told me that he had strongly disapproved of Guy's arrangement with me (though I had no doubt that it had the approval of their employers). The text of the book could not be changed: I had written it, a chapter a day, for a month, and presumably Guy had shown each chapter to his Soviet colleagues or superiors. But we had more time to talk privately now: he had lately moved into a new flat in Moscow, for which I had sent him a good deal of Scandinavian furniture from London, and I was also able to spend a weekend at his *dacha*, in a country village about an hour's drive (by official pool car) from the city; this I had not been allowed to do before, because the village was said to be in a restricted area. According to Guy, this did not necessarily mean that there were defence plants there – merely that a number of important people had houses in the neighbourhood.

The *dacha* had been allocated to him some time before. It had been taken over by the State because the Party official who had built and occupied it had been removed for embezzling Party funds. It was the largest house in the village and for this reason, and because it was State property, it was guarded constantly by four secret police, who lived in a cottage in a corner of the extensive grounds. This, at least, was the explanation that Guy gave me of these somewhat rigorous security measures: I do not know if he believed it himself, but I was not in a position to disprove it. He knew by certain means (I had better not, even now, say what they were) that these guards had to report, about once a fortnight, on his conduct and movements and on any visitors he might have. One of the guards became quite friendly with him, and told him that there was one room in the house, a small study, which was not 'miked'. As they were sitting in this room when the guard said this, and as he went on to make disparaging remarks about his own superior officers, Guy was inclined to believe him; but it could have been a trap. We did not, in any case, use this room when we wanted to talk privately; we thought it wiser to walk in the garden. (At his flat in Moscow we used to stand by a large radiogram and talk against the loudest possible music.)

The village of Guy's *dacha* was a small and pretty one, with an English-looking duck-pond and a typical onion-domed Orthodox church. Walking round it on the Saturday afternoon, I asked if there wasn't a bar we could go to in the evening, as one would go to a pub in England. Guy looked worried. 'There is one,' he said. 'But I can't go there now. Donald [Maclean] was staying here, and he had one of his drunken fits and wrecked the bar. There was a hell of a row about it. That was before he had his last cure.'

Then I worried him still more by saying that I thought I would go to the church in the morning: it would be interesting to see how many people – in particular, young people – still went to it. Guy said: 'I don't know which secret policeman will be on duty in the morning, but I don't think he'll like it. He'll probably feel he'll have to escort you, in case there are any hooligans around.' I pointed out that I had never, in any country, seen a village more tranquil and hooligan-free, and in the morning insisted on going to church, unescorted. (There were rather more people there than there would be in a comparable English village, but few young people.) The guard on duty saw me out of the big gate in the high wall surrounding the grounds, saluted, and locked it behind me – so that when I got back from the church I could not get in and had to go round to the corner of the grounds by the guards' cottage and shout to them to let me in.

Their reports on Guy's conduct would no doubt have included references in his drinking habits. These varied considerably. In Moscow he was alert in the morning but often, by the evening, getting a bit sozzled on vodka. At the *dacha* he kept only wine – usually a Georgian white wine – and drank no vodka. He led a solitary life there, occasionally talking to the friendly guard or to his elderly, devoted woman housekeeper, and doing a great deal of reading, chiefly of classic English literature. Occasionally he would sit down at a decrepit upright piano and strum a tune: at his request, I had got him a copy of the *English Hymnal*, and he would pick out with two fingers the hymns he had known at Eton, tears running down his cheeks. (As has been recorded before, he used to wear an Old Etonian tie in Moscow.) Many of his books were still in store in London. Some of them I retrieved and shipped to him, together with the furniture for his new flat. One book I gave, at his request, to the library of the Reform Club. It was Margot Asquith's autobiography, given to Guy by her, with marginal notes which she had scribbled, identifying some of the characters not named in the book – for instance, her first lover.

Naturally, I asked what his job in Moscow really was: his ostensible (and actual) work for the Foreign Literature Publishing House was hardly full-time. He recommended Western authors whom he thought worth translating into Russian, and was proud of having persuaded them to start on Graham Greene (not surprisingly, with *The Quiet American*), and, I think he said, E. M. Forster. Apart from this, he said, he sat on various committees concerned with international affairs, particularly Western policy, and wrote memoranda which, he claimed, were read at the highest level but one. That was when I first saw him. When I saw him again, some months later, the Suez crisis had occurred, and he said that he knew that his memoranda were now read at the highest level.

This was for an interesting reason. It is difficult to look back now and realise how almost universal was the belief that, after Eden's collapse, the next Prime Minister of Britain would be R. A. Butler. Apart from the Westminster commentators, that was the forecast communicated to Moscow by the Soviet Embassy in London. Only two men I know of – Randolph Churchill in London, Guy Burgess in Moscow – prophesied correctly that Macmillan would be the successor. Churchill had a special source of information in his father, whose dislike of Butler was well known. 'How on earth did you get it right?' I asked Guy. 'Oh,' he replied, 'from a study of the life of the great Lord Salisbury' – and, indeed, I remembered his saying that this Victorian statesman had been, to him, one of the most fascinating figures in modern political history.

I don't know how much of a handicap it was to him that he was not a fluent or correct Russian speaker: 'Kitchen Russian' was all that he said he could manage.

Guy's life in Moscow was somewhat restricted socially. He took me to spend an evening with two British Communists, a man and his wife, working there: it was a pleasant evening of serious talk, a good supper, and a splendid television performance of *Swan Lake* by either the Bolshoi or the Kirov ballet, but it hardly competed in excitement, for someone of Guy's temperament, with his much-publicised wild parties in London.

As we walked back from their flat, Guy said, doubtfully: 'Tell me . . . Are they as nice as I think they are?' I said: 'Yes, I like them both very much, but I don't think you'd ever have met them – or, at least, bothered to cultivate their friendship – if you'd still been in London.' While I was there we also saw, once or twice, the late Ralph Parker, a well-known British journalist who had been Moscow correspondent, successively, of *The Times* and of the *Daily Worker*. I had the impression that Guy did not care for Parker much. Indeed, he expressed mistrust in what was, for him, an odd remark: 'We all think he's an agent, but we can't make out whose side he's on' – adding that it was regarded as suspicious that Parker had his car serviced by a corporal at the American Embassy.

Wolfgang zu Putlitz

It was not long before I realised that I was well and truly caught up in the web of the British Secret Service.

The son of a famous aristocratic family from Potsdam, Wolfgang zu Putlitz sought to join the German diplomatic corps after his service in an Uhlan Guards regiment in Finland during the Great War. He already had a knowledge of French, but to improve his English he travelled to England in 1924 with an introduction to Jona von Ustinov, better known simply as Klop, who was then the London correspondent of a German newspaper and fulfilled the role of press attaché at the embassy. Zu Putlitz stayed with the Ustinovs and spent some weeks at Oxford where he became friendly with several undergraduates, including the young Graham Greene.

Upon his return to Berlin zu Putlitz passed the Foreign Ministry examinations and was posted to the German embassy in Washington DC. He was to spend five years in America, latterly as chargé d'affaires in Haiti, before he returned to Berlin to be put in charge of the press section dealing with British and American journalists.

When in June 1934 he was appointed press attaché in Ribbentrop's embassy in London, it was hoped by his British hosts that he might co-operate with SIS in much the same way as his predecessor; Klop Ustinov (his son Peter is the famous actor and writer) had been a valued source for MI5 and had later worked as an agent runner for SIS. After his defection, and his adoption of British citizenship,

Klop became a key figure in the recruitment of Germans disenchanted with the Nazi regime. The appointment of the aristocratic zu Putlitz, who was an active homosexual, was to prove a significant development for MI5 and SIS, for very soon he was being debriefed on a weekly basis. As he said in his memoirs, 'I would unburden myself of all the dirty schemes and secrets which I encountered as part of my normal daily routine at the Embassy.'

Zu Putlitz's MI5 case officer was the young Dick White, a future head of both MI5 and SIS who had himself only recently been recruited. As a window into the German regime's diplomatic manoeuvring, zu Putlitz was highly regarded and often held secret meetings with Sir Robert Vansittart of the Foreign Office.

Zu Putlitz eventually came under German suspicion as a traitor after he had been switched from London to The Hague in May 1938, and the Gestapo began to accumulate evidence of a highly placed leak. Tipped off to the investigation in October 1939, zu Putlitz demanded to be exfiltrated and Klop Ustinov helped Richard Stevens, the local SIS representative, supervise the escape, flying him and his valet to England. However, wartime London was no place for the defector, who – having been blown – no longer had any value to the intelligence services, and whose proposals for creating a German opposition among the Social Democrats exiled in Britain were politely ignored. One of the Cabinet ministers who received him, but rejected his ideas, was Sir Samuel Hoare.

After a period of frustration arrangements were made for him to be resettled with a new identity in Jamaica, but the temperamental German loathed the Caribbean and turned up in New York where the US Office of Strategic Services hired him to compile a comprehensive who's who of prominent figures in German politics. In January 1944 zu Putlitz returned to London where he was befriended by Anthony Blunt of MI5 and for the remainder of the war he helped in the preparation of propaganda broadcasts to Germany.

At the end of the war zu Putlitz returned briefly to Germany but he was no longer welcome. His family estates were in ruins and there was no job for a man widely regarded as a turncoat. Instead he returned to England to lecture German prisoners of war about democratic politics. In January 1946 Dick White helped him acquire British citizenship and later in the year he gave evidence for the prosecution at the Nuremberg war crimes trial.

Zu Putlitz revealed his Communist sympathies when, in 1952, he went to live in East Germany. He had first met Guy Burgess at a party at Cambridge in 1932 and they had remained close friends ever since. As he was to reveal in his autobiography, which included an acknowledgement to the kindness of Anthony Blunt, much to the latter's embarrassment, he had also been in touch with the Soviets since 1943. When Guy Burgess defected zu Putlitz felt compelled to follow, and in January 1952 he crossed into East Berlin. This was an odd move, considering that his brother had died in an East German prison in 1948, but zu Putlitz never gave a complete account of his motives, and he died in September 1975 leaving only his autobiography which had been published in England in

1957. In it he disguised the identities of Dick White (whom he referred to as 'Tom Allen'), Klop Ustinov ('Paul X'), Klop's wife Nadia Benois ('Gabrielle X') and their son Peter ('Hugo X').

Here zu Putlitz recalls an encounter with Major Richard Stevens, the SIS head of station in The Hague who disclosed that he was in contact with some dissidents in the Wehrmacht. Zu Putlitz immediately, and correctly, suspected a Gestapo trap (the Venlo incident – see pages 319–23) and alerted 'Paul'.

The zu Putlitz Dossier

Every possible precaution was taken to keep my presence in London [in 1939] a secret so that the Nazis would be in the dark as to what had become of me. But in London, of all places, the news was bound to leak out. Indeed, I had not been there two weeks before I ran into the Counsellor of the Dutch Embassy, Baron van Karnebeek. He was utterly astonished to meet me walking down Piccadilly and immediately began questioning me. I concocted some cock-and-bull story. Then he told me that he was leaving for The Hague the next day for a meeting with the Foreign Minister, van Kleffens. So I said quite frankly: 'Kaas, it's no use asking you to keep mum about our meeting. I've been a diplomat and I know that you'll tell van Kleffens, so I may as well ask you to do me a favour. Please ask van Kleffens to look after my personal belongings which I had to leave behind at Scheveningen, to see that they're not stolen by Butting's Gestapo men, and to send them to me here.'

Karnebeek promised to do his best, as well as not to tell anyone but his Minister that he had seen me.

About this time Paul [Klop Ustinov] returned from Holland, bringing with him Captain Stevens, and we all met again at the former's flat where the winter before I had had that fateful talk with Vansittart. They told me that on the evening of my flight they had had a celebration dinner of oysters and champagne at the famous Restaurant Royale at The Hague. They also told me that the Nazis had spread all sorts of conflicting stories about me. Some said that I had rejoined my regiment at Stahnsdorf, others that I had been killed in a motor accident on the Belgian border. But the story I liked best was that I had run off with all the cash from the Legation and bought a brothel in Rio de Janeiro.

Stevens had other interesting news. 'You'll be back in your country sooner than you think,' he said. 'Hitler is nearly finished.'

'Where on earth do you get that idea from!' I laughed. 'It doesn't look that way to me. He appears to be winning hands down. He's beaten

Poland and the German army in the West is more powerful than ever, but still the Allies do nothing.'

'There won't be any need for a military offensive. The Hitler régime is collapsing internally,' Stevens insisted with great conviction.

'Go on, tell me more. I'm curious to know,' I said cynically.

'I can't tell you everything, for obvious reasons,' he explained with an air of mystery. 'But you can take it from me that there is a lot hatching in the Wehrmacht which will soon flare up, and that will be the end of Hitler. Some of the top-ranking generals are mixed up in it. I'm in permanent radio contact with them from Holland. As soon as they've got rid of Hitler, they're going to sue for peace.'

I asked him the names of the generals. He was very guarded, but in the end mentioned General von Rundstedt. Immediately he did so, I remembered that two years before the Gestapo had used von Rundstedt's name as a decoy in abducting the former Reichs Chancellor, Bruening, from a Dutch monastery back to Germany. The plan only failed because Bruening had become suspicious at the last minute.

'Forgive me being sceptical,' I said, 'but you know that I've had some pretty nasty experiences myself with your so-called confidants. I'm afraid they'll lead you up the garden path.'

He gave me a rather lofty smile.

'I'm sorry I can't tell you more. But you'll soon see that I'm right.'

Some days later van Karnebeek returned from Holland and I went to see him about my belongings. He shifted uncomfortably in his chair, making excuses. Then at last he came out with the truth.

'Van Kleffens didn't consider he could risk quarrelling with the Third Reich over a pair of trousers belonging to Herr von Putlitz!' he said. 'Anyhow, your things had all been collected by Butting the day after you left.'

The only irreplaceable things that I really regretted were my father's gold watch and chain that my grandfather had bought in 1815 in the rue de la Paix when the Prussians had marched into Paris. The rest of my possessions I wrote off without tears.

In point of fact, I had not really expected any other treatment from the men in power in Holland at that time, for not long before a certain official of the Dutch Foreign Office had remarked to me: 'We Dutch are so sincerely neutral that we would like both sides to win.'

Not very long afterwards, Captain Stevens, too, had his own taste of Dutch neutrality. By the end of October, General von Rundstedt's plot was supposedly so far advanced that only one last personal conference remained to be held. Over the secret radio the anti-Hitler conspirators arranged to meet Stevens in a little café on the German border near Venlo. At an agreed time, Stevens, accompanied by a British colleague, Best, and a Dutch major, went to the rendezvous. But, instead of meeting von Rundstedt, they were confronted by a party of Gestapo thugs, who dragged them into Germany under the eyes of the Dutch frontier guards.

For two years Stevens languished in chains in solitary confinement before being sent to a concentration camp, where he had ample time to reflect on his credulity until the end of the war. The Germans made tremendous propaganda out this *coup de main*. They were even more pleased to announce that they now had proof of their claims that it was a member of the British Secret Service who had placed the mysterious bomb which exploded in the cellar in Munich on November 9th; a bomb which miraculously failed to kill the Führer, who had left the cellar ten minutes before.

As a result of the Stevens episode, it was quite obvious to me that the Gestapo knew that I was in England.

Guy Burgess

There is a danger, after this lapse of time, of forgetting just quite how violent and how arrogant was the attitude of reaction in this country to Russia.

Notorious as a Soviet mole who operated as a spy, first recruiting traitors at Cambridge in the 1930s, and later as a source in the Foreign Office, Guy Burgess worked for both SIS and MI5. By the time he was recruited into Section D of SIS in 1939 he had been operating on behalf of the Soviets for at least six years, and had organized a group of others, including Anthony Blunt and James Klugmann, to act as talent spotters. Burgess did not last long in SIS and his subsequent job was ostensibly that of a radio producer in the BBC's talks department, but in reality he was also employed by the Security Service. Unlike his younger brother Nigel and his wife, who also both worked for MI5, Guy was an agent runner. His most valued source was Eric Kessler, codenamed Orange, the first secretary in the Swiss embassy in London. Orange believed his information was going to the British authorities but in reality most went straight to Burgess's Soviet contacts.

Although Guy Burgess found time to moonlight for both MI5 and Section D while working at the BBC, he was regarded as one of the best, if also the most eccentric, of its talks producers. He had a talent for broadcasting the right expert at the right moment, and among his guests were MI5 and SIS colleagues, among them Roger Fulford, Tom Driberg, Hugh Seton-Watson, Anthony Blunt and David Footman. He also cultivated contacts in the Labour Party, one of whom, Hector McNeil, was later to become a Foreign Office minister and employ Burgess as his private secretary.

After the war, and despite his drunken behaviour and blatant homosexuality, Burgess was employed by the Foreign Office, his single overseas posting being to Washington DC where he stayed with his old Cambridge friend, the SIS head of station Kim Philby. In 1951 he was recalled to London in time to warn Donald Maclean that his arrest was imminent, and together the two diplomats fled to Moscow. Burgess found Soviet life far from his taste, and eventually died in 1963, soon after Philby's arrival.

Apart from correspondence retained by the BBC's archive, which covers the period Burgess worked as a radio producer, and the Foreign Office memoranda that have surfaced in the Public Record Office, no other material written by Burgess has been published. The book he was working on at the time of his defection, a biography of Lord Salisbury's daughter, Lady Gwendoline Cecil, was completed by James Pope-Hennessey. However, while working for Hector McNeil, he did ghost the letter's contribution to the Labour Party's official history, published in 1948 – a chapter entitled 'The Labour Party's Foreign Policy between the two Wars'. An extract follows.

The British Labour Party: Its History, Growth, Policy and Leaders

It was common ground that the war of 1914–18 had been produced by imperialism and that the result of an imperialist war was, inevitably, a peace full of imperialist features that if left unrevised would lead to further wars.

Thus as part of its fight for a world organisation the Labour Party put in the forefront the fight for the revision of the Peace of Versailles. And in 1924, after an election in which these two aims had been clearly placed before the country, the Labour Party was first in a position to put, as a Government, its policy before the world.

In its first short period in Office the Labour Party attempted to remedy some of the *basic* evils that the period of reaction which followed the first World War had created. First in point of time came Anglo-Soviet relations. It is odd that our friends of the Communist Party so rarely can think back (or at any rate express their views on) our record in 1919 and 1924.

On January 22, 1924, Ramsay MacDonald became the Prime Minister of the First Labour Government. On February 1, as Foreign Secretary, he despatched a note to the USSR. The message that the British representative in Russia was directed to hand to the Kremlin opened with these words: 'I have the honour by direction of my Government to inform your Excellency that they recognise the Union of Socialist Soviet Republics . . .'

I need not here go in detail through the appalling list of crimes committed by the Imperialist Powers against the Soviet Union since its establishment in 1917. Germany had begun it with a taste of the imperialist peace she would have imposed on the rest of the world had she won – Brest Litovsk. Winston Churchill had had to admit in the House of Commons that £100 million had been spent by Britain alone on intervention which, Germany having been defeated, could have and did have no other basic motive than the destruction of Socialism by panic-stricken reaction and bondholders. We of the Labour Movement can remember that it was the action of British dockers and transport workers, Ernest Bevin prominent among them, that finally put a stop to all that.

But even though military imperialism had been halted, financial imperialism and other forms of pressure had continued. Tsarist Russia had been a semi-colonial country, largely in the hands of Anglo-French finance-capital. In order to build up the military strength of her only ally against Germany before 1914, France had poured loans into Russia. Britain had done the same and held not only loans but vast concessions – the Lena goldfields, the oil of Baku.

From the time that military intervention had ceased, the refusal of the Soviet Government either to restore concessions, which was fairly absolute, or to recognise Tsarist indebtedness, which varied with the chance or otherwise of getting credits, had created a united front of imperialist bondholders against her. In our country there is no single example that shows more clearly than this the extent to which the Tory Party was bound to the great financial interests, and the sincerity with which the Labour Party fought them in the interests of 'one world'.

It is true that the British Government was not the first Government to recognise Russia. Mussolini, of all people, had anticipated MacDonald's action. But this is not so odd as it looks, for Italy alone amongst the victorious Powers had given no substantial loans to Russia.

The first action, then, of the Labour Government was to open negotiations. The Commercial Treaty was negotiated by Arthur Ponsonby and was signed during the lifetime of the Government. The first act of the succeeding Tory Government was to refuse ratification.

There is a danger, after this lapse of time, of forgetting just quite how violent and how arrogant was the attitude of reaction in this country to Russia and accordingly to overlook how courageous, for a minority Government with pressing internal affairs at home, was the action our Party took in 1924 in carrying out the foreign policy to which it was committed. So I re-record here two instances.

In *The Times* on April 14, 1924, appeared a manifesto by a number of leading British bankers addressed to the Prime Minister. The manifesto laid down the conditions on which British credit could be granted to Russia. The fifth condition ran: 'That bankers and traders and industrialists of this country should be able to deal freely without interference by Government authorities, with similar *private* institutions in Russia controlled by men of whom they have personal knowledge and in whose character, word and resources they have confidence.'

In other words British bankers demanded not only the restoration of capitalists in Russia but that the capitalists should be selected by British banks.

The second incident had happened a little while previously when Mr Shortt, a Liberal Home Secretary, had had to get up and admit to an astonished House of Commons that the British Government had fathered a fake edition of *Pravda*, printed in this country and sent abroad in the official bag. After that admission, Curzon's notes of frenzied protests to Russia on propaganda questions sound less convincing – and so not only in my opinion does the Zinoviev letter which lost the Labour Party the election.

There are, of course, other and rather convincing reasons for believing the Zinoviev letter to have been a forgery, but my concern here is with foreign policy. And so I ask: Would the Zinoviev letter have been forged, or alternatively, would *another* copy of what, assuming it was genuine, was a highly secret document have been sent to the *Daily Mail* unless the Labour Party had succeeded in carrying out its pledge to restore relations with Russia? For we must remember that it was on this issue, on the issue of the ratification of the Treaty, that our Party was preparing to fight the General Election before the Campbell case intervened.

So much for Russia. What about Europe? It is as put to the test there that we can see how soundly or otherwise the foundations of Labour Party foreign policy had been laid.

For Europe by 1924 had become a Europe in which the League might never have been thought of for all the collective security that existed.

France and Belgium had invaded the Ruhr as security for reparations. Invaded is scarcely too strong a word for the only reason the French Army was not engaged in actual war was that there was no German Army. Previously, the British and American Governments had tried to take reparations out of politics. A committee of experts had been sitting for some months, and when the Dawes Committee issued its report MacDonald at once declared that Britain accepted the plan. Of course this plan was not a specifically Labour Party plan. But it can be claimed that probably only the Labour Party by the policy of open diplomacy (MacDonald's correspondence with Poincaré), by the security it was known to be fighting for in France, and by the trust it had earned from its opposition to Versailles in Germany, could have brought the parties together. But this was done. An allied conference assembled in London on July 16, presided over by MacDonald. In a fortnight it was possible to invite the Germans, and six months after the Labour Party had come to power it was possible to say that reparations and all the bedevilment they caused were for the moment out of the way. Further, M. Herriot made an announcement on the evacuation of the Ruhr.

The achievements over Russia and reparations, however important, lay on the perimeter and not at the centre of Labour's proposal for security. Our main proposal was the Geneva Protocol. Here can be found in concentrated and analysable form, a controlled experiment in constructive international organization undertaken by a Party new to Office, inexperienced in the detailed handling of foreign affairs, which brought hope to a Europe in despair after only a few years of peace, a proposal whose lessons reached forward into the future, to Manchuria, to Abyssinia, to Czechoslovakia, to Poland, and to our own day, on the morrow of a second victory in a war that almost certainly could have been avoided.

In 1924, and subsequently, the hell's kitchen of fear between nations can be summed up by the dilemma: How can any Government responsible for the defence of its people disarm without security; yet how can security be achieved without disarmament? In any case, short of world government and the abolition of sovereignty, which was not in 1924 a dream worth gambling on, how in the last resort are you to settle international quarrels? That there would be such quarrels, given a peace treaty we thought unjust, our Movement was convinced.

Our contribution, and it is a general contribution not confined to the Europe of 1924, lay in linking together security and disarmament with arbitration as the solvent of the contradiction between them. This contradiction is one that a non-Socialist world is in danger of always finding insoluble and in fact no solution had been found until the initiative was taken by the First Labour Government at Geneva in 1924 (the point was again stressed by this Labour Government at the United Nations Assembly in 1946). Until the fifth session of the League Assembly, opened by MacDonald on September 4, security and disarmament had been pursued separately, while the attitude towards arbitration is best described by the adjective applied to the all-important paragraph 2 of Clause 36 of the Permanent Statute of the International Court of Justice. The adjective was 'optional.'

Here again I stress the theoretical difference between Labour Party theory and the Marxism of the National Communist Parties. The Communist Parties at this period remained in isolation from the League precisely because of this difference. They said, roughly, that until there is world Socialism there cannot be world peace. Therefore the only way to world peace is by the organisation, if necessary by forceful imposition, of world revolution (the Red Army's march into Poland). The British Labour Movement said then, as now: 'We will not impose Socialism on other countries, but we will not and cannot let the world organisation of peace wait until the nations of the world learn sense and choose Socialism.'

Roman Garby-Czerniawski

It was an immense relief to learn, as the months and years passed, that our agents were not shot, as happened with ordinary spies.

When Roman Garby-Czerniawski arrived in Britain in July 1942 he came with excellent credentials that should have ensured him a special welcome from SIS. Soon after the fall of France the Polish air force pilot had gone underground and had played a key role in a stay-behind network set up by the Polish Deuxième Bureau. Radio contact direct to London had been established in January 1941 with SIS, which had codenamed the organization Tudor.

At the time Tudor was virtually SIS's sole source of reliable information from occupied France, so Garby-Czerniawski was held in high regard in London and was given a hero's reception when he was flown over for secret consultations in October 1941. General Sikorski awarded him Poland's highest decoration for gallantry and for nine days he was fêted by SIS. Unfortunately, during his brief absence in England, his cipher clerk, who happened also to be his mistress, betrayed him to the Abwehr, and soon after his return he was arrested together with most of his group. This impressive coup allowed the Germans to continue to run the network with the intention of duping SIS, and for a period the deception succeeded. Meanwhile Garby-Czerniawski was offered a tempting proposal by his captors: if he would travel to England and spy for the Abwehr, the lives of his colleagues in prison in Paris would be spared and they would be treated as regular prisoners of war. Garby-Czerniawski accepted the deal and arrangements were made for him to make an authentic-looking escape from his incarceration in Fresnes.

In October 1942 Garby-Czerniawski reached Madrid where he was interviewed by Kenneth Benton, but he gave no clue that his dramatic escape had been anything other than genuine. However, by the time he reached London MI5 had heard from three other Polish officers that there was something fishy about his miraculous appearance in the Spanish capital. Challenged by his interrogators, Garby-Czerniawski revealed his secret compact with the Abwehr and he was enrolled as a double agent with the codename Brutus. He continued to maintain contact with his German controllers without arousing their suspicion until January 1945, and thereby saved the lives of his fellow workers in the Tudor network.

At the end of the war Garby-Czerniawski remained in London and worked as a printer in Fulham. He was also appointed minister of information in the Polish government-in-exile, a post that he held until his death in 1984.

In his memoirs Garby-Czerniawski gave his version of the events that led to the betrayal of the Tudor network in 1941. His cipher clerk, Mathilde Carré, had acquired considerable notoriety as a result of the publicity given to her trial in Paris on collaboration charges in 1945 but his name had not been revealed in open court. There had been much speculation about the identity of her lover, the mysterious Polish spy who had been the principal victim of her treachery, but Garby-Czerniawski was later to maintain that his friendship with her had been misrepresented. Several books were to be written about the episode, including an autobiography written by Carré herself after her release from gaol, and although Garby-Czerniawski was eventually to admit their relationship, he chose to draw a veil over his subsequent activities in London as a double agent for MI5.

In 1961 Garby-Czerniawski published a book about his SIS connections, discreetly leaving aside his role as one of MI5's star double agents. In this introduction he explains the background to his decision to write it. Note that the date in the first line should be 1944. The war finished in early May 1945 (hardly 'summer'), some time after the last flying bomb landed on UK soil.

The Big Network

On a Sunday afternoon in the summer of 1945, when flying bombs were roaring over London, I was lying on a small strip of common in Balham, in company with Colonel Wincenty Zarembski of the Polish General Staff.

Resting on the grass, we were lying faces up; talking, we could easily observe the tracks of the passing bombs – 'just in case', we agreed. A shelter was not far from us and we could run for it if necessary.

We were talking about our experiences in France a few years earlier; after Dunkirk and the collapse of France. Colonel Zarembski had directed at that time an Intelligence network in the unoccupied zone. I had joined him in his work in Toulouse, and had helped him in Marseilles until I left him for German-occupied Paris to start an Intelligence network covering the whole occupied zone.

Now on this Sunday we felt relatively safe from these noisy German intruders flying above us – when comparing the danger with another kind of 'close relations' with the Germans in France in 1940–42.

'Well, Roman,' said the Colonel, 'what about writing our respective stories?'

'Who would read these things?' I replied, shrugging my shoulders, 'it's all past already, and so many interesting things happen now;' I pointed to one of the bombs passing quite close to us, 'and there will be so many exciting and unusual developments of the war, described in so many different ways, that no publisher will accept any of our stories.'

We never spoke again about it, somehow. The war passed, and, of course, a number of most exciting true stories appeared. Reading some of them, especially those dealing with different aspects of activities on the Continent under German occupation, I was astonished first by mentions and then by growing comment about the activities of *our* organization. Details about our network started to appear in articles and books dealing with 'Underground War', and in the memoirs of some agents whose ways at one time or another crossed our paths.

Then more detailed information about our network was brought into the limelight for the first time, when the secretary of our organization was tried in Paris, after the war, for treason.

This woman, Mme Mathilde Lily Carré, better known as *La Chatte*, when arrested by the Germans in November 1941 after a year of very brilliant work in our organization, tried to save herself by betraying many people who worked in it.

Now at her trial, many details of our Intelligence network, Interallié, were brought to public knowledge. Sensational articles and serials appeared all over the world. Books were written on the subject: some largely fiction, like Soltikow's *The Cat*, some very serious, such as *The Cat with Two Faces* by Gordon Young; all of them based mostly on facts revealed during this famous trial, and on memoirs written in prison by the accused, or from interviews with some of the members of the network.

All these, for many reasons, were far from adequate to portray the true image of the life and work of this large network.

The agents could obviously see only tiny fragments of our activities, while the main source of information, the memoirs, reflected the image of the organization in what seemed to me to be a curved mirror! I had the chance to read these memoirs months only after they were written, when my own memories about the organization's life were still very fresh.

While writing my comments for the authorities on Mathilde Carré's memoirs, I was amazed by the number of inaccuracies, not only about persons, places and dates, which is easy to understand, but also about essential methods and ways of work. I could only think that the turbulent course of her life after her arrest by the Germans, her 'escapade' to England, her subsequent arrest by the British authorities and her life in prison, must somehow have veiled her memory.

We must also bear in mind that this story was written by a woman who, in our organization, was dealing mostly with the contact side of the work, and not with essential military matters; and this is reflected in her memoirs when she describes, in a rather chatty way, more of the people and her contacts with them, than the organization and its life and methods of work.

Yet she was, as secretary, the only person apart from myself, who had the chance of seeing the whole structure of the organization. The other people, as in all secret organizations, knew only small fragments of its activities.

I myself have been linked for some years with Intelligence work and bound by the Official Secrets Act not to speak or write on details of my work.

It is not easy for people concerned, like myself, to keep silence, especially when one is pressed for information by close friends, or when one reads, amused or angered, fantastic stories about one's activities, which appear from time to time in the press and in books.

Years ago, when pushed too much by some indiscreet or inconsiderate questioner, I used to reply:

'Look, my friend, before ever I told anyone my story, I had heard already about twenty fantastic versions. The story I tell myself is not true either!'

Still, after the publication of as many as four books in English [*The Cat* and *Cat with Two Faces* already mentioned, plus *Colonel Henri's Story* by Hugo Bleicher, and *I was The Cat* by Mathilde Lily Carré] which deal directly or indirectly with the story of the Interallié Network, I felt I could not, and should not, remain silent any more; not only from my own personal point of view but also in fairness to everyone engaged in the work of this Big Network.

I could no longer bear the inadequate or wrong pictures of the organization and the many people in it, nor the very inaccurate remarks about myself.

When, from lack of details or for sensational reasons, I was described, to the amusement of my friends, as 'tall and handsome' – which is definitely quite untrue! – when my love affairs were created or misrepresented; when some authors tried to make of me a double agent; and when all of them stated that nobody really knew what happened to me after the affair of Interallié (in reality I held high posts in the Polish General Staff and Polish Air Force Headquarters in London), it was becoming more than a strain.

While some people pressed me to write a story to clear, once and for all, these misrepresented facts, others pointed out the sensational angles of this 'unwritten story', such as: 'first organization which established complete dispositions of the German Army in France', 'first secret wireless working regularly in occupied France', 'first pick-up by British 'plane from German occupied territory', and many other unusual facts which would otherwise be entirely lost for any future student of the Underground activities of this war.

It all prompted me to write, finally, the story of the birth, growth and life of this great network, a story in which, while conforming to all the rules and etiquette of a former member of the Intelligence Service, I could still describe vividly the reality of life in this unique episode.

After so many years I cannot claim that I could avoid making some mistakes, although I have done everything possible to render the true picture and atmosphere of the work. I feel especially sorry that I have had to omit many brave acts of so great a number of people; but even if I had at my disposal all the reports it would be impossible to relate them now. At the time when these reports and information were arriving at our HQ we were inhumanly overworked, and of course our main preoccupation was to check the news and expedite it to London in the shortest possible time. One can only say that we were thrilled by the courage of all concerned, a feeling which was constantly renewed by frequent waves of details about new daring exploits. And just as we kept comprehensive records of German activities, so we had to refrain from keeping any records on our own people, for obvious reasons.

I apologize, therefore, to all these people whose personal exploits are for these reasons omitted from this book. But I would like to ask them to get in touch with me, reminding me of their stories, so that I might include them in a subsequent volume.

For a long time, even while amassing material for the book, harassed by my everyday business life, I could not find either the time or the right conditions in which to write. Then, fortunately, my whole family decided to help me in this respect, and started *Operation Big Network*. I signed a contract with my publisher, and was then invited by my parents-in-law to their lovely country house in Redruth in Cornwall, in order to be able to write quietly and undistured by my business problems. My dear wife, Thelma, offered to correct my far-from-good English, and to retype it!

This is how the first book on my Intelligence experiences became a reality.

Marie-Madeleine Fourcade

We were not spies but people who were fighting in the only way still feasible – with the only invisible weapon, intelligence.

After the French collapse in 1940 Marie-Madeleine Fourcade moved from Paris, where she was secretary to a group of magazines, to a small town near the foothills of the Pyrenees to be with her former boss, Georges Loustaunau-Lacau, who had been wounded.

Loustaunau-Lacau, who had an impressive record from the Great War, was a determined anti-Fascist and anti-Communist and, adopting the *nom de guerre* Navarre, began organizing an intelligence network in Vichy territory under cover of an ex-servicemen's group. His link with London depended on a Canadian diplomat based in Vichy but his refusal to work for de Gaulle's exiled intelligence apparatus brought him to SIS. In March 1941 he received a radio and operator from London and began operations with a measure of protection from the Vichy Deuxième Bureau. However, he was arrested in May 1941 while planning a scheme for an insurrection in North Africa, leaving Marie-Madeleine to take over the network. She re-established contact with SIS and travelled to Lisbon for a rendezvous with Kenneth Cohen. Until they actually met face to face SIS had no idea that their star agent was a glamorous thirty-two-year-old mother of two children. The circuit was known in London as Alliance but to Marie-Madeleine, who assigned the name of an animal to each of her agents, it was Noah's Ark, which subsequently became the title of her autobiography.

The Alliance network grew to include some 3000 members, operating about twenty wireless transmitters, and in July 1943 she reluctantly agreed to be flown out of France to escape the German net closing around her.

After the war Marie-Madeleine, who was a doughty supporter of President de Gaulle, became a member of the European Parliament. She died in July 1989. In this passage from her memoirs she describes the British traitor codenamed Bla, an SIS agent who was accepted for training despite his record as a Fascist. Although she did not reveal his true identity, his true name was Bradley Davis and when it became clear he had switched sides she was forced to have him assassinated.

Noah's Ark

The August moon renewed our preoccupation with the parachute drop that I had cancelled after Navarre's arrest. The British had almost stopped parachuting their agents blind, in the way they had done with my brother. They insisted on a 'reception committee' to lay out proper ground lights to mark the dropping zone and to give the prearranged light signal. The thought of receiving an Englishman made us wildly excited. Coustenoble suggested playing 'God Save the King' on the gramophone while the parachutist floated gently down to earth: 'After all, we can't receive him like a sack of peanuts!'

Everything was laid on for the special envoy. His false civilian papers had been sent to me. On the basis of this document we had also concocted a false identity card for Josette, who would assume the role of his lawful wedded wife.

The agents who were to learn the new ciphering methods were called to Pau and shown how to operate the new type of radio. Once the Englishman's job with us was finished, he was to be taken to Normandy, where he was to set up an independent sector. Later on I would have to send him money and receive his messages. He had his own personal code and radio. A second parachute would drop us spare parts, transmitting sets and a few weapons.

The drop on 5 August went well. In less than twenty-four hours Gavarni and Coustenoble were back. It was a fateful night when I was brought out of my lair to inspect the rare bird in the brilliantly lighted drawing-room of the Villa Etchebaster. Coustenoble, never at a loss for ideas, had me make my entrance to the first bars of 'God Save the King' followed by a resounding rendering of the Marseillaise. I stopped and gaped. Before me stood the most ridiculous, most grotesque parody of a 'typical' Frenchman. He was attired as if for a village wedding – short jacket and waistcoat, striped trousers, a spotted cravat, a stiff shirt with cutaway collar beneath a little goatee beard, a pair of pince-nez, and as a crowning glory, a bowler hat. Was this British Intelligence? The boys burst into roars of laughter.

The unhappy parachutist blinked his big, round, milky blue eyes at us. I decided to console him by saying a few welcoming words in English.

'Don't bother, Madame,' he answered in excellent French, but with a strong cockney accent. 'I've spent more of my life in France than in England.'

The new radios that had been dropped by parachute were much smaller than the first ones. Vallet was already fiddling about with his (OCK), intended for the Paris area, which Coustenoble was to smuggle into the occupied zone as quickly as possible in a cartload of vegetables. I admired the new office material: extra fine, silky paper for messages, more invisible ink, lots of little gadgets to make our job easier and to fox the enemy. I fingered the first envelope to come stamped with the royal coat of arms and containing a letter of encouragement addressed to 'POZ 55' and, couched in the politest possible vein, suggestions regarding the organization and its future work.

The sight of 'Bla' – our name for His Majesty's ambassador – and the sight of his lifeless face and defeated expression led me to end the session pretty quickly. I told him to take forty-eight hours' rest, get a complete change of clothes and shave off his beard.

The next day Lucien Vallet came to see me. I sensed that something was wrong. He came straight to the point: 'He's going to kick the bucket.'

'Who?'

'The Englishman.'

He explained. After I had left, Bla had started to complain of pains in the head and the stomach. Josette had taken his temperature. It had been 104. They at once diagnosed acute appendicitis.

'We can't let him die just like that. He must be looked after at once.'

Vallet's blue eyes went purple; he clearly felt no liking for Bla. 'He's a queer fish, Madame. You ought to let him go. He's already shown me the code. I can explain it to the others, there's nothing very difficult about it.'

I was very angry and gave orders that Bla should be taken to a hospital. We managed to save him. Josette stayed at his bedside and played the role of wife to perfection. When the patient came round and began talking in English she threw herself on him to stifle his Shakespearean moans and groans, covered him with resounding kisses and added her own cries to his, to the nurses' astonishment. A few days later everything was going well except that Bla, developing a taste for the game, pestered Josette with his demands and devoured everybody's rations on the quiet. Consequently Vallet's animosity towards him increased tenfold.

However, my radio operator was due to leave for Paris. He departed all smiles to take up his job in the occupied zone. The OCK set had arrived safely and was already installed where 'Tadpole', one of his friends, was living, and before leaving Pau Vallet carried what he called the 'flirtation' to the point of fixing a date in Paris with the British in London. I received an enthusiastic message of congratulations from British Intelligence when everything went off as planned and without a hitch. OCK was certainly one of the very first transmitters to operate in Paris and Vallet was a champion operator. The departure of this gay and inspiring fellow left a great void at our headquarters. We had been such a closely knit entity that I had the sad feeling we were cutting ourselves into pieces. Vallet's successor, who had been trained by him, took over the KVL transmitter at the Etchebaster. We called him 'Tringa'.

The appendicitis episode meant that I had to keep the parachutist in Pau longer than had been anticipated and his behaviour continued to worry me. Having presumably been properly trained, he should have known better than to give his coding lessons in a loud voice, sitting in the public park; nor should he have introduced himself to every visitor who came to the Etchebaster or exchanged names and addresses with all and sundry. Who would distrust an agent parachuted by the British? Although I had warned people to be careful, they were around him constantly.

The last straw was when my brother, whom I had called to the rescue, came and told me that, on learning he was a journalist, Bla had suggested buying from him, at a very good price, information for the British press. He said he would radio this information to London on a wavelength that British Intelligence knew nothing about. I was frightened. Was Bla here to test us, I wondered. The best thing was to get him to Normandy as quickly as possible, but he gave endless reasons why he should delay going. In the meantime he continued to offer his services to anyone and everyone and discovered more and more of the secrets of my organization.

One morning Antoine Hugon appeared from Paris. He was a garage owner and had the unusual distinction of having been awarded the Iron Cross for having saved the life of a drowning German soldier in the First World War. He made a point of wearing it openly, which presumably made his missions into the less accessible zones that much easier. He proudly unfolded a huge plan that he had wrapped round his body and smuggled across the demarcation line. It showed all the U-boat pens recently built at Saint-Nazaire, reproduced to scale, down to the last inch, by the engineer Henri Mouren.

Since the arrival of the Turenne patrol and Lucien Vallet, the Paris organization was expanding in a remarkable way. The only doubtful element was Armand Bonnet, the leader of the Guynemer patrol, who was cheerfully engaging in the black market. It was imperative that we should get rid of him and we agreed to remodel the organization. With the help of a post office official, Amedée Pautard, we would henceforth be able to address the mail to a fictitious name, care of the Post Office in Paris, without going through Bonnet, who would thus be automatically eliminated. Hugon, knowing all our sources, would take over the leadership of the Guynemer patrol.

This conversation with a sensible and intrepid man greatly cheered me. In spite of Schaerrer's disappearance and Bonnet's deficiency I would be able to equip the terrible occupied zone. I did not know that before leaving Antoine Hugon had, against my orders, arranged to meet Bla in the capital.

Everything comes to him who waits and Bla, looking very different from the day he first appeared, announced that he was ready to set off for Normandy. To get him there safely I detailed Jean Lefèvre, whose skill in crossing the demarcation line with the most compromising messages guaranteed the success of the operation, which was planned to the last detail.

Lefèvre returned forty-eight hours late. Throughout the whole trip his protégé, who was supposed to pretend he had a bad attack of toothache and was not to utter a word, had never stopped talking, asking stupid questions at the top of his voice and fooling with his transmitter, SHE. It was a miracle that they had got through safe and sound. Once there, Bla had vanished into thin air. And so Lefèvre, greatly concerned, had thought it wiser to come back and report. I congratulated him. Bla was in contact with London on SHE and with the network through the lawyer Bouvet at Dax. I would eventually find out what had happened to him. In actual fact, a short time later the British informed me that Bla had made contact with them by radio and they were delighted at this success. So Bla, for all his disconcerting antics, was perhaps fundamentally a sound man.

CHAPTER VIII

The Adventurers

For three days I was initiated into the mysteries of plastic high explosive, slow-burning fuses, detonators and primer-cord, and was given detailed instruction in the most effective method of blowing up a railway line. The knowledge that no railway existed in Crete did not dampen my immediate ardour.
Xan Fielding, Hide and Seek

During the Second World War the Secret Intelligence Service attracted a group of gallant young men who were willing to undertake missions of near-suicidal proportions into enemy-occupied territory. Some, like John Cross, who spent three years under appalling conditions in the Malayan jungle, were lucky to survive. Others, such as Patrick Whinney, who supervised the clandestine transport used to carry agents to their targets, only joined SIS after their wartime experience. In his memoirs Whinney recalls his work in the Mediterranean, ferrying saboteurs to Axis-occupied beaches for Special Operations Executive, but omits any reference to his post-war career in SIS.

Among the men who were recruited into SOE during the war and who later followed Whinney into SIS, were Adrian Gallegos, Xan Fielding and David Smiley. All of them later published accounts of their adventures behind German lines, drawing a discreet veil over their involvement in secret intelligence after the war.

All of those classified here as 'the adventurers' are swashbuckling, rather romantic figures who are easily recognizable as a type. They are to a man good-looking characters who have lived off their wits and for whom the war represented an opportunity to display extraordinary courage that each was later to downplay in an engagingly self-effacing way. There is no guile or conceit to be detected in these heroes, and perhaps their only disadvantage is that they have not all been able to adapt to the rather lesser challenges of the peace. However, as with every rule there is an exception, and Professor Robert Zaehner was arguably the most improbable secret agent to have undertaken clandestine missions. Where-as Xan Fielding's publishers would instantly recognize his ability to trek into enemy-held countries and live among local guerrilla bands, Zaehner the erudite Oxford don from All Souls hardly fitted the part. A brilliant linguist with a talent for picking up obscure Middle Eastern dialects, he was recruited by SIS from Oxford soon after the outbreak of war and in 1943 was posted to Tehran under press attaché cover. In reality he was to spend two years among the tribes of northern Persia, crossing over the frontier into Soviet territory and developing networks of saboteurs in a harsh, mountainous territory filled with hostile enemy agents.

After the war Zaehner remained in SIS and was posted to Malta to assist in the training of Albanian émigrés destined to return to their country in a fruitless attempt to topple the Communist regime. Although Zaehner knew no Albanian he soon learned the language and later, in 1950, transferred to Greece to supervise the teams of guerrillas infiltrated over the border from Macedonia.

Once it became clear that the Albanian operation had failed Zaehner was moved back to Tehran to help run a brilliant scheme designed to replace the anti-Western prime minister, Dr Mussadeq. Zaehner boasted many useful contacts in Iran, dating back to the networks he had recruited during the war, and they were to be of critical importance when the coup was eventually mounted, by which time Zaehner and the rest of Monty Woodhouse's SIS station had been evacuated.

Shortly before his death in November 1974, at the age of sixty-one, Zaehner was interviewed by Peter Wright, the MI5 molehunter who was on the trail of a Soviet spy partially identified by a defector. Some of the clues pointed to an SIS officer who had operated in Persia during the war and Zaehner was deeply wounded by the idea that his own loyalty should have come under suspicion. The irony is that whereas Peter Wright the molehunter dismayed his colleagues by his disclosures, Zaehner never wrote anything more controversial than *Dialectical Christianity and Christian Materialism, Evolution in Religion* and *The Catholic Church and World Religions*.

Adrian Gallegos

In my type of warfare I was dealing with people as human beings and individuals – not as cannon-fodder or just as a bolt or a nut in a complex fighting machine, but as complete units in themselves.

Originally recruited into SOE's H Section, Adrian Gallegos was intended to sabotage the bridges and railway lines of southern Spain in the event of a widely predicted Nazi thrust through Catalonia to Gibraltar. That attack never materialized and he was transferred to Algiers where, as a Lieutenant RNVR, he was assigned to a Special Forces unit in Sicily. After the island had been liberated he was sent as an advance party to Capri and began to plan operations against the Italian mainland, but during his first reconnaissance his fast motorboat struck a mine. Gallegos and the sixteen surviving crew climbed into three dinghies and were rescued by the German navy. Having spent much of his life in Italy, he pretended to be an Italian and was accepted as such by the Germans, and was sent as a prisoner of war to the Regina Coeli prison in Rome.

In December 1944 he was moved to a PoW camp near Munich where he attempted to escape but was caught while seeking new papers from the local Italian consulate. He made a second escape, from the train taking him to a concentration camp, but was intercepted close to the Swiss frontier. Imprisoned at the Reichenau Straflager, Gallegos persuaded his captors that he was a civilian worker who had lost his papers and, after five weeks, he was released to find a job in Innsbruck. Instead he took a train to Milan and, in September 1944, walked into the mountains to find the partisans. When he contacted them, the British Liaison Officer, Gordon Lett, signalled Gallegos's arrival and his identity was confirmed, although he had been reported lost, believed dead, more than a year earlier. Accompanied by a group of partisans and Allied ex-PoWs he then made his way to Rome where he reported to the local SOE commander, Gerald Holdsworth. He was flown back to London and posted back to Italy, to the Special Forces headquarters in Florence.

After the war Gallegos switched to SIS and operated under diplomatic cover in Madrid during the mid-1950s. In this passage from his war memoirs Gallegos recalls waiting, as a prisoner of the partisans, for confirmation of his real identity as a British officer.

From Capri into Oblivion

A week after my arrival in Partisan-land, Gordon Lett came down to Rossano. Together with Geoff [of SOE] we went for a stroll and, when we reached a secluded spot by a stream, we sat down and Lett pulled out of his pocket a few pieces of paper.

'I've received a few signals,' he said. 'Do you know anyone called Gerry, Adrian?'

I thought for a moment or two.

'Yes. . . . A man called Gerry was my chief in North Africa.'

That was a long time ago, it seemed to me.

'There's a signal here from him.'

I could hardly believe my ears. He handed me over the signal and I read:

Following for Gallegos stop Congratulations from us all on your escape stop All the best Gerry.

A flood of memories of happy days in North Africa surged in my mind – it seemed like another world which I had lost for ever. But it was a nice feeling knowing that my friends were still there and that perhaps I would be seeing them again some time. I was lost in thought for a few seconds and I was moved.

'Anything else of interest?' I asked.

'There's a signal confirming that you're not a fake and another one saying that Fifth Army would like us to blow up that fifteen-inch gun on the Pontremoli railway line – what a hope! And . . . just a minute – there's one here saying that an escape line to Allied-occupied territory is being started . . . Hm! Do you want to go?'

'It depends. Am I going to be of any use to you here?'

'You can be of great use to me and I should be very sorry to lose you, but they may want you over there for various reasons, such as telling what you've seen in your travels.'

'My information is stale. Besides, I've been out of things for too long. It seems to me that I can be more useful here than there, though it's up to them to decide, not me. Shall we ask for instructions?'

I drafted a signal giving the highlights of my activities from the day I sailed from Capri and ended:

Please instruct whether I am to remain here and in what capacity or to cross lines now that it is possible.

'And now tell me, Gordon,' I said. 'Are you connected with Special Forces?'

'Of course! They are my link in Allied Force Headquarters.'

'Well! And why didn't you tell me before?'

'Because I was waiting for official confirmation about you. And now I can give you another piece of information which I held back from you.'

'What's that?'

'Just before I first met you at Division HQ, a runner came up with a message saying that you were a well-known spy, an Italian naval commander, and please would we shoot you right away!'

'Indeed?'

'Yes. And you're lucky that I was there, otherwise poor old Adrian would now be resting under a heap of earth.'

'And, no doubt, you were not sure about me either, were you?'

'I was prepared to give you the benefit of the doubt because, I thought, a spy would hardly make up such a complicated story. But on the other hand the accusation against you in the runner's message was very definite and not to be ignored. Unbeknown to you I had your pockets searched by Mick once, but he found nothing of interest.'

'One way or another, it's surprising that my action in joining the partisans didn't end in failure or tragedy. First of all I picked on a day when there was a German drive on, then a partisan threatens to shoot me as a spy and then a runner comes up to the mountain with the same accusation. It's not an easy club to join, I must say.'

'And that's not all.'

'You don't say.'

'That priest you spoke to at Pian di Follo is a bad egg. He is a Fascist sympathizer and you're lucky he didn't give you away.'

'Well, well,' I laughed. 'It's indeed a miracle I am here!'

'Yes, you've had a number of narrow shaves, but now you can become a fully-fledged member of our Military Mission.'

'And I suppose that's why I haven't been sent on any operations and have been kept kicking my heels around here?'

'That's the reason.'

But my desire to become a fighting partisan was destined to remain unfulfilled. Two days later two signals arrived, one addressed to Lett and one to myself. Lett's signal read:

> On no account is Gallegos to be allowed to take part in activities involving danger stop You are to take all precautions regarding his safety and he should only attempt crossing lines when you are satisfied that it is reasonably safe.

My signal was in the same tone, but added at the end, 'When in Rome telephone number . . .'

'Well, Gordon,' I commented, 'I am sorry I can't stay on with you to the bitter end, but there it is. When is the first party going to cross the lines?'

'I am afraid you can't go on that one.'

'Why not?'

'The signal says "when you are satisfied that it is reasonably safe". I can promise you this much; you can go as soon as I receive a signal confirming that the first party has got through.'

I argued but it was no use. There was nothing for it but to wait and relax.

'Now you can tell me, Gordon,' I said, 'now that you know that I am not a spy. Between you and me, are these partisans any good?'

'Well . . . there are many good ones and there are many worthless ones. Some are incredibly brave and daring. But in judging them one must take in consideration several factors. You can't expect men to be good fighters if they've had no experience in fighting, and you can't have the experience unless you have the arms and the ammunition. We are hampered by lack of supplies; for instance we could do a lot of sabotage if we had the stuff to do it with: plastic, cordite, fuses and so on. I keep on asking for parachute drops but I've hardly had any so far. The men need boots, too, and clothing; many wear rags tied up with strings on their feet, for lack of boots. You can't expect men to be good fighters under such conditions, can you? It's not so bad in the summer – in the winter it will be impossible to carry on. I believe the raw material is there, provided the men can be properly equipped and trained. We are now reorganizing the formations after the disaster of the fourth of August.'

'What happened then?'

'The Germans sent up a large force, perhaps ten thousand men, and we were attacked simultaneously from all sides. It so happened that one month before two young German self-styled deserters volunteered to serve with the partisans. Stupidly, I realize now, we agreed to take them on. They found out all they wanted to know about us and then disappeared. The next time we saw them they were directing operations against us. What's more, they knew where our stocks of arms and ammunition were and made straight for them. Now you can realize why we are inclined to see spies everywhere! One or two properly-led detachments fought very well as, for instance, Ercole's detachment. The Beretta Brigade, six hundred strong, fought excellently. Otherwise it was complete chaos – many of them just dropped their arms and ran as far and as fast as they could.'

Patrick Whinney

The courageous few, who by acceptance of unremitting personal risk of death, of torture, or both, at the hands of an enemy both ruthless and efficient, gave such effective account of themselves in the provision of vital secret intelligence, help to escaping prisoners of war, sabotage and propaganda.

Patrick Whinney's introduction to unorthodox warfare came in 1940 when he was transferred to the Naval Intelligence sub-section known as DDOD(I) which, based in the Helford estuary, ran clandestine operations across the Channel in fishing boats and fast motor launches. A year later he was undertaking similar missions in the Mediterranean, first from Algiers and then from Tripoli. In 1943 he was in command of a flotilla of boats at Maddalena, Sardinia's most northerly port, transporting SOE and American OSS agents to the Italian coast.

After the war Whinney remained in SIS and in 1949 participated, as SIS's head of station in Athens, in the infiltration of guerrillas into Communist Albania, a task in which he was assisted by David Smiley and Robert Zaehner.

Whinney wrote an account of his experiences soon after the war, but it was to be more than forty years before it was published, by which time he had retired to the Channel Islands where he now lives. In this passage he recalls the arrival of a new operations officer.

Corsican Command

Operations were beginning to build up to a rate which ensured that we were kept rather more than busy when a welcome signal arrived announcing the appointment of another operational Lieutenant RNVR. Certainly we could do with the extra help. Reading the signal through a second time I noticed that his age was given as 38. This could be a mistake for 28 – or he might be somewhat special – or he might be quite unsuitable. Our average age, not including my own senile 32, was in the low twenties. I thought I knew the names of nearly all officers engaged in this particular work at that time, but I didn't know this one. Neither Prof, nor Tom had ever heard of him either. We waited with interest.

He arrived one evening without any warning from anyone, having apparently first gone to Maddalena. No one had told him we had moved. Prof shoved his head round the door just before dinner as I was finishing some reports.

'He's here,' said Prof.

I looked up. 'Who?'

'The new ops officer. Lieutenant Dow.'

He had spoken softly so I lowered my voice to little above a whisper. 'What's he like?'

Prof wagged his head from side to side in the lunatic manner he sometimes adopted when he wasn't sure of something, and grinned. 'I'll bring him in,' he whispered back, and vanished.

When a few minutes later Prof ushered in the new arrival he proved to be rather small, stockily built, with a lot of bristly hair beginning to go grey, a ruddy face, and pale blue eyes. Plainly he was tired after so much travelling and looked every day of his 38 years. When he apologised for being 'late' he spoke with a strong lowland Scottish accent. Coming round from behind my desk I shook his hand.

'Welcome, Colonel, you're just in time for dinner.'

Why I called him 'Colonel' I have no idea. But the name stuck thereafter. He blinked and looked a bit startled.

'Aye – sir.'

'Come and sit down, and have a cigarette.' I pushed a packet towards him and he helped himself.

'Aye. Thanks.'

'Care for a drink?'

'Aye. It's been a longish sort of day.'

I went out to the kitchen and asked Maria to bring us some wine. While I was away I had time to think, my God, he is old. When I went back he was sitting stiffly in his chair, staring at the opposite wall, looking, if anything, more grizzled than a minute or so earlier.

'Tell me, Colonel, what have you been doing up to now?' I asked resuming my seat behind the desk.

'Minesweeping.'

'Where?'

'Out of Liverpool.'

'And could you tell me what persuaded you to volunteer for this job?'

For a moment he looked away.

'It'll be a change,' he said in guarded tones.

'It should be that all right. What did they tell you before you left England?'

'Not much.'

We weren't getting along too well. Fortunately Maria came in at that moment. Putting the tray down on my desk she cast a swift gold-toothed smile at the newcomer. There was not a flicker of response, and she retired in what looked like a huff. I poured the wine and handed it to him.

'Your good health,' I tried.

'Cheers,' he replied and downed half the glass at a gulp.

'Did they tell you in London what you were coming out here to do?'

'Aye. Sort of. Landing operations, isn't it?'

'And picking up.'

'They mentioned that, too.'

'Have you ever been in fast craft? MTBs, that is?'

From his expression he appeared to consider this a trick question, and become ever more cautious. 'No,' he replied slowly, and to remove any lingering doubt on the matter, added, 'And I don't want to, either.'

'I see.' I found myself beginning to wonder about this taciturn little man. 'Tell me, what sort of boats d'you think we're operating?'

His eyes opened wide. 'What sort – ? Why, *feeshing* boats.' Indignantly he drained his glass. 'That's wha' I was told in London.'

To gain a little time for thought I filled him up again before continuing. 'I see. Well, Colonel, you'd better get it clear that we are not operating fishing boats any longer. We are now working from MAS boats – the Italian equivalent of our coastal forces' MTBs, MGBs and the like.'

'Oh.' He took a swig before peering into the depths of his glass while digesting this latest piece of information. When he looked up it was to fix me with a pebbly sort of stare. To emphasize the importance of his next question he spoke very slowly. 'An' wha' about the danger money?'

It was my turn to be baffled. 'Danger money? What d'you mean, danger money? Whatever for?'

His stare didn't waver as he pursued the subject. 'But I was informed there would be danger money – five shillings a day – in the fishing boats. The same as they get in submarines.'

'Good God. Who told you that?'

'They told me in London before I left.'

For the moment I could think of nothing to say. Someone in London had been filling the poor chap up with rubbish, or they'd been pulling his leg. While we sat, each pondering, he leaned forward and pinched one of my cigarettes. Well, evidently he wasn't one to lose his head in a crisis. I poured myself a glass.

A last try, then. 'Look Colonel, there has obviously been some serious misunderstanding. As I said just now, we do *not* operate fishing boats, although those which have arrived and come up from Maddalena, we now use for accomodation. We *were* to have used them, yes, but thank God, just in time the MAS boats have been turned over to us, and we use *them*. That's the first thing to get clear in your mind. And the second thing is – ' and I left a pause for what I hoped would be dramatic effect ' – the second thing is that there is *no* danger money.'

The dramatic effect was there all right, and it was instantaneous. Rising from his chair he stubbed out his cigarette, swallowed the rest of his drink, and said, 'Well – tha's simple. No fishing boats, an' no danger money. I'm away home.'

With that his pebbly stare turned to one of strong disapproval, and he made for the door.

'Sit down, Colonel.'

For a moment he hesitated, and I wasn't sure he would do as he was told. When he did he made it look as if it was a very temporary arrangement.

'Let us try to get this straight –' I started, but he interrupted immediately.

'It's straight enough, already. There's no fishing boats an' no danger money. I've been made a fule of. I'm off, I'm telling ye.'

'Was it,' I asked, 'the danger money you were after, or work in the fishing boats?'

'The two went together.'

'All right. Now listen to me. If you thought, or were led to believe that there was danger money attached to this job, then I agree you have been made a fool of. But there isn't any – and for a good reason.'

He was staring again. 'And what's that?'

'The work doesn't warrant it. That's why. It's a perfectly straightforward job, and simple. All of us are volunteers, agreed, but that doesn't make it dangerous. It's out of the rut, and just about as close to fun as you can get in wartime. There's no lack of volunteers. Understand that. Now –' and I got to my feet – 'we've talked enough. We'll have some dinner – you must be hungry, and probably weary, too – so for the rest of the evening you can get to know the others a bit. You and I will have another talk tomorrow.'

He was thoroughly unhappy and made no bones about it, which was hardly surprising, if what he had told me was true. It was such an improbable story as almost certain to *be* true; as an invention it was equally unlikely. On the other hand it was hard to guess who could have filled him up with such nonsense. I escorted him next door where Prof, Tom Maxted, and 'Cuzzie' Cosens – another experienced young ops officer – were gossiping before dinner. I said nothing of the meeting just finished, leaving the new arrival to sit between Prof and Tom. Watching from time to time during the meal he seemed to be getting on well enough for me to imagine a glimmer of interest beginning to develop from his previous grumpy attitude.

Prof was always an excellent talker, and with the occasional exercise of his more ghoulish wit usually managed to conjure a laugh from even the very dour. On the other side Tom was recounting one or two of the more amusing operational incidents. After dinner I contrived to catch Prof's eye; he and I then repaired to the office where I told him what had gone on earlier.

True to form Prof came straight to the point. 'D'you want to keep him?'

'We need him,' I replied.

'Not the same thing. We need another ops officer, right enough, but does it have to be him?'

'Oh, no. But I have a feeling – '

'Exactly.' Prof cut me short; perhaps he sensed that I might be about to waffle. 'So you do want to keep him.'

'I don't know about that. All I am sure of at the moment is that he won't be any use if he's going to have a permanent chip about fishing boats and danger money. Did he mention anything about it at dinner?'

Prof shook his head. 'No. He didn't say very much really, although I did get the impression that he still isn't too happy. The only thing I did was to tell him that we could have a yarn in the morning when I would show him round.'

The best answer seemed to be to return Lieutenant Dow to store with a rude message to whoever had been responsible for his original briefing but nothing could be decided that night, so we agreed to resume in the morning.

When I came down to breakfast Prof was already circling the table arms outstretched like an old vulture with an empty bowl in his hand. As I sat down he swooped on the cornflakes, then the sugar bowl, before settling himself, ruffling his feathers into a comfortable position, in front of the milk jug. He did the same thing pretty well every morning and it never failed to amuse me.

'Well,' he asked, splashing the milk lavishly in and around his plate, 'what are we going to do with your Colonel? Made up your mind yet?'

'Not yet. It depends largely on him.'

'It doesn't, you know, unless he opts firmly to go home. It's up to you – to decide whether you want to keep him.'

'Maybe you're right, Prof, but I don't care to have to admit it at breakfast.'

He bobbed his head up and down and grunted in amusement. 'Sorry – sir.'

'All right. You bring him along to the office at nine – and this time you stay and listen.'

'Aye, aye, sir.' He gave me a suspicious look and reached for the toast.

On the dot of nine o'clock there was a knock on the door and Prof and the Colonel came in. I waved them to chairs, preparatory to addressing the Colonel directly.

'Now you've had time to sleep on our conversation of yesterday, have you made up your mind what you want to do? D'you want to go home?'

For the first time a half smile flickered in his eyes. He spoke slowly, carefully. 'Well, it seems daft to come all this way to do a job and then go straight home.' So far so good. He waited a second before adding, 'But I'd like to know a wee bit more about what I'd be expected to do. I mean what's my part in such operations? There really are no feeshing vessels?'

'There are, but I wouldn't use them while we've got the MAS boats. Does that put your mind at rest?'

Again the trace of a smile. 'Aye. No fishing vessels.'

'As far as your job would be concerned you would be another operations officer – like Tom Maxted, or young Cosens – you've spoken to both of them – or like me. We all go to sea landing and embarking resisters in or from enemy territory.'

Immediate doubt showed in every line of his face, the protest came out quickly in very north-of-the-border tones. 'But I couldna dae tha'!'

'Why not?'

'I wouldna know how.'

Prof, who up to then had said nothing, leant forward in his chair and said quietly, 'There's nothing to it, you know. No magic.'

The unexpected corroboration seemed to have a calming effect. His next question was a genuine enquiry not a protest. 'But would I be expected to talk to these resister folk? I haven't a word of a foreign language, you understand.'

Step by step, between us, we took him through a typical operation while he listened attentively in silence. At the end he shook his head sadly and shrugged his shoulders.

'I couldna' do tha',' he said.

'Why not?' I asked.

'Oh, I'd need a lot o' practice first.'

We couldn't help laughing.

It wasn't so amusing, however, to hear Prof saying, 'But, my dear man, you don't seriously expect you would be let loose all by yourself *without* practice.' Then he turned to me. 'The CO will probably take you himself. Won't you – sir?'

There were times when I went off Prof.

'You can come with me tomorrow night.'

Relief was at last beginning to dawn in the Colonel's mind.

'You mean I really don't have to go off myself for some time yet? Is that it?' He was actually smiling.

'That,' I said, 'is, indeed, it. One thing must be understood, however, if you decide to stay then you stay for good. We can't afford to waste time training someone for them to leave immediately they're fully trained.'

'Aye. I understand that,' he said.

'Well? Yes or no?'

'I'll stay, if you'll have me.'

John Cross

We were spotted by some of our old friends in 3rd Indian Corps Signals and greeted with a derisive shout of – 'Here comes the Secret Service.'

In January 1942, shortly before the fall of Singapore, SIS's regional chief in Malaya, Major Rosher, inserted a group of volunteers into the Malayan jungle equipped with radios and instructions to report on enemy troop movements. The first party, led by Major James Barry, included a sergeant from the Royal Signals, Jack Cross, who had arrived in the Far East from Catterick only three months earlier. Cross had been called up, aged twenty-nine, when he was working for a firm of chartered accountants in London.

Operating under SIS's military cover of the Inter-Services Liaison Department, Rosher had established a training school designated STS 101 on an island off Singapore. There, in anticipation of a Japanese invasion, he had supervised the transformation of selected Chinese members of the Malayan Communist Party from political activists into well-armed saboteurs. The mission he entrusted to Major Barry was to lead a team of three SIS volunteers, assisted by some Chinese Communists chosen by the Malay Special Branch, into the forest to report on enemy troop movements. Known as Station A, it was to form a radio net with similar outposts on Java and in Rangoon, and make regular reports to SIS's main receiving centre at Kranji, near Singapore.

The plan went wrong almost from the beginning when the Japanese swept through the supposedly impenetrable jungle and outmanoeuvred the disorganized British defences. Kranji was evacuated, just before Singapore surrendered, leaving Barry and his mission isolated in the jungle for a harrowing three years. Racked by disease and cut off from the outside world, Barry slashed his wrists in mid-July 1944, leaving Cross in charge of what remained of his party. In April 1945 they eventually linked up with Major J. V. Hart of the MINT mission and re-established contact with Inter-Services Liaison in Ceylon, which had long given up Barry's mission for lost. By the end of the following month Cross and the survivors were aboard HMS *Thule* and heading for Fremantle where they received a hero's welcome and were decorated.

After a brief recuperation Cross was brought back to London and returned to civilian life. Although invited to remain in SIS and return to Malaya under cover, he declined to do so, and after the war he joined a firm of accountants and was assigned as company secretary to a property developer, Bernard Myers. He married Aileen Coles in 1948, adopted his stepson, and went to work in Northern Ireland as a management consultant.

A committed Socialist, he later ran a woodworking business in Abingdon, worked for a wire wholesalers in London and ended up as a credit controller in an employment agency he started in Bletchley.

Although self-educated, from a humble background in Acton, Cross was an exceptional man, but that was not his true name. He had been born Valentine Frederick Hegelund to a bigamous Dane, the manager of a cinema in North London who later ran off to California. His stepfather, determined to erase all trace of his natural parent, transformed him into John Cross.

Cross lived in the village of Dinton, Buckinghamshire, until 1979 when he contracted Parkinson's disease. He died in Stoke Mandeville Hospital in November 1981, and soon afterwards his papers were lodged with the Imperial War Museum.

He published an account of his gruelling experiences in 1957 and thereby became the first SIS agent of the Second World War to write about his contribution to the secret war. Here he describes his return to civilization by submarine after three years in the Malayan jungle.

Red Jungle

About 2 a.m. on the 2nd June the klaxon blared for a crash-dive. As I shook myself out of a heavy sleep the crew were leaping to their action stations, where they stood or sat silent and impassive, waiting for the next order. The little indicators flapped up and down, signalling 'Night Alarm', 'Night Alarm'. We 'passengers' could only keep out of the way and wait anxiously until the oppressive silence was broken by the captain's announcement over the inter-com that he had identified through the periscope a submarine five hundred yards away in the moonlight.

Two nights later we started the run-in for the passage through the Sunda Strait. A noisy propeller vibrated above the complete silence of the boat and that motor had to be stopped. Silently, on one motor, we passed beneath an enemy trawler and a large E-boat patrolling the narrows above us. After about sixteen hours of silent, sweating, carbon-monoxide-breathing vigil we were through and clear.

The rest of the twelve days was a pleasure-cruise for me. Day and night,

I spent every hour on the bridge for which I could get permission to stay up there, gulping down the fresh sea air and just gazing out across the vast empty seascape.

On the last morning at sea Wagstaff, Brian Smith, Jim Wright and I sat below in a little group. Dressed in our sail-cloth shirts and shorts and nursing our pathetic little bundles of possessions, we watched the submariners decking themselves out in their number ones for their ceremonial entry into Fremantle harbour. We were too expectant to talk. We started at the sudden explosion of a shell fired from the four-inch gun to clear the barrel of rust.

We seemed to be alone in the boat as the crew lined the casing above while the *Thule* went alongside the depot ship. Morter, still ill with fever, dressed and joined us and was led swaying across the narrow gangplank to the *Adamant*. He entered hospital and we didn't see him again for a month.

Lieutenant-Commander Mars left us in his cabin aboard the *Adamant* to await the arrival of two officers from our organization. I hope he has forgiven us our inroads on his box of Churchman's No. 1 in his absence!

The rest, the plentiful food, and the freedom from anxiety and the sea air during the second week of the voyage had put Wagstaff, Smith, Wright and me back on our feet. I was therefore taken aback when our two conducting officers joined us, to find them brimming with anxiety and compassion – they had even wondered about laying on ambulances!

We got into the waiting car and sped along the highway to Perth. After three and a half years all the amenities of civilization were plummeting into our laps!

We entered the Savoy Hotel and as we waited to be booked in I only half-noticed the discreetly curious glances from the Australians in the restaurant.

When we got upstairs to our two bedrooms, separated by a sumptuous bathroom, and saw ourselves in a full-length mirror for the first time, I wondered that the eyes of the visitors below hadn't popped – four bony figures, clad in sail-cloth and mud-caked jungle boots, with hollow eyes and long hair curling at the napes of our necks.

I was first in the bath and our conducting officers, who had got over their expectation of having four stretcher-cases on their hands, looked on wonderingly as the bath-water turned nearly black and exclaimed, 'Look at that bloody water!'

By evening we were fitted out in civilian clothes and looking for fun.

It was a queer fortnight's leave in Australia. We were thoroughly examined and X-rayed and pronounced fit for active service again. No medical treatment was found necessary other than being loaded with suppressive Atabrin to blot out the fever. This pigmented our skin and gave us a jaundiced look.

There were no facilities in Perth for a proper interrogation and it was decided to fly us to the headquarters of South-East Asia Command in Ceylon.

So each morning we were standing by in case an aircraft was available. Daily we declined invitations from Australians to their parties on the grounds that we were leaving the country, only to turn up unexpectedly in the evening – by the end of the fortnight I felt like a *prima donna* making her 'positively last performance'. On top of that, mention of Malaya was a hot-potato, with so many Australians missing at the fall of Singapore. We were absolutely forbidden to mention the place and our sealed lips act inhibited our relations with our hosts. But they were very kind, and stood us well.

We took off at 11 a.m. on Tuesday the 26th June. After tea at a lonely dust-blown airfield in the Australian desert we were airborne again for the fifteen and a half hours' non-stop flight to Colombo. The weather in Perth had seemed bitter, I had the most frightful cold and was glad to be back in the tropics again.

We were met by Major Boris Hembry and his FANY secretary. He was a planter in Malaya pre-war, who had been one of Major Spencer Chapman's behind-the-lines party of ten in January 1942. Separated from the main party in the Tanjong Malim area and with their equipment and stores lost, Hembry and two companions set off through the jungle and reached Singapore, where he went down with fever. After escaping from the Japs his two companions were recaptured and beheaded at Kuala Lumpur. Hembry made his escape to India. Since then he had been organizing clandestine forces in preparation for the liberation.

I had been longing to get out of Malaya and back to civilization but now, curiously, it was a pleasure to join up with this man with a Malayan background. He was in radio touch with Hart, he knew all about us, I could speak freely to him and he understood everything at once.

Our interrogation at Kandy followed. It took the form of a series of daily examinations by specialist officers in a hut at Supreme Allied Headquarters. I didn't feel it was a success. Perhaps I had developed some raw edges but the political affairs officer seemed to be haranguing rather than interrogating and I am afraid my hackles rose.

But the understanding Hembry gave me my head in a suggestion that

Wagstaff and I should sit quietly together in an office for two or three days while I made a written report of all our intelligence, which was a much more successful procedure.

The snippets of inside information I heard during our nearly three weeks in Ceylon added up to our being within three months of the Allied invasion of Malaya. The island was thronged with servicemen, most of whom had been, since VE day, itching to get the war over and go home. During my last two or three days I had nothing to do and I lazed about on the beach. Gazing east across the calm sea I grew melancholy, wondering how many of these chaps would shortly have to die on the beaches of Malaya.

We took off in a York from Colombo on Tuesday morning. Morter had been discharged from the Australian hospital and flown across to join us for the flight home. Brian Smith and Jim Wright had been posted to a regular Army unit for repatriation by sea. After short stops at Karachi, Shibah, Cairo and Malta we landed at Lyneham on the Thursday.

One of our jungle fantasies had been to imagine ourselves being parachuted down into Piccadilly Circus, dressed just as we were. This was nearly as good. Only six weeks away from the Malayan jungle and two days from the tropics, we were taking tea in a centuries-old English inn. Then the War Office car sped us towards London – along the Great West Road, through Ealing and Chiswick (where I had spent my embarkation leave), through Hyde Park into Whitehall. The suddenness of it all cast a quiet spell over the three of us.

That night we spent in a London hotel, thumbing through the directory and making telephone calls in all directions, telling relatives and friends we were back from the dead. Late next day we split up to go off home for a month's leave.

Under the necessity of keeping very 'mum' it was a lonely month. Everyone tried hard to make me feel at home but all conversation led to questions which I was not allowed to answer. Starved of emotion and colour for more than three years I was drawn to the cinema and the theatre – I sometimes went twice in one day. Inside, I was glad of the darkness which hid me from other patrons when the colourful scenes and music were too moving for me. By the end of the month, apart from an inability to sit with my back to a doorway, I was my pre-jungle self.

The surrender of Japan washed out any question of our returning to Malaya, and early 1946 found the three of us back in civilian life, with our recent experiences being crowded into the background.

Until, in May 1946, came a letter from Chai Chieh (Charlie). He was in

Kensington Gardens with the Malayan contingent for the Victory Parade. Delighted by the prospect of seeing him again I hurried along there. I had a job finding him because once again he had changed his name and was now Chen Tian – Captain Chen Tian, although I only learned this from the nominal roll because he and his comrades declined to use their ranks or wear insignia in public.

As a change from his officially-conducted tours the three of us separately got him out and about amongst the people. He developed a taste for a half-pint of bitter and lost his conception of most Englishmen being superior in attitude and bristling with racial prejudice. But his early indoctrination died hard. Morter got him an invitation into a modern council house in south London. Impressed by the appointments of the house, Charlie at first flatly refused to believe it was the home of a lorry driver!

I felt we had made some progress when he wrote me from Malaya in August 1946:

> During my stay which is very short of course, I study something and I learn something about the social life and the economic structure of Britain. . . .
>
> I see no reason why we can't build a country with its industry, agriculture and civil liberties full developed in the same way as Britain does. Don't you agree with me?
>
> Now I like to know something more about Britain. Can you send me regularly newspapers and periodicals such as *The Times*, *The Economist* and *New Statesman*.

We arranged a year's subscription to these three papers for him and I settled down to what I hoped would be a steady pen-friendship, especially as he wrote in December 1946:

> I agree with you entirely that we should maintain our friendship since we had been living a hard life during the past years. As you may have realized, we had really enjoyed the comradeship in spite of certain misunderstandings between you and me. Anyway those days are gone and I only look forward to a day when people throughout the world will enjoy that spirit of friendship which we had during those hard days. . . .

For more than a year he was silent, until he replied to a letter I wrote to him in 1948. He had visited Czechoslovakia, Yugoslavia and Paris and on the way back had stayed in London for a month awaiting a passage to Singapore. He had not contacted me while in London and I could only think that he had been on Party business and contact with me would have been an embarrassment to him.

The friendship seemed to have foundered on politics.

Xan Fielding

It was assumed, very properly, that anyone embarking on a clandestine venture into enemy-occupied territory would not wish to be hampered by supplies that were not absolutely essential, so that my equipment was reduced to the barest necessities: an electric torch, a small automatic pistol, a map of Crete printed on linen for discreet portability but of so small a scale as to be virtually useless, and a sum of money in currency so inflated that I found my total assets on landing amounted to little more than £16.

Xan Fielding was editing a newspaper in Cyprus when the war broke out. He was recruited into SOE in 1940, and in December 1941 was dropped on a beach in the south of Crete by HMS *Torbay* to join Monty Woodhouse. He was to remain on the island for nine months, organizing a series of resistance cells in the White Mountains before being evacuated to Beirut in August 1942. Decorated with a DSO, he was sent back to Crete in November on a second mission which was to last until February 1944.

Upon his return to Cairo Fielding obtained a transfer to SOE's French Section and in August he was dropped from Algiers into a resistance group in the south of France. Soon after his arrival he was arrested by the local *milice* but his freedom was negotiated by a member of his network. He was released from prison in Digne two days before that city's liberation. Withdrawn from France, he was sent on a mission to Greece, and was one of the first Englishmen to enter Athens after the German retreat. In December he returned briefly to Crete, and in the spring of 1945 was posted to the Far East prior to an assignment in Saigon.

After the Japanese surrender Fielding joined SIS in Europe and operated in Germany under British Control Commission cover. On his retirement he moved to Serrania de Ronda, in the south of Spain, and wrote a biography of his old friend Billy McLean of SOE, *One Man in His Time*, but died in August 1991, soon after its publication.

In his war memoirs, published in 1954, Fielding made no mention of his post-war role and instead gave a detailed account of his experiences in Crete, including this description of the internal conflict that dogged SOE's regional headquarters in Cairo. Brigadier Keble is the unnamed key figure who was the subject of much criticism, and his senior assistant was Colonel Guy Tamplin who died of a heart attack soon afterwards, having been removed from his command.

Hide and Seek

By this time [1942] our Headquarters, after its recent transfer to Jerusalem during the Great Flap caused by the German midsummer advance, had returned once again to Cairo; but the offices, though reinstalled as before in the block of flats called Rustom Building, were to me completely unrecognizable. The handful of experts who had welcomed me when I first joined the organization were now heavily outnumbered by a whole regiment of strangers, most of whom had recently arrived from England. The Colonel in charge had been replaced by a civilian director with authority equivalent to that of a general; and in close support was a formidable array of officers wearing red tabs, each responsible for departments, sections and sub-sections which previously had never existed. In this incessant gale of professional activity the building seemed to rock like a top-heavy transatlantic liner, and I regretted the milder climate of enthusiastic amateurism in which I had originally known it.

Through this confusing labyrinth, studded at every turn with code-names and cabalistic signs, Jack [Hamson] skilfully steered me, so that in a week or two I was able to find my way about the separate administrative and operational offices scattered throughout the building like the islands of a tropical archipelago. So much for the new constitution of our unit, to which Jack introduced me. For its internal politics – the departmental bickering, sectional jealousies and personal strife – my unofficial guide was Arthur Reade.

Arthur was probably better equipped than anyone else in the organization to provide an objective unbiased picture of its personalities and their functions. As head of a top-secret section responsible for the accommodation, employment and welfare of the agents and refugees from the various countries in which we were then operating, he was concerned less with the routine and mechanics of the firm than with its human aspect.

Though junior in rank, he was equal in years to the senior staff officer, a brigadier, but their age was the only thing they had in common. For the Brigadier [Keble], a globe-shaped choleric little militarist, did his best to conceal his natural and professional shortcomings by a show of blood-thirsty activity and total disregard for the agents in the field, whom he treated like so many expendable commodities. Arthur, on the other hand, whose duties and personal inclinations involved him in close companionship with the operational personnel, set out to prove that efficiency and decent behaviour were not necessarily incompatible.

Had he shared the Brigadier's mentality, he too, I suppose, might have allowed his physical eccentricity to affect his moral outlook and social conduct – for he was almost freakishly tall, with bright red hair falling over his forehead like a schoolboy's and a fulminatingly virile moustache which only stressed his excessively gentle expression. This sweetness of disposition immediately noticeable in his features and in every action of his daily life was to a certain extent mitigated by a razor-sharp critical faculty which made him fiercely opposed to any form of official negligence, malice or plain stupidity. In Rustom Building there was much for him to criticize.

The Brigadier's senior assistant was a middle-aged colonel [Tamplin] with lemon-coloured hair and eyebrows so fair as to be well-nigh invisible. He looked like a native of Esthonia and had, in fact, spent much of his life in that country. He was an expert on the Baltic States and so, in view of officialdom's geographical ignorance and passion for inappropriate postings, it was scarcely surprising that he should have been put in charge of the Balkan department. Nor was it, in consequence, surprising that our Greek and Jugoslav sections suffered from muddled policy and lack of direction. One frustrated agent accurately summed up the situation in these words, designed to be sung – but sung, of course, in secret – to the strains of a popular dance tune:

> We've the Partisan itch,
> But there's Mihailovic,
> And the Foreign Office doesn't seem to know which
>   is which . . .
> We'd better close down,
> We're the talk of the town,
> For nobody's using us now.
>
> We've got lots of mugs,
> Whom we've trained as thugs,
> But now they're at the mercy of the Greeks and the
>   Jugs . . .

The Colonel did not hold his unsuitable post for long. One morning, quite unexpectedly, he died at his desk. The news spread quickly through the building, and for the rest of the day the Brigadier was pestered on the internal telephone system by a succession of anonymous messages of sardonic congratulation. For it was known that with his usual interest in sudden death – other people's, not his own – he had been longing to determine the efficacy, by practical experiment, of a certain poison destined for operational use in enemy-occupied territory.

Such malignant insubordination could not, of course, be overlooked. The Brigadier at once undertook to discover the source of the libellous calls and ordered the Security Officer to unearth at least one culprit. But an investigation on these lines was not to the taste, even had it been in the power, of the elderly major who was affectionately known to all of us as 'Slyboots'. After several days devoted to padding up and down corridors, listening at keyholes and diving in and out of offices, he gave up the unrewarding search and, reduced by now almost to tears, sorrowfully confessed:

'I'm not a security officer at all; I'm just a very tired old man.'

David Smiley

Whereas at the end of the war SOE was completely disbanded and MI6 carried on its customary role of the British Secret Service, the Americans were different.

In 1940 David Smiley, a young Household Cavalry officer serving in Palestine, volunteered for the Somaliland Camel Corps. When he arrived in Egypt he persuaded General Wavell, who was a family friend, to help him transfer to No. 52 Middle East Commando, a unit operating behind the Italian lines in Abyssinia. In January 1943 he was recruited into SOE and briefed by Basil Davidson for a mission to Albania codenamed Consensus. The four-man team departed in April and were dropped by parachute into Greece where they were received by a group of guerrillas led by a British Liaison Officer. They trekked across the frontier into Albania and made contact with the local Communist partisans. Smiley remained in Albania until October when he was withdrawn by boat to Bari; after a brief rest in Italy he was flown to Cairo and then, in January 1944, was brought to London to report in person to Anthony Eden, the Foreign Secretary.

Early the following month Smiley returned to Cairo and prepared for a second mission to Albania, flying from Bari with Julian Amery. On this occasion they linked up with royalist supporters of King Zog who specialized in ambushing German road convoys. After many adventures Smiley's party was withdrawn by boat to Brindisi in October 1944.

Early in 1945 SOE sent him to the Far East, and in May he was dropped into north-eastern Siam. This mission was aborted after just three weeks when a booby-trapped case exploded, covering Smiley in flames. He was badly burned and was flown for medical treatment to Calcutta. He had recovered by August, and went on a second mission to Siam, accompanied by SOE's regional commander.

Smiley returned to London in November 1945 and was posted to Warsaw as assistant military attaché, but after nine months he was accused of espionage and declared *persona non grata*. He then spent a year with SIS in the Adriatic attempting to stem the flow of illegal Jewish refugees to Palestine, before returning to his regiment, the Royal Horse Guards, as second-in-command.

In July 1949 Smiley was invited to rejoin SIS, this time to supervise the training of Albanians who were to be infiltrated back into their country with the intention of subverting Enver Hoxha's hated Communist regime. A special school was established in conditions of great secrecy in Malta and several teams of agents were put ashore from fishing boats manned by SIS personnel. However, it soon became clear that the operation had been betrayed, for the local security apparatus seemed well prepared for their arrival. After working in Greece under the cover of an attachment to the British Military Mission, Smiley rejoined his regiment in 1952 and commanded it in Germany until 1955 when he was appointed military attaché in Stockholm. Three years later he went to Oman to command the Sultan's army, and in 1962 he became the military adviser to the Imam of Yemen and his guerrillas.

After four years in the Middle East Smiley retired to a farm near Alicante in Spain and wrote *Arabian Assignment* in 1975. His second volume of memoirs, *Albanian Assignment*, followed in 1984 shortly before his return to England. In this entertaining episode he recalls his conversations with the Albanian Communist leadership.

Albanian Assignment

Some days later [Billy] McLean returned and we received the first of many visits from the *Shtab* – the General Staff of the LNÇ, of whom the two leading members were Mehmet Shehu and Enver Hoxha. Mehmet Shehu was a short, wiry, dark, sallow-faced man of about thirty who seldom smiled except at other people's misfortunes. He spoke good English, was very capable, and had far more military knowledge than most other Albanians. After early education at the American school in Tirana he had attended a military college in Naples, from which he was expelled for Communist activities; a course at the Officers' School in Tirana was followed by Spain in 1938, where he joined the 'Garibaldi' International Brigade, and became Acting Commander of the Fourth Battalion. When the brigade withdrew into France in 1939 he was interned for three years. On his release he returned to Albania where he joined the partisan movement, shortly becoming a member of the Communist Party Committee in the Valona area. By the time we met him he was the commissar of all the partisan forces in the area.

He had a reputation for bravery, ruthlessness, and cruelty – he boasted that he had personally cut the throats of seventy Italian *carabinieri* who had been taken prisoner. I got on with him at first, for as soldiers we had something in common; but he did little to conceal his dislike of all things British, and my relations with him deteriorated. At one of our meetings with the *Shtab*, he made wild accusations against us, swearing that we had given all the arms dropped to us in Albania to the Balli Kombettar, leaving none for the partisans. In reply I drew out of my brief case a sheaf of lists of weapons I had handed over to the partisans, with the signed receipts attached; I took my time reading these out aloud in front of the *Shtab*, to Shehu's discomfort and fury, and he never forgave me. Later on, when the First Partisan Brigade put up as despicable an exhibition of cowardice as I had yet seen, I had my last words with Shehu, and they were far from polite. After the war he became Prime Minister of Albania and held that position until he was reported to have committed suicide in 1981.

Enver Hoxha was an entirely different character – a big man with too much flesh and a flabby handshake. He was not a military man although he had military pretensions, but he was more sociable than Shehu, and spoke with us in fluent French. He may have disliked us, but at least he concealed his feelings, whereas with Shehu you could feel the hostility.

Hoxha was about thirty-five years old. He had been educated in Gjirokaster Grammar School, the *lycée* in Korçë, and the University of Montpellier in France, which he was compelled to leave for failing his exams. He went on to Brussels and Paris to study law, though he never graduated, and returned to Albania to become a French teacher at the State Gymnasium in Tirana; he was later transferred to the *lycée* in Korçë, still as a teacher of French. We always knew him as 'Professor' Enver Hoxha – presumably he derived this title from his teaching appointments. He gave up teaching in 1940 to run a tobacconist's shop in Tirana which became a Communist cell and rendezvous for anti-government elements; after the founding of the Albanian Communist Party in 1941 he became the Secretary-General to the Party Central Committee, which was probably the position he still held when we first met him.

I got on well with Hoxha, even though he was inclined to bluster and lose his temper at our endless meetings. I took delight in teasing him about his politics, and the more Communist propaganda he aimed at me, the more right-wing, capitalist and imperialist I became. Once we were standing in front of a war map of the world while he lectured me on how he would like to see the world after the war – Communist, of course, all over. Turning to me he said, 'How would you like to see the world,

Monsieur le Capitaine?'; to which I replied, 'I too would like to see this map painted red all over, but not the sort of red you mean.' [Before the Second World War the British Empire was coloured red in maps of the world.] He seemed puzzled, but I let him think it out on his own. Hoxha had quite a sense of humour, and over a glass of raki could be cheerful and amusing, in contrast to his dour and morose companion Mehmet Shehu. He became President of Albania after the war.

CHAPTER IX

The Evaders

These were the days before Ian Fleming and John Le Carré had got down to the job of modernizing the intelligence services of the world.
J. M. Langley, Fight Another Day

After Dunkirk the Secret Intelligence Service belatedly recognized the need to establish escape lines through France to Spain and Portugal so as to repatriate the many stragglers abandoned on the Continent. Recognition was also given to the necessity of helping evading air crew to make their way home through hostile territory. Responsibility for setting up and managing the escape lines was given to a new sub-section of SIS, designated P15, and headed by a Coldstream Guards officer, Jimmy Langley, who had lost an arm during the retreat through France, been captured, had escaped from hospital and had been repatriated from Vichy France. The new department, with its network of agents across occupied Europe, was to operate separately from, but in parallel to, MI9, the military intelligence branch which liaised with British prisoners of war. Thus a strict demarcation line was introduced, with SIS organizing the secret business of the escape lines, leaving MI9 to brief and equip military personnel going into combat, to make contact with prisoners in enemy camps, and to debrief returning escapees.

One of the first to be enrolled into SIS's escape and evasion branch was Donald Darling who was posted to Lisbon, under consular cover, to develop escape lines over the Pyrenees. He was later to describe his experiences in *Secret Sunday*, the title having been taken from his codename, Sunday. Others in P15 adopted other days of the week as theirs: Airey Neave, the first British officer to make a 'home run' from Colditz, taking Saturday, P15's representative in Madrid, (Sir) Michael Cresswell, being Monday.

In May 1944 Jimmy Langley was appointed MI9's joint commander, thereby effectively combining MI9 and P15. That such an organization even existed remained a secret until the publication in 1969 of Airey

Neave's second volume of memoirs, *Saturday at MI9*. Neither *They Have Their Exits*, nor *Little Cyclone*, the story of Andrée de Jongh, a key figure in the Belgian escape lines, gave more than just a hint at the existence of MI9. The reason, explained Neave, was his belief that a similar organization might have to be used against a Soviet occupation of western Europe.

Jimmy Langley's autobiography, *Fight Another Day*, was published in 1974, and this was followed a year later by the memoirs of his subordinate, Donald Darling. The more authoritative official history *MI9: Escape and Evasion 1939–1945*, co-authored by Professor M. R. D. Foot and Jimmy Langley, was released five years later.

By D-Day in June 1944 some 4000 escapers and evaders had been returned to England, largely thanks to the combined efforts of MI9 and P15, although few of them had any idea of the secret agencies at work behind the scenes on their behalf. Agent-run escape routes apart, this took the form of much work by MI9 itself, including a whole range of sophisticated gadgetry, such as compasses disguised as buttons, smuggled into the camps concealed in Red Cross parcels and items of clothing. The agency also ran short courses for selected officers and NCOs on escape and evasion and gave briefings on methods of communicating with MI9 from a PoW camp. Special simple codes had been devised to facilitate clandestine communications and by as early as November 1940 the first sacks of PoW mail had been exchanged and contact had been established with the inmates of dozens of camps. One of those who had attended an MI9 course was John Brown whose book, *In Durance Vile*, was published after his death in 1964.

J. M. Langley

We are MI6, the Secret Intelligence Service of popular fiction, with the task of gathering information from all over the world about the intention, plans, etc. of any country that may be at war with Great Britain or may be a potential enemy.

The son of a high court judge, Jimmy Langley was badly wounded at Calais, was helped to escape from a hospital for prisoners of war in Lille, and was escorted to Paris. Later he crossed into the unoccupied zone and, declared unfit for future military service, was repatriated by the Vichy authorities.

Back in England Langley was recruited by SIS to organize a network of escape routes, managed by paid guides, a task that in early 1941 must have seemed impossible. However, Donald Darling had already made a start from Lisbon and an embryonic line of volunteers had been established from Belgium down to the Pyrenees. Posing as an architect assessing repairs needed to British diplomatic premises, Langley made an unsuccessful tour of MI9's assets in Lisbon and Madrid and swiftly fell foul of Sir Samuel Hoare, our ambassador in Spain, who greatly disliked any clandestine activity.

By September 1943 Langley had helped create a relatively sophisticated organization with agents and couriers running escape lines the length of occupied France, moving hundreds of evaders over the Pyrenees into Spain. At this point Langley passed the command of MI9 to Airey Neave and concentrated on the development of a special intelligence school where Allied personnel were trained in escape techniques in anticipation of the invasion of Europe. The course included simulated enemy interrogations and an introduction to some of the ingenious equipment that was concealed in ostensibly ordinary clothing for use in escapes.

Soon after D-Day Langley went to France to supervise the mobile interrogation teams created to screen returning Allied PoWs, and was in Paris as it was liberated. As 21st Army Group moved through Belgium and Holland, specialist MI9 groups made contact with evaders and returned them to their units. At the end of the war 'Intelligence School 9' had established itself in Bad Salzuffen, and was finally disbanded in July 1945 when Langley was appointed Town Major of Antwerp.

Langley was demobbed in 1946 and, although offered a permanent post in SIS, preferred to join Fisons to work on long-term surveys into agricultural raw materials. He attended the Harvard Business School in 1954, and in 1967 opened a bookshop. He later moved to Ipswich, where he took over another bookshop, and died there in April 1983.

He collaborated with Professor M. R. D. Foot on the official history of MI9, which was published in 1979. In this extract from his war memoirs Langley describes his first encounter with Claude Dansey, the SIS officer who masterminded the creation of MI9.

Fight Another Day

It was not my first visit to the Savoy Hotel. Father had given me a superb 21st birthday party there four years before and I had no difficulty in locating the man I was to meet who was dressed as described. He introduced himself as Colonel Claude Dansey, and my first impression was very much of a benign uncle, with his white hair, blue eyes and general air of benevolence; but this was quickly erased as he looked me sharply up and down and with a grunted 'Hm' said, 'F.O.L.'s son and wounded. What a bit of luck.'

I merely stared in amazement and he proffered me an explanation.

'Your father worked for me in Berne in 1917 and 1918. Some of my young men are finding it difficult to explain to their girl friends why they are not fighting. However, be that as it may, I am going to ask you the same question as I did your father when he joined my staff. What do you want?'

'I am sorry, sir, but I do not quite understand.'

'Surely I make myself plain. It is always much easier if you get what you want before you start working, then you don't spend half your time worrying about your possible award. Now an MC or an OBE? A DSO is more difficult and you are too young for a CBE. However, there are plenty of foreign decorations available. I am told that the Poles have the nicest ribbons – the Order of Stanislaus, or some such other outlandish name is very much sought after. I call it "Pologna Prostituta" as it is immensely popular with the women. Take your choice but be quick about it.'

I replied that I did not want anything.

'Just like your father. Well, do not come complaining to me that you have not been properly looked after. Waiter!'

The response to his call was as swift as a guardsman responding to a shout from the regimental sergeant-major.

'Two large dry martinis and tell Henry pre-war gin and none of that ersatz martini he dishes out to the Americans. I presume you drink dry martinis?' he asked as an afterthought. I assented in the certainty that if he had said strychnine and cyanide on the rocks my reply would have been the same.

'What am I to do?' I enquired, gaining courage from the dry martini.

'I never talk business in public. You do not know who is listening. Waiter! These were excellent, two more, please, and ask Mr Manetta to show us the menu in the Grill.'

Manetta, the maître d'hotel of the Grill, came over and whispered something in the colonel's ear.

'Excellent, you know how I like it.'

A further whisper. 'Yes, could not be better. How are your friends on the island?'

Manetta said they did not much like the food and were very homesick.

I was very much in the dark until the colonel condescended to explain. 'Most of the big boys in the restaurant world in London are Italians and when Italy declared war many of them were arrested and sent to the Isle of Man. I like them to think I was responsible and if I am not well looked after they will follow. Manetta says he has some excellent steak and a fresh Stilton, I hope they will be to your liking. Of course, I never would dream of taking any action however poor the food.'

No, I thought, I bet you wouldn't, but I should not like to be in their shoes after you had eaten a couple of bad oysters.

The colonel apparently preferred to eat in silence and our conversation was limited to queries by myself and short snapped answers which I felt would have been even more caustic had not the food and wine been excellent.

'When do I report to you?'

'Tomorrow, of course.' I ventured to point out that it would be Saturday and that I had only had five days' leave.

'All right, I suppose Monday will do, but don't forget we are at war.'

My next question as to where I was to be billeted was even less appreciated.

'Good God, man, you find your own accommodation. You will get a lodging allowance.'

'What uniform do I wear?' called for a further outburst.

'Plain clothes, of course. You are not in the army now. As far as I am concerned you can wear uniform to take out your girl friends but don't go telling them all about us or you will be in trouble.' I made a mental vow to imitate a Trappist monk.

'Well, off you go and report at 10 o'clock Monday morning at this address,' he said, scribbling on the back of a card. 'I have got some more work to do.'

I proffered my thanks and as I collected my hat I glanced at the card which was neatly inscribed 'Captain Charles Pomfret-Seymour, CBE, DSO, RN, The Naval and Military Club, Pall Mall'. On the back was written 'Admit, informing ACSS of arrival', followed by an address. I was later to learn that the colonel had a passion for aliases, the only difficulty being that he often forgot which one he had chosen for the day.

Broadway Buildings, opposite St James's Park Underground Station, where I duly reported was according to the brass plate at the entrance the head office of the Minimax Fire Extinguisher Company. A casual observer might well have wondered how on earth this company had managed to retain so large a staff in time of war and equally why there was a constant coming and going of uniformed despatch riders and military cars. The entrance hall was large enough to accommodate 15 or 20 people and it was frequently used by passersby to shelter from the rain. They were left undisturbed unless they tried to pass the reception desk, when they were politely asked their business by two middle-aged uniformed porters. However, these were the days before Ian Fleming and John Le Carré had got down to the job of modernizing the intelligence services of the world.

Uncle Claude, as Colonel Dansey was widely called, wasted no time in getting down to business. 'Just listen to me and don't ask any damned silly questions,' he said. 'The likes of you in France and Belgium are causing me considerable trouble, which is being made worse by the apparent inability of the RAF to remain airborne over enemy-occupied territory. My job, and that of my agents, is to collect information about the Germans' intentions and activities, not to act as nursemaids to people who seem totally incapable of doing much to get back on their own.' He pressed the bell for his secretary.

'Miss Reade, who controls Hengist?' The pretty red-headed girl replied 'Captain Caines, sir.'

'Right, ask him to come to my office, please.'

Captain Edward Caines was obviously somewhat apprehensive of the reason for this sudden summons.

'Good morning, Teddy. If I read your messages right Hengist has picked up another pilot. From the way he rakes them in you might think he is a homosexual. Rare I know in France but always possible. Is he one by any chance?'

'He is not a he, sir, he is a she.'

Uncle Claude slammed the desk with his fist.

'How many times have I told you not to go recruiting women and above all not without my agreement. A fine fool I would have looked if I had recommended him for the DSO and he turned out to be a woman.'

'I did not recruit her, she recruited herself when Horsa was caught.'

'That is beside the point. I will not have any of your organization run by a woman. They simply are not trustworthy. Do you understand?'

'Yes, sir.'

'Right. Now what are you going to do about the pilot?'

'I don't know.'

'I thought so. Well, this is Captain Langley who has recently escaped from Lille and knows all about the escape lines in France. His job will be to take over all British Service personnel who come into the hands of our people and arrange for them to be sent back here. Tell Hengist to hide the pilot for a couple of weeks when Langley will take him over.'

Teddy Caines withdrew and Uncle Claude turned to me. 'You understand now what you have to do?'

'Yes, sir.'

'Good, then let's get one or two further points clear. Theoretically you will be on loan from MI9, which is commanded by Colonel Crockatt. In practice you will be on my staff and under my orders in MI6. Is this clear?'

'Yes, sir.'

'While you will liaise with Colonel Crockatt on routine matters you will not give him any detailed report of your activities without my agreement.'

'Yes, sir.'

'Now I suppose we must fit you in here.'

He picked up the telephone and dialled a number.

'Good morning, Colonel. Dansey here. Have you still got any vacancies in your department?'

Colonel Heydon-Home, as I was to know him later, might be serving his country from an office but he addressed the telephone as though commanding a battalion on a ceremonial parade and his voice was clearly audible.

'Yes, IV Z never reported on mobilization.'

'What was he supposed to do?'

'How the hell do I know if he never turned up.'

'Well, he has now. Captain Langley is his name and he will be seconded to me.'

The telephone backfired several times and Uncle Claude said soothingly, 'I don't suppose you do want him. Don't worry, he will be paid by us. All you have to do is inform the War Office that IV Z has now turned up and has been seconded for special duties.'

The telephone emitted a low rumbling assent and Uncle Claude turned back to me.

'Well, there we are – all settled. Miss Reade will help you with any letters or reports you may have to write and will find you a room. I have already agreed your appointment with Colonel Crockatt but you had better go and see him in the next day or two. Don't hesitate to come and see me if there are any difficulties and don't forget to arrange with Captain Caines to remove that pilot off Hengist. I can't have sex interfering with our work.'

Miss Reade was most helpful, even though the only room available was used for making tea. 'After all,' as she remarked, 'you will at least get yours hot!' Colonel Heydon-Home might not approve of my appointment but nevertheless he wasted no time and I had hardly acquired a table, chair and blotting pad before a large file arrived labelled 'IV Z'.

I was duly impressed, until I started to read the contents of the file. The opening minute was dated April 1919 and requested advice as to the desirability or otherwise of permitting the Germans to manufacture Luger pistols for export. From then on until 1924 it had meandered round the War Office with occasional visits to the Foreign Office, the Board of Trade and the Home Office, collecting some interesting signatures, not least of which was that of Major Bernard Montgomery. As it had not been closed I could only assume that IV Z had died in harness at his desk and some vigilant clerk had awaited the appointment of his successor.

Well, IV Z was back in business and his first act was not going to be to let down his predecessor, so I addressed the file back to the War Office with the covering minute 'Closed pending outcome of present hostilities'.

Dealing with Teddy Caines' and Hengist's pilot was not so easy and I had to confess that there was no ready-made solution. All I could propose was that Hengist arrange for the pilot to be conducted to Marseilles and contact made with Ian Garrow through a mutual friend whom I knew would help. Teddy, however, was not prepared to ask his agents to have direct dealings with an escape organization. We compromised by agreeing that Hengist would be requested to arrange for the pilot to be passed into the unoccupied zone and put on a train to Marseilles with instructions to go to the Seamen's Mission and ask for Ian Garrow. Despite my apprehension all went well and in due course the pilot arrived safely in Spain and later in England.

All the talk of Hengist, Horsa, IV Z and the casual reference to MI9 and Colonel Crockatt left me completely confused. Major de Bruyne had said MI9 were responsible for helping POWs to escape and yet I was on loan from that organization to Uncle Claude who seemed to be taking a very direct interest in evasion, if only in France. I asked Teddy Caines what it was all about.

'Yes,' he said, 'I am not surprised you find everything a little confusing. I cannot myself quite understand why you have been sent here but, be that as it may, this is the background. We are MI6, the Secret Intelligence Service of popular fiction, with the task of gathering information from all over the world about the intention, plans, etc., of any country which may be at war with Great Britain or may be a potential enemy. My job here is to collect information from France and as you know, Horsa was one of my agents there. We have similar organizations in all enemy-occupied territories and we are all responsible in the first instance to Uncle Claude.'

'And Germany?' I queried.

He laughed. 'I simply do not know. We keep ourselves very much to ourselves. The less you know the less you can give away.

'MI9 with its headquarters in Beaconsfield and commanded by Colonel Norman Crockatt is responsible for helping and encouraging British POWs to escape. MI19, also at Beaconsfield, has the duty of interrogating and looking after German POWs.

'Then there is MI5 which deals with enemy spies, agents, call them what you like, in this country.

'Finally,' he heaved a sigh, 'there is the Special Operations Executive – usually shortened to SOE and commonly referred to as "The Baker Street Boys" since their offices are in that street. Sabotaging the enemy's war effort is their trade, though if you get Uncle Claude on the subject you would think their main efforts to date have been sabotaging our own.

'There you are, that's the background, no doubt you can fill in the gaps as you go along.'

I was very grateful for this information, but still not quite clear as to why I had been lent to Uncle Claude. I felt I must find out as soon as possible.

Donald Darling

P15's department was regarded by the Intelligence Service as 'chicken-feed'.

Donald Darling had worked for SIS's Z Organization in France before the war, so it was no surprise when in July 1940 Claude Dansey, the assistant chief of SIS, asked him to act as repatriation officer in the Iberian peninsula, shepherding British military personnel home. In his earlier connections with SIS he had occasionally undertaken small jobs for them while he was operating as a travel courier in France and Spain during the Spanish civil war. Once formally on SIS's books, Darling was attached to the British embassy in Portugal in the guise of a consular official handling refugee affairs, as one of Philip Johns's subordinates, and made a short visit to Madrid where he received a frosty welcome from Sir Samuel Hoare, the newly appointed ambassador. Hoare strongly disapproved of SIS operating on his territory and was convinced that their undiplomatic activities would jeopardize his task of keeping Spain neutral. Darling returned to Lisbon and was to spend the next two years based in the Portuguese capital, enabling Allied evaders to make the arduous journey from northern Europe, across enemy-occupied zones and over the Pyrenees.

One of the many agents Darling despatched into France was the oil magnate Nubar Gulbenkian who recalled his controller as 'a very cheerful, intelligent and dedicated man who lived for his job. When one met him alone, he was very witty and an excellent raconteur. In company he sat like a clam.'

In May 1942 Darling moved to Gibraltar which had become the focus of the escape lines. As a civilian assistant to the Governor he supervised the reception and interrogation of thousands of Allied personnel and arranged for their transport, either by ship or by air, back to England. Late in the summer of 1944 he moved to

Paris to supervise the winding-up of P15's networks, and later headed the awards office established to arrange for the organization's membership to receive the appropriate recognition and thanks.

After the war Darling retained his connections with SIS and in October 1946 undertook an assignment lasting five years to São Paulo in Brazil under consular cover. He was also in demand as a Portuguese interpreter, often receiving commissions to translate technical documents and contracts for the international diamond trade. Never having married, he died alone in London in reduced circumstances in December 1977.

Donald Darling's 1975 autobiography, *Secret Sunday*, was the first account of P15, a body that hitherto had been entirely unacknowledged. A second book, *Sunday at Large*, was published in 1977, covering his activities as MI9's representative in Gibraltar in more detail. In this passage from his first book he describes the lack of co-operation he received from Sir Samuel Hoare, himself a former SIS officer.

Secret Sunday

With communications by conventional channels completely severed between London and the Continent of Europe, Britain had once again become an off-shore island and if isolation had its distinct defensive advantages, it was also essential to know what was happening inside Europe. Since I spoke French and Spanish and had lived in those countries, besides having a practical knowledge of the Pyrenees, I had been selected as having more chance of succeeding than a newcomer to those areas.

Concurrently with lines for intelligence from France, I was to endeavour to set going an escape line into Spain for those members of the BEF who had evaded capture by the enemy after Dunkirk and who were beginning to congregate in the south of France, at Marseille. I was to offer guides a fixed fee per head, per man delivered at our Consulate at Barcelona, or elswhere.

Spain, as I was soon to see for myself, was only technically neutral (non-belligerent, to be more accurate) and was in fact under great pressure from Germany. General Franco's ability elegantly to procrastinate had successfully persuaded the German Government that he would cooperate with them, whilst not appearing to do so. The reverse in fact was his more probable intention, but hundreds of Germans and German agents who had been allowed to enjoy the greatest latitude in Spain and continued to do so, saw to it that German war requirements were forthcoming. Their 'emergency' usage of Spanish airfields was a constant cause of worry to the British Admiralty, for Spain had a long Atlantic and an even longer

Mediterranean coastline and attacks on British shipping in Spanish ports and at Gibraltar by Italian naval saboteurs were later to be made with tacit Spanish connivance, though officially 'regretted'.

In 1940 Spain was indeed very much a police state and a foreigner arriving in the frontier zones with France, with the private intention of organising a 'grapevine', would be constantly under surveillance and even if he had, as had I, diplomatic immunity and operated from a British Consulate, his movements could easily be watched and noted. His callers would be liable to arrest and questioning in Gestapo fashion. The only course would be to use trustworthy Spanish nationals, friends of Britain but not opponents of General Franco, who could make contact across the frontier to France.

The possibility of using radio communication for this purpose did occur to me, but first safe communications had to be established before transmitters and codes could be thought of. The outlook was not immediately promising.

After a few days looking round and talking to Embassy colleagues in Lisbon, I discovered that a number of refugee aid organisations were setting up offices there and from the general atmosphere I perceived that it would be from Portugal and not Spain, that British communications with France could best be renewed. I reported my findings to Colonel Dansey, through 4Z who made it known to me that the Colonel believed I should go at once to Spain to inspect the lie of the land and then send in a detailed report. Three days later I boarded the weekly Air France plane (the only alternative was to fly by Luft-Hansa) to Barcelona, landing at Madrid en route. From the air I was able to see something of the devastation caused by the recent Civil War. The environs of the University City at Madrid, the site of many bloody battles, which ebbed to and fro, reminded me of paintings I had seen of Flanders in 1916. Poor Spain, divided and impoverished after three and a half years of an internal war, which unofficially became an international conflict, was now again on the fringe of a world-wide upheaval which seemed almost certain to engulf her! At Barcelona airport, where we landed in the hot summer evening, I at once noticed unusual policing. The customs and passport men were sullen and unmannerly, staring at my diplomatic visa with suspicion. The city itself seemed to have lost its usual colour, noise and gaiety, as if stunned. Even the Ramblas, down which I strolled, had lost their animation and police patrolled up and down. There was a Kafka-like atmosphere of doom hanging over everything, even at the British Consulate General, when I called the following day. The Consul-General, though admitting that he had been informed of my pending arrival, was apprehensive and nervous. He asked me the nature of my business which, naturally, I could not tell him. 'We are constantly watched,' he said. 'You cannot stay here and I shall have to consult the Ambassador in Madrid.'

From the Majestic Hotel I telephoned an old friend, Jorge Taronja, at his office who, after expressing pleasant surprise at hearing my voice, said he would let me know when he could see me, from which I knew he was cautious about telephone eavesdroppers. He left a note at the hotel and that evening I called on him. He told me that things were very 'hot' and I should be careful. I gave him a general idea of what I hoped to do, after which, he said, 'I'll do all I can to help you, but it is not easy for anybody to avoid surveillance.' I explained that I had come to the conclusion that it might be easier to set up an organisation in Lisbon, to which he agreed. 'The Portuguese and Spanish security police are reputed to work closely together. But they despise each other and since the Portuguese are slovenly there is bound to be less vigilance there than here.'

Taronja warned me to burn all my notes in the lavatory pan and to pull the chain, to leave nothing in my suitcases of interest to the 'carrion crows' and always to carry my passport with me, all matters I had already attended to. 'You know where my feelings are,' he said giving me a hug as I left, escorted to the rear door by his clerk.

I called at the Consulate again the next morning when the jittery Consul-General told me coldly that the Ambassador had instructed him to request me to go to Madrid as soon as possible. In view of this situation, as maddening as it was incomprehensible, I took the 'Express' train the next morning. Spain's railway system had been badly crippled during the Civil War and this journey took twelve hours.

My hotel, where I had stayed before, seemed not to have suffered badly during the Civil War and to have survived occupation by foreign journalists, many of whom, in the bar, had compiled their 'reports from the front'. When I sat down in the restaurant, the head waiter came up with the meagre menu and he must have been advised of my arrival by the reception desk, since he said in a low voice 'Dichosos los ojos! I don't advise the soup, Sir, but the meat is good and is not horse.' His first words meant 'It does my eyes good to see you.' He only spoke to me formally after that.

The next morning I went to the British Embassy to call on Sir Samuel Hoare, who received me immediately. In the quiet of his office he told me nervously, 'You have come at a most embarrassing moment. You know that Colonel Martin and his secretary were expelled from Spain last night and you must leave as soon as I can arrange it.' Nonplussed I told him that I had never heard of Colonel Martin, to which he replied, 'Of course not. I didn't expect you would admit to knowing him'. I was at a loss to know how to deal with this scared man, whose political career had hardly inspired me in the past nor was to do so in the years to come, now in his capacity as Ambassador. He told me he regretted that all the spare beds in the Embassy were occupied but 'we can have something made up on the billiard table'! I told him I was staying at a hotel in the Castellana to which he replied, 'You cannot stay in a hotel. You must realise Madrid is a most dangerous place, particularly since this Colonel Martin scandal.'

I said I would prefer to say in the hotel and left his office feeling stymied. This reception certainly bore out my feeling that Lisbon and not Madrid would be more suitable for my operations. Although I was prepared to meet difficulties, I had expected them to be raised in Spanish, not British quarters! Sir Samuel told me that he had arranged for me to leave by road for Lisbon with a diplomat the next morning and I felt that he would be surprised if I were not murdered in my bed in the meantime.

I had not been murdered when the diplomat came to collect me the next morning.

The long journey through sun-parched Extremadura seemed endless and I was glad when we reached the Portuguese frontier at Elvas. The villages of Portugal, through which we then passed, with pleasant-looking people in the streets and cafes, contrasted strangely with the sad, dejected aspect of those I observed in Spain. I felt I had been right in my assessment of that country as unsuitable at that time for clandestine activities and that night I signalled to Colonel Dansey briefly, 'Returned Lisbon, letter follows'. The next day I enjoyed compiling that report, in which I did not mince my words. I felt certain that I had been royally railroaded by Sir Samuel, under the cover of the curious 'Colonel Martin' affair. There was to be a sequel to this story.

One afternoon late in 1940, I was bidden to our Embassy at Lisbon and wondering what this summons could mean, I went to the old mansion on the hill in the Lapa district. There I was told that Sir Samuel Hoare, on a brief visit to Lisbon from Madrid, wanted to see me and I was shown up to the glassed-in verandah where, on an antique sofa, he awaited me and bade me sit beside him. He was most effusive, as if greeting a long-lost friend, asked me about my affairs and how things were progressing. I told him everything was going very well but gave no details. He smiled and tapping my thigh with his grey cotton-gloved hands, assured me of his wish to cooperate in any way he could, within the confines of his diplomatic status. Feeling sickened by his insincerity and irritated by his gloved hand, I thanked him and to avoid yet further protestations on his part, took my leave.

Sir Samuel had clearly received a rocket from London for his performance over the 'Martin' affair, which had put paid to our plans in Spain.

Airey Neave

'Cover names' were often designed to protect intelligence departments against the curiosity of their rivals. If more time had been spent on the security of agents in the field than on internecine squabbles, fewer tragedies would have occurred.

Wounded during the bitter fighting for Calais in 1940, Lieutenant Airey Neave of the Royal Artillery was taken to hospital in Lille as a prisoner of war, and it was from there that he made his first escape bid. It was unsuccessful and he was transferred to Oflag IXa, a camp at Spangenburg near Kassel. From there he was moved to a camp at Thorn in Poland where he made a second escape, this one lasting just four days before being ended by the Gestapo.

In May 1941, following a period of detention, he was sent to Oflag IVc, a special camp for persistent escapers better known as Colditz Castle. From here, on his second try, he made it to the Swiss frontier in just four days. He arrived in Switzerland in January 1942 but he had to wait for a further three months before he was sent down an escape route through Vichy France to Spain, despatched by the British military attaché in Berne. Neave was unimpressed by the arrangements. 'It was all very well to have read Phillips Oppenheim. This was the real thing, and it seemed dangerously amateur. I had read Somerset Maugham's *Ashenden*, the master [fictional] British spy in Switzerland during the First World War. Surely he had been more professional?'

When he finally reached London he was invited to join MI9, the War Office organization created to brief soldiers on what to expect as prisoners of war. Through his own experience Neave knew that in addition to MI9, which also interrogated returning escapees, there was a separate organization run by SIS which managed the escape lines, but in his memoirs he implies that Donald Darling, who was an SIS officer, was actually MI9.

After the war Neave joined the prosecution staff at the Nuremberg war crimes trials, and in 1953 was elected the Conservative MP for Abingdon. He attained ministerial office in the Air Ministry, but was assassinated by an Irish nationalist terrorist group as he emerged from the Palace of Westminster underground car park in 1979, shortly before Mrs Thatcher's first General Election victory. Neave had been a close confidant of the Conservative leader and had been tipped to become her Secretary of State for Northern Ireland.

In his memoirs Neave recalls the reception he received in London after his escape from Colditz, and his introduction to MI9.

Saturday at MI9

When Woollatt and I reached Glasgow, no one seemed to believe we had really escaped from Germany. Our scruffy uniforms did not inspire confidence, and our attitude to authority was irreverent. We were constantly interrogated by the Military Police, who could not understand who we were. That evening they took us before a sallow, drooping, full Colonel dressed in a 'British Warm', from whom we demanded passes for the train to London.

'How do I know you are not enemy agents?' he said. 'Where are your papers?'

I produced a document signed by Donald Darling in Gibraltar and was grudgingly released.

When we reached Euston next morning it was raining hard. At the Station Hotel we breakfasted off toast with the consistency of flannel and the weakest tea.

Oh for the flat on the Quai Rive Neuve at Marseille and the cuisine of Madame Nouveau!

What was happening to these gallant people? And the girl in Annemasse who looked like Joan of Arc?

Our orders were to go to the Great Central Hotel at Marylebone for interrogation. So we took a taxi and found more Red Caps, sandbags and even bayonets. Had we really escaped? Or was I still dreaming in my two-tiered wooden bed at Colditz?

Before the war, the Great Central Hotel held a strong attraction for me. Not that there was any romantic experience to record – a drink or two, a hilarious bath at four o'clock in the morning before taking a milk train from Marylebone in white-tie and tails.

I was drawn to the magnificent dullness and solidity of the hotel. I liked the brass bedsteads, the marble figures on the stairs and the massive afternoon tea. Outside this refuge my young world was threatened by Hitler. Inside, I could pretend that I belonged to a safer age.

We were directed to the reception desk where two years before a splendid blonde in black had been on guard.

Now there was a sergeant at the desk.

'What is this place, sergeant?'

'The London Transit Camp, sir.' He studied me politely. 'Where are you from, sir?'

'Germany.'

He did not bat an eyelid.

'Quite so, sir. Then it will be MI9 you want. They are on the second floor.'

I climbed the wide stairs, with my cheap suitcase, still feeling I was a prisoner arriving at a new camp. The corridors were stripped and bleak. Everywhere I could hear the sound of typewriters and the bustle of troops in transit.

I entered what had been a large double-bedroom, which now served as an office for the interrogation of returned escapers by MI9. In place of the brass bedsteads were trestle tables and wire baskets. For half an hour, I gloomily watched the rain falling in Marylebone Road, and the mist obscuring the distant barrage balloons.

I wanted to get home. I had telephoned my father from Euston. He was shaving at the time and could think of little to say.

An earnest captain in the Intelligence Corps began to interrogate me. He was vastly interested in my 'Colditz story' and he would have kept me there much longer had I not shown my impatience. My adventures were taken down and reduced to War Office language. I could hardly recognise them. The account was far less exciting than a report by the CID on their observation of a public convenience.

He showed me the report he had written of my first escape from Stalag XXa at Thorn in April 1941 and my arrest and interrogation by the Gestapo.

It read as if I had been summoned for riding a bicycle without a rear light.

How the British glory in understatement!

Only the reference to a 'rubber truncheon' suggested something out of the ordinary.

I pretended not to care. I was young and lucky. The rubber truncheon had remained on the wall of the Gestapo office. But there was nothing to convey the sheer terror of being in their hands.

Then came a bald account of my escape from Colditz. How I 'entrained' at Leipzig and crossed the Swiss frontier. Luteyn and I had 'entrained' with a senior SS officer who offered us a place in his reserved compartment as 'Dutch allies' and 'detrained' at Ulm when we escaped from the German Railway police. These MI9 reports gave to high adventure the style of a Government circular.

The interrogation officer wanted me to continue with my story. Slowly he dragged the information out of me. Later I was to interrogate many returned prisoners myself and it was often very difficult to make them talk.

Writing of Charles II of England and his six weeks on the run after the battle of Worcester in 1651, Richard Ollard remarks that this great adventure became the central episode in the King's career.

It was his principal topic of conversation in after years.

In a modern comparison, Mr Ollard writes:

'People who have worked in resistance movements or prisoners-of-war do not care to dwell on their experiences. What is thrilling to the reader was frightening to the man he is reading about.'

This is profoundly true. The men, often very young, had been exposed to the feeling of being hunted, sometimes for several months. They hated this cross-questioning and a desire to sublimate their anxiety, added to the rather soulless War Office system, did not allay their fears. The shock of arrival, after weeks of danger and excitement, at the hideous Great Central Hotel increased their reticence.

Like King Charles too, in his flight from Boscobel to France, no man escapes without helpers and like the King, they never forgot the people who hid them at certain risk of execution. But in one's gratitude one was often afraid to give them away or to compromise them.

I was asked for the names of Pat O'Leary's organisation.

'They told me not to give their names.'

'Oh, we know them. We just want to confirm them for our records,' said the Intelligence Officer unconvincingly.

Reluctantly I gave him the names, not knowing which were code-names and which were real. For that May morning I knew nothing of the problems of MI9, of the need to learn more about the escape lines and to check the stories of suspicious arrivals.

'Captain Langley is waiting downstairs,' said the Intelligence Officer. 'He says you know him.'

I picked up my shabby suitcase, impatient to be gone, and went to the ground floor of the hotel in time to see Hugh Woollatt wave goodbye. I never saw him again.

A man was sitting in the lounge, now described as an Officers' Mess. It had awful brown armchairs and a coloured photograph of the King on the wall. I looked at my watch. It was eleven o'clock and the bar was still closed. When should I be allowed home to my family at Ingatestone in Essex?

I wanted to get the homecoming over and done with and then get back to London to make up for time lost. Besides the pleasures of the city, I had a list of relatives of fellow-prisoners to visit. In a moment of supreme confidence, I had collected them the night before my escape from Colditz.

The officer got up from his armchair, a small, moustached Captain in Coldstream Guards uniform with two decorations. He had lost his left arm, and the empty sleeve was sewn neatly to his tunic.

Jimmy Langley! Surely he was still in France?

Twenty months before, in the summer of 1940, I had been brought with other wounded from Calais to the Faculté Catholique, a school in Lille, converted into a hospital for British prisoners-of-war. A sombre, red-bricked affair with stone floors and a smell of wounds and disinfectant.

I could see Langley, pale and strained, playing cards in one of the wards. I remembered his high forehead and bright eyes as he sat on his bed dressed in a tattered shirt and trousers. Three months after our capture we were still in our bloodstained uniforms.

It astonished me that after the amputation of his arm, Langley had been able to escape from Lille. He had been put in touch with a shadowy organisation called the 'Institut Mozart' late in 1940 who aided his flight from the hospital and took him to Paris. He was then escorted over the demarcation line to unoccupied France. In the spring of 1941, the Vichy Armistice Commission declared him unfit for 'all future military service' and he was repatriated over the Spanish frontier by train.

Nubar Gulbenkian

There is nothing like a bold front when faced with adverse circumstances.

Often described in the press as the richest man in the world, Nubar Gulbenkian was an unlikely candidate for a secret agent, but his strongest asset was his diplomatic status. His father, Calouste Gulbenkian, the founder of the Anglo-Iranian Oil Company, was the Iranian ambassador in Vichy, a fact that allowed the diplomat's son to travel with the rank of commercial attaché to and from France's unoccupied zone without restriction. Accordingly Donald Darling, the SIS officer responsible for representing P15 in Lisbon, routinely used him as his courier, maintaining contact with the Allied escape lines.

It was because Gulbenkian was such an improbable secret agent that he was so successful. On every mission he was accompanied by his valet and became renowned for flourishing 500-dollar notes. He was later to remark that even his recruitment into SIS, by Captain Eddie Hastings while out cub hunting with the Old Berkeley near Bletchley Park, had been unorthodox.

Educated at Harrow, Bonn University and Trinity College, Cambridge, Gulbenkian was called to the Bar by the Middle Temple but devoted much of his life, as did his father, to the oil business, in which he was hugely successful. His first mission, after being briefed in Lisbon by Darling, was to travel, via Barcelona, to Perpignan where he made contact with a P15 agent, a garage proprietor, who was later to convey dozens of evaders across the French frontier.

In his memoirs, which were published seven years before his death in January 1972, Gulbenkian is discreet in identifying his SIS case officer only as 'Didi' which, to the *cognoscenti*, is recognizable as Donald Darling's initials. Note here the colourful version of the Venlo incident.

Pantaraxia

One day in the autumn of 1939 when I was out cub-hunting I saw at the covert-side a newcomer to the Hunt; I recognized his horse; he had hired it from a local Irish dealer friend of mine. He also had his spurs on upside-down; I remarked on this and started talking to him.

It came out that his name was Captain Eddie Hastings and he was stationed at Bletchley, a large country-house which had belonged to Lady Leon and had been taken over by the Government – for hush-hush work, it was said. No one knew exactly what went on there and everyone who did work there was very secretive about it. Captain Hastings was no exception; he was friendly, an agreeable conversationalist, but the model of discretion in his references to Bletchley. I told him of my difficulties in finding anyone who would let me do something for the war effort, of how eager and determined I was and how frustrated by official rejections.

'It seems there's always something not quite right,' I said. 'For one reason or another my Armenian origin goes against me.'

Captain Hastings nodded sympathetically. 'I know how you feel,' he said. 'I was talking to an Austrian the other day who has met the same kind of thing as you have. He felt pretty annoyed about it, too. He said he didn't see why he should be held responsible for being born in a particular bed in a particular place.'

After hunting I mentioned Captain Hastings to a friend, who said he knew him and quite a lot about the work he was doing at Bletchley. As soon as Hastings himself reached home I was on the phone to him. Without revealing my source of information, I told him what I had found out about him. He seemed impressed. We met a few times during the months that followed and he introduced me to others who worked with him at Bletchley, and a most interesting crowd they were. One was known as 'Christopher', another as 'Punch', a third as 'Uncle'. 'Punch' took me to lunch at the Thatched House Club at the bottom of St James's Street and discussed my feelings about the war very fully with me, enquiring about my past experience and what efforts I had made to join the orthodox services. 'Uncle' gave me lunch at Brown's Hotel and, wartime or no wartime, an excellent lunch it was. He suggested I should go to Berlin to see what I could find out. My cover story would be that I was there to sell oil from Iraq which could be shipped by neutral tanker, ostensibly to Rotterdam or some other neutral port, while destined in fact for Germany.

But this projected trip came to nothing when it was recognized that the Germans were neither fools nor squeamish in dealing with those who tried to outwit them. The newspapers at the time reported the misfortune which befell an English agent who had gone to Germany. It had been arranged that English colleagues in Holland should drive to the Dutch-German frontier to pick him up there on his way back from Berlin. Unfortunately, the Germans had already heard of the plan. The English-men drove, as arranged, to the Dutch frontier and went freely up to the customs post. The returning agent stepped forwards to meet them and the Germans pounced on the whole bunch. A Dutch Customs official who tried to protest was shot dead and the Germans carried off, back into Germany, a very important agent.

I learned later for myself just how thorough the German Secret Service could be. In that first autumn of 1939, I took a weekend off from London, spending it in Luxembourg. I went down along the Moselle to the point where the lines of French and German troops facing each other ended and motored through Luxembourg and on to Brussels. I was absent from London only two or three nights in all and was very quiet about my trip when I returned home. My journey had nothing to do with anyone else; but I travelled in my own name and signed my own name at the hotels. Soon after the Germans took over Paris in the middle of June 1940, the *Kommandantur* sent for my brother-in-law, Kevik Essayan.

'What,' they wanted to know, 'was your brother-in-law, Nubar Gulbenkian, doing in Brussels last autumn?' Of course, he, poor fellow, had never heard of my being there and said so quite truthfully to the Germans, but it took him some little time to convince them of his ignorance.

Although I did not attempt the Berlin trip, the Bletchley crowd soon appreciated my potential value, which lay in my special advantages as an official of a neutral legation and as the son of my father. The first gave me a diplomatic passport and a valid official excuse for going to consult with the Iranian Legation in Vichy; this in turn gave me excellent cover for going to Vichy to discuss business affairs with my father. Both in combination provided a first-class two-tier 'cover' for anything else afoot. And so began a phase of my life which bore many resemblances to a Phillips Oppenheim novel.

It was July 1940. France had fallen and the French Government, after being chased round France, had finally settled down in Vichy. My father had intended staying in Paris throughout the war, but had now followed the fleeing French Government down to Vichy; this gave me a convenient and valid excuse for going there. Even so, no one could travel out of England at that time unless he had a very good reason indeed and the reason had to be that the journey was in the national interest. Captain Hastings fixed things for me so that I could take my valet, Bailey, with me. (After leaving my service following his row with my second wife, Bailey had served the Crown Prince of Japan and had made enough money to set himself up in a pub at Ramsgate. When he was compulsorily evacuated from there after the fall of France, he rejoined me, taking my cottage at Weedon in hand with his wife, and allowing me, in effect, to be a guest in my own home. Many an official eyebrow was raised at the idea of my taking a valet with me in wartime, but Hastings justified it on the grounds that if Bailey could not go with me I would not go at all – which made Bailey a 'key person' in the whole operation.)

We travelled down to Bournemouth by car, arriving there in the middle of an air-raid, and then spent a short night at the Royal Bath Hotel before taking off by flying-boat from Poole at the crack of dawn. The flight to Lisbon took some nine hours. We flew down the Channel, well within sight of German-occupied France, but escorted by RAF Blenheims up to a point beyond the Scilly Isles where they peeled off and left us on our own.

We reached Portugal without incident. In the launch which took us from the flying-boat to the quayside, I came face to face with an old friend of my father's, a man I had not seen for years since he had given up his partnership in the firm of Bénard et Jarislowski. It was Jean Monnet, then on his way to America and now, of course, reputed throughout the world as the father of the famous Monnet Plan which has been the base of the whole revival of the French economy since the war.

Lisbon itself was a tragic sight, crowded with refugees from all over

Western Europe, people desperate to get to America. Here, in one place at one moment, was an image of a whole continent in turmoil and fear, a world whose orderly ways had been disrupted as by an earthquake. Terror was written on the faces of these refugees, the imagined terror of what would happen to them should Hitler's hordes catch up with them. Many of the Jewish families had arrived in Rolls-Royces, cars which had cost so much and had represented so much and which were now two a penny: scores of them, it seemed, had been abandoned on the quayside by people whose turn had come for a visa and a passage across the Atlantic to safety. There was, then, nothing more precious that money could buy them and they gladly left behind them the symbols of their former comfort and status in exchange for what they thought was the assurance of life itself.

I booked in for the night in the only place available to me in that overcrowded neighbourhood, a third-rate but very acceptable hotel at Sintra. At dinner in the restaurant that evening I mentioned to the waiter that I was flying on to Spain the next day. His reply was something of a shock. He pointed out three Italians who were enjoying a very jovial dinner, consuming large amounts of wine, and said: 'There is your tribulation. They are going to fly you tomorrow.' Judging from their happy state, I well believed they would indeed be a 'tribulation'. But my Portuguese at that time was rudimentary and the waiter's English was not that good and I found out later that he was translating the word *tripulação*, which is Portuguese for 'crew'.

Next morning, Bailey and I boarded an Italian plane bound for Madrid and Barcelona on its way to Corsica and Rome. On landing at Barcelona we repaired to the Ritz Hotel which, years later, I found to be one of the most comfortable hotels in Europe. But in 1940 conditions in Spain were appalling. Not only were they still staggering from the Civil War, but they were also under pressure to export what they could to their friends, the Germans. Even at the Ritz food was scarce and, to give an example of the way standards had deteriorated, there was a large ink-stain on the carpet of the best suite in the hotel.

One evening, the waiter came to me, beaming with pleasure, and said, 'Oh, señor, good news, good news, we have meat tonight, what would señor like?'

'What have you got?'

'Anything the señor would like. What about a fillet steak?'

I ordered a fillet steak and in due course three waiters arrived bearing a huge silver dish with a heater. The cover of the silver dish was removed with a flourish and, lo and behold, as they say, revealed beneath was a succulent and sizzling steak. We had had nothing like it for weeks and I set about it with relish. It was perhaps a trifle sweet but very good. I called the head waiter and asked him whether the steak was the end product of the bullfight that had taken place the day before. He held up his hands in horror.

'Oh, no, señor,' he said, 'a bull would be much too tough – that is a *caballito* – a little horse.'

Roland Rieul

This is a very dangerous game where your life will be continually in jeopardy.

A sergeant in the French army, Roland Rieul was taken prisoner by the Germans in 1940 and spent three years in captivity, including six months at the Henschel aircraft factory at Schoenfeld. After two unsuccessful escape attempts, he broke out of Stalag IIIb at Fürstenberg-an-der-Oder in May 1943 and made his way by train to the village of Besbach where he had a contact in the local school. Having been given shelter, he was escorted to the railway marshalling yards near by and instructed to climb on a train for Italy. He hid in one of the goods compartments and soon afterwards was in Basle. There he reported to the British consulate and was given a warm welcome by Tim Frenken, the consul, to whom he supplied a detailed description of the aircraft factory where he had worked.

Frenken also happened to be the local SIS head of station and once Colonel Cartwright, the British military attaché at the embassy in Berne, had confirmed his credentials, and also that his father was French and his mother British and that his English wife and two children were in England, Rieul was sent to Porrentruy to recover from the rigours of captivity. In July Rieul was taken to the French frontier by Sergeant Cartier, a member of the Swiss Border Police who was in Cartwright's pay, and safely despatched into enemy territory on his first mission to Paris, where he was to establish himself, carry out some minor assignements, and then return to Basle. He travelled by train and upon his arrival stayed with his uncle in Passy who introduced him to a friend who had access to the Ritz Hotel's guest list. As the hotel had been requisitioned for the use of senior German officers this information was regarded as significant, and Rieul returned to Switzerland to report a successful first mission.

Thereafter he made more than two dozen trips back to Paris, crossing the frontier in complete safety under the protection of the Swiss intelligence service with which SIS had reached an accommodation. The Swiss provided the facilities needed for clandestine infiltration into France, consisting of a farm near Boncourt that straddled the border, on condition that each agent report his arrival as soon as he had made the return journey.

At the end of the war Rieul was reunited with his family and they returned home to Paris where they lived until 1960 when, because of his wife's ill health, they moved to the Isle of Wight. Rieul has now retired as director of a fertilizer supply company and lives near Ryde. In this passage from his 1986 book he is told by Frenken – whom he calls 'Frank' – that SIS would prefer to send him to Paris as an agent than send him to England to join the Free French forces.

Soldier into Spy

Porrentruy was a small residential town very near the French border, closely resembling its counterparts in France. Whereas in Basle, Swiss-German is spoken, here one could only hear French coloured by bits of dialect.

René took me across the station square and introduced me to the *patron* of a hotel called Bienvenue des Voyageurs. A young porter took me to my room. It was very pleasant and had a window looking over the square.

I rejoined René in the bar where he stood me a glass of white wine and I said how pleased I felt at the prospect of spending a couple of months in such an attractive spot. My expressions of appreciation were interrupted by the arrival of two Swiss soldiers to whom René also offered a drink. I did not take in their names as I was so intrigued with the contrast of their appearance. They looked like Don Quixote and Sancho Panza, the only difference being that their roles were reversed, for it was the little fat one who wore the stripes. His name turned out to be Sergeant Cartier and it was his duty to be responsible for me throughout my stay at Porrentruy. Any requests or complaints were to be put through him. It was through him, too, that I should have to communicate if I wanted to get in touch with Frank, as all telephone calls direct to the Consulate were forbidden to me, but the sergeant undertook to make contact with me every day.

The time came for René to return to Basle and for the soldiers to take to their powerful motor-cycles. I went into the dining-room where there were only a few people left and had an excellent meal. Then I went out to get a breath of evening air in the deserted streets of this drowsy provincial town. I called in at a *guinguette* decorated with colourful bunting, to have a drink. There I sat and watched the dancers whirling round to the jaunty strains of an accordionist who sat perched high in one corner of the room. In the intervals we were entertained by various Tyrolean turns.

Thus ended the first day of my holiday at the expense of this mysterious 'fairy godmother'.

A few days spent with nothing to do but to eat and sleep soon began to fill out my face again. At mid-day the sergeant always called in for a drink to make sure that all was well and a week had passed before he brought me news of Frank, to the effect that he wished to see me on the following day. I was to take the 9.15 am train and go straight to his house for lunch.

I reached the Bahrfusser Platz almost at the same time that he did. He congratulated me on looking so well and offered me a whisky and water as an apéritif. We then had a very fine lunch and set off for the Consulate, Frank still not having explained why he had sent for me. However, as soon as I was settled in his office, he told me the reason.

'We have now completed our enquiries and I am pleased to tell you that we consider you above suspicion.'

'Thank you very much,' I retorted with some bitterness.

'Don't be offended. We are being subjected all the time to insidious manoeuvres on the part of the enemy and we have to take every possible precaution. So much for that. Now there is something I want to ask you to do for me.'

'Yes, with pleasure, what is it?'

'For reasons which I cannot explain, it's not possible for us to send you back to join up with the Allied Forces in North Africa. Moreover, even if this should become possible some day, in that position you would only be one of a number, whereas if you comply with our request, you could be a hundred times more useful to the Allied cause.'

'What do you mean?'

Frank paused for a long time before replying.

'Would you like to see Paris again?'

'Of course. Nothing would please me more, but how could I?'

'If you will agree to work as a British secret agent, I will send you to Paris. I don't want you to give me your answer now. Go back to Porrentruy and think it over carefully. Then come back and see me in two or three days' time. It's a very serious decision for you to make. You must bear in mind two things; first, this is a very dangerous game where your life will be continually in jeopardy, and secondly, if you accept, you will be rendering an inestimable service to the cause of the Allies who are struggling to free oppressed countries, France among them.'

Two days later I was back again sitting in the self-same chair.

'I accept your proposition on one condition; that I shall be freed from all commitments on the day when the last Boche is driven out of France.'

'I agree to that, I give you my word. I congratulate you on your decision. I think we can do a good job, together. I am going to send you to Paris, where, I'm sorry to say, our previous organisation has been completely wrecked by our opponents. There were too many contacts with the Resistance, which is fatal. Don't forget this when you are there, rule number one is have no contact with resistance groups.'

Frank went on to give me some preliminary tips and then announced that I must report to him every Tuesday and Friday to take a special course with an instructor. He also lent me a thick dossier containing copious information on German methods and organisation.

'Study this very carefully,' he said, 'and make a point of learning the military code system by heart, so that later on, once you have grasped it you will be able to identify at a glance the nature and strength of any enemy unit you may encounter.'

He warned me never to lose sight of the dossier, not to leave it in my hotel room but to take it with me wherever I went, even to the lavatory. I felt a bit dazed by all this and wondered if I hadn't plunged into the deep end a bit too hastily. I began to wonder whether I was up to this job. To learn a code by heart, when I had always had difficulty in memorising anything, was a lot to ask of me at the outset. However, having taken the plunge, I must sink or swim.

I went back to Porrentruy clutching the dossier tightly under my arm for fear someone should attempt to snatch it. It was not until I was safely locked into my hotel room that I dared open it. Then I began studying it page by page and to take in the good advice handed out to Intelligence Service apprentices.

From then on, I spent every morning in my room studying the dossier before parcelling it up and taking it to the dining-room at lunch time. One day, as I sat down to the meal, I took a quick look round the guests and caught sight of a very attractive blonde sitting at a table near the window. Throughout lunch I took an occasional look in her direction and finally managed to catch her eye. Fancying I saw a gleam of encouragement, I could not resist taking my coffee over to her table and saying, 'May I sit down?'

She made no protest, so I took a seat opposite her and embarked on small talk, but I had not been going for more than a couple of minutes, when the waitress passed me a saucer bearing an envelope addressed to 'Mr Roland Fournier'. I looked at it for a moment, thinking it was a mistake. Fournier was not my name, yet the Christian name was right. My hesitation did not escape my new acquaintance.

'Aren't you going to open it?'

Thus pressed, I became aware of a need for caution, so I opened it

454

taking care that she could not read the contents which were printed by hand in minute characters and consisted of three words: 'BEWARE OF ELIANE'.

Just as I was restoring the note to its envelope, my companion commented that I looked worried.

'It's nothing serious, I hope,' she said, in an enquiring tone.

'Yes and no. Just a reminder from the *patron* about my hotel bill.' I was pleased to have found such a prompt and plausible reply, but she had noticed the name on the envelope.

'So your name is Roland.'

'Yes, what's yours?'

'Eliane,' replied my peroxide panther!

That was enough for me. I knew where I stood. Gathering up the packet containing the famous dossier from between my feet, I made a pretext of an imaginary rendezvous at the bar and made a discreet withdrawal from the situation.

I stopped for a moment in the hall to catch the waitress as she went through, to enquire who had given her the letter which she brought to me.

'A customer.'

'Which one?' I asked.

'He's gone.'

At the bar where I ordered another coffee, I asked the barmaid if she knew Eliane and could tell me what she did.

'She's the tart of one of the watch-makers.'

I was no further forward in the matter, but at least, I knew now that I had embarked on my new career.

The next day was Tuesday, so I booked the first train to Basle to begin my course on espionage. Frank received me at his office and after asking me if I was enjoying myself at Porrentruy, he said:

'You must avoid that woman, Eliane. She is a very dangerous enemy spy. She tries to discover the destination to which our agents are bound in enemy territory. Then, by means of a photograph taken clandestinely by her or one of her acolytes, she gets them picked up by the Gestapo on arrival at their territory.'

With this advice, Frank took me into another room and presented me to my tutor, an Englishman with a military look. He was tall and thin, and very fair with a tooth-brush moustache. He was very pleasant to talk to and his course was instructive and interesting. I learnt what information was most vital and what was worthless and a waste of time to transmit.

After my interesting lesson, I spent the afternoon in a cinema before going back to Porrentruy. Days and weeks passed uneventfully. I had learnt my dossier by heart and thanks to my training course, I felt I knew what was expected of a secret agent. Only one incident upset the normal routine. One day wishing to stretch my legs, I left the hotel with my dossier under my arm as usual. I went round the block and was passing the rear of the hotel when I realised that I had left my cigarettes in my room. Using the service entrance, I ran up the four flights of stairs, let myself into the room and searched for the missing packet in the pockets of my coat and other suit. Suddenly, there was a knock at the door and as I happened to be standing just inside, I grabbed the handle and flung it open to find myself faced by a hotel porter, obviously taken aback to find the room occupied. He pulled himself together as much as he could and to explain his presence, he blurted out:

'Excuse me, have you got a light?'

This already seemed a very strange request on the part of a hotel employee. He was to become even more confused for as it so happened, I had just picked up my matches. I struck one, only to find that he was now without a cigarette and had to run off and collect one from his room before being able to take advantage of his premature request!

This marked my second contact with the enemy and this time, I had smelt him out myself. It was mostly due to luck and I had no real justification for being conceited about it, but could not help feeling very pleased to be able to make this incident the subject of my first report.

A few days later, in conversation with Frank, I learnt that my suspicions had been justified, that the porter was indeed an enemy agent but that by that time he was already safely in prison.

'When we came to make enquiries, following your report,' Frank told me, 'we discovered that he was an old lag, wanted by the police, so he won't be troubling us again for a long time!'

Although I was very pleased to hear this, I was never quite sure whether he was really after my dossier or only after my money. Having lived like a lord for five weeks, all the time at the expense of my mysterious Fairy Godmother, I was not at all surprised when the Swiss Sergeant Cartier arrived one day with the instruction that I was to take the dossier back to Basle. There, at the Consulate, Frank informed me that I was to undergo an oral examination that afternoon.

'This will be conducted by a high-ranking colleague of mine from Intelligence Service,' he explained, adding by way of encouragement, 'and if you give a satisfactory account of yourself, you will be registered in London as an official agent.'

My fears were quickly allayed when I saw my examiner. He was English and a young man with a disarming smile and no military pomp. His questions were not so much technical as framed to assess my personality and intelligence. I felt I came through all right, even on questions referring to the technicalities of German methods and administration, but was relieved to hear from Frank a few minutes later that I had been accepted and that application would be made to London straightaway for confirmation of my registration there.

After a few more days of vacation, I was recalled to Basle and told that my departure for Paris was imminent. I listened to a good deal of advice from Frank, warning me, especially, against the danger of getting in touch with 'resistance' groups and to beware of so called 'hidden Allied airmen'. On the other hand, my positive duties were once more impressed on me:

Firstly, I was to form an organisation for the purpose of supplying information at short notice on the strength and movements of German troops in the Paris region.

Secondly, on the day following an air raid, I was to transmit details of 'impact', the damage created and the effect that I estimated they would have on the enemy.

Thirdly, I was to ferret out any information which my espionage training made me deem useful.

John Brown

I had been expressly forbidden by MI6 officials from mentioning what I'd been doing.

After his return to England in 1945 Quartermaster-Sergeant John H. O. Brown of the Royal Artillery was decorated with the Distinguished Conduct Medal, an award that caused some surprise among the British prisoners of war with whom he had shared the previous five years. They remembered him as having often expressed pro-German sympathies and although he had never been a member of the notorious British Free Corps, he had been regarded as more likely to face a court martial when he was back in England than be the recipient of a medal. In reality Brown had undergone a lengthy debriefing at the hands of Len Burt of MI5 as soon as he had been repatriated, and his evidence, together with the secret messages he had succeeded in smuggling out of various German prison camps, ensured that none of those who had collaborated with their captors escaped justice.

The secret of John Brown's duplicity was finally revealed at the Old Bailey trial of Walter Purdy, a renegade Briton who was convicted of broadcasting propaganda for the Nazis. Both he and Tom Cooper, a leading recruiter for the British Free Corps, were sentenced to death after Brown had given damning testimony for the prosecution. Once Brown's role was made public he returned to civilian life and the full details of his extraordinary wartime adventure were only published after his death in 1964, when a manuscript was discovered among his possessions.

Educated at Cambridge and a man of deep religious beliefs, Brown had attended a course of MI9 lectures to prepare him for the possibility of capture. He memorized a simple code to use in his correspondence home and was taught to indicate the existence of a secret message by writing the date in a particular way and by underlining his signature. Scrutiny of the letters upon their arrival in London by British censors enabled those with secret messages to be diverted to MI9 where they were decoded.

Brown had been captured in France at the end of May 1940 with a dozen survivors of his battery. His first camp was Lamsdorf but he volunteered for a work camp at Blechhammer in Upper Silesia where he gathered information and conveyed it to MI9. Later, masquerading as a Nazi sympathizer, he switched to Berlin where he was approved for a special camp, Genshagen, which from June 1943 accommodated potential members of the British Free Corps. Brown was eventually liberated by American troops in April 1945 but was kept in custody as a suspected traitor until MI9 could confirm his credentials. Here Brown describes how, called to the Foreign Office in Berlin, he gained the trust of his Nazi captors.

In Durance Vile

We went by underground train to Potsdamer Platz, and were soon in the wonderful Chancellery building. I was ushered into a splendid room where I was introduced to a Dr Hesse and a Dr Ziegfeld. Dr Hesse told me he had been attached to the German Embassy in London before the war; and I later learned he was on Hitler's personal staff. Ziegfeld would be responsible to the German Foreign Office for Genshagen Camp.

'Mr Brown,' Dr Hesse began, 'we understand from our military authorities that you have been a most reasonable prisoner. You have been selected by us to run a special camp, the first of its kind in Germany. We feel the time has now come for a better English understanding of German policy, so that when we've won the war Englishmen will be more ready to co-operate with us in the struggle against communism.'

'If this is to be a political camp I wish to have nothing whatever to do with it!'

'You can rest assured on that point, Mr Brown. You will in no way be compromised, for we intend that you should be in charge of a genuine holiday camp. You should feel very honoured to be chosen. We have brought you here today to discuss the matter fully, and see if you have any ideas on how to run the camp.'

'What type of entertainment do you have in mind?'

'We hope to get the pick of the German artistes available in Berlin; and to make sure that nothing political is attempted we want you to meet each artiste beforehand and discuss his or her programme.'

'How often will these people be available?'

'Probably once a week.'

'Then I suggest that we get in touch with the YMCA to see if a talkie apparatus can be obtained with films, and also as much sports and games equipment as we can get.'

There was an awkward silence for a moment, then Dr Ziegfeld said, 'For the present we do not wish to have people outside know about the camp.'

'But if it is to be a genuine camp, surely there is nothing to hide – in fact exactly the reverse.'

'Very well then, the YMCA can be contacted.'

'And I think that in a camp of this nature a strong religious side is most important.'

'That is entirely up to you – we have nothing to say either way about that.'

'I think too we ought to have a permanent staff capable of providing good plays, and also have visits of dance and military bands from the other camps, so that we can give a show every night.'

'We are willing to agree to whatever you say. Can you tell us for certain now that you are willing to help us, or are we to send you away? Of course, you cannot go back to Prince Hohenlohe at Blechhammer, for he is now in Italy; and in any case we would not like to have our plans discussed. So it would be necessary to send you somewhere away from other prisoners.'

What a pleasant little threat, I thought; but I had to keep my temper, because if I played my cards correctly I could probably get all I wanted – so long as they thought I knew nothing of the British Free Corps scheme.

'I *am* willing to co-operate with you provided I can get my own staff to run the camp.'

'Are you not satisfied with the men already there?'

'They would not be of any use to me for entertainment or sports purposes.'

Hesse and Ziegfeld hastily conferred in whispers. Then Hesse said to me, 'We are willing to let you have your own staff, but now we must impose a special condition on you. We do not wish you to feel uncomfortable when you are with the German artistes in Berlin, so it is our desire that you should wear civilian clothes when you meet them.'

I could hardly believe my ears; this was too good to be true, though their intention was all to obvious: to compromise me from the very beginning. Whatever happened, I had to be careful not to appear over-eager.

'But it would be quite impossible for me to wear civilian clothes within the camp.'

Dr Hesse smiled slightly. 'You think your men might feel you are working on the German side?'

'It would destroy the idea of the camp being run straight without any attempt at propaganda.'

'Yes, we think you are quite right; and to cover yourself when you are alone in Berlin, we will give you an *Ausweis* [pass] which will be very useful to you. It will say that because you are friendly towards German politics you must be given every consideration, and when shopping must have every priority. It will mean that you will practically have the freedom of Berlin and be able to go where you will and meet whomever you wish, including women. We hope you will enjoy yourself, especially with the women; but do not of course take liberties.'

CHAPTER X

Post-war SIS

Meeting an old friend in a distant country is like finding refreshing rain after a long drought.
Chinese proverb

While the British authorities often suggest that nothing can safely be written about the world of secret intelligence, the reality is that several SIS and MI5 officers, who held senior positions in the post-war organization, have been allowed to go into print. Kenneth Benton, Alec Waugh and David Cornwell (John Le Carré), all former members of SIS, have written about espionage in fictional terms and found fame as thriller writers.

A further group of SIS officers have published books on subjects almost wholly unrelated to their previous occupation. Reading Brian Montgomery's books, for example, would give no clue to anyone except the *cognoscenti* that he had spent almost all his post-war career in SIS. The biographical data supplied by his publishers referred only to his military service. Equally, his chosen subjects of study, biographies of his elder brother the Field Marshal and Sir Shenton Thomas, the governor of Singapore at the Japanese invasion, scarcely betray a consuming preoccupation with intelligence. Ruari Chisholm, once SIS's head of station in Moscow, might also have adopted a retirement career as a historian, for his history of the siege of Ladysmith demonstrated his ability as a writer and researcher. Alas, he was to be struck down by illness while en route to London from his station-commander post in South Africa.

Another striking example of a talented historian to be found in SIS's ranks is that of Donald Prater, once the head of station in Stockholm, whose premature departure from 'the friends' was prompted by the embarrassing discovery that he had once been an active Communist. Nothing in the scholarly tomes that Prater has published even remotely suggests his true undercover role as an SIS officer. Prater's discretion, which may have been enforced by entreaties from his former employers, was certainly not matched by Monty Woodhouse who published his memoirs in 1982.

Another wartime intelligence officer who subsequently switched to SIS during the peace was Goronwy Rees, the Welsh academic and close friend of Guy Burgess, David Footman and Anthony Blunt. Rees's employment was hastily terminated after Guy Burgess's defection, but the closely guarded secret that Rees had worked for SIS was disclosed inadvertently by Malcolm Muggeridge who was mildly embarrassed to see him entering SIS's headquarters. Naturally, Rees's memoirs make no mention of this aspect of his troubled life. Before the war Rees had contributed to the leader column of the *Spectator*, the literary editor of which was Derek Verschoyle, who followed Rees into SIS and spent four years in Italy running clandestine operations, an occupation he omitted subsequently from his entry in *Who's Who*.

Similarly, the biographical details supplied by Charles Ransom hardly betray his life's work in the secret world. Ransom was the retired SIS officer chosen to join Professor Sir Harry Hinsley's team of Cambridge academics commissioned to prepare an official history of British Intelligence during the Second World War. His credentials, as an experienced SIS officer, are omitted from the biographical details which appear on the dustjacket. Hugh Seton-Watson is another author who preferred silence, and none of his many publications reveals his work for SIS which extended from the war into the peace as a consultant. Rather less prolific is Bunny Pantcheff, the SIS officer best known for extracting a confession from Dick Ellis. At the end of the war he investigated atrocities committed in Jersey and Guernsey during the German occupation and much later wrote the definitive account of the occupation of Alderney, where he eventually retired.

Before turning to the individual texts of these skilled intelligence officers, one unique case should be mentioned. Brian T. W. Stewart, SIS's Far East expert who operated in Burma, Hong Kong, the Philippines, Malaysia, Vietnam and China, spent more than three decades compiling an anthology of Chinese proverbs, *All Men's Wisdom*. A superficial study of his monograph, which was published in Hong Kong, might not lead anyone to believe that its author had devoted his career to working for SIS and had hoped to take the top job, yet there are some deliberate *double entendres*. SIS is known within the Allied intelligence community as 'the friends', and on the topic of friendship Stewart has chosen several proverbs which might well be understood to have a relevance to the British Secret Intelligence Service. 'A close friend is a jewel' is the Chinese version of the more familiar English expression 'A true friend is a man's most treasured possession'. Similarly 'Every place is equally delightful when friends are there' and 'Where your friends are there your riches are' could easily be fitting proverbs for an SIS station commander posted to some distant land, far from Whitehall.

Stewart's close colleague in the Far East was John Colvin who had the misfortune to be in Hanoi during the worst of the American bombing and subsequently wrote his autobiography, *Twice Around the World*. No doubt one of the titles on his reading list, before he took up his post in Vietnam, was the definitive study of the region, *The Emancipation of French Indo-China*, written by his SIS colleague Donald Lancaster.

More senior than all these officers, and the single author to boast in print of his position in the Secret Intelligence Service, was George Young, that organization's deputy chief until his decision in 1961 to follow the example of many colleagues and become a City banker. Waugh, Cornwell and Benton had all been Young's subordinates at various times in their SIS careers but none is mentioned by name in any of his books. While Young broke the convention that pretended SIS simply did not exist, he remained discreet about his former colleagues, even those that had also acquired a public persona.

Monty Woodhouse

Every left-wing Greek 'knew for a fact' that I had been sent to Greece in 1942 not to organise resistance but to undermine the 'people's struggle' as an agent of British imperialism, which meant the Foreign Office, the Intelligence Service and the City. I had a naive faith that if I steered clear of public life, these accusations would go away.

After a brilliant war with Greek guerrillas, operating in enemy-occupied territory for SOE, Woodhouse reopened SIS's Athens station and later joined SIS's post-war War Planning Directorate, preparing stay-behind networks across western Europe in anticipation of a Soviet invasion.

The younger son of Lord Terrington, he was educated at Winchester and New College, Oxford where he was awarded a double first. Commissioned as a gunner in 1939 he was recruited into SOE to train agents at the Special Training School at Haifa but was selected to join Operation Harling, a daring scheme to blow up a strategically important viaduct on the railway line used by the Germans to resupply Rommel. The plan was executed in November 1942 and Woodhouse remained in Greece to organize local partisans.

After the war Woodhouse was appointed secretary-general of the international commission supervising the Greek general election, and in 1946 he returned home to work in industry.

In 1951 he moved to the SIS station in Iran to supervise an ambitious scheme to remove Prime Minister Mussadeq from power. Codenamed Operation Boot, the plan was given Anthony Eden's approval after Woodhouse, accompanied by Robert Zaehner and George Young, had briefed him. Based in Cyprus, because of broken diplomatic relations, Woodhouse masterminded the coup in August 1953 and paved the way for the CIA to replace Mussadeq. One unforeseen development was the sudden flight of the young Shah, but he was quickly persuaded to return home from his refuge in Rome.

After Woodhouse's retirement from SIS he was elected Tory MP for Oxford, but lost his seat in 1966, only to recover it in 1970. He attained office in the Ministry of Aviation and the Home Office and retired from Parliament in September 1974. He has written extensively on Greece and his own account of his behind-the-lines adventures, *Apple of Discord*, was published in 1948.

In 1982 Woodhouse released his memoirs, *Something Ventured*, in which he recalled candidly his role in Boot and gave an entertaining account of how he had delayed relaying a signal from Tehran to Washington so as to give the CIA's revolution crucial additional time to rally its forces on the street in the face of stiff resistance from Mussadeq's Communist supporters. In this passage he describes his visit to Egypt in 1951 while undertaking a tour of SIS stations in the Middle East prior to taking up his post as head of station in Tehran.

Something Ventured

Soon afterwards it was settled that I should go to Tehran. On the way I spent a few weeks in other parts of the Middle East – Egypt, Cyprus, Lebanon and Turkey – to acclimatize myself afresh. It was a different world from the one I had known. Cairo had an especially changed aspect. All the British uniforms had disappeared into the Suez Canal Zone, but the surface of life seemed still intact. Shepeard's Hotel, where I spent my first few nights, was unchanged. So was the Gezira Sporting Club, where I lunched with Egyptian friends on the day after my arrival. But Shepeard's was soon to be burned to the ground, and Gezira went rapidly downhill.

My Egyptian friends were also in a mood of depression. Their conversation at lunch was a kind of threnody on Anglo-Egyptian relations. The British Embassy had once been the focus of social and intellectual life in Cairo, but now they no longer wanted to go there. It seemed that all the stories of decline centred upon the late Head of

Chancery, one Donald Maclean, whom I had never heard of. Mercifully he had already left Cairo, but the harm done by his reputation for drunken violence and insulting behaviour would not be forgotten for years.

Maclean had finally been sent home with what was called a nervous breakdown, and then rather oddly appointed head of the American Department in the Foreign Office. Some years later I met his Ambassador, by then retired, who told me that he had never had the slightest inkling that Maclean was anything but an admirable Head of Chancery. He seemed to think his own state of ignorance disposed of all the complaints, but I thought it made them worse.

As I left the club after lunch, I stopped to glance at the ticker-tape board in the hall. The date was 7 June. A three-line paragraph recorded, without comment, that two members of the Foreign Service had vanished. One of the names was familiar and notorious: I could believe anything of Guy Burgess. The other name was unfamiliar at first, but faintly rang a bell. When and where I heard of Donald Maclean before? Of course: at lunch ten minutes earlier. For the next few months I was to hear of very little else.

Both names came up again in Istanbul, where I was staying a month later with a friend in the Consulate-General. He drove me around in a jeep inherited from his predecessor, Kim Philby. Philby's name had not yet become famous, but the jeep was already a link in the Great Spy Mystery, for attached to the dashboard on the passenger's side was a short length of rope on a strong metal hook. It had been fitted there, I was told, when Burgess was visiting his friend Philby, so that he could hang on to it when rounding sharp corners, for he was seldom sober.

It would be interesting to know what Philby and Burgess talked about in their days together in Istanbul. Perhaps they chuckled over the fate of the British agents whom they had betrayed to the Soviet secret police. Later they were to meet again in Washington, where Philby gave the warning of impending discovery which enabled Burgess and Maclean to escape. By the time I grasped Burgess's length of rope on the jeep in Istanbul, he was already in Moscow, though the fact was not admitted until much later.

I spent only a week in Turkey, which was almost ceasing to be part of the Middle East. The Turks and the Greeks were on unusually good terms: both had taken part in the Korean War, both were being admitted to the Council of Europe and NATO. The United States' largest aircraft-carrier at anchor in the Bosphorus was a symbol of security and stability. When it performed the elegant manoeuvre of turning round by lining up all its aircraft on one side of the flight-deck and starting up their engines, the Turks were delirious with admiration. They even liked the Greeks for a time. I witnessed a parade of troops returning from Korea in which a Greek-speaking battalion marched as a unit.

Tehran, where I arrived in the middle of August, was a very different case, already on the brink of catastrophe. Negotiations with the AIOC [Anglo-Iranian Oil Co.] had finally broken down. The ill wind blew me a little good, since a comfortable house prepared for the negotiating delegation was empty and ready for me to take over, fully furnished and staffed. The house stood on the edge of the desert, north of Tehran, though like the house where we spent our honeymoon at Maroussi, it has long since been swallowed up in the expanding suburbs.

The Shah's father had decreed that no camels were to be allowed through the city, because he wanted Tehran to be more like Paris and he had been told that there were no camels in Paris. So the caravan routes passed round the edge of the desert. During many nights I heard the tinkle of their bells passing my house, and I was grateful to the old Shah. On some mornings I found merchants from central Asia camped beside my front gate. My children learned to ride camels before they ever sat on a pony.

My family joined me in October, just as the last of the AIOC withdrew from Iran, leaving the great refinery at Abadan idle and the oil wells practically out of production. A Minister in the Labour government, Richard Stokes, had come out to try to re-start negotiations, but with no success. On his return to London he made the unlucky remark in a speech that 'the grass is growing in the streets of Abadan'. That would have been one of the most startling miracles even in a region of miracles. But the idea of desolation which he wanted to convey was correct.

There seemed to be no prospect of a solution to the deadlock. To make matters worse, both Britain and the United States were very inadequately represented at this time of crisis. The British Ambassador, a dispirited bachelor dominated by his widowed sister, had been sent to Tehran for a rest after an arduous time elsewhere. The American was a business tycoon whom I had previously encountered in Greece. He was known (at any rate to his wife) as 'President Truman's trouble-shooter', which meant that he was being rewarded for his contributions to the Democratic Party. Fortunately he was soon replaced by an able career diplomatist, Loy Henderson, and he went off to shoot trouble elsewhere.

Musaddiq was riding high at the time, though with little sense of direction. About the time I arrived, he lodged a complaint against the

British government at the United Nations Security Council. The British government retaliated by bringing a case against Iran before the International Court. In New York Musaddiq had a personal triumph, though the Security Council decided to take no action pending the hearing at the International Court.

His popularity was enormous with the mobs in Tehran and other cities, where the Tudeh Party helped his own followers in organizing mass demonstrations, though with very different aims. He dominated the royal family, and forced first the Queen Mother and then Princess Ashraf to leave the country. Early in 1952 he closed all the British consulates. When the British Ambassador left, he publicly refused to accept his proposed successor – an insult without precedent. He wept and fainted in the midst of hysterically passionate speeches. He was the first great actor in the history of Iran. The Soviet Embassy loved him as much as the public.

'*C'est un pays où tout est toujours à refaire,*' the French military attaché told me when I asked him what Iran was like. In general he was right. Exceptions were those things which could not be done again because they had never been done at all, such as the water-supply and drainage system of Tehran. Excellent water flowed out of the mountains north of Tehran and through the city down open ditches known as *joobs* (from the Persian *jooi-ab* or water-course). So the rich people at the north end had good drinking water, and then used the *joobs* as their drains. The middle classes in the centre bought drinking water from travelling water-carts, and likewise used the *joobs* as drains. The slum-dwellers at the south end just had to use the *joobs* for both purposes.

A British firm of consulting engineers had been commissioned to install a modern system of water-supply and drainage. The pipes had been delivered and lay alongside the main streets, serving no purpose except as temporary housing for the homeless. The pipes could not be laid because the government had run out of money. This was naturally blamed on the imperialists, though the AIOC were almost the only people who regularly paid their taxes as well as the oil royalties.

Musaddiq then had a brilliant idea. Could not the total cost be halved by laying only one set of pipes, and using them to carry water by day and sewage by night? The consulting engineers thought not. All this was grist to the mill of the Tudeh Party. Everyone except themselves could be blamed for the hopeless situation. With such a social and political system, it was hardly necessary for the Soviet Embassy to waste any money on propaganda. The only member of the ruling class with a social conscience appeared to be the Shah. He was even trying to sell the royal estates to the peasants at knock-down prices. But Musaddiq, being a large land-owner himself, thought this a bad example.

I was convinced from the first that any effort to forestall a Soviet *coup* in Iran would require a joint Anglo-American effort. The Americans would be more likely to work with us if they saw the problem as one of containing Communism rather than restoring the position of the AIOC. Although some representatives of American oil companies seemed to be circling like vultures over Iran, American officials were inclined to be more co-operative. Averell Harriman, a roving Ambassador of great experience, had been associated with Stokes's negotiating mission. Loy Henderson changed the atmosphere in the US Embassy towards sympathy with the British case.

One of the Embassy officials who had already anticipated the change of his own accord was the head of the mission from the Central Intelligence Agency. He was a second-generation American of French descent, so he was both bilingual and quick to grasp a European viewpoint. The CIA was still a youthful organization which had a high regard for its British counterpart, although its confidence in us had naturally been shaken by the defection of Burgess and Maclean. I soon realized that liaison with my CIA colleague could be the key to success.

My own assets when I took up a nominal post in our Embassy were considerable, but demoralized by the setbacks of the past year. Three or four able young men in the Embassy specialized in intelligence on Iran and the Communists. Another cultivated leading Iranians who were hostile to Musaddiq. Another conducted a useful liaison, approved by the Shah, with the chief of the Security Police, who was well informed about the Tudeh Party.

The most striking figure of all was Robert Zaehner, later Professor of Eastern Religions at Oxford, who had arrived in the Embassy only a few weeks before me. He had worked in Tehran during the war, and acquired excellent contacts which he was now cultivating afresh. One was with a Swiss, Ernst Perron, who had formerly been the Shah's tutor and was still a close friend. Another was with a family of wealthy merchants, whose two leading figures were known to us simply as 'the Brothers'. It was through Zaehner also that I acquired the services of a young Parsee from Bombay, who had been a schoolfellow of the Shah. Although at the time his employment was humble, he later rose to fame through his services to Anglo-Iranian relations as Sir Shapur Reporter.

It was the Brothers who were to be the keystone of our plans. They had worked with Zaehner against the Germans and had kept their organization in good repair. Apart from their wealth, they had skills in two directions: they could influence opinions in the Majlis and the bazaars; and more important, they could mobilize street mobs, which were a powerful force in Iranian politics. Popular demonstrations often swayed political events in Tehran, but in recent years, thanks to the Tudeh Party and the Ayatullah Kashani, they had been effectively used to swing them against the West.

At first I was doubtful about using the Brothers, but gradually I became convinced that it would be possible to exploit the same popular forces in support of western policies. But there were difficulties. One was that the Brothers were strongly anti-American, while I was convinced that we needed American support. Another was that I had no direct contact with the Brothers, nor did I ever meet them: at least on the one occasion I did so, I was not aware of it. Liaison with them was the preserve of Zaehner, who was responsible to the Foreign Office, not to me.

It was an anomaly that the idea of organizing the downfall of Musaddiq was first formulated by the Foreign Office itself rather than entrusted to its so-called Friends. Still stranger was the fact that it was launched under a Labour government. But Herbert Morrison, like Ernest Bevin before him, was a pugnacious Foreign Secretary. Quite apart from sanctioning Zaehner's subversive activities. Morrison was willing to use force to recover the AIOC's rights and property, especially the great new refinery at Abadan.

George Young

It is doubtful whether the British intelligence interest is best served by maintaining the somewhat battered convention that SIS does not exist.

George Kennedy Young was a big bear of a Scot with a gruff manner that belied his intellectual prowess. After graduating from St Andrews University he studied at Giessen, Dijon and Yale, and went to work as a reporter on the *Glasgow Herald*. In 1940 he received a commission in the King's Own Scottish Borderers and saw action in East Africa where he was mentioned in despatches. Thereafter his proficiency in languages, which had won a double first at St Andrews, brought him into the Secret Intelligence Service which, after the invasion of Italy, opened a small branch in Bari to oversee its operations into Yugoslavia and Poland.

At the end of the war Young was posted to Vienna where he became the first post-war SIS head of station in the quadripartite city, liaising closely with his SIS colleagues at Klagenfurt where the British military base had been established. It was in Austria that Young saw the Cold War at close quarters, and handled Soviet defectors and the other flotsam of the intelligence conflict. After a three-year tour in Vienna Young returned to Broadway Buildings to head an economic intelligence unit, designated R8 and known as Economic Requirements, the principal objective of which was to identify certain industrial commodities that the Soviets were obliged to purchase on the world market. The intention was to monitor their production and, if it became necessary, intervene to deny them to the Eastern Bloc. This was a contingency plan that had failed to work against the Nazis who had continued to receive Swedish iron ore and Romanian oil after war had been declared in 1939. Young's plan was to ensure that in the event of hostilities key minerals would be denied to the Kremlin, thereby handicapping the Soviet military machine.

Two years later Young was appointed Controller, Middle East, and took a central role in the planning of Operation Buccaneer, a scheme to seize the assets of the Anglo-Iranian Oil Company which Mussadeq nationalized in 1951. It was rejected by the Cabinet, but within a few months the conditions had changed. Young had been promoted to vice-chief by Sir John Sinclair, and Britain had elected a new administration. The discarded Operation Buccaneer now became Boot and, with help from the CIA, was to prove a success, but only just. At a vital moment the US State Department lost its nerve and decided to abandon the project in mid-coup. However, all the CIA's communications to Tehran were being routed through the SIS station in Cyprus and Young engineered a delay so that the recall signal reached the agents in Iran only after Mussadeq had been overthrown and the Shah re-established.

Young always believed he was destined for the top, especially as his chief, Sir John Sinclair, had asked Anthony Eden, the Foreign Secretary, for permission to take early retirement. Young's hopes of succeeding him were dashed when Buster Crabb, a freelance diver, was killed while on a clandestine mission, specifically prohibited by the Prime Minister, against a visiting Soviet warship. A secret enquiry laid the blame on an unfortunate set of coincidences but, for the sake of the politicians, Sinclair agreed at least to appear to be a scapegoat. However, instead of appointing Young, Eden moved Sir Dick White from the Security Service into the chief's office. Young realized that even though he was five years younger he would never take the helm, and that in any event White would probably veto him. Disillusioned, he moved into merchant banking in 1961 and joined Kleinwort Benson. Significantly, his first book was entitled *Masters of Indecision: An Inquiry into the Political Process*, but he also wrote what is widely regarded as the standard textbook on merchant banking in London.

Young also moved into the political arena, considerably influenced by his wife Geryke who came from the Dutch East Indies and held strongly right-wing views. Although he stood unsuccessfully for Parliament in 1974 and was active in the Monday Club, he never held elected office. In this extract from *Subversion and the British Riposte* Young recalls Macmillan's distaste for a morsel of intelligence brought to him by SIS.

Subversion and the British Riposte

The Special Intelligence Service (SIS) which emerged from the Second World War, reorientated in 1945–46 to take on the Soviet challenge, was a well-trained corps speaking every known tongue and a few unknown ones, experienced in separating fact from forgery, and with specialist qualifications in the professional crafts ancient and modern. Fortunately Major General Stewart Menzies, its wartime chief, remained in the saddle until 1952, during the general rundown of defence and military organisations.

His successors benefited for at least a decade from his methods and influence. But it is doubtful whether the British intelligence interest is best served by maintaining the somewhat battered convention that SIS does not exist. Apart from Ministerial admissions to Parliament on several occasions over the Philby, Crabb and Blake affairs, its existence, its leading personnel and its general organisation are known to the intelligence services of NATO Allies and friendly powers, and as a result of the Philby and Blake defections, to the Russians. The 'D' Notice system, under which the Ministry of Defence notifies editors not to mention identities and locations connected with intelligence work, with the warning that to do so *may* lead to prosecution under the Official Secrets Acts, has long since broken down, and indeed since Communist journalists soon learn about the notices, the procedure is meaningless. Failures and scandals of the 'clandestine' services thus receive full publicity, while their successes go unrecognized.

And when British governments are pursuing 'know nothing' policies, it is not easy to be their eyes and ears. Clear policy objectives aid purposeful and discriminating intelligence gathering. Muddled thinking means muddled intelligence work. An advancing army collects its information as it advances, by obliging the adversary to reveal his hand in his reactions to initiatives forced upon him. When an army is static or retreating, the generals can only guess what is on the other side of the hill. Nor are the civil servants who are the first formulators of policy papers, necessarily looking for impartial evidence. They may be neutral in a political sense, but biased in matters where their own advancement clashes with the public interest. For instance a prospective High Commissioner to a Commonwealth country will not welcome adverse information upon its rulers. Macmillan's dislike of being bothered by unpleasant tidings was well served by a sycophantic staff under his Cabinet Secretary Sir Norman Brook. They all nodded in agreement when, after viewing vivid 'blow-ups' of the American U2 photographs showing the extent of Soviet missile installations, the Prime Minister commented, 'But what's the point of it all?'

Goronwy Rees

I believed myself to be a socialist and a Marxist, a worshipper at the shrine of what was sometimes familiarly referred to as the MCH; the Materialist Conception of History.

Until the defection of his friend Guy Burgess, Goronwy Rees was regarded by most of his friends as a lovable and highly intelligent Welsh rascal. Suddenly, overnight, his life changed and his friends turned on him, not so much because they believed he was still a Marxist or was implicated in espionage, but because of his bizarre behaviour in seeking to exploit the situation.

Born in Aberystwyth, Rees went to New College and All Souls, Oxford, and while still at university came under the spell of Guy Burgess who confirmed his commitment to Communism. They planned to visit the Soviet Union together but Rees instead began work on the *Manchester Guardian* and the *Spectator*. However, Burgess did confide in him that he was a Soviet agent, and that Anthony Blunt was also part of his ring.

Shortly before the outbreak of war Rees joined a territorial unit as a private soldier but in 1940 was sent to Sandhurst and was commissioned in the Royal Welch Fusiliers. Thereafter he spent much time on the staff in London, occasionally visiting Burgess at Victor Rothschild's flat. In 1944 he was transferred as an intelligence officer to the planning staff, 21st Army Group, in preparation for the Normandy landings. It was his duty to obtain signatures from Admiral Ramsay and Air Marshal Leigh-Mallory on the final sent of orders which sent Overlord into play. Rees recalls that moments before adding his name to the historic document Leigh-Mallory had proposed several slight alterations, and he was obliged to tell the most senior RAF officer in the country that it was too late for amendments. At the end of the war Rees went with the occupation forces to Germany, and then joined SIS.

According to his autobiography, *A Chapter of Accidents*, which was published in 1972, he became increasingly concerned that both Guy Burgess and Donald Maclean were still secret supporters of the Comintern, and this he reported to David Footman as soon as the news broke that Burgess had disappeared.

Five years after these events, as principal of the University College of Wales, Rees wrote a series of six anonymous articles for the *People* entitled 'Guy Burgess stripped bare – his closest friend speaks at last'. In it he implicated Anthony Blunt, although he was careful not to identify him by name, and smeared enough other people to spark a scandal. As soon as he was exposed as the author he was dismissed from his academic post and sued for libel. Among the few who stayed loyal to the tempestuous Welshman, and were named as such in his memoirs, were his former SIS colleagues, Robert Zaehner, A. J. Ayer and David Footman.

Having wrecked his careers in intelligence and academia, Rees took to writing novels and was mildly successful. He was, however, distrusted by the Security Service molehunters who were convinced he too had been a spy, and he was shunned by Blunt who thought Rees had betrayed him. Ironically, Rees died a few months before Blunt was exposed as a traitor by the prime minister in November 1979.

In this passage from his autobiography Rees gives his version of what happened immediately after Guy Burgess disappeared, and makes veiled references to David Footman, as the SIS man to whom he first turned, to Anthony Blunt, the former MI5 officer who nearly persuaded him to maintain his silence, and to Dick White as the Security Service officer who eventually interviewed him.

A Chapter of Accidents

I had never told my wife, or indeed anyone else except one other person, of my conversation with Guy before the war in which he had said he was a Comintern agent; even though I had so often wondered and speculated about it, I had regarded it as a thing of the past which was better forgotten. So it is not surprising that she could not have made much sense out of Guy's message [an almost incoherent phone call just hours before his disappearance]. And from her account of it, it was not easy for me to make out very clearly what Guy meant. But at least I made this out: that the message was a warning of some kind, and also a farewell. I was not sure what the warning was, but at least it meant that Guy was going away and that this involved some action which might be regarded as sensational even for Guy. I did not by any means think quite so consecutively, but having got so far I suddenly had an absolutely sure and certain, if irrational, intuition that Guy had gone to the Soviet Union.

I may say that in the weeks and months that followed I was never quite so certain of this again; but for a moment the confusion created by all the inconsistencies and aberrations of Guy's behaviour seemed to disappear, and the explanation seemed to be crystal clear. So much so that to my wife's utter bewilderment, and almost without thinking, I said: 'He's gone to Moscow.' Yet even as I spoke the words I felt how wildly improbable and fantastic they would sound to anyone else, and I had only to look at my wife's face to see that this was so. Indeed, when once we began to discuss Guy's absence and to consider all the other and far more plausible reasons why Guy should have gone away for a few days, the more improbable my initial conjecture became.

Yet, after so many years of doubt and speculation, I felt that this time it really was not for me to decide what was the truth of the matter, even though anything I did was likely to involve me in ridicule or perhaps worse. If I was right about what Guy had done, then it seemed to me that even the claims of friendship did not allow me to be silent any more, because the consequences of his action might be in innumerable ways disastrous. I had no choice, I felt, except to inform the proper authorities of Guy's absence, and of what I thought to be the reason for it, even though I didn't much look forward to the polite incredulity with which my story was likely to be received. I explained to my wife what I thought I should do and my reasons for doing it, and even then felt how very odd my explanation sounded, even to a sympathetic listener. It seemed to come out of a past that had vanished, and conjured up a present and a future that bore no relation to our own lives.

It was now late on Sunday night and I telephoned to a friend [Footman], who was also a friend of Guy's and a member of MI6, and told him that Guy had apparently vanished into the blue and that I thought MI5 ought to be told. When he asked why, I said I thought Guy might have defected to the Soviet Union. He was, naturally enough, incredulous, but I was insistent that something should be done and he promised, somewhat reluctantly, that he would inform MI5 of what I said. The next day I received a message from him saying that he had done so and that MI5 would be getting in touch with me.

On Sunday evening, however, I also told another friend of Guy's [Blunt], who had served in MI5 during the war, and still preserved close connections with it, of what I had done. He was greatly distressed, and said he would like to see me. On Monday he came down to my house in the country, and on an almost ideally beautiful English summer day, we sat beside the river and I gave him my reasons for thinking that Guy had gone to the Soviet Union; his violent anti-Americanism, his certainty that America was about to involve us all in a Third World War, most of all the fact that he may have been and perhaps still was a Soviet agent.

He pointed out, very convincingly as it seemed to me, that these were really not very good reasons for denouncing Guy to MI5. His anti-Americanism was an attitude which was shared by many liberal-minded people and if this alone were sufficient reason to drive him to the Soviet Union, Moscow at the moment would be besieged by defectors seeking asylum. On the other hand, my belief that he might be a Soviet agent rested simply on one single remark made by him years ago and apparently never repeated to anyone else; in any case, Guy's public professions of anti-Americanism were hardly what one would expect from a pro-fessional Soviet agent. Most of all he pointed out that Guy was after all one of my, as of his, oldest friends and to make the kind of allegations I apparently proposed to make about him was not, to say the least of it, the act of a friend.

He was the Cambridge liberal conscience at its very best, reasonable, sensible, and firm in the faith that personal relations are the highest of all human values. He reminded me of E. M. Forster's famous statement that if he had to choose between betraying his country or betraying his friend, he hoped he would have the courage to betray his country. I said that in the appalling political circumstances under which we lived, to betray one's country might mean betraying innumerable other friends and it might also mean betraying one's wife and one's family. I said Forster's antithesis was a false one. One's country was not some abstract conception which it might be relatively easy to sacrifice for the sake of an individual; it was itself made up of a dense network of individual and social relationships in which loyalty to one particular person formed only a single strand. In that case, he said, I was being rather irrational because after all Guy had told me he was a spy a very long time ago and I had not thought it necessary to tell anyone. I said that perhaps I was a very irrational person; but until then I had not really been convinced that Guy had been telling the truth. Now I was, and I was tired of the deceit he had practised over so many years and was only anxious to get rid of all my doubts and suspicions and speculations and pass them on to those whose business it was to say what they were worth.

He pointed out, with some force, that they were not likely to think them worth much; he even gently hinted, out of his own experience, that they might even wonder what on earth I was up to in coming to them with so curious a story. I could not help wondering if this would have been his own reaction when he was a member of MI5 himself and for a moment I had a sense of how profoundly English he was; but I repeated that I now felt that the only thing I could do was to tell the security authorities what I thought I knew as fully and precisely as I could and leave to them what use, if any, they might wish to make of it. At least it would not be my problem any more.

And so we left. He did not disguise his disapproval of what I was going to do. I spent the night in some misery and marvelled at the wonderful web of trickery and deceit Guy had woven around himself and wondered even now if I was not being foolish in believing a single word he had ever said. And yet, despite all this, and despite my conversation of that afternoon, I somehow recovered something of my conviction of the previous evening that Guy had, for whatever reason, gone to the Soviet Union, and rather irrationally this somehow cheered me up and I went to sleep.

Cheerfulness, however, did not last for long. I felt both alarmed and despondent when the next day I went up to London and made my way to MI5. I could not help reflecting on the process of events which, since my Oxford days, had finally brought me to the extraordinary position of laying information to the security authorities against one of my best friends, and on the almost total transformation in society, and perhaps in myself, this implied. It was as if somewhere along the line continuity had been broken and something new and strange had emerged, so that I hardly knew myself or the world I lived in.

At MI5 I was taken into the presence of an officer whom I had known during the war and who had also known Guy well [White]. For a moment this made things seem easier; it was as if it was all in the family. But it also made me feel even more foolish and the whole affair more improbable; this was not the kind of thing that happened between friends. I felt as if, from afar, Guy were exercising his gift of introducing the element of farce into everything he did, however serious or even disastrous it might be.

But this sense quickly passed when, after a few questions, I began my story and I became aware of the intense seriousness with which it was listened to. I had expected surprise or even incredulity rather than this atmosphere of concentrated, even strained, attention. After all, it was a very improbable story; all I really had to say was that Guy had been absent for four days and that from this I had deduced that he had gone to Moscow.

And here this particular story really ends, for what I had to tell them at MI5 was the same story that I have told here. But when I had finished, feeling, as one always does under such circumstances, that what I had to say sounded extraordinarily thin and unconvincing, there was a long silence. Then the officer, who was the head of the department concerned, gave me a curious look; I shall never be quite certain what it meant. After a moment he said, in a detached and matter-of-fact voice:

'Of course, you knew that Guy did not go alone?'

It was certainly the last question I had expected and for a moment I was too bewildered to reply. Then I said, rather foolishly:

'You mean that Guy really has gone?'

'Yes.'

'And that someone else has gone too?'

'Yes.'

'Who is it?' I said.

'Donald Maclean. They went together.'

Then I realized with a terrible sinking of the heart that everything I had thought about Guy was true; but that matters were even worse than I thought. They seemed even worse when I emerged from the office and in the street saw the headlines in the evening papers announcing that two British diplomats had vanished into thin air.

Brian Montgomery

Curiously enough, we Montgomerys have become distantly related, by marriage of Dean Farrar with a Cardew, to the infamous Russian spy and traitor 'Kim' Philby.

The youngest brother of the Field Marshal, Brian Montgomery was one of nine children born to the Bishop of Tasmania. After Sandhurst he was commissioned into the Royal Warwickshire Regiment and later served in East Africa with the King's African Rifles before transferring to the Indian Army.

During World War II Montgomery worked on Field Marshal Slim's staff and participated in the retreat from Burma. After the war, as a lieutenant-colonel, he commanded the 4th Battalion Baluch Regiment and upon the partition of India was recruited into the Secret Intelligence Service. He eventually retired in 1970 and was elected a councillor in the Royal Borough of Kensington and Chelsea, and with the publication of *A Field Marshal in the Family* established himself as a biographer. *Shenton of Singapore* followed in 1984 but neither volume betrays any details of Montgomery's quarter-century career in SIS. Nor, indeed, does he refer to SIS's role in the loss of Singapore, the military catastrophe for which Sir Shenton Thomas as governor was made a scapegoat.

In this passage Montgomery, who died in May 1989, reveals his distant kinship with Kim Philby, and the embarrassment this caused him when Harold Wilson's security adviser, Lord Wigg, started to investigate how many of Philby's relatives were still on SIS's payroll.

A Field Marshal in the Family

It was while he was at Harrow that Farrar [F. W. Farrar, later Dean of Canterbury, author of the notorious school story *Eric, or Little by Little*] married his wife, by whom he had a large family of five sons and five daughters. She was Lucy Mary, third daughter of Frederick Cardew, a judge in India, and she married my grandfather in 1860. The Cardews were an old family long settled at Truro in Cornwall. Curiously enough, we Montgomerys have become distantly related, by the marriage of Dean Farrar with a Cardew, to the infamous Russian spy and traitor 'Kim' Philby. It has happened in this way. H. St J. B. Philby, the famous explorer and Arabist, and the first European to cross Arabia from north to south via the Hadhramaut, was Kim's father. His (maternal) great-grandfather was Henry Clare Cardew whose sister was Mrs Farrar, my grandmother. Because of this Jack Philby wrote in his autobiography, *Arabian Days*, 'At Westminster I was encouraged to think that my childish delight in Greek verbs was but an echo of my kinship with the great Dean Farrar himself.' It was thus through my grandmother that the Philby family became known to my parents though Jack Philby never came to New Park. He was however well acquainted with my Field Marshal brother when they both served together in India, Jack in the Indian Civil Service and my brother with his regiment. In his *Arabian Days* the explorer wrote, 'In September (1910) I took ten days leave to get married at Murree with the support, as best man, of my cousin, Lieutenant Bernard Montgomery of the War-wicks.' After this marriage Kim, the traitor, was born in 1912. In this connection his father, friend of T. E. Lawrence and of the famous King of Saudi-Arabia, Abdul Aziz ibn Saud, had very early on showed signs of being a rebel against the establishment, which he certainly was. As long ago as 1908, in his last term at Cambridge, he was already a left-wing socialist. As he said himself, 'I was probably the first socialist to enter the Indian civil service, and I suppose I scandalised most of my friends by proclaiming from the beginning my adhesion to the ideal of Indian independence.' Later he became a firm supporter of the Labour party. But in the early part of the 1939–45 war he fell foul of the British authorities on account of his extreme views, which he voiced to all and sundry, and was imprisoned for some months under the Defence of the Realm Regulations. Looking back, with all the advantage of hindsight, it is perhaps permissible to wonder why, at the time, more thought was not given to the possible effects of heredity and environment, with special reference to the father's record, before admitting the son to the inner counsels of the British Secret Service. Be that as it may, in the late 1960s, Lord Wigg, then Paymaster General, and the Minister in the Cabinet responsible for security matters, saw fit to enquire about an alleged relationship between the traitor, Kim Philby, and Field Marshal Viscount Montgomery! This naturally caused no small stir and being then in the Diplomatic Service I was summoned, at a high official level, to explain matters precisely, including the fact that the Field Marshal had been best man to Kim's father. I heard no more about it!

John Colvin

The post was not accredited to anyone. Even the Mayor of Hanoi refused to receive me if I attempted to arrange a meeting.

After Dartmouth and London University John Colvin joined the Royal Navy and was an entirely conventional sailor until his transfer to the Adriatic during the war. There he ferried agents across to Yugoslavia on motor gunboats, but his clandestine career was to start in earnest when he joined SIS in 1951 and was posted to Oslo. In 1953 he was transferred to Vienna.

Colvin's first posting to the Far East, after three years in London, took place in 1958 when he went to Kuala Lumpur. During the height of the Vietnam war, between 1965 and 1967, he was in Hanoi as Consul-General, enduring the nightly American air raids.

Colvin's next appointment was as ambassador to the People's Republic of Mongolia, a post traditionally reserved for retiring SIS personnel, although in 1977 he went to Washington DC for his final posting as the SIS head of station. He now lives in London. His autobiography gives no hint of his *sub rosa* career, but this passage describes the difficulties of life in war-torn Hanoi.

Twice Around the World

The authorities did not allow me to ride a bicycle in Hanoi. The reason given was 'security' or, sometimes, 'protection', not wholly implausible among the dense files of somnambulist cyclists. The real concern of the External Affairs Bureau was, however, not my safety, but my mobility and the opportunities this would have afforded. When confronted with a refusal on similar grounds, one of my successors, Baroness Park, proposed that the difficulty be overcome by permitting a tandem with a militiaman on the pillion.

To walk – for time was of no account and Hanoi not enormous – was the most agreeable and, in the end, the most expeditious means of locomotion. It was certainly the most practical. The alleys, the deserted pagodas stained with damp and buried in untended growth, the brown faces, wary or curious, sharp-turned eyes toward one and as quickly away, the shops and abandoned craft streets, the parks and the lake would scarcely have become familiar from the back seat of a vehicle. The children played in one's path or scurried into doorways; the life of Hanoi, on broken, neglected tarmac or in the dark recesses of the little houses on each hand, was instantly accessible. The old women in black pyjamas selling their vegetables from wide straw baskets, the fierce harangue to his squatting back-street audience of a political instructor, the bougainvillea hanging in swags over a crumbled wall, discontented youths with sleek, if duck's-arse, hair cuts, and jeans acquired by what strange channel, the fight to board the trams, the filth, vigour and some of the meaning of this secret town were at least visible to the pedestrian.

And in the excited crowd at Tet around the Petit Lac, although myself as conspicuous as the Eddystone Light, I waited as the minutes ticked by for the blurred, mysterious explosion, through the surface of the water, of that turtle whose appearance had for centuries prophesied victory to the Tonkinese.

My destinations did not much vary. They included the State Department, the 'bizarrely named edifice' referred to by James Cameron, open daily from 5 to 8 in the morning. The State Department was, in fact, the State Shop. It was always crammed with customers, sometimes fifty to a line, for the meagre stock of goods dispensed by one or, rarely, two young female assistants to each counter, but it made a wartime British Woolworth's or the Balkans in 1945 seem like Asprey's.

Here I used, without the master's genius, to play Kim's Game. The goods available in November, 1966, included footballs, enamelled basins and chamberpots in immense quantity, a guitar or two, Bulgarian watches, Soviet and Chinese radios, hundreds of Chinese thermos flasks, two Czech bicycles and accessories, shelf upon shelf of torch batteries, one pair of Zeiss field-glasses, two crowded counters of foreign drugs (Caffein, Nivalin, Ematin, Philophran, Adrenalin, Progesterone), soap dishes, two or three showcases of local scent and soap, a few lipsticks, tin pots of face cream, one brand of tooth-paste, Soviet tinned and Chinese powdered milk, gumboots and poor-quality shoes, monocolour gabardine and other cloth, skimpy shirts and vests, face-flannels by the thousand, lightweight trousers. Clothes were sold at two prices, the lower by ten percent being for state employees.

Otherwise, apart from fairly good rubber sandals (not the famous 'Ho Chi Minhs') and what Lillywhite call 'yachting shoes', the stock consisted of ping-pong balls, repellent local lacquer and mother-of-pearl, vocational and polemical literature, shopping baskets, artificial flowers, bulldog clips, two self-coloured lady's bathing suits, three tennis rackets and a stimulating green bikini. A brave attempt had been made to lay out in window-dress this weird collection. Marked prices were the exception but, where shown, extraordinarily high.

An English traveller once defined a fully developed Socialist society as one where the lavatories at the airport did not function, and where hairpins were unavailable in the shops. The State Department had no hairpins.

The river bank near the house, with a little path running through high grass and not unlike the fen country, formed another of my regular 'constitutionals'. (In this barren stretch, young Vietnamese lovers, unlike their more controlled cousins in Peking, strolled hand in hand; but the girls, although racially akin to the ladies of Saigon, seemed of a different species. However much was owed by the erotic charm of the Saigonnaises to maquillage and to the high-slit Ao Dai, it was hard to believe that even those adjuncts could advantageously embellish the simple forms and faces of the austere northerners, asexual, even plain.) Other strolls, apart from daily visits to diplomatic missions, led me to the dyke walls, to the lake ablaze with flamboyants, to the clang and squalor of the inner city, the great French palaces and the leafy grandeur of the suburban boulevards, their villas now streaked by rain and leprous with inattention.

Sometimes when the city became too claustrophobic, we took the car a little way outside the town to drive slowly past the neat viridian squares of sunken padi and other fields of irrigated agriculture. Here, surrounded by the stooped figures of the cultivators among their endless rows of rice and vegetables ranged in military precision, was the permanent Asia. Here one could breathe, reacquire perspective, slough off metropolitan tensions.

We were not, on the other hand, permitted to drive to Haiphong, a privilege granted to the French, or for picnics to the enchanting Baie d'Along with its vast, conical rocks protruding out of the sea among fleets of square-sailed junks. On return journeys from these excursions, the Vietnamese militia required the French to open and unpack not only the picnic baskets themselves but individual items, including plastic containers, even removing bottles from their straw.

Sometimes, as on journeys to Gia Lam airport, the car was essential. On one occasion in 1967, because the Paul Doumer Bridge had been put out of action by bombing, we had to cross the river by ferry. Earlier crossings had been shambolic: most travellers had arrived at the airport after the aircraft had taken off, and one unfortunate Pole did not get back to Hanoi until the following morning.

Before Livesey's next bag run to Saigon, we therefore sought a priority permit from the Hanoi Security Commissariat earlier described in the old

French Sûreté building located, soberingly if logically, adjacent to the Tribunal and Gaol. After waiting for 30 minutes in the concierge's lodge among other lightly clad supplicants, I was escorted to the waiting room where my interlocutor, a Tonkinese police sergeant slightly resembling Gene Kelly, helpfully informed me that 'the present difficulties were the result of American bombing'. He added that he thought it unlikely that we should ever again reach the airport until the bombing stopped; two Flying Englishmen forever to cross the river and forever forlornly to return. The portrait of Ho Chi Minh opposite seemed, at that moment, to represent *schadenfreude* rather than benevolence. The functionary, however, promised to 'study the matter' with the Ministry of Transport. He replied to my thanks by expressions of his simple duty and by reassuring strokes and pats.

We eventually received an 'introduction', itself a form of permit, for the ferry. Armed with this and with travel permits, identity cards and passports, we then wasted the afternoon, on the incorrect advice of the French, in trying to secure ferry tickets from an office on the steps of the Cultural and Historical Museum which did not, in fact, open until 5 o'clock. When the officials arrived, we discovered that our applications had succeeded and that we were to be second vehicle on the 5.30 ferry. After many expressions of esteem but, alas, no buck-and-wing from the sergeant, we departed for the vessel.

The ferry, oddly referred to as the 'tourist ferry', was not far from the museum, by a small piece of inland water where fishing was in progress. At this point we opened the ice bucket, broached the gin and tonic, offered some beer to the driver, who shared it with his mates, and contemplated the sylvan and unaccustomed scene.

The Red River, actually pink, lay before us. MiGs roared overhead, explosions took place in the south-east every five minutes with high columns of smoke, the ground was pitted with air-raid shelters, every bush concealed an anti-aircraft weapon, militiamen freely employed their loud-hailers, but while in no way resembling a day at Southend, a fresh breeze blew from the river, and we were, at least temporarily, on our way out of Hanoi.

The cars then boarded the ferry, and we joined them on foot after a short period in a sort of sheep pen. The journey upstream lasted about 25 minutes, during which we had opportunity to regard the landscape, passing ferries, picturesque barques and lateen sails and the Bridge.

The latter looked, as has been well observed, like a horizontal Eiffel Tower (it was financed by the Compagnie Eiffel) and was largely obscured from the river by scrub jungle, but we were able to note that one section of about 50 yards, or almost half a span, was completely missing. The remaining western section of this span was about five feet out of true, and three lorries and about 40 workmen were seen near the spot. Oxyacetylene torches were in operation on my return journey, but it was difficult to believe that the section could be replaced at high water. Rumour asserted, however, that the bridge would be in operation by National Day: and indeed it was.

We were a jovial, even euphoric, ship's company. Smiles were exchanged, a hero of the Democratic Republic exhibited his wounds, laughter was general. A young woman in black silk trousers and purple shirt passed her time in shyly giving us the eye and scratching her initials on the bonnet of the car with her fingernails. On arrival at the East Bank, H. M. Consul-General made his contribution to the evening's entertainment by removing his shoes and socks, unique apparel at Hanoi, and unnecessarily wading ashore before the ferry had settled.

The remainder of the journey was accomplished by car, initially over a dusty road lined by unused pagodas, rice fields, water, anti-aircraft guns and bombed houses, accompanied by shouts of 'Harosho' from strolling yokels. We also observed numerous troupes of relatively ravishing girl workers returning home with spades, hoes, mattocks, shovels, picks, yoked baskets, etc., who, despite their rags, here compared well with the disturbing but factitious charms of the prettier ICC air hostesses. The Customs at Gia Lam spent their usual quarter of an hour unpicking the seams of Geoffrey Livesey's underwear, but he was, after all, almost their only airborne client, and I had by then unpacked the bar again.

Take-off was delayed, and apart from one short hold-up caused by bad traffic management, I reached the ferry in quick time on my return journey. Because the driver could not both drive and obtain the tickets, I was thus able to drive the car (illegally but unobserved) for the first time during my tour in the DRV, albeit for a few yards only. Unfortunately, owing to the sudden arrival of two high-level government vehicles, we were unable to get our car on to the first ferry; I went over by myself, leaving the driver to catch the next one. Seamanship was slovenly on arrival at the West Bank where, back to reality, I was refused a lift by the sullen Vietnamese drivers of the ICC and walked the short distance home.

Hugh Seton-Watson

Since the Second World War ended the world has not been at peace.

Educated at Winchester and New College, Oxford, Hugh Seton-Watson was the son of a prominent historian, R. W. Seton-Watson. An early recruit into Section D of SIS, he undertook missions in the Balkans while based in Belgrade and Bucharest. In 1941 he transferred to Cairo and worked in the Yugoslav Section of SOE until 1944. He then later returned to SIS before resuming his studies at University College, Oxford and in 1951 was appointed professor of Russian history at London University.

His first book, *Eastern Europe Between the Wars: 1918–1941*, was published in 1945; his own experience in central Europe provided much of the background for it and his second book, *The Eastern European Revolution*. He acquired a formidable reputation as a scholar and concentrated on nationalism and Communism, both topics in *The Pattern of Communist Revolution* and *The Decline of Imperial Russia 1855–1914*.

At the time of his death in December 1984 Seton-Watson was professor emeritus at the School of Slavonic and Eastern European Studies at London University, as well as a frequent lecturer in the United States.

Neither War nor Peace

The third long-term trend to be stressed is the evolution of the Soviet régime. We have noted elsewhere the pressure of both forces of reform and forces of revolution in Soviet society, the important role of the state *bourgeoisie* and the growing demands of the intellectual youth for freedom of thought. It is possible that these forces will influence Soviet governments of the future towards a more 'normal' type of foreign policy, towards less revolution-mongering and towards relatively greater concern for the state interests of Soviet Russia. It might be thought that a less ideological, more nationally-minded Soviet leadership would be easier for the West to live with – indeed, that such a leadership might recognize that it had a common interest with the West in maintaining, not only 'peace' in an abstract sense (this even Stalin admitted), but a mutually acceptable peace, an international order that would guarantee the interests of the West as well as of the Soviet Union. This is indeed possible, and it is a possibility which Western foreign policy should do what it can to bring about. But it is well to recognize that it does not depend only on the will of the Soviet leaders or the skill of Western statesmen, but will be determined above all by the general state of the world. A more nationally-minded Soviet government might co-operate peacefully with the West in a peaceful world. But if the world is not peaceful, if large parts of it are seething with unrest, the Soviet government is bound, however peaceful its general aims, to take an attitude towards the sources of unrest. And it would be very rash to assume that in crises arising in the Middle East or Eastern Europe, to take two obvious examples, the interests even of a much less ideologically-minded Soviet government would coincide with those of the West. In fact, the ability of the West and the Soviet Union to co-operate in future depends at least as much on the development of Asian and African nationalism, and on the relations of the Soviet Union to the subject states of Eastern Europe and of the East European communists with their subjects, as on the deliberate aims of the Western and Soviet governments with regard to each other.

Perhaps still more important is the future relationship between the Soviet Union and China. The potential sources of conflict between these great states have been briefly discussed above. It is necessary here to add only that, should serious conflict develop between them, this need not necessarily be to the advantage of the West. It is, of course, possible that, if the Soviet leaders anticipate danger from China, they will seek to protect themselves by coming to terms with the West. Equally possible, however, is that they will seek to strengthen themselves for future clashes with China by pushing ahead with their plans for the subjugation of the Middle East, Africa and Western Europe – in fact, that fear of China may drive them into a more adventurous and aggressive policy towards the West. Both are at the present stage mere hypotheses, but the one is as likely as the other.

The last problem on which a few words may here be permitted is the future of Western democracy itself.

What is called in Western countries 'democracy', Soviet and other Marxist-Leninists call '*bourgeois* democracy', and regard as a by-product of capitalism, performing a progressive function in human history in the period of capitalist strength, but bound to disappear when capitalism itself finally collapses, a process which they believe is now nearing its conclusion. In the place of capitalism will come socialism (whether by 'peaceful' or 'violent' revolution), which will in turn evolve into communism. Both economically and politically, they believe, socialism is incomparably superior to '*bourgeois* democracy', and communism is, of course, a still higher form of human organization.

One may believe that the whole Marxist-Leninist analysis of history is distorted, incomplete and unscientific; that capitalist economies have retained plenty of vigour and flexibility, and are at least as well designed to meet their needs as the Soviet economy to meet its different needs; and that the political system established by communist party totalitarianism is as odious as fascism and worse than most tyrannies known in the history of Europe and Asia; and yet one may have doubts about the present trend of democracy in the West. The Marxist-Leninist doctrines about the decay of capitalism and 'bourgeois democracy' may be wrong, but it does not follow from this that there is no decay.

The criticisms that are most heard, within Western countries, of Western democracy as it now is, concern inadequate progress towards equality and social justice. It is pointed out that there is still a great deal of miserable poverty (even in the United States); that there is still ostentatious luxury among the very rich; that power is still too much concentrated in rather small upper social strata; and that the ideal of equal opportunity for all to make a career according to their innate abilities and personal efforts is still far from realized. These arguments are without doubt largely justified. But two questions must here be put. The first is: should the present state of affairs be compared with an ideal state of perfect social justice, in which case it will be found lamentably deficient, or with the state of affairs a generation or a century ago, in which case it is clear that enormous progress has been made, and it is arguable that greater equality of opportunity, and a greater degree of social justice, have been achieved than ever in human history? The second question is: granted that these evils still exist, are they in fact the most dangerous evils that threaten Western societies and Western men and women?

We must here return to the problems, briefly mentioned in an earlier chapter, of authority and leadership in democratic societies, of the will of the rulers to exercise power and of the leaders to lead. The development of the modern democratic society may be regarded as progress towards social justice. This was a belief common to the pioneers of democratic ideas and policies in the past, however much they may have disagreed on the pace of progress. But another aspect of the same process, which some past enemies of democracy foretold and its champions repudiated as reactionary fantasy, is the widespread and increasing erosion of authority and abdication of responsibility. In the age of the other-directed man, popularity is the supreme criterion. By this standard, the best soap is the one which finds most buyers, and the best national policy is the one which finds favour with public opinion polls.

In a world of general security and affluence this system of values might work. Those who have kept their religious faith or hold to the morality derived from religious tradition, can never accept these values, but still society might be able to function without them. But the world is not secure, and affluence is confined to the 'north-west corner' of North America and Western Europe. In the rest of the world poverty is still the rule. What is more immediately important, poverty creates greater discontent than ever before, for the masses of Asia, Africa and Latin America are no longer willing to accept their wretched lot as a fact of nature. The peoples of the north-west corner are going to need all the skill and leadership they can find if they are to survive the dangers which press on them both from the 2,000 million who live in poverty, and from the ambitions of the totalitarians. The case for removing the remaining islands of wretched poverty within the affluent societies is, of course, unanswerable. But further pursuit in these societies of doctrinaire schemes of equality, and further increases in the consumption by all classes of ever more inessential luxuries, though not in themselves undesirable, must seem to anyone who seriously considers the world political scene today, to deserve a lower priority than is given them by their politicians, business-men and publicists. The question is not how much more affluent these societies can become, but whether they can survive at all.

What is needed, it would seem, is not so much more debunking, more undermining and derision of established traditions and loyalties, but a restoration of respect for authority, and greater encouragement to individual thought, achievement and leadership. This does not of course mean that the existing leadership in the West, or the existing means of recruiting leadership in either the political or the wider social field, are not capable of being vastly improved. Still less does it mean satisfaction with the snobbery and sanctimoniousness that are so marked a feature of Western societies (as, indeed, most stable societies in history). But it is surely possible, for example, to distinguish between the mass-produced quasi-religious adulation which surrounds the British monarchy, and the institution of monarchy itself; or to dislike the sycophancy that seems to flourish in the higher reaches of American business, without maintaining that industry can do without leadership. Democracy needs leaders, and leaders must not be afraid to give orders. To repudiate the very principle of hierarchy from hatred of complacency is to throw out the baby with the bath-water. The argument that no one who is not perfect has the right to find fault with others cannot be justified from any point of view, religious or secular, academic or political. All human action is imperfect and sinful, but within these limits choice is possible between good and evil and between greater and lesser evils. The process of letting social conscience make cowards of us all has been allowed to go too far. If consumers' sovereignty is to be extended to all political life, including the control of education, defence, finance and foreign affairs; if all original thought and all spontaneous initiative are to be treated as undesirable nonconformity, either comic or pernicious; if the only valid loyalty is loyalty to the clique – then the outlook for Western mass democracy is bleak. Yet it is still possible to reverse these trends and escape these perils.

There are no general answers to these problems. They have to be handled as they arise, and those whom fate or the vote has placed in positions which ought to (but do not always) require of their occupants the gifts of leadership, must decide on priorities (more money for defence or education, more financial aid for India or Brazil, greater military commitments towards Persia or Vietnam). These choices of priorities are the task of the practical politician. The politician is perhaps not a very popular, often not a very admirable figure. But he is what the voter has made him, no less than the voter is what the politician and the publicist have made him. The citizen who makes the politician a scapegoat for his frustrations is not helping democracy, and is not helping himself. The politician may be a cynical careerist: if so, it is the voter's fault for electing him, or for helping to create a climate of opinion in which cynical careerism can win. But the majority of democratic politicians, in whose characters personal ambition and honourable concern for the common weal are balanced in variable admixtures, must plot their course between two limits which are not easy to calculate – the most that they can demand of the people in sacrifices without being rejected by the voters, and the least that they can demand without betraying their country's interests. It is tempting for the exasperated citizen and the academic intellectual alike to inveigh against the democratic politician. But no one can begin to understand political reality who does not try sympathetically to grasp his predicament. It is not an easy one. This survey of the world political scene can best end with a prayer for the political leaders of the democracies, that they may find greater wisdom and courage than they have shown in the last fourteen years.

CHAPTER XI

Post-war MI5

I wasn't Mata Hari, and I wasn't Himmler's aunt, but it would be
stupid of me to pretend that I was not, like Somerset Maughan, Graham
Greene and lots of other writers, for a time engaged in that work.
John Le Carré, The South Bank Show, March 1983

While SIS regards a degree of hostile penetration and the employment of
the occasional oddball as an acceptable occupational hazard, the Security
Service is altogether more cautious and clings to the discredited belief that
even the slightest indiscretion could spell disaster, the Home Secretary
being far more likely to summon his Director-General to an awkward
interview than the Foreign Secretary is to carpet the chief of the Secret
Intelligence Service. Proof that MI5 was even prepared to accommodate
an officer with an alcohol problem and criminal convictions, rather than
risk a dismissal, was provided in the case of Michael Bettaney, a member
of MI5's counter-espionage branch who was convicted in April 1984 of
having passed secrets to the KGB. In his evidence to the Security
Commission the hapless Director-General, Sir John Jones, admitted that
he preferred to retain Bettaney with all his flaws rather than risk a
disgruntled ex-officer attracting the attention of the media to the organization.

The Bettaney episode proved exceptionally embarrassing to MI5, not
least because it was the first occasion in the eighty-year history of the
Security Service that one of its officers had been convicted of disloyalty.
To the dismay of the Directorate, Bettaney's performance during his trial
gained the sympathy of one of his former colleagues, Miranda Ingram,
who was prompted to write an article in *New Society*, pointing out what
she believed to be the essentially political nature of Bettaney's crime. Her
observations sparked something of a controversy and prompted another
former MI5 officer, Cathy Massiter, to write a letter in support of
Ingram's views. These developments were unusual because MI5 personnel rarely use the correspondence columns of fortnightly magazines to

air grievances. Nevertheless, both Ingram and Massiter did, and this led in March 1985 to the latter contributing to a television documentary on the subject of MI5's abuse of power.

This extraordinary episode, which provoked rage at MI5's head-quarters in Gower Street, became a precedent for other MI5 officers to express their opinions on sensitive issues in public. Alec McDonald, a retired director of MI5's counter-espionage branch, who had played a key role in the molehunts of the 1960s, not only participated in a television documentary which challenged many of Peter Wright's assertions, but also wrote a letter to *The Times* describing the terms of his contribution. Nor was he alone in going public in response to Wright's allegations. Tony Brooks, who had worked for SOE, SIS and MI5, also condemned his former colleague, although he did so through the medium of the autumn 1988 edition of the small-circulation quarterly newsletter of the Special Forces Club. Brooks objected to Wright's description of himself as 'assistant director of MI5' which gave a very misleading impression of his status. As he pointed out, there were more than a dozen officers of assistant-director rank in MI5's counter-espionage branch while Wright served there.

As has been seen, a large number of SIS officers who were operational in the post-war era have been published in book form, in sharp contrast with the relative handful of their counterparts in the Security Service who have ventured into print. Probably the best known of them all is David Cornwell (John Le Carré) whose reputation, paradoxically, is based on his SIS experience. However, before he switched to SIS he was an MI5 officer based in Curzon Street, learning his craft from John Bingham who was by then himself a successful thriller writer. Bingham's daughter Charlotte also worked briefly for MI5.

While the themes adopted by Cornwell and John Bingham are easily traced to their clandestine roles, the subjects chosen by Bill Magan and Charles Elwell hardly betray the authors' work in the secret world. After his retirement Magan wrote an account of his family's history and its Irish origin but he could not resist some additional observations about the campaign of terrorism waged in Ulster by the Republicans. Charles Elwell, an ace MI5 case officer in the counter-espionage branch, and latterly the Security Service's resident expert on subversion, wrote a fascinating travelogue of Corsica which made a short excursion into the counter-intelligence field with the story of Paolo Morati, a British agent who was left in Corsica when the Royal Navy withdrew in 1796, after an occupation lasting two years. He also published some monographs on the history of the Black Country and, in 1983, *Tracts beyond the Times*, a detailed guide to the 'Communist or Revolutionary' press.

Elwell's introduction to espionage came during the Second World War when, as a naval officer, he was posted to motor gunboats and routinely ferried SIS agents across the North Sea to the Dutch coast. On one occasion he rowed an agent to the beach and found that the sea was too rough to make his way back to his launch. A few hours later he was arrested and he spent the rest of the war in prison camps, ending up at Colditz.

After the war Elwell joined MI5 and, following a tour of duty in Malaya, was posted to the counter-espionage branch. Here he ran several successful anti-Soviet operations, the best known being the Portland case which ended in the arrests of Harry Houghton, Ethel Gee, Gordon Lonsdale, and the two Americans Morris and Lona Cohen. He also supervised the investigation in the Admiralty which resulted in the arrest and conviction of John Vassall.

Elwell retired from the Security Service in 1979 but followed the debate over the loyalty of his former Director-General, Sir Roger Hollis, with close interest, and in July 1984 wrote to *The Times*, in what amounted to an attack on his ex-colleague Arthur Martin, complaining that the proposition that MI5 had suffered hostile penetration was unsupported by the evidence. As a stern critic of Sir Roger's performance, Elwell's contribution was not without significance. He also wrote to the *Sunday Times* later the same year, criticizing journalist Chapman Pincher for poor research in his book *Their Trade is Treachery*.

Elwell and Magan were not the only post-war MI5 officers to go into print, albeit on slightly abstruse subjects. One of Britain's most distinguished modern historians, Alistair Horne, spent the better part of three years working for MI5's branch in the Middle East, and Maxwell Knight, after his retirement from MI5, developed an entirely new career in natural history.

For many years before the outbreak of the Second World War Max Knight enjoyed the status of being MI5's principal counter-espionage case officer. Although he never wrote his memoirs, he is to be found in print. Not only did he write a thriller, *Crime Cargo*. while he was working for the Security Service, but after his final departure from MI5 and in his new role as BBC's expert on animals, he wrote *Pets Usual and Unusual* and co-authored *The Senses of Animals*. Although somewhat discredited at the time of his retirement, having shouldered much of the blame for Harald Kurtz, the over-zealous agent, and having been ridiculed for his belief that MI5 had suffered Soviet penetration, Knight's achievements were to inspire his subordinates and successors, who included John Bingham, William Younger and David Cornwell.

A polio victim while still a child, Bill Younger suffered from restricted growth and a withered arm, and was therefore medically unfit to join the army so instead he worked for Knight, first as an agent and later as a full-time case officer. Younger was so secretive about his work for the Security Service that his family nicknamed him 'the bearded oyster'. He finally retired from MI5 in the late 1950s, having inherited a fortune and being determined to devote himself to writing. He originally concentrated on poetry, and his first book of verse, *Madonna and Other Poems*, was praised by the critics, Howard Spring saying that he 'is writing better poetry than Byron did at his age'. During the war he married Nancy Brassey, the widow of Wing Commander Reginald Leslie who was killed in the Mediterranean in 1943. She wrote novels, and together they produced *Blue Moon in Portugal*, a travelogue of their experiences in that country.

Younger died suddenly in early 1961 while on a visit to Sicily, where he contracted Asiatic flu, having recently completed *Gods, Men and Wine*, which was published posthumously.

As 'William Mole' Younger wrote several detective thrillers, the best of which was *The Hammersmith Maggot*. His first novel, *Trample an Empire*, released in 1952, was described by the publishers as 'above all a protest against earnestness and an assertion of the small man's rights to laugh at his ruler', perhaps a surprisingly iconoclastic approach for a serving MI5 officer. The same book was praised by Dennis Wheatley (who neglected to mention that Mole was his stepson) as 'quite out of the ordinary and exceptionally good'. In his murder mystery novel *The Skin Trap* Younger described the anguish of a murderer handicapped with a humpback, a result of spinal tuberculosis as a child. Considering that Younger was unable to use one arm, his description of and subsequent explanation for the strangulation of a beautiful woman may be seen to shed some light on his own disability. There may also be a connection between the hero of the book, a suave wine merchant, and the occupation of Younger's stepfather, Dennis Wheatley, who was also, briefly and unsuccessfully, in the licensed trade.

Another of Knight's wartime colleagues was George Leggett, who remained in the Security Service until 1971. Ten years after his retirement he published the standard work on *The Cheka: Lenin's Political Police*.

John Bingham

We used to call ourselves Knight's Black Agents after the passage from Macbeth.

John Bingham, quoted by Anthony Masters in Literary Agents

Best known as a thriller writer, Lord Clanmorris led a double life. He was one of MI5's star agent handlers, and had learned his trade while assisting Maxwell Knight. He once said that he joined MI5 from the Royal Engineers in 1940, aged thirty-two, after denouncing an entirely innocent German refugee to the authorities, but he had worked previously part-time as one of Knight's informants. Before the war he had been a journalist, first on the *Hull Daily Mail*, and then in London as a feature writer and then picture editor on the *Sunday Dispatch*. He recruited numerous beautiful women as his informants and helped run several that he would refer to as his 'bogies'.

After the war, and Max Knight's retirement, Bingham continued to operate as MI5's principal agent-runner. In Germany he operated under Control Commission cover, based in Hanover, and upon his return to London he headed MI5's anti-subversion operations unit, based in safe-houses around Knightsbridge. Both his wife and his daughter, Charlotte, also worked for MI5 and became authors. Upon the death of his father in 1960 Bingham inherited his Irish title, the seventh Baron Clanmorris, and a castle in Northern Ireland which later became Bangor's town hall.

Throughout his career in MI5, which lasted until 1977, Bingham was a prolific author, starting with his first spy novel, *My Name is Michael Sibley*, which was published in 1952. It was an unusual book in that it consisted almost entirely of the exchanges between a murder suspect and his interrogator. More than a dozen other crime mysteries were to follow, and *Fragment of Fear* was filmed in 1970. Of them all, *Night's Black Agent* and *The Double Agent* were probably based on his own experiences, the former title being a play on Max Knight's name and his own role as his principal assistant. In the foreword to the latter he observed, 'there are currently two schools of thought about our Intelligence Services. One school is convinced that they are staffed by murderous, powerful, double-crossing cynics, the other that the taxpayer is supporting a collection of bumbling, broken-down layabouts.' He strongly disapproved of the writing of his protégé David Cornwell, and observed, 'The belief encouraged by many spy writers that Intelligence officers consist of moles, morons, shits and homosexuals makes the Intelligence job no easier.'

When Madeleine Bingham announced she intended to publish an account of her husband's life the Security Service issued a stern warning that she should abandon the project immediately. He died in August 1988, not long after his wife. In this episode from one of his first spy thrillers, the title of which was a quotation from

Macbeth that to Bingham and his colleagues had a double meaning, the author describes a farewell party in an unidentified department of the civil service. The person named Macdonald, and described as head of section, may indeed have been Alec MacDonald, Bingham's branch director.

Night's Black Agent

One or two people from other sections drifted in to say goodbye and wish him well – people whom he had missed when he had gone on the usual ghastly routine round of farewell visits that it is normal to make before a civil servant leaves.

As six o'clock approached he heard footsteps tramping along the corridor outside and men's voices, and he recognised the Scottish tones of Macdonald, head of the section. Somebody said something he couldn't catch, and there was laughter. Then he heard women's footsteps, light and quick, and the tinkle of the glasses they had borrowed from the canteen. They would have bought the drink at lunch time. He'd seen it all before, many times, and it was all rather a bore for everybody.

He knew exactly what would happen. There would be Macdonald, making a three-minute speech, referring to his forty years of loyal service to the country di-da-di-da-di-da; wishing him a happy retirement; always glad to see him if he cared to pop in. (A lie of course: such visits held up the work and were tedious.) Somewhere at the end would come the little 'shop' joke about architecture – a coy, good-humoured reference to the famous day when he had passed a secretary's error in a Minute and had allowed himself to refer to the 'effect of myxomatosis upon the architecture of the nation' instead of upon the agriculture of the nation. Loud laughter.

Then would come a few brief words by the Assistant Secretary, who would be good enough to spare time to attend. Clap-clap-clap.

Then the parting presentation, from the section and a few others, and his own speech. Clap-clap-clap.

Macdonald would call him Harry Summers, and the Assistant Secretary would call him Mr Harold Summers.

He'd seen it all so often. People standing in little groups talking in desultory fashion. Secretaries glancing at their watches, wanting to dash home and change, wondering if they would catch their trains, grudging the minutes, calculating when they could reasonably leave. Men wondering if the gin would last out for another round.

That's the way it always went.

It meant nothing, nothing at all; it was a social formality devoid of any fundamental emotion whatever, and the parting present would either be useful but impermanent or dull and enduring. In either case, Elspeth would criticise it.

He heard more footsteps and voices outside in the corridor.

It meant nothing to them, he thought, and it meant nothing to him. It was something to be got through, that was all, and when he had got through it, there would still be Green.

He supposed he would have to go in now. Timing was important. If you weren't careful, either you went in early and stood about in the emptiness or you went in when the room was full and most people went on talking and you felt like a second-rate prima donna making an unimpressive entrance.

He thought that the room by now would be just right.

In-tray empty, Out-tray empty. He used to boast that he never had a Pending tray. He used to say it was bad psychologically; but he knew that, in effect, he had one all the same, because his secretary kept the pending files for him and brought them forward at appropriate intervals.

Drawers of his desk unlocked and empty except for odd paper clips, a few red 'Immediate' labels, bits of dusty paper, a pipe cleaner. On his desk the cheap ash tray his secretary had given him for Christmas. He put it in his pocket. She would be hurt if he left it behind.

All over now. The room dark except for the light from the desk lamp. Harold Summers, a Principal Officer of Her Majesty's Civil Service; top of his salary grade, £2,120; full retiring pension – fifty percent of his average salary over the previous three years, plus gratuity; and all the children off his hands, thank God. He pushed his chair back and walked to the door and along to the room where the party was being held.

They would all have subscribed for the present; and the men would have bought the drinks, because you couldn't charge it up to the Ministry. So they were entitled to see him off the premises, so to speak.

But it means nothing, he thought again, nothing to them and nothing to me, and I've seen it all before. Better get it over with. He quickened his pace, and straightened his tie, and went in.

Things didn't happen as he had expected, but the analytical side of his mind, the civil service-trained part, accustomed to viewing problems dryly and dispassionately, told him that it was always different when you yourself were the centre of the show. You saw all those people turned towards you, smiling, wishing you well, shaking you by the hand. You heard the compliments in the speeches, noted the raised glasses. You told yourself again and again that you'd seen it all before – the swiftly whipped up enthusiasm; the sudden, glowing appreciation of your work; the synthetic cheeriness – yet when you yourself were the centre of it all, you couldn't help wondering whether perhaps, just this time, there wasn't some sincerity in it.

After all, you had indeed served the country loyally for forty years; and worked hard and, on the whole, quite well; and you had, as far as you could recall, been good-tempered and helpful, as they said.

Vanity, whispered the civil servant part of Harold Summers' mind. Vanity, vanity, vanity – and this farewell drink is no different, no more sincere, than all the others.

Still, they had sung, 'For he's a jolly good fellow', and he couldn't remember that happening before; but immediately the objective counterpoise came into play, and he wondered coolly whether this would become a feature of all such occasions in future, whether it was a gimmick, a piece of showmanship thought up by somebody on the spur of the moment for the benefit of the Assistant Secretary.

If so, he wished they hadn't sung it just after he had been presented with the tape recorder, which had been hidden behind a screen. Two faint spots of pink coloured Harold Summers' heavy, putty-coloured cheeks as he thought of the neat little speech he had planned to make and of what he had actually said.

The Assistant Secretary had beamed and said that not only were they presenting him with the machine but, what was more, it had been running since the party began.

'So Mr Harold Summers will have a lasting record of what we think of him,' concluded the Assistant Secretary benevolently. He pulled aside the little screen on the table, and there was the machine, revolving smoothly and silently.

It was then that they had sung, 'For he's a jolly good fellow', and that had been recorded, too, of course; and then he'd had to reply, and all the while, as they sang, the thought had been running through his mind that this time it was a little different from other such occasions – this time they meant what they said.

So when he had to speak, all he said was what a pleasure it had been to work for so long among so many nice people. He had had plenty more to say, including one or two witty cracks about architecture, but he stopped abruptly and just added, 'Thank you – thank you.'

Fifteen minutes later the party was ending. One or two of the younger secretaries had already glanced at their watches and stolen quietly away. A couple of junior officers were edging towards the door. Harold Summers glanced down at the glass of gin and vermouth in his hand. There was nothing shameful about having a lump in your throat just when you had to speak, but it was disappointing. If your career has not been very distinguished, it is nice to leave with flying colours in an aura which might subtly hint that there were hidden depths in you that the hierarchy could have spotted earlier, had they been perceptive.

Well, it couldn't be helped.

David Cornwell

David Cornwell's first encounters with the intelligence world took place while he was still an undergraduate at Lincoln College, Oxford, reporting to a friend of his father's. After graduating he taught at Eton and then in 1958 joined MI5's F4 sub-section as a subordinate to John Bingham. By then he had completed his National Service which, thanks to his knowledge of German acquired during a year in Berne in 1948, had been spent with the Intelligence Corps in Germany screening refugees from the East.

Cornwell served his apprenticeship with Bingham and then transferred in 1960 to SIS which posted him to Bonn, the backdrop for several of his subsequent novels. His first, written under the pen-name John Le Carré while he was still operating for SIS under consular cover in Hamburg, was *Call for the Dead* which was published in 1961. This was followed the next year by *A Murder of Quality* which drew upon his experience as a schoolmaster at Millfield and Eton and introduced the character of George Smiley, the retired intelligence officer who, Cornwell later admitted, was based upon John Bingham. With the publication of *The Spy Who Came in from the Cold* in 1963, a typically bleak story of espionage and betrayal, Cornwell achieved worldwide recognition and won both the Somerset Maugham Prize and his early retirement from SIS. He compounded his success with *The Looking Glass War* and later developed George Smiley as the troubled, lonely spymaster in *Tinker, Tailor, Soldier, Spy* and *Smiley's People*.

Cornwell not only relied upon real people from his own past to use as characters in his books, but also extended the vocabulary of the intelligence community by describing authentic espionage tradecraft in unprecedented detail, referring to 'lamplighters' (known as 'the watchers' in the real world) and calling the guardians of safe-houses used to accommodate defectors 'babysitters'. In a remarkable example of life following art, he may have introduced the term mole and molehunter into the lexicon. Certainly Cornwell was keenly aware of his predecessors in both MI5 and SIS who had opted for a literary life. He recalled that in his day the Security Service had been hostile to Graham Greene and that

MI5's legal adviser, Bernard Hill, had considered urging the Attorney-General to prosecute Greene for disclosing inside information in *Our Man in Havana*. As he remarked in an interview,

> Writers are a subversive crowd, nothing if not traitors. The better the writer, the greater the betrayal tends to appear, a thing the secret community has learned the hard way, for I hear it is no longer quite so keen to have us abroad. Nevertheless, Mackenzie ended his days with a knighthood. Greene will end his with the Order of Merit at least, and if there is any justice at all in the secret world of literary awards, a Nobel prize.

Cornwell's success, due mainly to the compulsive power of his writing, is also due to his subject matter and the realistic atmosphere he creates.

Charlotte Bingham

I often heard my friend Mary telling her partners at coming-out dances that she worked for MI5. I would drag her off to the loo and remind her that our work was supposed to be terribly secret.

The daughter of Lord Clanmorris (novelist and agent runner John Bingham), Charlotte Bingham wrote the first volume of her autobiography aged nineteen while she was struggling with her shorthand and working during the day as a typist in MI5's Registry. *Coronet among the Weeds* was an instant and hilarious success. Soon afterwards she married the actor and writer Terence Brady and together they formed a successful writing partnership. *Lucinda* followed in 1966 and a second volume of autobiography, *Coronet among the Grass*, was released in 1974.

Educated at the Sorbonne, Charlotte's recruitment into MI5, as a filing clerk, was engineered by her father who was a close friend of the 'Registry Queen', Bunny, Lady Cadogan. After an introductory course at Leconfield House she was posted to C Branch in Cork Street where she found the work very uninspiring. Among MI5's more unconventional employees, she kept a bottle of champagne on her desk and photographs of film stars on the filing cabinets. She recalls that much of her time was spent typing letters with impossibly long Greek-Cypriot names and that she was really more interested in shopping at Fenwicks, the department store which was conveniently close, and in the weekend house parties which dominated the débutante season at that time. Her clandestine career was to be short-lived, partly owing to the reception of her first book, but also because of her poor typing and the increasingly long lunches with publishers. Her sense of security was also regarded as dubious, especially after an estimated twenty-nine files of classified atomic documents in her care were mislaid. As the Director of C Branch at the time remarked, 'We can only hope they haven't been lost on a Number 9 bus.'

Charlotte and Terence Brady continue a successful writing partnership, and live in Bruton, Somerset. In this extract from her autobiography Charlotte describes how her father found her a job although she is careful not to identify the nature of the work.

Coronet among the Weeds

I think me being hours on the telephone to that man really got my father down. Anyway he decided that finally he had to get me off his mind. And earning money. So he wrote to this office he knows very well and said, did they want any more secretaries? And they said yes. So I filled in all those forms they make you fill in. You know. What sex? What sex your parents? Are they sure? Are you a vampire? All that. Then this woman wrote and asked me to come for an interview. Only because she knew my father I think. Anyway I went.

Interviews are just as bad as you think they're going to be. First of all you don't know what to wear, then when you get there you can't remember whether you ate onions for lunch, so you spend the whole time mumbling sideways in case you did. Then you know you're going to hiccup so you have to cover it up with a coughing fit, and they ask you if you've had a medical, and, if you haven't, look doubtful about whether you're TB. And, when they tell you about what sort of job it is, you know you're going to hate every minute of it. And they usually say they only take on nice girls. So you try and look madly nice, and know you're going to loathe all the other nice girls. Sometimes I think I'd rather be a tart than go to another interview. Still I suppose even if you're a tart you have to be interviewed by a pimp. So you're back where you started.

By the time they said yes they would have me, it was the last thing I wanted to do, be a secretary in that old office. I nearly died when they said they'd have me. Still, my father was pushing really hard, so I'd had it. Anyway there's always the chance you might get run over on your way there. Or have a heart attack on the bus.

The first morning I went there that's what I did. I sat on the bus praying I'd have a heart attack. I didn't have one though, I spent most of the morning filling in more forms, then they sent me off to have lunch with this girl. I didn't know what to say to her. We had this ham salad so I talked about ham for quite a lot of the time. I could see she wasn't interested in ham, but I couldn't think of anything else.

Then we stomped along to this room where all these secretaries worked. And she introduced me to them all, one by one. They all tried to look as if they weren't very interested, but I knew they were. Not nice interested either. I knew they were all hating me before I even said hello, because they knew who my corney old father was. Honestly you die inside when you know people are hating you, because nothing you say seems to sound all right. So you end up not saying anything. Just smiling vacantly at your typewriter.

This girl who was in charge started telling me very quietly in a corner what the work was about, and what I had to do and everything. But I couldn't hear a word she was saying. The thing was she was saying all these things very quietly into my deaf ear. I've got this deaf ear, and when people say things very quietly into it I can't hear a thing. I didn't dare say I couldn't hear a thing she was saying. I thought she'd probably think I was being too grand to listen. So I sat the whole afternoon nodding and agreeing and not hearing a word. Honestly it was really embarrassing. Specially the next morning when I couldn't understand a word of what I was doing.

The first week they didn't put me to work for anyone. They just gave me things to type and letters to copy. That was embarrassing too, because I could only type terribly slowly because I hadn't done a job for such ages. And I knew they were all watching to see how fast I was going. So after every two lines I'd look round and give this shaky laugh. You try it, honestly it's no joke. Typing and giving shaky laughs all day long. You just think you'll never be able to stop. You think you're going to be there sweating and typing for the rest of your life. No really. Your whole life.

One thing about this office. They had terribly long coffee and tea breaks. Not just a cup at your desk, you went to this room and sat at tables and everything. 'Course the first week I was there no one much spoke to me, so I went to coffee and tea every day with these same two girls. It was much worse than typing. Honestly I used to sit there longing to be back sweating at my typewriter. The thing was I knew they were just dying to get me out of the way and say a few splendidly catty things about me and my typing. Only they couldn't because I was there and they were meant to be seeing I had someone to have coffee with.

You should have heard what they did talk about, these two girls. It was fantastic – day after day. They talked about how they washed their cardigans. And once they'd washed them they asked each other if they'd shrunk, and whether they should iron them. It wasn't that they couldn't talk about anything else, they just didn't want to. If I sort of murmured about something else they carried on talking about these old cardigans as if I wasn't there. Once I asked one of them if she had a boy friend, and she looked so offended you'd think I'd asked her if she was still a virgin. It would have killed me if she hadn't been. Though actually it's often the po-type girl that's swooniest about sex. They sit about looking very respectable and the next minute they're buying a smock.

'Course it's the old, old story when you get bags of women all working on top of each other. They just sit about knitting and talking about each other. If they haven't much imagination that's all they can think of doing. And once they've been doing it for a long time they couldn't stop if they wanted. Also they get this thing, like people in prison. They mind passionately about the tiniest things. Even things like whose turn to shut the window. And quarrel like anything for hours before they decide. It really matters to them whose turn it is. I don't think it does in the beginning, but I suppose after a bit they just get like everyone else. And they are in a prison. Only not the kind you can get out of.

None of those women liked me. I didn't really blame them. I don't think I'd have liked me if I'd been them either. It was awful at first because it was so lonely. When you've been a failure you mind about people not liking you. It really worries you. Because you're just a different kind of failure. But still a failure. Do you know I used to sit having coffee with those women, and sometimes I really wondered if we were all speaking English. No really. I could have been speaking Eskimo for all they knew or cared. And the awful thing was there was so many of them, and only one of me. You can scream with laughter if you've got someone else, but it's practically impossible to laugh by yourself. Every now and then I did though. Very privately behind my typewriter. But it was hardly living it up. I mean I can think of things I've done that were gayer.

Still, you can only mind about things up to a point. Once you've really done your nut about them, they cease to matter any more. Even being lonely you get like that. You mind like anything, then suddenly it just seems splendidly funny and you'd rather die than not be alone among a lot of tiny-minded women. I got more and more eccentric when I was in that office. I had to prove the whole day long that I wasn't like them. Honestly I'd have gone about naked to prove to myself I wasn't. Because every now and then I used to have awful nightmares that I was like them. Or I was becoming like them. Or I would become like them any minute. I'd wake up and find myself knitting and talking about Miss Smith's green hair. Gradually it would creep up on me. I wouldn't know it was happening but one day I'd wake up and I'd be a petty old thing sniping away making some poor little spotty secretary's life a misery. That's a feminine art that some women have to perfection. It's funny, it's nothing you can put your hand on. They don't swear and scream at you, but very quietly they make you suicidal. And yet you couldn't say what it was. You really couldn't. It's like that tap-dripping torture. I mean, what's an old tap dripping away?

Though it was all right for me. I had a cushy time of it compared to some people. I had weeds and parties and jokey parents and no spots. But imagine what it's like if you're weedless and parentless and you go home to your bed-sitter in the evening, only to eat, sleep and then take the tube again to face tiny minds for another eight hours. And on top of that you've got some old bitch sniping away at you. And you can't get another job, because you're afraid. I could have left any day, I only didn't because I wanted to prove I could stay in a job. I mean you feel sorry for those bitches till you see them torturing little asthmatic secretaries with runny noses. Hell, I was fair game.

I nearly went to live with an awful smooth man from working in that office. Honestly I was mad. I mean if you've got to live with someone it really shouldn't be some awful smooth slug. It was all part of proving madly that I wasn't becoming a net-curtain semi-detached typist. I wanted to be a bosomy sex symbol. One of those women from movie posters: 'Men loved and hated her. She was fire to the blood. No man had been known to forget her.'

I don't know why I even felt tempted to live with this slug. Except he wanted me to. But mostly when people ask me I scream with laughter. I didn't with him. He was the first weed who even tempted me. And yet I didn't love him in the least. I suppose I was flattered at being fire to someone's blood. Even a smooth slug. And he couldn't have been smoother. Honestly everything about him. He was good-looking, but in a very smooth way. He was smoothly intelligent, smoothly amusing, smoothly attentive. He had a smooth car and a smooth flat and he smoked smooth cigarettes.

Also he was smoothly seductive. He made you feel very silly because you wouldn't sleep with him. Not furious or anything. Just very silly. Actually it's funny about when men are trying to seduce you. You think up every reason. Like you're religious, your mother wouldn't like it, you respect them too much, all the corniest things. And the one thing you never think of is, you'd rather die than sleep with them and they make you feel quite sick anyway.

But this smooth man didn't make me feel sick. That was the trouble. It would have been easy if he'd made me feel sick. Not only didn't he make me feel sick, he made me laugh. When people make you feel a little foolish and make you laugh too it seems stupid. Particularly sometimes when you feel sad about not finding another superman. It was Migo who stopped me turning into a smooth mistress of a smooth slug. She said imagine if I got smoothly pregnant and had to get smoothly married and live smoothly ever after in that smooth flat. I couldn't take that. I really couldn't. Imagine having a smooth breakfast every morning. And watching him eat smooth boiled eggs. It would kill me.

Then Chloë came to work in this office. She was at school with Migo and me. She was going to be an actress, but she couldn't stand everyone stabbing everyone in the back. Anyway that's what she said. So she got down to being an old secretary like me. It made it much better Chloë being there actually, because she was pretty jokey. She couldn't do shorthand to save her life, and I don't think she knew how to wash a cardigan either. We both worked for two people in the same room, and we'd have secret signs to each other when we were taking dictation. Endless sunny afternoons we'd sit pretending we were in bikinis gambolling on beaches with bronzed men. That's one thing; if you've got imagination, they can never really stop you dreaming. It takes a bit of imagination to pretend you're on a beach when you're doing shorthand.

William Magan

In the Kremlin, at the heart of the Russian empire, there can hardly be men dreaming the dreams of Louis XIV and Philip II of Spain.

No history of the post-war Security Service would be complete without a reference to Brigadier William M. T. Magan, one of the most remarkable intelligence officers of his generation. Known to colleagues as Bill, he was born and brought up in Eire in an old Anglo-Irish family and became a Master of Foxhounds. He was a brilliant linguist and in later years was to be fluent in several dialects spoken in the Middle East. Commissioned from Sandhurst in 1928 he joined the Indian Cavalry and had many adventures in Persia and the North-West Frontier both before and during the war. In 1948 he joined MI5, rising to become the director of E Branch, responsible for liaison with Britain's colonies, for more than a decade until his retirement in 1968. During that period he supervised anti-terrorist operations in Cyprus and, at the request of Sir Martin Furnival Jones, undertook a detailed investigation into the possibility that his predecessor, Sir Roger Hollis, had been a Soviet mole. He also played a key role in anti-terrorist operations in Ulster.

After his retirement he and his wife Maxine, an artist of some note, started a successful pottery and he also turned his hand to his family history. His book,

Umma-More, is not merely the chronicle of an Irish family from its pre-Celtic roots in County Westmeath to the present day, but is a fascinating account of Ireland's rural history as seen through the experiences of the descendants of Humphry Magan, a landowner from Emoe in the parish of Ballymore, a place known in ancient times as Umma-More. Although Bill Magan now lives in Sussex he retains his strong Irish connections and several members of his family still live in Eire.

Virtually nothing in *Umma-More* would lead the reader to suspect that its author was a senior intelligence officer and he states that it was never his intention to take the narrative beyond his parents' generation but, as he says, the evolving relationship between England and Ireland 'is in one of its acute phases' and accordingly he added some 'current commentary' on recent events. This material is of considerable significance because it is the only example of a Security Service officer writing, in open literature, about the Provisional IRA.

Umma-More

The IRA, being an underground organisation, is necessarily secretive, and little enough is known about it even to the diligent press corps. The seemingly very efficient security authorities on both sides of the border are no less necessarily secretive about their knowledge of it. In these conditions no more than shadowy outlines of the IRA become discernible to the public.

The IRA of today appears to be an amalgam of four types of people:
(a) Genuine, if misguided, patriots.
(b) Modern, ruthless, international-type terrorists.
(c) Extreme militant Marxist-Leninists.
(d) Boys who fall into the clutches of the IRA at the dare-devil stage of life, and then cannot get out. They would be shot, or at least maimed, if they tried.

The genuine patriots in the IRA are misguided not only because they are breaking the law, and therefore acting contrary to the will of the great majority of their fellow citizens, but also because, in logic, the use of force can never succeed in bringing about what they claim to be their aim – a united Ireland. Violence can serve only to postpone the day when that may come about.

Moreover, growing repugnance at their increasing callousness and brutality progressively weakens even such limited sympathy and support as their patriotic claims have in the past engendered in extreme nationalist circles both at home and abroad. And it goes further than that. Their cowardly brutality brings the name and reputation of Ireland herself into world-wide disrepute. The IRA believes that its revoltingly barbarous acts bring it publicity. They do. But it is highly damaging publicity, both to themselves and to their country. The world supposes that the IRA in some measure reflects the temper and the colour of the government of the Republic, the people of Ireland, and the Irish Catholic Church. Thus the very name of Ireland is coming to be coupled with the taint of the IRA's crude and brutal savagery, and the people of Ireland sense it, and do not like it, and are finding it no longer tolerable. What Irishman, travelling abroad on the day following the unspeakably cowardly murder of the aged Lord Mountbatten and a boat full of women and children, and the carnage at Warren Point on the same day, would not have given his eyes not to have to display his Irish passport – a badge of shame upon that day, and the Irish, not excluding ardent nationalists, felt it to be so, and felt it deeply, and were determined in their hearts to see the end of the IRA.

Nevertheless, it is always the case in Ireland that the under-dog elicits sympathy, and particularly when the under-dog can claim to be a patriot suffering at the hands of the British. The IRA will therefore be liable from time to time to be able to arouse some public sympathy if they can put the British in the dock by events such as those of 'bloody Sunday', and their own callous sacrifice of ten of their members in the abortive 1981 hunger strike, and also in pockets of Catholic depression in the North. Their power to attract some public support should never, therefore, be over-looked. They will be concerned to foul Anglo-Irish relationships in any way they can.

But the people of Ireland will give support or encouragement to the IRA only at their own ultimate peril. The future lies in better relations with Britain, not in an IRA dominated Ireland. The enemy of Irish nationalists is not Britain. Britain would like nothing better than to be on terms of close friendship with them. When on British soil she extends her citizenship to them. And the British people treat the enormous number of Irish living in Britain with endless patience and good will. The real enemy of the Irish nationalists, and of true and loyal Irish nationalism, is the terrorism within their own body politic, an endemic Irish growth which, if they do not excise it, will inflict far more damage on Ireland than ever it will upon England.

Those members of the IRA who regard themselves primarily as patriots may argue that their grandfathers achieved the liberation of the twenty-six counties of the South by force of arms; and that what their grandfathers did in the South, they themselves can do in the North.

The Irish are addicted to mythology. It conforms to their romantic streak. Historical fact is, therefore, apt to reappear in mythological guise. Thus the mythology of what happened sixty years ago in Ireland has come to differ from the facts, and in this instance is dangerous to the Republic of Ireland itself, and to others.

The grandfathers of the present IRA did not set out to liberate the present Republic of Ireland. Their aim was an independent *united Republic of all Ireland*, which they determined to achieve by force and violence.

Politics being the art of the possible, every political realist was well aware that there was at that time no possibility that the Ulster loyalists would be prepared to accept a minority role in a united Ireland. But the leaders of the IRA (initially IRB – Irish Republican Brotherhood) were not political realists. They were romantic visionaries with, unfortunately, a brutal disregard for human life and suffering. Their campaign of violence did not, in the event, lead to a glorious victory. It failed, as it was inevitably bound to do. And what the IRA could not achieve sixty years ago with a much greater force, they cannot hope to achieve today with a lesser.

Nor is there any substance in the claim that the 1919–21 rebellion, even if did not achieve a united Ireland, did nevertheless bring about the independence of the twenty-six counties of the Republic of Ireland. That would have come about in any case through political negotiation.

Relations between Britain and the people of Ireland had probably never been better than they were during the first eighteen months of the 1914–18 Great War. The Home Rule bill had reached the Statute Book; and the British and Irish were united in a common war effort.

Then, during the Easter weekend of 1916, came the Sinn Fein rising. It was quickly crushed, but not before extensive damage had been done to the centre of Dublin city. Casualties, too, were high on both sides.

The rising had no public support. It was seen at the time by the people of Ireland as a futile, but damaging, affair. The rebels were treated with contempt – indeed with vilification by the Irish people.

After their surrender, they were jeered as they were taken through the streets to gaol. And the British soldiers who suppressed the rising received unstinting support from the civil population. The husbands, brothers and sons of many of the people of Ireland were at the war risking their lives alongside the British. A distraction in Ireland could only increase the danger for those at the front. So, 'down with the Sinn Feiners', was the overwhelming immediate reaction. It was not the Sinn Fein rebels who were then the heroes of Ireland. The heroes were men like Private Michael

Cassidy VC. His named rhymed with 'audacity', and his valour was the subject of a catchy ballad song that was on everyone's lips. And the most popular war song of all was, 'It's a long way to Tipperary'.

But during the next two years that mood was to change, and native Ireland was to revert to its more customary feelings of antipathy to England. Support fell away from the constitutionally elected political leaders of Ireland in the Whitehall parliament, and passed to the unconstitutional militant Sinn Fein leaders.

The execution in driblets over a period of ten days of some of the leaders of the 1916 Easter rising caused disquiet. After the first few were shot, responsible Irish leaders warned the British government that to continue the executions would have an adverse effect on the mood of the people of Ireland. But the executions went on. Fifteen were shot, including an infantile paralysis cripple, and one so badly wounded in the rebellion that he had to be carried to the execution ground on a stretcher and sat in a chair to be shot. There was public concern, and sympathy for the rebels began to be aroused.

There were probably three other principal factors which affected the temper of the people towards Britain.

Nearly a hundred rebels had been condemned to death. There was doubtless anxiety lest there be further executions.

Then, a large number of the captured rebels were taken out of Ireland and imprisoned in Britain. Who knew what might happen to them once across the water? More disquiet. When, after a short incarceration, they were brought back to Ireland and released, they were greeted rapturously, and treated as heroes.

The third factor was the threat of conscription which was widely regarded as unacceptable in Ireland. Many Irishmen were prepared to join the British forces voluntarily – and many were not. None were prepared to be dragooned into them.

The upshot was that by 1919, when the war was over, Sinn Fein had acquired overwhelming public support among Irish Catholics including the Catholic Church. And in January, 1919, they opened, with the brutal murder in cold blood of two policemen, the widespread and destructive – and altogether unnecessary – rebellion, known at the time, and ever since, as 'The Troubles', which was to last until mid-July 1921 when the IRA, having shot their bolt, were forced to come to the conference table where they should have come in the first place, instead of trying to bomb, murder and burn their way to their political objectives.

They had had their opportunity to act constitutionally and with political maturity and responsibility. Instead of refusing, Sinn Fein ought to have taken its seat at the 1917 Irish Convention. It had been called as a forum where Irishmen could negotiate between themselves the political future of Ireland. The nationalist Home Rule Party, the Ulster Unionists, and the Protestant Ascendancy were separately represented, but Sinn Fein stayed away. Had they attended, they would have had the full weight of the Catholic bishops, and the powerful Irish American lobby, behind them. That being so, there can be no doubt that, however protracted and difficult the negotiations, or whatever subsequent form they might have taken, the outcome would have been independence for the predominantly Catholic and nationalist parts of Ireland, without ever a shot being fired.

For half a century Britain had been moving towards Home Rule for Ireland. The 1912 Home Rule Bill was on the Statute Book. There can be no question that without the 1916 rebellion, and the subsequent 'Troubles', a degree of independence, probably well in excess of anything foreseen in the Home Rule bill, would have been granted to those parts of Ireland – the twenty-six counties of the South – where nationalist Catholics were in an enormous majority over loyalist Protestants.

It is no less inconceivable that nationalist Ireland could have failed to obtain a substantial measure of independence in consequence of the far-reaching discussions of the constitutional position of the White dominions during the 1920s which culminated in the Statute of Westminster, which, in effect, granted complete autonomy to the dominions in 1931.

Nor is it possible to suppose that, if never a shot had been fired, nationalist Ireland would have been any less independent today than she now is – any less independent, for instance, than Ghana or Jamaica, or many other imperial territories which received their freedom peaceably without ever a gun being drawn from the holster.

In nearly three centuries, since the 1641 rebellion, the only two significant occasions on which force had been used – the 1798 rebellion, and the Fenian outbreak in the mid-nineteenth century – it had achieved nothing. All the achievements – the amelioration and abrogation of the Penal Laws, the enfranchisement of Catholics, Catholic Emancipation, the disestablishment of the Church of Ireland, the succession of land laws whereby the lands of Ireland were being restored to the native Irish in an orderly and civilised manner, and finally the 1914 Home Rule bill – had been achieved by political processes, even though there had been occasional, sporadic, localised agrarian violence.

Although there could have been no possibility that Ulster would have joined a united Ireland, she would have been encouraged by Britain to develop such close relations with the South as might have seemed reasonable and possible. But the rebellion, followed by the Civil War among themselves of the Catholic nationalists in the South, in which they tore their country apart, and showed themselves hardly less merciful to each other than Cromwell had been, was no encouragement to the Ulster loyalists, Protestants or Catholic, to bed down with them.

The Irish Free State government which had been formed after the signing of the treaty with Britain in 1921, admitted officially to the execution during the Civil War of more than four times as many members of the IRA as the British 1916 executions. But that is probably only a fraction of the true figure, which is almost certainly unknown. The stories heard by those of us living in Ireland at the time of whole squads of IRA men caught with arms being secretly and summarily executed by the Irish army cannot have been without some foundation in fact. No graves were marked. No relatives were told. Numerous men who had taken up arms against the new Free State Government just disappeared. Ulster's distaste for a union with the South is understandable.

The later mythology, which raises the rebellions to heroic proportions, is indeed dangerous to Ireland. It would not have been approved by Daniel O'Connell, who would have no truck with violence. It endorses a precedent that threatens Ireland's own institutions. The rebellions of 1916, and 1919–21, did not usher in a glorious chapter of Irish history. They set the tone and the scene for a long period of lawlessness and violent crime, which continues to this day, and which has done much material damage to Ireland, caused great suffering to innocent people, dragged Ireland's name in the mud, and faced her today with a dangerous internal security problem.

There cannot be two standards of political morality. Laud the use of the gun as a political weapon, and you are setting the tone for all, and must not be surprised if others turn the gun on you to achieve their political ends. Praise the gun in the schools as a political weapon, and sign your own death warrant, and threaten Ireland with the standards of political morality of a banana republic. The schools themselves become the seed-bed for recruitment into the IRA of the enterprising, dare-devil boys. What they learn about the gunmen of the past may implant in their romantic young heads the notion that if they become the gunmen of today, they too will be the history book heroes of tomorrow. But that will not be their destiny. Instead, they will more than likely spend the best years of their lives all but forgotten in the Republic of Ireland's own gaols, instead of in useful service to their community. Is the land of saints and scholars bringing up its children in the right image?

Those of us who are living now are not responsible for what happened centuries ago. But we are responsible for what happens today. Let us consider what judgement history will pass on us in our turn. Teach history with understanding, and not with malice.

England unsettled Ireland; true. But the Romans, the Danes, the Anglo-Saxons, the French unsettled England; and much more recently Germany unsettled almost the whole of Europe. But sensible men all over Europe have been doing what they can to bury those old, and not so old, hatchets. The magnanimity of France, the Low Countries, Denmark and Norway towards Germany is an example worthy of study. Compare the EEC with the state of Western Europe in 1916, and in 1940. Fruitful and beneficial accommodation between old rivals is not impossible.

Alistair Horne

Judging from MI5's inept performance during the Hollis years, Hollis – an unforthcoming, reticent and retiring man – had at least a great deal to be reticent and retiring about. Macmillan regarded him dismissively as 'an insignificant man'.

In 1944, having already transferred from the Royal Air Force to the Coldstream Guards on the grounds of poor eyesight, Alistair Horne joined MI5's regional branch in Cairo, Security Intelligence Middle East. He had intended to drive tanks in the Guards Armoured Division but instead he was switched to intelligence duties which, at first, involved a reconnaissance of Transjordan to determine what area was accessible to Soviet T-34 tanks. He remained in SIME until he was demobbed in 1947.

Horne's work in SIME's Palestine branch was supervised by Maurice Oldfield, who was later to be appointed chief of SIS. He recalls that soon after the war SIS's cover name in the region changed from Inter-Services Liaison Department to the 'Combined Research Planning Office', known as 'Creepo', an acronym that was unfortunate as much of SIS's most secret correspondence was accidentally diverted to the Combined Regimental Pay Office, located in Jerusalem.

In 1952 Horne joined the *Daily Telegraph* as a foreign correspondent but left in 1955 upon the publication of his first book, *Back into Power*. Over the next twenty years he was to write more than a dozen important works of non-fiction, concentrating on military history and France. He was chosen by Harold Macmillan to be his official biographer, and in this passage (from Volume II) discusses the role of MI5 as the Profumo affair loomed.

Macmillan

Between the sentencing of the wretched Vassall [a homosexual Admiralty executive officer duped by the Russians into betraying secrets] in October 1962 and the publication of the Radcliffe Tribunal findings the following April [an investigation into all aspects of security in Britain following a succession of spy cases], Macmillan had no peace on the security front; the procession of spies continued. First, in November, there was Miss Barbara Fell, a senior official of the Central Office of Information, sentenced to two years' imprisonment for passing intelligence (of a fairly low order) to her young Yugoslav lover; 'apparently in the somewhat naive attempt to convert him to the Western way of life', commented Macmillan; 'not too bad', he wrote in his diaries, 'folly rather than treachery . . .' Next there came the final act in what Macmillan described as the 'almost historic' case of 'Kim' Philby. 'We think we have at last solved the mystery of who "tipped" off Burgess and Maclean,' he wrote in his diary for 19 February 1963:

> It was a man, much suspected at the time, but against whom nothing could be proved – one Philby. He was dismissed in 1951 from the service and has lived since in the Middle East, chiefly in the Lebanon, where he writes for the *Observer* and the *Economist*! In a drunken fit, he confessed everything to one of our men, so the whole thing is now clear. Maclean and Burgess were worse than mere *defectors* – they were spies, paid by Russians, over quite a number of years. This man Philby seduced them and recruited them to the Russian service. He has now disappeared from Beirut, leaving £2,200 in cash for his wife. Whether he will appear in Russia or not, we do not know. Anyway, it means more trouble . . .

Macmillan's diary entry described the details of the Philby story with fair accuracy, except that Philby had not been drunk when he had confessed to 'one of our men', Nicholas Elliott of MI6.

Macmillan seems to have been kept uninformed about the disappearance of Philby; this was consonant with his subsequent treatment by Hollis over Profumo, and almost certainly had something to do with his observations about 'shooting foxes' – which had become widely current in the Security Service. It was not until 29 March that Heath, speaking for the Foreign Office, announced it; on 1 July he stated categorically that Philby had been the 'Third Man', and was now presumed to be somewhere 'behind the Iron Curtain'. There was renewed storm in the press and a difficult passage for Macmillan in the Commons. He was agreeably surprised, however, at the staunch support he received from Gaitskell's successor, Harold Wilson. 'I had an hour with Harold Wilson,' Macmillan wrote in his diary for 11 July, 'and tried to explain to him how the so-called Security Services really worked. It seemed to me right to do so, and he took it quite well . . .' Macmillan recorded the gratitude he felt, after the Commons debate the following day, for Wilson's 'high sense of responsibility . . . at a period when I was very hard-pressed . . .'

From Philby the trail of powder led to Blunt. The last of a series of interrogations which led to Blunt's confession, and secret amnesty, apparently took place in 1964 – therefore after Macmillan's own resignation. When the revelations of Blunt's treachery first became known in 1979, Macmillan remarked,

> Yes, certainly we knew about it, but felt we couldn't do anything. Nothing to arrest the man on. No proof. If I'd said in the House, 'X was a traitor,' then I might have been called on to state this out of privilege, and suffer a monumental libel suit. Yes, we did suspect that Blunt was a wrong 'un . . .

'What was much more serious, in my time, and much more worrying,' Macmillan continued,

> was the warning we had of a possible traitor at the top of MI5. He'd been spotted wandering round the loos in the park . . . passing things, probably it was opium or something, he seemed to be somewhat unhinged, probably not working for the Communists. Fortunately he retired before we could do anything, but it was all a great worry . . .

He continued, eighteen months later, on the same theme:

> First of all we thought it was boys, then he was followed and was observed to meet a foreigner; I think he was probably Japanese, and we watched him.
> My impression was that he was – like so many people in that game – suffering from the fatigue of having been at it too long . . .

The wanderer-in-the-park was 'Peters', alias Graham Mitchell, Hollis's Deputy Director-General in MI5. On account of his strange activities, Mitchell had been under surveillance, under the codename of 'Peters', as a top-level mole at the head of MI5 since April 1963. Hollis had informed Macmillan about it shortly thereafter, evidently playing it down as much as possible, and refusing initially to request permission to tap 'Peters'' telephone. Mitchell then suddenly asked for early retirement; the mole-hunters were disconcerted, as this suggested that another mole might have tipped him off. By December 1963, after Macmillan had retired, 'Operation Peters' was abandoned for want of conclusive evidence. Mitchell died in 1984. The spotlight was then focused on Hollis himself, but on insubstantial and unsatisfying evidence. (Macmillan always held the opinion that Hollis was an inept and 'insignificant' head of MI5, but not a treacherous one.)

In April there were more security headaches for Macmillan. The first was a 'tiresome "leak" ' on Civil Defence, which had enabled the CND to print pamphlets:

> which purport to reveal the various Civil Defence measures, including the Regional HQs. It is *not* very serious from a practical point of view, but it's *another security failure* of the Government, and the Press – smarting under Vassall [Radcliffe had censured two newspapermen for alleged inaccurate reporting] – has grasped eagerly at a new chance of attacking me and the Home Secretary . . .

The second case, three days later and presumably related to the first, went unrecorded in Macmillan's memoirs:

> We have caught a spy (or rather a man 'getting ready to spy' – buying equipment etc.). He is an employee of Euratom, doing 'liaison' with the Atomic Energy Authority . . . It will be rather delicate with the Euratom authorities but rather a triumph for the Security Service. For once, we have 'got' a man *before* he has done us any injury . . .

This was all illustrative, Macmillan later thought, of how 'by an extraordinary combination of circumstances or an exceptional run of ill-luck, Parliament and the public were being continually stimulated into a sense almost of hysteria. Nor did our critics distinguish between the failures and the successes.' And he went on – perhaps rather revealingly: 'from my point of view, life would have been easier if the counter-espionage work had been less effective . . .'

It was against this essential backdrop that the Profumo case occurred.

Maxwell Knight

The type of man who lives in society by means of his wits and who is on the fringe of the underworld, is, perhaps, the most contemptible of all crooks. He is a man without morals or principles of any kind; he works alone, and owes allegiance to no boss.

Max Knight was probably MI5's least conventional, and most successful, case officer. He joined the organization in 1925, having been a naval cadet, and proceeded to recruit long-term sources in various political groups regarded as subversive. Perhaps his greatest coup was the insertion of Olga Gray into the Communist Party, and it was due to her evidence for the prosecution that a Soviet spy ring operating at Woolwich Arsenal was rounded up. Her appearance as a surprise witness led to the conviction in 1938 of Percy Glading, a veteran Communist activist, and three of his agents in the arsenal.

Knight's speciality was the cultivation of agents who could spend years manoeuvring themselves into a position of access. In Olga Gray's case it took nine years for her to accumulate sufficient information to call in the police. Similarly, Knight employed Joan Miller to ingratiate herself with a group of suspected Nazi sympathizers and in 1940 this led to the appearance of Anna Wolkoff and Tyler Kent at the Old Bailey on a charge of having stolen from the US embassy hundreds of secret telegrams that had been exchanged between the Prime Minister and President Roosevelt. Another of his agents was Tom Driberg who was eventually betrayed by Anthony Blunt and expelled from the CPGB, an incident that convinced Knight that the Soviets had penetrated MI5.

Knight enjoyed a wide circle of friends in London and used them as a useful pool from which to recruit informants and to obtain assistance. He approached Dennis Wheatley for permission to employ his stepson, William Younger, as an agent while he was still at Oxford. He also arranged for Wheatley to provide one of his other agents, Friedle Gaertner, with cover by hiring her as his secretary.

Although Knight enjoyed phenomenal success in counter-intelligence and trained a whole generation of case officers, his accomplishments were marred by the Benjamin Greene episode in which one of his agents, an Austrian named Harald Kurtz, concocted evidence against an espionage suspect who proved to be exceptionally well-connected. Greene and his family pursued Kurtz for years and eventually brought the case to the House of Lords. Greene was released from custody and Kurtz was exposed publicly as an unscrupulous Security Service stoolpigeon who had manufactured a spurious case against an innocent man for financial reward.

By any standards Knight was an unconventional man who commanded great loyalty from his subordinates and agents. He retired from MI5 in 1956 and established a reputation as a broadcaster, before succumbing to pneumonia in January 1968.

Fluent in German, Knight translated *A Confidential Matter: The Letters of Richard Strauss and Stefan Zweig, 1931-35*, and in 1934 wrote a melodramatic thriller, *Crime Cargo*, in which a newspaper reporter named Randall defeated a gang intent on robbing the passengers of a ship.

Crime Cargo

Elmer's pride had been mortally wounded by the succession of blows which had befallen him that day. To be turned down by a rich and lovely girl, put in one's place by a ship's captain, and finally to be laughed at by an assembly of one's fellow men and women might have a considerable effect on any man; on Elmer Courtney this combination of evils had produced a riot of savage resentment that threatened to rob him completely of his mental balance and control.

Almost the first thing he noticed when he entered his cabin was the folded paper which was propped up against the cigarette-box on the side table. Elmer frowned as he picked it up. For a wild moment he thought it might be a note of apology from Ailsa – the self-conceit of the man was colossal – but when he saw that the paper was soiled and creased, he dismissed the idea and proceeded to undo the crude fastenings. He gave a hurried glance at the contents, then crossed to the door and bolted it. He sat down on the bed and read it more carefully.

> We are all set for an early break. Be ready to help if required. You will be tipped off as to what you are to do. How would five grand suit you? Five more if the show's OK. Don't go looking for trouble – you'll find plenty if you do. There may be some rough stuff, so keep your nose clean and your mouth shut. If you agree and want to cash in, simply write the words: 'I agree to your terms' on a piece of paper *and sign it*. Then place it where you found this and it will be fetched and delivered safely. Don't wait. Do it at once and don't forget to tie up your tongue.

That was all. Courtney pulled at his lower lip and read it a third time. The idea of a possible ten thousand dollars appealed to him enormously; but the idea of writing out the reply did not. He could see how nicely it would place him in the hands of the gang.

Ten thousand dollars! Gosh, that sounded well. What on earth could the stunt be that they intended pulling, out here on the high seas? Robbery? Courtney did not think that there could be sufficient money or jewellery on board to make it worth while, and how would they make a getaway? Perhaps these fellows were mistaken in the amount they would get. He had always thought that the low roughneck type of crook was given to miscalculation – and if this was so, then there would be serious risk of his not getting his cut. On the other hand, this man Binetti was a real big shot, and big shots did not go in for speculative business. Again, was he in a position to refuse? He could, of course, go to Mr Holland and the captain straight away and expose the whole thing, but he knew enough about gangland to feel certain that even if the attempted hold-up, or whatever it was, failed, he would almost certainly be killed, and this was what mattered. After all, what use was it foiling the plot if he was not going to be alive to enjoy the fruits of his enterprise? No! There was no way out of it. He must send the reply. Damn the passengers and the captain and the blamed crew! He didn't owe them anything, and they'd laughed at him. Ailsa had treated him with contempt, and the two mates had skinned him at cards. Well, let them rot! He had a score to pay, and, by God, he'd pay it! Perhaps Ailsa would be only too glad to have him soon, in order to save herself from something worse.

With these pleasant thoughts coursing through his brain, Elmer picked up a piece of paper and took out his fountain-pen. His hand trembled, from suppressed rage rather than from fright, as he carefully proceeded to print the answer as directed. He was not going to have his writing give him away. Stay – what about the signature? Should he chance not signing it at all? No, that would be too risky. He would compromise. He placed a simple 'C' at the foot of the note and then put it into an envelope and set it up just as the other had been.

This done, he stubbed out the cigarette he had been smoking and placed the original note in his pocket. Then he smiled as he walked across the cabin, switched out the light, and slammed the door shut most ostentatiously. He turned and swiftly secreted himself behind a corner curtain which covered an arrangement for hanging coats, and stood motionless, hoping that he would not have too long a vigil. He might be forced into agreeing to sign the reply to the note, but at least he would take care to see who it was that came to call for the reply. This would satisfy his ever-present curiosity, and at the same time provide him with knowledge which he might usefully turn to his advantage at some future stage of the proceedings.

He had not long to wait, for he had hardly settled himself in the corner when he heard the sound of the door handle being softly turned. He held his breath, and moved aside the curtain just a fraction of an inch. The door was opening. The gap widened, and Elmer saw the outline of a man's figure. He had intended to lie low and just satisfy himself as to the messenger's identity. Would the man switch on the light or not? Elmer watched in some excitement, as the figure stood just a pace inside the doorway, listening. Then he closed the door behind him and, to the watcher's relief, switched on the light. Courtney could hardly suppress a gasp of surprise when he saw that the intruder was Randall.

Gosh! he thought. This was hot! A reporter, eh? So he'd taken them all in! Then why had he denounced the gangsters? Was he afraid, and did he hope to play a double game just as he himself was planning to do? If so, why was he acting as the messenger? It was all too confusing, and Elmer did not feel quite so happy about the affair. There were too many ramifications.

On Randall's part the going was easier. After closing the door he had at once seen the note in the plain envelope propped up so prominently. He debated as to whether he had time to open it carefully – it couldn't have been stuck down long – and so acquaint himself further as to the extent of Courtney's complicity. It would take him at least five minutes, though, and in that time there was risk of discovery by Luigi. Randall was thankful that Luigi was unknown to him as a gangster. He shivered as he thought of what the consequences might have been had they recognised each other the first day on board. It would have been Randall's last day, too!

On reflection, Randall decided that he would merely have a look round the cabin, in case there was any clue to be picked up that might throw light on this unholy alliance. He glanced about him and then he stiffened.

Beneath the corner curtain he could see a pair of shoes. Nothing much in that – but these shoes contained feet, and Randall felt that this was an unexpected and undesired development. Should he pretend he had not seen anything, and make his way out? All his news sense rebelled against this idea, and so, hoping that his ready wit would save him from any unpleasant consequences, he stepped quickly over and pulled aside the curtain.

Randall's first instinct was to laugh, so comical did Courtney look. He stood there gaping and confused. He strongly resembled a mummy in a museum. Then they both spoke, almost simultaneously.

'Great snakes! Diddled!'

'Oh! So it's the slick reporter, is it? Some reporter – huh!'

They stood still, eyeing one another closely. Their two brains wrestled with conflicting thoughts.

'What the hell,' thought Randall, 'was Courtney doing there? He must be crazy to try and find out the identity of the messenger. Did he not realise that too much knowledge, like too little, might be a very dangerous thing?'

Elmer's reactions were unpleasant. For a fourth time that day he had been made to look a fool.

Miranda Ingram

The danger is that officers are tempted to enjoy the secrecy surrounding their work and live the John Le Carré legend.

Twice during April 1983 Michael Bettaney smuggled top secret documents out of the Security Service headquarters in Gower Street and conveyed them to the home of the bemused KGB *Rezident* in London, Arkadi Gouk. Working in the élite counter-espionage K Branch, Bettaney was in an ideal position to identify the most appropriate member of London's Soviet community to receive the documents. He also knew exactly when Gouk's house in Holland Park would be free of MI5 surveillance, and he was confident that, considering the apparent paucity of MI5's information about the KGB, his treachery would go undetected. What he had not even considered was the existence of a British agent close to the heart of the local *Rezidentura*, in the form of Oleg Gordievsky, an SIS source since 1972. As soon as Gouk received his windfall he consulted Gordievsky who, instantly recognizing the danger of betrayal he faced, denounced the first package of K Branch secrets as an obvious provocation and promptly tipped off his SIS handlers.

Following an extended surveillance operation conducted by SIS, the field of suspects was narrowed to Bettaney and he was tried at the Old Bailey in April 1984 and sentenced to twenty-three years' imprisonment. One of those present in the gallery for the part of the prosecution which was conducted in public was one of his former K Branch colleagues, Miranda Ingram, who had recently left the Service following a disagreement with the management. She had become a journalist, and was later to work in Russia as the *Daily Mail*'s correspondent, but what she heard in court prompted her to write a fierce critique of the Security Service for *New Society* of 31 May 1984.

Trouble with Security

In my view, MI5, as a protector of our democracy against those who threaten it, has a valid role to play. But it should be, should be felt to be, and equally important should be seen to be, a body that is truly representative of the British people. Were it such, it is possible that the doubts and fears of Michael Bettaney might have been contained.

The intake is now broader than the old days, when one simply 'knew a chap'. However, the overall tone is right-wing. (This may be endemic in the nature of the work, although there is no reason why the protection of democracy, any more than patriotism, should be a right-wing concern.) Ideally the service is an apolitical body. And, indeed, most members are not political animals. A large majority are content just to 'do their job' and not to think any further. But the politically uninterested are – again maybe inevitably – conservative, and probably Conservative. Certainly, other views are not openly discussed. There is an absence of open political debate inside the service. In this atmosphere it is not only the socially inferior who can feel uncomfortable. Those who dissent from the overall tone are also faced with a problem.

Most of the work of MI5 would be seen as acceptable by most of the British public. The Russians are fair game. The glamour of MI5 in the public eye largely rests on the work of 'K', the counter-espionage branch, where both Michael Bettaney and I worked. Soviet spies, KGB, and so on: this is the stuff the thrillers are made of.

Within the service, too, a posting to this branch is much sought after. The enemy is professional, and there is a mutual respect between the two parties. The work is intellectually stimulating. It is a true battle of wits, with both sides willing participants in the game. 'K' branch is the acceptable face of MI5.

Likewise Libyans, IRA bombers and other terrorists are unquestionably acceptable targets. So are genuine 'subversives'. But it is in the area of domestic surveillance that problems can occur. This comes under 'F' branch. Working here means monitoring one's fellow-citizens.

'Subversive' is generally understood as meaning 'intending to subvert democracy by undemocratic or violent means'. 'Violent' is easy to define. 'Undemocratic' is obviously more open to differing interpretations. For example: are the miners currently [May 1984] trying to bring down the government by undemocratic means, or are they merely exercising their democratic right to strike? Furthermore, how does one determine whether or not a group or person is intending to be subversive without first monitoring it or him?

So where does one draw the line in domestic surveillance? Obviously each moderate and thinking man draws it at his own point. This inevitably becomes a political issue, as it did for Bettaney.

The concern of some officers is that there is a lack of flexible debate within the service about the interpretation of 'subversion' in the determining of policy. In the prevailing right-wing atmosphere, an officer who dissents from the official line does not feel encouraged to voice his concern. He feels that to do so would be futile, or, unfortunately, that it would be detrimental to his career. If he cannot discuss his doubts within the service, and he certainly cannot do so outside, he is faced with one of two choices. He can leave his job, or he can keep quiet. To leave one's job takes courage. At a time of extreme unemployment, it is certainly not an attractive idea. And, in the end, if he feels strongly enough about the issue, it is unconstructive.

So, initially, he keeps quiet. This is where the situation becomes dangerous. What might begin as a moderate dissent will be silently nurtured and will fester until it grows into a much more serious dissent. Because it is not drawn out into open debate, it may eventually seek a clandestine outlet. This might be a leak. Or, in a more extreme case, it can grow into a desire to seriously undermine the security service itself. The Bettaney case is an extreme manifestation of how dangerous this situation can become.

Cathy Massiter

In the course of my own career, I became increasingly at odds with myself over the nature of the work and its justifications.

Cathy Massiter's function in F Branch of the Security Service was, among other duties, to supervise the monitoring of political activists and organizations which were judged a threat to the state. Naturally the exact definition of what constitutes subversion is a highly political and subjective judgement, but this is a daily exercise in F Branch. Massiter became increasingly disenchanted with her work and, in the absence of a satisfactory safety valve within the structure of the Service where anxieties could be articulated without jeopardizing a promising career, she resigned.

The article written by Miranda Ingram in defence of Michael Bettaney proved to be a catalyst for Massiter. Having read 'Trouble with Security' she contributed a letter to *New Society* two weeks later which echoed some of the doubts her former colleague had expressed. Following its publication she was offered the opportunity to go into further detail on the subject of the intrinsic flaws of the Service. This television documentary was transmitted in March the following year amid much controversy. Today Cathy Massiter continues to live in East Sussex, having escaped unscathed after a series of disclosures about the performance and operations of the Security Service which led to litigation before the European Court.

New Society

SIR: As another ex-employee of MI5, I would like to congratulate Miranda Ingram on her courageous article on the Bettaney case ('Trouble with security', 31 May). I can only endorse fully her views on the general ethos of the security service and the steps which need to be taken if that organisation is to have credibility as a protector of a democratic society.

It seems to me particularly necessary to recognise that Michael Bettaney is not some kind of exceptional anomaly who got in because of the failure of recruitment/vetting procedures, but is to a large extent a product of the security service itself. Though his reactions were extreme, the conflicts and dissatisfactions which provoked them are far from rare.

In the course of my own career, I became increasingly at odds with myself over the nature of the work and its justifications, the problems becoming particularly acute in the last two to three years, which were spent in F Branch. Attempts to discuss its difficulties with senior officers were totally frustrating as one always arrived at the ultimate argument: 'It's the job – put up with it or get out.'

The system unfortunately has little capacity for dealing with such problems, and none at all for taking them seriously.

CATHY MASSITER

George M. Leggett

That there was a considerable basis of truth in certain of the Soviet allegations emerges clearly from accounts subsequently written by Reilly and his SIS colleague, Captain George Hill, who were rewarded for their exploits with an MC and a DSO respectively.

George Leggett began to research the Soviet intelligence and security apparatus when he joined MI5 from Trinity Hall, Cambridge in 1941. At the end of the war he spent two years in Germany under British Control Commission cover, and then returned to the Security Service. He was later posted to Canberra as MI5's Security Liaison Officer. He retired in 1971. The book he published in 1981, after years of research at the London School of Economics, where he still works, was drawn entirely from non-classified sources; nevertheless it provides an authoritative insight into British attitudes and SIS operations in the Soviet Union.

Leggett relied upon many academic sources for his study of Feliks Dzerzhinsky's secret police, and he has acknowledged the help he received from Ray Rocca, a senior member of the CIA's counter-intelligence staff, and Edward Ellis Smith, another CIA professional who had been the first chief of station in Moscow.

Leggett, who is married with a son, still lives in London and is researching a biography of Feliks Dzerzhinsky. In this extract he refers to Sidney Reilly and George Hill, both SIS agents of the early 1900s whose adventures have been described in these pages.

The Cheka: Lenin's Political Police

The anti-Bolshevik conspiracy, as reported in the Soviet press, consisted of two parts: the 'Lockhart case', involving Lockhart and Sidney Reilly in league with the Letts; and the 'envoys' plot', covering a much wider canvas, and based in the first instance on the revelations of René Marchand, former *Figaro* correspondent and trusted associate of the French diplomatic mission in Moscow. Marchand was sufficiently converted to Communism to give the Soviet authorities an account – in the form of a letter addressed to President Poincaré, conveniently 'found' in a Cheka search – of a meeting he had attended on 25 August [1918] at the office of the US Consul-General, de Witt Poole. The French Consul-General, Grenard, was also present, but not so Lockhart. This secret conclave decided that, after the impending departure of the remaining Entente staff from Russia, sabotage, espionage, and other disruptive work would be directed by stay-behind Allied intelligence representatives: Sidney Reilly for Britain, Colonel Henri de Vertement for France, and Kalamatiano for the USA. Bridges would be blown up on approaches to Petrograd, cutting off food supplies to the city, etc, etc. The purpose of these plots was to bring down the Bolshevik régime and to provoke renewal of hostilities on Germany's eastern front.

That there was a considerable basis of truth in certain of the Soviet allegations emerges clearly from accounts subsequently written by Reilly and by his SIS colleague, Captain George Hill, who were rewarded for their exploits with an MC and a DSO respectively. That is not to say that the conspirators necessarily proposed – as asserted by the Soviet press – to kill Lenin and Trotsky; more in character was Reilly's reported intention to march them trouserless, objects of derision, through the streets of Moscow. Zinoviev and Dzerzhinsky reached hysterical heights of absurdity in a statement published in *Izvestia* on 5 September, alleging: 'The English and French are the real murderers of Volodarskii and Uritskii, and the organisers of the attempts on the lives of Lenin and Zinoviev . . . The vile stranglers of freedom are ready to commit any crime. They have murdered Comrade Uritskii because he brought together the threads of an English conspiracy in Petrograd.'

More to the point was *Izvestia*'s allegation that 'representatives of the English and French Governments have entered into close contact with Tsarist generals . . . with the Kadet Party . . . and with the treacherous Socialist Revolutionaries and Mensheviks'. Lockhart, who in early April had begun to establish a rapport with anti-Bolshevik groups in Moscow – from monarchists to Mensheviks – had made contact in May 1918 with Savinkov's underground organisation, but was peremptorily ordered to discontinue this. The French were less diffident, and in early July subsidised the National Centre political resistance organisation – closely linked with Savinkov and with General Alekseev on the Don – to the amount of 2,500,000 roubles; Lockhart himself added one million roubles in mid-July, without authorisation. A little later Lockhart and his French colleagues despatched a courier carrying ten million roubles, with promises of much more to come, to General Alekseev. However, these secret subventions were probably not known to the Bolsheviks at the time.

The 'Lockhart case' and the 'envoys' plot' came up for open trial before the Supreme Revolutionary Tribunal in Moscow on 28 November 1918, lasting until 3 December and receiving wide coverage in *Izvestia*. Four of the principal accused, Lockhart, Reilly, Grenard and de Vertement, were outlawed *in absentia*, to be shot as enemies of the state if apprehended. Of the remaining accused, eight were pardoned, eight were committed to prison with hard labour for five years; only two were sentenced to death for spying, namely the US citizen of Russian-Greek parentage, Xenophon de Blumenthal Kalamatiano, and a Russian officer in Soviet Government service, Lieutenant Colonel Aleksandr Fride (or Friede), who was executed on 14 December 1918. Kalamatiano was twice taken out to be shot, in an endeavour to make him talk, and was each time temporarily reprieved. On 13 April 1919, Lenin brought Kalamatiano's case up for discussion at a meeting of the Party Central Committee, which pronounced: 'In view of the possibility of using him as a hostage in negotiations with the Americans, it has been decided not to shoot him for the time being, but to keep him in prison. In May 1920, Kalamatiano's death sentence was commuted; he was released in the summer of 1921, and returned to the USA.

The polyglot Sidney Reilly, described by Lockhart as a Jew from Odessa named Rosenblum, and as a Napoleonic character possessed of high ambition, superb courage, and a fertile imagination, eventually came to a tragic end. He continued to participate in anti-Bolshevik crusades, allowed himself to be lured back into Russia in 1925 by the bait of a highly sophisticated OGPU-controlled resistance organisation known as the *Trust*, and disappeared into limbo.

CHAPTER XII

Illicit Disclosure

_____

The whole crux of the issue, however, boils down to the government's contention that Secret Service officers owe the Crown (whatever that is) a lifelong duty of confidentiality. I was not advised of this either verbally or in writing – any more than I was asked when I joined the Service whether I was a Communist or a bugger. For that matter, neither was Kim Philby.
Anthony Cavendish, *Inside Intelligence*

The principle of banning the post-war memoirs of those who had enjoyed access to secret intelligence was established very soon after the Second World War. Ironically, one of the first victims of Whitehall's heavy-handed censorship was Sir Percy Sillitoe, MI5's first post-war Director-General. Sillitoe retired from MI5 in August 1953 and announced his intention to publish his memoirs, which prompted an instantaneous reaction from his successor, Sir Dick White. The new Director-General insisted that Sillitoe submit his entire manuscript for scrutiny before it went to the publishers, and the sanitized version that was eventually released in 1955 was almost completely emasculated. As the author said to his family, 'They've torn the bloody guts out of it, torn it to shreds.'

Sillitoe was luckier than Sir William Charles Crocker, the distinguished lawyer who served on the wartime Home Defence Security Executive, the powerful triumvirate consisting of himself, Sir Joseph Ball and Lord Swinton which effectively supervised MI5 during the first months of the war. Crocker was prohibited from describing any aspect of this secret work and remarks in his memoirs, *Far from Humdrum*, that 'this is a pity. I could have told a side-splitting yarn, but at the risk of being disbelieved.'

While Sillitoe and Crocker were prevented from making any worth-while disclosures, the traitors Kim Philby and George Blake suffered no penalty when they set pen to paper. Kim Philby's defection to Moscow in January 1963, prompted by Nicholas Elliott's dramatic confrontation in Beirut, was followed five years later by the publication of his autobiography, *My Silent War*. The announcement that SIS's most notorious traitor intended to release his memoirs caused consternation among his former colleagues but the government concluded that to ban the book would merely enhance its value and thereby its circulation. Philby's account, which went much further than his wartime experiences and gave details of his post-war activities, was published by a former member of the Communist Party of Great Britain, James MacGibbon, who had himself once been the subject of an MI5 investigation headed by Peter Wright. *My Silent War* became a best seller and did much to diminish SIS's reputation, but some well-informed insiders, principally Robert Cecil, were to question its accuracy and highlight areas where the author could be detected deliberately falsifying the record. Whatever its shortcomings, neither the author nor the publishers of *My Silent War* were prosecuted for breaching the Official Secrets Act. Among the disclosures made by Philby was the identity of one of his MI5 tormentors, Arthur Martin, who had by then transferred from the Security Service to SIS.

While Philby is best known in his role as traitor and author, before he fled to the Soviet Union, when he was at a low ebb, having been sacked from SIS, he ghosted a book for a friend. The result was *David Allens: The History of a Family Firm 1857–1957*.

Whatever the government's deliberations, a very similar process must have happened more than twenty years later when George Blake's autobiography, heavily edited by Tom Bower, was published in London. Unlike Philby, Blake had been convicted at the Old Bailey, and his defection to Moscow had taken place only after he had escaped from Wormwood Scrubs. Nevertheless, it is an unpalatable irony that the two senior SIS officers to betray their country received substantial royalties from British publishers for their memoirs, while three others, Joan Miller, Peter Wright and Anthony Cavendish, who all served their country faithfully, were to be harassed through the courts for attempting to do the same thing.

All three decided to publish accounts of their adventures while in the service of different branches of British Intelligence, and in doing so brought upon themselves the wrath of the Treasury Solicitor who, with varying degrees of success, obtained temporary injunctions to restrain publication. The reaction of the authorities, which ultimately proved counter-productive in every case, was entirely different when Greville Wynne released his memoirs *The Man from Moscow* which, for the first time, contradicted the official British line that he had been an innocent businessman when he was imprisoned in Moscow in 1963. In his book

Wynne confirmed that he had been an SIS courier operating in Eastern Europe, but instead of trying to prevent publication the Ministry of Defence merely commented that 'certain passages ... would almost certainly have been objectionable on security grounds, had they been true'.

Despite having been compromised by Philby, Arthur Martin's secret career as an MI5 molehunter was uninterrupted. He later fulfilled the same function for SIS where he teamed up with Stephen de Mowbray, formerly SIS's head of station in Washington DC, where both men fell under the spell of Anatoli Golitsyn. When the KGB defector came to publish the first volume of his Byzantine interpretations of the Kremlin's ambitions the book was edited by Martin, working with his old colleague de Mowbray.

Joan Miller

It's easy to see what made Max's department such a literary one; with so much dramatic material to hand, the impulse to make a high-class spy story out of it must have been pretty well irresistible to anyone with the least degree of narrative ability.

Joan Miller was the maiden name of Mrs Joanna Phipps, who was recruited into the Security Service in 1939 by MI5's legendary agent runner, Maxwell Knight. When she reported for work at Wormwood Scrubs, where MI5 established its early wartime headquarters, she had little idea that she would soon be deployed against Anna Wolkoff, a leading member of the anti-Semitic Right Club and a suspected Nazi spy. Joan's task was to penetrate this group of pro-Fascist activists and collect evidence against Wolkoff and the MP for Peebles, Captain Archibald Ramsay. Joan befriended Ramsay's wife and later provided crucial testimony against Wolkoff and her contact in the US embassy in London, Tyler Kent, both of whom were convicted and imprisoned.

Joan's memoirs, entitled *One Girl's War*, were ghosted by Pat Craig, an Ulster journalist who relied on notes written during Joan's declining years in Malta. The book was originally intended to be published in London by Lord Weidenfeld, but in November 1986 the Attorney-General, Sir Michael Havers, obtained an injunction to prevent its distribution in England. Joan had died in June 1985 but the next year her daughter Jonquil arranged for *One Girl's War* to be released in Ireland by a small publishing house, Brandon Books, based in Dingle, County Kerry. The Attorney-General then made an unsuccessful attempt in Dublin to obtain an injunction but the Irish High Court ruled that a ban would be a breach of Eire's constitution. It was not until March 1992 that the restriction in England was lifted. In this passage Joan recalls her attempts to collect incriminating information about Captain Ramsay.

One Girl's War

The Right Club, which bore certain similarities to Admiral Sir Barry Domvile's organization, The Link, had been founded in 1938 by Captain Archibald Maule Ramsay, Unionist member for Peebles since 1931. Its members – about three hundred altogether, peers and MPs included – professed a belief in the ideal of an Anglo-German fellowship, as well as nurturing vigorous anti-Semitic feelings. Captain Ramsay was a friend of Sir Oswald Mosley. The Ramsays had a house in Onslow Square, but the club usually held its meetings in a flat above a little restaurant in South Kensington. This restaurant was the Russian Tea Rooms.

Early in 1940 M [Maxwell Knight] decided I was ready to go ahead with the task he had set me. I had already met Mrs Amos (Marjorie Mackie), one of the other agents involved in the business (a cosy middle-aged lady who will always remind me of Miss Marple), and it was arranged that she should take me along to the tea-shop one evening, presenting me as a friend of her son who was serving with the RNR. The restaurant was on the corner of Harrington Gardens, directly opposite South Kensington tube station. It was owned and run by an émigré White Russian admiral and his wife and daughter. These people, whose name was Wolkoff, had been dispossessed as a consequence of the Bolshevik revolution – Admiral Wolkoff had been the Tsar's naval attaché in London at the time – and understandably took a fervent anti-Communist line. Anna, the daughter, in particular, had come to revere the policies of Nazi Germany. From its inception, she had been among the leading activists of the Right Club.

It was a cold windy evening when I came out of the underground with Mrs Amos and crossed the road to the tea-rooms. The doors opened straight on to the street. Mrs Amos had described the old admiral to me, and, as we entered, I saw and recognized him at once: an upright, dignified, white-haired figure sitting aloof at a table, observing with detachment the comings and goings of his customers. He gave the impression of someone brought to a state of impassivity by the experience of countless vicissitudes.

The place was fairly crowded that evening, but we found an empty table, sat down and ordered tea. (You could actually get vodka here, long before it became a fashionable drink in this country, and also Russian foods like riaptchiki and caviar.) People around us were discussing the kinds of minor accident that occurred in the blackout, or lamenting in rueful voices the impossibility of obtaining certain necessities. These were among the standard topics of wartime conversation; you heard such unembittered complaints all over the place. Presently Anna Wolkoff came across the room, making her way through the polished tables, and stopped to speak to Mrs Amos who soon found an opportunity to bring me into the conversation, mentioning my supposed association with her son. Anna, who seemed prepared to be friendly in a guarded sort of way, asked what I did. I told her I worked at the War Office, laughed and added that really my job was a very boring one in a filing department. She nodded once or twice and passed on to something else. I could only hope I'd impressed her sufficiently to ensure that she remembered me when I next appeared.

The Russian Tea Rooms, with its polished wooden furniture, panelled walls and open fireplace, was the sort of café you could visit unescorted without jeopardizing your reputation. Over the next few weeks I made a habit of dropping in at all hours of the day, sometimes bringing along an innocent friend to lend colour to the deception I was engaged in. The old admiral used to join me quite often at my table where he would sit reminiscing about the past in Russia. 'No nonsense like these absurd licensing laws you have in England,' he would say, when his mood was jovial. I got to know Anna too, and whenever I spoke to her I put on a show of opposition to Britain's involvement in the war and support for the Fascist cause – not too emphatically at first, of course, but more openly as time went on. I invented a pre-war romance with a Nazi officer to account for these aberrant views. Anna, who was as wary and suspicious as a wildcat, listened to all this without giving anything away. When I insinuated that her experiences must have left her with strong opinions on these matters, she only smiled. I could sense that she approved of what I was saying, though. (I was learning!)

Anna Wolkoff had been born in Russia in 1902 or thereabouts, into a privileged family; and this made her the right age to suffer the fullest effects of enforced exile and impoverishment, with stories of Bolshevik atrocities to keep her indignation active. After 1917 the Wolkoffs found themselves among the numerous other White Russian families dispersed all over Europe. They were never in a frame of mind to relish the colourful reversals of fortune that overtook so many of their compatriots, refusing to have any truck with a system that could allow a grand duke, for example, to wind up as a gigolo or a waiter. Anna found as much solace as she could in politics, becoming a right-wing agitator and crypto-fascist. If it hadn't been for the war she might have gone on in this way, unedifying as it was, without ever finding herself in a position to do much damage.

But in the peculiar conditions that prevailed in 1940, her pro-Nazi sympathies acquired a very dangerous outlet.

She was short and dark-haired, not very impressive in appearance, and displayed the intensity of manner which is often associated with those of a fanatical disposition. She took herself and her causes very seriously indeed. It was difficult to get close to her as she was filled with mistrust, but, once she'd accepted you, Anna was capable of impulsive and generous acts. In spite of her upbringing she was a good cook and this skill, I imagine, helped to keep the restaurant in business; dressmaking, however, was her principal occupation (one of her clients was the Duchess of Windsor). She owned the flat that served as headquarters for the Right Club, as well as another one in Rowland Gardens.

One evening I was invited upstairs to eat one of Anna's special omelettes with a small group of friends. To reach the flat you had to climb a narrow flight of stairs behind a door in the tea-shop to the left of the entrance. I came up these stairs with quaking knees. I was about to be vetted, I knew, and if I failed to give a convincing performance I would not only ruin the whole enterprise but also implicate an agent greatly valued by M. I knew it was Mrs Amos's testimony as much as anything else that had got me this far. All this time she had been recommending me, with my War Office connections, as a particularly useful recruit. At last it seemed the point had been taken.

Mrs Amos was among the group of ten or twelve assembled in the cramped sitting-room of Anna's flat, and so was Mrs Ramsay, wife of the misguided MP. I was introduced to her, and to a number of her friends. No men were present, partly because a lot of Right Club members had already been rounded up under Regulation 18b, and also because this was only an unofficial gathering. The women here were mostly senior club members and wives of internees. They were all considerably older than I was and regarded me, I thought, with a certain amount of curiosity.

'Joan has a great deal of common sense about political matters,' Mrs Amos said. 'She finds the War Office a bit of a bore.'

'Actually, I'm not too keen on war either,' I added. I didn't want to utter too many grotesque untruths, so I kept reiterating the same naïve illiberal sentiments, which went down well enough, as far as I could judge. I said the disaster for this country had been embarking on the war. I deplored the decision to jettison our policy of appeasement. I blamed the Government for its wrong-headed revulsion over Germany's imperialist ambitions. I complained about feeling cut off from the sense of being morally in the right that made things tolerable for everyone else. This elicited some sympathetic murmurs. Then, to my relief, the conversation became general and I was able to lapse into silence while I gathered my wits.

The next day M reported that I had passed the test: the ladies of the Right Club had taken my assertions at face value. Soon I was invited to join the organization: Mrs Ramsay put it to me that here was a way to help England. (These people all believed, sincerely I imagine, that they had the country's best interests at heart. Even the Wolkoffs weren't in the least anti-British; they simply associated the Nazi movement with the possible liberation of Russia and supported it partly for this reason.) I assured her that nothing would please me more. 'I've felt so futile,' I said. A silver badge in a red case was found for me, and I began to attend meetings in the Harrington Gardens flat. (The badge depicted an eagle in the process of putting paid to a viper, the latter standing for the Communist and Jewish element in British society.)

How did these people set about obstructing the war effort? They used to sneak about late at night in the blackout groping for smooth surfaces on which to paste the pro-German, anti-Semitic notices they carried. There were certain precautions one could take to lessen the likelihood of being arrested. Anna instructed her helpers to keep to the dark side of the road, paying particular attention to shadowy doorways where an alert police-man or air-raid warden might lurk, and to carry out the sticking while continuing to walk. These guidelines were issued to each member in the form of a printed sheet. Passersby who observed the Right Club's papers adhering to lamp posts, telephone kiosks, belisha beacons [illuminated (in peacetime) pedestrian crossing markers named after Sir Leslie Hore-Belisha, pre-war transport minister], church boards and so on, were informed that the war was a Jews' war. This was the Right Club's famous 'sticky-back' campaign. They also used greasepaint to deface ARP and casualty station posters. Jeering at Winston Churchill when he appeared on cinema newsreels was another of their practices. None of this could be said to constitute a serious threat to Londoners' morale; but there were, as it turned out, more sinister aspects to the organization.

By now I knew the identity of the third MI5 agent whom M had planted on the spot: this was Helen, a young, convent-educated Belgian girl. I'd seen her quite a few times at the Russian Tea Rooms, but for obvious reasons we had very little to do with one another. Helen, who had known Admiral Wolkoff since 1936, had also become friendly with Anna, on M's instructions.

Helen was in the habit of visiting relatives in Belgium, and Anna, knowing that she was about to make one such trip (this was in April

1940), gave her the task of consulting one of the Right Club's agents in Brussels about the trustworthiness of another. Anna presented her with a typewritten list of questions for the agent drafted in inferior French, which she was to learn by heart and then tear up. Helen proceeded to translate the document, which requested information about the progress of 'our work in Belgium', as well as containing encouraging news about the way things were going for the Right Club in England. She handed the translation to M, before leaving for Brussels where she dutifully performed all the tasks Anna had set her. On her return, a few days later, she was able to assure Anna that the agent she had doubted was completely loyal. She also passed on a message from her contact to the effect that Anna would do well to stop involving herself in such a devious and dangerous game. Probably Anna brushed this unwanted advice to one side; but undoubtedly she was very pleased with Helen's performance as an emissary.

M saw to it that I was kept in touch with these events. Through Mrs Amos, too, he had received information about the Right Club's plans for me. They hoped I might succeed in getting myself transferred to a department offering greater scope for sabotage. When Mrs Ramsay invited me to tea, I guessed the suggestion was about to be made. (The Ramsays' telephone line was tapped, but when the tape came through I learnt nothing of interest about the household, beyond the fact that the cook was helping herself to a good supply of sugar and butter.) It occurred to M that the machinations of this lady might be stopped once and for all if she were to make her seditious proposals in front of an audience. By this time my office had a good enough case to approach the Special Branch for their help. They agreed to co-operate and it was decided that I should change the rendezvous to a flat that could be wired and occupied by a couple of Special Branch men in advance. I dialled the Onslow Square number.

'Mrs Ramsay? Joan Miller here. I'm sorry to change the arrangement, but as it happens I've to got to stay at home this afternoon to take an important telephone call. Perhaps you wouldn't mind joining me here for tea?' After a pause she said that would suit her quite well; I gave her the address of Philip Brocklehurst's flat in Pond Place which I arranged to borrow.

I collected the keys and dashed to the Fulham Road in time to admit the two large Special Branch men who had been detailed for the job. (As far as Mrs Ramsay was concerned, this was my day off.) They set to and wired the sitting-room, before clearing a convenient cupboard and arranging themselves inside it with a machine, ear-phones and shorthand pads. We tested the system and found that, with the window open, you could hear nothing but the traffic in the Fulham Road. This was no good at all. The window had to be kept closed however stifling the room became. It was an exceptionally warm day, I remember. When my guest arrived, wearing a hat, gloves, a dress and jacket, it was as if she'd stepped into a greenhouse. 'Oh, my dear, can't we have the window open?' she asked at once.

'I'm sorry,' I cried. 'The cat might jump on the window-sill and fall into the street.' There was no cat, of course, but I hoped she'd assume it was a timorous animal that kept well away from strangers, and put my anxiety down to over-protectiveness.

'Two inches?' she suggested. I told her the sashcords were faulty, speaking with more vehemence than the occasion required. She didn't persist, but sat pointedly fanning herself with an old theatre programme someone had left on the table. It wasn't a good beginning. I felt as inadequate as an understudy unexpectedly thrust into the limelight on an opening night – I knew the performance was doomed to failure. What the policemen were going through in the cupboard I hardly dared imagine. It was up to me to direct the talk into productive channels, but all I could do was babble uselessly about the dreariness of my job and the awfulness of my employers. My prudent visitor didn't rise to the bait. 'I'm sorry you're unhappy in your work, Joan,' she said ironically.

I was actually quite relieved when she took herself off; nervous tension was making me overact to a dangerous degree. But how was I to placate two hot policemen whose time had been wasted? (In those days it was difficult to get the Special Branch to do this sort of thing.) They emerged from the cupboard mopping the sweat from their faces. Fortunately, after I'd given them some tea and made suitable apologies, they were ready to see the funny side of Mrs Ramsay's obstinate discretion. 'Not giving much away, was she?' they joked. 'You won't catch that old bird in a hurry.' I was grateful for their forcbcarance as well as being charmed by their jocularity, after all the quasi-Teutonic intensity I'd been subjected to lately.

Next day I had to report to Brigadier 'Jasper' Harker, Deputy Director of MI5, who agreed I'd been unlucky and told me to try again. (He also sent me along to Special Branch Headquarters to apologize. They said, 'Don't worry, just give us a pin-up photograph of yourself – so I did, and they kept it on the wall throughout the war.)

Arthur Martin

It was the evidence of continued penetration of the service after Blunt retired in 1945 until at least the early 1960s which carried complete conviction among those working on the case.

Arthur Martin in The Times, *19 July 1984*

Mole-hunting is one of the loneliest professions and there is a belief among some counter-espionage practitioners that no one can spend more than five years investigating the loyalty of his colleagues without losing his perspective. One senior SIS officer was always referred to as 'Harpic' because 'he went clean round the bend' while pursuing suspected leaks. As with any rule, there is an exception, and Arthur Martin must be one of the few who has dedicated much of his life to preserving the integrity of Britain's security apparatus without compromising the quality of his judgement.

Martin's first involvement with the secret world occurred during the war when he was transferred from the Royal Signals to a unit in the Middle East known as the Special Wireless Group. This was a radio interception organization which monitored the enemy's transmissions and sent them on to the cipher experts at Bletchley Park. Similar units operated in all theatres of war.

Although Martin did not prove an exceptional wireless operator he did sufficiently well in the SWG to be offered a permanent position with GCHQ at the end of the war, and in 1949 he was assigned to London as a liaison officer with the Security Service. He played a key role in preparing the cryptographic evidence that was to form the basis of the identification and subsequent interrogation of the atom spy Klaus Fuchs, and soon afterwards he joined MI5 to work on the investigation of wartime leaks from the British embassy in Washington DC, an enquiry that was to prove the catalyst for the defection of Guy Burgess and Donald Maclean in May 1951.

It was Arthur Martin whom Sir Percy Sillitoe selected to accompany him to Washington in June of that year when he tried to explain to the US authorities how Burgess and Maclean had managed to elude MI5. Later Martin was to participate in the cross-examination of Kim Philby who was sacked from SIS because of his suspected involvement with the two traitors. Soon after this episode Martin was sent to Singapore to report on conflicts that had emerged within the Malayan security structure during the Emergency and he remained there for two years as Director of Intelligence in Kuala Lumpur.

Upon his return to London Martin concentrated on counter-espionage cases but it was not until the defection of Anatoli Golitsyn in December 1961 that MI5 and the CIA suddenly acquired an unprecedented KGB source. Golitsyn defected in Helsinki and was promptly flown to the US where Martin debriefed him. Not only did he provide sufficient new clues for Martin to conclude some old cases, but he promised a new insight into the KGB's operations in England and, in particular, details of Soviet penetration of the British security apparatus.

Once Martin and Stephen de Mowbray, the local SIS head of station, had listened to Golitsyn they were convinced that he represented a genuine opportunity to combat the KGB. Both reported to London that Golitsyn's allegations of hostile penetration should be taken seriously and thereafter both men became involved in the lengthy molehunts that purged their respective services of suspected Soviet spies. Both were to play vital roles in the Fluency Committee investigations of Sir Roger Hollis and other possible moles, including Donald Prater, but their careers were not advanced by their new preoccupation. Martin was transferred from MI5 to SIS, where he was appointed to the largely administrative function of Head of Registry, while de Mowbray was transferred to South America.

Arthur Martin's role as an MI5 molehunter was first disclosed by Kim Philby who referred to him briefly in *My Silent War* as 'a quiet young man'. Thereafter he avoided the limelight but his determination to learn the extent to which the KGB had gained access to MI5's secrets gave him a notoriety that he and his wife Joan, who had been secretary to the Deputy Director-General of the Security Service, Guy Liddell, both abhorred.

In 1984, after his retirement from SIS and at the conclusion of his post-retirement job as a clerk in the House of Commons, Martin joined forces with his SIS colleague Stephen de Mowbray to find a publisher for *New Lies for Old*, Golitsyn's analysis of the Kremlin's Machiavellian plotting. This was eventually released in 1984, with Martin and de Mowbray collaborating with two senior CIA officers, Scott Miler and Vasia Gmirkin, to write an 'Editors' Foreword'. Curiously, although Gmirkin signed the foreword, and had spent three years as Golitsyn's CIA case officer, he never subscribed to the defector's labyrinthine theories.

New Lies for Old

EDITORS' FOREWORD

Very rarely disclosures of information from behind the Iron Curtain throw new light on the roots of communist thought and action and challenge accepted notions on the operation of the communist system. We believe that this book does both these things. It is nothing if not controversial. It rejects conventional views on subjects ranging from Khrushchev's overthrow to Tito's revisionism, from Dubcek's liberalism to Ceausescu's independence, and from the dissident movement to the Sino-Soviet split. The author's analysis has many obvious implications for Western policy. It will not be readily accepted by those who have for long been committed to opposing points of view. But we believe that the debates it is likely to provoke will lead to a deeper understanding of the nature of the threat from international communism and, perhaps, to a firmer determination to resist it.

The author's services to the party and the KGB and the unusually long periods he spent in study, mainly in the KGB but also with the University of Marxism-Leninism and the Diplomatic School, make the author uniquely well qualified as a citizen of the West to write about the subjects covered in this book.

He was born near Poltava, in the Ukraine, in 1926. He was thus brought up as a member of the postrevolutionary generation. From 1933 onward he lived in Moscow. He joined the communist youth movement (Komsomol) at the age of fifteen while he was a cadet in military school. He bcame a member of the Communist Party of the Soviet Union (CPSU) in 1945 while studying at the artillery school for officers at Odessa.

In the same year he entered military counterintelligence. On graduation from the Moscow school of military counterespionage in 1946, he joined the Soviet intelligence service. While working in its headquarters he attended classes at the University of Marxism-Leninism, from which he graduated in 1948. From 1948 to 1950 he studied in the counterintelligence faculty of the High Intelligence School; also, between 1949 and 1952 he completed a correspondence course with the High Diplomatic School.

In 1952 and early 1953 he was involved, with a friend, in drawing up a proposal to the Central Committee on the reorganization of Soviet intelligence. The proposal included suggestions on the strengthening of counterintelligence, on the wider use of the satellite intelligence services, and on the reintroduction of the 'activist style' into intelligence work. In connection with this proposal, he attended a meeting of the Secretariat chaired by Stalin and a meeting of the Presidium chaired by Malenkov and attended by Khrushchev, Brezhnev, and Bulganin.

For three months in 1952–53 the author worked as a head of section in the department of the Soviet intelligence service responsible for counterespionage against the United States. In 1953 he was posted to Vienna, where he seved for two years under cover as a member of the *apparat* of the Soviet High Commission. For the first year he worked against Russian émigrés, and for the second against British intelligence. In 1954 he was elected to be a deputy secretary of the party organization in the KGB residency in Vienna, numbering seventy officers. On return to Moscow he attended the KGB Institute, now the KGB Academy, as a full-time student for four years, graduating from there with a law degree in 1959. As a student of the institute and as a party member, he was well placed to follow the power struggle in the Soviet leadership that was reflected in secret party letters, briefings, and conferences.

From 1959 to 1960, at a time when a new long-range policy for the bloc was being formulated and the KGB was being reorganized to play its part in it, he served as a senior analyst in the NATO section of the Information Department of the Soviet intelligence service. He was then transferred to Finland, where, under cover as vice-consul in the Soviet embassy in Helsinki, he worked on counterintelligence matters until his break with the regime in December 1961.

By 1956 he was already beginning to be disillusioned with the Soviet system. The Hungarian events of that year intensified his disaffection. He concluded that the only practical way to fight the regime was from abroad and that, armed with his inside knowledge of the KGB, he would be able to do so effectively. Having reached his decision, he began systematically to elicit and commit to memory information that he thought would be relevant and valuable to the West. The adoption of the new, aggressive long-range communist policy precipitated his decision to break with the regime. He felt that the necessity of warning the West of the new dimensions of the threat that it was facing justified him in abandoning his country and facing the personal sacrifices involved. His break with the regime was a deliberate and long-premeditated political act. Immediately on his arrival in the United States, he sought to convey a warning to the highest authorities in the US government on the new political dangers to the Western world stemming from the harnessing of all the political resources of the communist bloc, including its intelligence and security services, to the new long-range policy.

From 1962 onward the author devoted a large proportion of his time to the study of communist affairs as an outside observer reading both the communist and Western press. He began work on this book. While working on the book he continued to bring to the attention of American and other Western authorities his views on the issues considered in it, and in 1968 allowed American and British officials to read the manuscript as it then stood. Although the manuscript has since been enlarged to cover the events of the last decade and revised as the underlying communist strategy became clearer to the author, the substance of the argument has changed little since 1968. Owing to the length of the manuscript, a substantial part of it has been held over for publication at a later date.

With few exceptions, those Western officials who were aware of the views expressed in the manuscript, especially on the Sino-Soviet split, rejected them. In fact, over the years it became increasingly clear to the author that there was no reasonable hope of his analysis of communist affairs being seriously considered in Western official circles. At the same time, he became further convinced that events continued to confirm the validity of his analysis, that the threat from international communism was not properly understood, and that this threat would shortly enter a new and more dangerous phase. The author therefore decided to publish his work with the intention of alerting a wider sector of world public opinion to the dangers as he sees them, in the hope of stimulating a new approach to the study of communism and of provoking a more coherent, determined, and effective response to it by those who remain interested in the preservation of free societies in the noncommunist world.

In order to give effect to his decision to publish, the author asked the four of us, all former US or British government officials, for editorial advice and help. Three of us have known the author and his views for twelve years or more. We can testify to his Sisyphean efforts to convince others of the validity of what he has to say. We have the highest regard for his personal and professional integrity. The value of his services to national security has been officially recognized by more than one government in the West. Despite the rejection of his views by many of our former colleagues, we continue to believe that the contents of this book are of the greatest importance and relevance to a proper understanding of contemporary events. We were, therefore, more than willing to respond to the author's requests for help in editing his manuscript for publication, and we commend the book for the most serious study by all who are interested in relations between the communist and noncommunist worlds.

The preparation of the manuscript has been undertaken by the author with the help of each of us, acting in an individual and private capacity.

The author is a citizen of the United States of America and an Honorary Commander of the Order of the British Empire (CBE).

Stephen de Mowbray

Stategic political deception exists as a weapon in the Soviet political armoury over and above the more generally recognized tactical techniques of disinformation (such as the circulation by the KGB in Africa and elsewhere of forged British or American official documents).

A graduate of New College, Oxford, Stephen de Mowbray joined SIS in 1950, aged twenty-five, and two years later was posted to Cairo. In 1953 he undertook a two-year tour in Baghdad, and then returned to Broadway. In 1957 he was appointed head of station in Montevideo and was back in London in 1961.

During his period in SIS's counter-intelligence branch he was inducted into the molehunts that had beset the Security Service, and he acted as one of SIS's two representatives on the Fluency Committee which investigated Soviet spy suspects. One of the cases he pursued was that of Donald Prater, whom he interviewed in New Zealand after the latter's retirement from SIS, ostensibly on health grounds. De Mowbray transferred to Washington DC in 1964 and succeeded the head of station in 1966. He remained in the States for a further two years before returning to London.

In June 1974 he became concerned that evidence of Soviet penetration of the Security Service was being overlooked and decided to alert the Prime Minister. His visit to Downing Street, where he was received by the Cabinet Secretary, sparked off the enquiry conducted by Lord Trend into the allegations made against Sir Roger Hollis. At the conclusion of his investigation, about which de Mowbray expressed severe reservations, Trend concluded that there was no compelling evidence against Hollis, or even that MI5 had suffered hostile penetration.

De Mowbray retired in 1975 to start a new family in Kent, where he now lives, and he has helped edit Anatoli Golitsyn's book *New Lies for Old* and embarked on an ambitious project to record a comprehensive chronology of the Soviet Union. This extract is taken from an article he wrote for *Encounter* in the July/August 1984 issue.

Soviet Deception & the Onset of the Cold War

On 27 October [1943], the British Legation in Stockholm reported that Willi Boehm (a prominent Hungarian socialist exile who worked in the Press Reading Bureau attached to the Legation as a Hungarian press reader and source of political intelligence on Hungary) had spent four days in Scotland on his way back from London to Sweden in the company of Razin, the newly appointed First Secretary at the Soviet Embassy in Stockholm. Asked by Boehm if the NKFD was a political or a propaganda weapon, Razin replied that it was both. From the propaganda point of view, it was very valuable for demoralising the German army. From a political point of view, it was a defence against the misuse of Germany against the Soviets.

Razin went on to say that the Soviets had no intention of 'bolshevising' Germany or South-eastern Europe. On the contrary, every disorder in Europe would be against Soviet interests, which demanded that Europe should resume production immediately after the War and that all anarchy should be avoided. The Soviet Union was resolved that both in Germany and in other states pro-Soviet elements should always be in power. After victory, the Soviets would possess a strong army; but the Soviets' economic foundation grew weaker with every day of the War. The machinery of production was going to pieces. The Soviets needed the help of England and America. Preconditions for collaboration were that friendship towards the Soviet Union should be sincere, that there should be no intrigues, and that a second front in Europe should be opened.

Such was the dearth of unofficial expressions of view by Soviet officials at the time, that this account of a conversation with Razin was minuted all the way up through the professional Foreign Office hierarchy. Particular attention was paid to Razin's remarks about the Soviet Union's post-War economic weakness. There were reservations about whether Razin was trustworthy and had been correctly reported. Northern Department commented that what he said about economic weakness was not altogether true; at the same time, the department had always taken the view that Russia would need Anglo-American assistance after the War, and that Soviet energies would largely be absorbed in the task of reconstruction.

What the Foreign Office did not know was that Razin was the chief representative in Sweden of Soviet Intelligence. He is described in some detail in *Empire of Fear* (1956) by Vladimir and Evdokia Petrov, the Soviet Intelligence couple who had worked under Razin in Sweden, and who received asylum in Australia in 1954. What was also not appreciated at the time by the Foreign Office was that the 'weakness of the Soviet Union' was a theme that had been used by the Soviets in the 1920s for deception purposes. Razin's remarks are, in fact, a good example of what Anatoly Golitsyn had called the 'weakness and evolution' pattern of disinformation. Two themes in particular, used by Smollett in his paper for the Special Issues Committee – the thriving of the 'small man' in Russia, and the replacement of ideologues by managers and technicians – had also been used in the 1920s. In the 1960s and '70s more was to be heard of this second point.

The overwhelming impression left by all the available evidence in 1943 was that the Russians were neither interested in nor capable of dominating a large part of post-War Europe. Once they had achieved security, they would be more interested in retiring into their own camp, healing their wounds with the help of Anglo-American poultices and, by and large, leaving the rest of the world to sort out its own problems. The British view of Soviet policy in Europe was set out in a draft Cabinet paper drawn up by the Foreign Office in July 1944. It said that Britain had a vital interest in the independence of the European nations and in the avoidance of domination of them by either Germany or Russia. The foundation of Britain's post-War European policy must be the Anglo-Soviet alliance, based on a joint interest in preventing the recurrence of German aggression. It should not be assumed that a conflict of interests between ourselves and the Russians was inevitable in any region of Europe.

The main Soviet interest in Central Europe was to prevent Germany from ever again threatening Russian security. Although the Soviets were hostile to the pre-War, semi-authoritarian régime in Poland, they were now ready to see a new régime there with a broad basis of popular support in the democratic Peasant and Socialist parties. There was, therefore, reason to hope that Poland would be left with genuine independence and free from excessive Russian interference. Equally, the Soviets had disliked the pre-War oligarchy in Hungary. There was danger of a recurrence there of the excesses of the (Communist) Béla Kun régime of 1919 – but it did not follow that the Soviet Union would necessarily foster such developments.

Indeed, there had been no signs of any Soviet desire to impose Communist régimes in any of the Central European countries. Russian relations were in fact closest with Czechoslovakia, a *petit-bourgeois* country with a capitalist structure. The USSR seemed perfectly prepared to accept the present social structure there. And there was no reason to suppose that there would be any clash between Soviet and British interests in Austria. As *The Times* put it on 30 September 1943:

> No essential differences of interest or purpose divide the three great nations. Unity between them is the only foundation on which both a sound British foreign policy and the hopes of lasting peace can be built.

It is not fanciful to suppose that Stalin appreciated at an early stage that the Second World War would present opportunities for a rapid expansion of the Communist world. Louis Fischer, for example, recorded in *The Soviets in World Affairs* (1930) that, after it had become apparent in the 1920s that the Revolution was not going to spread like wildfire as Lenin had hoped, expectations of future revolutions tended to be associated with the next world war. The MI5 paper already quoted had referred to Lenin's dictum that 'wars cause revolutions and revolutions lead to wars.'

Peter Wright

I carried the burden of so many secrets that lightening the load a little could only make things easier for me.

In September 1955 the directorate of the Security Service decided to recruit a scientist, and their candidate was Peter Wright, a Marconi wireless specialist who had recently achieved a remarkable breakthrough in the field of clandestine eavesdropping. A captured Soviet listening device, although of quite simple construction, was highly sophisticated and had been small enough to be concealed inside the great seal which had hung in the office of the American ambassador in Moscow. This was at the height of the Cold War in 1952, and the self-contained, remote-controlled unit – a combined microphone and transmitter apparently operating without its own power supply – was a considerable improvement on anything the West could produce, but the CIA had been unable to learn how it worked. Eventually they reluctantly admitted defeat and passed it over to their British counterparts. It landed on Peter Wright's workbench at Marconi's factory at Great Baddow in Essex, and he accomplished what the other boffins had failed to do. Not only did he establish the microwave principle behind the device, but he also got it to work and gave a practical demonstration to MI5's senior management in their Mayfair offices.

Wright's reputation was established by this success, and his work in A2, the technical resources sub-section of MI5's Administration Branch, concentrated on the development of similar equipment for the Security Service. In practical terms this meant constructing and placing sensitive microphones into diplomatic premises in London where the conversations of hostile intelligence personnel, masquerading as diplomats, could be monitored. Wright's undoubted skill in this arcane field made him a valuable asset for the Service and he was to travel extensively to advise Allied security agencies on how to plant and detect telephone intercepts and bugs.

Wright's career would probably have gone unrecorded if, in May 1963, he had not been loaned to MI5's counter-espionage branch for a particularly secret investigation. The molehunters had come to suspect that Graham Mitchell, the Deputy Director-General, was leaking details of anti-Soviet operations to the KGB, and Wright was brought in to insert a microphone in Mitchell's home and a camera in his office. This enquiry, though inconclusive, was Wright's initiation into molehunting and for the next twelve years he was to study the phenomenon of treachery in high places. He began (where better?) with the interrogation and debriefing of Anthony Blunt, who had been persuaded in April 1964 to give a detailed confession in return for a formal immunity from prosecution. Thereafter Wright became obsessed with the knowledge that dozens of well-placed civil servants, politicians, intelligence officers and senior members of the Establishment had wormed their way into positions of influence so they could betray as much as they could to Moscow. Some he interviewed, while others like Tom Driberg and John Cairncross he attempted to run as double agents.

When Wright eventually retired from the Security Service in January 1976, with the rank of Assistant Director, he moved to Australia to breed horses and acquired Australian citizenship. As well as being exhausted by the burden of secrets he had learned over two decades, he was also embittered because his pension had been calculated without taking account of his Admiralty service before he had joined MI5. His appeal to the Cabinet Office had been rejected on the grounds that to accommodate him would require an Act of Parliament, but Wright insisted that he had been assured in 1955 that his transfer to the Security Service would not financially disadvantage him.

While in Australia Wright had prepared some notes of his experiences, and these he supplied to Chapman Pincher in 1980, having been introduced to the journalist by Lord Rothschild. He had been prompted to make his disclosure following Margaret Thatcher's statement to the Commons in November 1979 about Blunt's treachery in which she suggested that Soviet penetration of MI5 had only occurred during the war. Wright knew from his own investigations that there was evidence of Soviet penetration eighteen years *after* Blunt had left MI5 and, enraged, was determined to set the record straight. Dismayed by Chapman Pincher's distorted account in his book *Their Trade is Treachery*, Wright collaborated with a television reporter, Paul Greengrass, to produce his notorious autobiography, *Spycatcher*.

The book acquired its notoriety only because the British government unwisely decided to prevent its publication on the grounds that Wright owed a duty of confidentiality to his former employers and thus turned a mediocre book, of only marginal accuracy, into a worldwide bestseller. In this passage, which is typical, Wright recalls an episode which occurred within a few months of his arrival at MI5's headquarters. He misspells Lionel Crabb's name, and those who can recall Khrushchev's billiard-ball-like baldness will wonder at the reference to the intelligence Wright says he obtained from a microphone concealed in the Soviet Premier's suite at Claridge's. Wright had no hesitation in naming all his colleagues, and here he correctly identifies Nicholas Elliott as a key figure in the fiasco that was to cause Commander Crabb's death, embarrass the Prime Minister Anthony Eden and lead to the Director-General of MI5, Sir Dick White, moving to SIS.

Spycatcher

Ethics, as far as I could ascertain, were displayed by MI6 purely for Whitehall or MI5 consumption. In fact MI6, under its chief, Sir John Sinclair, had become a virtual liability. It still refused to face up to the appalling consequences of Philby's being a Soviet spy. It was operating in the modern world with 1930s attitudes and 1930s personnel and equipment. It was little surprise to me when they stumbled, in April 1956, into their greatest blunder of all, the Crabbe affair.

The Soviet leaders Khrushchev and Bulganin paid a visit to Britain on the battleship *Ordzhonikidze*, docking at Portsmouth. The visit was designed to improve Anglo-Soviet relations at a sensitive time. MI5 decided to operate against Khrushchev in his rooms at Claridge's Hotel. Normally Claridge's has permanent Special Facilities installed on the hotel telephone system, because so many visitors stay there who are of interest to MI5. But we knew the Russsians were sending a team of sweepers in to check Khrushchev's suite before he arrived, so we decided it was the right time to use for the first time the specially modified SF which John Taylor had developed in the Dollis Hill Laboratory. The new SF did not require a washer to be fitted, so it was virtually undetectable. The telephone could be activated over short distances using shortwave high-frequency megacycles. We set the SF activation up in an office of the Grosvenor Estates near Claridge's. It worked perfectly. Throughout Khrushchev's visit his room was permanently covered. In fact, the intelligence gathered was worthless. Khrushchev was far too canny a bird to discuss anything of value in a hotel room. I remember sitting up on the seventh floor with a transcriber translating loosely for me. We listened to Khrushchev for hours at a time, hoping for pearls to drop. But there were no clues to the last days of Stalin, or to the fate of the KGB henchman Beria. Instead, there were long monologues from Khrushchev addressed to his valet on the subject of his attire. He was an extraordinarily vain man. He stood in front of the mirror preening himself for hours at a time, and fussing with his hair parting. I recall thinking that in Eden, Khrushchev had found the perfect match. Both were thoroughly unscrupulous men, whose only interest lay in cutting a dash on the world stage.

But while MI5 were discreetly bugging Krushchev, MI6 launched a botched operation against the *Ordzhonikidze*. The operation was run by the MI6 London Station, commanded by Nicholas Elliott, the son of the former headmaster of Eton. MI6 wanted to measure the propeller of the Russian battleship, because there was confusion in the Admiralty as to why she was able to travel so much faster than had originally been estimated by Naval Intelligence. Elliott arranged for a frogman, the unfortunate Commander 'Buster' Crabbe, to take on the assignment.

In fact, this was not the first time MI6 had attempted this operation. A year before, they tried to investigate the hull of the *Ordzhonikidze* while she was in port in the Soviet Union. They used one of the X-Craft midget submarines which MI6 kept down in Stokes Bay. These had dry compartments to enable a diver to get in and out and were small enough to pass undetected into inshore waters. A Naval frogman had attempted to enter the harbour, but security was too tight and the mission was aborted.

The second attempt in Portsmouth ended in disaster. Crabbe was overweight and overage. He disappeared, although a headless body which was later washed up was tentatively identified as his. John Henry, MI6 London Station's Technical Officer, had informed me that MI6 were planning the Crabbe operation, and I told Cumming [of MI5] . He was doubtful about it from the start. It was a typical piece of MI6 adventurism, ill-conceived and badly executed. But we all kept our fingers crossed. Two days later a panic-stricken John Henry arrived in Cumming's office telling us that Crabbe had disappeared.

'I told Nicholas not to use Buster; he was heading for a heart attack as it was,' he kept saying.

We were highly skeptical of the heart attack theory, but there was no time for speculation. The secret MI6 parlour game was at risk of becoming embarrassingly public. Crabbe and his MI6 accomplice had signed into a local hotel under their own names.

'There'll be a fearful row if this comes out,' snapped Cumming. 'We'll all be for the pavilion!'

Cumming buzzed through to Dick White's office and asked to see him immediately. We all trooped upstairs. Dick was sitting at his desk. There was no hint of a welcoming smile. His charm had all but deserted him, and the years of schoolmaster training came to the fore.

'The Russians have just asked the Admiralty about the frogman, and they've had to deny any knowledge. I'm afraid it looks to me rather as if the lid will come off before too long,' he said tersely.

'John, how on earth did you get yourself into this mess?' he asked with sudden exasperation.

Henry was chastened, but explained that the Navy had been pressing them for months for details of the *Ordzhonikidze*'s propeller.

'You know what Eden is like,' he said bitterly, 'one minute he says you can do something, the next minute not. We thought it was an acceptable risk to take.'

White looked unconvinced. He smoothed his temples. He shuffled his papers. The clock ticked gently in the corner. Telltale signs of panic oozed from every side of the room.

'We must do everything we can to help you, of course,' he said, finally breaking the painful silence. 'I will go and see the PM this evening, and see if I can head the thing off. In the meantime, Malcolm will put A2 at your disposal.'

A thankful John Henry retreated from the room. Cumming telephoned the CID in Portsmouth and arranged for the hotel register to be sanitized. Winterborn and Henry rushed down to Portsmouth to clear up any loose ends. But it was not enough to avert a scandal. That night Khrushchev made a public complaint about the frogman, and a humiliated Eden was forced to make a statement in the House of Commons.

The intelligence community in London is like a small village in the Home Counties. Most people in the senior echelons know each other at least well enough to drink with in their clubs. For some weeks after the Crabbe affair, the village hummed in anticipation at the inevitable reckoning which everyone knew to be coming. As one of the few people inside MI5 who knew about the Crabbe affair before it began, I kept my head down on John Henry's advice.

'There's blood all over the floor,' he confided in me shortly afterward. 'We've got Edward Bridges in here tearing the place apart.'

Shortly after this, Cumming strode into my office one morning looking genuinely upset.

'Dick's leaving,' he muttered. 'They want him to take over MI6.'

The decision to appoint Dick White as Chief of MI6 was, I believe, one of the most important mistakes made in postwar British Intelligence history. There were few signs of it in the mid-1950s, but MI5, under his control, was taking the first faltering steps along the path of modernization. He knew the necessity for change, and yet had the reverence for tradition which would have enabled him to accomplish his objectives without disruption. He was, above all, a counterintelligence officer, almost certainly the greatest of the twentieth century, perfectly trained for the Director-General's chair. He knew the people, he knew the problems, and he had a vision of the sort of effective counterespionage organization he wanted to create. Instead, just as his work was beginning, he was moved on a politician's whim to an organization he knew little about, and which was profoundly hostile to his arrival. He was never to be as successful there as he had been in MI5.

But the loss was not just MI5's. The principal problem in postwar British Intelligence was the lack of clear thinking about the relative role of the various Intelligence Services. In the post-imperial era Britain required, above all, an efficient domestic Intelligence organization. MI6, particularly after the emergence of GCHQ, was quite simply of less importance.

But moving Dick White to MI6 bolstered its position, stunted the emergence of a rationalized Intelligence community, and condemned the Service he left to ten years of neglect. Had he stayed, MI5 would have emerged from the traumas of the 1960s and 1970s far better equipped to tackle the challenges of the 1980s.

Anthony Cavendish

An SIS officer lies from his first day in the Service. It is part of his cover.

The Bulgarian who changed his name to Anthony Cavendish first came to public attention in 1986 when he wrote to *The Times* to protest that Chapman Pincher could never have conducted an interview with Sir Maurice Oldfield on the latter's deathbed, as claimed by the veteran *Daily Express* journalist. Cavendish insisted that he had been at Oldfield's bedside continuously and Pincher's claim was untrue. The background to the challenge was extraordinary. Oldfield, who had been chief of the Secret Intelligence Service, and later Director of Intelligence in Northern Ireland, had been posthumously denounced by Pincher as an active homosexual who had first lied to the authorities about his illicit proclivities and then confessed to them. A former SIS officer, Cavendish was outraged by Pincher's allegation and was prompted to publish his own memoirs, entitled *Inside Intelligence*, in defence of his friend and ex-colleague. His account traced his work as a case officer with Security Intelligence Middle East, as an SIS officer in post-war Germany, and recalled his involvement with one of SIS's first Soviet intelligence defectors. However, far from welcoming his intervention, the British government responded with an injunction against publication which was later overturned in the Scottish courts. When the book was eventually released, in 1990, it contained a foreword by George Young, formerly SIS's vice-chief.

Educated in Switzerland, Cavendish was commissioned into the Intelligence Corps at the end of the war and sent to Cairo where he joined SIME. There he met Maurice Oldfield, and they served together in Egypt and Palestine until Oldfield's transfer to SIS in London. In July 1948 Cavendish was demobbed and, following an interview with Frank Slocum, Dick Brooman-White and Tim Milne, invited to join R5, the counter-intelligence 'requirements' section where Oldfield also worked.

In the summer of 1950 Cavendish was posted to Hamburg under Control Commission cover as one of John Bruce Lockhart's subordinates, and helped run agents across the Baltic into eastern Europe. Later he was moved to Berlin and then, having fallen out with Donald Prater, transferred to the SIS station in Vienna. Cavendish's promising SIS career came to an end soon afterwards when he was recalled to London following a late-night motor accident.

In this extract Cavendish describes how his prospects were ruined by Donald Prater and another former Communist, Andrew King, both of whom he refers to by pseudonymous Christian names.

Inside Intelligence

'Tony, get over here.'

The weekend of 25 to 27 May 1951 proved to be a memorable one. May is always a beautiful time of the year in Berlin, and in those days West Berliners, though surrounded by the Soviet zone, often took picnics to the Grunewald and the Waansee to enjoy the perfections of nature which even Russian occupation could not spoil. The brief telephone call to my flat near the Blue and White tennis club summoned me to the Olympic Stadium; which was not only British military headquarters but also the main office of SIS. I arrived and was surprised to find that all the officers of the station were assembling. But then our Station Commander began handing out photographs of two men. They were, he explained, two British diplomats, Donald McLean and Guy Burgess who, it was believed, intended to defect and might well pass through Berlin.

Each of us was detailed to watch a specific crossing point to see if we could recognize them. I do not recall that we were instructed to stop them but, in any event, after forty-eight hours and a sleepless weekend, we were all called off and learnt in due course that the two had defected without coming anywhere near Berlin.

Early in June I received a message from my Station Commander that I was to travel from Berlin down to the British zone as Big John wanted to see me. I decided to drive down the autobahn – which the occupying powers were allowed to do – and I remember the journey well because I used our 'military' jeep for the trip. A short way out of Berlin I came to the first Soviet checkpoint, where I was stopped by a rather young, sullen Red Army sentry with rifle and fixed bayonet and a sergeant with a machine pistol. The sergeant carefully read my inter-zonal pass and waved me through. Then I drove down the autobahn towards Helmstedt, at the statutory fifty miles an hour, noting mentally the large number of Red Army vehicles going about their duties, most of them carrying armed troops. At Helmstedt another, more cursory check and I drove on into the British zone and down towards Herford.

Next morning I reported to John's office and had to wait. When he arrived he asked me gruffly to sit down. He was sorry, he said, but he had some bad news. London had received a confidential report written on me after my first three years in the Service and had decided on the basis of the report that I was not suitable to be confirmed as a 'long-term' SIS officer.

This was a bitter blow.

I immediately protested and John said that my report had been compiled by Derek [Donald Prater], who had written that he was unable to make up his mind about me and thus felt that, if he could not himself be certain about my suitability, it would be wrong to give me the benefit of the doubt.

Had I known then what I know now I would have played my hand very differently. Some years after I eventually left the Service I was informed by a serving member that Derek had been a former member of the Communist Party, had lied during his vetting procedure and about whom the truth was only later discovered during an intensive shake-up of SIS that happened when Sir Dick White took over as Chief. Derek was then sacked but this did not undo what he had already done to me.

I left Germany bitter but determined to fight the decision. It was probably as well that Maurice [Oldfield] was in the Far East or, upset as I was, I might well have embarrassed him by asking him for friendship's sake to fight my battle.

Taking my courage in my hands, I demanded to see Commander Kenneth Cohen, the Chief Controller for Europe and the man under the Chief, directly responsible for activities in the whole of Europe. I decided that this was not a time for modesty and gave him a summary of my achievements, emphasizing not only that I was an outstanding linguist but also that what seemed mostly to be held against me was that I was still considerably younger than anybody else that I worked with. Cohen told me to go away and come back and see him twenty-four hours later. When I did so, he announced that he was revoking the decision made on the basis of Derek's report, that I would be posted to Vienna and the future was up to me. The Controller under Cohen responsible for Austria was called Philip [Andrew King], and I had to report to him for my instructions. (Again, it is only in recent years that I have discovered that Philip too was a one-time member of the Communist Party.)

There were similarities between the Berlin station and the Vienna station, since both cities were then occupied by the four powers even though well behind the Iron Curtain. But the SIS operation in Germany was large and supported by occupation costs, while the operation in Vienna was small and based at the British Embassy.

I had already had a serious fight with the Station Commander in Vienna during my time in R5, over one of his pet agents known as 'Dandelion'.

This agent having been fairly successful for us as a double agent had suddenly announced that his Russian case officer was pushing him to move to South America. If we wanted him to go this would involve the Service providing him with a new passport and also a considerable amount of money.

Both my colleague in R5 dealing with South America and I were convinced that Dandelion was a fraud, who was using us to pay for his resettlement plans. We opposed the project and it went up to ACSS [Assistant Chief Secret Service] Air Commodore Jack Easton for a decision. He overruled us and supported the Station Commander.

It was therefore somewhat gratifying, in a bizarre way, that a few months later, after Dandelion had arrived in Venezuela, he gave the station two fingers and the Vienna Station Commander reluctantly had to accept that we had been tricked. I had been right but that did not endear me to the Vienna station.

Since I was to take the Service car supplied to me up to Vienna, I planned a week's trip that would take me through Cologne, Munich and Salzburg, and then on to Vienna.

I felt that I wanted to thumb my nose at Derek so I arranged my route to take me past the German station and stopped off to spend a night there with them. Derek quickly told me how delighted he was that I was still in the Service, and had he only known how London would react to his report he would have worded it in an entirely different manner. Privately I doubted this.

I had not been briefed on my cover before leaving for Vienna but had assumed I would be in the Embassy, although I knew there was currently no diplomatic slot available. In the event, I was told I was to be Int. Org., the intelligence organization of the Austrian Control Commission. The Embassy had an Embassy Liaison Officer to Int. Org. and, for cover purposes, I was to be the Int. Org. Liaison Officer with the Embassy. My office, therefore, was in Schoenebrun Barracks and a new SIS secretary for me was posted out from London with Int. Org. cover.

My main assignment was to establish a war plan system as I had done in Berlin and to run two agents, one who supplied information on the Soviet Army and Air Force and one who supplied us with economic information, mainly on Austrian oil production and its shipment to the East.

I took rooms in the Park Hotel in Schoenebrun, which, at that time, was requisitioned for use by British officers. My accommodation was extremely comfortable and my stay there started a love affair which still continues with the Wiener Schnitzel. I would order a Wiener Schnitzel at the drop of a hat, particularly relishing them when put in brown Austrian peasant bread as a makeshift sandwich. My friends point to my time in Vienna as the beginning of my corpulent build-up!

The Station Commander in Vienna and I did not instantly take to each other, but that did not worry me since he was at the end of his tour and was shortly to be replaced. My colleagues numbered four at the Embassy and another two with me under Control Commission or military cover. Luckily, the officer I dealt with most at the Embassy was a woman, a former ATS officer who was our expert on Soviet forces. What did surprise me was that some of them appeared to me to be homosexuals. I have since discovered that most homosexuals in the Service are almost invariably prima donnas in their attitude to their work.

While I was not particularly close to the Station Commander who was about to leave, I was made no happier by the news that he was to be replaced by Philip from London; the former Communist who gave the impression of being homosexual as well. The two agents I had to run had already been recruited, and it was therefore only a question of them being handed over to me, but the stay-behind network I was to manage had to be set up from scratch.

By its very nature, and the fact that a stay-behind network has to remain asleep until needed, stay-behind agents cannot be recruited through agents with whom one is already in contact. The reason is obvious. If a current agent were caught he or she could blow part of the stay-behind network if the network had been based on an agent recruited through him.

My immediate task was the control of my two active agents; Hans, an Austrian, had been an officer in the German army and consequently had a mastery of things military, while Edgar, a Doctor of Economics, worked in the main office of the Austrian oil company on the other side of the Danube at Zisterdorf. Hans was about thirty-five, blond, blue-eyed and a great, though almost obsessive, athlete. He strode around in leather knickerbockers, heavy walking shoes and a thick white pullover; summer and winter, morning and evening. At that time, apart from the usual troop-watching activities (which to a large extent consisted of taking down and identifying vehicle numbers), our priority was to get clear photographs of the Russian MIG fighter plane.

Head Office had developed an automatic robot camera with a sight through the lens which enabled agents to pan the camera on an aeroplane in flight, even when the camera was equipped with a 175mm telephoto lens. Of course, when these aircraft flew over Vienna, they were always so high that even a good telephoto lens could not give a satisfactory picture.

The trick, therefore, was to take the photographs near a Russian airfield, and one of the main ones was at Wiener Neustadt, about forty miles south of Vienna on the way to Graz and Klagenfurt. It was understandably dangerous to be caught loitering near a Soviet airfield, and to do so would be perilous with the type of camera we were using.

Hans tried first. He used to set off with a rucksack, on foot as though enjoying the wildlife. Unfortunately, although he knew various hides in which to wait close to the airfield at Tulln, we were not getting good enough pictures. After a while, when we were still not getting the pictures we needed, I decided to try for some myself.

Members of the British Occupational Forces in Vienna were allowed to leave Vienna by the road to the Semmering, provided they were in possession of a grey pass. Grey passes had to be signed by the Soviet Kommandetura and it obviously drew suspicion if one person kept going up and down without good reason.

I have always been interested in fishing and just over the Semmering Pass, and in what was the British zone, the river Murz is close to a small village called Kindberg. There was a superb pub and guest house at Kindberg and since the military were given Wednesday afternoons off for recreation, I took to spending Wednesday afternoons, Saturdays and sometimes Sundays at Kindberg ostensibly for the purpose of fishing. I had the special camera with me. Whenever I saw any MIGs I would lift the bonnet of my car and then peer under it, but in such a way that I could hold the camera and focus it for the shot I wanted, and photograph whatever MIGs were in sight. I eventually got so daring (or reckless) that I began pulling up as close to the airfield as I could and photographing MIGs on the ground; although some time during this activity the Russians took to building blast shelters for the jets until all I could see of them were the tips of the tails.

In Melk I discovered a nice little beer shop with seats on its terrace where Soviet officers gathered. Melk, the site of an early Benedictine Abbey whose situation compared with that of Monte Cassino, was not far from St Poelten, which was the Headquarters of the Soviet army in Austria. Thus my interest in church architecture developed quickly, just as my interest in fishing waned, and most weeks I would apply for a grey pass to travel into the Soviet zone to visit the abbey at Melk. After a cursory visit to the abbey I would sit myself on the terrace of the little pub and, whenever Soviet officers appeared, would seek to get into conversation with them if it could be done unobtrusively. I always used German. Sometimes it was obvious that they were suspicious and did not wish to talk, but eventually a young Russian Artillery Captain struck up conversation with me which, in due course, led to him proposing a drinking competition.

Draught beer was served in various sizes of glass at the pub, including a vast glass holding two litres which was called a *Stiefel*, a riding boot. The glass was made in that shape and in that size. My new Russian friend challenged me to drink a *Stiefel* of beer and a glass of vodka if he would do the same. Then we would repeat the process until the one who gave up first was the loser. I imagine the Russian officer had had a bad night or had been out on the town the evening before because, as our contest continued he had to leave the table and rush to the lavatory. He looked rather green on his return and we both decided the contest was over.

Tactfully, I did not insist I had won but said rather that ill health caused us to call it off. I added we should try again on another occasion, at which my Russian friend told me that he normally came into Melk if not on duty and said he thought he would be in again the Sunday after next. I could not make any preparation for my next meeting with him as I did not know his name, only his first name and patronymic which were Grigori Vassilevitch, and those were not sufficient to see if there was any trace of him in SIS records.

A fortnight later I returned to Melk and was slightly surprised to see that Grigori was already there, sitting in the pub drinking a beer. He was on his own. I assumed, since it was a beautiful day, that the reason he was sitting inside and by himself was because he was meeting me.

This was dangerous. Either it meant he was out to entrap me or it meant that he wanted to talk to me knowing me to be British, with the British Commission and therefore, to the suspicious mind of a Soviet officer, possibly a spy.

I drew up a chair and ordered a beer, a small one. Grigori told me he wanted to apologize for his behaviour the previous time we had met. Something he had eaten the evening before had not agreed with him and this accounted for his impolite behaviour. I commiserated, in a fully-understanding manner, and said we had been silly to drink so much even though it was obvious that we were both good drinkers. At this we clinked glasses.

From then on I carried on a conversation discussing everything and anything except matters to do with the Soviet forces or his work. We talked about our families, home life, what we had done as children, what brothers and sisters we had, what our parents did, and so on. In order to ingratiate myself I told him that my father had been a factory worker, who had been unemployed for a long time, and after he had died I had been brought up by my mother. He told that his father had been killed in the war by the Germans and that he, himself, had been in the Red Army for the famous advance on Berlin, and that he planned to stay in the army. He was now a captain in the Artillery with an office job in St Poelten, the Soviet Military Headquarters.

I said immediately that, in this case, it might be difficult for him if he were seen talking to a foreigner for too long, but he dismissed this saying that he knew what he could and could not do.

The obvious thought to me was that if I could continue and build on my acquaintanceship with Grigori I might, at some later time, be able to recruit him as a source – a Staff Officer from Soviet Military Headquarters in Austria would be worth his weight in gold.

I introduced myself using a pseudonym, I think it was probably Paul Carpenter at this time. He told me his name. Hoping I was on my way to something big as we bade each other farewell, I returned to Vienna to plan my next move.

We had agreed to meet again a fortnight later, same place, same time. I arrived as arranged but there was no sign of Grigori and though I waited as long as I dared he did not arrive. I waited until early evening and then set off back to Vienna feeling rather depressed. A fortnight later I went to the pub again and this time saw three Soviet officers drinking on the terrace. I had seen two of them previously as part of the group when I first saw Grigori. I sat down and ordered a drink, waiting to see if they would say anything to me. When they did not, I was faced with deciding whether to risk approaching the officers myself to ask after Grigori, or else finding another way.

The first was too risky, so I went into the pub to the kitchen and explained to the proprietor, who knew me now from my several visits, that I was anxious to enquire after Grigori but for various reasons did not want to approach the Russians myself. I asked him politely if he would mind enquiring after Grigori, saying that the last time Grigori had been he had left behind a box of cigarettes, which fortunately the landlord had picked up.

Some other Russian visitor had left his cigarettes behind and I had pocketed them. I gave them to the landlord and waited inside while the landlord performed his charade. He came back shortly telling me that one of the Russians, who had been rather angry at the question, had told him that Captain Grigori would not be coming for his cigarettes because he had been posted back to the Soviet Union.

The fact that the Russians gave this information indicated that alcohol was already loosening their tongues, but what was even more clear was that any plans we had to recruit Grigori were over. He was the first of three Russian officers whose acquaintance I made and who then disappeared.

My second Soviet contact came as a result of a visit to the opera. During a break in a performance of *Boris Godounov*, with George London singing the main part, I went for a drink in the bar. As I stood at the bar alone I found in fact that I was standing close to a Russian Army Colonel whose shoulderboards told me he was in the Artillery. It was easy, when he turned around glass in hand, to ensure that in doing so he made me spill some of my drink. He apologized immediately and insisted with a smile on buying me a fresh drink.

'I would be delighted,' I replied, but only on condition that I could reciprocate. He hesitated and when the bell rang for an end to the interval he agreed to meet for the second interval at the same spot.

Naturally, my thoughts were not with the opera for the next fifty minutes or so. I was excited and expectant when I moved back to the bar for my second encounter with the Colonel. He arrived as agreed and I ordered our drinks. We began by talking about the opera and moved on to exchanging personal details. He was on the staff at Soviet Headquarters in Vienna, which were in the Imperial Hotel a short way down the Ring from the Opera House.

I told him in return that I was in the Control Commission. He did not enquire further as to what my job was, though mentally I had determined that I would tell him I was an historian if asked.

His friendliness and openness were such that I felt safe in asking him to have lunch with me. He accepted readily enough and we arranged to meet in the basement brasserie of a local brewery, the Goesserbrau, three days later.

Next morning I discussed the whole matter in detail with Philip who decided that London's guidance should be sought. Unfortunately, it being a first meeting, I had only got the first name of my colonel and we were therefore unable to pass his full name through our records to see if we already had trace of him.

A signal sped back from London authorizing me to continue the contact, and Philip said that I would be kept under observation while with Nikolai. The fact that we were meeting in a dimly lit restaurant meant that concealed photography would be difficult.

I was impatient for the day of the lunch to arrive. The thought that we might be at the start of an enterprise which, if handled well, could land us a defector from Soviet Headquarters in Vienna was exciting for everybody.

I arrived at the Goesserbrau about ten minutes before the appointed time and chose a table between two others that were unoccupied. The tables with benches were set in the centre of three-sided stalls and, in the normal Austrian tradition, if the place got full, strangers could ask if they might take a spare place at a table.

Nikolai arrived punctually at 12 o'clock and joined in a beer and also ordered himself an iced schnapps to go with it. We tucked into the special dish of the day, which was boiled beef and dumplings, and as we ate we discussed Vienna, occupied Austria, the world situation and then the war. Nikolai was an intelligent man, with some personal knowledge of life outside occupied territory since he had visited France with some kind of Soviet military mission. Towards the end of the meal he told me his full name, and it was easy to remember because his last name was the same as the well-known General of Polish origin, Rokossowski.

We had a longish meal and shortly after 2 o'clock he said he must return to his office. I took care to pay for the lunch at which he asked if I would join him the following week for a meal as his guest.

I accepted as casually as I knew how, and he mentioned that he knew a very good little restaurant called the Bulgar, off the Graben in the centre of Vienna. We agreed to meet there, just before eight in the evening in a week's time.

Now that we knew Nikolai's full name we were able to pass him through our records and confirm that he was indeed a Staff Officer in the Soviet Commander-in-Chief's secretariat. He was thus an extremely valuable contact, either as a potential defector or, better still, as a potential source.

However, a complication now arose. In naming that particular restaurant the Russian Colonel had given us a problem. The Bulgar was in the international sector of Vienna, where the Soviets had as much right to operate as any of the other occupying powers. It would not therefore be very difficult for them to arrange to kidnap me on a pretext of first arresting me, in company with the Austrian police, based on a complaint lodged by my Soviet friend. For, if he was in touch with Soviet intelligence or indeed was himself a KGB officer, he could be playing exactly the same game as I was. It was decided, therefore, that we would have to stake out the restaurant so that help would be at hand in the event of anything untoward happening.

I arrived in the restaurant at about ten past eight, giving Nikolai – as host – the chance to get there first. After half an hour we started to get worried and decided after an hour that he was not coming. We assumed either that something had come up which prevented him from keeping the dinner date, or that he had mentioned meeting me to a colleague and that the KGB had forbidden him to attend.

We had given each other a private telephone number on which we could be reached. So the next morning I arranged for a colleague, an émigré whose Russian was perfect, to ring the number and ask for Colonel Nikolai. My émigré friend called me later to say that when the telephone was eventually answered a brusque voice announced that Colonel Nikolai had recently returned to the Soviet Union.

Kim Philby

One does not look twice at an offer of enrolment in an élite force.
My Silent War

Contrary to public belief, Harold Adrian Russell Philby was never tipped to be a future chief of SIS. He was a philandering drunk whose career was destined to be curtailed by the knowledge, acquired secretly by MI5, that he had once been a member of the Communist Party of Great Britain. His first wife, Litzi Friedman, was a known Soviet agent and three of his children had been born out of wedlock which, in the 1940s, was something of a social stigma. His heavy drinking, together with a stutter, made him an unlikely candidate for SIS's top post, although that myth continues to be perpetuated even after his death.

Philby joined SIS from Special Operations Executive in September 1941 and was to work closely with Graham Greene in Section V's Iberian sub-section. He spent his wartime service with SIS in St Albans and London but in 1944 he travelled abroad, to Paris, where he spent a memorable evening with Malcolm Muggeridge. In November 1951, after foreign postings as SIS's representative in Istanbul and Washington DC, Philby was cross-examined about his links with Burgess and Maclean, and sacked. In the unhappy months that followed he tried to eke out an existence as a journalist and many of his friends, who believed he had been treated unfairly, rallied to his support. He worked temporarily for Jack Ivens, a fruit importer who had worked for SIS's Section V in Madrid during the war, and then was commissioned to ghost a history of the publishing firm David Allen. For this task Philby moved to Ireland, abandoning his wife and family at their home in Crowborough.

Philby eventually defected to Moscow in January 1963, after having been confronted with evidence of his duplicity by his old colleague Nicholas Elliott. In the safety of the Soviet Union he prepared his autobiography, *My Silent War*, which was published in London in 1968 and was described by Graham Greene as 'more gripping than any novel of espionage I can remember'. He died in Moscow in May 1988 having betrayed his sister Helena, who also worked for SIS, his family, his friends and his country. He even denounced Tim Milne, one of his closest friends from their school days at Westminster, as a Soviet spy. His legacy was one of lasting bitterness which extended beyond those who knew or worked with him. His illegitimate son Alan Young was abandoned by his parents and was brought up in children's homes. In 1984, when he was sentenced to a term of imprisonment, this time on a charge of blackmail, the court in London was told that Young's discovery that his true father had been the notorious traitor had marked a deterioration in his criminal conduct.

In this passage from the company history he ghosted, Philby describes David Allen's private commitment to Chartism and radical politics.

David Allens: The History of a Family Firm

Some time in 1847 David Allen left Belfast for Liverpool. There is a legend that he broke his [printing] apprenticeship agreement, but it would seem that in 1847 he should have completed, or almost completed, the seven years begun in 1840. The breach of an agreement is scarcely in keeping with the character for integrity attributed to him by all his generation in Belfast.

There is no hint that boyish involvement with the Young Ireland movement, then sliding towards the perilous crisis of 1848, suggested a rapid move; yet this could explain David's leaving James Macauley (perhaps with the latter's implicit consent) before his term was up. And David's drifting life in Liverpool, and his return to Belfast after a lapse of two years, can suggest the possibility of the passage of an awkward situation. In those days boys were committed very young in the dangerous politics of Ireland and it is clear that James Allen had started taking his eldest son to the wild meetings of Meagher, Mitchell and Smith O'Brien at the early age of ten. David's movements in 1847–8 are almost as obscure as those of the young Samuel Johnson in 1745; and it is possible that his shyness of public life in later years and his acid view of politics covered some secret enthusiasm of his youth.

On the other hand, David, like so many of the Young Irelanders, had to earn his meagre living, and he had a mother and younger brothers and sisters looking to him for contributions. It would seem reasonable, therefore, that having completed his apprenticeship, he should decide to widen his experience by seeking employment over the water. Indeed, in the famine years in Ulster, he may simply have been forced to go further afield to find work. At seventeen, he was doubtless already determined to succeed in his trade, and he was confident that he could work his way out of the ruck. There is no indication that he ever contemplated going to America; he seldom showed interest in travel for its own sake. But other openings lay closer at hand. There was Clydeside, for instance, along which his ancestors had passed on their way to Ireland; there was Liverpool, with an Irish population already large and still growing. Doubtless it was mainly chance that determined David's choice, perhaps some casual connection scraped at the docks or an introduction from a fellow apprentice. One day, probably in 1847, he carried his bag on board the Liverpool steampacket.

We may wonder whether David found Liverpool as strange as he had expected, and perhaps hoped. Its population, well over 300,000 at that date, was four times that of Belfast. Otherwise the two ports were in many ways alike. The prosperity of Liverpool in the eighteenth century had rested largely on privateering and the slave trade; by the late 1840s its energies had turned into more acceptable channels, mainly into trade with the western hemisphere. Cotton, grain, foodstuffs and tobacco from America, sugar and rum from the West Indies, were imported against textiles, machinery, coal and salt. The port was growing, like Belfast, at the feverish rate characteristic of the Industrial Revolution in Britain, and when David arrived, the urban authorities had only just begun to face the pressing problems of street maintenance, housing and sewerage. At the end of the Napoleonic wars, Liverpool was notorious for the bad condition and wretched lighting of its streets. They were paved with large boulder stones, and drainage channels ran down the middle. 'Even judged by contemporary standards, Liverpool was very unhealthy . . . Figures published in 1844 by the Registrar of Births, Marriages and Deaths showed that out of every 100,000 children . . . 51,739 died before reaching the age of ten. The corresponding figure in London was 35,079.' Houses were built with little regard for drainage or ventilation. About a quarter of the population lived in stinking courts and alleys, which the municipal scavengers ignored. The only lavatories were privies – one to about eight houses. 'The few sewers that existed were never cleaned except by rain.' In the 1840s and 1850s, the vigorous efforts of a handful of reformers bore fruit; a number of Bills were passed empowering the Corporation to improve the standards of housing, sanitation, water supply and other services. But progress was slow. As late as 1864 there were still over 18,000 houses in Liverpool with bad sanitation or none at all. The dwellers in these slums were largely Irish. Hardship, then famine, had driven them over in alarming numbers. Hungry and almost penniless, they drifted into the cellars and courtyards.

It is probable that David was earning enough before setting out from Belfast to avoid the extremes of misery. Yet he was certainly moved by the fate of the Irish in Liverpool, and the Radical tradition which the family had brought from Randalstown gave him a personal interest in working-class politics. The printers were beginning to play a leading part in the growth of trade unionism; their occupation gave them wider horizons than most. The ancient institution of the printers' 'chapel', with its 'father' and 'clerk', was dying out. Its place was being taken by trade unions organized on an urban, regional or national basis. The printers, like the Dorsetshire labourers, had their martyrs. In 1810, a group of journeymen, after a dispute with *The Times*, were tried and sentenced by Sir John Sylvester, the Common Serjeant of London, otherwise known as Bloody Black Jack. Despite such setbacks, the movement spread. In 1845, many London and provincial societies of compositors joined forces in the National Typographical Society, an ambitious organization grouped into sixty branches under five District Boards. But its membership never matched its ambitions, and after a series of abortive small strikes it broke up in 1847. During the next two years – the years of David's sojourn in Liverpool – there were attempts to revive it, with limited success.

David's first Liverpool job was a mere stop-gap. A theatrical manager named Kiernan had bought the old Unitarian Church in Paradise Street, and had converted it into a music-hall which he called Kelly's Theatre. The Kiernan family used the vestry as a bedroom, and printed their playbills in the vaults. So far as is known, it was David's first contact with the theatre. Perhaps, like some of his fellow apprentices, he supplemented his daytime earnings as printer's devil by acting as a call-boy at night, either at Kelly's or at the Adelphi. After a short time, he left Kiernan for McCall's, a printing house in Hunter Street, which, as we shall see, was to play a small part in the Allen history many decades later, and a few months later he was on the move again, having found a post with the *Liverpool Mercury*, a bi-weekly newspaper of good standing. Here his experience with *The Vindicator* must have helped him; here also he discovered unionism in England. In general, the printers' unions belonged to the moderate wing of the working-class movement. Their meetings were orderly, even solemn. Nevertheless, it was through unionism in the printing trade, as well as through his Irish friends, that David made his first contact with Chartism. Although few knew it at the time – and David was certainly not among the few – the Chartist movement was near its end. The fiasco at Newport, where a few ragged volleys had dispersed several thousand rioters, had betrayed its weakness. Its political aims were clearly formulated in the Charter itself; but there clarity ended. Its organization was loose, the dispute over methods chronic. It stood no chance against the forces of the state, provided the Government stood firm against the torchlight processions, the garrulous conventions and the monster petitions. When David toyed with Chartism, its ranks were already riven by the same issue which had split the Irish repeal movement – the choice between moral and physical force. While extremists like Feargus O'Connor and Julian Harney threatened violence the moderates worked for the total renunciation of physical force. The moderates had already left the movement by 1848, when O'Connor presented to Parliament the last 'monster' petition. It was found to contain less than two million signatures, among them such as Queen Victoria, Wellington and Pug Nose. Within a few months, Chartism had disappeared, leaving the field free for trade unionism and, much later, the Labour Party.

David's flirtation with Chartism is one of the obscurest chapters of his life. It was surely a deep impulse that caused him to throw up his job with the *Liverpool Mercury* and move to the Isle of Man, then a stronghold of Radical journalism. Newspapers on the mainland were still carrying the burden laid on them by the Stamp Act, first levied in 1712 at the rate of 1*d.* for a one-sheet paper. In the hundred years after its first imposition, the 'tax on knowledge', as its enemies called it, was steadily raised until it reached 4*d.* at the end of the Napoleonic wars. The result was a flood of illicit unstamped sheets, some of them wearing an oddly modern look in their single-minded preoccupation with crime and vice. Stricter regulation and government action in the courts did little to stem the tide. The cure clearly lay in the direction of freedom rather than restriction – freedom for the better papers to expand in an age of enlightenment. But it was not until 1855 that stamp duty on the press was abolished. Up till that date, many newspaper managements resorted to publication in the Isle of Man, where the Stamp Act did not run. Among them was the Chartist sheet on which David was employed in 1849. Its name is not known; in any case it cannot have survived long after the collapse of the movement in England. Towards the end of 1849 or early in 1850, David was at a loose end again. He was already half-way from Liverpool to Belfast and he went home.

George Blake

I had of late suspected and hoped that the job for which I was being interviewed had something to do with 'Intelligence'. But that I would actually become an officer in the British Secret Service, the legendary centre of hidden power, commonly believed to have a decisive influence on the great events of this world, was something that far exceeded my wildest expectations.

Born George Behar in Rotterdam, Blake possessed British nationality through his father, who had become a naturalized citizen following service in the Great War. He was educated in Holland and Egypt, and joined his mother and sister in London after an escape from the Nazi occupation of the Netherlands. In 1943 Blake anglicized his name by deed poll and the next year was recruited by SIS as a conducting officer in the Dutch Section.

At the end of the war Blake remained in SIS and, having completed a Russian language course, was posted to Seoul where he was interned at the outset of the Korean War. In captivity he volunteered to spy for the KGB and did so upon his release and until he was finally denounced in 1961. At his trial he received a record sentence of forty-two years' imprisonment, but in October 1966 he escaped and defected to Moscow.

Blake still lives in Russia, having written an autobiography entitled *No Abiding City*. It was read by a few Western publishers but rejected on the grounds that it was too boring, so he prepared a second memoir, *No Other Choice*. Despite the British government ban on former intelligence personnel disclosing details of their professional work, Blake's book was released in England, and it named many of his former SIS colleagues whose identities had never previously been published. Surprisingly, no action was taken to prevent the book's circulation.

In recent times there have been two disclosures from Moscow that shed new light on his case. The first is the admission that one of his KGB contacts in London was Vasili A. Dozhdalev who, by coincidence, happened to be conveniently on hand in Berlin on the very night Blake turned up, ostensibly without warning: the implication being that even if the Soviets had not played a direct role in engineering his escape from Wormwood Scrubs they would appear to have had foreknowledge of his arrival in Germany. The second is the claim made by Lieutenant-General K. Grigoriev, a retired KGB officer, that Blake's recruitment in Korea had not been an example of ideological conversion, but rather one of manipulation; apparently KGB Colonel Nikolai Loyenko befriended Blake by slipping him bread and chocolate, and was quoted subsequently as having concluded that 'the way to an intelligence officer's heart is through his stomach'.

Royalties from Blake's autobiography have been blocked by the Treasury

Solicitor in order to prevent a criminal from profiting from crime but this appears to have been the only disadvantage to the release of *No Other Choice*. In this scene Blake recalls the circumstances of his interrogation at the hands of his SIS colleagues. His claim that he was trapped into confessing his duplicity by a skilful interrogator who suggested that he had been coerced into becoming a spy contrasts with the memory of one of those present at the time, who insists that Blake was spotted by surveillance experts whilst trying to telephone his Soviet contact in the apparent hope of a rescue.

No Other Choice

The next morning, it being the Tuesday after Easter, I reported to the Personnel Department in Petty France, shortly after ten, as instructed. I was shown into the room of Ian Crichley, the Deputy Head of the Department. There an old acquaintance of mine, Harry Shergold, one of the SIS experts on Soviet affairs, was already waiting for me. They both welcomed me in a friendly manner and Shergold suggested that I should come with him as he wanted to discuss certain questions which had arisen in connection with my work in Berlin. Instead of taking me to Head Office in Broadway, a stone's throw away, he led me across St James's Park to the house in Carlton Gardens, so familiar to me from the days when I worked there in Section 'Y'. We were shown into the rather splendid reception room on the ground floor. At a large table two of my colleagues were seated. I knew them both since they also worked in the Soviet field, but their names, I must admit, I have now forgotten. They got up to greet me and then we all sat down round the table. After some general conversation, they got down to business. Shergold did most of the talking. He began to tell me about an event which had happened in Berlin, some time after I left.

As I have already mentioned, the agent Mickey – his real name was Horst Eitner – was married to an attractive, young woman who had spent five years in a prison camp in Siberia, having been sentenced by the Soviet authorities in East Germany to twenty-five years' imprisonment for espionage on behalf of the Americans and subsequently been amnestied. I have also mentioned how Mickey and his wife were recruited by the Soviet Military Intelligence service so that both were, in fact, double agents.

Mickey and his wife were in the habit of celebrating every year her release from Soviet imprisonment with a dinner in one of Berlin's many restaurants in the company of one of her girlfriends who had been an inmate in the same camp as she and had been released on the same day. It was, as always, a very convivial party and all concerned had more to drink than was good for them. In the course of the evening, Mickey started making passes at his wife's girlfriend which, of course, Mrs Mickey did not like. She showed her irritation and asked him to stop. He ignored her entreaties and went on with his flirtatious behaviour. At last, driven to exasperation, Mrs Mickey threatened to go to the police and tell them that her husband was a Soviet agent. Mickey didn't take this threat seriously and told her to do what she liked. Without another word, she got up and went straight to the nearest police station. They thought at first that she had had too much to drink and did not want to believe her story. To prove that she was telling the truth, she asked them to accompany her to her flat. There she showed them two hidden microphones, installed by the Soviets. Mickey was arrested the same evening and Mrs Mickey herself the next day.

What had happened was this. While I was in Berlin and Mickey's case officer, there had been no need for the Soviets to listen in to what passed between us. But when I left and handed him over to Johnny Spears, another expert on Soviet affairs, they became interested in my successor. They therefore asked Mickey if he would allow them to put microphones in his flat so that they could monitor the conversations between him and his case officer. Mickey agreed to this and two microphones were installed.

Having told me this story in some detail, Shergold began by asking me why I thought the Soviets had wanted to install microphones only after I had left and another officer had taken over. To this I could only answer that I did not have the faintest idea.

It was now also clear – Shergold continued – that, since Mickey had been a Soviet agent, Boris, the Soviet Comecon official, must have been a plant. How could I explain that? I agreed that the evidence pointed to Boris having been planted on us, but as to why, well, all I could say was that Mickey had obviously been a convenient link for this purpose.

Thus the discussion went on till lunchtime. When we broke up, nobody suggested, as would normally have been the case, that we should have lunch together. I thought this was a bad sign. I walked alone to Soho and had lunch in a small Italian restaurant I sometimes used to go to. I can't say that I had much appetite. My thoughts were on other things.

By itself, of course, the fact that the Soviets had placed microphones in Mickey's flat only after my departure could quite easily be explained as pure coincidence. That Boris was, in all probability, a plant followed from the fact that Mickey, as was now known, had been a Soviet agent. But in all this there was nothing criminal. These things could happen and did happen in the career of any intelligence officer, especially in a place like Berlin where many agents were double or even triple agents. If they had no more than this circumstantial evidence, I had not much to worry about. On the other hand, would I have been called back from Beirut, at a particularly crucial point in my studies, just to discuss this in Carlton Gardens and not in Shergold's room in Head Office, which would have been more normal, and why was it necessary to have three people there?

When I returned to Carlton Gardens, my three colleagues resumed their questioning. The subject now shifted from Berlin to Poland. They said that they had evidence that certain important SIS documents, bearing on Poland and with a very restricted distribution list which included me, had found their way into the hands of the Polish Intelligence Service. How could I account for this? I said I couldn't and that their guess was as good as mine.

In the course of further questioning, it became clear to me that they must have a source in the Polish Intelligence Service at a pretty high level. Many years later, I found confirmation of this in Peter Wright's book *Spycatcher*, in which he relates how one Michael Goleniewski (codename Sniper), allegedly a deputy head of the Polish Intelligence Service, who defected in 1959 to the Americans, had reported to the CIA that the Russians had two very important spies in Britain, one in the British Intelligence Service and one somewhere in the Navy. This report eventually led to the arrest, first, of Gordon Lonsdale and his group and then, a few months later, of myself. I also discovered in this book that I had been given the codename 'Lambda 1' and Lonsdale that of 'Lambda 2'. The questioning went on all through that afternoon, in ever decreasing circles, till, towards the end of the day, my interrogators – for that is what they were more and more becoming – openly accused me of working for the Soviet Intelligence Service. This I flatly denied. At six o'clock we broke up and they asked me to come back the following morning at ten. On the way back to Radlett [where he was staying in his mother's flat], I kept on turning over in my mind all that had been said that day. Of one thing I was no longer in any doubt – SIS knew that I was working for the Soviets. Otherwise such a grave accusation would never have been levelled against me.

Thinking back now, that evening and the two following evenings were, without doubt, the most difficult hours in my life. Knowing that I was in serious danger, that, whatever happened, life would never be the same again for any of us, I had to pretend to my mother that all was well and continue to discuss with her the plans for her forthcoming trip and all the purchases we had to complete before the end of the week. I remember in particular how one item, high on my wife's shopping list, was mosquito nets. My mother had found out that these could only be bought at Gamages and she instructed me to make sure to go there the next day and order them so that they could be delivered in time.

To cut a long story short, all the next day my interrogators continued to accuse me of being a Soviet agent, revealing little bits of additional evidence in the process, and all the next day I stubbornly continued to deny this. At lunch time, though my mind was on quite different matters, I managed to go to Gamages and order the mosquito nets and some other items. That evening, I went home again to my mother and her cosy flat seemed to me cosier and safer than ever. It became increasingly difficult however to pretend that I did not have a worry in the world and I pleaded a busy day ahead to go to bed early and be alone with my thoughts.

The next morning found us again, all four, sitting round the table in the sumptuous ground-floor room in Carlton Gardens. One of the reasons this venue had been chosen, I now realised, was that recording apparatus was installed in the next room so that everything that was said could be taken down. Round and round we went over the same ground, without getting any further. I must stress, however, that, throughout, the tone remained courteous and no threats of any kind were made.

When we resumed after lunch, my interrogators changed tack. Looking back now, I don't think this was only a ploy on their part. It seemed to me that they themselves genuinely believed that it had all happened the way they suggested and it was this that lent special weight to their words. Be that as it may, the fact remains that, whether by luck or by planning, they hit upon the right psychological approach. What they said was this: 'We know that you worked for the Soviets, but we understand why. While you were their prisoner in Korea, you were tortured and made to confess that you were a British intelligence officer. From then on, you were blackmailed and had no choice but to collaborate with them.'

When they put the case in this light, something happened which to most people would seem to go against all the dictates of elementary common sense and the instinct of self-preservation. All I can say is that it was a gut reaction. Suddenly I felt an upsurge of indignation and I wanted my interrogators and everyone else to know that I had acted out of conviction, out of a belief in Communism, and not under duress or for financial gain. This feeling was so strong that without thinking what I was doing I burst out, 'No, nobody tortured me! No, nobody blackmailed me!

I myself approached the Soviets and offered my services to them of my own accord!'

A gut reaction this outburst may have been, but it amounted well and truly to a confession. Having now admitted to my interrogators – as unexpectedly to them, I am sure, as to myself – that I was a Soviet agent, I now went on to explain exactly the reasons that impelled me to become one. They listened to me in amazed silence, but their courteous attitude to me did not change nor did they question, either then or afterwards, that I had acted for other than ideological motives. At no time, then or later, did they offer me immunity from prosecution in return for what I might have been able to tell them. My reaction in the end was no different from that of my friends Michael Randle and Pat Pottle when it became known, in 1989, that they were the people who had helped me to escape and had been named in the press. They wrote a book *The Blake Escape* in which they admitted their role in the escape. What was important to them was that everyone should know exactly why they had done it. They chose to face the danger of prosecution and a prison sentence rather than have the wrong motives ascribed to them.

By the time I had finished it was nearly six o'clock and time to go home. It was arranged that a chauffeur-driven car should take me to Radlett where I could spend the night at my mother's. I was not to say anything to her, however, only that my return to Beirut had been postponed as I had to attend an urgent conference which would take me away from London for a few days.

The next morning, another chauffeur-driven car came to collect me and I said goodbye to my mother as if I really was going away for a few days. As I waved to her from the car window, I wondered if and when I would see her again. At Carlton Gardens, Harry Shergold, one of the other interrogators whose name I have forgotten and John Quine, an old friend of mine were waiting for me. I had known the latter well in the Far East, where he had been Head of Tokyo station at the time that I was in Korea. He had on two or three occasions visited me there and I had stayed at his and his charming wife's hospitable house in the Embassy compound whenever I had been in Tokyo for consultation or to deliver the diplomatic bag. Now he was there, partly because he was head of R5, the counter-espionage department in SIS which worked closely with MI5, and partly, I think, because he was a friend of mine.

With a police car ahead and another following the party then drove in two cars to a small village in Hampshire – I have forgotten its name – where Harry Shergold had a cottage. There we were met by his wife and his mother-in-law, a charming old lady with snow-white hair, who reminded me of my grandmother. It was now Friday, the day I had hoped to return to Shemlan.

The next three days had something surreal about them with everyone pretending that this was just an ordinary weekend party among friends. The only difference was that the house was surrounded by Special Branch officers and, every time we went out for a walk, a police car drove slowly behind us. It was a bizarre situation which struck me as very English – I should say endearingly English. I particularly remember one afternoon which I spent in the kitchen making pancakes with the old grandmother. I am something of a specialist in this and when it was suggested that we should eat pancakes, I offered to make them. At night John Quine shared a bedroom with me, and when we were alone he spoke a lot about my family and wanted me to tell him again what had been my motives for doing what I did. I had a feeling he was trying hard to understand. During the day, there were frequent telephone conversations with London, conducted in another room so that I could not hear what was being said. In the course of the weekend it became clear to me that we were all waiting for something, though for what I had no idea.

Somehow, I felt no longer worried about my own fate, but all my thoughts were with my wife and children, my mother and my sisters. How would they be told, how would it affect them and what would now become of them?

Sir Percy Sillitoe

I find now that my acquaintances cherish a fond belief that it must many times have fallen to my lot to take part in Bulldog Drummond-like adventures in connection with my work in MI5. I am sad to disappoint them, though I must confess I have never fancied myself as that type of hero.

In 1946 the new Prime Minister Clement Attlee invited Sir Percy Sillitoe, who was then Chief Constable of Kent, to become the Director-General of the Security Service to replace Sir David Petrie who was retiring. A professional police officer with experience that dated back to the British South African Police in 1908, Sillitoe had made his reputation as a gang-buster in Glasgow and a no-nonsense copper with few intellectual pretensions. During the war he had written a report for the Home Office on Communist agitation and this may have brought him to the attention of the incoming Home Secretary, Chuter Ede.

While he was Director-General Sillitoe authorized two of his officers to indulge in literary pursuits. Courtney Young helped write *Handbook for Spies*, the autobiography of a Briton, Allan Foote, who had defected from the Soviet GRU, and Jim Skardon was encouraged to collaborate with Alan Moorehead who wrote *The Traitors*, a study of the atom spies Allan Nunn May, Bruno Pontecorvo and Klaus Fuchs. None of this help was acknowledged publicly but both books served MI5's purposes.

Sillitoe remained as Director-General until August 1953, and during that turbulent period he was to oversee some of MI5's more notorious investigations, including the arrest of Fuchs and the defections of Burgess and Maclean. The former case was to be traumatic for Sillitoe because, reluctantly, he allowed himself to be persuaded to lie to the Prime Minister in order to conceal the appalling blunder of a subordinate. Sillitoe accordingly said that MI5's identification of Fuchs as a traitor in 1949 had been the culmination of a lengthy investigation which had been conducted properly at every stage, and when challenged by Attlee he denied that Fuchs should have been caught years earlier. The truth was that the Americans had acquired enough evidence to incriminate the scientist from cryptographic sources and had simply passed it on. Further, a dossier had been compiled on Fuchs as a likely Soviet spy immediately after the war, and Michael Serpell, an officer whose suspicions had been aroused, attached a note to the file drawing attention to the need for further enquiries to be made urgently. The then director of the counter-espionage division had ignored the recommendation and thus had enabled Fuchs to continue operating for a further three years.

Sillitoe was bitter that he had been corrupted by what he regarded as an unhealthy coterie of Security Service intellectuals, and he promised a group of senior staff that he would not repeat the exercise to save their skins, but he never alluded to the incident again. Even in his memoirs, ghosted largely by Russell Lee, his personal assistant, he gives the official version of MI5's investigations into Fuchs, and omits any reference to Michael Serpell's comments being overlooked, which had caused him such anguish.

Cloak without Dagger

In the case of Fuchs, the circumstances were unusual. He was born in Germany and his youth was spent in the troubled post-war period of upheaval. His father was a Lutheran clergyman who became a Quaker and taught his two sons and two daughters firmly that it was not enough to know what was right, but that one must always act according to one's conscience, no matter what the cost.

The result of this teaching, when it coincided with the Nazi régime, was that one daughter committed suicide after Nazi persecution, another daughter and the elder son were driven into exile, and the younger son –

Klaus – had to go underground to hide from the Brownshirts among the Communists. The good clergyman's wife committed suicide and the pastor himself was thrown into prison. Those were unhealthy days, in Germany, for men, women, and children who possessed independent consciences.

Klaus Fuchs had, whilst a student at Kiel University, crossed swords with the Nazi Party and had published a pamphlet when he was twenty years old, condemning it. The next year Hitler became Chancellor, and the Nazi students in Kiel joined up with the Brownshirts in a victory parade before the classrooms. Klaus Fuchs chose that moment to walk out amongst them and damn them to their faces. He was lucky not to be killed, but he was savagely beaten and flung into the river.

At that time the only party in Germany that did anything at all to oppose the Nazis was the Communist Party. Klaus Fuchs joined it, and wore the hammer-and-sickle badge boldly in his lapel until he knew the Gestapo were after him; then he pinned it inside his jacket and became a member of the anti-Nazi resistance group.

Fuchs was exceptional in the extent of the damage he did, but he was not alone in the dilemma which resulted in his treachery. When he betrayed the atomic secrets to Russia, he did so because he believed sincerely that the Communist way of life was more admirable than our own. It was at first as a matter of simple conviction that he decided to place his own scientific findings at the disposal of the Russians, thinking them worthy recipients of his knowledge. His position became more and more complicated as the information at his disposal grew increasingly important and he realized that his giving or withholding of it might substantially alter the fate of all the peoples of the world. He was exceptional in having such information to dispose of, yet one must recognize that in the workings of his mind which persuaded him that he was justified in disposing of it against the interests of his adopted country, he was not alone. Since the end of the last war MI5 has been constantly aware that in this country it is by no means impossible for men in positions of trust and authority to become enamoured of Communist doctrine to the point where they will spy on behalf of the Russians and feel no shame in doing so.

These men who betrayed us were unlike any earlier spies or traitors in history. They did not want money, nor personal glory, nor were they lured into espionage for any reasons of adventure, so far as one can see. They were men who had come via the quiet and unpurposeful ways of scholarship into sudden possession of powerful, terrible knowledge. By their very remoteness from the ordinary human ways of life and the struggles and bewilderments of their neighbours, these men were lured to make the mistake of thinking that they and their private decisions were beyond our ordinary law. It was the same with Fuchs as with Dr Nunn May; although these two men were markedly different in personality, each felt that he was not to be bound by any declarations made under the Official Secrets Act, nor to be swayed by any emotions such as normal loves and loyalties.

The Fuchs family was not Jewish. But Pastor Fuchs, his elder son and two daughters organized escapes for Jewish refugees from Nazi terrorism. Eventually, they had to scatter and flee. In Berlin, Klaus Fuchs, the younger son, was advised by the anti-Nazis to escape from Germany and continue his studies abroad, so that he could return one day to help rebuild his country when Hitler had fallen from power.

Fuchs, aged twenty-one, arrived in England, ragged, pale, and hungry, with all his property in a small canvas bag, on 24th September 1933, and was registered as an alien – one of hundreds who were arriving daily. Fourteen months later the German consulate at Bristol reported unofficially to the Bristol police that Fuchs was a Communist, wanted by the Gestapo.

This information was correctly passed by the Bristol police to London, with the comment of the Chief Constable that Fuchs, as an alien, had been checked three times at intervals, was behaving himself, and was not taking any part in Communist activities in Bristol.

The British security authorities were at this time taking a somewhat cynical view of such Gestapo denunciations, for it was Nazi practice to declare almost every refugee a Communist, and to agitate for him to be sent back to Germany if the man were at all important. The only variation was for them to accuse a refugee of being a wanted criminal. In the case of Fuchs, they did not demand his return nor brand him a criminal. By comparison with many other Gestapo incriminations, young Fuchs's denunciation was very mild.

For the next six years Fuchs lived a withdrawn, studious life with Quaker families in England, and was assisted by the Society for the Protection of Science and Learning to complete the studies that had been so violently interrupted at Kiel. He went first to Bristol University upon a scholarship grant, and afterwards to Edinburgh, where he won the Carnegie Research Scholarship. All this time – and up to 1939 – there was an unrestricted and eager interchange of reports between the scientists of every nation of the world, upon progress in nuclear physics.

In July 1939 Fuchs applied for British naturalization, probably not so much because of any overwhelming loyalty at this time to us, but because life as an alien held certain disadvantages. Before naturalization could be granted, however, war was declared and after two months he was brought before the Aliens' Tribunal at Edinburgh for investigation. Contrary to suggestions that have since been made, he did not declare any Communist sympathies before this Tribunal, nor did he say that he had at any time been a member of the Party. His excellent record whilst in Britain ensured that he was permitted to return to his work at the university.

But at the Dunkirk crisis Fuchs was scooped into internment with thousands of other refugees from Nazidom. He was sent first to the Isle of Man, and thence to Canada, under what were, beyond denial, conditions of extreme haste and discomfort. Unfortunately the Canadians were ill-informed as to the precise status of these internees, and subjected them to somewhat contemptuous treatment, believing them to be Nazi spies. Fuchs, wearing the uniform of a prisoner of war with a big coloured patch on the back, was by further mischance sent to a camp for particularly belligerent Nazis. It was January 1941 before his scientist and university friends obtained his release and he was able to return to England, where he joined Professor Peierls at Birmingham in the first wartime research upon the atomic bomb.

The salary was £275 a year, and Fuchs was not told more about the job than that it was urgent, secret, and had to do with the war effort. He accepted the post, and Professor Peierls applied to the department concerned – the Ministry of Aircraft Production – for authority to employ him. The report of MI5 was required, but all the Department knew that might be significant was that the Gestapo had said several years before that he was wanted as a Communist. He had been seven years in England without flaw in his behaviour, and had applied for naturalization. He was a proven enemy of the Nazis, and the war we were fighting at that time was against nobody but the Nazis and their friends. The security advice given on Fuchs was that he was an acceptable risk on a low security rating, to have restricted access to confidential information.

It is not the job of MI5 to dictate whether or not a man or woman shall be given a particular job. MI5 merely advises the government department concerned, and requires to have a final say in such decisions only when candidates for MI5 itself are being considered.

At this time Mr Churchill and his Cabinet had stated most emphatically that anybody who could help us win the war should be employed. So Fuchs was employed.

He signed the declaration required by the Official Secrets Act and at this point loses all logical claim to sympathy for what he afterwards did. For the present, however, he worked under Professor Peierls, living in his household; and he continued to do so without incident or any suspicious action, for the next two years. The Peierls sewed on his buttons and helped him buy his Christmas gifts, and sent his shoes for repair; occasionally they took him to the cinema, but usually he came straight from the laboratory to his bedroom where he continued to work until midnight.

After six months, another great wartime secret came into being. It was the 'firm' registered as Tube Alloys, and in reality it was the clearing house for atomic bomb research. The head of staff was Sir Wallace Akers of Imperial Chemical Industries, who was directly answerable to Sir John Anderson and the Prime Minister, and whose job it was to co-ordinate work on the atom bomb at the various laboratories and secret research plants. All the scientists at Oxford, Cambridge, Birmingham, Edinburgh, and elsewhere, were to send in monthly reports so that the main effort could be clarified and no work wasted or duplicated.

One man became outstanding. One man sent in reports punctually, never pleading petulantly that he was too busy. Always his reports were models of clear thinking, accuracy, and simplicity, despite the deep and abstruse subjects he was exploring. And whenever called upon to explain his reports to scientists and others engaged in different lines of work, he showed a remarkable flair for reducing them to simple, easily understandable language. This man was Dr Klaus Fuchs, among the youngest of the scientists who had now come to the forefront in the vital work of separating uranium isotopes, and by 1942 he had become recognized throughout Britain and America as a scientist who excelled at solving intricate problems, and whose results could be utterly depended upon.

Greville Wynne

I have no serious loyalty to my country now because they put me into this affair.

> *Greville Wynne to Nikolai Chistiakov,*
> *his KGB interrogator, 22 November 1962*

Born in South Wales in 1919, Greville Wynne came to public attention when he was arrested in Budapest on 2 November 1961. At his trial, held in Moscow in May the following year, he was convicted of espionage and sentenced to eight years' imprisonment, five of which were to be spent in a labour camp. His co-defendant, Colonel Oleg Penkovsky, was executed by firing squad.

The British government's reaction to these events was one of feigned innocence. In the West Wynne was portrayed as a businessman who had been incarcerated on trumped-up charges and this impression was sustained even after his release in April 1964 in exchange for Gordon Lonsdale, the KGB illegal caught in England. The charade continued until 1967 when Wynne's brother-in-law, the novelist John Gilbert, ghosted *The Man from Moscow*. Far from being an ordinary trade representative peddling the wares of British engineering companies behind the Iron Curtain, Wynne revealed himself as an SIS courier of long standing who had recruited and run Penkovsky as a source for eighteen months before the latter was finally tracked down by the KGB.

Encouraged by the success of *The Man from Moscow*, and disappointed by the failure of his marriage and his ventures in property development overseas, Wynne cooperated with another author, Bob Latona, and produced *The Man from Odessa* in 1981. In this second volume of memoirs Wynne portrayed his connection with British Intelligence as going back to 1938, when he was allegedly instrumental in entrapping a Nazi spy, and divulged details of an earlier SIS operation which had enabled a GRU defector named Sergei Kuznov to be exfiltrated from Odessa. In fact this second book, which was used as the basis of a BBC television series, was almost entirely fiction. He not only exaggerated and misrepresented his own role in the Penkovsky case, but actually invented the figure of Sergei Kuznov.

The reality was that Wynne had been recruited, unwisely, by SIS as part of its 'directed traveller' project under which visitors to the Soviet Union authorized to move around the Eastern Bloc were either alerted to what to look for, or were debriefed upon their return. By the time Wynne met Penkovsky the latter had already made several approaches to Western students and diplomats, but on each occasion he had been rejected as a crude provocation. SIS accepted Penkovsky as genuine and proceeded to milk him as a source of unprecedented importance. However, the operation became complicated by Wynne's determination to maintain contact with the GRU officer, even after Penkovsky's CIA case officers had demanded his removal from the scene. Hopelessly indiscreet and a near alcoholic, Wynne was entirely out of his depth in the life-and-death game played out between the professionals of the CIA, SIS and KGB in classic tradecraft on the streets of Moscow. Even after the British had undertaken to withdraw Wynne he made a final attempt to meet Penkovsky in a Moscow restaurant, thereby exposing him to KGB surveillance and endangering himself.

Whether Wynne's embarrassingly insecure behaviour contributed to Penkovsky's exposure and arrest is uncertain, but it is clear that his account of their relationship was sheer fantasy, as was so much else in Wynne's life. In this characteristic passage from *The Man from Odessa*, Wynne describes his implausible diversion to allow Sergei Kuznov to escape from Odessa. Among the many discrepancies in the tale is the fundamental one that the ship used in the operation, the *Uzbekistan*, had not even been built at the time Wynne described. Wynne, who rarely hesitated to bring defamation proceedings against anyone who doubted his version of events, was never contradicted by his former SIS contacts, but his extravagant assertions were eventually ridiculed by exasperated CIA officers who grew tired of his preposterous claims. He died in February 1990, having been forced to abandon his last libel action when the disclosure of his wartime army record disproved his claim to have held the rank of major.

The Man from Odessa

One of these snippets of information was that Kuznov had learned of the first factory in the Soviet Union to manufacture Wellington boots. To begin with the output would be limited to one hundred pairs a month, and one of the bright central planners in the Kremlin had decided that KGB officers were to have the first priority in receiving these boots as they came off the production line. When Kuznov told this to my colleagues in London, our agents throughout the Soviet Union were alerted, and as soon as the first snowfall came that autumn, they were out in the streets clicking away with hidden cameras at anyone wearing the tell-tale gum boots.

It was interesting to compare these photographs with the ones of known KGB agents in the files. Many matched, and those that did not enabled MI6 to extend their list of known or suspected Soviet agents.

A similar thing, Kuznov revealed, happened with the introduction of trilby hats in the Soviet Union. In this case, local Party officials and government functionaries had been given the pick of the production, but the funny thing was that nobody generally seemed to have noticed that in the West, these hats were generally worn with a dip in the centre. So it was simple to pick these chaps out of a crowd when they went around with their comical-looking headgear.

Also included in the package Kuznov passed to me was a list giving hundreds of names of Soviet agents from both the KGB and the GRU currently undergoing special training prior to being posted to embassies and commercial delegations in European, African and Asian capitals. He had made careful note of their cover identities and special duties. There was no possibility of my memorizing these names, which made it imperative to get the originals back to London at any cost.

'I'll see that these get to where they're going,' I told Kuznov. 'But you still haven't explained how you've worked the rest of it out. I can't have this package on me when I take that tumble from the ship.'

'Of course not.' Kuznov nodded vigorously. 'You must hide it in a safe place immediately after you come on board the *Uzbekistan*. I think I can tell you where. There are lavatories for men and women outside the entrance to the bar. What I suggest you do is conceal the documents in one of the ventilation ducts in there. The grille comes off easily – it's only held in place with self-tapping screws. You'll find some heavy-duty adhesive tape in the package. Use that to secure the package to the inside surface of the duct. The tape is strong enough to withstand the vibrations from the engine once the ship gets underway, so you needn't worry on that account.'

'Then I'll have to embark a little earlier than I'd been planning,' I said. 'Your friends from the KGB will probably have my baggage searched when I'm out of the cabin.'

'That's possible, though I don't think at this point you'll have any trouble. As long as there's no evidence linking the package to you, I'm fairly sure you won't be in any personal danger even if something goes drastically wrong, and the package is discovered. The ship's security officer will have to radio for instructions and by that time you'll be safe in Turkey.'

'Anything else?'

'No.' The players were jogging off the field now. Major Kuznov got to his feet and looked me in the eye. 'Greville, the French say *Au Revoir*, let that be the word for us.' He turned and joined the spectators impatiently filing past us, melting into the crowd.

I still had hours to wait. The *Uzbekistan* was due to lift anchor at half past midnight. I went back to the hotel, packed and had a fine meal. My two English friends didn't turn up at the restaurant that evening, but I convinced myself it was nothing to be alarmed about. At nine o'clock exactly, the Zil pulled up by the hotel, with my Intourist guide in the front passenger's seat. She accompanied me as far as the gangway, shook hands politely, and walked back to the car.

The looming bulk of the ship was lit up like a Christmas tree. Mercury-arc floodlamps focused in an ellipse of light at the spot where the passengers embarked, but the rest of the dock was poorly illuminated. A half-dozen men at the fantail end were unloading crates from a truck and placing them on a conveyor belt that led to an open cargo hatch halfway up the hull. I didn't see any passengers in the vicinity; it was still a bit early for that. Starlight glinted on the choppy surface of the water; the Black Sea never looked blacker than it did to me then.

I started up the gangway. The purser on duty at the top end, looking bored and idle, took my suitcase – I wasn't expecting that in the Soviet Union – and summoned a steward who showed me to my cabin. It was ten o'clock by my watch. More than two hours before she sailed.

Act naturally, I had to keep repeating to myself. What would you ordinarily do? Hang up my clothes. I hung my clothes and washed my hands. The cabin windows stayed open with the curtains apart and fluttering, so the guards would know I was in my cabin and had nothing to hide.

Two hours or a little less, now. Better get rid of the packet before the ship fills up with people. Nobody met me in the corridor and the lavatory was empty when I got there. Thank God for that. I gave the four cubicles a quick glance and for no particular reason chose the second one on my right. By standing on the seat I could reach the air vent and still not be seen outside the cubicle, if anyone suddenly came in.

I had a tiny screwdriver taken from my electric razor repair kit. The grille came loose without difficulty; it was a fairly new ship, and hadn't been long enough at sea for the fixtures to get rusty. I noticed the draught when I put my hand in the vent. It didn't seem too strong, but just to make sure I took a sheet of lavatory paper and let it dangle in the airstream. Only the gentlest tug. Good. A little cool air could only help the adhesive retain its hold.

More lavatory paper to wipe away the dust from inside the galvanized metal shaft. I then took the packet from my back pocket and reached in as far as I could with a five-inch strip of the Major's adhesive tape across its length. A few tugs to make sure it was securely attached. Then I waited, listening for approaching footsteps. Nothing. This part of the ship seemed deserted. I screwed the grille carefully back into place trying not to scratch the paintwork. In case a search was made, it would have to be a damned thorough one. I balanced myself with a hand on the cistern, stepped down and wiped the sweat from my forehead.

More than anything else I wanted a drink, and wanted it badly. It's only on television you see secret agents with nerves of steel nonchalantly complete their mission, grab the girl, and shoot their way to safety. My nerves had been on edge ever since I had met the Major at the football game and now they were stretched absolutely taut. I was all too conscious that the information I was now carrying about in my head was of the very highest priority. That, along with the imminent swan dive onto the sandpile made me feel like a man with a worm coiling in his stomach.

'I've got to be sober when I make the jump,' I reminded myself. But there was still another hour until the curtain went up for the final act. In the bar, I caught sight of the purser who had greeted me earlier when I came on board. Somehow I managed to get a normal conversation going with him about the *Uzbekistan* and how he liked his job. He was thirty years old and his wife had just had a baby; I can't remember where he said he was from. Finally, he downed his beer and excused himself saying that he had to check off the passengers who were just now starting to board. Except for the barman scrubbing glasses, I now had the place to myself.

I lingered for as long as I could over my drink, eyes glued to the clock on the wall. Assuming the merchantman weighed anchor at the scheduled time, my jump would take place at about a quarter to twelve. At half past eleven, I left the bar and strolled along the deck. It didn't take long to find the spot. I saw where the bulkhead light was out of commission and ran my hand along the railing until I came to a section that wiggled like a loose tooth. Who had seen to these arrangements, I did not know, nor was I in the mood to speculate just then.

I was very conscious as the seconds ticked by that I had to look out to sea and identify the foreign ship moving slowly out of the harbour to synchronize my leap. The experts in London had it worked out that I was to jump the moment the bow of the outgoing merchantman was directly in line with the edge of the *Uzbekistan*'s single funnel. I heard pacing footsteps on the deck overhead. Guards? Quite possibly. I lit a cigarette and stepped back from the doctored railing. I concentrated on the light-speckled silhouette of the foreign merchantman. Another few seconds . . . there, that's it! Now do it!

I swallowed hard and launched myself over the side of the cruise ship.

The concussion of impact shattered me into a million pieces. I screamed as the overwhelming spasms of pain consumed my body, and screamed again, shrilly at the top of my lungs. No sand. Where was the sand? Damn it, I thought fiercely, what did they do with the sand. I heard myself whimper faintly. Shouts, running footfalls. Searchlights probed the darkness until their beams picked me out and converged on the china doll that was me, writhing and screaming as the impassive Black Sea lapped at the pilings a few feet away.

Somebody hastily threw a blanket over me. My arm reached out to cling to the leg of his trousers. 'Don't move, don't move,' a voice said, and I knew it was the officer I'd been chatting with in the bar. Then he bent over and whispered, 'Don't say you've been drinking with me, *please* . . . !'

That was all I could remember. When I came round again, I was lying on a hospital table, recurrent waves of throbbing agony kept at bay by a drug-induced numbness in all my limbs. An elderly man in a white smock fastened to the back of his shirt with adhesive straps was talking to a pair of white-turbaned female colleagues. The blonde Intourist girl stood at the right of the table. She drew back in surprise when my eyes flickered open.

'Mr Veeny . . . ?' she said in a soft drawl. 'Mr Veeny. You are feeling better now, I hope.'

I tried to answer but only a sound halfway between a moan and a croak came from my throat.

'Please don't try to move,' the girl said. 'The doctor wants that you know you have broken your femur in two places. Your spine may have been twisted when you hit the ground.'

Then it started coming back to me. All I could think about was the bloody sand. What went wrong? The pile of sand that could have made it the simplest thing for me to pick myself up from the quay and complain loudly about my bruises. Probably free drinks for the rest of the cruise, profuse apologies. Now I realized the Department slipped up somewhere. Damn them, I thought. Damn them to hell. This has spoiled everything.

Postscript

I remained, as I still am, under the constraint of the Official Secrets Act.
Anthony Blunt, 20 November 1979

The British secret services continue to maintain their mystique, apparently as determined as ever to preserve their unique status as government organizations that operate under the jurisdiction of the European Convention on Human Rights, yet without the same degree of parliamentary accountability that most of their Western counterparts have come to accept. Although the names of the chief of the Secret Intelligence Service and the Director-General of the Security Service are now routinely released by Whitehall, usually upon their appointment, evidently that is the limit of the public's right to know about the remarkable personalities who inhabit Britain's secret establishment. Certainly it is clear from the stature of the literary figures who have worked in both agencies that their colleagues are no ordinary bureaucrats or mindless automatons, despite the occasionally barbed comments of critics like Malcolm Muggeridge and Hugh Trevor-Roper. As we have seen, there is a long tradition, stretching back to the Great War, of talented young men and women being drawn into the world of espionage. Some, like Dennis Wheatley, Valentine Williams and Somerset Maugham, were already well known as novelists before their recruitment. Others, such as David Cornwell, Graham Greene and John Bingham, have capitalized on their own experiences, but few members of the reading public would ever have suspected that Brian Montgomery, Nubar Gulbenkian or Freddie Ayer had operated under cover.

The paradox at the heart of the knowledge that so many distinguished authors have pursued classified careers and participated in clandestine operations is the discipline of silence which they are supposed to have accepted. Criminal statute, in the form of the much-discredited Official Secrets Act, and the principles of breach of confidence enshrined in English common law, are weapons that have been deployed with varying degrees of success against Compton Mackenzie, Eddie Chapman, Peter Wright, Joan Miller and Anthony Cavendish. Mackenzie and Chapman were convicted but given only nominal fines; Wright, Miller and Cavendish saw their autobiographies achieve unexpectedly high sales because of the counter-productive tactics adopted by an ill-advised and reluctant Attorney-General.

The spectacle of the Crown's senior law officer failing in his attempt to suppress the most innocuous of books is unpalatable to all, especially to the supporters of a liberal democracy. Quite apart from the appalling waste of public money, there is also the issue of human rights. Why should intelligence personnel be subject to more restrictions than the holders of other, equally sensitive posts? As lawyers acting for Wright, Cavendish and Miller argued, none had ever taken a vow of silence. Indeed, when the matter was considered by the courts, and in the absence of any supporting documentation, the Crown was obliged to fall back on the dubious proposition that all the defendants had committed themselves to secrecy under the terms of an *implied* contract. What is an implied contract? It is the kind of agreement that is never written on paper, cannot be signed, but can be litigated in England, if not in America.

In response to the failure of its civil suits against Peter Wright's *Spycatcher* the British government introduced a further Official Secrets Act in 1989 to prohibit all intelligence officers from disclosing any aspect of their service, irrespective of its nature or when it took place. This had the effect of imposing a duty of discretion retrospectively on those who had never previously given undertakings, and in many cases had retired decades earlier. To obtain a conviction under the law the Crown merely had to demonstrate that an individual who was or who had once been employed by the security or intelligence services had revealed information. The issue of whether the data was already in the public domain, or perhaps was of a trivial nature, was deemed irrelevant. There was no qualitative assessment allowed; the Act recognized only the absolute offence of unauthorized disclosure and even encompassed fiction that might be taken by the public to be authentic. However, even if the law failed to accommodate the novelist and the insider who purveyed innocuous gossip, it was recognized that juries would be reluctant to convict unless the offence was demonstrably damaging. Not surprisingly therefore no prosecution has been brought under the new Act, although several books have been published recently by retired intelligence officers, none of whom has even received a warning.

Retired senior intelligence personnel in Australia (Harvey Barnett;

Michael Thwaites), Canada (Cliff Harvison; James Dubro), Israel (Isser Harel), France (Comte de Marenches; Jean Rochet) and Germany (Reinhard Gehlen) have been allowed to publish memoirs without their respective agencies sustaining much embarrassment or damage. In the United States there is a veritable industry centred on the recollections of former CIA officers, with no less than four Directors (Allen Dulles, William Colby, Stansfield Turner and William Casey) choosing to release their stories, and dozens of their subordinates have followed their example. If so many countries can enable their retirees to publish autobiographies without compromising security, why is it that their British counterparts cannot do the same? Even the totalitarian German Democratic Republic allowed its legendary spymaster Markus Wolf to write *Die Troika*, his family's history. In contrast SIS professionals of the calibre of John Colvin and Nicholas Elliott, who have both produced highly entertaining books filled with harmless anecdotes, are obliged to adhere to the ludicrous pretence that they were simply diplomats.

SIS and MI5 argue that any admission, however banal, might be of help to a hostile intelligence agency or to a terrorist. Whilst this thesis might have been tolerable at the height of the Cold War, or in the midst of a conflict fought against urban guerrillas, neither scenario is realistic in Britain at the end of the twentieth century, after the collapse of the Soviet Bloc. Certainly there remain significant challenges to the West's security, posed not least by the proliferation of nuclear technology, nationalist extremism and Islamic fundamentalism, but none of the groups which constitute a threat can really be said to be in a position where they might exploit a minor, inadvertent indiscretion embedded deep in a vintage case history dating back some thirty years or so. How might a terrorist like Abu Nidal benefit from the revelation that a particular molehunt had been conducted in England in 1963? The purists would assert that any discussion of intelligence methodology is unhelpful in that it might, for example, alert unsuspecting terrorists to the dangers of technical surveillance, or tip off an assassin to the need for caution when using a telephone. Whilst the operational targets of security agencies inevitably will change, the principles and techniques employed will remain much the same.

Undoubtedly there are dangers in unauthorized disclosure. Peter Wright dismayed his former colleagues in MI5 by his frequent and uninhibited reference to authentic codenames. Similarly Victor Ostrovsky, the author of *By Way of Deception*, incurred the wrath of Mossad by his identification of Yasser Arafat's chauffeur as a key Israeli asset inside the Palestine Liberation Organization. It is bad enough when an overzealous newsman stumbles across a current source and jeopardizes it. Such is the hazard of running an intelligence service in a free society, as Bill Casey discovered in 1986 when he tried to persuade the American media to keep silent about a highly profitable interception programme codenamed Ivy Bells which was tapping an underwater cable in the Sea of Okhotsk off the extreme north-east corner of the former USSR. Casey failed, just as his predecessor Bill Colby had been unable to prevent details of Jennifer, the salvage of a Soviet Golf class submarine from the Pacific in 1974, from appearing in the *New York Times*. The occasional leak is inevitable but there are others, orchestrated by insiders, that are considered avoidable. One of the first of the genre was Victor Marchetti's *The CIA and the Cult of Intelligence*, which was released after a lengthy legal battle in 1974. This book proved doubly embarrassing for the CIA because not only was it published with more than three hundred blank spaces, where the text had been deleted by order of the Agency's lawyers, but some of the material was printed in bold, to indicate where the CIA had opposed the inclusion of the passage but had seen its objections overridden by the courts.

The CIA's efforts to restrict Marchetti turned his book into a best seller, a lesson that was not learned by the British Security Service which experienced a humiliating defeat in the Australian courts a decade or so later when it sought belatedly to stop the distribution of *Spycatcher*. Incredibly, the Israelis made the same mistake when they sought and lost an injunction in the Canadian courts to prevent the circulation of Victor Ostrovsky's autobiography in 1990, thereby proving its authenticity beyond doubt to hitherto sceptical reviewers.

Spy fiction and non-fiction will continue to be popular for as long as there are secrets to be kept and plans to be betrayed. The public's appetite for tales of the British Secret Service will probably prove equally enduring, just so long as its traitors remain as colourfully prestigious as Guy Burgess and Anthony Blunt, and while it engenders mystification by declining to submit to any kind of external or parliamentary scrutiny.

Bibliography

Agar, Augustus, *Baltic Episode* (Conway Maritime Press, 1963)
– *Showing the Flag* (Evans Brothers, 1962)
– *Footprints in the Sea* (Evans Brothers, 1959)
Amery, Julian, *Approach March* (Hutchinson, 1973)
Ayer, A. J., *Part of My Life* (Collins, 1977)
Benton, Kenneth, *Sole Agent* (Collins, 1970)
– *The Twenty-Fourth Level* (Thriller Book Club, 1969)
– *Spy in the Chancery* (1972)
– *Craig and the Jaguar* (Macmillan, 1973)
– *Craig and the Tunisian Tangle* (1974)
– *Death on the Appian Way* (Chatto & Windus, 1974)
– *Craig and the Midas Touch* (Macmillan, 1975)
– *A Single Monstrous Act* (Macmillan, 1976)
– *The Red Hen Conspiracy* (Anchor Press, 1977)
– *Ward of Caesar* (1986)
Best, Sigismund Payne, *The Venlo Incident* (Hutchinson, 1950)
Bingham, Charlotte, *Coronet among the Weeds* (Heinemann, 1963)
Bingham, John, *Night's Black Agent* (Dodd, 1961)
– *A Fragment of Fear* (Victor Gollancz, 1965)
– *The Double Agent* (Victor Gollancz, 1966)
– *Vulture in the Sun* (Victor Gollancz, 1971)
– *Brock and the Defector* (Doubleday, 1982)
Bingham, Madeleine, *Peers and Plebs* (Allen & Unwin, 1975)
– *Scotland under Mary Stuart* (Allen & Unwin, 1971)
– *Sheridan* (St Martin's, 1972)
– *Masques and Façades: Sir John Vanbrugh* (Allen & Unwin, 1974)
Blunt, Anthony, *Tomas Harris* (Courtauld Institute)
Brown, John, *In Durance Vile* (Robert Hale, 1981)
Burt, Leonard, *Commander Burt of Scotland Yard* (Heinemann, 1967)
Cairncross, John, *After Polygamy was Made a Sin* (Routledge)
Carew-Hunt, Robert, *The Theory and Practice of Communism* (Geoffrey Bles, 1950)
Carr, John Dickson, *Top Secret* (Hamish Hamilton, 1964)

Cavendish, Anthony, *Inside Intelligence* (Collins, 1990)

Cawelti, John G., *The Spy Story* (University of Chicago Press, 1987)

Cecil, Robert, *A Divided Life* (Bodley Head, 1988)

Chapman, Eddie, *The Eddie Chapman Story* (Library 33, 1966)

Chaucer, Eve, *Silksheets & Breadcrumbs*

Childers, Erskine, *The Riddle of the Sands* (Blackie, 1961)

Chisholm, Roderick, *Ladysmith* (Osprey, 1979)

Clive, Nigel, *A Greek Experience 1943–48* (Michael Russell, 1985)

Colvin, John, *Twice around the World* (Leo Cooper, 1991)

Cookridge, E. H. (Edward Spiro), *The Third Man* (Arthur Barker, 1968)

Cottenham, Earl of (Mark Pepys), *Steering Wheel Papers* (privately)

– *Motoring without Fear* (Methuen & Co, 1928)

Crocker, Sir William, *Far from Humdrum* (Hutchinson, 1967)

– *Tales from the Coffee House*

Cross, John, *Red Jungle* (Robert Hale, 1957)

Darling, Donald, *Secret Sunday* (William Kimber, 1975)

– *Sunday at Large* (William Kimber, 1977)

Davidson, Basil, *Special Operations Europe* (Gollancz, 1980)

– *Partisan Picture* (Bedford Books, 1946)

De Mowbray, Stephen, *Key Facts in Soviet History* (Pinter, 1990)

Driberg, Tom (Lord Bradwell), *Ruling Passions* (Jonathan Cape, 1977)

– *Guy Burgess* (Weidenfeld, 1956)

Dukes, Sir Paul, *The Story of ST-25* (Cassell, 1938)

– *Epic of the Gestapo* (Cassell, 1940)

– *Come Hammer Come Sickle* (Cassell, 1947)

Elliott, Nicholas, *Never Judge a Man by his Umbrella* (Michael Russell, 1991)

Ellis, C. H. Dick, *Transcaspian Episode* (Hutchinson, 1963)

Elwell, Charles, *Corsican Excursion* (Bodley Head, 1954)

Fielding, Xan, *Hide and Seek* (Secker & Warburg, 1954)

– *One Man in His Time* (Macmillan, 1990)

Fleming, Ian, *Casino Royale* (Signet, 1953)

Fletcher, Reginald (Lord Winster), *The Air Defence of Britain* (Penguin, 1938)

Footman, David, *Dead Yesterday* (White Lion, 1974)

– *Red Prelude* (Cresset Press, 1944)

– *Civil War in Russia* (Faber & Faber, 1961)

– *The Yellow Rock* (Jenkins, 1929)

– *A Pretty Pass* (Morrow, 1933)

– *Balkan Holiday* (Heinemann, 1935)

– *Pig and Pepper* (Heinemann, 1936)

– *Pemberton* (Cresset Press, 1943)

– *Half Way East* (Heinemann, 1935)

– *Better Forgotten* (Heinemann, 1938)

– *The Primrose Path* (Cresset Press, 1946)

Footman, David, *In Memoriam Archie, 1904–64* (privately, 1967)
– *The Last Days of Kolchak* (St Antony's, 1953)
Fourcade, Marie-Madeleine, *Noah's Ark* (Allen & Unwin, 1973)
Fulford, Roger, *Queen Victoria* (Collins, 1951)
Gallegos, Adrian, *From Capri to Oblivion* (Hodder & Stoughton, 1959)
Garby-Czerniawski, Roman, *The Big Network* (George Ronald, 1961)
Gibson, William, *Wild Career* (Harrap & Co, 1935)
Glover, Sir Gerald, *115 Park Street* (Gerald Glover, 1982)
Golitsyn, Anatoli, *New Lies for Old* (Bodley Head, 1984)
Grant, Joan (Joan Wheatley), *Return to Elysium* (Methuen, 1957)
Greene, Graham, *The Confidential Agent* (1939)
– *This Gun for Hire* (1936)
– *Ministry of Fear* (1943)
– *Brighton Rock* (1938)
– *The Heart of the Matter* (1948)
– *The Tenth Man* (Bodley Head, 1985)
– *Our Man in Havana* (1958)
Gulbenkian, Nubar, *Pantaraxia* (Hutchinson, 1965)
Hart, H. L. A., *Law, Liberty and Morality* (OUP, 1963)
Hastings, Stephen, *The Murder of TSR 2*
Hill, George, *Go Spy the Land* (Cassell, 1932)
– *Dreaded Hour* (Cassell, 1936)
Hoare, Sir Samuel (Lord Templewood), *The Fourth Seal* (Heinemann, 1930)
Horne, Alistair, *Macmillan* (Macmillan, 1991)
Household, Geoffrey, *Against the Wind* (Michael Joseph, 1958)
– *Rogue Male* (1939)
Hyde, Harford Montgomery, *Secret Intelligence Agent* (Constable, 1982)
Johns, Philip, *Within Two Cloaks* (William Kimber, 1979)
Jones, Aubrey, *The Pendulum of Politics* (Faber & Faber, 1946)
Jones, R. V., *Most Secret War* (Hamish Hamilton, 1978)
– *Reflections on Intelligence* (Heinemann, 1989)
Kirton, James (Kenneth Benton), *A Time for Murder* (1985)
Knight, Maxwell, *Crime Cargo* (Philip Allan, 1934)
– *Gunman's Holiday* (Philip Allan, 1935)
– *Pets and their Problems* (Heinemann, 1968)
– *Be a Nature Detective* (Warne, 1969)
– *The Young Naturalist's Field Guide* (G. Bell, 1952)
Knightley, Philip, *The Second Oldest Profession* (André Deutsch, 1986)
Knoblock, Edward, *Round the Room* (Chapman & Hall, 1939)
Kurtz, Harald, *The Empress Eugénie* (Hamish Hamilton, 1964)
Lancaster, Donald, *The Emancipation of French Indochina* (OUP, 1961)
Landau, Henry, *All's Fair* (Putnam, 1935)
– *Secrets of the White Lady* (Putnam, 1933)

Landau, Henry, *The Enemy Within* (Putnam, 1937)
– *Spreading the Spy Net* (Jarrolds, 1938)
Langley, J. M. *Fight Another Day* (Collins, 1974)
Langley, J. M. & Foot, M. R. D., *MI9: Escape and Evasion 1939–1945* (Bodley Head, 1979)
Le Carré, John (David Cornwell), *Call for the Dead* (Victor Gollancz, 1961)
– *A Murder of Quality* (Victor Gollancz, 1963)
– *The Spy Who Came in from the Cold* (Victor Gollancz, 1963)
– *The Looking Glass War* (Heinemann, 1965)
– *The Naive and Sentimental Lover* (Hodder & Stoughton, 1971)
– *Tinker, Tailor, Soldier, Spy* (Hodder & Stoughton, 1974)
– *The Honourable Schoolboy* (Hodder & Stoughton, 1977)
– *Smiley's People* (Hodder & Stoughton, 1980)
– *The Little Drummer Girl* (Hodder & Stoughton, 1983)
– *A Perfect Spy* (Hodder & Stoughton, 1986)
Leggett, George, *The Cheka: Lenin's Political Police* (OUP, 1981)
Lyall, Archie, *The Balkan Road* (Methuen, 1930)
– *25 Languages of Europe* (Sidgwick & Jackson, 1932)
– *Russian Roundabout* (Douglas Harmsworth, 1933)
MacInnes, Helen, *Cloak of Darkness* (Ballantine, 1982)
Mackenzie, Compton, *Greek Memories* (University Publications of America, 1987)
– *Sinister Street* (1913)
– *Greek Memories* (Cassell, 1932)
– *First Athenian Memories* (Cassell, 1928)
– *Water on the Brain* (Chatto & Windus, 1933)
Magan, William, *Umma-More* (Element Books, 1983)
Marshall-Cornwall, Sir James, *Wars and Rumours of Wars* (Leo Cooper, 1984)
Mason, A. E. W., *The Summons* (Hodder & Stoughton, 1920)
– *The Four Corners of the World* (Hodder & Stoughton)
Masterman, J. C., *The Double Cross System of the War of 1939–45* (Yale, 1972)
– *On the Chariot Wheel* (OUP, 1975)
Masters, Anthony, *Literary Agents* (Basil Blackwell, 1987)
Maugham, W. Somerset, *Ashenden* (Heinemann, 1928)
Miller, Joan (Joanna Phipps), *One Girl's War* (Brandon Books, 1986)
Mills, Cyril, *Bertram Mills Circus: Its Story* (Hutchinson, 1967)
Moe, John, *John Moe: Double Agent* (Mainstream, 1986)
Mole, William (William Younger), *The Hammersmith Maggot* (Eyre & Spottiswoode, 1955)
– *Skin Trap* (Eyre & Spottiswoode, 1957)
Monkhouse, Allan, *Moscow 1911–33* (Gollancz, 1933)
Montgomery, Brian, *A Field Marshal in the Family* (Constable, 1973)
– *Shenton of Singapore* (Leo Cooper, 1984)

Moorehead, Alan, *The Traitors* (Harper & Row, 1952)
Muggeridge, Malcolm, *Chronicles of Wasted Time* (Morrow, 1974)
Neave, Airey, *Saturday at MI9* (Hodder & Stoughton, 1969)
– *They Have Their Exits* (Hodder & Stoughton, 1953)
Nicholson, Leslie (John Whitwell), *British Agent* (William Kimber, 1966)
O'Brien-ffrench, Conrad, *Delicate Mission*
Owen, Frank, *The Eddie Chapman Story* (Julian Messner, 1954)
Pantcheff, Theodore, *Fortress Island* (Phillimore & Co, 1981)
Philby, H. A. R. (Kim), *My Silent War* (MacGibbon & Kee, 1968)
– *The David Allens: The History of a Family Firm*
Popov, Dusko, *Spy CounterSpy* (Weidenfeld & Nicolson, 1974)
Prater, Donald, *A Ringing Glass* (Clarendon Press, 1986)
Pujol, Juan, *GARBO* (Weidenfeld & Nicolson, 1985)
Putlitz, Wolfgang zu, *The Zu Putlitz Dossier* (Allan Wingate, 1957)
Ransom, Charles, *British Intelligence in the Second World War* (HMSO, 1979)
Reilly, Sidney, *Sidney Reilly: Britain's Master Spy* (Harper, 1933)
Rees, Goronwy, *A Chapter of Accidents* (Chatto & Windus, 1972)
Rickman, Alexander, *Swedish Iron Ore* (Faber, 1939)
Rieul, Roland, *Soldier into Spy* (William Kimber, 1986)
Rothschild, Lord, *Meditations on a Broomstick* (Collins, 1977)
– *Random Variables* (Collins, 1984)
Sergueiev, Lily, *Secret Service Rendered* (William Kimber, 1968)
Seton-Watson, Hugh, *Neither War nor Peace* (Methuen, 1960)
Sillitoe, Sir Percy, *Cloak without Dagger* (Cassell, 1955)
Simkins, Anthony, *British Intelligence in the Second World War* (HMSO, 1990)
Sinclair, Ronald (Reginald Teague-Jones), *Adventures in Persia*
Smiley, David, *Arabian Assignment* (1975)
– *Albanian Assignment* (Chatto & Windus, 1984)
Stewart, Brian, *All Men's Wisdom* (ed.) (River Bank Culture Enterprise, 1985)
Stirling, Walter, *Safety Last* (Hollis & Carter, 1953)
Sweet-Escott, Bickham, *Baker Street Irregular* (Methuen, 1965)
Tangye, Derek, *The Way to Minack* (Michael Joseph, 1978)
Teague-Jones, Reginald, *The Spy Who Disappeared* (Gollancz, 1990)
Trevor-Roper, Hugh, *The Philby Affair* (William Kimber, 1968)
Verschoyle, Derek, *The English Novelists* (1933)
– *The Balcony* (1949)
Walker, David E., *Lunch with a Stranger* (W. W. Norton, 1957)
Watts, Stephen, *Moonlight on a Lake in Bond Street* (W. W. Norton, 1961)
Waugh, Alec, *A Spy in the Family* (W. H. Allen, 1970)
Weldon, L. B., *Hard Lying* (Herbert Jenkins, 1925)
West, William J., *Spymaster* (Wynwood Press, 1989)
Wheatley, Dennis, *Drink and Ink* (Hutchinson, 1979)
– *Red Eagle* (1937)

Wheatley, Dennis, *The Eunuch of Stamboul* (1935)
– *The Deception Planners* (Hutchinson, 1980)
– *Stranger than Fiction* (Hutchinson, 1959)
Whinney, Patrick, *Corsican Command* (Patrick Stephens, 1989)
Whitwell, John (Leslie Nicholson), *British Agent* (William Kimber, 1966)
Williams, Valentine, *The Man with the Clubfoot* (Herbert Jenkins)
– *The Return of Clubfoot* (Herbert Jenkins)
– *The World of Action* (Hamish Hamilton, 1938)
Winterbotham, F. W., *The Ultra Secret* (Weidenfeld & Nicolson, 1974)
– *Secret and Personal* (William Kimber, 1969)
– *The Ultra Spy* (Macmillan, 1989)
Wolfe, Peter, *Corridors of Deceit* (Bowling Green State University, 1987)
Woodhouse, Hon C. M., *Something Ventured* (Granada, 1982)
Wright, Peter, *Spycatcher* (Heinemann Sydney, 1987)
Wynne, Greville, *The Man from Moscow* (Hutchinson, 1967)
– *The Man from Odessa* (Robert Hale, 1981)
Young, George K., *Who is My Liege?* (Gentry Books, 1972)
– *Subversion and the British Riposte* (Ossian, 1984)
Younger, Kenneth, *Changing Perspectives in British Foreign Policy* (OUP, 1964)
Younger, William and Elizabeth, *Blue Moon in Portugal* (1956)
Zaehner, Robert, *Hinduism* (OUP, 1966)

Acknowledgements

For permission to reprint copyright material the publishers gratefully acknowledge the following:

AUGUSTUS AGAR: from *Footprints in the Sea* (Geoffrey Bles Ltd, 1959) by permission of HarperCollins Publishers Ltd.

JULIAN AMERY: from *Approach March* (Hutchinson, 1973), © Julian Amery 1973, reproduced by permission of Curtis Brown London Ltd on behalf of Julian Amery.

A. J. AYER: from *Part of My Life* (Collins, 1977) by permission of HarperCollins Publishers Ltd.

SIGISMUND BEST: from *The Venlo Incident* (Hutchinson, 1950) by permission of Random House UK Ltd.

CHARLOTTE BINGHAM: from *Coronet Among the Weeds* (Heinemann, 1963) by permission of the Peters Fraser & Dunlop Group Ltd.

JOHN BINGHAM: from *Night's Black Agent* (Dodd Mead & Co, 1961) © The Estate of John Bingham.

GEORGE BLAKE: from *No Other Choice* (Cape, 1990) by permission of Random House UK Ltd.

JOHN BROWN: from *In Durance Vile* (1981) by permission of Robert Hale Ltd.

JOHN BRUCE LOCKHART: from 'Intelligence: A British View' by permission of the author.

LEONARD BURT: from *Commander Burt of Scotland Yard* (1967), by permission of William Heinemann Ltd.

ROBERT CAREW-HUNT: from *The Theory and Practice of Communism* (Geoffrey Bles Ltd, 1950) by permission of HarperCollins Publishers Ltd.

ANTHONY CAVENDISH: from *Inside Intelligence* (Unwin Hyman, 1990) by permission of HarperCollins Publishers Ltd.

ROBERT CECIL: from *A Divided Life* (Bodley Head, 1988) by permission of Andrew Lownie, Literary Agent.

EDDIE CHAPMAN: from *The Real Eddie Chapman Story* (1966), © Eddie Chapman, by permission of the author.

NIGEL CLIVE: from *A Greek Experience 1943–48* (1985) by permission of Michael Russell (Publishing) Ltd.

JOHN COLVIN: from *Twice Around the World* (Leo Cooper, 1991) by permission of Leo Cooper.

E. H. COOKRIDGE: from *The Third Man* (Arthur Barker, 1968) by permission of George Weidenfeld & Nicolson Ltd.

JOHN CROSS: from *Red Jungle* (Robert Hale, 1957) by permission of David Higham Associates.

DONALD DARLING: from *Secret Sunday* (1975) by permission of William Kimber, an imprint of HarperCollins Publishers Ltd.

BASIL DAVIDSON: from *Special Operations Europe* (Gollancz, 1980) by permission of Victor Gollancz, an imprint of Cassell.

TOM DRIBERG: from *Ruling Passions* (Cape, 1977) by permission of David Higham Associates.

SIR PAUL DUKES: from *The Story of 'ST-25'* (Cassell, 1938) © The Estate of Sir Paul Dukes.

NICHOLAS ELLIOTT: from *Never Judge a Man by his Umbrella* (1991) by permission of Michael Russell (Publishing) Ltd.

DICK ELLIS: from *Transcaspian Episode* (Hutchinson, 1963), © The Estate of C. H. Ellis.

XAN FIELDING: from *Hide and Seek* (1954), by permission of Martin Secker & Warburg Ltd.

IAN FLEMING: from *Casino Royale*, © 1953 by Glidrose Productions Ltd; from *Dr No*, © 1958 by Glidrose Productions Ltd, by permission of Glidrose Publications.

REGINALD (REX) FLETCHER: from *The Air Defence of Britain* (Penguin, 1938).

ADRIAN GALLEGOS: from *From Capri into Oblivion* (1959) by permission of Hodder and Stoughton Ltd.

ROMAN GARBY-CZERNIAWSKI: from *The Big Network* (George Ronald Publisher, 1961) © The Estate of Roman Garby-Czerniawski.

WILLIAM J. GIBSON: from *Wild Career* (Harrap, 1935) by permission of Chambers Publishers.

GERALD GLOVER: from *115 Park Street* (Gerald Glover, 1982) by permission of Lady Susan Glover, OBE.

GRAHAM GREENE: from *The Tenth Man* (Bodley Head) © 1985 Verdant SA, by permission of David Higham Associates.

NUBAR GULBENKIAN: from *Pantaraxia* (Hutchinson, 1965) by permission of Random House UK Ltd.

GEORGE HILL: from *Go Spy the Land* (Cassell, 1932) © The Estate of George Hill.

SIR SAMUEL HOARE (Viscount Templewood): from *The Fourth Seal* (William Heinemann, 1930) by permission of Mrs Paul Paget.

GEOFFREY HOUSEHOLD: from *Against the Wind* (Michael Joseph, 1958) by permission of A. M. Heath on behalf of the estate of the late Geoffrey Household.

HARFORD MONTGOMERY HYDE: from *Secret Intelligence Agent* (Constable, 1982), © Estate of Montgomery Hyde 1982, by permission of Curtis Brown Ltd, London.

MIRANDA INGRAM: from 'Trouble With Security', *New Society*, 31 May 1984, © New Statesman & Society, by permission.

EDWARD KNOBLOCK: from *Round the Room* (Chapman & Hall, 1939) © The Estate of Edward Knoblock.

HENRY LANDAU: from *Secrets of the White Lady* (G. P. Putnam's Sons, 1935) © Captain Henry Landau.

GEORGE LEGGETT: from *The Cheka: Lenin's Political Police* (1981), © George Leggett 1981, by permission of Oxford University Press.

ARCHIE LYALL: from *Russian Roundabout* (Douglas Harmsworth, 1933) © The Estate of Archie Lyall.

WILLIAM MAGAN: from *Umma-More* (1983) by permission of Element Books Ltd.

SIR JAMES MARSHALL-CORNWALL: from *Wars and Rumours of Wars* (Leo Cooper, 1984) by permission of Leo Cooper.

ARTHUR MARTIN: from the Editors' Foreword from Anatoli Golitsyn: *New Lies for Old* (Bodley Head, 1984) by permission of Random House UK Ltd.

ERIC MASCHWITZ: from *No Chip on My Shoulder* (Herbert Jenkins, 1957), © The Estate of Eric Maschwitz.

A. E. W. MASON: from *The Four Corners of the World* by permission of A. P. Watt Ltd on behalf of Trinity College, Oxford.

CATHY MASSITER: letter, *New Society* 14 June 1984, © New Statesman & Society, by permission.

SIR JOHN MASTERMAN: from *On the Chariot Wheel* (OUP, 1975) © The Estate of Sir John Masterman by permission of Curtis Brown London Ltd.

W. SOMERSET MAUGHAM: from *Ashenden* (1928), by permission of William Heinemann Ltd.

ACKNOWLEDGEMENTS

JOAN MILLER: from *One Girl's War* (1986) by permission of Brandon Books Publishers Ltd.

JOHN MOE: from *John Moe: Double Agent* (1986) by permission of Mainstream Publishing Co. (Edinburgh) Ltd.

BRIAN MONTGOMERY: from *A Field Marshal in the Family* (1973) by permission of Constable Publishers.

STEPHEN DE MOWBRAY: from 'Soviet deception and the onset of the Cold War', *Encounter* July/August 1984, © Stephen de Mowbray 1984.

MALCOLM MUGGERIDGE: from *Chronicles of Wasted Time: The Infernal Grove* (William Morrow, 1974).

AIREY NEAVE: from *Saturday at MI9* (1969) by permission of Hodder & Stoughton Ltd.

JUAN PUJOL: from *Garbo* by Juan Pujol with Nigel West (1985) by permission of Weidenfeld & Nicolson Ltd.

WOLFGANG ZU PUTLITZ: from *The zu Putlitz Dossier* (Allan Wingate, 1957), © The Estate of Wolfgang zu Putlitz.

RONALD REED: 'Technical Problems Affecting Radio Communications by the Double-Cross Agents' from *British Intelligence in the Second World War* by permission of the Controller of Her Majesty's Stationery Office.

GORONWY REES: from *A Chapter of Accidents* (Chatto, 1972) by permission of David Higham Associates.

ALEXANDER RICKMAN: from *Swedish Iron Ore* (1939) by permission of Faber and Faber Ltd.

ROLAND RIEUL: from *Soldier into Spy* (William Kimber, 1986), © 1986 by Roland Rieul, by permission of Mark Paterson and Associates on behalf of Roland Rieul.

LORD ROTHSCHILD: from *Meditations on a Broomstick* (Collins, 1977) by permission of HarperCollins Publishers Ltd.

ANTHONY SIMKINS: 'Security against Germany in the United Kingdom to the End of the War' from *British Intelligence in the Second World War Vol. 4* by permission of the Controller of Her Majesty's Stationery Office.

DAVID SMILEY: from *Albanian Assignment* (Chatto & Windus, 1984) by permission of Random House UK Ltd.

EDWARD SPIRO *see* COOKRIDGE

WALTER STIRLING: from *Safety Last* (Hollis & Carter, 1953), © The Estate of Walter Stirling.

DEREK TANGYE: from *The Way to Minack* (Michael Joseph, 1978) by permission of the Peters Fraser & Dunlop Group Ltd.

ACKNOWLEDGEMENTS

REGINALD TEAGUE-JONES: from *The Spy Who Disappeared* (Gollancz, 1990) by permission of Victor Gollancz, an imprint of Cassell.

HUGH TREVOR-ROPER: from *The Philby Affair* (William Kimber, 1968) by permission of the Peters Fraser & Dunlop Group Ltd.

DAVID E. WALKER: from *Lunch With a Stranger* (Norton, 1957), © David E. Walker 1957, reproduced by permission of Curtis Brown London Ltd.

STEPHEN WATTS: from *Moonlight on a Lake in Bond Street* (Bodley Head, 1961) by permission of Random House UK Ltd.

L. B. WELDON: from *Hard Lying: Eastern Mediterranean 1914–1919* (Herbert Jenkins, 1935), © The Estate of L. B. Weldon.

DENNIS WHEATLEY: from *The Time Has Come: Pen and Ink* (Mandarin) by permission of the publisher.

F. W. WINTERBOTHAM: from *The Ultra Secret* (1974) by permission of George Weidenfeld & Nicolson Ltd.

PETER WRIGHT: from *Spycatcher* (1987) by permission of William Heinemann Australia, an imprint of Reed International Books Australia Pty Ltd.

GREVILLE WYNNE: from *The Man from Odessa* (1981) by permission of Robert Hale Ltd.

GEORGE YOUNG: from *Subversion and the British Riposte* (1984) by permission of Ossian Publishers Ltd.

Faber and Faber Limited apologize for any errors or omissions in the above list and would be grateful to be notified of any corrections that should be incorporated in the next edition or reprint of this volume.

Index